ENCYCLOPEDIA OF EDUCATION

SECOND EDITION

EDITORIAL BOARD

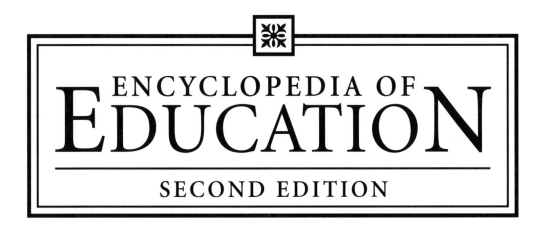

ENCYCLOPEDIA OF EDUCATION

SECOND EDITION

James W. Guthrie, Editor in Chief

VOLUME

1

AACSB–Commerce

**MACMILLAN
REFERENCE
USA™**

New York • Detroit • San Diego • San Francisco • Cleveland • New Haven, Conn. • Waterville, Maine • London • Munich

Encyclopedia of Education, Second Edition

James W. Guthrie, Editor in Chief

For permission to use material from this product, submit your request via Web at http://www.gale-edit.com/permissions, or you may download our Permissions Request form and submit your request by fax or mail to:

Permissions Department
The Gale Group, Inc.
27500 Drake Road
Farmington Hills, MI 48331-3535
Permissions Hotline: 248-699-8006 or
800-877-4253 ext. 8006
Fax: 248-699-8074 or 800-762-4058

LIBRARY OF CONGRESS CATALOGING-IN-PUBLICATION DATA

Encyclopedia of education / edited by James W. Guthrie.—2nd ed.
   p. cm.
Includes bibliographical references and index.
  ISBN 0-02-865594-X (hardcover : set : alk. paper)
1. Education—Encyclopedias. I. Guthrie, James W.
  LB15 .E47 2003
  370'.3—dc21   2002008205

ISBNs
Volume 1: 0-02-865595-8
Volume 2: 0-02-865596-6
Volume 3: 0-02-865597-4
Volume 4: 0-02-865598-2
Volume 5: 0-02-865599-0
Volume 6: 0-02-865600-8
Volume 7: 0-02-865601-6
Volume 8: 0-02-865602-4

Printed in the United States of America
10 9 8 7 6 5 4 3 2 1

CONTENTS

EDITORIAL AND PRODUCTION STAFF

Linda S. Hubbard, *Editorial Director*

Deirdre Graves, Anjanelle M. Klisz, Jennifer Wisinski, *Project Editors*

Monica M. Hubbard, John Krol, Angela Pilchak, Beth Richardson, Nicole Watkins, *Editorial Support*

Pamela Willwerth Aue, Allene M. Goforth, Peter Jaskowiak, Katherine Moreau, David E. Salamie, *Copy Editors*

Mary Russell, Eleanor Stanford, *Proofreaders*

Jennifer Farthing, Katherine Taylor Haynes, *Appendix Editors*

Laurie Andriot, *Indexer*

Michelle DiMercurio, *Art Director*

Datapage Technologies International, Inc., *Typesetter*

Mary Beth Trimper, *Manager, Composition*

Evi Seoud, *Assistant Manager, Composition*

Rita Wimberley, *Buyer*

MACMILLAN REFERENCE USA

Frank Menchaca, *Vice President*

Jill Lectka, *Director, Publishing Operations*

PREFACE

At its Greek and Latin roots, the word *education* refers to a "bringing forward" or "flowering." The idea is to reach inside and withdraw the potential for understanding. Thus, education can be defined as the process by which individuals come to understand a topic or condition more fully.

There are many avenues by which individuals come to be educated. People learn at home, from their friends, and from their many formal and informal associations with businesses, religious organizations, or social clubs. People also learn at school. This formal instruction is what is called schooling.

The purpose of the *Encyclopedia of Education*, first published by Macmillan/The Free Press in 1971, is to provide a comprehensive description of the enterprise of education, both within the United States and throughout the world. The 1971 edition was the first reference work to offer a view of the institutions, people, processes, roles, and philosophies found in educational practice. While the second edition retains the mission and organizational structure of the 1971 edition, it has been rewritten to reflect the societal and resulting institutional changes that have occurred over the past thirty years.

Education and Its Evolution

From the chronological vantage point of the turn of the twenty-first century, and through the lens of historical perspective, one can see that modern societal conditions are reshaping education, both in the United States and abroad, in a rapid and profound manner. Modern technologies, coupled with global economic forces, have contributed to an intense and pervasive level of individual, organizational, and international interdependence. These new societal dynamics are altering education every bit as much as they are changing the home life, workplace, lifestyle, and political economy of virtually every person, in every village, in almost every nation.

In response, education, as we know it, is evolving in several ways. First, formal educational institutions are more intertwined with society than ever before. Almost a third of the American population is linked tightly to formal schooling, either as a student or as a parent of an enrolled student.

Serving this extensive clientele requires a huge workforce. Educational institutions in the United States currently employ more individuals than are engaged directly in agriculture. The United States now spends more money annually on education than it spends on any other publicly subsidized practical activity, except health care. Not even national defense spending exceeds the $3 billion per operating day the nation appropriates to support its schools and colleges. Not surprisingly, given the number of individuals whose lives are immediately touched by schooling, the significance of the activity for the larger society, and the magnitude of resources involved, political leaders and the policy community spend more time deliberating and acting upon education matters than almost any other subset of public issues.

Second, education is itself more complicated and its various components are more reciprocally linked than previously acknowledged. For example, what happens to a child before going to school and outside of school is now recognized as influencing student success. Events in preschool and kindergarten are known to influence the effectiveness of elementary school; student success in elementary school influences success in high school; college admission procedures shape high school curricula; graduate school admission standards shape college undergraduate courses of study.

Finally, the interconnected and global nature of the larger society renders American education unusually susceptible to comparison with and influence by other national school and college systems. How children in Singapore learn mathematics, what Muslim children are taught regarding America, and how the British Open University operates are seen as issues that matter in profound ways. Also, through student exchange, branch campuses, and distance education, education has risen to be among the nation's largest overseas export categories.

These three conditions expand the utility of a compendium and synthesis such as this second edition of the *Encyclopedia of Education*. Interested readers, parents, teachers, administrators, media researchers, scholars, policymakers and their staffs, administrative branch personnel, private sector executives, and informed citizens can benefit from an understanding of modern education and its society-wide significance as portrayed in the articles of this encyclopedia.

A Societal Perspective

The thirty-year period between publication of the first and second editions of the *Encyclopedia of Education* represents one of the most formative and fluid periods in American life and world history. A detailed discussion of the forces shaping the development of American education can be found in the article "Educational Policy, United States." Key elements of the article are synthesized in this preface.

In a prior era, it was possible for an individual in the United States to forego formal schooling and still own land, acquire relatively well-paying employment, participate as an informed citizen, and achieve a substantial degree of personal fulfillment. For the most part, these circumstances have changed. Modern economics renders formal education crucial for individual success, social mobility, and engagement with the demands of the workforce, the environment, and democratic government.

Education is an important element in national economic progress. People once flourished or floundered based on what they could extract from the ground. Today, a nation is more likely to survive and prosper based on the minds of its people.

The world and America's position in the world have changed profoundly since the publication of the encyclopedia's first edition. Here are a few illustrations of the global changes and resulting challenges that have emerged since 1971:

- The post–World War II cold war rivalry between East and West is over. Democratic capitalism has generally replaced totalitarian socialism to become the world's dominant political economy. Modern communication and transportation technologies have contributed to globally oriented, highly mobile, and rapidly paced societies. Economic developments have created a heretofore unknown degree of individual, organizational, and international interdependence.

- The United States has emerged as the leading economic and political power in the world. This condition, coupled with globalization, generates added diplomatic, military, and humanitarian responsibilities for the nation and its citizens.

- America is fortunate to have vast resources. These resources, however, are increasingly deployed in other regions of the world. Issues of health in Africa, overpopulation in Asia, political instability in Latin America, religious conflict in the Middle East, trade restrictions in Europe, ozone depletion in Antarctica, overfishing in the North Atlantic, or ice cap reductions in the Arctic are no longer remote issues. The eventual outcome of these conditions now matters as much for a child being raised on a family farm in South Dakota as for a recently liberated farm family in South Africa.

This new and fast-paced world has dampened some old issues. Widespread fears of nuclear annihilation, pestilence, and global famine are now ameliorated. Nevertheless, age-old concerns regarding religious and racial intolerance, social injustice, economic inequality, and discouraging instances of inhumanity have by no means been eliminated.

A few new issues have evolved, such as the fear of widespread environmental degradation and uneven economic development between nations in the northern and southern hemispheres. Solutions rest not simply upon good intentions but also upon good ideas. Therefore, regardless of what else may prove predictable for the twenty-first century, the policy and practical significance of education is assured. Both the transmission of existing knowledge and the discovery of new knowledge will occupy a more prominent place in the spectrum of public issues and the search for productive practices. The educational consequences of these economic, technological, demographic, and ecological challenges are substantial.

American Education in the Nineteenth and Twentieth Centuries

A brief history of American education suggests that the nineteenth century was occupied with constructing a system of schooling, principally elementary and later secondary education. The fundamental components of U.S. formal schooling—local schools, school districts, school boards, land-grant colleges, an agrarian base to the school calendar, and reliance upon locally determined property taxes for financing schools—were shaped during this period.

The twentieth century, or at least the latter half of it, was occupied with equalizing access to and expanding schooling itself. After World War II, the United States made a number of changes to its education system. Through judicial fiat, legislative enactment, and administrative actions the nation eliminated legally sanctioned racial segregation, mandated inclusion of disabled students, rendered schools more accessible to non- and limited-English-speaking students, imposed equal treatment for women, made preschool and kindergarten more widely available at public expense, and encouraged students to persist through high school to graduate and get a diploma.

The nation also vastly expanded its postsecondary education system, moving from elite to mass higher education. Community colleges enjoyed great growth, and public institutions of higher education grew in number and enrollments. And, finally, the United States enhanced its network of research universities capable of linking knowledge discovery to the nation's economic, health, and defense needs.

These were the societal shifts and public policy currents shaping education at the time the first edition of the *Encyclopedia of Education* was issued. The contributions of its editors and authors understandably reflected the issues and institutions of their time.

A Nation at Risk

Since the appearance of the first edition of the *Encyclopedia of Education,* the United States has been engaged in one of the most sustained periods of educational change in the nation's history. These changes establish a likely trajectory for the foreseeable future.

The reform period of the late twentieth and early twenty-first centuries was launched by the 1983 appearance of a highly visible national report, *A Nation at Risk.* As explored in the article "Educational Policy, United States," many educators and educational researchers believe that the fundamental thesis of this document was inaccurate. Paradoxically, seldom has a blue-ribbon report had such a widespread and long-lasting consequence and had such a profound and lasting impact on public opinion and policy.

The report asserted that America's preeminent positions in defense, technology, economics, science, and industry were threatened by the mediocrity of its public education system. The report left the impression that the United States was about to succumb to a deluge of foreign dominance, unless its schools were rapidly rendered more rigorous.

But twenty years later, as this preface is written, it is easy to see that the economic slump in which the United States found itself at the time of the report's issuance was far more a consequence of inefficient management practices than of the nation's ineffective education system. Also in the intervening period, the Japanese economy plummeted and its once vaunted education system was unable to protect it from its inefficient financial practices and protectionist trade policies. Indeed, beginning in 2000, Japan took steps to pattern its education system more after that of the United States.

Rightly or wrongly, however, *A Nation at Risk* launched two decades of reform in America, and the call for change shows no signs of subsiding. However inaccurate its analysis, the message of *A Nation at Risk* captured the importance of education to a modern society. Its message, even though flawed, was right for the time.

U.S. education, both higher and lower, has been changing dramatically ever since. More important, the forces symbolized by *A Nation at Risk* are everywhere still in operation and are likely to influence education in America and around the world for decades yet to come.

Educational Effectiveness

One can reasonably ask: "So what?" What specifically has changed since publication of the first edition? The answer is that because education now matters in new and more intense ways for individuals and societies, there is far greater interest in ensuring that education is effective.

High performance schools, high-stakes testing, academic accountability, school effectiveness, organizational efficiency, teacher productivity, performance financing, charter schools, alternative schools, break-the-mold schools, privatizing, outsourcing, and *pay for results* are illustrative of the slogans, issues, and topics that dominate American education policy and practice at the onset of the twenty-first century.

Two major change strategies have evolved. One is called the standards movement. The other travels under the banner of "competition" or "privatization." The two strategies are not mutually incompatible. Each necessitates government specification of learning standards or curricula goals that schools are expected to meet.

The standards movement suggests that textbooks and other instructional materials, teacher training, professional licensing, financial arrangements, statewide achievement testing, and performance awards and penalties should be made consistent with these standards.

Advocates for the second strategy, competition, contend that schools, like American automobiles in the 1970s, will improve only under the threat of competition. Proponents of this strategy argue that only when the current public school monopoly is severed will professional educators be motivated to try harder and teach better. Competition or privatization advocates seek magnet schools, charter schools, voucher plans, parental choice, and smaller schools and school districts.

As of this writing, the standards movement holds the upper hand. Literally thousands of legislative enactments, commission reports, gubernatorial campaigns, and regulatory activities have been constructed in its support. It is too early to judge its effects.

Competition has yet to be fully implemented and perhaps never will. In *Zelman v. Simmons-Harris* (2002), the U.S. Supreme Court upheld the constitutionality of an Ohio education provision permitting public funds to be used by parents to pay the private school tuition of their children. This case may eventually prove to be a substantial benefit to advocates of greater K–12 school competition. The Supreme Court decision is thought, however, to have little short-run consequence.

Historically, colleges and universities were seldom subjected to the same societal forces as the lower schools. But this too is changing and changing fast. The twentieth-century movement toward universal public higher education has rendered colleges and universities more vulnerable to political dynamics. College presidents, especially those serving public institutions, no longer have the luxury of simply hiring scholarly superstars, ensuring admission of athletes, and satisfying influential alumni. They must constantly ensure that powerful legislators and governors are informed about and supportive of higher education. The same demands for efficiency, effectiveness, affordability, and performance and value-added expectations now being faced by K–12 school administrators are just over the horizon for college administrators in the twenty-first century.

There is little evidence that public desire for better education is waning. Congressional enactment in 2002 of the No Child Left Behind Act was symbolic of the reform quest. The United States is on a sustained and intense path seeking means for rendering the education system more effective.

Capturing These Changes in the Encyclopedia

Although the enterprise of education has changed since the first edition, the format of the encyclopedia remains the same. An alphabetized list of articles and a thorough index are still the stable tools by which users can seek the information they need.

Nor has the encyclopedia format been altered to contain separate sections connected explicitly with modern developments such as globalization, information technology, accountability, or efficiency. Modern topics, as well as important historic issues and unusually influential individuals, are arrayed within the previously mentioned alphabetical arrangement.

Our understanding of the societal forces coalescing to reshape education has had an influence on the content and context of the second edition. With the exception of the biographies of John Dewey, William James, and Edward Thorndike, every article was newly commissioned, and a great majority of the articles in the second edition have been completely rewritten. The rapidly changing world conditions served as a road map guiding the selection of associate editors, the construction of broad topical areas to be covered, and the commissioning of individually written articles.

The editor in chief made a conscious decision to select associate editors who encompassed the many significant and rapidly evolving facets of education, formal and informal, institutional and instructional, historic and contemporary, contextual and content.

Planning Procedures and Associate Editors

An editorial board meeting with the editor in chief, the associate editors, and Macmillan officials was convened in Nashville, Tennessee, during the summer of 2000. Content domains were specified, individual responsibilities agreed to, and time schedules constructed.

The editor in chief and seven associate editors, assisted by Macmillan editorial officials, were responsible for conceptualization of the second edition's modern content, specification of article topics and biographies, identification of (and later selected communication with) authors, and approval of the content of manuscript submissions.

A great deal of responsibility resided with associate editors. They were not ornaments included because of their academic notoriety.

In alphabetical order, the associate editors and their areas of encyclopedia responsibility were as follows:

- Dr. John Braxton: Dr. Braxton oversaw issue analysis and institutional descriptions connected with postsecondary education. He is a professor of higher education at Peabody College, Vanderbilt University, and president of the American Association for the Study of Higher Education. His research specialization is academic and scientific norms and professional misconduct.

- Dr. James Cooper: Dr. Cooper is a professor of education, and former dean, at the Curry School of Education at the University of Virginia. He specializes in issues and institutional arrangements associated with elementary and secondary education, curricular issues, and teacher education.

- Dr. Susan Goldman: Dr. Goldman is a professor of psychology and education at the University of Illinois, Chicago. She is among the nation's leading psychologists concerned with human development and cognitive science. She was responsible for the construction of articles and commissioning of authors related to human development, intelligence, cognitive processes, and learning and instruction.

- Dr. James Guthrie: Dr. Guthrie, in addition to his role as editor in chief, assumed encyclopedia responsibilities for matters related to education policy, governance, finance, and politics.

He is a professor of public policy and education at Peabody College, Vanderbilt University.

- Dr. Stephen Heyneman: Dr. Heyneman was a World Bank education and economic development official for twenty years. During this time he had program officer and area expert responsibility for geographic regions such as Northern Africa, Eastern Europe, and the Middle East. He currently is a professor of international policy at Peabody College, Vanderbilt University. For the encyclopedia, he assumed responsibility for education issues and institutions outside the United States.

- Dr. Julia Koppich: Dr. Koppich is a principal in an educational consulting firm specializing in teacher policy and labor-management issues in education. She is best known for her research and writing on the future of teacher unions and the relationship of unions to modern education reform. These and out-of-school influences on children were areas of her encyclopedia responsibility.

- Dr. Craig Kridel: Dr. Kridel is a professor of educational research and foundations at the University of South Carolina. He specializes in the history of education and is the curator of the highly regarded Education Museum at his institution. He assumed encyclopedia responsibility for selecting and commissioning biographical sketches of significant historic education figures.

- Dr. Claire Smrekar: Dr. Smrekar is a professor of public policy and education at Peabody College and an assistant to the provost at Vanderbilt University. Her research focuses on out-of-school influences on children and families. She assumed responsibility for these and related topics in the encyclopedia.

About the Second Edition of the Encyclopedia

The second edition of the *Encyclopedia of Education* represents a large undertaking. Its eight volumes contain 3,000 pages covering more than 850 articles, ranging in length from 500 to 5,000 words. The project took several years to complete, from conceptualization to distribution.

Entries address such items as K–12 education, higher education, international education, educational policy and legislation, learning and instruction, out-of school influences, teacher preparation, and testing. In addition, the second edition includes

121 biographical sketches of influential educators, ranging historically from Plato to Alice Miel.

The encyclopedia's first edition included 100 articles about education systems in individual nations. A surprising number of these nations no longer exist. The world is simply too fluid any longer to focus upon individual polities. Consequently, the second edition provides descriptions and comparisons of global regions. Additionally, this edition provides cross-national comparisons of education systems in selected articles throughout the overall text.

Education technology is also treated throughout the entire set of volumes as well as being described and analyzed in nine specific articles.

Special Features of the Encyclopedia

Articles are signed by the authors and include cross-references to related articles in the encyclopedia. Cross-references facilitate use of the entire set and make the encyclopedia's total content more accessible.

Articles conclude with a bibliography, the length of which varies according to the length of the article. When relevant, websites are included in bibliographies.

Volume 1 includes both an alphabetical list of articles and an alphabetical list of contributors with affiliations and the titles of articles written.

Volume 8 of the encyclopedia is a substantial departure from past efforts. It includes a thematic outline of content that takes all entry terms and regroups them in logical categories. This feature should prove valuable to teachers preparing lesson plans and to students and lay readers alike who may desire assistance in connecting ideas and disciplines.

Volume 8 also contains a selection of primary source documents pertaining to the field of education—essential tools and natural complements to the scholarship delivered in the main part of the work. These documents include abridged versions of U.S. Supreme Court cases, legislation pertaining to education, and international education agreements.

Other features of volume 8 include (1) an alphabetical list of commonly administered standardized tests along with the address and website for the testing organization; (2) a list of state departments of education addresses and websites; (3) a list of recommended websites in the field of education; and (4) a bibliography listing classic works in the field.

Volume 8 also features a comprehensive index of concepts, names, and terms designed to enable readers to locate topics throughout the encyclopedia. Many subjects will not be treated in separate articles but are instead covered within the context of comprehensive articles. The index will guide readers to discussions of these subjects.

Acknowledgments

An undertaking of this magnitude obviously necessitated the participation of literally hundreds of individuals—editors, authors, production staff, printers, and others.

At the peril of overlooking some individuals whose contributions are greater than I fully understand, I would like to express my particular appreciation to each of the associate editors whose understanding of education, in the United States and throughout the world, was individually and collectively awe inspiring.

To each individual author, I wish to say, "Thank you." Obviously without your contributions there would be no content.

I am also deeply indebted to Macmillan Reference officials Jill Lectka, Deirdre Graves, Jan Klisz, and Jennifer Wisinski for judgment, patience, detailed record-keeping, and selflessness beyond easy description.

I wish to express my gratitude to Peabody College and Vanderbilt University, specifically Dean Camilla Benbow, Provost Nicholas Zeppos, former Provost Thomas G. Burish, Chancellor Emeritus Joe B. Wyatt, and current Chancellor E. Gordon Gee, without whose support and resources my contributing colleagues and I would have been vastly inconvenienced.

My administrative assistant, Joyce Hilley, somehow kept records straight, deadlines clear, and schedules flexible, all the while maintaining a stalwart sense of perspective in the face of periodic frustrations.

Finally, those whose names I have mentioned above and I are indebted to Elly Dickason, the former publisher of Macmillan Reference, who oversaw the birth of this idea and retired before the project's completion. She set the course by articulating high hopes and high standards. It was our goal to create an encyclopedia that exceeded these expectations.

James W. Guthrie
Editor in Chief
Nashville, Tennessee
June 2002

LIST OF ARTICLES

LIST OF AUTHORS

Charles M. Achilles
Eastern Michigan University
CLASS SIZE AND STUDENT LEARNING

Paul Ackerman
University of Maryland
SPECIAL EDUCATION
INTERNATIONAL CONTEXT

Jacob E. Adams Jr.
University of Washington
EDUCATION REFORM
OVERVIEW

Robert H. Adams
Austin Peay State University
ACCOUNTING SYSTEMS IN HIGHER EDUCATION

Susan A. Adler
University of Missouri-Kansas City
SOCIAL STUDIES EDUCATION
PREPARATION OF TEACHERS

Bruce Alberts
National Academy of Sciences
NATIONAL ACADEMY OF SCIENCES

Patricia A. Alexander
University of Maryland, College Park
READING
PRIOR KNOWLEDGE, BELIEFS, AND LEARNING

Richard L. Alfred
University of Michigan
FINANCE, HIGHER EDUCATION
COMMUNITY AND JUNIOR COLLEGES

Dwight W. Allen
Old Dominion University
MICROTEACHING

Diane Allensworth
Kent State University
HEALTH EDUCATION, SCHOOL

Philip G. Altbach
Boston College
HIGHER EDUCATION, INTERNATIONAL ISSUES
HIGHER EDUCATION IN CONTEXT

Donna E. Alvermann
University of Georgia
LITERACY AND READING

Jo-Ann Amadeo
University of Maryland
INTERNATIONAL ASSESSMENTS
POLITICAL DEMOCRACY AND THE IEA STUDY OF
CIVIC EDUCATION

Gordon M. Ambach
Council of Chief State School Officers and
New York State Commissioner of Education
COUNCIL OF CHIEF STATE SCHOOL OFFICERS

John Ambrosio
University of Washington, Seattle
MULTICULTURAL EDUCATION

Lorin W. Anderson
University of South Carolina
BLOOM, B. S.
HAVIGHURST, ROBERT J.
PRESSEY, SIDNEY L.
TAXONOMIES OF EDUCATIONAL OBJECTIVES

Robert H. Anderson
NONGRADED SCHOOLS

Ronald E. Anderson
University of Minnesota, Minneapolis
INTERNATIONAL ASSESSMENTS
IEA STUDY OF TECHNOLOGY IN THE CLASSROOM

Richard I. Arends
Central Connecticut State University
INSTRUCTIONAL STRATEGIES

Gordon B. Arnold
  Montserrat College of Art
  UNIVERSITY PRESSES

Robert F. Arnove
  Indiana University
  INTERNATIONAL ISSUES OF SOCIAL MOBILITY OF
    UNDERPRIVILEGED GROUPS

Brenda Ashford
  American Association of Collegiate Registrars
    and Admissions Officers
  ACADEMIC CALENDARS

John G. Augenblick
  Augenblick and Myers, Inc.
  FINANCIAL SUPPORT OF SCHOOLS
    CAPITAL OUTLAY IN LOCAL SCHOOL SYSTEMS

Carol J. Auster
  Franklin and Marshall College
  ETHICS
    HIGHER EDUCATION

Bill Ayers
  University of Illinois, Chicago
  HORTON, MYLES

Charles Baffi
  Virginia Polytechnic Institute and State
    University
  HEALTH SERVICES
    SCHOOL

Richard D. Bagin
  National School Public Relations Association
  NATIONAL SCHOOL PUBLIC RELATIONS
    ASSOCIATION

Ronald C. Baird
  National Sea Grant College Program
  SEA GRANT PROGRAM

David P. Baker
  The Pennsylvania State University
  INTERNATIONAL EDUCATION STATISTICS
    THE USE OF INDICATORS TO EVALUATE THE
      CONDITION OF EDUCATION SYSTEMS

Eva L. Baker
  University of California, Los Angeles
  STANDARDS FOR STUDENT LEARNING

Roger G. Baldwin
  Michigan State University
  FACULTY MEMBERS, PART TIME
  TECHNOLOGY IN EDUCATION
    HIGHER EDUCATION

Kathryn A. Balink
  Vanderbilt University
  COLLEGE ADMISSIONS

Mark Bandas
  Vanderbilt University
  RESIDENTIAL COLLEGES

James A. Banks
  University of Washington, Seattle
  MULTICULTURAL EDUCATION

Anne K. Barkis
  Augenblick and Myers, Inc.
  FINANCIAL SUPPORT OF SCHOOLS
    CAPITAL OUTLAY IN LOCAL SCHOOL SYSTEMS

Henry Barnes
  Association of Waldorf Schools in North
    America; Anthroposophical Society in
    America
  STEINER, RUDOLF

Melissa K. Barnes
  Allegheny College
  CAREER COUNSELING IN HIGHER EDUCATION

Lisa R. Barnicoat
  University of South Carolina
  CAPSTONE COURSES IN HIGHER EDUCATION

Robert D. Barr
  Boise State University
  ALTERNATIVE SCHOOLING

Helen Vrailas Bateman
  Vanderbilt University
  ADOLESCENT PEER CULTURE
    OVERVIEW
  ADOLESCENT PEER CULTURE
    PARENTS' ROLE

Bradley James Bates
  Vanderbilt University
  COLLEGE ATHLETICS
    ATHLETIC SCHOLARSHIPS
  COLLEGE ATHLETICS
    COLLEGE STUDENTS AS ATHLETES
  COLLEGE ATHLETICS
    THE ROLE AND SCOPE OF INTERCOLLEGIATE
      ATHLETICS IN U.S. COLLEGES AND
      UNIVERSITIES

Michael T. Battista
  Kent State University
  MATHEMATICS LEARNING
    MYTHS, MYSTERIES, AND REALITIES

Patricia J. Bauer
  University of Minnesota
  MEMORY
    DEVELOPMENT OF

Sandy Baum
  Skidmore College
  COLLEGE FINANCIAL AID

Steven R. Baum
Granberg Elementary School
OPEN CLASSROOM SCHOOLS

Margaret E. Bausch
University of Kentucky
ASSISTIVE TECHNOLOGY

Melissa L. Beall
University of Northern Iowa
SPEECH AND THEATER EDUCATION

John P. Bean
Indiana University
COLLEGE STUDENT RETENTION

Albert E. Beaton
Boston College
INTERNATIONAL ASSESSMENTS
IEA THIRD INTERNATIONAL MATHEMATICS AND
SCIENCE STUDY

Barbara Beatty
Wellesley College
BLOW, SUSAN
PUTNAM, ALICE

Isabel L. Beck
University of Pittsburgh
LITERACY
VOCABULARY AND VOCABULARY LEARNING

Joseph Beckham
Florida State University
SCHOOL BOARDS
DUTIES, RESPONSIBILITIES, DECISION-MAKING,
AND LEGAL BASIS FOR LOCAL SCHOOL BOARD
POWERS

John Beineke
Arkansas State University
KILPATRICK, WILLIAM H.

Robert Belton
Vanderbilt University Law School
SEGREGATION, LEGAL ASPECTS

Camilla Benbow
Vanderbilt University
SUMMER ENRICHMENT PROGRAMS

Ron Bennett
School Services of California, Inc.
STUDENT ACTIVITIES
FINANCING

Carl Bereiter
KNOWLEDGE BUILDING

Joseph B. Berger
University of Massachusetts
HIGHER EDUCATION IN THE UNITED STATES
SYSTEM

Robert J. Berk
Vanderbilt University
JEWISH EDUCATION, UNITED STATES

Jane Bernard-Powers
San Francisco State University
TABA, HILDA

Barnett Berry
Southeast Center for Teaching Quality
TEACHER EMPLOYMENT

Sue Berryman
The World Bank
EASTERN EUROPE AND CENTRAL ASIA

Michael J. Berson
University of South Florida
SOCIAL STUDIES EDUCATION
OVERVIEW

Anthony K. Betrus
State University of New York at Potsdam
INDIVIDUALIZED INSTRUCTION

Leonard Bickman
Vanderbilt University
MENTAL HEALTH SERVICES AND CHILDREN

Katerine Bielaczyc
Harvard University
INSTRUCTIONAL DESIGN
LEARNING COMMUNITIES

Peter Biella
San Francisco State University
COLLIER, JOHN, JR.

Jeffrey Bisanz
University of Alberta
DEVELOPMENTAL THEORY
COGNITIVE AND INFORMATION PROCESSING

Daniel Bjork
St. Mary's University
SKINNER, B. F.

April Bleske-Rechek
Vanderbilt University
INTELLIGENCE
MEASUREMENT

Gregory S. Blimling
Appalachian State University
COLLEGE AND UNIVERSITY RESIDENCE HALLS
LIVING AND LEARNING CENTER RESIDENCE HALLS

Harland G. Bloland
University of Miami
AMERICAN COUNCIL ON EDUCATION
AMERICAN ASSOCIATION OF STATE COLLEGES AND
UNIVERSITIES
ASSOCIATION OF AMERICAN UNIVERSITIES
NATIONAL ASSOCIATION OF INDEPENDENT
COLLEGES AND UNIVERSITIES
NATIONAL ASSOCIATION OF STATE UNIVERSITIES
AND LAND-GRANT COLLEGES

David M. Bloome
Vanderbilt University
LANGUAGE AND EDUCATION
LITERACY
INTERTEXTUALITY

Jackie M. Blount
Iowa State University
YOUNG, ELLA FLAGG

Elena Bodrova
George Mason University
DEVELOPMENTAL THEORY
VYGOTSKIAN THEORY

Bennett G. Boggs
Kentucky Council on Postsecondary
Education
BUTLER, NICHOLAS M.

Kimberly M. Bonner
University of Maryland
INTELLECTUAL PROPERTY RIGHTS

Geoffrey D. Borman
University of Wisconsin
COMPENSATORY EDUCATION
UNITED STATES

Gilbert J. Botvin
Cornell University
DRUG AND ALCOHOL ABUSE
SCHOOL

Ed Bouchard
Independent Education Consultant
READING
COMPREHENSION

Tammy Bourg
California State University, Sacramento
RESEARCH METHODS
VERBAL PROTOCOLS

Candace Perkins Bowen
Kent State University
JOURNALISM, TEACHING OF
JOURNALISM EDUCATION ASSOCIATION

B. Ann Boyce
University of Virginia
PHYSICAL EDUCATION
OVERVIEW

William Lowe Boyd
The Pennsylvania State University
WALLER, WILLARD W.
INTERGOVERNMENTAL RELATIONS IN EDUCATION

Christy Brady-Smith
Columbia University
POVERTY AND EDUCATION
CHILDREN AND ADOLESCENTS
POVERTY AND EDUCATION
OVERVIEW

Margaret Stimman Branson
Center for Civic Education
CIVICS AND CITIZENSHIP EDUCATION

Mark Bray
The University of Hong Kong
SMALL NATIONS
TUTORING
INTERNATIONAL TRENDS

Nathaniel J. Bray
Virginia Polytechnic Institute and State
University
CHIEF ACADEMIC AFFAIRS OFFICERS, COLLEGE AND
UNIVERSITY

Mary E. Brenner
University of California, Santa Barbara
MATHEMATICS LEARNING
NUMERACY AND CULTURE

William F. Brewer
University of Illinois
LEARNING THEORY
SCHEMA THEORY

Derek C. Briggs
University of California, Berkeley
TESTING
TEST PREPARATION PROGRAMS, IMPACT OF

Jeanne Brooks-Gunn
Columbia University
POVERTY AND EDUCATION
CHILDREN AND ADOLESCENTS
POVERTY AND EDUCATION
OVERVIEW

Jere Brophy
Michigan State University
SOCIAL PROMOTION

Sean Brophy
Vanderbilt University
ASSESSMENT TOOLS
TECHNOLOGY BASED

M. Christopher Brown II
The Pennsylvania State University
AFFIRMATIVE ACTION COMPLIANCE IN HIGHER
EDUCATION
AFRICAN-AMERICAN STUDIES

Mary T. Brownell
University of Florida
SPECIAL EDUCATION
PREPARATION OF TEACHERS

Anne L. Bryant
National School Boards Association
NATIONAL SCHOOL BOARDS ASSOCIATION

Glenn R. Bucher
Messiah College
BOYER, ERNEST

Francis J. Buckley
University of San Francisco
TEAM TEACHING

Kermit G. Buckner Jr.
East Carolina University
COMMENCEMENT
PRINCIPAL, SCHOOL

Juanita F. Buford
Meharry Medical College
DENTISTRY EDUCATION
MEDICAL EDUCATION

Robert V. Bullough Jr.
Brigham Young University
ALBERTY, H.B.
BODE, BOYD H.

Linda K. Bunker
University of Virginia
MOTOR LEARNING

Nicholas C. Burbules
University of Illinois, Urbana-Champaign
PHILOSOPHY OF EDUCATION
CURRENT TRENDS

Barbara B. Burn
University of Massachusetts, Amherst
STUDY ABROAD

M. Susan Burns
George Mason University
DEVELOPMENTAL THEORY
VYGOTSKIAN THEORY

Heidi Legg Burross
University of Arizona
PEER RELATIONS AND LEARNING

Timothy C. Caboni
Vanderbilt University
INSTITUTIONAL ADVANCEMENT IN HIGHER
EDUCATION

Bruce T. Caine
Vanderbilt University
MILITARY PROFESSIONAL EDUCATION SYSTEM
MILITARY TRAINING DOCTRINE, PHILOSOPHY, AND
PRACTICE
U.S. WAR COLLEGES

James Calderhead
University of Bath, England
TEACHING
METHODS FOR STUDYING

Maria Vita Calkins
University of Massachusetts
HIGHER EDUCATION IN THE UNITED STATES
SYSTEM

Carolyn M. Callahan
University of Virginia
ADVANCED PLACEMENT COURSES/EXAMS

David A. Campaigne
Georgia Southern University
CONANT, J. B.

Stephen Michael Campbell
Iowa State University
AGRICULTURAL EDUCATION

Mark Cannon
Vanderbilt University
EMPLOYMENT
EMPLOYERS' PERCEPTIONS OF EMPLOYMENT
READINESS

Colleen A. Capper
University of Wisconsin, Madison
SEXUAL ORIENTATION

Denise Cardinal
National Education Association
NATIONAL EDUCATION ASSOCIATION

John R. Carnaghi
Florida State University
RESOURCE ALLOCATION IN HIGHER EDUCATION

James C. Carper
University of South Carolina, Columbia
PRIVATE SCHOOLING
PROTESTANT SCHOOL SYSTEMS

Carole F. Cashion
Ursuline College
NURSING EDUCATION

Sharon Castle
George Mason University
INSTRUCTIONAL STRATEGIES

Elizabeth B. Castor
National Board for Professional Teaching
Standards
NATIONAL BOARD FOR PROFESSIONAL TEACHING
STANDARDS

Claudio De Moura Castro
The Advisory Council of Faculdade Pitágoras
VOCATIONAL AND TECHNICAL EDUCATION
INTERNATIONAL CONTEXT

Cynthia A. Cave
Virginia Department of Education
COMPULSORY SCHOOL ATTENDANCE

Lori J. Cavell
George Washington University
GRADUATE RECORD EXAMINATION

Marta Cehelsky
National Science Foundation
NATIONAL SCIENCE FOUNDATION

John A. Centra
Syracuse University
FACULTY TEACHING, ASSESSMENT OF

Stephen Chaikind
Gallaudet University
FEDERAL SCHOOLS AND COLLEGES

J. J. Chambliss
Rutgers University
ARISTOTLE

Marilyn J. Chambliss
University of Maryland, College Park
READING
LEARNING FROM TEXT

Jie-Qi Chen
Erikson Institute, Chicago
INTELLIGENCE
MULTIPLE INTELLIGENCES

John J. Cheslock
University of Arizona
RESEARCH GRANTS AND INDIRECT COSTS

George W. Chilcoat
Brigham Young University
MISSISSIPPI FREEDOM SCHOOLS

Laura Blackwell Clark
Sacred Heart School; Vanderbilt University
MEDIA, INFLUENCE ON CHILDREN

Richard E. Clark
University of Southern California
MEDIA AND LEARNING

Roseanne Clausen
American Speech-Language-Hearing
Association
SPEECH AND LANGUAGE IMPAIRMENT, EDUCATION
OF INDIVIDUALS WITH

Alma R. Clayton-Pedersen
Association of American Colleges and
Universities
MULTICULTURALISM IN HIGHER EDUCATION

Margaret M. Clements
Indiana University
INTERNATIONAL ISSUES OF SOCIAL MOBILITY OF
UNDERPRIVILEGED GROUPS

James Coaxum III
Rowan University
HISTORICALLY BLACK COLLEGES AND UNIVERSITIES

Marilyn Cochran-Smith
Boston College
TEACHER LEARNING COMMUNITIES

Ronald D. Cohen
Indiana University Northwest
GARY SCHOOLS

Carol L. Colbeck
The Pennsylvania State University
TEACHING AND RESEARCH, THE RELATIONSHIP
BETWEEN

Angelo Collins
Knowles Science Teaching Foundation
SCIENCE LEARNING
STANDARDS

Richard Colwell
University of Illinois
MUSIC EDUCATION
OVERVIEW

Kate Connolly
Concordia University
RECREATION PROGRAMS IN THE SCHOOLS

Clifton F. Conrad
University of Wisconsin, Madison
CURRICULUM, HIGHER EDUCATION
TRADITIONAL AND CONTEMPORARY
PERSPECTIVES
HONORS PROGRAMS IN HIGHER EDUCATION
MASTER'S DEGREE, THE

David R. Conrad
University of Vermont
BRAMELD, THEODORE

Bradley J. Cook
Utah Valley State College
ISLAM

Thomas J. Cooney
University of Georgia
MATHEMATICS EDUCATION, TEACHER
PREPARATION

Bruce S. Cooper
Fordham University
COLEMAN, JAMES S.

Harris Cooper
University of Missouri
HOMEWORK

Bruce S. Cooper
Fordham University
PUBLIC SCHOOL BUDGETING, ACCOUNTING, AND
AUDITING

David E. Copeland
University of Notre Dame
MEMORY
MENTAL MODELS

James M. Copeland
National Forensic League
YOUTH ORGANIZATIONS
NATIONAL FORENSIC LEAGUE

David S. Cordray
Vanderbilt University
RESEARCH METHODS
OVERVIEW

David P. Cordts
National Association of Secondary School
Principals
NATIONAL HONOR SOCIETY

Dinka Corkalo
University of Zagreb, Croatia
PEACE EDUCATION

Catherine Cornbleth
University at Buffalo
CURRICULUM, SCHOOL
HIDDEN CURRICULUM

Dewey G. Cornell
University of Virginia
ADOLESCENT PEER CULTURE
GANGS
JUVENILE JUSTICE SYSTEM
JUVENILE CRIME AND VIOLENCE

Lyn Corno
Columbia University
INDIVIDUAL DIFFERENCES
AFFECTIVE AND CONATIVE PROCESSES

Monica Farmer Cox
Vanderbilt University
ENGINEERING EDUCATION

Bruce C. Craig
Smithsonian Center for Education and
Museum Studies
SMITHSONIAN INSTITUTION, EDUCATION
PROGRAMS

Tena B. Crews
State University of West Georgia
BUSINESS EDUCATION
SCHOOL

Johanna V. Crighton
University of Cambridge, England
TESTING
STANDARDIZED TESTS AND EDUCATIONAL
POLICY

Christopher T. Cross
Center on Education Policy
COUNCIL FOR BASIC EDUCATION
SCHOOL REFORM
U.S. DEPARTMENT OF EDUCATION
OVERVIEW

Patricia Crosson
University of Massachusetts
FACULTY SERVICE ROLE, THE

Robert L. Crowson
Vanderbilt University
NEIGHBORHOODS
SCHOOL-LINKED SERVICES
TYPES OF SERVICES AND ORGANIZATIONAL
FORMS

Kathleen Cruikshank
Indiana University
HERBART, JOHANN
MCMURRY, CHARLES

Bárbara C. Cruz
University of South Florida
SOCIAL STUDIES EDUCATION
OVERVIEW

Judith J. Culligan
BETHUNE, MARY MCLEOD

Anne Cunningham
University of California, Berkeley
READING
VALUE OF READING ENGAGEMENT FOR
CHILDREN

Reagan Curtis
Northwestern State University of Louisiana
MATHEMATICS LEARNING
NUMERACY AND CULTURE

Willard R. Daggett
International Center for Leadership in
Education
VOCATIONAL AND TECHNICAL EDUCATION
CURRENT TRENDS

Carol Ann Dahlberg
Concordia College
FOREIGN LANGUAGE EDUCATION

David Yun Dai
State University of New York at Albany
GIFTED AND TALENTED, EDUCATION OF

Susan Dalebout
University of Virginia
HEARING IMPAIRMENT
SCHOOL PROGRAMS

D. Jack Davis
University of North Texas
ART EDUCATION
PREPARATION OF TEACHERS

Houston Davis
Austin Peay State University
ACCOUNTING SYSTEMS IN HIGHER EDUCATION
STATES AND EDUCATION
STATE GOVERNMENTS IN HIGHER EDUCATION

Gedeon O. Deák
University of California, San Diego
CATEGORIZATION AND CONCEPT LEARNING

David Dean Jr.
Columbia University
SCIENCE LEARNING
EXPLANATION AND ARGUMENTATION

Elizabeth H. DeBray
Brown University
FEDERAL EDUCATIONAL ACTIVITIES
HISTORY

Larry E. Decker
Florida Atlantic University
COMMUNITY EDUCATION

Erik De Corte
University of Leuven, Belgium
MATHEMATICS LEARNING
WORD-PROBLEM SOLVING

Magdalena H. de la Teja
Austin Community College
COLLEGE STUDENTS WITH DISABILITIES
SPECIAL LEARNING NEEDS

Marietta Del Favero
Louisiana State University
ACADEMIC DEAN, THE
FACULTY RESEARCH AND SCHOLARSHIP,
ASSESSMENT OF
ACADEMIC DISCIPLINES

Noah de Lissovoy
University of California, Los Angeles
FREIRE, PAULO

William DeLoache Jr.
Beacon Education Management, Inc.
BEACON EDUCATION MANAGEMENT, INC.

Lawrence J. Dennis
Southern Illinois University
CHILDS, JOHN L.

Laura Desimone
Vanderbilt University
RESEARCH METHODS
SCHOOL AND PROGRAM EVALUATION

Douglas M. DeWitt
Minnesota State University
SUMMER SCHOOL

Deborah DeZure
University of Michigan, Ann Arbor
CURRICULUM, HIGHER EDUCATION
INNOVATIONS IN THE UNDERGRADUATE
CURRICULUM

Katinka Dijkstra
Florida State University
LITERACY
NARRATIVE COMPREHENSION AND PRODUCTION

Anne DiPardo
University of Iowa
WRITING, TEACHING OF

Andrea A. diSessa
University of California, Berkeley
SCIENCE LEARNING
KNOWLEDGE ORGANIZATION AND
UNDERSTANDING

Carol N. Dixon
University of California, Santa Barbara
LITERACY
WRITING AND COMPOSITION
RESEARCH METHODS
QUALITATIVE AND ETHNOGRAPHIC

Beth Donaghey
Claremont McKenna College
LEARNING THEORY
HISTORICAL OVERVIEW

Saran Donahoo
  University of Illinois at Urbana-Champaign
  AFFIRMATIVE ACTION COMPLIANCE IN HIGHER
    EDUCATION

Eileen F. Donoghue
  City University of New York, College of
    Staten Island
  FAWCETT, HAROLD P.
  SMITH, DAVID EUGENE

David Dorn
  American Federation of Teachers
  INTERNATIONAL TEACHERS ASSOCIATIONS

Malcolm P. Douglass
  Claremont Graduate University
  GEOGRAPHY, TEACHING OF

Edward R. Ducharme
  University of Vermont; Drake University
  TEACHER EDUCATION
    HISTORICAL OVERVIEW

Mary K. Ducharme
  Drake University
  TEACHER EDUCATION
    HISTORICAL OVERVIEW

Karen Duderstadt
  University of California, San Francisco
  MANAGED CARE AND CHILDREN

Alan P. Duesterhaus
  Tennessee Independent Colleges and
    Universities Association
  BOARD OF TRUSTEES, COLLEGE AND UNIVERSITY
  PRESIDENCY, COLLEGE AND UNIVERSITY

Molly Black Duesterhaus
  Vanderbilt University
  GENERAL EDUCATION IN HIGHER EDUCATION
  HEALTH SERVICES
    COLLEGES AND UNIVERSITIES

Charles R. Duke
  Appalachian State University
  AMERICAN OVERSEAS SCHOOLS

Michael J. Dunkin
  University of Western Sydney, Australia
  TEACHER EDUCATION
    INTERNATIONAL PERSPECTIVE

James A. Duplass
  University of South Florida
  SOCIAL STUDIES EDUCATION
    OVERVIEW

Anthony Gary Dworkin
  University of Houston-University Park
  SOCIAL ORGANIZATION OF SCHOOLS

Jason R. Edwards
  University of Kentucky
  COLLEGE ATHLETICS
    HISTORY OF ATHLETICS IN U.S. COLLEGES AND
      UNIVERSITIES
  ELIOT, CHARLES
  HARPER, WILLIAM RAINEY
  HIGHER EDUCATION IN THE UNITED STATES
    HISTORICAL DEVELOPMENT
  JOHNS HOPKINS UNIVERSITY
  UNIVERSITY OF CHICAGO
  UNIVERSITY OF VIRGINIA

Arthur D. Efland
  The Ohio State University
  BARKAN, MANUEL
  LOWENFELD, VIKTOR

Howard Eichenbaum
  Boston University
  LEARNING
    NEUROLOGICAL FOUNDATION

David Elkind
  Tufts University
  PIAGET, JEAN

Kirsten M. Ellenbogen
  King's College, London
  MUSEUM AS AN EDUCATIONAL INSTITUTION, THE

Catherine Engstrom
  Syracuse University
  LEARNING COMMUNITIES AND THE
    UNDERGRADUATE CURRICULUM

Erwin H. Epstein
  Loyola University of Chicago
  GLOBALIZATION OF EDUCATION

Joyce L. Epstein
  Johns Hopkins University
  FAMILY, SCHOOL, AND COMMUNITY CONNECTIONS

K. Anders Ericsson
  Florida State University
  EXPERTISE
    DOMAIN EXPERTISE

Amber M. Esping
  Indiana University
  GODDARD, HENRY H.

Suzanne E. Estler
  University of Maine
  COLLEGE ATHLETICS
    NCAA RULES AND REGULATIONS

Carolyn M. Evertson
  Vanderbilt University
  CLASSROOM MANAGEMENT

Jenesse Wells Evertson
University of Virginia
READING
TEACHING OF

Janet Eyler
Vanderbilt University
SERVICE LEARNING
HIGHER EDUCATION

Thomas K. Fagan
The University of Memphis
PSYCHOLOGIST, SCHOOL

Gahan Fallone
Brown Medical School; E. P. Bradley Hospital
SLEEP AND CHILDREN'S PHYSICAL HEALTH

George Farkas
The Pennsylvania State University
SCHOOL READINESS

Art Farlowe
University of South Carolina
TUTORING
HIGHER EDUCATION

Joseph P. Farrell
University of Toronto
TEACHING AND LEARNING
INTERNATIONAL PERSPECTIVE
TEXTBOOKS
OVERVIEW

Alan E. Farstrup
International Reading Association
INTERNATIONAL READING ASSOCIATION

Rebecca C. Fauth
Columbia University
POVERTY AND EDUCATION
CHILDREN AND ADOLESCENTS
POVERTY AND EDUCATION
OVERVIEW

Rachelle Feiler
San Diego State University
CHILD DEVELOPMENT, STAGES OF GROWTH

Sharon Feiman-Nemser
Brandeis University
TEACHING
LEARNING TO TEACH

Leonard S. Feldt
University of Iowa
LINDQUIST, E. F.

Peter Felten
Vanderbilt University
CENTERS FOR TEACHING IMPROVEMENT IN
COLLEGES AND UNIVERSITIES

Charlie Ferguson
University of California at Berkeley
FAMILY COMPOSITION AND CIRCUMSTANCE
FOSTER CARE

Emilia Ferreiro
Departamento de Investigaciones Educativas,
Cinvestav, Mexico
LITERACY
EMERGENT LITERACY

Michael Feuer
National Academy of Sciences
NATIONAL ACADEMY OF SCIENCES

Andrew J. Finch
Vanderbilt University
INTERNATIONAL DEVELOPMENT AGENCIES AND
EDUCATION
BILATERAL AGENCIES
INTERNATIONAL DEVELOPMENT AGENCIES AND
EDUCATION
REGIONAL INSTITUTIONS
INTERNATIONAL DEVELOPMENT AGENCIES AND
EDUCATION
UNITED NATIONS AND INTERNATIONAL
AGENCIES
NEIGHBORHOODS

Dorothy E. Finnegan
The College of William and Mary
ACADEMIC LABOR MARKETS

William Firestone
Rutgers University
EDUCATIONAL ACCOUNTABILITY

Donald Fisher
University of British Columbia
CANADA

Ann E. Flanagan
RAND
TESTING
NATIONAL ACHIEVEMENT TESTS,
INTERNATIONAL

Lamont A. Flowers
University of Florida
RACE, ETHNICITY, AND CULTURE
RACIAL AND ETHNIC MINORITY STUDENTS IN
HIGHER EDUCATION

Patrick N. Foster
Central Connecticut State University
TECHNOLOGY EDUCATION

Robert A. Forsyth
University of Iowa
LINDQUIST, E. F.

Tony Fowler
Federal Interagency Committee on Education
FEDERAL INTERAGENCY COMMITTEE ON
EDUCATION

Robert D. Fox
University of Oklahoma, Norman
CONTINUING PROFESSIONAL EDUCATION
UNITED STATES

Carol Frances
Claremont Graduate University
FACULTY CONSULTING

Barry M. Franklin
Utah State University
BOBBITT, FRANKLIN

Cheryl A. Franklin
University of Virginia
LOOPING

Phyllis Franklin
Modern Language Association of America
MODERN LANGUAGE ASSOCIATION OF AMERICA

Donald J. Fraynd
University of Wisconsin, Madison
SEXUAL ORIENTATION

Debra M. Freedman
Pennsylvania State University
HOLT, JOHN
NEILL, A. S.

Sarah Warshauer Freedman
University of California, Berkeley
WRITING, TEACHING OF

Margaret Freedson-Gonzales
Harvard University
BILINGUALISM, SECOND LANGUAGE LEARNING,
AND ENGLISH AS A SECOND LANGUAGE

John Fremer
Educational Testing Services
TESTING
INTERNATIONAL STANDARDS OF TEST
DEVELOPMENT

Susan H. Frost
Emory University
ACADEMIC ADVISING IN HIGHER EDUCATION

Gary R. Galluzzo
National Board for Professional Teaching
Standards
NATIONAL BOARD FOR PROFESSIONAL TEACHING
STANDARDS

Lenore Yaffee Garcia
U.S. Department of Education
U.S. DEPARTMENT OF EDUCATION
INTERNATIONAL ROLE

Sidney L. Gardner
Children and Family Futures
SCHOOL-LINKED SERVICES
OUTCOMES

David C. Geary
University of Missouri
DEVELOPMENTAL THEORY
EVOLUTIONARY APPROACH

Dedre Gentner
Northwestern University
LEARNING
ANALOGICAL REASONING

Lisa Geraci
Washington University
MEMORY
IMPLICIT MEMORY

Elizabeth Gilbert
University of New Mexico, Gallup
SPORTS, SCHOOL
ROLE IN STUDENT'S SOCIAL AND EMOTIONAL
DEVELOPMENT

Leigh Z. Gilchrist
Vanderbilt University
DRUG AND ALCOHOL ABUSE
COLLEGE
PERSONAL AND PSYCHOLOGICAL COUNSELING AT
COLLEGES AND UNIVERSITIES
PERSONAL AND PSYCHOLOGICAL PROBLEMS OF
COLLEGE STUDENTS

Dwight E. Giles Jr.
University of Massachusetts, Boston
INTERNSHIPS IN HIGHER EDUCATION

Rick Ginsberg
Colorado State University
EDUCATION REFORM
REPORTS OF HISTORICAL SIGNIFICANCE

Drew H. Gitomer
Educational Testing Services
INDIVIDUAL DIFFERENCES
ABILITIES AND APTITUDES

Thomas E. Glass
University of Memphis
SCHOOL BOARD RELATIONS
RELATION OF SCHOOL BOARD TO THE
SUPERINTENDENT
SUPERINTENDENT OF LARGE-CITY SCHOOL SYSTEMS

Judith Glazer-Raymo
Long Island University
CONSORTIA IN HIGHER EDUCATION

Charles L. Glenn
Boston University
IMMIGRANT EDUCATION
INTERNATIONAL
IMMIGRANT EDUCATION
UNITED STATES

Don Glines
Educational Futures Projects
YEAR-ROUND EDUCATION

Shelley Goldman
Stanford University
INSTRUCTIONAL DESIGN
LEARNING THROUGH DESIGN

Susan R. Goldman
Vanderbilt University
LITERACY
INTERTEXTUALITY

Ellen Goldring
Vanderbilt University
JEWISH EDUCATION, UNITED STATES

Fredrick L. Golladay
The World Bank
POPULATION AND EDUCATION

Allan E. Goodman
Institute of International Education
INSTITUTE OF INTERNATIONAL EDUCATION

Elana B. Gordis
University of Southern California
VIOLENCE, CHILDREN'S EXPOSURE TO
GENERAL EFFECTS

Howard R. D. Gordon
Marshall University
VOCATIONAL AND TECHNICAL EDUCATION
HISTORY OF

Arthur Graesser
University of Memphis
DISCOURSE
COGNITIVE PERSPECTIVE
INSTRUCTIONAL DESIGN
PEDAGOGICAL AGENTS AND TUTORS

Sandra Graham
University of California, Los Angeles
MOTIVATION
OVERVIEW

Michael A. Grandillo
Tiffin University
COLLEGE RECRUITMENT PRACTICES
SOCIAL FRATERNITIES AND SORORITIES

Brad Gray
Vanderbilt University
VOLUNTEER WORK

John Gray
School Services of California, Inc.
STUDENT ACTIVITIES
FINANCING

Madison Gray
Vanderbilt University
LAW SCHOOL ADMISSION TEST

Vincent Greaney
The World Bank
INTERNATIONAL ASSESSMENTS
IEA AND OECD STUDIES OF READING LITERACY

Gilbert R. Gredler
University of South Carolina
BINET, ALFRED

Margaret E. Gredler
University of South Carolina
ERIKSON, ERIK
VYGOTSKY, LEV

Christopher S. Greeley
Vanderbilt University
RISK BEHAVIORS
SMOKING AND ITS EFFECT ON CHILDREN'S
HEALTH

Judith L. Green
University of California, Santa Barbara
RESEARCH METHODS
QUALITATIVE AND ETHNOGRAPHIC

Brian Greer
San Diego State University
MATHEMATICS LEARNING
WORD-PROBLEM SOLVING

Kenneth W. Griffin
Cornell University
DRUG AND ALCOHOL ABUSE
SCHOOL

Thomas D. Griffin
University of Illinois at Chicago
LEARNING
REASONING

Pamela L. Grossman
Stanford University
ENGLISH EDUCATION
PREPARATION OF TEACHERS

Pamela J. Grotz
National PTA
NATIONAL PTA

John W. Groutt
>   The Pell Institute for the Study of
>   Opportunity in Higher Education; University
>   of Maryland
>   UPWARD BOUND

Thomas R. Guskey
>   University of Kentucky
>   GRADING SYSTEMS
>   SCHOOL

Gerald L. Gutek
>   Loyola University of Chicago
>   ELEMENTARY EDUCATION
>   HISTORY OF
>   FROEBEL, FRIEDRICH
>   PESTALOZZI, JOHANN

James W. Guthrie
>   Vanderbilt University
>   EDUCATIONAL POLICY, UNITED STATES
>   NO CHILD LEFT BEHIND ACT OF 2001
>   STATE EDUCATIONAL SYSTEMS

William N. Haarlow
>   Independent Scholar, Chicago, Illinois
>   COMMON SCHOOL MOVEMENT

Thomas J. Haas
>   U.S. Coast Guard Academy
>   MILITARY ACADEMIES
>   U.S. COAST GUARD ACADEMY

Martin Haberman
>   University of Wisconsin, Milwaukee
>   STRATEMEYER, FLORENCE
>   URBAN EDUCATION

Paul D. Hain
>   Vanderbilt University Medical Center
>   NUTRITION AND CHILDREN'S PHYSICAL HEALTH

Horace R. Hall
>   University of Illinois at Chicago
>   DU BOIS, W. E. B.

Daniel P. Hallahan
>   University of Virginia
>   ATTENTION DEFICIT HYPERACTIVITY DISORDER
>   HEARING IMPAIRMENT
>   LEARNING DISABILITIES, EDUCATION OF
>   INDIVIDUALS WITH
>   TEACHING METHODS
>   VISUAL IMPAIRMENTS, EDUCATION OF
>   INDIVIDUALS WITH

Denise Dion Hallfors
>   University of North Carolina
>   RISK BEHAVIORS
>   HIV/AIDS AND ITS IMPACT ON ADOLESCENTS

Carolyn Tucker Halpern
>   University of North Carolina
>   RISK BEHAVIORS
>   HIV/AIDS AND ITS IMPACT ON ADOLESCENTS

Diane F. Halpern
>   Claremont McKenna College
>   LEARNING THEORY
>   HISTORICAL OVERVIEW

Florence A. Hamrick
>   Iowa State University
>   FACULTY ROLES AND RESPONSIBILITIES

Jane Hansen
>   University of Virginia
>   READING
>   TEACHING OF

Janet S. Hansen
>   Committee for Economic Development
>   EARLY CHILDHOOD EDUCATION
>   OVERVIEW

Hobart L. Harmon
>   Education Consultant
>   RURAL EDUCATION
>   OVERVIEW

Edward D. Harris Jr.
>   Stanford University; Alpha Omega Alpha
>   HONOR SOCIETIES
>   ALPHA OMEGA ALPHA

Amy Harris-Solomon
>   Vanderbilt University
>   CHILD CARE
>   AVAILABILITY AND QUALITY
>   CHILD CARE
>   COST AND FINANCING

Ted S. Hasselbring
>   University of Kentucky
>   ASSISTIVE TECHNOLOGY

Giyoo Hatano
>   University of the Air
>   EXPERTISE
>   ADAPTIVE EXPERTISE

Willis D. Hawley
>   University of Maryland, College Park
>   TEACHER UNIONS
>   INFLUENCE ON INSTRUCTION AND OTHER
>   EDUCATIONAL PRACTICES

Jennifer Grant Haworth
>   Loyola University of Chicago
>   HONORS PROGRAMS IN HIGHER EDUCATION
>   MASTER'S DEGREE, THE

Mary C. Hayden
University of Bath, England
INTERNATIONAL BACCALAUREATE DIPLOMA

David E. Hayes-Bautista
University of California, Los Angeles
RACE, ETHNICITY, AND CULTURE
LATINO GROWTH

Katherine Taylor Haynes
Vanderbilt University
NONGOVERNMENTAL ORGANIZATIONS AND
FOUNDATIONS
INTERNATIONAL DEVELOPMENT AGENCIES AND
EDUCATION
REGIONAL INSTITUTIONS
INTERNATIONAL DEVELOPMENT AGENCIES AND
EDUCATION
UNITED NATIONS AND INTERNATIONAL
AGENCIES

Marilyn Heath
HUNTER, MADELINE CHEEK

John M. Heffron
Soka University of America
LINCOLN SCHOOL

Patricia A. Helland
Vanderbilt University
DOCTORAL DEGREE, THE
GRADUATE SCHOOL TRAINING
POSTDOCTORAL EDUCATION

Donald E. Heller
The Pennsylvania State University
FEDERAL FUNDS FOR HIGHER EDUCATION

Joshua A. Hemmerich
University of Illinois, Chicago
LITERACY
LEARNING FROM MULTIMEDIA SOURCES

Jennifer Henderlong
Reed College
MOTIVATION
INSTRUCTION

Leslie Henrickson
University of California, Los Angeles; Second
Site Consulting for Education
COMMERCE OF EDUCATION

Jean M. Henscheid
University of Idaho
CAPSTONE COURSES IN HIGHER EDUCATION

Joan L. Herman
CRESST, University of California, Los Angeles
ASSESSMENT
PORTFOLIO ASSESSMENT

Carolyn D. Herrington
Florida State University
IMPACT AID, PUBLIC LAWS 815 AND 874
STATE DEPARTMENTS OF EDUCATION
ROLE AND FUNCTION

Frederick M. Hess
University of Virginia
HOME SCHOOLING

Brian Lloyd Heuser
Vanderbilt University
DIVINITY STUDIES

Stephen P. Heyneman
Vanderbilt University
INTERNATIONAL EDUCATION
MISCONDUCT IN EDUCATION
SOCIAL COHESION AND EDUCATION

Suzanne Hidi
University of Toronto
READING
INTEREST

Stephen J. Hiemstra
Purdue University
SCHOOL FOOD PROGRAMS

Erik Hilgendorf
Vanderbilt University
MIDDLE EAST AND NORTH AFRICA

E. D. Hirsch Jr.
University of Virginia
CURRICULUM, SCHOOL
CORE KNOWLEDGE CURRICULUM

Amy Hirschy
Vanderbilt University
CARNEGIE CLASSIFICATION SYSTEM, THE
NATIONAL MERIT SCHOLARSHIPS

Peter Hlebowitsh
University of Iowa
BENJAMIN, H.R.W.
HARRIS, WILLIAM T.
TYLER, RALPH W.

Cindy E. Hmelo-Silver
Rutgers University
INSTRUCTIONAL DESIGN
PROBLEM-BASED LEARNING

Elaine Ho
University of Alberta
DEVELOPMENTAL THEORY
COGNITIVE AND INFORMATION PROCESSING

Hsiu-Zu Ho
University of California, Santa Barbara
INDIVIDUAL DIFFERENCES
ETHNICITY
INDIVIDUAL DIFFERENCES
GENDER EQUITY AND SCHOOLING

Sui Chu Esther Ho
The Chinese University of Hong Kong
SOCIAL CAPITAL AND EDUCATION

Harold Hodgkinson
Center for Demographic Policy
YOUTH DEMOGRAPHIC TRENDS

Robert R. Hoffman
Florida State University
EXPERTISE
DOMAIN EXPERTISE

Janet M. Holdsworth
University of Minnesota
TITLE IX
INTERCOLLEGIATE ATHLETICS
TITLE IX
SCHOOL SPORTS

Thomas W. Holdsworth
SkillsUSA-VICA
YOUTH ORGANIZATIONS
SKILLSUSA-VICA

Brian Holland
Government Partnerships, Frontline Global
Resources
CONTINUING PROFESSIONAL EDUCATION
INTERNATIONAL CORPORATIONS

Mary S. Holm
University of Virginia
LOOPING

Donald B. Holsinger
Brigham Young University
SECONDARY EDUCATION
INTERNATIONAL ISSUES

Thomas B. Horton
University of South Carolina
MANN, HORACE

Don Hossler
Indiana University
COLLEGE SEARCH AND SELECTION
ENROLLMENT MANAGEMENT IN HIGHER
EDUCATION

Paul D. Houston
American Association of School
Administrators
AMERICAN ASSOCIATION OF SCHOOL
ADMINISTRATORS
SUPERINTENDENT OF SCHOOLS

Kenneth R. Howey
University of Wisconsin, Milwaukee
ELEMENTARY EDUCATION
PREPARATION OF TEACHERS

Anita Woolfolk Hoy
The Ohio State University
EDUCATIONAL PSYCHOLOGY

Wayne K. Hoy
The Ohio State University
SCHOOL CLIMATE

Bruce W. Hozeski
Ball State University
HONOR SOCIETIES
LAMBDA IOTA TAU

Angela Huang
University of North Carolina, Chapel Hill
IMMUNIZATION AND CHILDREN'S PHYSICAL
HEALTH
RISK BEHAVIORS
SEXUALLY TRANSMITTED DISEASES

Kathryn Dey Huggett
University of Wisconsin, Madison
CURRICULUM, HIGHER EDUCATION
TRADITIONAL AND CONTEMPORARY
PERSPECTIVES

Dana Hughes
University of California, San Francisco
HEALTH CARE AND CHILDREN
MANAGED CARE AND CHILDREN

Katherine L. Hughes
Columbia University
EMPLOYMENT
GENERAL IMPACT ON STUDENTS
EMPLOYMENT
REASONS STUDENTS WORK

Michelle Hughes
James Madison University
MENTORING

William G. Huitt
Valdosta University
CHARACTER DEVELOPMENT

Debra Humphreys
Association of American Colleges and
Universities
ASSOCIATION OF AMERICAN COLLEGES AND
UNIVERSITIES

E. Stephen Hunt
National Library
ACCREDITATION IN AN INTERNATIONAL CONTEXT,
HIGHER EDUCATION

Thomas C. Hunt
University of Dayton
PRIVATE SCHOOLING

Mary Stuart Hunter
University of South Carolina
COLLEGE SEMINARS FOR FIRST-YEAR STUDENTS

Philo Hutcheson
Georgia State University
ACADEMIC FREEDOM AND TENURE
AMERICAN ASSOCIATION OF UNIVERSITY
    PROFESSORS
BOWEN, HOWARD

Cynthia Hynd
University of Georgia
READING
    CONTENT AREAS

David G. Imig
American Association of Colleges for Teacher
    Education
AMERICAN ASSOCIATION OF COLLEGES FOR
    TEACHER EDUCATION

Scott R. Imig
University of Virginia
TEACHER EVALUATION
    OVERVIEW

Marcia Invernizzi
University of Virginia
READING
    TEACHING OF

Bonita Iritani
University of North Carolina
RISK BEHAVIORS
    HIV/AIDS AND ITS IMPACT ON ADOLESCENTS

M. René Islas
Council for Basic Education
COUNCIL FOR BASIC EDUCATION
SCHOOL REFORM
U.S. DEPARTMENT OF EDUCATION
    OVERVIEW

Irene V. Jackson-Brown
NTL Institute for Applied Behavioral Science
NTL INSTITUTE FOR APPLIED BEHAVIORAL SCIENCE

Stacy A. Jacob
Indiana University
LIBERAL ARTS COLLEGES

Robert Jaeger
U.S. Department of Education
SPECIAL EDUCATION
    INTERNATIONAL CONTEXT

Jennifer J. Jakubecy
University of Virginia
SPECIAL EDUCATION
    CURRENT TRENDS
SPECIAL EDUCATION
    HISTORY OF

Dean T. Jamison
University of California, Los Angeles
HEALTH AND EDUCATION

Barbara J. Johnson
University of New Orleans
FACULTY DIVERSITY

Bonnie C. Johnson
University of Kentucky
INTERGOVERNMENTAL RELATIONS IN EDUCATION

Christopher Johnston
University of California, Santa Barbara
LITERACY
    WRITING AND COMPOSITION

J. Howard Johnston
University of South Florida
SOCIAL STUDIES EDUCATION
    OVERVIEW

Donna Redmond Jones
University of Maryland, College Park
TEACHER UNIONS
    INFLUENCE ON INSTRUCTION AND OTHER
        EDUCATIONAL PRACTICES

Jane A. DeShong Jones
SkillsUSA-VICA
YOUTH ORGANIZATIONS
    SKILLSUSA-VICA

Lisa M. Jones
University of Minnesota, Minneapolis
UNIVERSITY-INDUSTRIAL RESEARCH
    COLLABORATION

Roger E. Jones
Lynchburg City Schools
STUDENT ACTIVITIES
    OVERVIEW

Gerald W. Jorgenson
John Carroll University
GRAY, WILLIAM SCOTT

Troy R. Justesen
U.S. Department of Education
COLLEGE STUDENTS WITH DISABILITIES
    ACCOMMODATING
PEOPLE WITH DISABILITIES, FEDERAL PROGRAMS
    TO ASSIST

Melissa Kachan
University of Alberta
DEVELOPMENTAL THEORY
    COGNITIVE AND INFORMATION PROCESSING

James M. Kauffman
University of Virginia
EMOTIONALLY DISTURBED, EDUCATION OF
PHYSICAL DISABILITIES, EDUCATION OF
    INDIVIDUALS WITH
SPECIAL EDUCATION
    CURRENT TRENDS
SPECIAL EDUCATION
    HISTORY OF

Thomas Kellaghan
St. Patrick's College, Dublin
INTERNATIONAL ASSESSMENTS
    IEA AND OECD STUDIES OF READING LITERACY

Luke E. Kelly
University of Virginia
ADAPTED PHYSICAL EDUCATION

Vera Kemeny
Northwestern University
MATHEMATICS LEARNING
    GEOMETRY

Nancy Kendall
Stanford University
EDUCATION DEVELOPMENT PROJECTS

Louise Kennelly
New American Schools
NEW AMERICAN SCHOOLS

Lori Kenschaft
PALMER, ALICE FREEMAN

George Kersey Jr.
Phi Delta Kappa International
HONOR SOCIETIES
    PHI DELTA KAPPA INTERNATIONAL

Trina C. Kershaw
University of Illinois-Chicago
CREATIVITY

Maureen Kessenich
Loyola University Chicago
DEVELOPMENTAL THEORY
    HISTORICAL OVERVIEW

Adrianna Kezar
University of Maryland
GOVERNANCE AND DECISION-MAKING IN
    COLLEGES AND UNIVERSITIES

Barbara Z. Kiefer
Columbia University
CHILDREN'S LITERATURE

Edward Kifer
University of Kentucky
HUTCHINS, ROBERT

Sally B. Kilgore
Modern Red SchoolHouse Institute
MODERN RED SCHOOLHOUSE

Anneka L. Kindler
The George Washington University
MIGRANTS, EDUCATION OF

Kenneth King
University of Edinburgh
VOCATIONAL SCHOOL FALLACY

Douglas B. Kirby
ETR Associates
RISK BEHAVIORS
    TEEN PREGNANCY

David W. Kirkpatrick
Pennsylvania State Education Association
TEACHER UNIONS
    OVERVIEW

Joanna Kister
Consultant, Education and Workforce
    Development
STATE DEPARTMENTS OF EDUCATION
VOCATIONAL EDUCATION

Kenneth F. Kitchell Jr.
University of Massachusetts
LATIN IN SCHOOLS, TEACHING OF

Terry L. Kline
Eastern Kentucky University
DRIVER EDUCATION

Kathy Klock
Bill and Melinda Gates Foundation
EDUCATIONAL LEADERSHIP

Clifford E. Knapp
Northern University
OUTDOOR AND ENVIRONMENTAL EDUCATION

Michael Knoll
Schloss-Schule Kirchberg, Germany
HAHN, KURT
KERSCHENSTEINER, GEORG
PROJECT METHOD
PROSSER, CHARLES
SNEDDEN, DAVID

Paul Koehler
WestEd Regional Education Laboratory
PUBLIC EDUCATION, CRITICISM OF

Thierry G. Kolpin
Stanford University
GUIDANCE AND COUNSELING, SCHOOL

Janet L. Kolodner
    Georgia Institute of Technology
    INSTRUCTIONAL DESIGN
        CASE-BASED REASONING

Julia E. Koppich
    Julia E. Koppich and Associates
    OUT-OF-SCHOOL INFLUENCES AND ACADEMIC
        SUCCESS
    SHANKER, ALBERT

Timothy Koschmann
    Southern Illinois University
    COMPUTER-SUPPORTED COLLABORATIVE LEARNING

Richard J. Kraft
    University of Colorado, Boulder
    SERVICE LEARNING
        SCHOOL

David R. Krathwohl
    Syracuse University
    TAXONOMIES OF EDUCATIONAL OBJECTIVES

Ken Krehbiel
    National Council of Teachers of Mathematics
    NATIONAL COUNCIL OF TEACHERS OF
        MATHEMATICS

Craig Kridel
    University of South Carolina
    EIGHT-YEAR STUDY
    HARVARD UNIVERSITY
    TAYLOR, HAROLD

Robert F. Kronick
    University of Tennessee
    FULL-SERVICE SCHOOLS

John D. Krumboltz
    Stanford University
    GUIDANCE AND COUNSELING, SCHOOL

Deanna Kuhn
    Columbia University
    SCIENCE LEARNING
        EXPLANATION AND ARGUMENTATION

Patrick C. Kyllonen
    Educational Testing Services
    INDIVIDUAL DIFFERENCES
        ABILITIES AND APTITUDES

Jeffrey A. Lackney
    University of Wisconsin, Madison
    SCHOOL FACILITIES
        OVERVIEW

Berta Vigil Laden
    University of Toronto
    AMERICAN ASSOCIATION OF COMMUNITY
        COLLEGES
    HISPANIC-SERVING COLLEGES AND UNIVERSITIES
    TRIBAL COLLEGES AND UNIVERSITIES

Susanne P. Lajoie
    McGill University
    MATHEMATICS LEARNING
        LEARNING TOOLS

Teruni Lamberg
    Vanderbilt University
    MATHEMATICS LEARNING
        NUMBER SENSE

Judith J. Lambrecht
    University of Minnesota
    BUSINESS EDUCATION
        PREPARATION OF TEACHERS

Mary Lamon
    University of Toronto
    LEARNING THEORY
        CONSTRUCTIVIST APPROACH

Roderic R. Land
    University of Illinois, Urbana-Champaign
    AFRICAN-AMERICAN STUDIES

Kurt Landgraf
    Educational Testing Service
    EDUCATIONAL TESTING SERVICE

Timothy J. Landrum
    University of Virginia
    EMOTIONALLY DISTURBED, EDUCATION OF

Janet Fentress Laster
    Ohio State University
    FAMILY AND CONSUMER SCIENCES EDUCATION

Kathy Howard Latrobe
    University of Oklahoma
    SCHOOL LIBRARIES

Lisa R. Lattuca
    The Pennsylvania State University
    CURRICULUM, HIGHER EDUCATION
        NATIONAL REPORTS ON THE UNDERGRADUATE
            CURRICULUM
        INTERDISCIPLINARY COURSES AND MAJORS IN
            HIGHER EDUCATION

Nancy C. Lavigne
    University of Pittsburgh
    MATHEMATICS LEARNING
        LEARNING TOOLS

Janet H. Lawrence
University of Michigan
FACULTY PERFORMANCE OF RESEARCH AND
SCHOLARSHIP

Stephen B. Lawton
Northern Arizona University
STATES AND EDUCATION
STATE ADMINISTRATIVE SERVICES IN EDUCATION

Margaret D. LeCompte
University of Colorado-Boulder
SOCIAL ORGANIZATION OF SCHOOLS

Carol D. Lee
Northwestern University
LITERACY AND CULTURE

Stephanie D. Lee
Union University
STUDENT ORIENTATION PROGRAMS

James I. Lengle
Georgetown University
HONOR SOCIETIES
PI SIGMA ALPHA

Timothy Leonard
Saint Xavier University
AUGUSTINE, ST.

Deborah J. Leong
George Mason University
DEVELOPMENTAL THEORY
VYGOTSKIAN THEORY

Mark R. Lepper
Stanford University
MOTIVATION
INSTRUCTION

Nancy Lesko
Columbia University
HALL, G. STANLEY

Henry M. Levin
Columbia University
ACCELERATED SCHOOLS
COST EFFECTIVENESS IN EDUCATION

Joel R. Levin
University of Arizona
MNEMONIC STRATEGIES AND TECHNIQUES

Marsha Levine
National Council for Accreditation of Teacher
Education
PROFESSIONAL DEVELOPMENT SCHOOLS

Keith M. Lewin
University of Sussex, England
EAST ASIA AND THE PACIFIC

Joy W. Lewis
WestEd Regional Education Laboratory
PUBLIC EDUCATION, CRITICISM OF

Betty J. Liebovich
University of Illinois at Urbana-Champaign
EARLY CHILDHOOD EDUCATION
PREPARATION OF TEACHERS

Jerry A. Ligon
National-Louis University
MISSISSIPPI FREEDOM SCHOOLS

Carrie W. Linder
University of South Carolina
COLLEGE SEMINARS FOR FIRST-YEAR STUDENTS

Alfred A. Lindseth
Sutherland, Asbill, and Brennan, LLP
CONSTITUTIONAL REQUIREMENTS GOVERNING
AMERICAN EDUCATION

Marcia Linn
University of California, Berkeley
SCIENCE LEARNING
TOOLS

Deandra Little
Vanderbilt University
FUTURE FACULTY PREPARATION PROGRAMS

Valinda Littlefield
University of South Carolina
CLARK, SEPTIMA POINSETTE
JEANES TEACHERS

Jeffrey Loewenstein
Northwestern University
LEARNING
ANALOGICAL REASONING

Paulo N. Lopes
Yale University
INTELLIGENCE
EMOTIONAL INTELLIGENCE

Catherine Gavin Loss
University of Virginia
PROGRESSIVE EDUCATION

Christopher P. Loss
University of Virginia
COLLEGES AND UNIVERSITIES, ORGANIZATIONAL
STRUCTURE OF
PROGRESSIVE EDUCATION

Patrick Love
New York University
ADJUSTMENT TO COLLEGE
GAY AND LESBIAN STUDIES

Chris Lowber
Vanderbilt University
MATHEMATICS LEARNING
NUMBER SENSE

John W. Lowery
University of South Carolina
RISK MANAGEMENT IN HIGHER EDUCATION

David Lubinski
Vanderbilt University
INTELLIGENCE
MEASUREMENT

Ton Luijten
International Association for Educational
Assessment
INTERNATIONAL ASSESSMENTS
INTERNATIONAL ASSOCIATION FOR
EDUCATIONAL ASSESSMENT

Pamela B. Lutz
AEL, Inc.
REGIONAL LABORATORIES AND RESEARCH AND
DEVELOPMENT CENTERS

Susan L. Lytle
University of Pennsylvania
TEACHER LEARNING COMMUNITIES

William R. Maas
Centers for Disease Control and Prevention
DENTAL HEALTH AND CHILDREN

Victoria-María MacDonald
Florida State University
IMPACT AID, PUBLIC LAWS 815 AND 874

Douglas Mac Iver
Johns Hopkins University
MIDDLE SCHOOLS

Reynaldo F. Macías
University of California, Los Angeles
LANGUAGE MINORITY STUDENTS
IMPACT ON EDUCATION
LANGUAGE MINORITY STUDENTS
SCOPE

Linda J. Mack
University of Wisconsin, Milwaukee
SCHOOL-BASED DECISION-MAKING

Padraic MacLeish
Deep Springs College
MEIKLEJOHN, ALEXANDER

Brian MacWhinney
Carnegie Mellon University
LANGUAGE ACQUISITION

Rachel M. Madsen
California Institute of Technology
COLLEGE ATHLETICS
INTRAMURAL ATHLETICS IN U.S. COLLEGES AND
UNIVERSITIES

William H. Maehl
The Fielding Graduate Institute
LIFELONG LEARNING
NONTRADITIONAL STUDENTS IN HIGHER
EDUCATION

Gene I. Maeroff
Columbia University
CARNEGIE UNITS

Joseph P. Magliano
Northern Illinois University
LEARNING
CAUSAL REASONING

Robert M. Malina
Michigan State University
SPORTS, SCHOOL
OVERVIEW

Heinz Mandl
University of Munich, Germany
KNOWLEDGE MANAGEMENT

Gayla Margolin
University of Southern California
VIOLENCE, CHILDREN'S EXPOSURE TO
GENERAL EFFECTS

Elizabeth J. Marsh
Washington University
MEMORY
MYTHS, MYSTERIES, AND REALITIES

J. Dan Marshall
Pennsylvania State University
HOLT, JOHN
NEILL, A. S.

Robert Allen Martin
Iowa State University
AGRICULTURAL EDUCATION

Elizabeth A. Martinez
University of Virginia
HEARING IMPAIRMENT
TEACHING METHODS
LEARNING DISABILITIES, EDUCATION OF
INDIVIDUALS WITH

John Maslyn
Vanderbilt University
EMPLOYMENT
EMPLOYERS' PERCEPTIONS OF EMPLOYMENT
READINESS

Patricia G. Mathes
University of Texas, Houston
READING DISABILITIES

Alexei G. Matveev
College of William and Mary
FACULTY AS ENTREPRENEURS

Richard E. Mayer
University of California, Santa Barbara
LEARNING
PROBLEM SOLVING

Bruce McCandliss
Cornell University
BRAIN-BASED EDUCATION

Jane McCarthy
University of Nevada, Las Vegas
ELEMENTARY EDUCATION
CURRENT TRENDS

Mary McCaslin
University of Arizona
PEER RELATIONS AND LEARNING

N. L. McCaslin
The Ohio State University
VOCATIONAL AND TECHNICAL EDUCATION
PREPARATION OF TEACHERS

Shederick A. McClendon
Vanderbilt University
RACE, ETHNICITY, AND CULTURE
RACIAL AND ETHNIC MINORITY STUDENTS IN
HIGHER EDUCATION

Jacquelyn McCroskey
University of Southern California
FAMILY SUPPORT SERVICES
OVERVIEW

Steven A. McFadyen-Ketchum
Vanderbilt University
AGGRESSIVE BEHAVIOR

Margaret G. McKeown
University of Pittsburgh
LITERACY
VOCABULARY AND VOCABULARY LEARNING

Peter McLaren
University of California, Los Angeles
FREIRE, PAULO

Timothy J. McManus
National Association of Secondary School
Principals
NATIONAL ASSOCIATION OF SECONDARY SCHOOL
PRINCIPALS

Danielle S. McNamara
Old Dominion University
LEARNING
KNOWLEDGE ACQUISITION, REPRESENTATION,
AND ORGANIZATION

Robert F. McNergney
University of Virginia
TEACHER
TEACHER EVALUATION
OVERVIEW

Anna Marie Medina
University of Southern California
VIOLENCE, CHILDREN'S EXPOSURE TO
GENERAL EFFECTS

Howard D. Mehlinger
Indiana University
TECHNOLOGY IN EDUCATION
SCHOOL

M. David Merrill
Utah State University
INSTRUCTIONAL DESIGN
DIRECT INSTRUCTION

Debbie Miller
Vanderbilt Institute for Public Policy Studies
CHILD ABUSE AND NEGLECT
FAMILY COMPOSITION AND CIRCUMSTANCE
OVERVIEW
VIOLENCE, CHILDREN'S EXPOSURE TO
DOMESTIC VIOLENCE

Janet L. Miller
Columbia University
MORRISON, HENRY C.
NEWLON, JESSE
RICE, JOSEPH MAYER

Catherine M. Millett
University of Michigan, Ann Arbor
GRADUATE STUDY IN EDUCATION

Henry L. Minton
University of Windsor
TERMAN, LEWIS

Susan L. Mintz
University of Virginia
SECONDARY EDUCATION
HISTORY OF

Murray Mitchell
University of South Carolina
PHYSICAL EDUCATION
PREPARATION OF TEACHERS

Dorothy I. Mitstifer
Kappa Omicron Nu Honor Society
HONOR SOCIETIES
KAPPA OMICRON NU

Gregory Mixon
University of North Carolina at Charlotte
WASHINGTON, BOOKER T.

Devery R. Mock
University of Virginia
ATTENTION DEFICIT HYPERACTIVITY DISORDER
SPECIAL EDUCATION
CURRENT TRENDS
SPECIAL EDUCATION
HISTORY OF
VISUAL IMPAIRMENTS, EDUCATION OF
INDIVIDUALS WITH

Luke Moissinac
Clark University
AFFECT AND EMOTIONAL DEVELOPMENT

E. Jennifer Monaghan
Brooklyn College of The City University of
New York
CHALL, JEANNE
WEBSTER, NOAH

David H. Monk
The Pennsylvania State University
EFFICIENCY IN EDUCATION

M. Kristiina Montero
University of Georgia
LITERACY AND READING

Christopher C. Morphew
University of Kansas
RESEARCH UNIVERSITIES

Jerome E. Morris
University of Georgia
RACE, ETHNICITY, AND CULTURE
CULTURAL EXPECTATIONS AND STUDENT
LEARNING

Peter E. Morris
Lancaster University
MEMORY
STRUCTURES AND FUNCTIONS

Robert C. Morris
State University of West Georgia
GOSLIN, WILLARD E.

Frederick J. Morrison
University of Michigan
DEVELOPMENTAL THEORY
HISTORICAL OVERVIEW

Gary R. Morrison
Wayne State University
MEDIA AND LEARNING

Eric Moyen
University of Kentucky
ELIOT, CHARLES
HIGHER EDUCATION IN THE UNITED STATES
HISTORICAL DEVELOPMENT
JOHNS HOPKINS UNIVERSITY
UNIVERSITY OF CHICAGO
UNIVERSITY OF VIRGINIA

Kenneth K. Muir
National School Public Relations Association
NATIONAL SCHOOL PUBLIC RELATIONS
ASSOCIATION

Robert J. Mulvaney
University of South Carolina
WHITEHEAD, ALFRED NORTH

Meaghan E. Mundy
Vanderbilt University
HONOR SOCIETIES
PHI BETA KAPPA
HONOR SOCIETIES
SIGMA XI
HONOR SOCIETIES
TAU BETA PI

Karen Mundy
Stanford University
EDUCATION DEVELOPMENT PROJECTS

Linda L. Murphy
University of Nebraska
BUROS, OSCAR KRISEN

P. Karen Murphy
The Ohio State University
READING
PRIOR KNOWLEDGE, BELIEFS, AND LEARNING

Caryn McTighe Musil
Association of American Colleges and
Universities
MULTICULTURALISM IN HIGHER EDUCATION

Daniel C. Murrie
University of Virginia
ADOLESCENT PEER CULTURE
GANGS
JUVENILE JUSTICE SYSTEM
JUVENILE CRIME AND VIOLENCE

Robert G. Myers
Consultative Group on Early Childhood Care
and Development
EARLY CHILDHOOD EDUCATION
INTERNATIONAL CONTEXT

Na'ilah Nasir
Stanford University
LEARNING
TRANSFER OF LEARNING

Mitchell J. Nathan
University of Colorado
MATHEMATICS LEARNING
ALGEBRA

Gary Natriello
Columbia University
DROPOUTS, SCHOOL

Peter M. Neal
Corporation for Public Broadcasting
EDUCATIONAL BROADCASTING, FEDERAL SUPPORT

Murry Nelson
The Pennsylvania State University
HANNA, PAUL
RUGG, HAROLD

Stephen D. Nelson
American Association for the Advancement of
Science
FEDERAL FUNDING FOR ACADEMIC RESEARCH

Rafael Michael Nevarez
U.S. Department of Education
U.S. DEPARTMENT OF EDUCATION
INTERNATIONAL ROLE

L. Jackson Newell
Deep Springs College
CAMPBELL, ROALD F.
MEIKLEJOHN, ALEXANDER

Joseph W. Newman
University of South Alabama
JOHNSON, MARIETTA PIERCE

John Nietfeld
University of West Georgia
MEMORY
METAMEMORY

David W. Noble
University of Minnesota
CURTI, MERLE

James A. Noseworthy
General Board of Higher Education and
Ministry, The United Methodist Church
COLLEGES AND UNIVERSITIES WITH RELIGIOUS
AFFILIATIONS

Larry Nucci
University of Illinois at Chicago
MORAL DEVELOPMENT

J. Wesley Null
University of Texas
BAGLEY, WILLIAM C.

Graham Nuthall
University of Canterbury, New Zealand
DISCOURSE
CLASSROOM DISCOURSE

Philip H. Nisonoff
Emerson Public Schools
PUBLIC SCHOOL BUDGETING, ACCOUNTING, AND
AUDITING

Jean Fox O'Barr
Duke University
WOMEN'S STUDIES

Angela M. O'Donnell
Rutgers University
COOPERATIVE AND COLLABORATIVE LEARNING

Kwabena Dei Ofori-Attah
Cumberland College
BUSINESS EDUCATION
COLLEGE AND GRADUATE STUDY
INSTITUTIONAL RESEARCH IN HIGHER EDUCATION

Christine A. Ogren
University of Iowa
SHELDON, EDWARD

Stellan Ohlsson
University of Illinois-Chicago
CREATIVITY

Yukari Okamoto
University of California, Santa Barbara
MATHEMATICS LEARNING
NUMERACY AND CULTURE

Joleen R. Okun
University of Virginia
HOME SCHOOLING

Phyllis M. Olmstead
Magnet Schools of America
MAGNET SCHOOLS

Larry Olsen
New Mexico State University
HEALTH EDUCATION, SCHOOL

KerryAnn O'Meara
University of Massachusetts
FACULTY SERVICE ROLE, THE

Harold F. O'Neil Jr.
University of Southern California
STANDARDS FOR STUDENT LEARNING

Banu Öney
University of Illinois at Chicago
READING
BEGINNING READING

Kirsten A. Peterson
Allegheny College
MEDICAL COLLEGE ADMISSION TEST

N. Andrew Peterson
University of Iowa
YOUTH DEVELOPMENT PROGRAMS

Lawrence O. Picus
University of Southern California
DECISION-MAKING IN SCHOOLS, APPLYING
ECONOMIC ANALYSIS TO
FINANCIAL SUPPORT OF SCHOOLS
STATE SUPPORT
SCHOOL FACILITIES
MAINTENANCE AND MODERNIZATION OF

Bradford H. Pillow
Northern Illinois University
LEARNING
CAUSAL REASONING

Ellen E. Pinderhughes
Vanderbilt University
FAMILY COMPOSITION AND CIRCUMSTANCE
ADOPTION

Allison Pingree
Vanderbilt University
CENTERS FOR TEACHING IMPROVEMENT IN
COLLEGES AND UNIVERSITIES

Paul R. Pintrich
University of Michigan, Ann Arbor
MOTIVATION
SELF-REGULATED LEARNING

Georgine M. Pion
Vanderbilt University
RESEARCH METHODS
OVERVIEW

Barbara S. Plake
University of Nebraska
BUROS, OSCAR KRISEN

Tjeerd Plomp
University of Twente, the Netherlands
INTERNATIONAL ASSESSMENTS
INTERNATIONAL ASSOCIATION FOR THE
EVALUATION OF EDUCATIONAL ACHIEVEMENT

Jonathan A. Plucker
Indiana University
GODDARD, HENRY H.
WATSON, JOHN B.

Hudi Podolsky
Coalition of Essential Schools
COALITION OF ESSENTIAL SCHOOLS

Howard R. Pollio
University of Tennessee, Knoxville
GRADING SYSTEMS
HIGHER EDUCATION

Andrea S. Polster
Loyola University of Chicago
MASTER'S DEGREE, THE
HONORS PROGRAMS IN HIGHER EDUCATION

Diane M. Porter
NTL Institute for Applied Behavioral Science
NTL INSTITUTE FOR APPLIED BEHAVIORAL SCIENCE

Michael I. Posner
Sackler Institute, New York; University of
Oregon, Eugene
ATTENTION

Linda M. Post
University of Wisconsin, Milwaukee
ELEMENTARY EDUCATION
PREPARATION OF TEACHERS

Michael Potashnik
e-Learning Associates, LLC
INTERNATIONAL GAP IN TECHNOLOGY, THE

Russell Poulin
Western Cooperative for Educational
Telecommunications
DISTANCE LEARNING IN HIGHER EDUCATION

F. Clark Power
University of Notre Dame
KOHLBERG, LAWRENCE

Susan M. Powers
Indiana State University
TECHNOLOGY IN EDUCATION
SCHOOL

Harold Pratt
National Science Teachers Association
NATIONAL SCIENCE TEACHERS ASSOCIATION

George Psacharopoulos
Member of Parliament, Greece
ECONOMIC BENEFITS OF EDUCATION INVESTMENT,
MEASUREMENT

Brian Pusser
University of Virginia
COLLEGES AND UNIVERSITIES, ORGANIZATIONAL
STRUCTURE OF

Ralph T. Putnam
Michigan State University
TEACHING
KNOWLEDGE BASES OF

LeAnn G. Putney
  University of Nevada, Las Vegas
  RESEARCH METHODS
    QUALITATIVE AND ETHNOGRAPHIC

Linda F. Quinn
  University of Nevada, Las Vegas
  ELEMENTARY EDUCATION
    CURRENT TRENDS

Therese Quinn
  University of Illinois, Chicago
  HORTON, MYLES

Gabriel A. Radvansky
  University of Notre Dame
  MEMORY
    MENTAL MODELS

Mary Ann Rafoth
  Indiana University of Pennsylvania
  INDEPENDENT STUDY, SCHOOLS

Jason Duque Raley
  University of California, Santa Barbara
  INDIVIDUAL DIFFERENCES
    ETHNICITY

James L. Ratcliff
  Performance Associates Postsecondary
    Consultants
  ACADEMIC MAJOR, THE
  COMMUNITY COLLEGES

Charles H. Rathbone
  Wheaton College
  OPEN EDUCATION

Kerry Redican
  Virginia Polytechnic Institute and State
    University
  HEALTH SERVICES
    SCHOOL

Tony Reid
  Hansen Elementary School, Cedar Falls, Iowa
  ZIRBES, LAURA

Charles M. Reigeluth
  Indiana University
  INSTRUCTIONAL DESIGN
    OVERVIEW

Fernando Reimers
  Harvard University
  COMPENSATORY EDUCATION
    POLICIES AND PROGRAMS IN LATIN AMERICA

David Reinking
  University of Georgia
  LITERACY
    MULTIMEDIA LITERACY

K. Ann Renninger
  Swarthmore College
  EFFORT AND INTEREST

Joseph S. Renzulli
  National Research Center on the Gifted and
    Talented
  GIFTED AND TALENTED, EDUCATION OF

Katherine C. Reynolds
  University of South Carolina
  BUCHANAN, SCOTT
  RICE, JOHN A.
  ST. JOHN'S COLLEGE

John J. Rieser
  Vanderbilt University
  LEARNING
    PERCEPTUAL PROCESSES

Sara E. Rimm-Kaufman
  University of Virginia
  INFANT SCHOOLS IN ENGLAND

Christopher L. Ringwalt
  Pacific Institute for Research and Evaluation
  RISK BEHAVIORS
    DRUG USE AMONG TEENS

Patrick A. Roberts
  National-Louis University
  MACDONALD, JAMES

Terry Roberts
  National Paideia Center
  PAIDEIA PROGRAM

U. Monique Robinson-Wright
  Vanderbilt University
  STUDENT SERVICES
    COMMUNITY COLLEGES

Thomas W. Roby IV
  City Colleges of Chicago
  SCHWAB, JOSEPH

Monica Rodriguez
  Sexuality Information and Education Council
    of the United States
  SEXUALITY EDUCATION

Carlos Xavier Rodriguez
  University of Iowa
  MUSIC EDUCATION
    PREPARATION OF TEACHERS

Henry L. Roediger III
  Washington University
  MEMORY
    IMPLICIT MEMORY

Everett M. Rogers
University of New Mexico
TECHNOLOGY TRANSFER

R. Anthony Rolle
North Carolina State University
EDUCATIONAL EXPENDITURES, PROJECTING

Mary K. Rothbart
Sackler Institute, New York; University of
Oregon, Eugene
ATTENTION

Robert Rothman
Brown University
TESTING
STATEWIDE TESTING PROGRAMS

Kate Rousmaniere
Miami University
HALEY, MARGARET

Allen Ruby
Johns Hopkins University
MIDDLE SCHOOLS

Karen D. Rudolph
University of Illinois, Urbana-Champaign
STRESS AND DEPRESSION

Russell W. Rumberger
University of California, Santa Barbara
STUDENT MOBILITY

John L. Rury
DePaul University
KEPPEL, FRANCIS

Leanna Blevins Russell
University of Virginia
STRATEGIC AND LONG-RANGE PLANNING IN
HIGHER EDUCATION

Val D. Rust
University of California, Los Angeles
WESTERN EUROPE

Kevin Ryan
Boston University
MORAL EDUCATION

Mary Ryan
Institute for Experiential Learning
INTERNSHIPS IN HIGHER EDUCATION

David Sadker
American University
CLASSROOM QUESTIONS

Laura Hersh Salganik
Education Statistics Services Institute
INTERNATIONAL EDUCATION STATISTICS
OVERVIEW

Pasi J. Salhberg
University of Helsinki, Finland
EDUCATIONAL CHANGE

Peter Salovey
Yale University
INTELLIGENCE
EMOTIONAL INTELLIGENCE

Ginger Sampson
NCSL Public Affairs
NATIONAL CONFERENCE OF STATE LEGISLATURES

Ted Sanders
Education Commission of the States
EDUCATION COMMISSION OF THE STATES

Kyle J. Scafide
University of New Orleans
FACULTY DIVERSITY

Marlene Scardamalia
The Ontario Institute for Studies in Education
of the University of Toronto
KNOWLEDGE BUILDING

Ernesto Schiefelbein
Centro de Investigacion y Desarrollo de la
Educacion, Chile
LATIN AMERICA AND THE CARIBBEAN

Paulina Schiefelbein
Centro de Investigacion y Desarrollo de la
Educacion, Chile
LATIN AMERICA AND THE CARIBBEAN

Judith Ann Schiff
Yale University
YALE UNIVERSITY

Patricia A. Schmuck
Lewis and Clark College
GROUP PROCESSES IN THE CLASSROOM

Richard A. Schmuck
University of Oregon
GROUP PROCESSES IN THE CLASSROOM

Gail T. Schneider
University of Wisconsin, Milwaukee
SCHOOL-BASED DECISION-MAKING

Alan H. Schoenfeld
University of California, Berkeley
MATHEMATICS LEARNING
COMPLEX PROBLEM SOLVING

Gregory Schraw
University of Nevada, Las Vegas
MEMORY
METAMEMORY

Gwen Schroth
Texas A&M University, Commerce
SCHEDULING

William H. Schubert
University of Illinois, Chicago
HOPKINS, L. THOMAS
MACDONALD, JAMES

Daniel L. Schwartz
Stanford University
LEARNING
TRANSFER OF LEARNING

Robert A. Schwartz
Florida State University
HARVARD UNIVERSITY

John Schwille
Michigan State University
INTERNATIONAL ASSESSMENTS
POLITICAL DEMOCRACY AND THE IEA STUDY OF
CIVIC EDUCATION

Timothy David Seldin
Montessori Foundation
MONTESSORI, MARIA

Susan F. Semel
The City College of New York
DALTON SCHOOL

Priti Shah
University of Michigan
MEMORY
GRAPHICS, DIAGRAMS, AND VIDEOS

Steven B. Sheldon
Johns Hopkins University
PARENTAL INVOLVEMENT IN EDUCATION

Anuradha Shenoy
University of Maryland, College Park
INTERNATIONAL STUDENTS
THE GLOBAL COMMERCE OF HIGHER
EDUCATION

Lorrie A. Shepard
University of Colorado at Boulder
TESTING
STANDARDIZED TESTS AND HIGH-STAKES
ASSESSMENT

Peter L. Sheras
University of Virginia
RISK BEHAVIORS
SUICIDE

John Sherfesee
U.S. Air Force Academy
MILITARY ACADEMIES
U.S. AIR FORCE ACADEMY

Jody Sherman
University of Alberta
DEVELOPMENTAL THEORY
COGNITIVE AND INFORMATION PROCESSING

Sharon L. Shields
Vanderbilt University
SPORTS, SCHOOL
ROLE IN STUDENT'S SOCIAL AND EMOTIONAL
DEVELOPMENT
VOLUNTEER WORK

Catherine Dunn Shiffman
Vanderbilt University
WELFARE REFORM
EFFECTS ON FAMILIES AND CHILDREN

Smita Shukla-Mehta
University of Texas at Tyler
PHYSICAL DISABILITIES, EDUCATION OF
INDIVIDUALS WITH

Lee Shumow
Northern Illinois University
CLUBS
TUTORING
SCHOOL
LATCHKEY CHILDREN
YOUTH ORGANIZATIONS
GIRL SCOUTS OF THE USA
YOUTH ORGANIZATIONS
BOY SCOUTS OF AMERICA

J. Eagle Shutt
University of South Carolina
CUBBERLEY, ELLWOOD

Jane Rodgers Siegel
Columbia University
HANDWRITING, TEACHING OF

Edward A. Silver
University of Michigan, Ann Arbor
ASSESSMENT
PERFORMANCE ASSESSMENT

Justin R. Silverstein
Augenblick and Myers, Inc.
FINANCIAL SUPPORT OF SCHOOLS
CAPITAL OUTLAY IN LOCAL SCHOOL SYSTEMS

Katherine G. Simon
Coalition of Essential Schools
COALITION OF ESSENTIAL SCHOOLS

Robert J. Simpson
University of Miami
AMERICAN OVERSEAS SCHOOLS

Pearl Sims
Vanderbilt University
WELFARE REFORM
MOVING MOTHERS FROM WELFARE TO WORK

Paul T. Sindelar
University of Florida
SPECIAL EDUCATION
PREPARATION OF TEACHERS

Theodore R. Sizer
Brown University
COALITION OF ESSENTIAL SCHOOLS' COMMON
PRINCIPLES

Kathryn Gray Skinner
Belmont University
INTERNATIONAL STUDENTS
U.S. COLLEGES AND UNIVERSITIES

Robert E. Slavin
Johns Hopkins University
SUCCESS FOR ALL PROGRAMS

Anne Smith
U.S. Department of Education
SPECIAL EDUCATION
INTERNATIONAL CONTEXT

Carol L. Smith
University of Massachusetts at Boston
LEARNING
CONCEPTUAL CHANGE

Louis M. Smith
Washington University in St. Louis
ROGERS, CARL

Lydia A. H. Smith
Simmons College
OPEN EDUCATION

Nora C. Smith
University of Wisconsin, Madison
CURRICULUM, HIGHER EDUCATION
TRADITIONAL AND CONTEMPORARY
PERSPECTIVES

Sonya G. Smith
Vanderbilt University Law School
STUDENT SERVICES
COMMUNITY COLLEGES

Susan E. Smith
University of Southern California
FAMILY SUPPORT SERVICES
INCOME SUPPORT SERVICES FOR CHILDREN AND
FAMILIES

Thomas M. Smith
National Science Foundation
INTERNATIONAL EDUCATION STATISTICS
THE USE OF INDICATORS TO EVALUATE THE
CONDITION OF EDUCATION SYSTEMS

Claire Smrekar
Vanderbilt University
PARENTING
HIGH-RISK NEIGHBORHOODS
PARENTING
INFLUENCE OF PARENTS' LEVEL OF EDUCATION
PARENTING
INFLUENCE ON CHILD'S EDUCATIONAL
ASPIRATIONS AND ATTAINMENT

John A. Smyth
United Nations Educational, Scientific, and
Cultural Organization
INTERNATIONAL EDUCATION AGREEMENTS

Martha E. Snell
University of Virginia
AUTISM, EDUCATION OF INDIVIDUALS WITH
MENTAL RETARDATION, EDUCATION OF
INDIVIDUALS WITH
SEVERE AND MULTIPLE DISABILITIES, EDUCATION
OF INDIVIDUALS WITH

Catherine E. Snow
Harvard University
BILINGUALISM, SECOND LANGUAGE LEARNING,
AND ENGLISH AS A SECOND LANGUAGE

William G. Spady
HeartLight International
OUTCOME BASED EDUCATION

Paul W. Speer
Vanderbilt University
COMMUNITY-BASED ORGANIZATIONS, AGENCIES,
AND GROUPS

Erin Spinello
American Speech-Language-Hearing
Association
SPEECH AND LANGUAGE IMPAIRMENT, EDUCATION
OF INDIVIDUALS WITH

Carmen Rasmussen
University of Alberta
DEVELOPMENTAL THEORY
COGNITIVE AND INFORMATION PROCESSING

Michele Spitulnik
University of California, Berkeley
SCIENCE LEARNING
TOOLS

Sam Stack
West Virginia University
BEREA COLLEGE
CLAPP, ELSIE RIPLEY

Frances K. Stage
New York University
COLLEGE STUDENTS WITH DISABILITIES
SPECIAL LEARNING NEEDS

Robert E. Stammer Jr.
Vanderbilt University
COLLEGE ATHLETICS
ACADEMIC SUPPORT SYSTEMS FOR ATHLETES

Rebecca M. Starr
University of Minnesota
MEMORY
DEVELOPMENT OF

Robert J. Starratt
Boston University
SUPERVISION OF INSTRUCTION

Judith S. Stein
Magnet Schools of America
MAGNET SCHOOLS

Laurence Steinberg
Temple University
PARENTING
OVERVIEW

Nicholas H. Steneck
University of Michigan
RESEARCH MISCONDUCT

Robert J. Sternberg
Yale University; American Psychological
Association
INTELLIGENCE
TRIARCHIC THEORY OF INTELLIGENCE

Richard Stiggins
Assessment Training Institute
ASSESSMENT
CLASSROOM ASSESSMENT

Wanda L. Stitt-Gohdes
University of Georgia
BUSINESS EDUCATION
SCHOOL

John A. Stoops
Commission on Elementary Schools of MSA;
Commission on International and
Transregional Accreditation
ACCREDITATION IN THE UNITED STATES
SCHOOL

C. Carney Strange
Bowling Green State University
COLLEGE AND ITS EFFECT ON STUDENTS

Kenneth A. Strike
University of Maryland
ETHICS
SCHOOL TEACHING

Nelly P. Stromquist
University of Southern California
GENDER ISSUES, INTERNATIONAL

Stephen D. Sugarman
University of California, Berkeley School of
Law
SUPREME COURT OF THE UNITED STATES AND
EDUCATION, THE

Larry Suter
The National Science Foundation
INTERNATIONAL ASSESSMENTS
OVERVIEW

Randy Swedburg
Concordia University
RECREATION PROGRAMS IN THE SCHOOLS

Mary Kay Switzer
California State Polytechnic University
Pomona
HONOR SOCIETIES
ASSOCIATION FOR WOMEN IN
COMMUNICATIONS

Daniel Tanner
Rutgers University
TEXTBOOKS
SCHOOL TEXTBOOKS IN THE UNITED STATES
WASHBURNE, CARLETON

Alton L. Taylor
University of Virginia
STRATEGIC AND LONG-RANGE PLANNING IN
HIGHER EDUCATION

Stephen Tchudi
University of Nevada, Reno
ENGLISH EDUCATION
TEACHING OF

Shane Templeton
University of Nevada, Reno
SPELLING, TEACHING OF

Terry D. TenBrink
INSTRUCTIONAL OBJECTIVES

Amy M. Tenhouse
Vanderbilt University
COLLEGE EXTRACURRICULAR ACTIVITIES
COMMUTER STUDENTS

Sevan G. Terzian
University of Florida
COMENIUS, JOHANN
PLATO
ROUSSEAU, JEAN-JACQUES

Martha May Tevis
University of Texas Pan-American
SANCHEZ, GEORGE I.

Bill Tharp
Nashville Metropolitan Government
WELFARE REFORM
MOVING MOTHERS FROM WELFARE TO WORK

H. S. Thayer
City University of New York
THAYER, V. T.

Michael Theall
Youngstown State University; CATALYST
COLLEGE TEACHING
TEACHING AND LEARNING
HIGHER EDUCATION

John R. Thelin
University of Kentucky
COLLEGE ATHLETICS
HISTORY OF ATHLETICS IN U.S. COLLEGES AND
UNIVERSITIES
ELIOT, CHARLES
HARPER, WILLIAM RAINEY
HIGHER EDUCATION IN THE UNITED STATES
HISTORICAL DEVELOPMENT
JOHNS HOPKINS UNIVERSITY
UNIVERSITY OF CHICAGO
UNIVERSITY OF VIRGINIA

Keith Thiede
University of Illinois at Chicago
LEARNING TO LEARN AND METACOGNITION

P. L. Thomas
Woodruff High, Woodruff, South Carolina
LABRANT, LOU L.

Scott L. Thomas
The University of Georgia
FINANCE, HIGHER EDUCATION
OVERVIEW

Charles P. Thompson
Kansas State University
MEMORY
AUTOBIOGRAPHICAL MEMORY

Gordon Thompson
University of Saskatchewan
CORPORATE COLLEGES

Cheri Tiernan
Boys and Girls Clubs of America
YOUTH ORGANIZATIONS
BOYS AND GIRLS CLUBS OF AMERICA

Jandhyala B. G. Tilak
National Institute of Educational Planning
and Administration, India
SOUTH ASIA

Vincent Tinto
Syracuse University
LEARNING COMMUNITIES AND THE
UNDERGRADUATE CURRICULUM

Gerald N. Tirozzi
National Association of Secondary School
Principals
SECONDARY EDUCATION
CURRENT TRENDS

Barbara F. Tobolowsky
University of California, Los Angeles
COLLEGE RANKINGS

Heather A. Tomlinson
University of California, Santa Barbara
INDIVIDUAL DIFFERENCES
GENDER EQUITY AND SCHOOLING

Dana Tomonari
Vanderbilt University
CHILD DEVELOPMENT, STAGES OF GROWTH

James Tooley
University of Newcastle; Institute for
Economic Affairs
GOVERNMENT AND EDUCATION, THE CHANGING
ROLE OF

Judith Torney-Purta
University of Maryland
INTERNATIONAL ASSESSMENTS
POLITICAL DEMOCRACY AND THE IEA STUDY OF
CIVIC EDUCATION

Steve Tozer
University of Illinois at Chicago
BENNE, KENNETH D.
BROUDY, HARRY S.

Tom Trabasso
University of Chicago
READING
COMPREHENSION

Susan Traiman
The Business Roundtable
BUSINESS INVOLVEMENT IN EDUCATION

Franklin I. Triplett
Mount Union College; Alpha Mu Gamma
HONOR SOCIETIES
ALPHA MU GAMMA

Mun C. Tsang
Columbia University
DECISION-MAKING IN DEVELOPING NATIONS,
APPLYING ECONOMIC ANALYSIS TO

Marc S. Tucker
National Center on Education and the
Economy
STANDARDS MOVEMENT IN AMERICAN EDUCATION

Harlan Tull
National Association of State Directors of
Pupil Transportation Services
TRANSPORTATION AND SCHOOL BUSING

David Turner
Illinois Principals Association
RECORDS AND REPORTS, SCHOOL

James B. Tuttle
Dickinson College
GENERAL EDUCATIONAL DEVELOPMENT TEST

David Tzuriel
Bar-Ilan University, Israel
ASSESSMENT
    DYNAMIC ASSESSMENT

Julie K. Underwood
National School Boards Association
LIABILITY OF SCHOOL DISTRICTS AND SCHOOL
    PERSONNEL FOR NEGLIGENCE

Wayne J. Urban
Georgia State University
BOND, HORACE MANN

Michael D. Usdan
The Institute for Educational Leadership
SCHOOL BOARD RELATIONS
    CONTROL OF THE SCHOOLS
STATES AND EDUCATION
    STATE BOARDS OF EDUCATION

U.S. Naval Academy Publications Office
MILITARY ACADEMIES
    U.S. NAVAL ACADEMY

Jennifer A. Vadeboncoeur
University of Queensland, Australia
EXPERIENTIAL EDUCATION

Timothy S. Valentine
Fordham University
COLEMAN, JAMES S.

Gilbert A. Valverde
State University of New York, University at
Albany
CURRICULUM, INTERNATIONAL

Donna Van Alst
Rutgers University
YOUTH DEVELOPMENT PROGRAMS

Lynda Van Kuren
Council for Exceptional Children
COUNCIL FOR EXCEPTIONAL CHILDREN

James J. Van Patten
University of Arkansas; Florida Atlantic
University
LAW EDUCATION

Tom Vander Ark
Bill and Melinda Gates Foundation
EDUCATIONAL LEADERSHIP

Bruce A. VanSledright
University of Maryland
HISTORY
    LEARNING
HISTORY
    TEACHING OF

Lieven Verschaffel
University of Leuven, Belgium
MATHEMATICS LEARNING
    WORD-PROBLEM SOLVING

Adriaan M. Verspoor
Management and Design of Educational
Development Projects
SUB-SAHARAN AFRICA

Deborah A. Verstegen
University of Virginia
G.I. BILL OF RIGHTS

Gordon G. Vessels
Atlanta Public Schools
CHARACTER DEVELOPMENT

Eleanora Villegas-Reimers
Wheelock College
TEACHER PREPARATION, INTERNATIONAL
    PERSPECTIVE

Lois J. Voigt
Loyola University Chicago
INTERDISCIPLINARY COURSES AND MAJORS IN
    HIGHER EDUCATION

Nancy J. Vye
Vanderbilt University
INSTRUCTIONAL DESIGN
    ANCHORED INSTRUCTION

Jennings L. Wagoner
University of Virginia
COMMON SCHOOL MOVEMENT

Kimberly B. Waid
University of Virginia
TEACHER

Timothy Walch
U.S. Catholic Historian
CATHOLIC SCHOOLS

Donald R. Waldrip
Magnet Schools of America
MAGNET SCHOOLS

Joan M. T. Walker
Vanderbilt University
PARENTING
INFLUENCE OF PARENTS' LEVEL OF EDUCATION
PARENTING
INFLUENCE ON CHILD'S EDUCATIONAL
ASPIRATIONS AND ATTAINMENT

James M. Wallace
Lewis and Clark College
DE LIMA, AGNES

Donovan R. Walling
Phi Delta Kappa International
ART EDUCATION
SCHOOL

Kenneth A. Wallston
Vanderbilt University
HUMAN SUBJECTS, PROTECTION OF

Daniel J. Walsh
University of Illinois at Urbana-Champaign
EARLY CHILDHOOD EDUCATION
PREPARATION OF TEACHERS

Jason L. Walton
Vanderbilt University
FEDERAL EDUCATIONAL ACTIVITIES
SUMMARY BY AGENCY
FINANCIAL SUPPORT OF SCHOOLS
HISTORY

Jia Wang
University of California, Los Angeles
HEALTH AND EDUCATION

Weiping Wang
Taiyuan Normal University, China
MICROTEACHING

Nell Northington Warren
Vanderbilt University
LIFE EXPERIENCE FOR COLLEGE CREDIT

John W. Warren
Tennessee Tech University; Association of
College Honor Societies
HONOR SOCIETIES
ASSOCIATION OF COLLEGE HONOR SOCIETIES

William H. Watkins
University of Illinois at Chicago
DU BOIS, W. E. B.
MAYS, BENJAMIN
WOODSON, CARTER GODWIN

Hersh C. Waxman
University of Houston
CLASSROOM OBSERVATION

Kent M. Weeks
Vanderbilt University
SCHOOL BOARDS
SELECTION AND EDUCATION OF MEMBERS
STATES AND EDUCATION
LEGAL BASIS OF STATE RELATIONS TO
NONPUBLIC SCHOOLS

Sheldon G. Weeks
University of Botswana, South Africa
RURAL EDUCATION
INTERNATIONAL CONTEXT

Brenda Lilienthal Welburn
National Association of State Boards of
Education
NATIONAL ASSOCIATION OF STATE BOARDS OF
EDUCATION

Amy E. Wells
University of New Orleans
FLEXNER, ABRAHAM

Traci Wells
University of California, Los Angeles
WESTERN EUROPE

Bette Weneck
Columbia University
MCCALL, WILLIAM A.

Susan West
Vanderbilt University
COLLEGE ADMISSIONS TESTS

Ian Westbury
University of Illinois, Urbana-Champaign
CURRICULUM, SCHOOL
OVERVIEW

Joel Westheimer
University of Ottawa
COUNTS, GEORGE S.

Steven C. Wheatley
American Council of Learned Societies
AMERICAN COUNCIL OF LEARNED SOCIETIES

Angela D. Whipple
University of California, Santa Barbara
INDIVIDUAL DIFFERENCES
ETHNICITY
INDIVIDUAL DIFFERENCES
GENDER EQUITY AND SCHOOLING

Kathleen Whitmire
American Speech-Langauge-Hearing
Association
SPEECH AND LANGUAGE IMPAIRMENT, EDUCATION
OF INDIVIDUALS WITH

Alan Wieder
University of South Carolina
GOODMAN, PAUL

Vanessa Wigand
Virginia Department of Education
DRIVER EDUCATION

Jennifer Wiley
University of Illinois, Chicago
LITERACY
LEARNING FROM MULTIMEDIA SOURCES

Barbara Willer
National Association for the Education of
Young Children
NATIONAL ASSOCIATION FOR THE EDUCATION OF
YOUNG CHILDREN

Amber M. Williams
Messiah College
BOYER, ERNEST

Susan M. Williams
University of Texas at Austin
TECHNOLOGY IN EDUCATION
CURRENT TRENDS

Roger L. Williams
University of Arkansas
LAND-GRANT COLLEGES AND UNIVERSITIES

Barbara Klaymeier Wills
Florida State University
SCHOOL BOARDS
DUTIES, RESPONSIBILITIES, DECISION-MAKING,
AND LEGAL BASIS FOR LOCAL SCHOOL BOARD
POWERS

Christopher Wilson
University of Virginia
G.I. BILL OF RIGHTS

Mark Wilson
University of California, Berkeley
ASSESSMENT TOOLS
PSYCHOMETRIC AND STATISTICAL

Maureen E. Wilson
Bowling Green State University
COLLEGE ENTRANCE EXAMINATION BOARD, THE
STUDENT SERVICES
COLLEGES AND UNIVERSITIES

Donald Winkler
The World Bank
DECENTRALIZATION AND EDUCATION

Katrin Winkler
KNOWLEDGE MANAGEMENT

Arthur E. Wise
National Council for Accreditation of Teacher
Education
NATIONAL COUNCIL FOR ACCREDITATION OF
TEACHER EDUCATION

Jean Wode
Magnet Schools of America
MAGNET SCHOOLS

Jenny T. Wojcik
National-Louis University
HOPKINS, L. THOMAS

Lisa Wolf-Wendel
University of Kansas
SINGLE-SEX INSTITUTIONS

Christine E. Wolfe
University of Iowa
SHELDON, EDWARD

Michael B. W. Wolfe
Grand Valley State University
READABILITY INDICES

Michael P. Wolfe
Kappa Delta Pi Honor Society
HONOR SOCIETIES
KAPPA DELTA PI

Mimi Wolverton
University of Nevada
DEPARTMENT CHAIRPERSON, THE

Kenneth K. Wong
Vanderbilt University
EDUCATIONAL INTEREST GROUPS
SCHOOL BOARD RELATIONS
RELATION OF SCHOOL BOARD TO THE
COMMUNITY

Margo Wood
University of Southern Maine
LANGUAGE ARTS, TEACHING OF

Maureen Woodhall
University of Wales, Aberystwyth; University
of London
STUDENT LOANS IN AN INTERNATIONAL CONTEXT

Katherine J. Workman
AEL, Inc.
REGIONAL LABORATORIES AND RESEARCH AND
DEVELOPMENT CENTERS

William G. Wraga
  University of Georgia
  BESTOR, A. E., JR.
  CHARTERS, W. W.
  KANDEL, ISAAC L.
  ZACHARIAS, JERROLD

Robert E. Yager
  University of Iowa
  SCIENCE EDUCATION
    PREPARATION OF TEACHERS
  SCIENCE EDUCATION
    OVERVIEW

Elizabeth Anne Yeager
  University of Florida
  MIEL, ALICE

Nancy K. Young
  Children and Family Futures
  FAMILY COMPOSITION AND CIRCUMSTANCE
    ALCOHOL, TOBACCO, AND OTHER DRUGS

Michelle D. Young
  University Council for Education
    Administration
  UNIVERSITY COUNCIL FOR EDUCATIONAL
    ADMINISTRATION

Steven P. Young
  Vanderbilt University
  FACULTY SENATES, COLLEGE AND UNIVERSITY

Nancy F. Zelasko
  The George Washington University
  BILINGUAL EDUCATION

Arthur Zilversmit
  Lake Forest College
  ADDAMS, JANE

Stephen A. Zuniga
  University of California, Los Angeles
  ASSESSMENT
    PORTFOLIO ASSESSMENT

Rolf A. Zwaan
  Florida State University
  LITERACY
    NARRATIVE COMPREHENSION AND PRODUCTION

A

AACSB INTERNATIONAL

AACSB International—The Association to Advance Collegiate Schools of Business is a nonprofit association of approximately 900 educational institutions, corporations, and other organizations dedicated to the promotion and improvement of higher education in management, accounting, and business administration. AACSB International serves as a professional association for college and university management education and as the leading accrediting agency for bachelor, master, and doctoral degree programs in business administration and accounting around the world.

Program

One of the primary functions of AACSB International is the accreditation of undergraduate and graduate degree programs in business administration and accounting. The association's demanding accreditation process begins with institutional self-evaluation, whereby a school assesses its own accomplishments relative to its stated mission and AACSB's accreditation criteria. AACSB International accreditation also requires a peer review, during which external analysts examine and evaluate the school's education programs, curriculum and faculty, assessment systems, and plans for growth and improvement.

In addition to its accreditation program, AACSB organizes and conducts a variety of professional development programs for faculty and staff of management and business administration schools. AACSB International also sponsors an annual two-day conference attended by more than 1,000 educators from around the world. The conference includes exhibits,

presentations, special events, affinity-group meetings, and discussions of important issues in management, business administration, and accounting education. Other AACSB International meetings include the Dean's Conference and the New Deans Seminar for deans and other administrators of business schools; a two-day biennial Public and Media Relations Conference for business school public relations personnel; and the Business School Development Conference, which trains business school administrators about strategies for raising funds from foundational and corporate sources. AACSB International also helps organize the Global Forum on Management Education. Held every five years, this conference brings together administrators and educators from business schools around the world, heads of corporate education and training programs, and corporate executives to discuss the advancement and practice of business and management education worldwide.

AACSB International's Knowledge Services program collects, collates, and disseminates statistical and analytical information about business schools around the world. Information available from Knowledge Services includes salary surveys and demographic analyses of business school faculty and staff; student, staff, and alumni satisfaction surveys; and Effective Practice reports featuring analyses and comparisons of the career services, curriculum, and instruction offered by various MBA programs.

AACSB International also sponsors affinity groups to facilitate the communication and networking of member institutions with common interests and goals. Affinity groups meet at AACSB International conferences and seminars, establish e-mail networks, schedule their own meetings at times and locations convenient to group members, and post information on the AACSB web site. Each affinity group is also assigned an AACSB International staff liaison to help with record-keeping, program and meeting planning, and communications. In 2001, AACSB International affinity groups included the Small School Network group, the Metropolitan Schools group, the Woman Administrators in Management Education group, the MBA for Working Professionals group, and the Associated New American Colleges group. Institutions which are not members of AACSB International may participate in affinity groups if they are sponsored by an AACSB member.

AACSB International maintains relationships with business and management organizations around the world, and sponsors periodic educational exchange programs. Since 1993, AACSB International and Keizai Koho Center, a Japanese business organization, have sponsored an annual ten-day tour of Japan, during which AACSB members can study Japanese management techniques, corporate reforms, industrial technology, and business traditions. Tour participants also meet with Japanese business leaders, academics, and government officials.

AACSB International issues numerous print and electronic reports, surveys, accreditation manuals, curriculum guides, and guides to undergraduate and graduate business and management programs. Other publications include *Newsline,* the association's monthly newsletter, and *BizEd,* a bimonthly magazine that covers trends, practices, and issues in management education and training. AACSB also sponsors the Management Education Career Marketplace, an online job search and placement service with listings of open positions and resumes from those seeking jobs in business and management education.

History

AACSB International was organized in 1916 by seventeen leading American colleges and universities. The new organization began its accreditation function in 1919 when it adopted its first standards for business degree programs. AACSB standards for programs in accountancy were established in 1980, with new standards and a peer review process adopted in 1991. By 2002, AACSB International membership included about 650 American institutions of higher education, nearly 200 institutions of higher

education in forty-nine foreign countries, and about fifty corporate and nonprofit organizations around the world. Formerly known as the International Association for Management Education or American Assembly of Collegiate Schools of Business, the association officially changed its name to AACSB International—The Association to Advance Collegiate Schools of Business in April 2001.

See also: BUSINESS EDUCATION.

INTERNET RESOURCE

AACSB INTERNATIONAL. 2002. <www.aacsb.edu>.

JUDITH J. CULLIGAN

ACADEMIC ADVISING IN HIGHER EDUCATION

The role of the academic adviser shifts as student populations and administrative conditions in universities change over time. Faculty members are increasingly committed to teaching undergraduates, and academic advising is an innovative form of teaching that helps students become involved in their own choices. Instilling students with a sense of commitment to their future plans and responsibility for their decisions is the cornerstone of the academic adviser's work.

Developmental Advising

Traditionally, faculty advisers simply helped students choose courses in a prescriptive approach to advising. Since the 1970s, however, scholars and faculty members have redefined the academic adviser's task to include guidance as well as imparting information. Developmental academic advising evolved out of this process; faculty advising took on importance as an experience that contributes to a student's personal growth. In two seminal works on academic advising, both published in 1972, Burns B. Crookston and Terry O'Banion targeted three goals, or vectors, for developmental academic advising: developing competence, developing autonomy, and developing purpose in the undergraduate student. Using this approach, advisers ask students to become involved in their own college experiences, explore with students the factors that lead to success, and show interest in both the students' academic progress and extracurricular achievement. As they urge students to take responsibility for their own learning, developmental advisers avoid simply providing answers and instead ask open-ended questions. Developmental advising provides advantages not only for the student, but for the university as well: the school's academic community benefits from an advising process that bridges institutional divisions between academics and student affairs.

Differences between Developmental and Prescriptive Approaches

Perhaps the most important part of any successful adviser/student relationship is a sense of shared responsibility: Students learn by taking control of their own choices and finding ways to handle the consequences of those decisions. Traditional or prescriptive advising situations, however, tend to emphasize the authority of advisers and the limitations of students. Prescriptive advisers supply answers to specific questions but rarely address broad-based academic concerns. An adviser using the prescriptive approach supplies information to the student, giving out information about campus resources. The developmental approach, on the other hand, urges students to take responsibility for their own college experience and career goals. In a developmental advising relationship, students and faculty share responsibility. This form of advising contributes to students' rational processes, environmental and interpersonal interactions, and behavioral awareness, as well as problem-solving, decision-making and evaluation skills. The relationship between adviser and student is vital, and both long-term and immediate goals are important. Successful advising functions first as a means of exploring careers and majors, and second as a method for selecting courses and arranging schedules. Most academic advising programs clarify their approach with a mission statement, which helps both advisers and students to understand their roles and responsibilities.

A Brief History of Academic Advising

The historical aims of undergraduate education—involving students with learning and involving students with teachers—pertain to academic advising. The role of the academic adviser has shifted with cultural and historical changes. Before academic advising became a defined part of the university experience, formal divisions often kept students and faculty apart and limited interaction between the two groups. In the late 1930s many colleges and universities developed formalized but unexamined advising systems, which focused solely on the academic aspects of student life. By the 1950s federal funding for education resulted in an emphasis on accommodating new student populations, and universities began implementing freshman orientation programs.

Changes in the advising process result primarily from shifts in the undergraduate student population. In the twentieth century, new populations gained access to colleges and universities, demanding innovative responses from faculty and administrators. After the passage of the Servicemen's Readjustment Act of 1944 (commonly known as the G.I. Bill), higher education became a possibility for students from a variety of backgrounds and age groups. As women, multicultural students, students with disabilities, and transition students began to matriculate, institutes of higher learning responded with changes in their approaches to student support structures such as academic advising. In the late twentieth and early twenty-first century, technological communication has signaled another major shift in the adviser/student relationship. Academic advisers are able to contact students through e-mail, and students are also able to seek out academic advisers through electronic communication. As online education has affected university classes and research, academic advising has also had to adjust, and advisers have had to meet the challenges of using online communication to strengthen, not diminish, their interactions with students.

Peer Advisers, Professional Advisers, and Faculty Advisers

The adviser population is diverse; faculty from all disciplines advise students, and many schools, both colleges and universities, hire professional advisers and implement peer-adviser programs as well. Because faculty members often know the culture and requirements of both their own disciplines and the university as a whole, their expertise strengthens their relationships with the students they advise. Often, institutional recognition for faculty advising is limited on college and university campuses, and adviser/student relationships can suffer from a faculty member's busy schedule. Developing useful methods for evaluating academic advising helps faculty advisers receive credit for this important aspect of their work as teachers.

Many schools hire outside professional advisers to handle freshman orientation and other academic advising needs. Professional advisers tend to bring useful counseling experience to the advising process. These advisers, however, need training to understand the university's program and the role of academic advising in the institution. The primary role of the academic adviser is to offer support, encouragement, and information to improve a student's academic life and create a sense of responsibility in an undergraduate. Students should discuss personal, emotional, and mental health problems, however, with a trained counselor.

Many colleges and universities have implemented peer-adviser programs. Peer advisers tend to understand a fellow student's position and the undergraduate culture at their institution better than either faculty or professional advisers. Because peer advisers often know less than the faculty about college requirements and academic issues, however, training is an important part of any peer-advising program. Colleges and universities that offer peer advising usually require the student advisers to take part in extensive training programs, such as retreats, workshops, and meetings.

These three types of academic advisers work with either individual advisees or groups of students. With successful group facilitation, advising groups can provide students with an academic adviser as well as a sympathetic peer group. Discussion among members of an advising group is important, and students in the group need to learn effective ways of exchanging ideas and interacting with others.

Student Populations and the Adviser/Student Relationship

Academic advising has evolved with academic trends and, most important, with student populations. Research shows that interaction between students and faculty increases student involvement on campus and makes students more likely to remain in school. These advantages of the academic adviser system are particularly valuable for the increasingly diverse student populations attending U.S. universities. Interested and informed advisers work with all students, not only to help them stay in school but also to help them become contributing members of the college or university community. Students with particular advising needs include academically underprepared students, students with disabilities, student athletes, students in transition, and international students.

Some student populations benefit from intrusive advising; academic advisers of academically underprepared students, for example, often initially assume responsibility for sustaining the advising relationship by contacting students frequently and encouraging them to succeed. Started out of concern for freshmen and sophomores who were unsuccessful in college, intrusive advising employs some prescriptive advising tools. The field of academic advising continues to react to changes in student populations. In meeting the needs of students, academic advisers must tailor their approaches in the increasingly diverse undergraduate student population.

Conclusion

As college graduates face new expectations from the workplace, academic advisers can help them learn to take responsibility for their decisions. Academic advising, in developing these valuable relationships between teachers and students, becomes an important form of teaching. Academic advisers help undergraduates understand their choices as students and the effect of those decisions on their future plans. Through open-ended questions and discussions, academic advisers develop a valuable relationship with undergraduate students, helping them to become more responsible members of college or university communities and to develop a lasting sense of personal responsibility.

See also: ADJUSTMENT TO COLLEGE; CAREER COUNSELING IN HIGHER EDUCATION; COLLEGE STUDENT RETENTION; FACULTY ROLES AND RESPONSIBILITIES; GUIDANCE AND COUNSELING, SCHOOL.

BIBLIOGRAPHY

CROOKSTON, BURNS B. 1972. "A Developmental View of Academic Advising as Teaching." *Journal of College Student Personnel* 13:12–17.

FROST, SUSAN H. 1991. *Academic Advising for Student Success: A System of Shared Responsibility.* Washington, DC: George Washington University, School of Education and Human Development.

FROST, SUSAN H. 1994. "Advising Alliances: Sharing Responsibility for Student Success." *NACADA Journal: The Journal of the National Academic Advising Association* 14(2):54–58.

FROST, SUSAN H. 2000. "Historical and Philosophical Foundations for Academic Advising." In *Ac-*

ademic Advising: A Comprehensive Handbook, ed. Virginia Gordon and Wesley R. Habley. San Francisco: Jossey-Bass.

GORDON, VIRGINIA, and HABLEY, WESLEY R., eds. 2000. *Academic Advising: A Comprehensive Handbook.* San Francisco: Jossey-Bass.

SUSAN H. FROST

ACADEMIC CALENDARS

Academic calendar use at the higher education level has followed a consistent and non-varied path over the last few decades. Five types of calendars have been principally used. These include the early semester, traditional semester, quarter system, trimester, and "4-1-4" calendars. A longitudinal review of use patterns revealed that the traditional semester (a calendar that divides the academic year into two terms of 15 to 17 weeks) was the dominant calendar used by U.S. colleges and universities from the 1950s to the early 1970s. The early semester (a variant of the traditional semester that divides the academic year into equivalent terms but begins and ends about two weeks earlier) replaced the traditional semester in prevalence in the mid-1970s and has remained the dominant calendar used since that time.

The American Association of Collegiate Registrars and Admissions Officers (AACRAO) conducted an analytical study of calendar use in 2001 to gauge the extent of change that has occurred. The study, based on data sets from the National College Stores, Oberlin, Ohio, and literature and institutional practice reviews, examined calendar use and conversions at 4,100 colleges and universities during the 2000–2001 academic year. Principal findings from the study and evaluative information on the impacts of calendar use or conversion on higher education instruction follow.

Calendar Use during the 1990–2000 Decade

Marginal variations occurred in calendar use over the 1990–2000 decade. Most institutions used the early semester calendar; its use actually increased by 8 percent over the ten-year period. Use of the quarter calendar decreased cumulatively by 9 percent, while use of the traditional semester experienced a zero level of net change. Modest shifts occurred in use of the trimester and 4-1-4 systems.

Current Calendar Use

A significant majority of higher education institutions currently use the semester calendar (either the early or traditional semester). The AACRAO study found that 70 percent of all institutions that participated in the study and 77 percent of the degree-granting institutions used a semester calendar for academic year (AY) 2000–2001. Two-thirds of the institutions used the early semester calendar and 4 percent used the traditional semester. Fifteen percent used the quarter system, few institutions used the 4-1-4 calendar, and the trimester was the least frequently used.

The pattern (i.e., predominance) of calendar use was consistent across institutions even when adjustments for basic indices such as institutional sector and size were made. Disaggregation by these institutional indices, in fact, yielded statistically similar results.

Calendar use by institutional level or sector. The early semester was the dominant calendar used across all institutional sectors. Eighty-three percent of the community colleges used it, along with 71 percent of the four-year doctoral and nondoctoral granting institutions, and 52 percent of the junior colleges. Fifty-nine percent of the professional schools (law/medical schools) and 40 percent of the graduate schools also used the early semester calendar. Trade schools, by contrast, used the quarter system more frequently than other calendars (with a use rate of 39%).

Calendar use by enrollment size. Again, because of its generalized high frequency of use, the early semester was the primary calendar used across all enrollment variants. Sixty-four percent of schools with small enrollments (total enrollments under 5,000) used it, as well as 68 percent of medium-sized schools (those with enrollments of 5,000 to 19,999), and 77 percent of schools with larger enrollments (equaling or exceeding 20,000 students).

Calendar Conversions

Three hundred and eighty-five of the institutions participating in the AACRAO 2001 study changed their calendar during AY 2000–2001 (a conversion rate of 9.2%). This conversion rate is historically significant because it constitutes a rate that is four times the conversion rate that occurred in AY 1990–1991 and more than twice the rate that occurred in AY 1997–1998 (the last time the AACRAO study was conducted).

Prevalent conversions. The majority of the conversions entailed changes to the semester calendar; 55 percent of the converting institutions made this change (48% converted to the early semester system and 7% to the traditional semester). Seventeen percent of the institutions converted to the quarter calendar and 12 percent converted to the 4-1-4 calendar. Other conversions were nonconsequential.

Conversion paths. The most frequent change entailed institutions converting from the traditional semester to the early semester system; fifty-eight institutions (or 15% of those converting) made this change. Fifty-five institutions (14%) converted from the quarter calendar to a semester calendar (primarily to the early semester); and forty-four institutions (11%) converted from the semester to the quarter calendar.

Conversions by institutional type or level. Conversion rates by institutional level were again fairly consistent. Professional schools (law/medical schools) converted at a rate that was marginally higher than other school types (13%). Junior colleges, trade schools, and graduate schools converted at rates of 12% each. Community colleges and four-year doctoral and nondoctoral colleges and universities converted at lower rates (8% respectively).

Conversions by institutional size. Rates of conversion were also consistent across enrollment variants. Smaller institutions (those with enrollments of less than 5,000) converted slightly more frequently than institutions of other sizes (13%). Medium-sized schools (enrollment size of 5,000 to 19,999) and schools with larger enrollments (20,000 or more students) converted at a rate of 8 percent.

Effects of Calendar Use and Conversion on Instruction and Curriculum

The AACRAO study did not address the impacts of calendar use or conversion on higher education instruction. An examination of these issues, especially effects on degree requirements, time-to-degree completion, course load/credit hour requirements, and curriculum restructuring, would have enhanced the study but were considered to be beyond its scope.

A review of institutional policy documents, technical approaches, and working papers from the Ohio State University, University of California at Davis, and other institutions did, however, provide the following evaluative assessments:

> Most of the college and university administrators who have participated in imple-

menting calendar changes have had varied assessments of its impact. Administrators at some of the larger research institutions have suggested that the impact of conversion on teaching load, class size and staffing needs will vary depending on the conversion model adopted (typically the Constant Format model, the Constant Content model, or a hybrid of the two). Faculty and administrators of other institutions suggest that most of the models proposed are too inflexible and will ultimately have negative consequences on college curriculum. Most agree that the various models utilized or proposed either expand or shorten the length of instruction time but generally have a neutral effect on course content. Many also agree that rigidly defined schemes of assigning semester credits to courses must be considered and justified as part of the implementation process that precedes the calendar change; and that any conversion model adopted ensures that program instructional time and hours are maintained over the course of the academic year. (The Ohio State University 2001 Ad Hoc University Calendar Committee, n.p.)

The administrators at the Ohio State University (when considering a quarter to semester calendar conversion) admonished that the conversion would result in a reduction of the total credit value of curricula by approximately one third (as the total number of credits to graduate increases from 180 to 120) but felt that it was actually the distribution and "packaging" of the course content that would actually change, as a result of the reduction in the number of courses and credits offered per course. They further suggested that there are two primary issues to consider when contemplating a quarter to semester conversion: (1) the use of a semester calendar will bring institutions into conformity with 85 percent of the U.S. research institutions (most of the highly ranked institutions are on the semester calendar); and (2) consideration of a calendar change must occur simultaneously with the institution's curricular review, including reviews of credits-to-graduate and general education curriculum requirements. The following assessments were offered in regard to effects on course load and time-to-degree completion:

A lack of documentation on this subject precluded a detailed discussion of the issue. Literature reviews provided little if any substantive or empirical information on these outcomes. Information from institutions that have made conversions suggest that the outcomes for students at these institutions are not well defined. The semester system, for example, reduces the number of terms per year but lengthens the span of each term imposing greater commitments on students. Students will be forced to make greater commitments to each term because failure to complete a term will delay degree completion by a full semester. There may, however, be a tendency for students to remain enrolled in a two semester system to avoid that delay. The lengthened commitment represented by semesters may have a particularly negative impact on the enrollment of students who are part-time, older, non-traditional, university employees, or public school teachers taking evening courses. The increased commitment necessary may cause scheduling difficulties for these students and result in delayed graduation or program completion. The quarter calendar may extend time-to-completion for more students than the semester system because students may be able to skip a quarter and delay their academic progress by only three months. Students on quarters can also change majors more casually than students on semesters because required courses in program majors can begin in the subsequent quarter. (The Ohio State University 2001 Ad Hoc University Calendar Committee, n.p.)

Advantages and Disadvantages of Specific Calendars

Reports from the University of California at Davis and Ohio State University that examined the merits of calendar system use addressed the issue of quarter versus semester system advantages and suggested the following. Some of the advantages of the semester calendar cited are that: (1) it provides an opportunity for more thorough examination of subjects, research assignments, and term papers; (2) it increases time spent in each course, making it possible to receive in-depth learning and a better opportunity for students to "rebound" from a poor start in a course; (3) it promotes greater interaction between faculty and students; (4) it reduces the tendency towards course fragmentation; and (5) for transfer students, it offers greater compatibility with other institutions' calendars and curriculums.

Some advantages cited in favor of the quarter system include its ability to: (1) afford departments greater flexibility in providing course offerings and availability; (2) allow students increased flexibility in selecting majors and arranging class schedules; (3) allow fundamental, introductory courses to be offered more frequently, making scheduling easier and classes smaller; (4) allow students to receive instruction from more instructors; (5) provide opportunities to retake failed courses sooner; (6) allow students who miss terms to resume college enrollment sooner; and (7) provide more opportunities for students to drop in and out, possibly shortening time-to-degree for part-time and transient students.

See also: ACADEMIC MAJOR, THE; CURRICULUM, HIGHER EDUCATION; GENERAL EDUCATION IN HIGHER EDUCATION.

BIBLIOGRAPHY

AMERICAN ASSOCIATION OF COLLEGIATE REGISTRARS AND ADMISSIONS OFFICERS and STATE HIGHER EDUCATION EXECUTIVE OFFICERS. 1998. "Postsecondary Student Data Handbook (Internal Review Draft)." Washington, DC: National Center for Education Statistics and U.S. Department of Education.

NATIONAL ASSOCIATION OF COLLEGE STORES. 2000. *Schedule of College and University Dates, 2000–2001.* Oberlin, OH: National Association of College Stores.

NATIONAL CENTER FOR EDUCATION STATISTICS. 1995. *Integrated Postsecondary Education Data System, Glossary.* Washington, DC: U.S. Department of Education.

OVERTURF, L. L.; FRAZIER, J. E.; and BAKER, R. D. 1977. "The Process of Calendar Conversion." *College and University* 52:724–734.

INTERNET RESOURCES

CUYAHOGA COMMUNITY COLLEGE. 1997. "Semester Conversion Frequently Asked Questions." <www.tri-c.cc.oh.us/FAQ/docs/Conver.htm>.

OHIO STATE UNIVERSITY 2001 AD HOC UNIVERSITY CALENDAR COMMITTEE. 2001. "The University Calendar Study." <www.osu.edu/calendar study/report.html>.

UNIVERSITY OF CALIFORNIA AT DAVIS SEMESTER COMMITTEE. 1993. "Semester Conversion Task Force Report." <http://chancellor.ucdavis.edu/resource/commun/1997/semester/sctfrep.cfm>.

UNIVERSITY OF GEORGIA SEMESTER CONVERSION COMMITTEE. 1995. "Basic Guiding Principles for Curriculum Conversion to the Semester System." <www.uga.edu/vpaa/planprio/convsem.html>.

BRENDA ASHFORD

ACADEMIC DEAN, THE

Academic deans are typically the highest ranking academic officials in an institution, next only to the president or chancellor and the provost or chief academic officer. Academic deans preside over colleges, schools, or divisions comprised of a cluster of disciplines or disciplinary specialties, such as arts and sciences, engineering, fine arts, business, natural sciences, education, and health sciences. Most academic deans are situated in the institutional hierarchy as reporting to vice presidents or provosts; however, some hold the dual title of dean and vice president, a situation that is often an artifact of institution size and type. Smaller liberal arts institutions and community colleges, where numbers of faculty are fewer, may have a dean of faculty or academic dean who has jurisdiction over faculty in all disciplines. Deans' roles frequently vary according to academic field, institution type, and institutional context. In institutions marked by higher levels of disciplinary specialization, such as research and doctoral institutions, the number of academic deans is larger so as to accommodate the unique leadership demands of the diverse disciplinary programs housed in the institution.

Drawn from the senior faculty ranks, academic deans are seen by many as serving a dual role, that of scholar and administrator, particularly in institutions that place high value on research and publication in assessing faculty performance. Terms of appointment are typically in the range of five to seven years, and while appointments may be extended, very few serve more than ten years in a deanship position. This is no doubt due to the demands inherent in the role and the associated stress characteristic of the management environment. Deans answer to a variety of constituents, including faculty, the central campus administration, students, and alumni, and in order to be effective must be capable of understanding and serving their often disparate interests and conflicting goals.

Deans serve both academic and administrative purposes in that they are responsible for hiring department chairs and providing management oversight to bureaucratic processes within the unit. Depending on unit size, deans often have some number of associate and assistant deans to whom they delegate responsibilities associated with administrative functions related to finances, facilities, personnel, and management of academic or curricular programs. The position's uniqueness lies in its routine contact with a broad range of institutional constituents—the president or chancellor, the chief academic affairs officer, the faculty, students, external stakeholders such as donors and corporate supporters, and in some cases the boards that provide institutional or unit oversight. The unique position occupied by academic deans places them at the forefront of institutional change.

Decision-making responsibilities of academic deans typically encompass the following areas: (a) educational program/curriculum; (b) faculty selection, promotion, and development; (c) student affairs; (d) finance; (e) physical facilities development; and (f) public and alumni relations. Given the comprehensiveness of responsibility, it is not uncommon for the role of academic deans in larger, more complex institutions to resemble that of a chief executive officer of a moderately sized business enterprise. Resources under their control are often into the tens, sometimes hundreds of millions of dollars in large research institutions. With diminishing state support of higher education and increased operational costs, the need to identify new sources of revenue has increased considerably, and the work of garnering such support has become a primary function of academic deans in most institutional settings. Responsibilities associated with fundraising, the increasingly complex financial environment presented by issues of student access and equity, and increasing numbers of part-time faculty has made the role of the academic dean far more complex than it has been in the past.

Typical Characteristics of Academic Deans

The press of responsibility and the critical role assumed by academic deans is reflected in the increasing skills required for the position. Typically, academic deans are not only required to be scholars of highest repute but also to possess some measure of managerial and leadership talent. Communication with faculty is a central activity to the deanship and one that often provokes disagreement, if not conflict. Faculty interactions often involve sensitive issues, such as tenure decisions and salary concerns, demanding an acute sensitivity to faculty needs and skills in problem-solving and conflict management. The most effective deans are skilled in building consensus, influencing outcomes in support of academic programs in a context of disparate goals, and in negotiating for resources in an increasingly scarce resource environment. On a university-wide level, many of the rivalries among academic units are resolved in the relationship between the dean and the central administration. Thus, persuasiveness and ability to navigate the political environment are essential. Effective deans also possess skills in collaboration and integration that facilitate development and implementation of new academic programs and cultivation of new opportunities for research and student learning.

Possibly one of the biggest challenges of academic deans is enacting leadership in a context where those being led neither believe they need to be led, nor are predisposed to succumb to administrative policy and procedural dictates. Such is the case with the typical faculty collective. To complicate matters further, faculty believe the kind of work in which they are engaged—teaching and research—does not require extensive bureaucratic structures, thus the administrative apparatus that demands their conformity is viewed as a nuisance and a diversion of resources. Consequently, deans must operate in an environment within which their authority is subject to ongoing challenge, making fortitude, perseverance, and humility important attributes for survival.

Career Path to the Academic Deanship

One typically ascends to the full-time administrative post of the deanship through the academic ranks, having achieved success as a scholar and teacher. This particular path often includes time spent in a previous administrative role such as department chair and an assistant or associate deanship. An alternative route, and one which is less characteristic of deans in research and doctoral institutions where scholarly performance is typically the primary prerequisite for candidacy, is that of the trained administrator. These individuals specialize in the practice and study of institutional management and have made a career in institutional administration. Another route that is becoming more common, particularly in professional schools such as business and engineering, is via the corporate world. The experience of the seasoned business executive is viewed as bringing added value in the development of important linkages with business and industry.

See also: BOARD OF TRUSTEES, COLLEGE AND UNIVERSITY; CHIEF ACADEMIC AFFAIRS OFFICERS, COLLEGE AND UNIVERSITY; COLLEGES AND UNIVERSITIES, ORGANIZATIONAL STRUCTURE OF; FACULTY SENATES, COLLEGE AND UNIVERSITY; GOVERNANCE AND DECISION-MAKING IN COLLEGES AND UNIVERSITIES; PRESIDENCY, COLLEGE AND UNIVERSITY.

BIBLIOGRAPHY

DIBDEN, ARTHUR J. 1968. *The Academic Deanship in American Colleges and Universities.* Carbondale: Southern Illinois University Press.

GRIFFITHS, DANIEL E., and McCARTY, DONALD J. 1980. *The Dilemma of the Deanship.* Danville, IL: The Interstate Printers and Publishers.

MORRIS, VAN CLEVE. 1981. *Deaning: Middle Management in Academe.* Urbana: University of Illinois Press.

TUCKER, ALAN, and BRYAN, ROBERT A. 1991. *The Academic Dean.* New York: ACE and Macmillan.

WOLVERTON, MIMI, WOLVERTON, MARVIN L., and GMELCH, WALTER H. 1999. "The Impact of Role Conflict and Ambiguity on Academic Deans." *Journal of Higher Education* 70(1):80–106.

MARIETTA DEL FAVERO

ACADEMIC DISCIPLINES

Discipline is defined by the *Oxford English Dictionary* as "a branch of learning or scholarly instruction." Fields of study as defined by academic discipline provide the framework for a student's program of college or postbaccalaureate study, and as such, define the academic world inhabited by scholars. Training in a discipline results in a system of orderly behavior recognized as characteristic of the discipline. Such behaviors are manifested in scholars' approaches to understanding and investigating new knowledge, ways of working, and perspectives on the world around them. Janice Beyer and Thomas Lodahl have described disciplinary fields as providing the structure of knowledge in which faculty members are trained and socialized; carry out tasks of teaching, research, and administration; and produce research and educational output. Disciplinary worlds are considered separate and distinct cultures that exert varying influence on scholarly behaviors as well as on the structure of higher education.

The number of disciplines has expanded significantly from those recognized in early British and German models. Debates are ongoing about the elements that must be present to constitute a legitimate disciplinary field. Among such elements are the presence of a community of scholars; a tradition or history of inquiry; a mode of inquiry that defines how data is collected and interpreted, as well as defining the requirements for what constitutes new knowledge; and the existence of a communications network.

Disciplines and the Structure of Higher Education

Influence in the academic profession is derived from disciplinary foundations. A hierarchical structure of authority is not possible in colleges and universities given the autonomy and expert status of faculty with respect to disciplinary activities. Consequently, the structure of higher education is an associational one based on influence and persuasion. Interaction between the professor and the institution is in many ways shaped by the professor's disciplinary affiliation. This condition is not only a historical artifact of the German model of higher education that was built on the "scientific ethos" from which status in the profession has been derived, but it also results from faculty members having their primary allegiance to a discipline, not to an institution. Disciplinary communities establish incentives and forms of cooperation around a subject matter and its problems. Disciplines have conscious goals, which are often synonymous with the goals of the departments and schools that comprise an institutional operating unit.

Colleges and universities are typically organized around clusters of like disciplines that have some cognitive rationale for being grouped together. The seat of power for decisions on faculty promotion, tenure, and, to some extent, support for research and academic work, lies in the academic department. Thus discipline as an important basis for determining university structure becomes clear. In institutions placing lesser emphasis on research and in institutions more oriented toward teaching, the faculty may adopt more of a local or institutional orientation than a cosmopolitan or disciplinary orientation. In these institutions faculty performance and recognition may be based on institutional as opposed to disciplinary structures. Therefore, the strength of discipline influence on organizational structure in research institutions, liberal arts colleges, and community colleges, for example, can be expected to vary.

Discipline Classification Systems

Numerous analytical frameworks are evident in the literature for classifying academic disciplines for purposes of comparative study. Four of these frameworks have drawn much of the focus of empirical work in the study of discipline differences. These are codification, level of paradigm development, level of consensus, and the Biglan Model. Each of these frameworks is reviewed in turn with relevant commentary on categorical variation determined through empirical study.

Codification. Codification refers to the condition whereby knowledge can be consolidated, or codified, into succinct and interdependent theoretical formulations. As a cognitive dimension, codification describes a field's body of knowledge as opposed to behavioral attributes of scholarly activity. Use of the codification framework in the study of discipline has essentially been displaced by the use of the high-low consensus concept, because consensus, or level of agreement among scholars, has been determined to be a function of codification.

Paradigm development. Paradigm development, as first developed by Thomas S. Kuhn, refers to the extent to which a discipline possesses a clearly defined "academic law" or ordering of knowledge and associated social structures. "Mature" sciences, or those with well-developed paradigms such as physics, are thought to have clear and unambiguous ways of defining, ordering, and investigating knowledge. At the opposite end of the scale are fields such as education and sociology, which are described as pre-paradigmatic. These fields are characterized by a high level of disagreement as to what constitutes new knowledge, what are appropriate methods for inquiry, what criteria are applied to determine acceptable findings, what theories are proven, and the importance of problems to study. The terms *paradigm development* and *consensus* are thought to be interchangeable as they describe a common dimension of disciplinary fields—the extent of agreement on structure of inquiry and the knowledge it produces.

Consensus. The core of the paradigm development concept is the degree of consensus about theory, methods, techniques, and problems. Consensus implies unity of mind on elements of social structure and the practice of science. The indicators of consensus in a field are absorption of the same technical literature, similar education and professional initiation, a cohesiveness in the community that promotes relatively full communication and unanimous professional judgments on scientific matters, and a shared set of goals, including the training of successors. Researchers commonly attribute high levels of consensus to the physical sciences, low levels to the social sciences, and even lower levels to the humanities.

Greater particularistic tendencies, that is, judgments based on personal characteristics, have been exhibited by low-consensus disciplines. For example, in award structures in the sciences, the lower the consensus level the more awards are based on personal characteristics. With respect to the peer-review process, low-consensus editorial board members have been shown to be more likely to accept publications from their own universities. Also, in selection of editorial board members, low-consensus journals put more emphasis on personal knowledge of individuals and their professional associations.

The Biglan Model. Anthony Biglan derived his taxonomy of academic disciplines based on the responses of faculty from a large, public university and a private liberal arts college regarding their perceptions of the similarity of subject matter areas. His taxonomy identified three dimensions to academic disciplines: (1) the degree to which a paradigm exists (paradigmatic or pre-paradigmatic, alternatively referred to as hard versus soft disciplines); (2) the extent to which the subject matter is practically applied (pure versus applied); and (3) involvement with living or organic matter (life versus nonlife systems). The natural and physical sciences are considered to possess more clearly delineated paradigms and are in the "hard" category. Those having less-developed paradigms and low consensus on knowledge bases and modes of inquiry (e.g., the social sciences and humanities) are considered "soft." Applied fields tend to be concerned with application of knowledge, such as law, education, and engineering. Pure fields are those that are viewed as less concerned with practical application, such as mathematics, history, and philosophy. Life systems include such fields as biology and agriculture, while languages and mathematics exemplify nonlife disciplines. Biglan's clustering of thirty-three academic fields according to his three-dimensional taxonomy is displayed in Table 1.

Subsequent work by Biglan substantiated systematic differences in the behavioral patterns of faculty with respect to social connectedness; commitment to their teaching, research, and service roles; and publication output. Biglan concluded that the three dimensions he identified were related to the structure and output of academic departments. Specifically, hard or high-paradigm fields showed greater social connectedness on research activities. Also, faculty in these fields were committed more to research and less to teaching than faculty from soft or low-paradigm fields. Those in hard fields also produced more journal articles and fewer monographs as compared to their low-paradigm counterparts. Greater social connectedness was exhibited by scholars in high-paradigm fields, possibly as a result of their common orientation to the work. Applied fields showed greater commitment to service activities, a higher rate of technical report publication, and greater reliance on colleague evaluation. Faculty in life system areas showed higher instance of group work with graduate students and a lesser commitment to teaching than their counterparts in nonlife systems areas. Empirical research applying the Biglan Model has been consistent in supporting its validity.

Discipline Differences

While the disciplines may share a common ethos, specifically a respect for knowledge and intellectual inquiry, differences between them are vast, so much

TABLE 1

Biglan's clustering of academic areas in three dimensions

Task Area	Hard		Soft	
	Nonlife System	Life System	Nonlife System	Life System
Pure	Astronomy	Botany	English	Anthropology
	Chemistry	Entomology	History	Political science
	Geology	Microbiology	Philosophy	Psychology
	Mathematics	Physiology	Communications	Sociology
	Physics	Zoology		
Applied	Ceramic engineering	Agronomy	Accounting	Educational administration
	Civil engineering	Dairy science	Finance	Secondary/Continuing education
	Computer science	Horticulture	Economics	Special education
	Mechanical engineering	Agricultural economics		Vocational/Technical education

SOURCE: Based on Biglan, Anthony. 1973. "Relationships between Subject Matter Characteristics and the Structure and Output of University Departments." *Journal of Applied Psychology* 57(3):204–213.

so in fact that discipline has been referred to as the major source of fragmentation in academe. Disciplines have been distinguished by styles of presentation, preferred approaches to investigation, and the degree to which they draw from other fields and respond to lay inquiries and concerns. Put simply, scholars in different disciplines "speak different languages" and in fact have been described as seeing things differently when they look at the same phenomena.

Differences in discipline communication structures, reward and stratification systems, and mechanisms for social control have been observed. In addition to these variations in structure of disciplinary systems, variations at the level of the individual scholar, the departmental level, and the university level, summarized in a 1996 work by John M. Braxton and Lowell L. Hargens, are drawing a good bit of scholarly attention. To illustrate the extent and content of differences reflected in the literature, a comparative review of discipline differences, based on nature of knowledge, community life and culture, communication patterns, and social relevance or engagement with the wider context, has been synthesized from the work of Tony Becher in Table 2.

It is important to note that the differences captured here encompass both epistemological and social characteristics of each of the four discipline groups. Much of the early study of disciplinary variation focused primarily on the epistemological or cognitive aspects, and it was essentially studies in the sociology of science that brought attention to the social aspects of disciplinary work. Indeed the social

factor is becoming more a focus of study with increased attention to the disciplinary impacts on academic organization and leadership. In better understanding how social and epistemological characteristics are manifested in disciplinary groups, scholars will move closer to a theory of discipline differences.

See also: FACULTY PERFORMANCE OF RESEARCH AND SCHOLARSHIP; FACULTY ROLES AND RESPONSIBILITIES.

BIBLIOGRAPHY

BECHER, TONY. 1987. "The Disciplinary Shaping of the Profession." In *The Academic Profession: National, Disciplinary, and Institutional Settings,* ed. Burton R. Clark. Berkeley: University of California Press.

BECHER, TONY. 1989. *Academic Tribes and Territories: Intellectual Enquiry and the Cultures of the Disciplines.* Bury St. Edmunds, Eng.: Society for Research into Higher Education, Open University Press.

BEYER, JANICE M., and LODAHL, THOMAS M. 1976. "A Comparative Study of Patterns of Influence in United States and English Universities." *Administrative Science Quarterly* 21:104–129.

BIGLAN, ANTHONY. 1973. "The Characteristics of Subject Matter in Different Academic Areas." *Journal of Applied Psychology* 58:195–203.

BIGLAN, ANTHONY. 1973. "Relationships between Subject Matter Characteristics and the Structure

TABLE 2

Characteristics of discipline groups

Discipline Group	Category	Description
Hard-Pure	Nature of knowledge	Cumulative; atomistic (crystalline/tree-like); concerned with universals, quantities, simplification; resulting in discovery/explanation
	Community life/culture	Competitive, gregarious social patterns; politically well-organized; high publication rate; task-oriented
	Communication patterns	1. Social interaction in the context of teams; high people-to-problem ratio; rapid pace; demand for progress reporting strong 2. Leadership qualities include tough-mindedness, organizing ability, and entrepreneurial flair
	Social relevance/wider context	1. High prestige 2. Commonly held to be intellectually demanding and attracting individuals of high ability 3. Substantial dependence on external sponsorship 4. Research funding requirements call for effective professional political lobby
Hard-Applied	Nature of knowledge	Purposive; pragmatic (know-how versus hard knowledge); concerned with mastery of the physical environment; resulting in products/techniques
	Community life/culture	Entrepreneurial, cosmopolitan; dominated by professional values; patents substitutable for publications; role-oriented
	Communication patterns	1. Comparatively less teamwork in research; modest pace; time to publication of new knowledge not seen as crucial; contact maintained by correspondence 2. Leadership qualities include tough-mindedness, organizing ability, and entrepreneurial flair
	Social relevance/wider context	1. Research promise often assessed by utilitarian criteria instead of theoretical purity 2. Political insistence often required to promote favor of applied work 3. Active competition for research funds 4. Substantial dependence on goodwill of public and private support for research
Soft-Pure	Nature of knowledge	Reiterative; holistic (organic/river-like); concerned with particulars, qualities, complication; resulting in understanding/interpretation
	Community life/culture	Individualistic, pluralistic; solitary social patterns; loosely structured; low publication rate; person-oriented
	Communication patterns	Pace of interchange leisurely; public networks are more symbolic (show of social solidarity) than for sharing of ideas; occasional conference attendance, stay in touch by reading what others publish; no strong requirement for rapid publication
	Social relevance/wider context	1. Knowledge largely atheoretical involving the study of the particular rather than general and the search for empathetic understanding not causal explanation 2. Forms of knowledge viewed ambivalently by the external world 3. Large monetary investment unneeded and consequently little demand on the public for support 4. Individualism is an inherent feature of research 5. Relatively weak professional organizations
Soft-Applied	Nature of knowledge	Functional; utilitarian (know-how versus soft knowledge); concerned with enhancement of professional or semiprofessional practice; resulting in protocols/procedures
	Community life/culture	Outward-looking; uncertain in status; dominated by intellectual fashions; publication rate reduced by consulting activity; power-oriented
	Communication patterns	Pattern comparable to soft-pure; no strong requirement for rapid publication; relatively few conferences
	Social relevance/wider context	1. Research agenda susceptible to nonacademic interests 2. Comparatively less autonomy because of strong influence of practitioner associations 3. Relevance and usefulness of topics is often called into question by government and client interests

SOURCE: Courtesy of author.

and Output of University Departments." *Journal of Applied Psychology* 57(3):204–213.

BRAXTON, JOHN M., and HARGENS, LOWELL L. 1996. "Variations among Academic Disciplines: Analytical Frameworks and Research." In *Higher Education: Handbook of Theory and Research*, Vol. XI, ed. John C. Smart. New York: Agathon Press.

CLARK, BURTON R., ed. 1987. *The Academic Profession: National, Disciplinary, and Institutional Settings.* Los Angeles: University of California Press.

KOLB, DAVID A. 1981. "Learning Styles and Disciplinary Differences." In *The Modern American College*, ed. Arthur W. Chickering. San Francisco: Jossey-Bass.

KUHN, THOMAS S. 1996. *The Structure of Scientific Revolutions,* 3rd edition. Chicago: University of Chicago Press.

LADD, EVERETT C., and LIPSET, SEYMOUR MARTIN. 1975. *The Divided Academy: Professors and Politics.* Berkeley, CA: Carnegie Commission on Higher Education.

LIGHT, DONALD, JR. 1974. "Introduction: The Structure of the Academic Professions." *Sociology of Education* 47(winter):2–28.

LODAHL, JANICE B., and GORDON, GERALD. 1972. "The Structure of Scientific Fields and the Functioning of University Graduate Departments." *American Sociological Review* 37(February):57–72.

RUSCIO, KENNETH P. 1987. "Many Sectors, Many Professions." In *The Academic Profession: National, Disciplinary, and Institutional Settings,* ed. Burton R. Clark. Los Angeles: University of California Press.

MARIETTA DEL FAVERO

ACADEMIC FREEDOM AND TENURE

Professors have a variety of responsibilities, which generally fall within one of three main areas: research, teaching, and service. In research and teaching, and sometimes in service, inquiry is the key aspect of what professors do. In research, professors examine traditional and new ideas and draw conclusions; in teaching, professors share information and knowledge with students, raising questions and at times offering answers about issues. And, in service, professors bring their expertise to a problem, using inquiry to aid in the solution. These fundamental activities give rise to complex concepts: academic freedom and tenure.

Roots of Academic Freedom

Academic freedom in the United States derives its conceptual basis from nineteenth-century German conceptions of freedom for professors in research and teaching. These conceptions, called *Lehrfreiheit,* offered legal protections for professors, who were employed as civil servants in German universities. U.S. professors who had studied in Germany in the 1800s (the most popular location for graduate study at the time) returned home focused on research as a search for truth. As American professors increasingly challenged a variety of economic, political, and social tenets, a need for academic safeguards soon arose. By the early 1900s, a few nationally recognized professors had been dismissed by their universities because of their findings on such issues as the abuse of immigrant labor, unions, and administrative control of universities.

Initially, disciplinary societies investigated these dismissals, although they had virtually no power to sanction institutions, other than through public discussion of institutional errors of judgment. A national professorial organization, the American Association of University Professors (AAUP), was founded in 1915 in an effort to provide opportunities for professors to influence, if not control, colleges and universities. Association leaders found, however, that the most pressing challenge was the protection of academic freedom, and the AAUP became the primary national group dedicated to the preservation of academic freedom. Although German professors were protected as civil servants, United States professors have had to rely on the activity of organizations such as AAUP. In 1915, 1925, and 1940, the AAUP developed national policy statements on academic freedom, and the 1940 *Statement on Principles of Academic Freedom and Tenure* has been endorsed by a wide range of educational organizations, whose membership ranges from mostly professors to mostly administrators. The statement provides a definition of academic freedom, including that:

1. The teacher is entitled to full freedom in research and in the publication of the results, subject to the adequate performance of his other academic duties; but research for pecuniary return should be based upon an understanding with the authorities of the institution.

2. The teacher is entitled to freedom in the classroom in discussing his subject, but he should be careful not to introduce into his teaching controversial matter that has no relation to his subject. Limitations of academic freedom because of religious or other aims of the institution should be clearly stated in writing at the time of the appointment.

The AAUP proposed that institutions assure such freedom through the device of academic tenure, and the 1940 statement outlined specific procedures in regard to the award and removal of tenure, indicating that "teachers or investigators should have permanent or continuous tenure, and their service should be terminated only for adequate cause, except in the retirement for age, or under extraordinary circumstances because of financial exigencies" (p. 4), and that moral turpitude may be cause for dismissal. The statement also indicates that professors should exercise restraint in their public utterances, in view of their special position as experts. Tenure is a device that protects, to some degree, professors' academic freedom.

Thus, academic freedom is the freedom to inquire and to communicate the results of that inquiry both in publication and in the classroom. The AAUP definition has important exceptions to such freedom, including for institutions with religious aims since these institutions often require statements of faith that preclude unfettered inquiry, with truth defined by a church or denomination. However, a 1970 interpretation addressed this exception, indicating that church-related institutions, which were becoming increasingly secular, needed to address the principle of academic freedom.

Restrictions on Academic Freedom

Other organizations have also developed statements on academic freedom, including the American Federation of Teachers (AFT), the National Education Association (NEA), and in the 1950s, the Association of American Universities. The AFT and NEA issued a joint statement in the 1990s, one that reflects much of the sentiment of the 1940 AAUP statement. The statement of the Association of American Universities on academic freedom in 1953, however, placed substantial restrictions on professors, claiming, for example, that membership in the Communist Party warranted dismissal. Such a claim was in the context of McCarthyism, when much of the nation was gripped with fear about Communist infiltration of political and intellectual sectors of society, yet the claim also put academic freedom in conflict with the First Amendment of the United States Constitution. The AAUP itself, in a 1956 statement on academic freedom, indicated that it was legitimate to question the competence of professors who were Communists. As several scholars have noted, restrictions on public utterances are, in fact, restrictions on freedom

of speech as constructed in the First Amendment of the U.S. Constitution. Thus, statements on academic freedom are not necessarily absolute statements of principle.

Nor does academic freedom exist outside the social characteristics of the academy. An empirical analysis of AAUP academic freedom cases involving dismissed professors in the 1980s indicated that there was a gendered bias in academic freedom and tenure issues, for institutions often removed women professors before considering the removal of other faculty members. This finding suggests that women occupy an especially vulnerable place in the academy, regardless of the protections offered by academic freedom and tenure. Throughout the 1970s, 1980s, and 1990s, the AAUP leadership and membership debated the relationships of academic freedom to such issues as race, ethnicity, and gender, and the association has addressed these relationships through a variety of policy statements.

In addition, academic freedom entails areas of behavior with important nuances. Examinations of professors in times of specific societal concerns about patterns of thought—such as McCarthyism or the segregation in the deep South—indicate that professors may restrict their work without acknowledging any restriction on their academic freedom. Any such apprehensions about academic freedom (which scholars have documented as a key issue of academic freedom) reflect external pressures and, perhaps just as important, individual professors' hesitancy to challenge the status quo.

Finally, in view of the challenges to society and institutions that occur as a result of inquiry in the academy, there are disparate views regarding academic freedom, and there is even a tendency to individual interpretation. While the AAUP statements on academic freedom have been central points of reference, other organizations have added to the meanings of academic freedom, and individual colleges and universities may also develop their own definitions of the concept. In general, it represents the freedom of the professor to do research and to teach on matters of expertise, but specific characteristics often vary depending on the era, the topic of concern, the individual professor, and the institutions involved. Academic freedom is also dependent on a college or university's willingness to protect the professor, especially by guaranteeing his or her appointment. Tenure is the primary device for such guarantees.

Tenure

Tenure, in general, provides a lifetime contract between a professor and an institution, and as such serves as the primary safeguard for academic freedom. The AAUP initiated negotiations with the Association of American Colleges in the 1930s in order to develop its 1940 statement, and a central goal of the AAUP leadership was to ensure procedures, through the use of tenure, that would protect academic freedom. Careful processes for the dismissal of a tenured professor are offered in detail in the 1940 statement, with several subsequent interpretations to further the right of professors to due process. Institutions do dismiss professors with tenure, although far less often than they dismiss professors without tenure, since the dismissal of a tenured professor can be a protracted experience and may include lawsuits as well as lengthy institutional procedures.

Tenure often requires a probationary period of seven years, during which the professor is expected to develop the patterns of productivity, especially in scholarship and teaching, that will characterize his or her work for the remainder of the career. In the last year or so of the probationary period, the tenure candidate proceeds through a review process, which usually includes fellow professors as well as administrators and culminates in a decision to award or deny tenure. Professors who do not receive tenure may leave higher education, or move to another college or university—sometimes in a tenure-track position, and other times in a position that will never offer tenure.

There are a variety of arguments about the worth of tenure, including many opposing views. It is unclear whether institutions spend more or less money when they have tenured faculty members, as the condition of tenure is a device for recruiting potential professors at less than pure market competitive conditions, but then requires an institution to maintain its contract—and increases in salary and benefits—with the tenured professor. Some institutions have used contracts (often in three- or five-year sequences), rather than tenure, as a way of establishing flexibility. These institutions have often found, however, that it is extremely rare for them to dismiss any of the contracted professors. Additionally, tenure does not protect the academic freedom of untenured professors, an issue that became extremely important in the 1990s, when the number of part-time and non-tenure-track professors surged.

Nevertheless, tenure remains a dominant characteristic of the U.S. professoriate. For several decades, from two-thirds to half of all full-time professors have held tenure, and the national faculty associations continue to place considerable emphasis on tenure. Despite arguments against tenure, colleges and universities have not found any compelling substitutes that offer professors some security when they pursue controversial topics in their research and teaching.

Academic freedom is a cornerstone of the role of higher education, offering professors the opportunity to investigate issues, including highly controversial ones, in the ongoing search for truth. Tenure offers protection for professors who voice unpopular ideas. Neither academic freedom nor tenure, however, operates in a pure sense, as both are subject to social and institutional pressures.

See also: FACULTY PERFORMANCE OF RESEARCH AND SCHOLARSHIP; FACULTY RESEARCH AND SCHOLARSHIP, ASSESSMENT OF; FACULTY ROLES AND RESPONSIBILITIES.

BIBLIOGRAPHY

AMERICAN ASSOCIATION OF UNIVERSITY PROFESSORS. 1984. "1940 Statement of Principles and Interpretive Comments." *Policy Document Reports*, 1940 edition. Washington, DC: American Association of University Professors.

GRUBER, CAROL. 1975. *Mars and Minerva: World War I and the Uses of Higher Learning.* Baton Rouge: Louisiana State University Press.

HOFSTADTER, RICHARD, and METZGER, WALTER P. 1955. *The Development of Academic Freedom in the United States.* New York: Columbia University Press.

HUTCHESON, PHILO A. 2000. *A Professional Professoriate: Unionization, Bureaucratization, and the AAUP.* Nashville, TN: Vanderbilt University Press.

SLAUGHTER, SHEILA. 1994. "Academic Freedom at the End of the Century: Professional Labor, Gender, and Professionalism." In *Higher Education in American Society,* 3rd edition, ed. Philip G. Altbach, Robert O. Berdahl, and Patricia J. Gumport. Buffalo, NY: Promotheus Books.

PHILO HUTCHESON

ACADEMIC LABOR MARKETS

The process by which colleges and universities acquire qualified applicants and hire faculty members, and by which academics seek and gain academic employment, is known as the academic labor market. Few general elements characterize the academic labor market. Depending on their mission, colleges and universities seek faculty with diverse backgrounds to perform different institutional roles. Likewise academics seek different positions depending upon their aspirations and education. The academic labor market fluctuates by demographics, the demands created by student preferences, and alterations in society's employment opportunities. Finally, the academic labor market is also influenced by social norms.

In the mid-nineteenth century American colleges tended to look very much the same. Led by an academic president, colleges employed a handful of faculty members who taught several subjects. In the twenty-first century postsecondary institutions range from community colleges that offer two-year associate degrees in the liberal arts and technical and pre-professional fields to research universities (often called *multiversities*) that provide baccalaureate through doctoral education, as well as televised football games. The distinction among these diverse institutions resides in their missions. Many colleges and smaller universities are dedicated primarily to teaching, whereas others attach great significance to their research output. Thus, the institutional mission defines the role of the faculty at a particular institution.

Teaching institutions search for and hire faculty members who are oriented primarily to the student and the classroom. In community colleges, instructors teach approximately fifteen hours, or five courses, per semester. At liberal arts (only baccalaureate degrees) and comprehensive (both baccalaureate and master's degrees) colleges, faculty members teach three or four courses per term. At the other end of the spectrum research universities seek academics who spend as much, if not more, of their time producing scholarship as they do in instructional activities. Since research university faculty members are expected to conduct and publish research results regularly, their teaching load generally consists of two courses each term.

Community colleges, therefore, tend to hire faculty members who are more interested in teaching than in research. Approximately two-thirds of the faculty in these two-year colleges have earned master's degrees, while only 15 percent possess the doctorate. In almost all other types of collegiate institutions, the doctorate, which educates recipients to a life of research, is a requirement for entry. Most four-year and master's degree institutions seek faculty members for their interest in teaching. As a result of their doctoral education, these faculty also often engage in research and publication. However, except for prestigious liberal arts colleges, most do not exist in a "publish or perish" environment.

The competition for faculty appointments at research universities extends beyond the possession of the doctorate. Those aspiring to a faculty position are rarely selected for an interview if they have not published several articles and given several presentations at professional meetings. In days gone by the prestige of a particular dissertation mentor brought a young scholar to the attention of a research university department seeking a new hire. Today, however, while a renowned mentor may still be helpful, an applicant's publishing career is just as important.

Supply and Demand

The institutional demands and professional preferences of faculty applicants are compounded by issues of supply and demand. The faculty supply depends in part on the output of graduate programs across the nation. When faculty positions are plentiful, students flock to graduate school—as they did in the late 1960s, when college enrollments soared. However, faculty members are not interchangeable across their specialties. If enrollment demands shift away from or towards certain academic programs, as they did in the mid-1970s, colleges and universities must respond by adjusting the distribution of faculty positions. By 1975 the supply of liberal arts faculty overwhelmed demand; thus many new Ph.D.s had to seek nonacademic employment and institutions hired instructors with more prestigious credentials than previously.

The supply of potential faculty members also depends on the professional interests and aspirations of graduate students. In 2000 there were 41,368 doctoral degrees awarded across the various fields, but these were not evenly distributed. Twenty-one percent of the doctorates were awarded in the life sciences, including biology and zoology, while only 2.5 percent were awarded in business. The number of graduates is only half the equation, however. The graduates' aspirations and the availability of nonacademic professional employment further reduce the supply. In engineering, for example, 5,330 doctorates were awarded in 2000, but 70 percent of these graduates intended to enter industry research positions rather than education. Nonacademic employment opportunities are uneven across fields, and thus create either expanded or limited career choices for doctoral graduates. Of all doctoral graduates in 2000, only 38 percent intended to seek a teaching position. The rest planned to enter research and development (31 percent), administration (12 percent), or professional services, such as counseling (12.5 percent). By field, graduates in the humanities aspired to teaching positions most often (74 percent), while only 11 percent of doctoral engineers planned to teach.

Gender and Ethnicity

The supply of faculty also involves gender and ethnicity differentials. Fields differ in attracting men and women, as well as members of various ethnic groups. In the early twenty-first century men continued to dominate some fields, such as engineering, physical science, and, to a lesser degree, business. In the year 2000 women earned 65 percent of the doctorates in education. Some other fields, such as humanities, social sciences, and life sciences, awarded doctorates in even proportions. All fields attract predominately white aspirants, but some fields appear to be slightly more attractive (or receptive) to members of certain ethnic groups. African Americans are slightly more likely to enter education (12.4 %) than other fields, while Asian Americans lean more toward engineering (17.5%).

On the demand side, social norms have affected the hiring of women and ethnic minorities in colleges and universities. The proportion of women within American faculties increased throughout the 1990s. By 1997, women composed 36 percent of all full-time instructional faculty; however, women are more likely to be employed as full-time faculty members within two-year (47%), rather than four-year (33%), colleges. The gender distribution among all part-time faculty gives a slight advantage to men (53%).

Institutions of higher education attempted to recruit faculty of color to campuses throughout the 1980s and the 1990s through affirmative action programs. However, the ethnic distribution still does not reflect national demographics. In 1998, 85 percent of the faculty were white, 6 percent were Asian, 5 percent were African American, and 3 percent were Hispanic. Colleges and universities with enrollments consisting predominantly of one ethnic group (e.g., African American, Hispanic, Native American) tend to employ higher percentages of that ethnic group than other institutions. Approximately 16 percent of African-American faculty members teach in historically black institutions. This pattern reduces the distribution of faculty of color within the general labor market. Finally, high-demand labor markets support the hiring of minorities, whereas a high-supply market merely creates more competition across ethnic lines and seems to favor white candidates.

Salary Issues

Salaries offered to faculty recruits largely depend on the type of institution, the rank at which a faculty member is hired, the field, and, to some degree, gender and ethnicity. Faculty members in public institutions receive 22 percent less compensation than their private-institution colleagues. On the whole, faculty members earn an average of $8,600 more at four-year institutions than at two-year institutions, and two-year college faculty average 55 percent less than doctoral university faculty. Those who work in research earn higher salaries than faculty in teaching institutions. The salary differentials between institutional types largely spring from the imperative to recruit and retain faculty members who are at the forefront of knowledge in their fields.

Although 69 percent of American faculty teach in four-year colleges, 82 percent of Asian-American faculty members are employed at these institutions. Two-thirds of the Asian-American faculty are men. Not surprisingly then, Asian-American faculty average higher salaries than any other ethnic group. Full-time Hispanic faculty members earn slightly below-average salaries, in part because 43 percent of all Hispanic faculty teach in two-year colleges and 48 percent are part-time faculty.

Men still take home more money than women do, regardless of rank. The gender differentiation in salary is sometimes explained by the short length of time women have served as faculty, or by their lower publication rates, resulting in employment at lower ranks. Indeed, only 16 percent of all full-time women faculty are full professors, while 32 percent of all full-time men have attained this rank. However, men comprise 80 percent of all full professors. In

1998 the average female professor earned $8,500 less than her male counterpart. This pay inequity crosses ethnic lines as well. Seventy-one percent of all professors are white men. Within the other ethnic groups, men also dominate the highest rank: 63 percent of all black professors, 85 percent of all Asian professors, and 73 percent of all Hispanic professors are men. Thus, women across all ethnic groups have yet to emerge proportionately into the highest ranks, and thus receive higher salaries.

Salary is also associated with field differentiation. Humanities and education, which attract significant numbers of women, are among the lower-paying fields, whereas engineering, law, and business, fields still dominated by men, produce higher salaries. In the 1999–2000 academic year, the salary difference between high-paying fields and low-paying fields, on average, was $24,000 for professors and $16,000 for assistant professors.

At the beginning of the twenty-first century few institutions are experiencing the rapid growth in enrollment, and thus the massive faculty hiring, of the late 1960s. Tight institutional finances and the need for flexibility have also changed the demand for faculty. As states cut back their support of public institutions, and as private institutions attempt to hold down escalating tuition costs, the sizable group of retiring faculty has enabled institutions to establish new hiring patterns. Rather than automatically replacing retirees with tenure-track assistant professors, many institutions have instituted non-tenure-track positions or hired part-time faculty to fill the classrooms. In 1997 only 73 percent of the faculty in public four-year colleges were full-time employees, while 59 percent of those at private four-year colleges were full-time. Students are more likely to be taught by part-time faculty at community colleges, where 66 percent of the faculty have part-time status. Private colleges and universities appear to have more opportunity to experiment with non-tenure-track and part-time positions than public institutions. Only 58 percent of their faculty are tenured, as opposed to 66 percent in public colleges and universities.

In ways similar to other labor markets, academe is composed of various types of organizations with differing needs. Its academic staff and its hiring patterns are changing as society changes its demands for education and its norms for equality.

See also: COLLEGE TEACHING; FACULTY MEMBERS, PART TIME; FACULTY PERFORMANCE OF RESEARCH AND SCHOLARSHIP; FACULTY RESEARCH AND SCHOLARSHIP, ASSESSMENT OF; FACULTY TEACHING, ASSESSMENT OF.

BIBLIOGRAPHY

BALDWIN, ROGER, and CHRONISTER, JAY. 2001. *Teaching without Tenure: Policies and Practices for a New Era.* Baltimore: John Hopkins University Press.

FAIRWEATHER, JAMES S. 1996. *Faculty Work and Public Trust: Restoring the Value of Teaching and Public Service in American Academic Life.* Boston: Allyn and Bacon.

FINKELSTEIN, MARTIN J., and SCHUSTER, JACK H. 2001. "Assessing the Silent Revolution." *AAHE Bulletin* 54(2):3–7.

FINKELSTEIN, MARTIN J.; SEAL, ROBERT K.; and SCHUSTER, JACK H. 1998. *The New Academic Generation: A Profession in Transformation.* Baltimore: Johns Hopkins University Press.

FINNEGAN, DOROTHY E.; WEBSTER, DAVID; and GAMSON, ZELDA F., eds. 1996. *Faculty and Faculty Issues in Colleges and Universities.* ASHE Reader Series. Needham Heights, MA: Simon and Schuster Custom Publishing.

GLAZER-RAYMO, JUDITH. 1999. *Shattering the Myths: Women in Academe.* Baltimore: Johns Hopkins University Press.

MANRIQUE, CECILIA G., and MANRIQUE, GABRIEL G. 1999. *The Multicultural or Immigrant Family in American Society.* Lewiston, NY: The Edwin Mellen Press.

INTERNET RESOURCE

NATIONAL CENTER FOR EDUCATIONAL STATISTICS. 1997–1998. *Integrated Postsecondary Data System.* <www.nces.ed.gov/ipeds>.

DOROTHY E. FINNEGAN

ACADEMIC MAJOR, THE

The major field of study is the most prominent and significant structural element of the American baccalaureate degree. For students it is often a key to choosing which college or university to attend. College catalogs frequently claim certain types of learning result from study in a particular academic major. They also often suggest that study in specific majors prepares individuals for graduate education and for specific jobs and careers, and that it can impart certain specialized knowledge. Research affirms that the academic major is the strongest and clearest curricular link to gains in student learning.

Across higher education there is a tremendous variety of academic majors—ranging from art history to political science to zoology. Collectively these represent several hundred fields and subfields of study. The major field of study is often thought of synonymously with academic disciplines (e.g., history, physics, music); however majors also represent professional fields (e.g., education, engineering) and interdisciplinary fields (e.g., African-American studies, ecological studies). Employers interview students at specific institutions based on the perceived match between their needs and a corresponding major program. A significant portion of the gifts and grants given to colleges and universities come based on the rank, reputation, or perceived quality of one or more academic majors.

The major provides in-depth study in one of the fields in which an institution awards a degree. General education imparts knowledge, skills, and abilities drawn from the various realms of liberal learning and is the *breadth* component to the undergraduate degree. The major, on the other hand, is the *depth* component, providing the student with (a) terms, concepts, ideas, and events pertinent to the field; (b) models, frameworks, genres, theories, and themes that link phenomena and give them meaning; (c) methods of research and modes of inquiry appropriate to the area of study; and (d) criteria for arriving at a conclusion or making generalizations about that which is studied.

An academic major may serve multiple purposes. The major may represent specialization in a disciplinary or interdisciplinary field attendant to liberal learning, and as such can be regarded as nonpreparatory specialization. It may also serve as the student's first introduction to a field of study that is manifested in postgraduate study as well. In addition, the major serves as preparation for one or several professional fields. Thus, a student may choose to study biology for its own merits, in preparation for graduate work in the biological or life sciences, or as preparation for entry into medicine or health-

related fields. In some instances students may create their own majors reflecting their own interests or the specific competencies they wish to develop. Aside from such instances, the faculty with expertise in the field of study prescribe the entrance qualifications for students, the number of courses or credits required to complete the major, the content of those courses, the number and sequence of courses, and the requirement of exams, papers, or theses associated with satisfactorily completing study in the subject area.

The Rise of the Disciplines and Majors

Major fields of study emerged in the nineteenth century as alternative components of the undergraduate degree. In 1825 the University of Virginia offered students eight programs from which to choose, including ancient languages, anatomy, and medicine. Following the American Civil War, academics increasingly received their advanced training in continental Europe. Specialization at the undergraduate level and in graduate and professional studies developed quickly in the latter half of the nineteenth century. The term *major* was first used in the 1877–1878 catalog of Johns Hopkins University, as was the term *minor,* signifying a course of specialized study less lengthy than the major—the major required two years of study, while the minor required but one. From 1880 to 1910, institutions offering the American baccalaureate degree widely adopted the free elective system, whereby a student might choose from the courses offered by the institution to amass credits necessary for degree completion.

In research universities particularly, the German concepts of *Lernfreiheit* and *Lehrfreiheit* were freely interpreted by American academics as the professors' freedom to teach and to conduct research as scholarly interest and inquiry dictated, and as the students' freedom to select those courses, seminars, and topics that propelled the individual's intellectual development and curiosity. Majors and minors became widely adopted in such institutions, providing prescription and socialization of students to the language, perspectives, and values of disciplinary inquiry.

The development of academic majors deeply structured not only the curriculum but also the organization of institutions. Nearly all colleges and universities have academic departments that reflect the primary academic disciplines and applied fields of study, such as English, education, mathematics, and sociology. The department is often thought to be synonymous with the discipline or field of study, yet a department may offer several academic majors representing various subfields of study. Proponents of the department and the major argue that they enable an academic community to foster the development, conservation, and diffusion of knowledge. In contrast, critics claim that they promote intellectual tribalism, where specialization receives favor over the mastery of multiple epistemologies, where broader values of liberal learning and of campus unity are lost, and where innovation is inhibited due to parochial opposition to new subspecialties and research methods.

Structure

Most colleges and universities offer majors, though they are more common in professional and technical colleges than in liberal arts colleges. While they are common features of baccalaureate-granting institutions, majors are frequently only present in the pre-professional, technical, and vocational subjects of associate degree (two-year) colleges. Credits required for the major represent 20 to 50 percent of the bachelor of arts degree and 20 to 40 percent of the associate of arts degree. Study in a professional field may require more credits and a greater proportion of the overall degree within the major than study in a liberal arts field. Also, professional majors may be subject to professional accreditation and state licensing.

Courses within disciplinary, applied, field, and professional studies majors possess an inherent coherence generated by the knowledge structures and paradigms of that single discipline or field. While such courses may be highly bounded by the way knowledge is organized within a given discipline, they possess a certain inherent coherence as a result. Interdisciplinary majors possess a coherence represented in the theme or focus to which they are addressed, although they are more permeable to the addition of subjects or topics than traditional disciplinary majors. Thus, the American studies major may incorporate relevant courses from history and literature, but may also include art or architecture. Coherence is found in the interdisciplinary focus on American society and culture.

Interdisciplinary Majors

One innovation that draws upon the disciplines is the interdisciplinary major. One of the earliest interdisciplinary majors was American studies. Arising in the 1930s, its organizers and proponents used the concept of culture to serve as one of its organizing principles. Other areas, such as Russian studies and Latin American studies, developed later, primarily due to government and foundation interests in foreign relations. Majors, like individual courses, come into existence in response to social, intellectual, or technical issues and interests. In the early 1970s, new interdisciplinary majors, such as women's studies and black studies, derived their interest from the civil rights movement. These majors relied on cultural issues for content and ethnography for method. Interdisciplinary majors often rely on related disciplines for their teaching faculty, and the interdisciplinary majors often use what may constitute electives in traditional disciplinary fields. Thus, a course in women's literature may serve as an elective in an English major and a required course in a women's studies major.

Students, Academic Majors, and Disciplinary Knowledge

Disciplinary inquiry often supersedes institutional goals in defining the direction and purpose with which undergraduates study. A discipline is literally what the term implies. When one studies a discipline, one subjugates the ways one learns about phenomena to a set of rules, rituals, and routines established by the field of study. A student learns to study according to these rules, classifying phenomena according to commonly adopted terms, definitions, and concepts of the major field. Relationships among phenomena are revealed through the frames provided by the discipline, and the researcher or student arrives at conclusions based on criteria for truth or validity derived from the major field.

Disciplines can provide conceptual frameworks for understanding what knowledge is and how it is acquired. Disciplinary learning provides a logical structure to relationships between concepts, propositions, common paradigms, and organizing principles. Disciplines develop themes, canons, and grand narratives to join different streams of research in the field and to provide meaningful conceptualizations and frameworks for further analysis, and they impart a truth criteria used globally to define differences in the way knowledge is acquired and valued. They also set parameters on the methods employed in discovering and analyzing knowledge, and how they affect the development of students' intellectual skills.

Not only are the paradigms of inquiry imparted by disciplines, but so too are values and norms regarding membership and scholarly conduct within the major field, as well as the preferred modes of learning (canonized texts, methods of investigation, and schools of interpretation). Disciplines provide much structure and coherence to learning. It is easy to underestimate their power and importance in the advancement of knowledge and understanding at the undergraduate level. It is not clear whether a student or a faculty member can be truly interdisciplinary without first mastering one or more disciplines. The ascendancy of the disciplines in the late nineteenth century and their continuing dominance throughout the twentieth century have left an indelible imprint on the shape and direction of the academic major. It also has subjugated the aims of general and liberal studies to the perspectives and political rivalries of individual departments and specialized fields. It was only in the late 1980s and 1990s that interdisciplinary studies, multiculturalism, feminist pedagogy, and a renewed concern for the coherence and direction of the undergraduate program began to assail the baccalaureate degree dominated by the academic major.

Evaluation of Programs and Majors

Academic majors are subject to review as part of the institutional accreditation process. Specialized accrediting bodies, such as the Accrediting Board for Engineering and Technology and the American Occupational Therapy Association, also evaluate many majors in applied and professional fields. Finally, institutions themselves often insist on periodic reviews of academic programs and their majors. Regional, specialized, and institutional program reviewers most frequently rely on the judgments and observations of peers in conducting these evaluations. Peer reviewers who visit a department or program as part of the accreditation process often praise those units that use their own statement of purpose and educational objectives to frame its description of the characteristics and competencies it intends its student to acquire in the given major. Such reviewers also expect the teaching faculty to establish measurable learning objectives for what they expect their student to learn—not only in specific courses, but in the major field as a whole.

Conclusions

At the outset of the twenty-first century, students, teachers, employers, parents, and lawmakers often ascribe a liberal arts education largely to the academic major studied; i.e., they believe the major and the degree are largely one in the same. Majors, at least conversationally, have become more imitative of graduate study. Until the rise of the universities, the elective system, and the academic major, most—if not all—of undergraduate courses were taken by all of the students at an institution. The academic major, a twentieth-century phenomenon, implies a uniformity of curriculum for any group of students; however, that uniformity has become the major more than the institution in which it resides. That the academic major is a powerful and predominant tool of the baccalaureate degree is both its strength and its limitation.

See also: CURRICULUM, HIGHER EDUCATION; FACULTY PERFORMANCE OF RESEARCH AND SCHOLARSHIP; FACULTY ROLES AND RESPONSIBILITIES.

BIBLIOGRAPHY

BECHER, TONY. 1989. *Academic Tribes and Territories: Intellectual Enquiry and the Cultures of Disciplines.* Bristol, PA: Open University Press.

BECHER, TONY, and KOGAN, MAURICE. 1992. *Process and Structure in Higher Education,* 2nd edition. London: Routledge.

BIGLAN, ANTHONY. 1973. "The Characteristics of Subject Matter in Different Academic Areas." *Journal of Applied Psychology* 57:195–203.

BIGLAN, ANTHONY. 1973. "Relationships between Subject Matter Characteristics and the Structure and Output of University Departments." *Journal of Applied Psychology* 57:204–213.

CARNOCHAN, W. B. 1993. *The Battleground of the Curriculum: Liberal Education and American Experience.* Stanford, CA: Stanford University Press.

CONRAD, CLIFTON F. 1978. *The Undergraduate Curriculum: A Guide to Innovation and Reform.* Boulder, CO: Westview Press.

DONALD, JANET G. 1986. "Knowledge and the University Curriculum." *Higher Education* 15:267–282.

HOLLAND, JOHN. 1963. "Explorations of a Theory of Vocational Choice and Achievement II: A Four Year Predictive Study." *Psychological Reports* 12:547–594.

HUTCHINSON, PHILO A. 1997. "Structures and Practices." In *Handbook of the Undergraduate Cur-*

riculum: A Comprehensive Guide to Purposes, Structures, Practices, and Change, ed. Jerry G. Gaff and James L. Ratcliff. San Francisco: Jossey-Bass.

KOLB, DAVID A. 1981. "Learning Styles and Disciplinary Differences." In *The Modern American College: Responding to the New Realities of Diverse Students and a Changing Society,* ed. Arthur W. Chickering et al. San Francisco: Jossey-Bass.

KOLB, DAVID A. 1984. *Experiential Learning: Experience as the Source of Learning and Development.* New York: Prentice-Hall.

LEVINE, ARTHUR M. 1978. *Handbook on Undergraduate Curriculum.* San Francisco: Jossey-Bass.

PASCARELLA, ERNEST T., and TERENZINI, PATRICK T. 1991. *How College Affects Students: Findings and Insights from Twenty Years of Research.* San Francisco: Jossey-Bass.

RUDOLPH, FREDERICK. 1977. *Curriculum: A History of the American Undergraduate Course of Study Since 1636.* San Francisco: Jossey-Bass.

SHULMAN, LEE S. 1987. "Knowledge and Teaching." *Harvard Educational Review* 57:1–22.

JAMES L. RATCLIFF

ACADEMIC RESEARCH

See: ACADEMIC DISCIPLINES; ACADEMIC FREEDOM AND TENURE; FACULTY PERFORMANCE OF RESEARCH AND SCHOLARSHIP; FACULTY RESEARCH AND SCHOLARSHIP, ASSESSMENT OF; FACULTY ROLES AND RESPONSIBILITIES; FEDERAL FUNDING FOR ACADEMIC RESEARCH; RESEARCH GRANTS AND INDIRECT COSTS; RESEARCH UNIVERSITIES; TEACHING AND RESEARCH, RELATIONSHIP BETWEEN; UNIVERSITY-INDUSTRIAL RESEARCH COLLABORATION.

ACCELERATED SCHOOLS

Accelerated Schools emerged from a national school reform movement established in 1986 to replace academic remediation for at-risk students with academic enrichment. Research studies done in the 1980s documented a growing population of students who were at risk of educational failure because they lacked the experiences in their homes, families, and communities on which school success is based. These students were heavily concentrated among minority, immigrant, and single-parent families—and those with low parental education and income. Studies of the schools such students attended found heavy reliance on repetition and drill, as well as a glacial instructional pace, compared to schools with more advantaged pupils. The consequences of this uninspiring instruction, with its low expectations and stigmatization of students in at-risk situations, were viewed as contributing to an achievement gap for at-risk students that led to failure and dropping out of school.

Accelerated Schools were designed to bring all students into the academic mainstream through academic enrichment and acceleration by replacing remediation with gifted and talented instruction. In the fall of 1986 two schools were established as pilot schools in the San Francisco Bay Area to implement the ideas that had been derived from the earlier research. The goal was to transform these schools from an emphasis on remediation to an emphasis on acceleration. The schools were exposed to the ideas behind the project and asked to consider if they wanted to move forward with them. Both schools agreed to work with teams from Stanford University to implement Accelerated Schools at their sites. From this initial work on implementation, replication, and research, considerable development has taken place in terms of the knowledge base, the process of transformation, and the expansion of Accelerated Schools. In 2001 there were about 1,000 Accelerated Schools enrolling almost half a million children in forty-one states and in several foreign countries.

The Accelerated Schools approach aims to make all students academically able at an early age through *Powerful Learning,* an approach to enrichment that integrates curriculum, instructional strategies, and school context. Powerful Learning is embodied in student research activities, artistic endeavors, community studies, and a range of applications where knowledge is applied to real-world activities. Students are expected to generate authentic ideas, products, artistic performances, and problem solutions across subjects that can be assessed directly for quality, rather than assuming that examination scores will be adequate assessment instruments.

The conversion to acceleration requires an internal transformation of school culture. The Accelerated School incorporates a model of governance and operations built around three principles that empower the school community to adopt accelerated strategies: (1) *Unity of Purpose* refers to consensus by school staff, parents, and students on common goals, a search for strategies for reaching them, and accountability for results; (2) *Empowerment with Responsibility* refers to the establishment of the capacity of the participants to make key decisions in the school and home to implement change and to be accountable for results; and (3) *Building on Strengths* refers to the identification and utilization of the strengths of all of the participants in addressing school needs and creating powerful learning strategies.

Accelerated Schools Process

Accelerated Schools require the training and support services of both an external coach and internal facilitators to assist the school in following the model of transformation. External coaches are usually drawn from the central office staff of each district, and are given a day or more a week to work with the school. Internal facilitators are teacher leaders who are provided with time to assist the external coach in providing training and follow-up guidance. Both coaches and facilitators are trained at regional centers of the Accelerated Schools Project (ASP) through an intensive initial session of five days, followed by subsequent monthly training sessions of one or two days. Staff from regional centers train and communicate with coaches on a regular basis through telephone follow-up and school visits to provide support for coaches and facilitators and feedback to the school. Schools are provided with an Internal Assessment Toolkit to check implementation progress as well as guidelines for end-of-year assessment.

The transformation process puts great emphasis on placing school governance and decision-making in the hands of school staff, parents, and students so that they can take responsibility for transforming their own culture and practices. School staff and other members of the school community begin by taking stock of school strengths, challenges, and operations. This is done through initiating members into small research groups. Taking stock is followed by a community-wide effort to set out a future vision for the schools with specific goals. The results of the taking-stock summary are contrasted with the future vision to set out areas of priority that the school

must address. Governance at the school site is structured through cadres working on these priorities, a steering committee, and an overall decision-making body called *school as a whole* (SAW) that includes all school staff, parents, other community members, and student representatives. Each of these entities is guided through problem solving and decision making by a specific inquiry process that carefully defines each challenge and generates hypotheses on why the challenge exists. Hypotheses are tested, and solutions are sought that match those that are supported by data. Powerful learning approaches are developed to address learning challenges, and overall school results are evaluated periodically.

Both time and district support are major challenges. School staff and other participants need regular meeting times to do the research that taking stock, inquiry, and evaluation require, and to receive and apply training. Powerful Learning requires teamwork in constructing units, lessons, and learning experiences and sharing them—with the intent of always finding new ways to strengthen them. Governance can only be done through careful reflection and consideration of the usefulness of recommendations and the evidence that supports them. Appropriate time requirements include a minimum of six full days per year for staff development, as well as a weekly early-release day or its equivalent for governance, inquiry, and planning activities. Coaches and facilitators need time to plan and monitor school progress and provide additional training and support. District support includes not only meeting these time requirements, but also providing a coach with appropriate skills and the stability to enable the school to master the ASP process.

Results have been encouraging. Schools have reported substantial increases in student achievement, parent participation, community projects, student research, and artistic endeavors. Third-party evaluations have shown gains in student achievement of 8 percentiles in a national evaluation and about 40 percentiles in an urban sample of six schools when compared with similar schools not undertaking reforms. The accomplishments suggest that a school based on acceleration is superior to one using remediation for students in at-risk situations.

See also: ELEMENTARY EDUCATION, *subentry on* CURRENT TRENDS; SCHOOL REFORM; SECONDARY EDUCATION, *subentry on* CURRENT TRENDS.

BIBLIOGRAPHY

BLOOM, HOWARD; HAM, SANDRA; KAGEHIRO, SUSIE; MELTON, LAURA; O'BRIEN, JULIEANNE; ROCK, JOANN; and DOOLITTLE, FRED. 2000. *Evaluating the Accelerated Schools Program: A Look at Its Early Implementation and Impact on Student Achievement in Eight Schools.* New York: Manpower Development Research Corporation.

FINNAN, CHRISTINE, and SWANSON, JULIE D. 2000. *Accelerating the Learning of All Students.* Boulder, CO: Westview Press.

HOPFENBERG, WENDY; LEVIN, HENRY M.; CHASE, CHRISTOPHER; CHRISTENSEN, S. GEORGIA; MOORE, MELANIE; SOLER, PILAR; BRUNNER, ILSE; KELLER, BETH; and RODRIGUEZ, GLORIA. 1993. *The Accelerated Schools Resource Guide.* San Francisco: Jossey-Bass.

LEVIN, HENRY M. 1987. "New Schools for the Disadvantaged." *Teacher Education Quarterly* 14:60–83.

LEVIN, HENRY M. 1998. "Accelerated Schools: A Decade of Evolution." In *International Handbook of Educational Change,* Part Two, ed. Andy Hargreaves, Ann Lieberman, Michael Fullan, and David Hopkins. Boston: Kluwer.

NATRIELLO, GARY; MCDILL, EDWARD M.; and PALLAS, AARON M. 1990. *Schooling Disadvantaged Children: Racing Against Catastrophe.* New York: Teachers College Press.

ROSS, STEVEN M.; WANG, L. WEIPING; SANDERS, WILLIAM L.; WRIGHT, S. PAUL; and STRINGFIELD, SAMUEL. 1999. *Two- and Three-Year Achievement Results on the Tennessee Value-Added Assessment System for Restructuring Schools in Memphis.* Memphis, TN: University of Memphis, Center for Research in Educational Policy.

HENRY M. LEVIN

ACCOUNTING SYSTEMS IN HIGHER EDUCATION

The objectives of colleges and universities differ from those of commercial enterprises for which profit is the primary motive in that colleges and universities seek to provide educational services within the existing levels of revenues available, although a slight level of excess revenue may be desired by some governing boards. A balanced budget where expenditures remain within available revenues is always expected of a financially responsible college or university. A major reduction in the net assets of an institution should be cause for concern and may be a sign of financial instability.

Revenue and Assets

The primary sources of revenue vary depending on whether an institution is public or private. Most private institutions depend heavily on student tuition as the major source of revenue, while public institutions receive a mixture of state appropriations and student tuition. The portion of the budget that comes from state appropriations may vary from state to state depending on the policy position of each state as to the percentage of the budget that tuition is expected to support.

According to 1996–1997 data from the National Center for Education Statistics, fund revenues for public institutions came from four primary sources: tuition and fees (19%), federal funds (11%), state funds (36%), and sales and services (22%). Private institutions also received the majority of total revenues from these four sources but had different percentages in each category: tuition and fees (43%), federal funds (14%), state funds (2%), and sales and services (21%). As noted, state appropriations are particularly important to public institutions and, in fact, represent the majority of revenues available to the overall higher education enterprise. In the academic year 1995–1996, direct general expenditures of state and local governments for postsecondary education totaled $100.7 billion. Of this total, $89.7 billion were appropriated for educational and general expenditures and $11.0 billion for capital outlay. Without the state funding of public institutions, private colleges and universities have greater reliance upon tuition and fee revenue. In 1999–2000, the total tuition, room, and board per private institution student was $20,277, while the same fees for public school students averaged $7,302. Public and private institutions are all facing an increased reliance upon those tuition and fees for any level of improvement funding. Even within the public sector with its government funding, revenues from tuition and fees increased 318 percent from 1980 to 1996 while revenues from government appropriations during that time only increased 125 percent. Little evidence exists that this trend will change between now and 2010.

Other important sources of revenue include grants and contracts, private gifts, endowment income, investment income, and sales and services of auxiliary enterprises. Auxiliary enterprises include such operations as student housing and campus bookstores that are expected to be service components that finance their own operations. Some institutions also have teaching hospitals that are major financial component units. In addition to these revenue categories, higher education institutions must also account for sizable property holdings. The total value of higher education property in 1995–1996 was $220.4 billion. Of this amount, $11.4 billion was represented by land, $150.5 billion by buildings, and $58.5 billion by equipment inventory.

Expenditures

Higher education institutions are very labor intensive, with the major portion of expenditures being devoted to salaries and benefits. Other expenditure requirements include such items as utilities, travel, scholarships and fellowships, communication costs, debt service on capital assets, supplies, and contractual services. In 1999–2000, total expenditures in higher education were $257.8 billion. Of this total, public institutions accounted for $159.7 billion and private institutions for $98.1 billion.

As a foundation of the accounting system, most higher education institutions maintain expenditures by functional classification. These classifications include instruction, research, public service, academic support, student services, institutional support, operation and maintenance of plant, scholarships, and auxiliary enterprises. Current operating activities are further identified and separated depending on whether the source of revenue is unrestricted or restricted. Unrestricted revenues are presumed to be available for current operations without specific external restrictions being placed on the use of the revenues. Restricted revenues, which are available for current operations, must be used for the purpose designated by the donor or granting entity.

Colleges and universities also have other specialized accounts that are used for the unique functions of those institutions. Loan accounts are used to record loans to students, faculty, and staff. Specific reporting requirements may be imposed on loan funds (such as the Federal Perkins Loan Program) depending on the source of funding. These accounts function on a revolving basis accounting for principal, interest, and amounts available for new loans. An-

other special set of accounts are agency accounts that are used for resources held by the institution strictly in a custodial role.

Many institutions are the recipients of gifts and donations for which the donor stipulates that the principal be invested with the earnings available for designated purposes. Endowment accounts are used for these types of purposes. The account is deemed to be a true endowment if only the earnings can be spent with the principal remaining intact. A term endowment allows the principal to be used after some period of time or specified event. Governing boards may designate funds to function as endowments, but the board may rescind these decisions.

Three specialized types of accounts are used for plant activities. These types include accounts for the construction or acquisition of capital assets, resources set aside for the repair and replacement of capital assets, and resources set aside for the repayment of principal and interest (debt service) on capital assets.

The three financial statements required of higher education include the *Statement of Net Assets,* the *Statement of Revenues, Expenses, and Changes in Net Assets,* and the *Statement of Cash Flows.* Accounting standards are established for private institutions by the Financial Accounting Standards Board (FASB) and for public institutions by the Governmental Accounting Standards Board (GASB). Major new reporting requirements were established for public institutions effective with fiscal years beginning after June 15, 2001.

See also: GOVERNANCE AND DECISION-MAKING IN COLLEGES AND UNIVERSITIES.

BIBLIOGRAPHY

NATIONAL CENTER FOR EDUCATION STATISTICS. 2000. *Digest of Education Statistics.* Washington, DC: National Center for Education Statistics.

INTERNET RESOURCES

FINANCIAL ACCOUNTING STANDARDS BOARD (FASB). 2002. <www.fasb.org/main.html>.

GOVERNMENTAL ACCOUNTING STANDARDS BOARD (GASB). 2002. <www.gasb.org/main.html>.

HOUSTON DAVIS
ROBERT H. ADAMS

ACCREDITATION IN AN INTERNATIONAL CONTEXT, HIGHER EDUCATION

The United States, and a small but increasing number of other countries, use the process of voluntary accreditation to assure minimum standards of quality in the operation and delivery of educational services. The idea of having institutions do self-policing through accrediting associations is not universal, and most countries accomplish quality assurance via recognition or approval by a government agency, or a government-approved quality assurance authority, or both.

Voluntary accreditation is a product of America's decentralized and market-oriented higher education system with its large private sector component. Accreditation by nongovernmental (or at least noncentral) bodies has happened in other situations: (1) in other federal states, such as Belgium, Canada, and Russia; (2) in countries that have consciously adopted parts of the American model, such as the Philippines and parts of eastern Europe; and (3) in countries where the formal regulation of quality assurance is a new development, such as Australia. Even in these countries, however, the requirement of quality assurance is not often totally voluntary, but usually proceeds from a national mandate or set of laws. This is due to historical traditions of state control or leadership in education; to the nature of the chartering and control of institutions; and to the lack of diversity, collegial traditions, and the small and elite character of the higher education sector in most national systems. Relatively few higher education systems in the world have a large or vigorous private sector, and many have laws or policies that restrict private institutions or make it difficult for them to operate. All these factors contribute to the tendency of institutional recognition and accreditation to be a traditional monopoly of the state in most parts of the world.

Globalization has challenged this status quo in two major ways. First, the increased cross-border movement of people, and the evolution of multistate agreements, such as the European Union, MERCOSUR, and the North American Free Trade Agreement (NAFTA), have caused national authorities and educators to have to develop mechanisms for the international recognition of legitimate institutions, diplomas, and credits. The old informal arrangements between friendly institutions and faculty no longer suffice to assure either recognizable quality or adequate legal protection for institutions, graduates, or employers. Second, the rise of the multinational private commercial and professional sectors has created a whole universe of qualifications and educational providers. These vary widely in quality, and lie outside the regulatory reach of national authorities whose mandates focus on—and often restrict—their attention to public higher education and state sector jobs. The concept of voluntary accreditation is frequently better suited to quality assurance in this fluid transnational environment than are traditional methods, particularly as these are often restricted by laws and practices that ignore private institutions and limit the acceptance of foreign institutions and degrees. Accreditation is also a means for devoting serious attention to quality assurance by organizations that prefer to keep governmental regulation limited. It also allows governments that would prefer to limit their regulatory regimes to accommodate both the public's need for quality assurance and a desire to work via consensus with educational providers.

International organizations such as the United Nations Educational, Scientific and Cultural Organization (UNESCO), the Council of Europe, the European Union, the Association of Southeast Asian Nations (ASEAN), and the Asia-Pacific Economic Corporation (APEC) have recognized the need for transparent and reliable procedures for recognizing institutions and degrees across borders, and even across global regions. These organizations have incorporated international educational mobility (of students, faculty, and institutions) and the mutual recognition of nationally accredited or approved institutions and qualifications (degrees and diplomas) into their treaties and other agreements. Examples of agreements in this area include the Lisbon Convention on the Recognition of Qualifications Pertaining to Higher Education in the European Region (UNESCO and the Council of Europe, 1997), the Bologna Process (European Union, 1999), the APEC Education Dialogue and Knowledge Sharing Network, and the education and professional mobility components of NAFTA. Except for the European Union's Bologna Process, none of these agreements binds national authorities or educational institutions to preset standards or commitments. They do contribute to an evolving international consensus on the need for information systems, agreed procedures, and quality assurance mechanisms for higher education: Business and government need to assure educational quality; and this will occur voluntarily, through accreditation-like mechanisms, or it will be regulated in other ways.

See also: ACCREDITATION IN THE UNITED STATES, *subentries on* HIGHER EDUCATION, SCHOOL; HIGHER EDUCATION, INTERNATIONAL ISSUES.

E. STEPHEN HUNT

ACCREDITATION IN THE UNITED STATES

SCHOOL
  John A. Stoops
HIGHER EDUCATION
  Michael D. Parsons

SCHOOL

The word *accreditation* is derived from the Latin *credito* (trust). Its application to American schools dates from 1871, when, on the basis of on-site visits by representatives of its faculty, the University of Michigan began "accrediting" secondary schools entrusted with providing adequate preparation for university studies. The practice was soon taken up by universities in nearby states, and in 1884 was adopted by the University of California. In 1899, graduates of 187 high schools in fifteen different states were eligible, by diploma alone, for admission to the University of Michigan.

A Community of Trust

Between 1895 and 1917, American colleges and secondary schools came together in five (later six) regional associations for consensus-building discussions about the developing system of American education. The movement of students from school to school, school to college, and college to college was on the agenda, along with other transactions that depended upon trust among institutions. The regional associations sought a voluntary method for identifying institutions capable of their objectives and worthy of trust, and accreditation became the preferred name of this process.

The diversity of sponsorship and purpose among educational institutions prohibited equating accreditation with advocacy. The regional associa-

tions simply wanted to establish that accredited institutions were what they said they were, had what they said they had, and did what they said they did in accordance with standards approved by the American academic community. Anything an accredited institution might say about its staff, facilities, curricula, services, or the accomplishments of its students was presumed to be true. Credibility was therefore essential for successful participation in the free American system. Institutions unwilling or unable to establish credibility through accreditation had to use some other means—none could prosper without it.

Regional School Accrediting Commissions

School accreditation moved from the West and South toward the Northeast. The North Central Association of Colleges and Schools (NCA) was founded in 1895 by educational leaders already involved in school accreditation. In 1904, NCA published a list of accredited schools. Also founded in 1895, the Southern Association of Colleges and Schools (SACS) established a commission for secondary school accreditation in 1912. The Northwest Association of Schools and Colleges (NASC) began accrediting colleges and schools in 1917, the year it was founded. It formed a secondary school commission in 1927.

Established in 1887, the Middle States Association of Colleges and Schools (MSA) was initially preoccupied with its successful effort to establish the College Entrance Examination Board. Consequently, MSA did not form a Commission on Secondary Schools until 1922. The New England Association of Schools and Colleges (NEASC), which dates from 1885, began accreditation of private secondary schools in 1927, and later public secondary school accreditation moved under the control of the Association. In 1962, California and Hawaii separated from the Northwest Association to form the Western Association of Schools and Colleges (WASC) and an accrediting commission for secondary schools.

After the middle of the twentieth century, all regional associations extended accreditation to other kinds and levels of schools. Commissions for elementary schools were established by the Southern Association in 1953, by the Middle States Association in 1978, and by the New England Association in 1987. After 1960, the original commissions for secondary schools of the other three associations were renamed Commissions on Schools, and they extended their missions to include the accreditation of elementary schools. In 1968, The New England Association had begun a commission on vocational and technical education, so by 1990 the American school accreditation establishment included a total of eleven regional commissions.

The Eight-Year Study

In 1932 the young and developing secondary school commissions of the (then) five regional associations implemented a nationwide eight-year study aimed at establishing standards for secondary school accreditation. The study culminated in 1940 with publication of the *Secondary School Evaluative Criteria,* in which hundreds of the *parts* of a secondary school were organized and listed, each to be evaluated separately against the backdrop of a community study and the school's philosophy. The intense rigor of the listing commanded wide respect. It appealed to the prevailing mind-set of the industrial age and encouraged the growth and embellishment of the apparatus of secondary education. Even its few critics agreed that *the instrument* (as it was often called) offered a useful indication of the effort a community was making.

After 1940 the study was incorporated and lived on as the National Study of School Evaluation (NSSE). Governed by the accrediting school commissions, NSSE revised the *Criteria* every ten years and published other support materials. Despite the growing diversity of accredited schools, the dominance of the *Criteria* was not challenged until 1980 when a new generation of leaders, influenced by postindustrial models of thought, insisted school evaluations should center on the processes by which the resources given to a school were transformed into desired results.

From Parts to Processes

Moving from disembodied parts to (results-oriented) processes proved to be more than just a bend in the road; it was an entirely different road. Parts no longer had relevance apart from processes, and processes drew relevance only from results. This conversion entailed retraining thousands of schools, commissioners, and evaluators. NSSE and the commissions published new support materials on topics such as strategic planning, cyclical improvement, paradigmatic alignment, energy auditing, impact analysis, critical description, scenario analysis, and synergy development. Some commissions evaluated

schools more frequently, using fewer evaluators, and the periodic reports required of accredited schools became action-based, focusing on their movement toward goals that can be empirically defined and verified.

Accreditation standards were also revised. With total acceptance of the ubiquity of change, the commissions reasoned that status quo was incompatible with merit. Accordingly, schools were to be judged on the quality of their movement towards desired goals, and not of their current standing. Standards for accreditation became measures of school improvement activity. Regardless of prior accomplishments, schools had to demonstrate continuous improvement for continuous accreditation. In 1990 the sixth and last edition of the *Criteria* was published. By 1997 all commissions were using process-oriented protocols, and the methods for school accreditation that had prevailed from 1940 had expired.

National and International Activity

As transportation improved, educators moved most of their deliberations from regional to national venues. Only accreditation, which had prospered from regional governance, continued to be regional. The regional commissions became the sole custodians of its meaning and traditions. They remained connected by their responsibility for NSSE; and, from 1968, they met annually for an exchange of information as part of the Council of Regional School Accrediting Commissions (CORSAC). There was no interest in establishing a national school accreditation authority.

However, American families were becoming increasingly mobile, and the public media were becoming nationally focused. After 1950 some commissions began serving American schools overseas, but efforts to establish regional jurisdictions abroad proved acrimonious. New national educational corporations with schools spread across all regions objected to dealing with different accreditation authorities. So the regional commissions began seeking ways to provide national and international services while preserving the independence they all cherished.

In 1994 the commissions established a "legal platform" for combined activities by replacing CORSAC with a corporation named the International Council of School Accreditation Commissions, Inc. (ICSAC). The first project on this "platform" was conversion of the International Registry of Accredited Schools into a searchable database that is available online. The second was the establishment of a quadrennial international convocation, with the recurring theme of Peace and Justice through Education (Atlanta, 1996 and Chicago, 2000). The third was an umbrella accreditation authority named The Commission on International and Trans-Regional Accreditation (CITA). Designed to accredit kinds and configurations of schools in the United States not easily served by one commission, CITA also accredits the growing number of indigenous schools of foreign nations that have been converting to the American plan of education. (American overseas schools and Department of Defense schools that are overseas continue to be accredited by the separate regional commissions as before.) CITA began operations in 1996. By 2000 the number of schools continuously engaged in CITA accreditation protocols approached 1,000. Its name recognition had become so widespread that, in 2000, ICSAC was renamed CITA, Inc.

Cooperative Activities

The flexibility of process protocols and school improvement standards presented the possibility that school improvement programs and accreditation could be synchronous. After 1985 some systemwide improvement programs for public and Catholic diocesan schools were redesigned as accreditation protocols. Similar collaborations developed between the regional commissions and organizations of special purpose and method schools (e.g., Christian, hearing impaired, Montessori) that enhanced the special rigors of these organizations and schools by offering special accreditation.

To avoid forcing these schools to choose one or the other accreditation (or do both), the commissions exercised their flexibility in designing protocols leading to both regional and special accreditation. In 1993, thirteen of these organizations came together as the National Council for Private School Accreditation (NCPSA), which soon established a working relationship with CITA. In 1999, CITA and NCPSA jointly began the International Academy of Educational Accreditors (IAEA), an agency designed to assist other nations establish accreditation systems.

These cooperative undertakings were fruits of the century-long growth of school accreditation, and

of perceptions of its modern potential. It began with secondary schools only and spread to schools of all kinds and levels. At a critical point it moved from assessing effort to examining processes aimed at results. It originated within separate commissions that later acquired the means and determination to combine for national and international endeavors. Positive relations with special accrediting organizations broadened its foundations. By 2001 its voluntary, peer-governed, internally driven, and externally monitored methods were spreading abroad, and its regional commissions were equipped to combine with others as needed.

See also: ACCREDITATION IN AN INTERNATIONAL CONTEXT, HIGHER EDUCATION; ACCREDITATION IN THE UNITED STATES, *subentry on* HIGHER EDUCATION; SCHOOL REFORM.

BIBLIOGRAPHY

BAKER, STEVE. 1999. *The Quality School Improvement Process for Elementary and Middle Schools.* Decatur, GA: The Southern Association of Colleges and Schools.

BEMIS, JAMES F. 1991. *The Northwest Association of Colleges and Schools 75-Year History, 1917–1991.* Boise, ID: The Northwest Association of Colleges and Schools.

BROOME, EDWIN CORNELIUS. 1903. *A Historical and Critical Discussion of College Entrance Requirements.* New York: Columbia University Press. Reprinted by The College Entrance Examination Board, 1963.

CARROTHERS, GEORGE E.; GREZZEL, E. DUNCAN; and ROMER, JOSEPH. 1939. *How to Evaluate a Secondary School.* Schaumburg, IL. The National Study of School Evaluation.

CHALLENDER, RICHARD D. 1987. *The Middle States Association: The Last Twenty-Five Years, 1962–1987.* Philadelphia, PA: The Middle States Association of Colleges and Schools.

DAVIS, CALVIN O. 1945. *A History of the North Central Association of Colleges and Secondary Schools.* Tempe, AZ: The North Central Association of Colleges and Schools.

FITZPATRICK, KATHLEEN. 1997. *Indicators of Schools of Quality.* Schaumburg, IL: The National Study of School Evaluation.

GEIGER, LOUIS. 1970. *Voluntary Accreditation: A History of The North Central Association 1945–1970.* Menasha, WI: George Banta.

JONES, ADAM LEROY, and GREZZEL, E. DUNCAN. *The Middle States Association: A Seventy Five Year Review, 1887–1962.* Philadelphia, PA: The Middle States Association of Colleges and Schools.

MILLER, JAMES D. 1985. *A Centennial History of the Southern Association of Colleges and Schools, 1885–1985.* Decatur, GA: The Southern Association of Colleges and Schools.

NEWMAN, MARK. 1996. *Agency of Change: One Hundred Years of the North Central Association of Colleges and Schools.* Tempe, AZ: The North Central Association of Colleges and Schools.

O'DONNELL, ROBERT. 1986. *Development of the Commission on Public Secondary Schools: The First Hundred Years, 1885–1985.* Bedford, MA: The New England Association of Colleges and Schools.

PETRY, DONALD. 1999. *The Commission on Standards and Review.* Virginia Beach, VA: The National Council for Private School Accreditation.

REYNOLDS, MICHAEL. 1987. *The Middle States Association: An Annotated Chronology of School and College Relations 1887–1987.* Philadelphia: The Middle States Association of Colleges and Schools.

SIVERSON, LYLE. 1987. *A History of the Western Association of Schools and Colleges, 1962–1987.* Burlingame, CA: The Western Association of Colleges and Schools.

SNAVELY, E. GUY. 1945. *A Short History of the Southern Association.* Decatur, GA: The Southern Association of Colleges and Schools.

STEADMAN, DAVID. 1997. *School Improvement Process.* Boise, ID: Northwest Association of Colleges and Schools.

STOOPS, JOHN A. 1998. *CITA and The New Education.* Tempe, AZ: The North Central Association of Colleges and Schools.

STOOPS, JOHN A., ed. 1993. *The International Registry of Regionally Accredited Schools.* Tempe, AZ: The North Central Association of Colleges and Schools.

WEST, RALPH O. 1985. *A Half-Century and More of Independence: A History of the New England Commission on Independent Schools.* Bedford, MA: The New England Association of Colleges and Schools.

INTERNET RESOURCE

COMMISSION ON INTERNATIONAL AND TRANSREGIONAL ACCREDITATION (CITA). 2002. "International Registry of Accredited Schools." <www.accreditedschools.org>.

JOHN A. STOOPS

HIGHER EDUCATION

One of the primary differences between higher education in the United States and other countries is that there is no centralized government control in the United States. The types of review, oversight, and quality control performed by national education ministries in other nations is performed by private, not-for-profit accrediting agencies in the United States. Accreditation is a process that recognizes a postsecondary institution or a program of study within the institution as having met accrediting standards and qualifications.

Historical Development

In the second half of the nineteenth century, Americans were building colleges and universities at a rate unmatched in the history of humankind. While the numbers were impressive, few of these institutions could meet the loosest definition of a college, and many could not match the quality of today's American high schools. Teachers' colleges, land-grant colleges, women's colleges, black colleges, research universities, and various specialized institutions were developing without anyone being able to answer the basic question, "What is a college?" Not only could this question not be answered, but potential students and their parents could not find an answer to questions about commonly accepted standards for admission to college and for completing a degree once the student was admitted.

The rapid, unregulated, growth helped produce public pressure for some type of rating or evaluation system. Higher quality colleges and universities called for government evaluation as a way to limit competition with what they correctly saw as inferior institutions. In 1870 the U.S. Bureau of Education listed the nation's colleges but did not offer an evaluation of the institutions. The bureau asked the Carnegie Foundation to evaluate the institutions. The foundation completed the study but refused to release the results for fear that the information would be misused. If colleges and universities wanted to be evaluated, then they would have to take up the task themselves.

It was a group of secondary school masters in New England who took the initiative. In 1884 members of the Massachusetts Classical and High School Teachers Association, in cooperation with Harvard University President Charles Eliot, formed the New England Association of Schools and Colleges. This marked the beginning of what would come to be known as the regional accrediting associations. In order of development the six associations were: (1) New England Association of Schools and Colleges, 1885; (2) Middle States Association of Colleges and Schools, 1887; (3) Southern Association of Schools and Colleges, 1895; (4) North Central Association of Schools and Colleges, 1895; (5) Northwest Association of Schools and Colleges, 1917; and (6) Western Association of Schools and Colleges, 1923.

The regional agencies provide what is known as regional or institutional accreditation for member institutions. While the six regional associations differ in size, traditions, and character, they provide the basic framework for accreditation. Institutional accreditation focuses on issues such as: appropriateness of the institutional mission and objectives; effectiveness of the institution in meeting its mission and objectives; adequacy of financial and physical resources including library holdings, instructional space, laboratories, and offices; quality of faculty; effectiveness of management, including administrative structure and function; and adequacy of personnel and student services offered by the institution.

The basic framework developed over a period of time, as regional associations saw the need to cooperate and negotiate common standards. In 1949 the Federation of Regional Accrediting Commissions in Higher Education (FRACHE) was created. As an association of regional accrediting associations, FRACHE was succeeded by other institutional accrediting associations, and today the regional accrediting associations are represented by the Council for Higher Education Accreditation (CHEA). From FRACHE to CHEA, the associations have attempted to provide coherence and continuity to the rapidly changing accreditation process, serve as a communication and discussion forum for the regional associations, and provide guidance in the revision of regional accreditation policies.

Regional versus Specialized Accreditation

Accreditation arose in the United States as a means of conducting peer evaluation of higher education institutions and programs. In its simplest form, accreditation can be defined as quality control. It is also a way to protect against governmental interference and to ensure academic freedom. In a more complex form, accreditation can be defined as a process in which an institution evaluates its educational mission, goals, objectives, and activities and seeks an independent peer judgment to confirm that it is achieving its goals and objectives and that it is equal to comparable institutions. There are two major types of accrediting associations: regional or institutional accreditation associations and specialized or programmatic accreditation associations.

A regional or institutional accreditation review offers an assessment of the overall quality and integrity of the institution. A team sent from the institution's regional association conducts the assessment. The team spends several days at the institution meeting with its officials, observing classes, and evaluating its facilities and programs. The institution will have prepared its own self-study as part of the preparation for the accreditation review. This report will also help guide and inform the assessment team.

Following the visit, the team writes an evaluation report, which includes an assessment of the institution, a rundown of its strengths and weaknesses, and suggestions for improvement in its curriculum, faculty, and other areas. Generally, institutions are reaccredited for ten years, but accreditation is not a guaranteed outcome when a team visits. If an institution has significant deficiencies, the accreditation association may withhold a decision on its status until the weaknesses have been corrected. The association may schedule return visits to check on the status of improvements and corrections. Finally, in extreme cases, the association may withhold accreditation.

While regional accreditation is responsible for a broad assessment of an institution's quality and integrity, specialized or programmatic accreditation focuses on academic programs that offer curricula in professional and technical fields. The intent is to ensure that graduates entering an accredited professional or technical field possess the necessary skills, knowledge, and competencies required to practice in that field. The earliest specialized accreditation occurred when the American Medical Association

(AMA) established the Council on Medical Education and Hospitals in 1904. In 1905 the council adopted standards for medical schools and published its first classification of these schools based on the performance of graduates in licensing examinations. Other professional education programs quickly followed the AMA starting with dental education in 1918 and then legal education in 1923, engineering education in 1936, and pharmaceutical education in 1940.

Today, specialized accreditation is the subject of some controversy as institutions are faced with a proliferation of programmatic accrediting agencies with each making demands on an institution's limited resources. For example, a large public institution such as Indiana University or the University of Illinois might face accreditation visits for business, teacher education, counseling education, education psychology, dental education, law, nursing, occupational therapy, physical therapy, library sciences, pharmacy, social work, journalism, optometry, psychology, and more. Institutions are concerned about the rising costs and the inflexibility of the specialized accreditation process. Institutional leaders are also concerned about what they see as the self-serving nature of some policies and practices of the specialized associations that seek to expand the associations' authority over institutional resources and policies. This is why some institutions are now rethinking the need for specialized accreditation.

In the meantime, specialized accrediting associations continue to function in much the same way that regional accrediting associations function but on a more limited and focused scale. Students entering programs accredited by specialized associations will know that the program has established appropriate goals and objectives, can provide evidence that these goals and objectives are being met, and has sufficient resources to ensure that the current level of quality will be maintained in the future. Students will also benefit in that accredited programs make it easier for graduates to move from one state to another. For example, graduates of programs accredited by the National Council for Accreditation of Teacher Education (NCATE) can more easily move their teaching licenses from one state to another. This is possible because many states have reciprocity agreements based on graduation from NCATE-accredited schools.

Accreditation and the Federal Government

It is unlikely that accreditation is high on a student's list of concerns when selecting an institution. It is only when an institution is not accredited that a student becomes concerned. One reason is that lack of specialized accreditation will hamper a student's career after graduation. Another more immediate reason is that the federal government uses accreditation as a criterion for student financial aid. A student cannot use federal financial aid to attend an institution that is not accredited by a federally approved accrediting association. Accreditation is part of what is commonly called the "triad" and is a way for the federal government to use existing, nongovernmental agencies to fulfill public policy goals.

The triad establishes relationships between the federal government and eligibility for funding, state government and its responsibility for chartering institutions, and voluntary membership associations that require accreditation for membership. The triad evolved from the passage of the Higher Education Act of 1965, which provided the first broad-based, permanent, federally funded student financial aid programs for students in public and private universities. This act is an authorization statute that must be renewed after a fixed number of years. In the various renewals since 1965, accreditation has taken on an increased role as part of the oversight triad.

In 1992 the Higher Education Act gave the Department of Education increased authority over the accreditation process. Specifically, the Education Department was to require that all regional and specialized associations assess thirteen specific criteria in their reviews:

- academic calendars, catalogs, publications, grading, and advertising
- curricula
- faculty
- facilities, equipment, and supplies
- student support services
- recruiting and admissions practices
- fiscal and administrative capacity as appropriate for the scale of the institution
- program length and tuition and fees in relation to the subject matter taught and the objectives of the degree
- measures of program length in clock hours or credit hours
- student outcome measures

- default rate
- record of student complaints received by the accrediting association or state agency
- compliance with program responsibilities under Title IV of the Higher Education Act

The intent of these new requirements was to address concerns of fraud and abuse in the federal student aid program. The primary targets of the new requirements were proprietary and vocational schools, but the new rules applied to traditional colleges and universities as well.

The 1998 reauthorization of the Higher Education Act reversed some of the 1992 requirements, thereby returning some control and administrative discretion to the accrediting associations. Still, the reauthorization did not reverse the trend of the federal government taking an increasingly interventionist approach toward the associations. Over a three-decade period, the federal government had become a major investor in higher education with billions of dollars going to student financial aid yearly. The federal government was no longer willing to simply let the voluntary accrediting associations establish the rules of accreditation. The decreased number of fraud and abuse cases has reduced federal pressure on the associations, but the triad will never return to its old relationship of three independent parties acting together to ensure institutional integrity.

Future Issues

Accreditation will remain a defining characteristic of American higher education. The federal government is unwilling to take on the task of accrediting public and private institutions of higher education. Even if there were such a movement, it would not survive institutional, state, and constitutional challenges. This is not to say that accreditation will remain static. Regional accreditation will continue to evolve to meet the needs of institutions just as it has for more than 100 years. Specialized accreditation will face stiffer challenges. It is probable that more and more major universities will discard specialized accreditation. In some fields, teacher education for example, new specialized associations are attempting to challenge NCATE. The federal government will continue to use the associations as part of the triad but will continue to try to intervene in the accreditation process to ensure that federal interests are protected.

Regardless of the accuracy of these predictions, the primary differences between higher education in the United States and other countries will continue to be that there is no centralized control in the United States. The types of review, oversight, and quality control performed by national education ministries in other nations will continue to be performed by private, not-for-profit accrediting agencies in the United States.

See also: ACCREDITATION IN AN INTERNATIONAL CONTEXT, HIGHER EDUCATION; ACCREDITATION IN THE UNITED STATES, *subentry on* SCHOOL.

BIBLIOGRAPHY

ABERNATHY, DONNA J. 2001. "Sizzlin' Sites for Accreditation." *Training and Development* 55(1):21.

BLAISE, CRONIN. 2000. "Accreditation: Retool It or Kill It." *Library Journal* 125:54.

BLOLAND, HARLAND G. 1999. "Creating CHEA: Building a New National Organization on Accrediting." *Journal of Higher Education* 70:357.

BUCK, SUE, and SMITH, ERSKINE. 2001. "The Integrity of the Council for Accreditation Process." *Journal of Family and Consumer Sciences* 93(3):52.

CROSSON, FREDERICK J. 1987. "The Philosophy of Accreditation." *North Central Association Quarterly* 62:386–397.

DILL, WILLIAM R. 1998. "Specialized Accreditation: An Idea Whose Time Has Come? Or Gone?" *Change* 30(4):18–25.

EATON, JUDITH. 2001. "Regional Accreditation Reform: Who Is Served?" *Change* 33:38–45.

HOLMBERG, SELBY. 1997. "Is Accreditation Worth the Trouble?" *Education Weekly* 16:32.

JACOBY, BARBARA, and THOMAS, WILLIAM L., JR. 1991. "Professional Standards and the Accreditation Process." *New Directions for Student Services* (53):19–28.

LEATHERMAN, COURTNEY. 1991. "Specialized Accrediting Agencies Challenged by Campus Officials." *Chronicle of Higher Education* September 18.

MANGAN, KATHERINE S. 1998. "Education Department Threatens to Revoke Bar Association's Accreditation Authority." *Chronicle of Higher Education* September 18.

MILLARD, RICHARD M. 1987. "Relation of Accreditation to the States and Federal Government." *North Central Association Quarterly* 62:361–379.

NEWMAN, MARK. 1996. *Agency of Change: One Hundred Years of the North Central Association of Colleges and Schools.* Kirksville, MO: Thomas Jefferson University Press.

PARSONS, MICHAEL D. 1997. *Power and Politics: Federal Higher Education Policymaking in the 1990s.* Albany: State University of New York Press.

RATCLIFF, JAMES L.; LUNINESCU, EDWARD S.; and GAFFNEY, MAUREEN, eds. 2001. *How Accreditation Influences Assessment.* San Francisco: Jossey-Bass.

MICHAEL D. PARSONS

ACCREDITING COMMISSION OF CAREER SCHOOLS AND COLLEGES OF TECHNOLOGY

The Accrediting Commission of Career Schools and Colleges of Technology (ACCSCT), formerly known as the Accrediting Commission for Business Schools, is the accrediting authority for private postsecondary technical and vocational schools, colleges, and programs of instruction. Its more than 700 participating institutions of various types range from one-year vocational programs to continuing education programs, to full four-year undergraduate degree programs in qualified fields of study. The goal of the commission is to ensure the highest standard of career-oriented education for over 350,000 students in the United States and in Puerto Rico, and it is recognized as the accreditation authority in its area of expertise by the U.S. Department of Education.

Program

On the request of an interested postsecondary institution, the commission first requires proof that the school or program is legally established and properly licensed by the state in which it operates. Once this has been proved, the person responsible for managing the program to be accredited must attend a workshop in which he or she learns the philosophy behind accreditation and the procedures by which to achieve it. During this workshop, information on resources, publications, and other aids that may help in the accreditation process are also made available.

After attending the mandatory workshop, the administrator of the petitioning institution must file a detailed self-evaluation report. In this document, the school sets forth its mission statement and the plan by which it fulfills this mission. It must provide course syllabi, financial statements, an organizational chart documenting its administrative hierarchy, a list of faculty along with each instructor's educational and professional qualifications to teach, copies of all advertising and promotional materials, catalogs and brochures, and copies of all state and federal reviews of the program to be accredited. In addition, the institution must provide a statement of its graduation and job-placement rates, a description of the physical facilities available, and a statement of the student services offered and procedures used in handling student grievances. Finally the report must document student recruitment and admissions policies as well as the requirements students must fulfill to qualify for the degree or certification offered by the program.

Once this report is filed, the commission sends a team of investigators to verify the information. The team consists of an administrative expert, who evaluates the administrative and financial practices of the institution; an occupational specialist, who examines the equipment and practical instruction offered by the program; and an educational specialist, who investigates the quality and sufficiency of the faculty teaching the program. In addition the team includes a representative from the commission, whose role is to help both the investigative team and the institution fully understand and comply with accrediting requirements. In some cases a representative from the relevant state licensing or oversight board may also join the team.

After completing its survey, the team prepares a Team Summary Report and makes a copy for the institution so that it may address any questions or issues that arose during the investigation. The whole file then goes to the commission, which makes the determination as to whether or not to grant accreditation.

For a first-time applicant, the commission may make one of four decisions: to grant accreditation (for a period not to exceed five years); to accredit the institution "with stipulations"; to defer its decision pending receipt of additional information; or to deny accreditation. An institution accredited with stipulations is one that essentially meets the commission's standards but falls short in one or more aspects of its program. The stipulations provide the institution with accredited standing, while giving it an opportunity (usually with a strict deadline) to rectify any such problems. If accreditation is denied, the institution must wait nine months before reapplying for consideration by the commission.

Even if accreditation is granted, however, the institution must maintain an ongoing dialog with the commission. It must file annual reports to show that it continues to maintain the commission's standards, and it must reapply for accreditation once the five-year term (or less, in some cases) is up. Failure to file the annual report, or to pass muster during the re-accreditation process, can result in an institution being put on probation or even being stricken from the list of accredited institutions.

Once accredited, member schools are a valued resource to the commission, which seeks their advice and cooperation in the ongoing process of establishing standards that reflect changes in technology and in educational and employment policies and standards. In return, member schools gain access to commission resources and advisors as they seek to improve their programs and remain abreast of the changing world of vocational and technical education.

Although accreditation is voluntary, it is necessary if a school wishes to participate in federally administered student grant and loan programs. Accreditation also serves as a sign of quality, making accredited schools more attractive to potential students and to the high school guidance counselors who advise them on career and postsecondary educational choices.

Organization

The commission is made up of thirteen members, each of whom has been elected to serve a single four-year term. Six of the members are drawn from the public sector, representing government, the business and industrial communities, and the public postsecondary educational community. The remaining seven members are drawn from the private institutions served by the commission. The election of this latter group is done by direct vote of the commission's more than 700 member institutions, whereas the public representatives are selected by the commission itself, from a list drawn up by its own nominating committee.

The committee meets every four months to review applications for accreditation and to discuss possible changes in the standards or process used to guarantee continuing improvement in postsecondary education. It also publishes a quarterly newsletter, *The Monitor,* and maintains a website to circulate information of interest to professionals in the field of vocational and technical education.

Financial Support

As an independent organization, the commission receives no public funds or outside financing. Instead it supports its activities entirely from its own income. Its income includes the fees it charges for its workshops and application process, as well as the annual dues it collects from the institutions it has accredited. Dues are calculated based on the number of students enrolled in the program, school, or institution and adjusted according to the amount of tuition charged per student.

History

Although the ACCSCT only became an independent entity in 1993, it got its start in the early 1950s. At this time a number of groups became concerned about establishing professional standards for business schools, which were increasing in number and popularity. In 1952 the U.S. Office of Education (now the Department of Education) set up the National Association and Council of Business Schools to administer the accreditation process for the whole nation, and in 1956 this became the single accrediting authority of career schools in the nation. One of the earlier independent groups, the American Association of Business Schools, soon merged with the national organization, and together they formed the Accrediting Commission for Business Schools.

At about the same time, an organization was formed to evaluate the programs available from trade and technical schools offering postsecondary programs. Advancements in technology during the ensuing three decades blurred the once clear distinction between business and technical training, and the two accrediting organizations ultimately merged into the ACCSCT, a division of the National Association of Trade and Technical Schools. In 1993, as a result of provisions contained in 1992 amendments to the Higher Education Act, the Accrediting Commission became an independent organization.

INTERNET RESOURCE

ACCREDITING COMMISSION OF CAREER SCHOOLS AND COLLEGES OF TECHNOLOGY. 2002. <www.accsct.org>.

HAROLD B. POST
Revised by
NANCY E. GRATTON

ADAPTED PHYSICAL EDUCATION

Adapted physical education (APE) is specially designed instruction in physical education intended to address the unique needs of individuals. While the roots of adapted physical education can be traced back to Swedish medical gymnastics in the 1700s, adapted physical education, as practiced today, has been significantly shaped by the mandates of the Individuals with Disabilities Education Act (IDEA). This act, enacted in 1997, amended the Education for All Handicapped Children Act, which was enacted in 1975 and stipulated that all children with disabilities had a right to special education.

The IDEA Mandates

Specifically, IDEA defined special education as "specially designed instruction, at no cost to parents or guardians, to meet the unique needs of a child with a disability, including—(A) instruction conducted in the classroom, in the home, in hospitals, and institutions, and in other settings; and (B) instruction in physical education." The inclusion of physical education in the definition of special education is significant for two reasons. First, it identified physical education as a direct service that must be provided to all students who qualify for special education services as opposed to related services, such as physical or occupational therapy, that are required only when they are needed for a child to benefit from a special education service. Second, it highlighted the importance of physical education for students with disabilities.

IDEA also defined physical education, mandated that all special education services be delivered in the least restrictive environment (LRE), and prescribed a management document called an Individualized Education Program (IEP). Physical education was defined as "the development of: (A) physical and motor fitness; (B) fundamental motor skills and patterns; and (C) skills in aquatics, dance, and individual and group games and sports (including intramural and lifetime sports." IDEA further delineated that "physical education services, specially designed if necessary, must be made available to every handicapped child receiving a free appropriate public education" and that "if specially designed physical education is prescribed in a child's individualized education program, the public agency responsible for the education of that child shall provide the service directly, or make arrangements for it to be provided through other public or private programs."

With respect to LRE, IDEA stated the following: "To the maximum extent appropriate, children with disabilities, including those in public or private institutions or other care facilities, are educated with children who do not have disabilities; and . . . special classes, separate schooling, or other removal of children with disabilities from the regular educational environment occurs only when the nature and severity of the disability is such that education in regular classes cannot be achieved satisfactorily."

To ensure that IDEA was implemented as intended, the act required that IEPs must be developed and monitored for all students who qualify for special education. The IEP is developed by a team and includes the student's present level of performance; annual goals and short-term instructional objectives; specific educational services that will be provided and the extent to which the student will participate in regular education programs; any needed transition services; the projected dates for the initiation and duration of services; and objective criteria and procedures for evaluating, at least annually, progress on the stated goals and instructional objectives.

Finally, IDEA mandated that qualified personnel deliver special education instruction. In this context, "qualified" meant that a person has "met State educational agency approved or recognized certification, licensing, registration, or other comparable requirements which apply to the area in which he or she is providing special education or related services."

In summary, the legal basis for adapted physical education results from the mandates that require that all students who qualify for special education must receive physical education. If specially designed physical education is required, then these services must be stated in the IEP, delivered in the LRE, and provided by a qualified teacher.

It is important to note that while IDEA requires that all students who qualify for special education have a right to adapted physical education if needed to address their unique needs, adapted physical education is, can, and should be provided to all students who have unique physical and motor needs that cannot be adequately addressed in the regular physical education program. It is not uncommon, for example, for many students to have temporary orthopedic disabilities such as sprained ankles, broken limbs, or muscle strains during their school years. Short-term APE programs would be appropriate for these students both to assist in the rehabilitation of their injuries and to minimize any fitness and/or skill deficits that may occur during their recovery. Other students may have mild physical or health impairments, such as asthma or diabetes, that do not interfere with their educational performance enough to qualify them for special education but that are severe enough to warrant special accommodations and considerations in physical education.

In the United States physical education and most major sport/recreation programs for youth are school centered, hence the emphasis on education in the terms *physical education* and *adapted physical education*. In other countries, physical education, recreation, and sport are commonly conducted independent or outside of the schools and sponsored by other organizations and agencies. In these settings, the term *adapted physical activity* may be used instead of adapted physical education.

Trends and Issues

Although IDEA has provided a sound legal basis for adapted physical education, there are still a number of issues that need to be resolved by the profession to ensure that the physical and motor needs of all students with disabilities are appropriately addressed. Two major issues relate to who is qualified to provide APE services and how decisions are made regarding the appropriate physical education placement for students with disabilities.

Who is qualified? While IDEA specified that physical education services, specially designed if necessary, must be made available to every child with a disability receiving a free appropriate education, it stopped short of defining who was qualified to provide these services. IDEA stated that it was the responsibility of the states to establish teacher certification requirements. Unlike other special education areas (e.g., teachers of individuals with mental retardation or learning disabilities), most states did not have in place defined certification requirements for teachers of adapted physical education. Given the fiscal constraints placed on schools by the mandates of IDEA, most states were reluctant to place additional demands on their schools by forcing them to hire APE specialists. As a result, by 1991 only fourteen states had actually defined an endorsement or certification in adapted physical education.

The existence of a mandate that required that services be provided but that did not define who was qualified to provide these services created a dilemma for both teachers and students. In many cases, regular physical educators with little or no training related to individuals with disabilities and/or therapists with no training in physical education were assigned the responsibility of addressing the physical education needs of students with disabilities. Since these teachers do not have the prerequisite skills to address the needs of these students, these needs are largely going unaddressed. To respond to this situation, the National Consortium for Physical Education and Recreation for Individuals with Disabilities (NCPERID) created national standards and a voluntary national certification exam for adapted physical education. The adapted physical education national standards (APENS) delineate the content that adapted physical educators should know across fifteen standards. The national exam has been administered annually since 1997 at more than eighty test sites in the United States.

While the creation of the APE national standards and the national certification exam have been significant steps toward addressing the issue of who is qualified to teach APE, much more work still needs to be done. The NCPERID is working with a small number of states on developing a process through which states can adopt the NCPERID APE standards and APE national certification exam as their state credential. It is hoped that a uniform certification similar to the APENS exam will be adopted by all states by 2010, and this issue will be resolved.

How are placement decisions made? The intent of defining physical education as a direct service, specially designed if necessary, in IDEA was to ensure that the physical and motor development needs of these students were not ignored or sacrificed at the expense of addressing other educational needs. This emphasis was warranted given the extensive research documenting marked physical and motor development delays and increased health risks (e.g., coronary heart disease and obesity) in many children with disabilities. There is also a wealth of research that has shown that well-designed and implemented physical education programs can reduce both physical and motor delays and many health risks in students with disabilities. While the intent of the law was clear, how it has been implemented has been less then optimal.

What has happened in many schools is that the majority, if not all, of the students with disabilities are being dumped into regular physical education classes. The justification for this practice can be linked to a number of subissues. First, like many other problems in the schools, most schools were not provided with sufficient resources to implement the mandates of IDEA. Given the need to comply with legal mandates and limited resources, many schools were forced to look for ways to meet the letter of the law using their existing resources. Two particular mandates shaped this behavior. First, part of the LRE mandate stated that students with disabilities be educated in the regular education environments to the maximum extent appropriate. Second, the IEP mandates required only that specially designed services be defined and monitored in the IEP. Many schools therefore deduced that if they put all the students with disabilities in regular physical education, then they would be addressing part of the LRE mandate and at the same time avoiding the additional time, effort, and costs related to actually creating specially designed physical education programs. Fiscally this solution was very attractive given that most schools lacked qualified personnel who were trained to assess the physical and motor needs of students with disabilities and who could make appropriate decisions regarding what would be the most appropriate (LRE) physical education environment in which to address their needs.

Ideally, this practice would have been identified and stopped during the early years of implementing the law via the required state and federal monitoring procedures. Unfortunately, it was not for a number of reasons. One of the reasons was that the IEP document was used as the primary monitoring document. Because physical education was not identified as a needed specially designed service, it was not monitored. In the rare cases in which parents understood their rights and demanded specially designed physical education to meet the unique needs of their child, schools tended to handle these requests on an individual basis and subcontract to have these services delivered.

The approach to stopping the practice of placing all students with special needs in regular physical education must be multifaceted. The ideal solution would be simply for schools to hire qualified adapted physical educators as intended by the law. This solution, however, is not as simple as it may initially appear. First, schools would have to recognize that their current physical education placement practices were wrong and then be motivated to make a change. In many schools these practices have gone on unquestioned for more than twenty years. In addition, there are no new fiscal resources to hire the additional teachers needed to correct this problem. To obtain additional public monies to fund these positions, schools would have to explain why these new teachers were needed and why they had not provided these appropriate services in the past.

Resolving the problem of inappropriate placement of students with disabilities into regular physical education is important not only for the students with disabilities but also for the regular education students and the regular physical education teachers. Research in the field has repeatedly shown that many regular physical educators feel unprepared to address the needs of students with disabilities and that trying to accommodate the needs of these students has a negative impact on all the students in their classes.

Recognizing the dilemma schools face in resolving this problem, the issue is being addressed at two levels. The first level is to educate schools and state departments of education about this problem and recommend that they develop both long- and short-term solutions. An example of a long-term solution would be to require schools to hire certified adapted physical educators as replacements when existing physical educators retire or leave for other positions. An example of a short-term solution would be to use in-service training programs for school administrators and regular physical educators. These programs would focus on educating them on what is appropriate physical education and then providing them with some of the fundamental skills needed to offer a continuum of alternative placements in physical education as intended by the LRE requirements. The second level is to educate parents via the various parent advocacy organizations regarding their rights and what should be involved in making an appropriate placement decision in relation to physical education. This information would allow parents to make more informed decisions and to advocate for appropriate physical education services for their children.

Training

Through competitive grant provisions associated with the Education for All Handicapped Children Act and subsequently IDEA, a number of colleges and universities have developed pre-service adapted physical education teacher-training programs. Because adapted physical education training builds upon the traditional teacher training in physical education, most adapted physical education training occurs at the master's level. Most undergraduate physical education teacher preparation programs now include at least one APE course as part of their required curriculum. In recent years, many regular physical education teacher-training programs have also started to offer three- to twelve-credit emphases or minor areas of study in adapted physical education as part of their undergraduate programs. These emphasis areas typically are composed of one to three theory courses and one to two practical experiences where the students can apply their APE course work.

See also: MOTOR LEARNING; PHYSICAL DISABILITIES, EDUCATION OF INDIVIDUALS WITH; PHYSICAL EDUCATION, *subentries on* OVERVIEW, PREPARATION OF TEACHERS; SPECIAL EDUCATION.

BIBLIOGRAPHY

Education for All Handicapped Children Act of 1975. U.S. Public Law 94-142. *U.S. Code.* Vol. 20, secs. 1401 et seq.

Individuals with Disabilities Education Act of 1997. U.S. Public Law 105-17. *U.S. Code.* Vol. 20, secs. 1400 et seq.

KELLY, LUKE E., ed. 1995. *Adapted Physical Education National Standards.* Champaign, IL: Human Kinetics.

RIMMER, JAMES H. 1994. *Fitness and Rehabilitation Programs for Special Populations.* Dubuque, IA: Brown and Benchmark.

SHERRILL, CLAUDINE. 1998. *Adapted Physical Activity, Recreation, and Sport: Crossdisciplinary and Lifespan,* 5th edition. Dubuque, IA: MCB/McGraw-Hill.

WINNICK, JOSEPH P., ed. 2000. *Adapted Physical Education and Sport,* 3rd edition. Champaign, IL: Human Kinetics.

INTERNET RESOURCES

INTERNATIONAL FEDERATION FOR ADAPTED PHYSICAL ACTIVITY. 2002. <www.per.ualberta.ca/rhc/IFAPA/mainframe.htm>.

NATIONAL CONSORTIUM FOR PHYSICAL EDUCATION AND RECREATION FOR INDIVIDUALS WITH DISABILITIES. 2002. <ncperid.usf.edu>.

NORTH AMERICAN FEDERATION ON ADAPTED PHYSICAL ACTIVITY. 2002. <ed-web3.educ.msu.edu/nafapa>.

SPORTIME. 2002. "Adapt-talk." <www.lyris.sportime.com/>.

TEXAS WOMAN'S UNIVERSITY. 2002. "Adapted Physical Education National Standards." <www.twu.edu/APENS>.

LUKE E. KELLY

ADDAMS, JANE (1860–1935)

Founder and driving force behind Hull-House, the pioneer American settlement house, Jane Addams is best known for her contribution to urban social service; however, she was also an important and influential educator who espoused Progressive educational ideas and practice.

Born in the small northern Illinois village of Cedarville, Addams was deeply influenced by her father, John Huy Addams, a successful self-made businessman and a strong supporter of Abraham Lincoln, with a dedication to public service. Although her father was wealthy, Addams found a genuinely democratic community in Cedarville, where members of different classes mingled freely—an ideal that she would strive for in her adult career. As a child, she steeped herself in literary classics and she was a highly successful student at Rockford Seminary. Like others of this first generation of college women she was, as her biographer Allen F. Davis points out, "self consciously a feminist, not so much concerned with women's suffrage as women's role in the world" (p. 19).

Discovering her own role after graduation did not come easily. She suffered a long period of illness, partly physical and partly psychological. Her depression was exacerbated by the sudden death of her beloved father. She briefly attended medical school but dropped out because of illness. For eight years Addams searched for an appropriate career. Two trips to Europe were influential in her search. In London she was shocked by the poverty she observed and deeply impressed by Toynbee Hall, England's first settlement house. In Germany she was stunned by the tasks of working women she observed. Her new observations led her to question her own education. In her autobiography, *Twenty Years at Hull-House,* she referred to it as a "Snare of Preparation." The first generation of college women, she now believed, had been educated away from life; "somewhere in the process of 'being educated' they had lost that simple and almost automatic response to the human appeal, that healthful reaction resulting in activity from the mere presence of suffering or of helplessness . . ." (p. 44). She was convinced that an adequate education should not be "disconnected from the ultimate test of the conduct it inspired" (p. 46).

This was to be the philosophy of education that inspired the rest of her career. By 1889 Addams had discovered her true role when she, with her friend Ellen Gates Starr, founded Hull-House in an impoverished section of Chicago that was home to many immigrants. Hull-House was, from its very beginning, dedicated to education. One of its first activities was a nursery school. Addams pursued not only the education of her poor neighbors; an important role of this new institution was the education of the middle-class women who resided within the house. In her influential essay, "The Subjective Necessity for Social Settlements," she argues that the function of social settlements is to extend democracy beyond the political democracy envisioned by the founding fathers into a form of social democracy. Working with the poor, middle-class men and women could connect with the vitality of working people while, at the same time, sharing their knowledge and culture with others. She saw Hull-House as a place "in which young women who had been given over too exclusively to study might restore a balance of activity along traditional lines and learn of life from life itself . . ." (1910, p. 51). Hull-House, like other settlements, was an educational institution that protests "against a restricted view of education."

John Dewey was a trustee and a frequent visitor at Hull-House. He credited conversations with Addams as highly influential in developing his own philosophy of education. Addams and Dewey shared a vision of education as the basis for producing a democratic community. They also shared a conception of education that went well beyond formal learning in classrooms. Hull-House itself was an educational setting, furnished as a middle-class home, with fine art and fashionable furniture, because Addams believed that in a truly democratic society the poor needed to have access to a setting that enriched the lives of the upper classes. Beyond the setting, Hull-House featured art and literature classes, political discussion groups, plays by Shakespeare and Sophocles, and lectures by prominent intellectuals, including Henry Demarest Lloyd and the radical African-American leader W. E. B. Du Bois.

Agreeing with Dewey and William James, Addams believed that knowledge should not be separated from its consequences. Education's role, therefore, was to provide the knowledge that would improve the life of all of the participants in the community. Unlike the formal education provided by the public schools and the universities, this education would not be abstract and focused on future goals, but would, rather, be an effort to relate to the needs and interests of the participants, both the children and adults who came to Hull-House. Like the university, Hull-House conducted social research but unlike the university, its aim was to use this knowledge for the improvement of community life.

Among the first activities of the new settlement were clubs in which children were organized in groups rather than conventional classes. "The value of these groups," she recalled in her autobiography, "consisted almost entirely in arousing a higher imagination and in giving the children the opportunity which they could not have in the crowded schools, for initiative and for independent social relationships . . ." (p. 63). These clubs provided opportunities for creative activities, absent from the rigid, public schools' curriculum.

Addams was inspired by the idea that education could ameliorate the sharp divisions in the new industrial society. As a way of overcoming the split between immigrant parents and their Americanized offspring, she created the Hull-House Labor Museum in which immigrants were given the opportunity to practice the handicrafts they had learned in their home countries, demonstrating to their children the skills they retained despite the difficulties of acculturation in this strange new society.

Addams's view of education was broad, involving not only the Hull-House neighborhood, but also the larger Chicago community and eventually the world. Although she was not a radical feminist, in her neighborhood she worked to educate the women to extend their traditional duties of maintaining their households and protecting the health of their children to a broader concern for community cleanliness and hygiene. Hull-House inspired a drive, led by the Hull-House Women's Club, to improve the health of the neighborhood by securing better garbage removal and an improved sewage system, an effort that eventually led Addams to an appointment as garbage inspector for the ward.

Addams was less successful when she was appointed to the Chicago School Board in 1905 by reformer Mayor Edward F. Dunne. She was at first identified as an ally of the Chicago Teachers' Federation's dynamic leader, Margaret Haley. She supported the reformers on the board in an effort to improve tax assessments to support public education through higher teacher salaries and the construction of new schools. These efforts alienated powerful business interests and especially the *Chicago Tribune*. But she also isolated herself from the reformers by her willingness to compromise on the controversial issue of removing political influence from the process of teacher promotions. When the other school board reformers were removed by a new mayor, to their dismay, Addams did not resign in protest. Addams' deep belief that she could promote social harmony through dialogue and compromise resulted in a conspicuous failure.

This search for harmony and reconciliation was to meet its biggest challenge when Addams became one of the leading opponents of World War I. Her efforts to induce the combatants to confer instead of continuing to fight and, most important, her efforts to keep her own nation out of the war led to a rapid decline in her reputation and influence. Addams, who had been widely regarded as an American heroine, was reviled and denounced during these years (as were the immigrants she defended).

The rapid decline of Addams' reputation in these difficult years was a severe challenge to her philosophy. Like Dewey, Addams had a deep and abiding faith in reforming society through a new kind of education—an education related to the lives and interests of the people it served. But, as Christopher Lasch has pointed out, "The leap from the school and the settlement to the reform of the social structure as a whole was a much greater leap than the progressives imagined" (1965b, p. 201).

Addams' efforts to avoid war were integral to her constant vision of building a better, more democratic society by educating people to appreciate their common interests and participating in a broader sense of community, an effort that was more deeply appreciated in the postwar years. In 1931 she was finally awarded the Nobel Peace Prize. Characteristically, she distributed the monetary reward to the Women's International League for Peace and her Hull-House neighbors.

See also: DEWEY, JOHN; IMMIGRANT EDUCATION, *subentry on* UNITED STATES; MIGRANTS, EDUCATION OF.

BIBLIOGRAPHY

ADDAMS, JANE. 1910. *Twenty Years at Hull-House, with Autobiographical Notes.* New York: Macmillan.

ADDAMS, JANE. 1930. *The Second Twenty Years at Hull-House: September 1909 to September 1929 with a Record of Growing Consciousness.* New York: Macmillan.

DAVIS, ALLEN F. 1973. *American Heroine: The Life and Legend of Jane Addams.* New York: Oxford University Press.

ELSHTAIN, JEAN BETHKE. 2002. *Jane Addams and the Dream of American Democracy: A Life.* New York: Basic Books.

LASCH, CHRISTOPHER. 1965a. *The New Radicalism in America.* New York: Vintage.

LASCH, CHRISTOPHER, ed. 1965b. *The Social Thought of Jane Addams.* Indianapolis: Bobbs-Merrill.

ARTHUR ZILVERSMIT

ADHD

See: ATTENTION DEFICIT HYPERACTIVITY DISORDER.

ADJUSTMENT TO COLLEGE

Pursuing a college education requires adjustment on the part of all students, though the type and degree of adjustment experienced by each student will vary depending on background, experience, and prior schooling. Adjustment to college will also vary depending on the size, mission (e.g., research intensive versus teaching intensive), affiliation (e.g., religiously affiliated institutions), and control (e.g., public versus private) of the institution in question. Arthur Chickering and Nancy Schlossberg (1995) point out that students who are leaving high school, attending college full-time, and living on campus tend to experience the most dramatic adjustment. Younger commuter students who are still living at home and maintaining high school friendships will experience slightly less change, and adult students who are attending part-time and are balancing school, work, and family may require the least adjustment.

Types of Adjustment

Ernest Pascarella and Patrick Terenzini (1991) assert that adjusting to college entails the complementary processes of desocialization and socialization. Desocialization is the changing or discarding of selected values, beliefs, and traits one brings to college in response to the college experience. Socialization is the process of being exposed to and taking on some of the new values, attitudes, beliefs, and perspectives to which one is exposed at college. It is also the process of learning and internalizing the character, culture, and behavioral norms of the institution one is attending. Pascarella and Terenzini describe the transition from high school as a "culture shock involving significant social and psychological relearning in the face of encounters with new ideas, new teachers and friends with quite varied values and beliefs, new freedoms and opportunities, and new academic, personal and social demands" (pp. 58–59). This culture shock is especially acute for those students who do not have siblings or parents who attended college.

Specific types of collegiate adjustment involve changes in roles, relationships, academic demands, and social demands. In addition, some subpopulations of students will face specific adjustment issues depending on the institution in question.

Roles. Taking on the new role of college student often brings new challenges and forces adjustment in existing roles, such as those of son/daughter, friend, partner, spouse, and parent. This is especially the case for part-time adult students with full-time jobs and families. Adjustment also involves disengaging from old roles that no longer exist for the student in the collegiate environment, such as athlete (for those not participating in college athletics), or

social leader (a role often lost for students moving from small high schools to large colleges).

Relationships. New college students need to adjust to changes in their relationships. Students make new friends and develop new peer groups in college. In fact, students who remain preoccupied with friends from home tend not to adjust well to college. Students often need to renegotiate existing relationships, especially with their parents and family. However, while remaining preoccupied with friends from home detracts from adjustment, students who maintain compatible relationships with their families are more likely to experience success in college. College is often a place where one is more likely to meet people who are different from oneself in terms of ethnicity, race, and socioeconomic status.

Establishing relationships may be a struggle for students who do not fit the institution's norms, such as students of color (at predominantly white institutions), international students, students with disabilities, adult students, and gay, lesbian, and bisexual students. For these students this situation often results in initial feelings of marginalization and isolation. In college (depending on the particular type of institution), there also are often different types of relationships with faculty than students may have experienced in previous educational settings. On the one hand, students are expected to be independent learners, yet there also exists the possibility of developing intellectual, collaborative, and social relationships with faculty.

Academic demands. For most college students, the transition to the college classroom requires an adjustment of academic habits and expectations. They often must study harder, improve their study habits, and take school more seriously. Classes are larger, instructors have differing teaching styles, the pace is faster, written work is more frequent, reading assignments are lengthier, standards are higher, and the competition is more acute. Students need to learn to set and balance priorities, and for commuter and adult students this includes balancing work, home, and school.

Social demands. The social environment of college requires adjustment on the part of new college students. Students must learn to balance the many social choices they have with their academic responsibilities. Developing new relationships represents an important element of social adjustment. Other social issues that require adjustment include negotiating dating in an era of sexually transmitted diseases, homesickness, shifts in daily routines, and the lack of externally imposed structure on their lives.

Student subpopulations. There are specific adjustment issues for students of color; women students; gay, lesbian, and bisexual students; students with disabilities; and adult students—and especially for students who are members of more than one of these groups. For example, at predominantly white institutions, students of color (especially those from homogenous living environments) will face attitudes, belief systems, and power structures that often work against people of color. In classes, students of color may be asked to speak for their entire ethnic group on matters of race. Especially acute social adjustment issues for students of color include dealing with depression and stress, managing cross-cultural relationships, and adjusting to the campus racial/cultural climate. Some classroom environments will be experienced by women students as "chilly"; that is, women students may be addressed inappropriately and treated as less competent than male students.

College is the time when many gay, lesbian, and bisexual students choose to come out publicly for the first time. The homophobia and heterosexism they experience will require an enhancement of coping skills. Students with disabilities, depending on the type and severity of their disability, will also face a host of adjustment issues, including perhaps being independent for the first time and finding and establishing support services. Finally, older students may face issues of low confidence, low self-esteem, identity adjustment, and role stress to a more severe degree than traditional-age students.

Services Available to Assist with Adjustment

American colleges and universities have taken on the responsibility of assisting students with their adjustment to college in multiple ways. Many standard services contribute to the positive adjustment of students, including academic support programs, counseling services, academic and career advising, living-learning centers, residence halls, campus activities, and health and wellness programs. In addition, there are also services specifically designed to aid in adjustment to college, including new student orientation programs, University 101 courses, freshman interest groups and learning communities, developmental/remedial courses, and early warning systems.

New student orientation programs. The primary purpose of new student orientation programs is to help students successfully adjust to college. The programs do this by connecting students to the institution, helping them to set and reach goals, and making them successful in the classroom. While new student orientation programs vary in length, scope, purpose, timing, and content, most aim to give students information about facilities, programs, and services and to give them a chance to meet and make connections with faculty, staff, and students.

University 101. Freshmen orientation seminars, or University 101, proliferated on college campuses in the 1980s and 1990s. These are often weekly seminars co-instructed by faculty and students. They serve to extend new student orientation activities throughout the first semester or first year.

Freshmen interest groups. Freshman interest groups (FIGs) are a form of learning community through which students take a series of linked courses as a cohort group (typically between twenty and thirty students). The courses that make up a FIG are chosen to reflect a general theme and frequently include some type of composition or writing course. There is often a common discussion section for these students led by another student or by one or more of the faculty teaching the courses in the FIG. The faculty work together to coordinate assignments and link and connect specific course subjects across classes. The emphasis in a FIG is on active and collaborative learning. The purpose of the program is to assist students' academic adjustment by providing a "small college experience" (i.e., the small cohort) while taking courses that often have hundreds of other students.

Remedial/developmental courses. These courses are designed to help students who are not fully prepared for the college academic experience. They seek to help students gain the skills they need in order to succeed, and are typically focused in the areas of mathematics, English, and writing.

Early warning systems. These systems are designed to identify students who are having difficulty adjusting to the academic and behavioral expectations of college. It is important to identify such adjustment problems early enough in the student's first semester in order to have some chance for a successful intervention. Examples include providing midterm grade reports early in the semester and having advisers or other staff follow up with all students who fall below a certain cutoff point in grade point average. Early warning systems can be incorporated into FIGs or academic advising relationships.

See also: COLLEGE STUDENT RETENTION; STUDENT ORIENTATION PROGRAMS.

BIBLIOGRAPHY

CHICKERING, ARTHUR W., and SCHLOSSBERG, NANCY K. 1995. *Getting the Most out of College.* Needham Heights, MA: Allyn and Bacon.

ERICKSON, BETTE L., and STROMMER, DIANE W. 1991. *Teaching College Freshmen.* San Francisco: Jossey-Bass.

EVANS, NANCY J., and D'AUGELLI, ANTHONY R. 1996. "Lesbians, Gay Men, and Bisexual People in College." In *The Lives of Lesbians, Gays, and Bisexuals: Children to Adults,* ed. Ritch C. Savin-Williams and Kenneth M. Cohen. Fort Worth, TX: Harcourt Brace.

LEVEY, MARC; BLANCO, MICHAEL; and JONES, W. TERRELL. 1998. *How to Succeed on a Majority Campus: A Guide for Minority Students.* Belmont, CA: Wadsworth.

LOVE, PATRICK G., and GOODSELL LOVE, ANNE. 1995. *Enhancing Student Learning: Intellectual, Social, and Emotional Integration.* ASHE-ERIC Higher Education Report Series 4. Washington, DC: George Washington University, Graduate School of Education and Human Development.

PASCARELLA, ERNEST T., and TERENZINI, PATRICK T. 1991. *How College Affects Students.* San Francisco: Jossey-Bass.

PAUL, ELIZABETH L., and BRIER, SIGAL. 2001. "Friendsickness in the Transition to College: Precollege Predictors and College Adjustment Correlations." *Journal of Counseling and Development* 79:77–89.

SANDLER, BERNICE R. 1996. "The Chilly Classroom Climate: A Guide to Improve the Education of Women." *AWIS Magazine* 25(5):10–11.

SCHWITZER, ALAN M.; GRIFFIN, ORIS T.; ANCIS, JULIE R.; and THOMAS, CELESTE R. 1999. "Social Adjustment Experiences of African American College Students." *Journal of Counseling and Development* 77(2):89–197.

TINTO, VINCENT. 1993. *Leaving College: Rethinking the Causes and Cures of Student Attrition,* 2nd edition. Chicago: University of Chicago Press.

UPCRAFT, M. LEE, ed. 1984. *Orienting Students to College.* San Francisco: Jossey-Bass.

UPCRAFT, M. LEE, and GARDNER, JOHN, N. 1989. *The Freshman Year Experience: Helping Students Survive and Succeed in College.* San Francisco: Jossey-Bass.

PATRICK LOVE

ADMINISTRATION, EDUCATIONAL

See: AMERICAN ASSOCIATION OF SCHOOL ADMINISTRATORS; EDUCATIONAL LEADERSHIP; NATIONAL ASSOCIATION OF ELEMENTARY SCHOOL PRINCIPALS; NATIONAL ASSOCIATION OF SCHOOL ADMINISTRATORS; NATIONAL ASSOCIATION OF SECONDARY SCHOOL PRINCIPALS; PRINCIPAL, SCHOOL; SCHOOL BOARD RELATIONS, *subentry on* RELATION OF SCHOOL BOARD TO THE SUPERINTENDENT; SUPERINTENDENT OF LARGE-CITY SCHOOL SYSTEMS; SUPERINTENDENT OF SCHOOLS.

ADMISSIONS, COLLEGE

See: COLLEGE ADMISSIONS.

ADOLESCENT PEER CULTURE

OVERVIEW
  Helen Vrailas Bateman
GANGS
  Dewey G. Cornell
  Daniel C. Murrie
PARENTS' ROLE
  Helen Vrailas Bateman

OVERVIEW

The view that peers play a central role in adolescence is widely accepted as fact. In the popular image of adolescence, however, adolescent peer groups often play a negative role in adolescent development. Traditionally, the adolescent peer culture of modern society has been perceived as a primarily negative influence, separate from that of adults and often leading to problem behaviors. Alcohol abuse, drug use, truancy, and premarital pregnancy are attributed to a separate youth culture. There are, however, an increasing number of researchers who object to this negative image of adolescent culture and who argue for a more positive image of adolescent culture in modern society, its unique and important contributions, and its robust relationship with and similarities to adult culture. In the following section, these disparate points of view and the evidence for them are briefly examined.

What Is Meant by Peer Culture?

The term *peer culture,* as introduced in 1988 by William Corsaro, was derived through Corsaro's study of children in nursery settings and contains the following aspects of social interaction:

1. Children in these settings appear to adhere to and behave according to a set of "social rules" and behavioral routines. If such rules and routines are breached, then comments and negotiations between children follow.

2. Children in these settings share a mutual understanding of actions and norms for procedures. This shared framework of understanding enables children to systematically interpret novel situations.

3. Children in these settings engage in activities that focus on themes that are repeated and that all members of the peer group recognize.

Corsaro also examined the relationship between the social systems shared by children and the culture of adults (namely, teachers and parents). Corsaro suggested that there was a dynamic interchange of elements between the two cultures, with elements that appeared in one culture reappearing in the other. In 1994 Corsaro and Donna Elder discussed how this interchange between cultures is particularly interesting in adolescence, during which the adolescent peer culture, while maintaining its own unique social system, introduces rules and systems that facilitate belonging in the adult society. Other researchers have shared this view of a distinct adolescent peer culture with its own structure. Support for this view of adolescent peer culture comes from a variety of sources.

Societal Factors Contributing to Adolescent Peer Culture

While contact between adolescents and their peers is a universal characteristic of all cultures, there is a great deal of variability in the nature and the degree of such contact. In American contemporary society, adolescents spend significantly more time with their peers than with younger children or adults. The pattern of age segregation in American society did not become the norm until the onset of the industrialized society. Changes in the workplace separated children from adults, with adults working and children attending school. The dramatic increase of mothers in the workplace has further contributed to the reduction in the amount of time adolescents spend with adults. School reform efforts during the nineteenth century, which resulted in age-segregated schools and grades, have reduced the amount of time adolescents spend with younger children. Finally, the changes in population are considered a factor that may have contributed to the emergence of adolescent peer culture. From 1955 to 1975, the proportion of the population that was adolescent (between the ages of fifteen and nineteen) increased dramatically, from 11 percent to 20.9 percent. This increase in the number of adolescents might be a contributing factor to the increase in adolescent peer culture both in terms of growth in size as well as in terms of its impact on society's other cultures (adults, younger children).

Research supports the view that adolescents spend a great deal of time with their peers. In 1977 Mihaly Csikszentmihalyi, Reed Larson, and Suzanne Prescott examined adolescent's daily activities and found that they spend more time talking to their friends than engaging in any other activity. In a typical week, high school students will spend twice as much time with their peers as with adults. This gradual withdrawal from adults begins in early adolescence. In sixth grade, adults (excluding parents) account for only 25 percent of adolescent social networks. Another important characteristic of adolescent peer culture is its increasingly autonomous function. While childhood peer groups are conducted under the close supervision of parents, adolescent peer groups typically make an effort to escape adult supervision and usually succeed in doing so. (Note, importantly, that this is in reference to informal peer groups.)

Adolescent peer culture also differs from that of younger-age children in the patterns of relationships between peers. Adolescence is characterized by the emergence of crowds as an important social context of development. This is a departure from the peer culture of younger children, which is defined by dyadic (two-person) and small-group relationships. Another unique characteristic of adolescent peer culture is the increasing contact with peers of the opposite sex. Unlike younger children, who adhere to sex-segregated groups, adolescents steadily increase their levels of association with members of the opposite sex. Adolescence is marked by the increased need and ability for intimate relationships both in the form of friendships and in the form of romantic relationships such as dating.

Are Peer Relations Necessary for Development?

The question of the role that peer culture plays in adolescent development has to start with the issue of the necessity of peer relations in human development. Research using monkeys that were reared without peer monkeys showed that growing up peerless resulted in monkeys that were socially disadvantaged and depressed. Studies with humans suggest that lack of harmonious peer relations during adolescence is related to poor mental health later in life. Evidence from follow-back studies of adults consistently supports the view that psychological and educational maladjustment in adulthood is associated with histories of problematic childhood peer relationships. Longitudinal prospective studies also indicate that children who were identified as socially rejected by their peers in fifth grade were twice as likely to be delinquent as adolescents. Researchers found that children who had poor peer relationships at the age of nine were more likely to develop into adolescents who engaged in higher levels of substance abuse, had more conduct problems such as aggression and attentional problems, and committed more delinquent offenses. In 1995 Virginia Burks, Kenneth Dodge, and Joseph Price reported that children who were rejected by their peers in middle childhood had higher rates of depression and loneliness six year later. A large body of research therefore indicates that peer relationships are a very important factor in human development.

The Nature of Adolescent Peer Culture

James Coleman's work on adolescent peer culture was extremely influential in shaping views on modern adolescent culture. In 1961 Coleman suggested that an adolescent subculture had emerged in industrialized societies that was distinct from that of more agrarian cultures (such as the Amish culture). According to Coleman, social and economic forces that encourage age segregation shape the socialization of adolescents in industrialized societies. In a rapidly changing society, parents' skills easily become obsolete. Parents therefore cannot transmit their accu-

mulated knowledge to their children, and hence they have fewer opportunities for direct influence over their children's development. Education takes place in school settings, for longer periods, further reducing the influence that family-centered learning has on adolescents. The period of schooling required in modern societies is becoming lengthier, and even within schools, children are segregated according to age in separate grades. These age-segregation patterns, according to Coleman, precipitate the creation of a separate adolescent culture in which adolescents speak a "language" increasingly different from that of adults. Modern industrialized societies encourage this "separate adolescent culture" by creating specialized marketing that cultivates and targets the adolescents' unique taste in music, clothes, and entertainment.

Such isolation from adults, Coleman claimed, results in the creation of adolescent societal standards and behavioral norms that are far removed from those of adult society. Adolescents look to their peers rather than to their parents and teachers for guidance and approval, thereby diminishing the ability of adults to influence adolescents' development. Coleman suggested that because of the aforementioned conditions, examining adolescent culture within the schools, its compositions and characteristics, is the only way in industrialized societies to understand and influence contemporary adolescents and their development.

Coleman's influential study examined adolescents and their parents in ten schools. Coleman found that on the average high school students are not very interested in academic goals but rather tend to focus more on social and athletic goals. This lack of focus on academic achievement, coupled with the decreased influence that parents and teachers have on adolescents' decision-making processes, led Coleman to declare that the existing school climate and culture was inadequate in addressing adolescent needs in industrialized societies. Coleman suggested that changes in the school culture should include a schoolwide emphasis on scholastic achievement as being the most desired outcome for students (rather than the present emphasis and glorification of athletic accomplishments) as well as an educational system that enables adolescents to become "active" rather than "passive" learners. Coleman argued that by becoming active participants in their learning processes, adolescents can assume roles of responsibility and leadership that are more appropriate to their developmental needs and are therefore more likely to result in higher levels of engagement in academics and adherence to school norms. High school teachers should encourage creative, hands-on learning activities in high schools and engage in teaching practices that focus on intrinsic rather than on extrinsic motivation.

Subsequent research, for the most part, has supported Coleman's findings of the central role that peer culture plays in adolescent development. Some critics, however, object to the "oversimplification" of peer culture that is depicted by Coleman's work, calling into question his unidimensional description of adolescent culture. Instead, these critics argue that research supports the view that there are multiple adolescent cultures that can be very different from each other. For example, a 1968 study of Canadian adolescents conducted by David Friesen contradicted Coleman's work by finding that most students preferred to be remembered as outstanding scholars rather than as outstanding athletes or as popular students. Other studies suggest that there are significant differences in the importance adolescents place on grades, athletic ability, and appearance based on adolescents' gender and grade level. Critics also suggest that the nature of adolescent peer culture also changes over time, reflecting social, economical, and historical changes in society. Subsequent examination of the proposed lack of influence of parents on adolescent culture has also yielded mixed findings, with some studies suggesting that parental values remain very influential in shaping adolescent behavior such as the patterns of friendships adolescents have with their peers.

Adolescent Peer Crowds and Cliques

In 1990 Bradford Brown suggested that, rather than having a monolithic approach to adolescent culture that depicts it as primarily "deviant," it is more appropriate to examine and understand the multiplicity of adolescent peer cultures and the factors that influence such variability in values and aspirations.

When examining peer groups, a distinction should be made between cliques (small, highly interactive groups) and crowds (large groups with more emphasis on reputation than on interaction). As noted earlier, peer groups and peer group membership change from childhood to adolescence. Some of the changes already mentioned are that adolescents spend more time interacting with their peers than younger children do, less time interacting with

adults, and more time interacting with opposite-sex peers. Adolescents also seem to gravitate more toward group and crowd membership. Research supports the view of an adolescent culture comprising very different groups and cliques, each with a unique blend of behavioral norms and beliefs. In 1975 Leo Rigsby and Edward McDill proposed categorizing the various crowds along two orthogonal dimensions: the degree to which they are committed to the formal (adult-controlled) reward system of school and the degree to which they are committed to the informal (peer-controlled) status system. In 1998 Margaret Stone and Bradford Brown further developed this categorization axis and found that all adolescent groups could be categorized across the two orthogonal axes of academic engagement and peer status. Within these axes various groups were formed (the "rebels," the "jocks," the "populars," the "normals," the "brains," the "black crowd," and the "wannabe black crowd"). The broad range of crowds had well-differentiated norms, beliefs, and goals and lent support to an image of adolescent culture that is far from monolithic and static. Stone and Brown also cautioned against generalizing their findings across all settings. Cultural and socioeconomic conditions can alter the type of groups that comprise a given adolescent culture.

Reasons for such changes in peer relationships can be attributed to multiple aspects of adolescent development. The need to establish a unique and autonomous identity different from that of one's parents is one of the driving forces behind adolescents' need to reduce their psychological dependency on their parents as well as on other adults. An additional benefit to belonging in various crowds and cliques is the opportunity to explore different value systems and lifestyles in the process of forming one's identity. Adolescents' social-cognitive maturation enables them to seek groups that can meet their emerging social and cognitive needs as well as their emerging values and beliefs.

Biological changes also play an important role in adolescents' need to form relationships with the opposite sex—both friendships and dating relationships. Finding the "right" clique to belong to can provide adolescents with a very much needed emotional and social support that can help them successfully navigate the demands of adolescence. Finding the "wrong" clique, on the other hand, can lead to maladaptive consequences that can include deviant behavioral patterns. The question of the direction of peer group influence on adolescents, however, is not a simple one. The traditional way of thinking about peer influence is that it is unidirectional and direct; that is, the peer group exerts a direct and overt influence on the adolescent's behavior. Research indicates, however, that the influence is interactional. Adolescents tend to choose peer groups that share their own beliefs and norms. Conversely, peer groups tend to approach like-minded adolescents to join their group. While peer culture tends to influence adolescent behavior, it has become clear that peer culture accounts for only part of the variation in adolescent behavior. For example, adolescents' smoking and alcohol drinking patterns are attributed to peer pressure only 10 to 40 percent of the time. It is also important to note that peer culture influences are not limited to deviant behavior. As discussed above, many peer groups have positive influences on adolescents regarding academic achievement. When adolescents were asked to describe the degree and direction of peer pressure from their friends, the most commonly mentioned and strongest pressure adolescents reported was to stay in school and to finish high school. An interesting aspect of this bidirectional influence between cliques and individuals is the issue of the similarity between participants of adolescent cliques. Research indicates that cliques typically comprise adolescents who are similar in multiple dimensions, such as age, socioeconomic status, and race. Moreover, some research indicates that adolescents can be members of multiple groups and that there are similarities across group boundaries, reinforcing the image of adolescent culture—even within a homogeneous group of adolescents—as a complex system of multiplicity of styles and relationships not unlike adult society.

Changes in Peer Culture during Adolescence

During adolescence, important changes take place in the structure of the groups and cliques that adolescents belong to. In early adolescence, adolescents tend to form cliques with same-sex individuals. The same-sex cliques evolve into mixed-sex cliques during middle adolescence. Finally, in late adolescence and early adulthood, these cliques gradually give way to dyadic dating relationships. This development parallels the increasing ability and need for intimacy that develops during adolescence. Even the nature and boundaries of the groups and cliques change during adolescence, with the groups becoming less important to adolescents' self-image and less insular

by the end of high school. In 1994 Brown, Mory, and David Kinney presented evidence that outlines the developmental trajectory of adolescent crowds. In middle school, the crowd system consists of only two crowds—the "trendies" (students who have high status) and the "dweebs" (lower-status students). The "dweebs" comprise the majority of the student body. The boundaries of these two middle school crowds are fairly rigid. As adolescents transition to high school a more elaborate social structure that is comprised of many different groups appears, thus enabling the majority of students (who had previously been classified as "dweebs") to seek membership in groups such as the "normals" or the "punkers." Status differences between the groups are fairly salient during the early years of high school. By the end of high school, however, the boundaries between some of these groups seem to disappear, and status differences seem to diminish. This study illustrates very well the dynamic and changing nature of peer groups and peer culture during adolescence.

Adolescent Peer Culture and School

Peer acceptance and membership in a clique is an important aspect of becoming an adolescent. Peer crowds and cliques can have a profound influence on how adolescents adjust to a school setting. As noted earlier, adolescents in school settings can become members of various cliques each with unique norms and beliefs. Laurence Steinberg, in his 1996 book *Beyond the Classroom,* reported the alarming results of studies that suggest that in today's schools, less than 5 percent of all students are members of a high-achieving crowd that sets high academic standards. Even more alarming is that in most schools there appears to be a great deal of pressure from the "prevailing" peer culture to underachieve in school. Steinberg reported that one out of six students deliberately hides her intelligence and interest in doing well in class out of the desire to be accepted by her peers. When adolescents were asked which group they would like to belong to, five times as many students selected the "populars" or the "jocks" as selected the "brains." Moreover, an additional indication that high-achieving students with aspirations to academic excellence are not popular in schools today came from the fact that, when asked, the "brains" were least happy with the group they belonged to (nearly half wished they could be in a different crowd). Longitudinal data confirms the fact that initial membership in a peer group that is academically oriented is correlated with higher grades, more time spent on homework, and more involvement in extracurricular activities. Beyond significantly lower academic achievement, adolescents whose friends in school were members of a "delinquent" crowd were more likely to exhibit more negative behaviors inside and outside the classroom (including conduct problems and drug and alcohol use).

The strong relationship between a positive and supportive peer culture in school and classroom settings and students' academic, emotional, and social adjustment is also evident in research that examines students' sense of belonging and sense of community in a school setting and their academic, social, and emotional adjustment. In 2002 Helen Bateman found that students define a supportive peer community as one that:

1. Shares their values and educational goals.
2. Actively supports their learning needs.
3. Provides a safe and pro-social environment in which adolescents can learn.
4. Values their contributions.

Students with a higher sense of community in the school and classroom have higher grades and higher academic self-esteem. Students with a higher sense of community also display higher levels of learning orientation and greater interest in complex problem-solving tasks. Finally, students with high sense of community also display higher levels of social skills and pro-social behavior.

Conclusion

It is clear that convergent evidence from many different areas of research suggest that peer culture has a very strong influence on students' adjustment to school during adolescence. Given the sensitivity of adolescents to peers, the effects of this informal social organization of the school community in crowds and cliques can surpass and counteract the effects of any formal school norms (such as regular attendance, the importance of academic achievement, and proper conduct). The issue of adolescents belonging to "positive" peer communities that encourage academic engagement and pro-social behavior should therefore become a central point of concern for parents and educators during the period of adolescence.

See also: PEER RELATIONS AND LEARNING.

BIBLIOGRAPHY

BATEMAN, HELEN VRAILAS. 2002. "Sense of Community in the School: Listening to Students' Voices." In *Psychological Sense of Community: Research, Applications, and Implications,* ed. Adrian T. Fisher, Chris C. Sonn, and Bryant J. Bishop. New York: Kluwer Academic/Plenum Publishers.

BROWN, B. BRADFORD. 1990. "Peer Groups and Peer Cultures." In *At the Threshold: The Developing Adolescent,* ed. Shirley S. Feldman and Glen R. Elliott. Cambridge, MA: Harvard University Press.

BROWN, B. BRADFORD; MORY, MARGARET S.; and KINNEY, DAVID A. 1994. "Casting Adolescent Crowds in a Relational Perspective: Caricature, Channel, and Context." In *Personal Relationships during Adolescence,* ed. Raymond Montemayor, Gerald R. Adams, and Thomas P. Gullotta. Thousand Oaks, CA: Sage.

BURKS, VIRGINIA S.; DODGE, KENNETH A.; and PRICE, JOSEPH M. 1995. "Models of Internalizing Outcomes of Early Rejection." *Development and Psychopathology* 7:683–696.

COLEMAN, JOHN S. 1961. *The Adolescent Society.* New York: Free Press of Glencoe.

CORSARO, WILLIAM A. 1988. "Routines in the Peer Culture of American and Italian Nursery School Children." *Sociology of Education* 61(1):1–14.

CORSARO, WILLIAM A., and ELDER, DONNA. 1990. "Children's Peer Cultures." *Annual Review of Sociology* 16:197–220.

CSIKSZENTMIHALYI, MIHALY; LARSON, REED; and PRESCOTT, SUZANNE. 1977. "The Ecology of Adolescent Activity and Experience." *Journal of Youth and Adolescence* 6:281–294.

FRIESEN, DAVID. 1968. "Academic-Athletic-Popularity Syndrome in the Canadian High School Society." *Adolescence* 3:39–52.

RIGSBY, LEO C., and MCDILL, EDWARD L. 1975. "Value Orientations of High School Students." In *The Sociology of Education: A Sourcebook,* ed. Holger R. Stub. Homewood, IL: Dorsey Press.

STEINBERG, LAURENCE. 1996. *Beyond the Classroom: Why School Reform Has Failed and What Parents Need to Do.* New York: Touchstone.

STONE, MARGARET R., and BROWN, B. BRADFORD. 1998. "In the Eyes of the Beholder: Adolescents'

Perceptions of Peer Crowd Stereotypes." In *Adolescent Behavior and Society: A Book of Readings,* ed. Rolf E. Muuss and Harriet D. Porton. Boston: McGraw-Hill.

U.S. Bureau of the Census. 1996. *Statistical Abstract of the United States.* Washington, DC: U.S. Bureau of the Census.

Helen Vrailas Bateman

GANGS

Gangs pose a serious problem for many schools. Students at schools with gangs are more than twice as likely to be victims of violent crimes than students at schools without gangs, they report greater access to illegal drugs, and they are four times more likely to report seeing a student with a gun in school. Gangs generate an atmosphere of fear and intimidation that pervades the school environment. Schools with gangs are much more likely to employ security measures such as guards, metal detectors, and locker checks. Gangs are reported by nearly 40 percent of students in U.S. public schools, including 25 percent of students in rural areas and more than 50 percent of students in communities with more than 50,000 residents. Nearly two-thirds of Hispanic students, almost one-half of African-American students, and one-third of white students report gangs in their schools.

What is a *gang*? Definitions vary widely, but usually refer to a self-formed group of individuals who identify themselves by a name and engage in recurrent criminal activity. Gangs typically have recognized leaders, membership requirements and initiation rituals, and an identified territory. Youth gangs contain adolescents, but often also include young adults (persons age eighteen or older). This definition distinguishes youth gangs from other types of groups, such as ideological groups, motorcycle gangs, and organized crime groups, that are primarily adult organizations.

Gangs are not new to the United States, and they have long been associated with unfavorable social and economic conditions experienced by immigrants in urban neighborhoods. Most historians agree that the economic difficulties and sociocultural stresses experienced by immigrant groups of many ethnic backgrounds have generated gang activity. Following a wave of Irish immigration in the 1820s, New York City was plagued by gangs such as the Bowery Boys, the Dead Rabbits, and the Plug Uglies, who marched brazenly through the streets in distinctive dress and confronted one another in armed combat. Mexican youth formed gangs when their families migrated to the southwestern United States in the early 1800s. More youth gangs followed waves of immigration to major industrial centers during the late 1800s and early 1900s. Many gangs were on the payroll of politicians and union leaders—or worked as junior confederates to organized crime. Frederic Thrasher's classic 1929 study of youth gangs in Chicago focused on the effects of poverty, immigration status, poor parental supervision, and lack of recreational opportunities among ethnic minorities, including Polish, Italian, Irish, Jewish, and other immigrant groups. Thrasher identified more than 1,300 youth gangs, although his definition emphasized allegiance among members and did not require criminal activity.

According to a national law enforcement survey, there were approximately 28,700 gangs and 780,200 gang members active in the United States in 1998. Gangs increased rapidly during the 1980s and early 1990s. There is considerable research and debate on reasons for the increase in youth gangs; among the most likely factors are the emergence of the crack cocaine market, an influx of Asian and Latin American immigrants who had few employment opportunities, the proliferation of gang federations and alliances, and a sustained, national surge of single-parent households. Gangs are most prevalent in the western United States and least prevalent in the Northeast. Youth gangs are most common in large cities, especially Los Angeles, New York, Chicago, Detroit, and Houston. Ninety-four percent of U.S. cities with populations of more than 100,000 report youth gangs, though gangs are also present in smaller communities. Half of all suburban counties, one-third of all small cities, and one-fifth of rural counties report active youth gangs. Although gang membership declined nationwide from 1996 to 1998, the number of gang members in rural counties increased by 43 percent.

Gang Characteristics

In his studies of Detroit gang activity in the 1980s, Carl Taylor distinguished three types of gangs. *Scavenger gangs* are informal groups that come together periodically and commit opportunistic, impulsive crimes. They are not well organized, leadership is variable, and the existence of the gang may be short-lived. In contrast, *territorial gangs* have many of the features commonly associated with gangs: a well-defined territory or turf that they defend from outsiders, membership requirements and initiation rituals, leadership by an individual or core group of members, distinctive dress, and use of symbols or hand signs for covert communication. Taylor used the term *corporate gang* to characterize highly organized and profit-oriented gangs engaged in extensive, well-defined criminal enterprises, such as drug dealing and extortion. Such gangs display a corporate-like structure in the differentiated assignment of roles and responsibilities to members, who may be involved in marketing, sales, or distribution, or in more specifically criminal activities such as enforcement.

Although media accounts sometimes refer to "gang migration" from larger to smaller cities, research suggests that organized migration is rare. When it does occur, it is generally the result of families moving from one city to the next for mundane reasons. In some cases, a youth who moves to a new city may claim membership in a well-known hometown gang in order to bolster his or her status in the new community. Most small-town and rural gangs are homegrown independent groups, and some may take on the name of nationally known gangs in an effort to gain prestige and status. Many gangs are poorly organized and short-lived, and such a gang's reputation may generate unwarranted public fear and concern.

Although gangs are often referred to as *youth gangs,* law enforcement estimates in 1998 suggested that 60 percent of gang members were adults (over age seventeen). Youth gangs have often been ethnically or racially homogeneous, although during the 1990s more than one-third of gangs were reported to have a racially mixed membership. Nationally, in 1998, 46 percent of gang members were Hispanic, 34 percent were African American, 12 percent were white, and 6 percent were Asian.

Most studies report that fewer than 10 percent of gang members are girls, although some studies have found rates as high as 30 percent, perhaps suggesting a trend toward greater female involvement in gangs. Early studies suggested girls formed auxiliary groups to male gangs, but in the 1990s many gangs had mixed gender membership, and 1 to 2 percent of gangs had more than 50 percent female membership. Gender studies indicate that girl gang members commit more crimes than girls who are not in gangs, but fewer crimes than boy gang members.

Gangs and Crime

Gang membership substantially increases a youth's involvement in criminal activities, even though youths who join gangs tend to be predisposed to delinquency and often have previous arrest records. Youths who join gangs engage in more crime than youths with similar backgrounds, even if those youths do associate with delinquent peers. Association with gang members is linked to greater involvement in delinquent activity than association with delinquent nongang peers.

Gang members commit a disproportionate share of juvenile crime, especially serious crime. In some studies, gang members were found to commit crimes at twice the rate of other arrested youths. Gang crimes vary over time and across gangs, but most frequently involve weapons offenses, drug sales, assault, and auto theft. Shootings, particularly drive-by shootings, are strongly associated with gang conflicts. Violent gang crime is more common in large cities, while gang involvement in breaking and entering and other property crimes is relatively more common in rural and suburban areas.

Although many youths join gangs for protection, studies show that gang membership greatly increases the risk of violent injury or death. Gang members are more likely than other youths to carry concealed weapons, and gang rivalries often lead to violent feuds and turf battles. Informal codes of honor in many gangs demand that members respond aggressively to perceived acts of disrespect so as to protect and bolster their reputation. Acts of aggression often stimulate vengeful counter-attacks, followed by further retaliation in an escalating pattern.

Drug trafficking is commonly associated with gangs, and economic rivalries over drug markets, as well as disputes over drug deals and sales, can lead to violence. Many authorities believe that the development of lucrative crack cocaine markets in the 1980s stimulated the growth of gangs and led to a dramatic increase in violent crimes, particularly firearm-related homicides in large cities. Law enforcement surveys indicate that approximately one-third of youth gangs are specifically organized for drug trafficking, although members of other gangs frequently participate in drug sales in a less systematic manner. Gang involvement in drug sales is common in rural and suburban areas as well as major cities. Nevertheless, the role of drug sales in homicides has proven to be smaller than expected, with substantial numbers of gang-related homicides associated with interpersonal conflicts and gang disputes over status and territory.

Why Do Young People Join Gangs?

Historically, sociologists have contended that gang involvement is associated with membership in an underclass—that youths who join gangs tend to be members of racial or ethnic minorities from economically deprived and socially disadvantaged areas. Indeed, young gang members are often poor, minority youth from disorganized neighborhoods. However, membership in the underclass is not a sufficient explanation for gang involvement, since the majority of such youths do not join gangs. Likewise, youths from less disadvantaged backgrounds also join gangs.

Ask a young gang member why he joined a gang, and the most frequent answer will be that his friends are in the gang. Friendship patterns are powerful influences on gang membership, as is the excitement of involvement in delinquent activity. Gangs grow and spread largely through individual contacts between gang members and prospective members. The appeal of belonging to a powerful, seemingly prestigious group is strong in adolescence, and young teens may aspire for acceptance into a group led by older teens and young adults. Many young teens are characterized as gang "wannabes," and researchers recognize a continuum of gang membership ranging from nonmembers to hardcore members. Although some gangs report lifelong membership, even devoted gang members usually cease active involvement in their gangs during their twenties. Longitudinal studies have found that more than 50 percent of gang members drop out of their gangs within a year of joining.

Gangs are appealing because they offer a sense of identity and social recognition to adolescents who feel marginalized in society and regard their future as bleak or uncertain. Conventional opportunities through education and employment may seem remote or unattainable to minority youth living in impoverished communities. Gangs offer opportunities for excitement, feelings of power and status, and defiance of conventional authority. Gangs also provide a well-defined, reliable peer group for recreation and

affiliation, which is a compelling concern during the teenage years. On a more practical level, gang involvement may provide financial opportunities through drug dealing and other criminal endeavors. In many neighborhoods gang membership offers protection from bullying or assault, and some youths may feel pressured to join a gang simply because they reside within the gang's territory.

Though it may be tempting to speculate about the psychological profile of a gang member, there is no simple explanation. Gangs offer a variety of roles and opportunities: one youth may aspire to lead others or serve as protector to his or her neighborhood; another may seek financial gain through crime, while still another may be drawn into the pattern of violence and neighborhood warfare that characterizes some gangs.

Family factors such as parental absence or inadequate supervision play a role in some cases, but in other cases parents may encourage gang involvement because of their own history of criminal activity or gang membership. Some large, well-established gangs claim generations of gang members within families. Popular culture may also encourage gang membership by promoting positive images of gangs—such as the Jets and Sharks of the Broadway musical *West Side Story* or movies that glamorize gang feuds similar to that between the Crips and Bloods, gangs that originated in Los Angeles. Many celebrities in music and professional sports proudly display their gang affiliation through tattoos, dress, and gestures.

Prevention and Intervention

The risk factors for gang membership are generally the same as for delinquency, and gang members are usually delinquent before they join gangs, suggesting that prevention efforts aimed at delinquency are relevant to preventing gang involvement as well. Although several strategies have been found to prevent or reduce general delinquency, programs aimed specifically at gangs have not met with much success. On an individual level, parental supervision and an emphasis on keeping youths from associating with delinquent peers is critically important.

One of the oldest gang prevention strategies attempts to alter the socioenvironmental factors presumed to produce gangs through community interventions such as increased recreational activities, neighborhood improvement campaigns, and direct assistance to gang members in seeking employment, vocational training, health care, and other services. Despite the best of intentions, however, such programs have not demonstrated evidence of reducing gang activity. On the contrary, some critics have reported that such programs tend to increase gang cohesiveness.

In 1991 the Phoenix Police Department introduced the school-based Gang Resistance Education and Training (GREAT) program, modeled on the Drug Abuse Resistance Education (DARE) program and subsequently supported by the U.S. Bureau of Alcohol, Tobacco, and Firearms. The GREAT curriculum consists of nine weekly lessons taught to middle school students by law enforcement officers. The GREAT curriculum is used in schools in all fifty states, but has not been extensively evaluated. Two studies suggest that the program has modest short-term effects in improving student attitudes and reducing self-reported delinquency, but long-term, rigorously controlled outcome studies are needed.

Some demonstrable success in the war against gangs has come through law enforcement efforts leading to the long-term incarceration of gang leaders. Gang intelligence, intensive investigation, and well-planned prosecution have disrupted, and in some cases eliminated, gangs. However, high-profile, intensive policing efforts to suppress gang activity by saturating a neighborhood with law enforcement officers and generating numerous arrests on minor charges have not been successful.

See also: JUVENILE JUSTICE SYSTEM.

BIBLIOGRAPHY

BATTIN-PEARSON, SARA R.; THORNBERRY, TERENCE P.; HAWKINS, DAVID, J.; and KROHN, MARVIN D. 1998. "Gang Membership, Delinquent Peers, and Delinquent Behavior." *Juvenile Justice and Delinquency Prevention Bulletin* October 1998. Washington DC: Office of Juvenile Justice and Delinquency Prevention.

CHANDLER, KATHRYN A.; CHAPMAN, CHRISTOPHER D.; RAND, MICHAEL R.; and TAYLOR, BRUCE M. 1998. *Students' Reports of School Crime: 1989 and 1995.* Washington, DC: National Center for Education Statistics.

ESBENSEN, FINN-AAGE. 2000. "Preventing Adolescent Gang Involvement." *Office of Juvenile Justice and Delinquency Prevention Bulletin* September 2000. Washington DC: Office of Juvenile Justice and Delinquency Prevention.

ESBENSEN, FINN-AAGE, and OSGOOD, D. WAYNE. 1997. *National Evaluation of GREAT.* Washington DC: National Institute of Justice.

HOWELL, JAMES C. 1998. "Youth Gangs: An Overview." *Office of Juvenile Justice and Delinquency Prevention Bulletin* August, 1998. Washington DC: Office of Juvenile Justice and Delinquency Prevention.

HOWELL, JAMES C., and LYNCH, JAMES P. 2000. "Youth Gangs in Schools." *Office of Juvenile Justice and Delinquency Prevention Bulletin* August 2000. Washington DC: Office of Juvenile Justice and Delinquency Prevention.

HUFF, C. RONALD, ed. 1996. *Gangs in America,* 2nd edition. Thousand Oaks, CA: Sage.

MILLER, WALTER B. 2001. *The Growth of Youth Gang Problems in the United States: 1970–1998.* Washington DC: Office of Juvenile Justice and Delinquency Prevention.

MOORE, JOAN, and HAGEDORN, JOHN. 2001. "Female Gangs: A Focus on Research." *Office of Juvenile Justice and Delinquency Prevention Bulletin* March 2001. Washington DC: Office of Juvenile Justice and Delinquency Prevention.

NATIONAL YOUTH GANG CENTER. 2000. *1998 Youth Gang Survey.* Washington DC: Office of Juvenile Justice and Delinquency Prevention.

SPERGEL, IRVING A. 1995. *The Youth Gang Problem: A Community Approach.* New York: Oxford University Press.

TAYLOR, CARL S. 1989. *Dangerous Society.* East Lansing: Michigan State University Press.

THORNBERRY, TERENCE P. 1998. "Membership in Youth Gangs and Involvement in Serious and Violent Offending." In *Serious and Violent Juvenile Offenders: Risk Factors and Successful Interventions,* ed. Rolf Loeber and David P. Farrington. Thousand Oaks, CA: Sage.

THRASHER, FREDERIC M. 1929. *The Gang: A Study of 1,313 Gangs in Chicago.* Chicago: University of Chicago Press.

DEWEY G. CORNELL
DANIEL C. MURRIE

PARENTS' ROLE

The pivotal role that parents play in a child's development is undisputed. Researchers have shown that differences in parenting practices can have profound and lasting effects on all aspects of development—cognitive, social, physical, and emotional. Differences in parenting styles translate to differences in a myriad of outcomes, such as academic achievement, self-esteem, deviant behavior, autonomy, emotional maturity, and leadership ability, to name just a few. It would be safe to say that while poor parenting practices can lead to adolescents who are experiencing multiple problems, good parenting practices can lead to well-adjusted and successful adolescents. But what are the mechanisms through which parents can positively impact adolescent development? And what is the degree to which parents can remain influential in the face of the increasing influence of peers in adolescence?

Different Types of Parenting Styles

Due to the well-documented importance of parenting practices on children's development, much research has been conducted in the area. In 1978 Diana Baumrind introduced one of the most influential theories of parenting styles. Baumrind suggested that parenting styles can be classified under four general patterns that differ along two dimensions: parental *responsiveness* and parental *demandingness.* Parental responsiveness entails the ability to respond to a child's evolving needs in a warm and flexible manner. Parental demandingness entails the ability to set rules and standards that a child has to respect and follow. Parents who are both demanding and responsive are characterized as *authoritative.* Parents who are demanding and directive but not responsive are characterized as *authoritarian.* Parents who are responsive but not demanding are characterized as *permissive.* Finally, parents who are neither responsive nor demanding are characterized as *rejecting-neglecting.*

The relationship between parenting styles and developmental outcomes has been well documented by Baumrind and many other researchers. Overall, adolescents whose parents are authoritative have the most positive outcomes—namely, higher levels of autonomy, confidence, maturity, social skills, and academic achievement. They are also more able to successfully adapt to life's challenges. Children of authoritarian parents tend to become more timid, less socially competent, and more dependent as they grow up. However, under certain circumstances, such as those of African-American families living in poor, high-crime areas, the authoritarian parenting

style seems to be most beneficial. Children of permissive parents tend to become adolescents that are lacking in maturity, self-discipline, leadership skills, and in the ability to stand up to bad peer influences. Finally, children of rejecting-neglecting parents seem to suffer the most serious problems—namely, poor academic skills, more deviant behavior (including drug and alcohol abuse), and an inability to control impulsive behavior.

Differences in parenting styles translate to different family environments with different family dynamics. Families in which there is an ongoing dialogue, good conflict-resolution practices, mutual respect, and flexibility are families in which adolescents seem to have more positive outcomes. Beyond parenting styles, the modeling of parental behavior inside and outside the family and the type of relationship between the parents is another factor that can influence adolescent development.

Peer Influence and Parents

During adolescence, peers become increasingly important—adolescents spend more time with their peers then with any other group. Given the important role that peer culture plays in adolescents' lives (primarily in the form of groups and cliques), the degree to which parents can remain influential during this period is, and has been, an issue of scientific inquiry and debate.

Patricia Noller suggests that adolescents who are able to talk to their parents about issues that are important to them and who get emotional support from their parents are less likely to rely on peers for advice on important issues. They are less likely to succumb to peer pressure as it relates to using alcohol and drugs as means of coping with the pressure of adolescence. This leads to the conclusion that adolescents who already have, and can maintain, an open, positive, honest, flexible, and emotionally supportive relationship with their parents are more likely to take their parents' advice under serious consideration, and to better withstand pressure to participate in undesirable behaviors. On the other hand, adolescents that already have problematic relationships with their parents—characterized by lack of communication—are likely to become more dependent on their peers for advice and for emotional support.

Bradford Brown and colleagues suggest that rather than assuming that parental influence will be reduced during adolescence due to the increasing influence of peer groups and cliques, the specific environmental conditions that might facilitate and/or hamper parental influence should be examined. They report that specific parenting practices are significantly related to specific adolescent behaviors, and that they are also associated with specific patterns of group or clique membership. However, this relationship is mediated (in most cases) by adolescent behavior. Brown and colleagues suggest that it is unlikely that peer groups and cliques are going to counteract parental norms. Adolescents tend to select peer groups that have goals, behavioral patterns, and value norms that are similar to their own (and which parental behavior has helped shape). Parents directly influence adolescents' behaviors and value systems, and thus are able to exercise a significant but indirect effect on peer group and clique influence and membership.

The selection of an appropriate environment (schools and neighborhood) is another way that parents can exert an indirect influence on adolescents' peer affiliations. The composition of cliques and groups, as well as their relative influence, can vary greatly from school to school and from neighborhood to neighborhood. In some high schools, students who aspire academic excellence are ridiculed and isolated from the predominant peer culture in the school, which may value truancy, alcohol and drug use, early sexual activity, and a lack of academic engagement. Conversely, there are schools in which academic excellence is valued by the peer culture.

Parents should try to place their children in schools in which positive peer groups and cliques are influential in the community culture of the school, while avoiding schools in which negative peer groups that advocate deviant behaviors are predominant. The degree to which an adolescent will continue to be influenced by parents is directly related to the type of group or clique he or she belongs to. If the adolescent is a member of groups in which parents and their advice are considered valuable resources, then a parent will continue to be very influential during adolescence. If, however, the adolescent becomes a member of a group that promotes deviant behavior, then the ability of the parents to exert influence on the adolescent's behavior is greatly diminished.

See also: PARENTAL INVOLVEMENT IN EDUCATION; PARENTING.

BIBLIOGRAPHY

BAUMRIND, DIANA. 1978. "Parental Disciplinary Patterns and Social Competence in Children." *Youth and Society* 9:239–276.

BAUMRIND, DIANA. 1991. "The Influence of Parenting Style on Adolescent Competence and Substance Abuse." *Journal of Early Adolescence* 11:56–95.

BROWN, B. BRADFORD, and HUANG, BIH-HUI. 1995. "Examining Parenting Practices in Different Peer Contexts: Implications for Adolescent Trajectories." In *Pathways through Adolescence,* ed. Lisa J. Crockett and Ann C. Crouter. Mahwah, NJ: Erlbaum.

BROWN, B. BRADFORD; MOUNTS, NINA; LAMBORN, SUSIE D.; and STEINBERG, LAWRENCE D. 1993. "Parenting Practices and Peer Group Affiliation in Adolescence." *Child Development* 64:467–482.

NOLLER, PATRICIA. 1994. "Relationships with Parents in Adolescence: Process and Outcome." In *Personal Relationships during Adolescence,* ed. Raymond Montemayor, Gerald R. Adams, and Thomas P. Gullotta. Thousand Oaks, CA: Sage.

STEINBERG, LAWRENCE D. 1996. *Beyond the Classroom: Why School Reform has Failed and What Parents Need to Do.* New York: Touchstone.

HELEN VRAILAS BATEMAN

ADOPTION

See: FAMILY COMPOSITION AND CIRCUMSTANCE, *subentry on* ADOPTION.

ADULT EDUCATION

See: CORPORATE COLLEGES; CONTINUING PROFESSIONAL EDUCATION; DISTANCE LEARNING IN HIGHER EDUCATION; LIFE EXPERIENCE FOR COLLEGE CREDIT; LIFELONG LEARNING; NONTRADITIONAL STUDENTS IN HIGHER EDUCATION.

ADVANCED PLACEMENT COURSES/EXAMS

Development of the Advanced Placement program came about because of a perceived need to provide motivated high school students with an opportunity to earn college credit. In 1954 the Educational Testing Service (ETS) was given a contract to develop exams in a group of experimental high schools and to compare the results of the high school students' scores on the exams to those of freshmen in twelve colleges. The resulting favorable comparison gave impetus to an expansion of efforts to further develop additional courses and examinations across the disciplines; this evolved into a program of the College Entrance Examination Board (College Board), with technical aspects of test administration and scoring handled by ETS. Advanced Placement courses are designed to mirror the introductory level college courses offered in the major discipline areas.

The most frequently cited reason for enrollment in AP courses has been the greater rigor and challenge of AP courses compared to traditional high school offerings. Successful candidates also gain the advantage of being allowed to take more advanced courses at the beginning of their college careers and to select more elective courses.

AP courses and examinations, which were initially developed for the highest-achieving 5 percent of high school seniors, were widely available to juniors and seniors (10 to 20 percent of such students in many schools) by the beginning of the twenty-first century, and AP courses in calculus and physics were being taken via computer by students as young as those in eighth grade. In 2000, 768,586 students from 13,253 schools (out of approximately 22,000 high schools nationwide) took 1,272,317 exams. The students had the option of submitting their scores to 3,070 colleges.

Students are not required by the College Board to take an exam if enrolled in an Advanced Placement course. About one-third of students enrolled in the courses take the exam. But individual schools may, and sometimes do, require enrolled students to take the exam. Students may also elect to take an AP exam without enrolling in the course in high school. There is no predetermined number or pattern of courses or exams students must take during their high school careers. Not all high schools offer Advanced Placement courses and some offer only one or two courses. Table 1 lists the Advanced Placement courses and examinations available in 2002.

In addition to creating the examinations used to assess students' mastery of college-level subject matter, the College Board provides schools with course

TABLE 1

Advanced Placement courses and examinations

Art	Art History Studio Art: General Studio Art: Drawing
Computer science	A level (half-year course) B level
Economics	Microeconomics (half-year course) Macroeconomics (half-year course)
English	English Language and Composition English Language and Literature International English Language
French	Language Literature
German	Language
Government and politics	U.S. Government (half-year course) Comparative Government (half-year course)
History	European History U.S. History World History
Latin	Literature Vergil
Mathematics	Calculus AB Calculus BC Statistics (half-year course)
Music	Theory
Psychology	Psychology (half-year course)
Science	Biology Chemistry Environmental Science (half-year course) Physics B Physics C, Electricity and Magnetism (half-year course) Physics C, Mechanical (half-year course)
Spanish	Language Literature

SOURCE: Courtesy of author.

syllabi, including topical outlines and recommended texts. Examinations are developed in consultation with college faculty and high school teachers who are experienced in Advanced Placement teaching.

Grading of AP examinations is done independently by trained examiners. Exam results are assigned a rating with the College Board between 1 and 5. A 3 means the student is qualified to earn college credit and/or advanced placement in "virtually all four year colleges and universities, including the most selective." A 5 is deemed "extremely well qualified." The American Council on Education has also recommended, as a general rule, that colleges and universities award credit for grades of 3 or better on AP examinations. The College Board, however, does not assign college credits. Credits are assigned according to the policy of the college or university to which the student applies for credit. At a particular college, the required score for credit and/or advanced standing is determined by the faculty of that college and may vary from examination to examination. William Lichten reported in 2000 that even though two-thirds of test takers earn a score of 3 or higher, only 49 percent receive college credit based on Advanced Placement exam scores. Lichten further noted that while a majority of colleges still award credit for scores of 3 or higher, many highly selective colleges and universities require at least a 4, and there is an increased tendency for institutions of higher education to require higher scores in some areas (e.g., English literature, foreign language) than in others. Some colleges do not accept credit for advanced placement courses or success on the exam at all, rejecting the assertion that the AP and college courses are equivalent. Information on the level of success required for earning college credit at a specific college or university based on the results of a particular AP exam is provided by the College Board at its website.

There is no fee for enrolling in Advanced Placement courses, but students must pay a fee to take the examination. Twenty-six states use state funds to support AP programs either through subsidizing exam fees, subsidizing the costs of teacher training, providing funds for materials and supplies for AP courses, offering incentives for providing AP courses or hosting training sessions, encouraging universities to accept AP credit, and encouraging the offering of professional development opportunities. Eighteen of these states provide direct assistance to students by paying for exam fees. The federal government has also provided funds to pay either partial or full examination fees for minority and low-income students, and in some cases individual school systems have taken the initiative to pay for the examination.

According to the College Board, college admissions personnel view AP courses as one indicator of future success at the college level. Participation in AP courses, therefore, is considered an advantage to a student who wishes to attend a highly selective college. The importance of AP programs in the college admissions process has even been the basis underlying a lawsuit filed in 1999 in California claiming bias because fewer Advanced Placement programs are offered in schools with higher percentages of minority and low-income students.

See also: CURRICULUM, SCHOOL, *subentry on* OVERVIEW; SECONDARY EDUCATION, *subentry on* CURRENT TRENDS; STANDARDS FOR STUDENT LEARNING.

BIBLIOGRAPHY

COLLEGE ENTRANCE EXAMINATION BOARD AND EDUCATIONAL TESTING SERVICE. 1999. *Facts about the Advanced Placement Program, 2000.* New York: College Entrance Examination Board and Educational Testing Service.

RAVALGLIA, RAYMOND; DEBARROS, J. ACACIO; and SUPPES, PATRICK. 1995. "Computer-Based Instruction Brings Advanced-Placement Physics to Gifted Students." *Computers in Physics* 9:380–386.

ROTHCHILD, ERIC. 1995. "Aspiration, Performance, Reward: The Advanced Placement Program at Forty." *College Board Review* 176–177:24–32.

SINDELAR, NANCY W. 1988. "English Curriculum and Higher Education." *Journal of College Admissions* (summer):2–5.

INTERNET RESOURCES

COLLEGE BOARD. 2001. "AP Central." <http://apcentral.collegeboard.com>.

LICHTEN, WILLIAM. 2000. "Whither Advanced Placement?" *Education Policy Analysis Archives* 8(29). <www.epaa.asu.edu/epaa/v8n29.html>.

VIADERO, DEBORAH. 2001. "AP Program Assumes Larger Role." *Education Week* <www.edweek.org/ew/ewstory.cfm?/slug=32ap.h20>.

CAROLYN M. CALLAHAN

AFFECT AND EMOTIONAL DEVELOPMENT

Affect is a general term that encompasses mood and emotions. *Mood* is a feeling state that extends over a protracted period of time and is not about any particular object. An *emotion* is generally considered a transient feeling state that is usually about one particular object. Beyond these generalities, the definition of emotions and their development depends on whether one takes a functional perspective, a process viewpoint, or considers emotions to be discrete biophysiological states.

Functionalist Perspectives

From a functionalist perspective, an emotion entails a readiness to adjust one's relationship to the environment with respect to something that is of importance to the person. The adjustment can be one of maintenance or change. Hence, this approach emphasizes the idea that emotions function to focus action that achieves personal goals. In doing so, emotions exert bidirectional influences on cognitive processing, social interaction, and physical experience. In addition, emotions play an important role in the emergence of self-awareness, because the interest and excitement that infants display when interacting with novel objects helps them develop a sense of self-efficacy. Within the functionalist approach, development entails the progressive ability to regulate emotions according to the demands of the physical and social worlds. In addition, children are socialized into knowing the appropriateness of different emotional displays in the culture in which they grow up. Concurrent to this, development also increases the range of responses that a person is able to mount to environmental changes, resulting in the emergence of families of emotions with differing nuances, which are centered on the commonly recognized emotions, such as joy, sadness, shame, and pride. Each family of emotions provides a range of behavior-regulatory, social-regulatory, and internal-regulatory functions for the person as well as action tendencies that match situational demands. Although functional theorists include many components in the generation of particular families of emotions—for example, concerns, cognitive appraisals, bodily reactions, and action tendencies—they emphasize that these components are organized around functional significances for the person. These theorists would also be careful to differentiate between different nuances of a particular emotion, such as discriminating between the fear of being robbed and the fear of dying from cancer, although these nuances may belong to the same emotion family. Hence, according to functional theorists, emotional processes are evoked with reference to motives and concerns of the developing person and as such undergo quantitative and qualitative change in development.

Emotions as Discrete States

From this perspective, emotions are viewed as patterns of configurations in the brain, accompanied by particular neurochemical processes that result in subjectively experienced feeling states, which are accompanied by automatic changes in bodily function as well as changes in behavior. These nonreducible affective states are taken to be distinguishable from each other, giving rise to the distinct basic emotions of happiness, interest, surprise, fear, anger, sadness, and disgust. Evidence for such a position is accumulating more from a cognitive neuroscience direction, which emphasizes the central circuitry of different emotional states, than from a search for unique configurations of autonomic nervous system arousal in peripheral bodily processes. Thus, the amygdala has been found to be important in the experience of fear and the left prefrontal cortex is associated with positive emotions while the right prefrontal cortex seems to be implicated in negative affect and withdrawal. In accordance with the assumption that the basic emotions are innate to all humans, discrete-state theorists posit a maturational timetable for their emergence, which can be observed through the initial occurrences of their expression in infants: Happiness, interest, sadness, and anger emerge from the first weeks to the fourth month of life, while fear begins to emerge only between the seventh and ninth months. In addition, the discrete-state view assumes the evolutionarily adaptive functionality of the basic emotions, that is, their provision of adaptive value for the organism. For example, happiness would motivate repeated encounters with a particular situation, interest would motivate exploratory behavior, and fear would motivate avoidant responses. Because they are deemed nonreducible states, these basic emotions do not undergo transformation in development. Development mainly entails the formation of links between emotion and cognition so that affective–cognitive structures are fashioned according to learning in new situations. In this way, new emotional experiences that are dependent on cognition can emerge, for example shame and pride, although these are not defined as new emotions but rather new couplings between thought and emotion. In addition, cognitive development will also give rise to new abilities to understand and self-regulate the basic emotions.

Process Viewpoints

Although neither disclaiming the functional utility of emotions nor their grounding in feeling states, process views of the emotions and emotional development focus on how the different components that make up an emotional experience interact in order for the subjective sense of the emotion to emerge. *Process viewpoints* are also known as systems perspectives, and their defining feature is that they do not privilege any one component of the emotional process, instead focusing on how emotions emerge from the self-organizing tendencies of interacting components. These components include felt experiences, cognitive appraisals, motivations, functions, and control elements. The number of ways in which these interacting components can coalesce to give rise to an emotional experience is assumed to be infinitely large. On the other hand, normal developmental trajectories result in a finite number of stable emotional patterns that are called *attractors*. It is these attractors that are commonly recognized and labeled with the terms that have become familiar, such as happiness, anger, surprise, and disgust. However, the infinite possibilities of combinations allow for infinitely different nuances of particular emotions to emerge as well as leaving open the possibility that new emotions may arise. Development in this type of paradigm allows for an open system of transformations, which can include both qualitative and quantitative change. From a dynamic systems perspective, cognitive and emotional systems continuously interact throughout development, giving rise to emotional interpretations that are similar to the affective–cognitive structures proposed by the discrete-state theorists. These emotional interpretations are situation specific, complex, and provide the bases of the self and personality. Examples include anxiety, pride, and humiliation. In common with functionalist and discrete-state theorists, systems theorists maintain that emotions serve adaptive functions for the person, especially in social contexts.

Emotional Milestones

No matter to which paradigm one subscribes, there have been research findings that document emotional milestones in expressiveness and understanding that are generally agreed on, although individual differences exist. Right from birth until about six months of age, infants display signs that indicate the presence of all the basic emotions. In this period the social smile and laughter appear, the infant appears happier when interacting with familiar people, and emotional expressions are related to social events. In terms of understanding, the infant seems to come into the world already able to be receptive to the subjective states in other people, being able to match the feeling tone of caregivers in face-to-face communication. Between seven and twelve months, negative emotions such as fear and anger become more prominent in parallel to an increasing fear of strangers. Concurrently, the infant begins to use the primary caregiver as a secure base for exploration while becoming more able to self-regulate his or her emotions. In this period social referencing develops, that is, the infant checks the emotional display/reaction of the caregiver to obtain guidance on how to act. In the second year of life, the self-conscious emotions (including pride, shame, guilt, envy, and embarrassment) emerge. In tandem, empathy with others' emotions begins to be displayed while an understanding of the difference between one's own and another person's emotions appears, a sort of emotional decentration. As cognitive development accelerates between the ages of three and six, the child also develops increasing linkages between cognition and emotion, which give rise to better emotional self-regulation, to the extent that a positive emotional display can be achieved without a concomitant positive feeling state. The increasing affective–cognitive links also foster a better understanding and interpretation of the emotional displays of others. After age six until about age eleven, emotional development involves the integration of the self-conscious emotions with a developing moral code, emotional self-regulation becomes more internalized and situation specific, and the ability to conform to the rules of emotional display improves. Emotional understanding also expands to take in multiple sources of information when interpreting the emotions of others and the realization that emotional displays may be deceptive. Naturally, further development is a lifetime affair.

Emotions and Learning

There is recent evidence to show that emotional understanding in children relates positively to adaptive social behavior and negatively to measures of internalizing behavior that may index feelings of anxiety, depression, and loneliness. Furthermore, emotion knowledge has also been found to mediate the effect of verbal ability on academic competence. The ability to detect and react to emotion cues seems to be important to the maintenance of rapport between teachers and peers in school. This would encourage closer and more effective educational interchanges with teachers as well as guard against the morale decrements that accompany poor relations with peers.

See also: AGGRESSIVE BEHAVIOR; MORAL DEVELOPMENT; INTELLIGENCE, *subentry on* EMOTIONAL INTELLIGENCE; STRESS AND DEPRESSION.

BIBLIOGRAPHY

DAMON, WILLIAM, and EISENBERG, NANCY, eds. 1998. *Handbook of Child Psychology, Vol. 3: Social, Emotional, and Personality Development,* 5th edition. New York: Wiley.

DAVIDSON, RICHARD, J.; JACKSON, DAREN, C.; and KALIN, NED H. 2000. "Emotion, Plasticity, Context, and Regulation: Perspectives from Affective Neuroscience." *Psychological Bulletin* 126:890–909.

EKMAN, PAUL, and DAVIDSON, RICHARD J., eds. 1994. *The Nature of Emotion: Fundamental Questions.* New York: Oxford University Press.

IZARD, CARROLL; FINE, SARAH; SCHULTZ, DAVID; MOSTOW, ALLISON; ACKERMAN, BRIAN; and YOUNGSTROM, ERIC. 2001. "Emotion Knowledge as a Predictor of Social Behavior and Academic Competence in Children At Risk." *Psychological Science* 12:18–23.

LEWIS, MARC D. 1995. "Cognition-Emotion Feedback and the Self-Organization of Developmental Paths." *Human Development* 38:71–102.

MASCOLO, MICHAEL, F., and GRIFFIN, SHARON, eds. 1998. *What Develops in Emotional Development?* New York: Plenum.

SALOVEY, PETER, and SLUYTER, DAVID J., eds. 1997. *Emotional Development and Emotional Intelligence.* New York: Basic Books.

SHARMA, DINESH, and FISCHER, KURT W., eds. 1998. *Socioemotional Development Across Cultures.* San Francisco: Jossey-Bass.

TREVARTHEN, COLWYN, and AITKEN, KENNETH J. 2001. "Infant Intersubjectivity: Research, Theory, and Clinical Applications." *Journal of Child Psychology and Psychiatry* 42:3–48.

LUKE MOISSINAC

AFFIRMATIVE ACTION COMPLIANCE IN HIGHER EDUCATION

Affirmative action is a government policy that seeks to remedy long-standing discrimination directed at specific groups, including women and racial and ethnic minorities. The basic purpose of affirmative action policies and programs is to increase access to, and ensure the equitable distribution of, opportunities in higher education, employment, government contracts, housing, and other social-welfare areas. To this end, affirmative action provides regulations, procedures, and guidelines to assure that eligible and interested citizens receive equal consideration regardless of their race, ethnicity, gender, religion, or age. Affirmative action does not fully restrict all forms of discrimination or make them illegal. Rather, it attempts to redress historical inequities by providing traditionally underrepresented groups with more equal access to most public and private arenas. This access is regarded as "more equal" since it attempts to address years of inequities and inequalities within a short amount of time.

The civil rights innovations outlined in the U.S. Constitution were not available to all of the inhabitants of the new nation. Prior to 1865, most African Americans were slaves, and they were considered property and counted for census purposes as three-fifths of a person. For the most part, Native Americans received no consideration at all. Women, although counted as full persons in census data, had very few rights. In spite of a variety of legal and social changes, these groups continued to suffer blatant discrimination well into the second half of the twentieth century.

The Fourteenth Amendment to the Constitution provides the legal basis for affirmative action policies. Added to the Constitution in 1868, this amendment extends legal protection to all U.S. citizens. Specifically, the equal protection clause of the Fourteenth Amendment asserts that, "No state shall . . . deny to any person within its jurisdiction, the equal protection of laws." Although the language is clear, this legislation was infrequently enforced.

It was not until the Supreme Court ruled in the case of *Brown v. Board of Education* (1954) that the notion of equal protection received serious national consideration. Specifically citing the Fourteenth Amendment, the Court held that racial segregation in elementary and secondary education is unconstitutional because it promotes an unequal educational system. Following this ruling, President John F. Kennedy issued Executive Order 10925 in 1961, which asked federal contractors to adopt diversity programs in an effort to help end segregation. (This order provides the legal foundation for affirmative action programs.)

In the spirit of the equal protection clause, the Civil Rights Act of 1964 bans discrimination on the basis of race, color, religion, sex, or national origin. To ensure compliance, federal funds are denied to those institutions that violate this mandate. More specifically, Title VII of the Civil Rights Act of 1964 states that:

> It shall be an unlawful employment practice for an employer (1) to fail or refuse to hire or to discharge any individual, or otherwise to discriminate against any individual with respect to his compensation, terms, conditions, or privileges of employment, because of such individual's race, color, religion, sex, or national origin; or (2) to limit, segregate, or classify his employees or applicants for employment in any way which would deprive or tend to deprive any individual of employment opportunities or otherwise adversely affect his status as an employee, because of such individual's race, color, religion, sex, or national origin.

Compliance

To ensure compliance, the federal government established the Office of Federal Contract Compliance Programs (OFCCP) and the Equal Employment Opportunity Commission (EEOC). Established in 1965 under Executive Order 11246, the OFCCP reviews, monitors, and enforces an institution's affirmative action plan. The OFCCP posits that each employment agency is responsible for designing an "acceptable" affirmative action program, which "must include an analysis of areas within which the contractor is deficient in the utilization of minority groups . . . and further, goals and timetables to which the contractor's good faith efforts must be directed to correct the deficiencies, and thus to achieve prompt and full utilization of minorities . . . at all levels and in all segments of its work force where deficiencies exist" (41 C.F.R. Sec. 60-2.10).

Similar to the OFCCP, the EEOC also helps to enforce antidiscrimination laws and regulations. Created by Title VII of the Civil Rights Act of 1964, the EEOC also enforces other related legislation, including the Equal Pay Act of 1963, the Age Discrimination in Employment Act of 1967, and Title I of the Americans with Disabilities Act of 1990. The EEOC investigates discrimination charges filed by individuals. If an employer is in violation, the EEOC first attempts to bring about voluntary resolution. If this fails, the EEOC may choose to file suit against the employer in federal court. At the conclusion of such a case, the EEOC issues a "notice of the right to sue," which allows an individual to file an additional suit in federal court.

To comply with affirmative action regulations, most colleges and universities reformed their admissions and hiring practices. Throughout the 1970s, higher education institutions established affirmative action programs and antidiscrimination policies designed to increase the number of women and minority students and faculty members in all fields and disciplines. These activities included actively encouraging women and minorities to apply for faculty and administrative positions, aggressively recruiting students from traditionally underrepresented groups, and offering support programs to help at-risk students succeed. Even so, affirmative action programs did not resolve all of the discrimination problems affecting higher education. Instead, it became one of them. In fact, white women received the greatest benefit from these programs, and many people questioned the constitutionality of affirmative action.

Court Cases Affecting Affirmative Action

Since the late 1970s, several cases have challenged the constitutionality and legality of affirmative action mandates. The earliest and most influential of these cases was *Bakke v. Regents of the University of California* (1978). Alan Bakke, a white male who was twice denied admission to the University of California–Davis Medical School, charged the institution with practicing reverse discrimination because it reserved certain positions for disadvantaged students. In this case, the Supreme Court held that it is lawful to consider race or ethnicity as one factor in making admission decisions. The opinion also supported the goal of striving to create a diverse student body. At the same time, the Court also stated that the use of racial distinctions is highly suspect and requires meticulous judicial review. Regarding University of California–Davis Medical School's specific program, the Court rejected it as unlawful because it used a fixed quota, or set-asides, in order to attain diverse enrollment.

Rather than settle the constitutional debate surrounding affirmative action, the *Bakke* decision made it more muddled and confused. In this ruling, the Supreme Court seemed to support the goal of affirmative action programs, while simultaneously making most of them illegal. In *Wygant v. Jackson Board of Education* (1986), the Court further limited an institution's ability to act on affirmative action legislation by developing the *strict scrutiny* test. Seeming to clarify the *Bakke* decision, *Wygant* required that the use of racial classification both support a compelling interest of state and be narrowly tailored to satisfy that particular interest. The Court's ruling in this case also stated that historic social discrimination was not by itself a compelling reason for an affirmative action policy, and that a public employer should only enact such a policy if it is indeed needed.

In the cases of *Kirwan v. Podberesky* (1994) and *Hopwood v. State of Texas* (1994 and 1996), U.S. circuit courts applied the Supreme Court decisions in *Bakke* and Wygant. In *Kirwan,* the U. S. Court of Appeals for the Fourth District ruled that a scholarship program for African-American students at the University of Maryland did not serve a compelling state interest, and therefore failed the strict scrutiny test. In 1994, the U.S. District Court of Appeals for the Fifth Circuit held that the University of Texas School of Law's admission policy of accepting less qualified minority applicants was unlawful because it was a quota system. In 1996, this same court also held that the equal protection clause of the Fourteenth Amendment did not permit the University of Texas to establish admissions policies that gave preferential treatment to one race over another.

As a result of the 1996 *Hopwood* decision, many people have concluded that affirmative action programs are unconstitutional, and many states have begun to rethink their use of affirmative action programs. Most notably, in 1996, California voters approved a law banning the use of such programs in state and local agencies, including the state's public colleges and universities. Yet, because many states are not bound to follow the Fifth Circuit's 1996 decision, the national debate over affirmative action continues.

The confusion the Supreme Court created in the *Bakke* decision continues to make it difficult for lower courts to rule on issues related to affirmative action programs. In 2000, the state of Michigan became a battle site for this debate. Highlighting the two-faced approach used by the Supreme Court in its *Bakke* ruling, the cases of *Gratz v. Bollinger* (2000) and *Grutter v. Bollinger* (2001) first upheld, and then

rejected the use of affirmative action programs in college admissions. In the *Gratz* case, the U.S. District Court for the Eastern District of Michigan, South Division ruled that the University of Michigan College of Literature, Science and Arts' consideration of race as a factor in its admission of undergraduate students was both a lawful and "narrowly tailored" way of achieving diversity in its student population. However, in the Grutter case, the same court ruled that the University of Michigan Law School's use of race in its admission decisions violated both the Fourteenth Amendment and Title VI of the Civil Rights Act of 1964, and was therefore unconstitutional.

The Supreme Court has yet to hear either case involving the University of Michigan. And as of March 2002, the Court has thus far refused to hear a case challenging the validity of California Proposition 209. Until these cases are heard the future of affirmative action programs and policies remains unknown.

Timeline of Affirmative Action Legislative and Judicial Developments

1787 U.S. Constitution is drafted, including Article I, Section 2, which counts each African-American slave as three-fifths of a person.

1862 The Morrill Act establishes sixteen higher education institutions specifically dedicated to the education of African Americans.

1863 The Emancipation Proclamation is issued, ending slavery in the Confederate States.

1865 The Thirteenth Amendment is added to the U.S. Constitution, abolishing slavery throughout the nation.

1868 The Fourteenth Amendment is added to the U.S. Constitution, guaranteeing equal protection under the law.

1870 The Fifteenth Amendment is added to the U.S. Constitution, extending the right to vote to all male citizens.

1896 In Plessy v. Ferguson, the U.S. Supreme Court establishes the doctrine of "separate but equal," helping to promote segregationist laws and policies.

1948 President Harry S. Truman issues Executive Order 9981, which ends segregation in the U.S. Armed Forces.

1948 In *Sipuel v. Board of Regents*, the Supreme Court orders the University of Oklahoma to admit an African-American law student because the state does not provide a separate law school for African Americans.

1950 In *McLaurin v. Oklahoma State Regents*, the Supreme Court rules that it is unconstitutional for an African-American student to be physically segregated from other students because of his race.

1950 In *Sweatt v. Painter*, the Supreme Court rules that the state of Texas's newly established law school for African Americans does not provide separate but equal facilities. As such, it cannot deny the petitioner the right to attend the University of Texas Law School.

1954 The Supreme Court reverses its doctrine of separate but equal established in *Plessy v. Ferguson*. In *Brown v. Board of Education*, the Court holds that state laws mandating or permitting segregation are unconstitutional under the equal protection clause of the Fourteenth Amendment.

1964 The Civil Rights Act of 1964 is passed. This legislation includes Title VI, which prohibits public and private institutions receiving public funds from discriminating on the basis of "race, color, religion, sex, or national origin," and Title VII, which provides for the establishment of the Equal Employment Opportunity Commission (EEOC).

1965 President Lyndon B. Johnson issues Executive Order 11246, requiring organizations that receive federal contracts of $50,000 or more and have fifty or more employees to develop affirmative action plans. The Office of Federal Contract Compliance Programs (OFCCP) is developed to monitor compliance with these regulations.

1967 President Lyndon B. Johnson issues Executive Order 11375, which amends and extends Executive Order 11246 to include women.

1972 Title IX of the Education Amendments of 1972 is passed, prohibiting gender-based discrimination in the programs and employment practices of federally funded organizations.

1978 In *Bakke v. Regents of the University of California*, the U.S. Supreme Court rules that University of California–Davis Medical School's special admissions program is unlawful.

1981 In *DeRonde v. Regents of the University*, the Supreme Court of California rules that the affirmative action plan in place at the University of California–Davis Law School violates of the equal protection clause of the Fourteenth Amendment.

1986 In *Wygant v. Jackson Board of Education*, the U.S. Supreme Court holds that the school board's plan to consider race in laying off teachers violates the equal protection clause of the Fourteenth Amendment. In this case the Court also established the *strict scrutiny* test.

1992 The U.S. Department of Education and the University of California, Berkeley establish an agreement ending the admissions practice of placing applicants into separate pools on the basis of race.

1994 In *Kirwan v. Podberesky*, the U.S. Circuit Court of Appeals for the Fourth Circuit holds that the University of Maryland's Banneker Scholarship Program unlawfully violates the equal protection clause of the Fourteenth Amendment.

1994 In *Hopwood v. State of Texas*, the U.S. District Court for the Western District of Texas holds that the admissions policy of the University of Texas School of Law established an unlawful quota system.

1996 The U.S. Circuit Court of Appeals for the Fifth Circuit holds that the equal protection clause of the Fourteenth Amendment does not permit an institution to establish preferential, race-based admissions policies. The Fifth Circuit also rules that the University of Texas Law School may no longer consider race in its admissions decisions.

1996 California Proposition 209, also known as the California Civil Rights Initiative, is voted into law, eliminating the use of affirmative action programs throughout state and local agencies, including public colleges and universities.

2000 In *Gratz v. Bollinger,* the U.S. District Court for the Eastern District of Michigan, Southern Division rules that the University of Michigan College of Literature, Science and Arts' use of race in its admissions decisions is a lawful and "narrowly tailored" way of achieving diversity.

2001 In *Grutter v. Bollinger,* the U.S. District Court for the Eastern District of Michigan, Southern Division holds that the University of Michigan Law School's use of race in its admissions decisions is unconstitutional, stating that the university's policies violate both the equal protection clause of the Fourteenth Amendment and Title VI of the Civil Rights Act of 1964. The court also rules that diversity is neither a "compelling interest" of the state nor a remedy for past discrimination.

Since the *Bakke* decision, some public and private entities have either chosen or been forced to abandon affirmative action programs. Rather than resolve issues surrounding the validity of these programs, this decision has actually caused more controversy. The legal challenges that resulted from the Supreme Court's ambiguous decision in this case suggest that the Court will soon be expected to make a final determination regarding the constitutionality of these programs.

See also: FACULTY DIVERSITY; MULTICULTURALISM IN HIGHER EDUCATION; RACE, ETHNICITY, AND CULTURE, *subentries on* CULTURAL EXPECTATIONS AND STUDENT LEARNING, RACIAL AND ETHNIC MINORITY STUDENTS IN HIGHER EDUCATION.

BIBLIOGRAPHY

BOWEN, WILLIAM, and BOK, DEREK. 1998. *The Shape of the River: Long-Term Consequences of Considering Race in College and University Admissions.* Princeton, NJ: Princeton University Press.

CENTER FOR INDIVIDUAL RIGHTS. 1998. *Racial Preferences in Higher Education: A Handbook for College and University Trustees.* Washington, DC: Center for Individual Rights.

FEINBERG, WALTER. 1998. *On Higher Ground: Education and the Case for Affirmative Action.* New York: Teachers College Press.

FLEMING, JOHN E.; GILL, GERALD R.; and SWINTON, DAVID H. 1978. *The Case for Affirmative Action for Blacks in Higher Education.* Washington, DC: Howard University Press.

GARCIA, MILDRED. 1997. *Affirmative Action's Testament of Hope: Strategies for a New Era in Higher Education.* Albany: State University of New York.

POST, ROBERT, and ROGIN, MICHAEL, eds. 1998. *Race and Representation: Affirmative Action.* New York: Zone.

M. CHRISTOPHER BROWN II
SARAN DONAHOO

AFRICAN-AMERICAN STUDENTS

See: AFFIRMATIVE ACTION COMPLIANCE IN HIGHER EDUCATION; AFRICAN-AMERICAN STUDIES; HISTORICALLY BLACK COLLEGES AND UNIVERSITIES; INDIVIDUAL DIFFERENCES, *subentry on* ETHNICITY; LITERACY AND CULTURE; MISSISSIPPI FREEDOM SCHOOLS; MULTICULTURAL EDUCATION; MULTICULTURALISM IN HIGHER EDUCATION; RACE, ETHNICITY, AND CULTURE.

AFRICAN-AMERICAN STUDIES

African-American studies (also known as black studies) is an inter/multidisciplinary field that analyzes and treats the past and present culture, achievements, characteristics, and issues of people of African descent in North America, the diaspora, and Africa. The field challenges the sociohistorical and cultural content and definition of western ideology. African-American studies argues for a multicultural interpretation of the Western Hemisphere rather than a Eurocentric one. It has its earliest roots in history, sociology, literature, and the arts. The field's most important concepts, methods, and findings to date are situated within these disciplines.

More than one hundred and fifty years after the signing of the Emancipation Proclamation, African Americans still struggle for a space in academia for a legitimate voice to express their interpretations and perspectives of their historical and contemporary experiences in Africa, the diaspora, and North America. Those in African-American studies argue not only that their voices have been marginalized, but that the history of African Americans' experiences and contributions to the United States has historically and systematically been missing from the texts and the curricula. Thus, African-American studies functions as a supplementary academic component for the sole purpose of adding the African experience to traditional disciplines.

Implicit to African-American studies is the notion that the black diasporic experience has been ignored or has not been accurately portrayed in academia or popular culture. From the earliest period of the field to the present, this movement has had two main objective: first, to counteract the effects of white racism in the area of group elevation; and second, to generate a stronger sense of black identity and community as a way of multiplying the group's leverage in the liberation struggle.

The Foundations of African-American Studies

The Atlanta University Conferences held from 1898 to 1914, under the auspices of W. E. B. DuBois, marked the inauguration of the first scientific study of the conditions of black people that covered important aspects of life (e.g., health, homes, the question of organization, economic development, higher education, common schools, artisans, the church, crime, and suffrage). It was during this period that African-American studies was formally introduced to the university and black academics initiated research studies.

One of the important goals of the scholars of this period was to counteract the negative images and representations of blacks that were institutionalized within academia and society. This was in response to the major tenet of social science research at this time that argued blacks were genetically inferior to whites and that Africa was a "dark continent" that lacked civilization. The American Negro Academy, founded in 1896, set as one of its major goals to assist, by publications, the vindication of the race from vicious assaults in all areas of learning and truth. In 1899 DuBois published a sociological study, *The Philadelphia Negro*. This landmark study highlighted the conditions of blacks in Philadelphia in the Seventh Ward. The study investigated the black experience as reflected in business, public education, religion, voluntary associations, and public health.

In 1915 the founding of the Association for the Study of Negro Life and History (ASNLH) by Carter G. Woodson marked the beginning of a new era in African-American studies. The ASNLH was founded to promote historical research; publish books on black life and history; promote the study of blacks through clubs and schools; and bring harmony between the races by interpreting the one to the other. In 1916, Woodson founded the *Journal of Negro History* and served as its editor until his death. This was perhaps one of Woodson's greatest contributions to the area of African-American studies.

In 1926 Woodson and his colleagues launched Negro History Week. This event, which later evolved into a whole month, was not intended to be the only time of the year in which Negro history was to be celebrated and taught. Woodson and his colleagues viewed this as a time to highlight the ongoing study of black history that was to take place throughout the year.

It was during this time that historically black colleges and universities (HBCUs) began to respond to the scholarly activities in history and social science. It was becoming clear that black education should conform to the social conditions of black people. Black colleges began to add courses in black history to their curricula; this corresponded with the call by black college students for a culturally relevant curriculum, a theme that reoccurred later with greater political influence.

In 1919, prior to the influx of HBCUs offering black history courses as a part of their curriculum, Woodson issued the first report on African-American studies courses offered in Northern colleges. He reported the following courses:

1. Ohio State University, *Slavery Struggles in the United States*

2. Nebraska University, *The Negro Problem Under Slavery and Freedom*

3. Stanford University, *Immigration and the Race Problem*

4. University of Oklahoma, *Modern Race Problems*

5. University of Missouri, *The Negro in America*

6. University of Chicago, *The Negro in America*

7. University of Minnesota, *The American Negro*

8. Harvard University, *American Population Problems: Immigration and the Negro*

Furthermore, Woodson reported that a small number of HBCUs were offering courses in sociology and history pertaining to the Negro experience. Woodson stated that in spite of the lack of trained teachers,

Tuskeegee, Atlanta University, Fisk, Wilberforce, and Howard offered such courses, even at the risk of their becoming expressions of opinions without the necessary data to support them.

The period from approximately 1940 to the mid to late 1960s marked yet another era of African-American studies in history and the social sciences, characterized by an growing legitimacy and an increasing number of white scholars entering the field. Prior to this time, black scholars did the majority of the research conducted on African-American studies.

The Emergence of African-American Studies Departments

The student strike of 1968–1969, held at San Francisco State University (SFSU), forced the establishment of the Division of Ethnic Studies and departments of Black, Asian, Chicano, and Native Studies. The Black Student Union at SFSU drafted a political statement, "The Justification for African-American Studies," that would become the main document for developing African-American studies departments at more than sixty universities. The demands/objectives within this document included the opposition of the "liberal-fascist" ideology that was rampant on campus (as shown by college administrations who had attempted to pacify Black Student Union demands for systemic curriculum by offering one or two courses in black history and literature); the preparation of black students for direct participation in the struggles of the black community and to define themselves as responsible to and for the future successes of that community; the reinforcement of the position that black people in Africa and the diaspora have the right to democratic rights, self-determination, and liberation; and opposition to the dominant ideology of capitalism, world imperialism and white supremacy. During this period, Nathan Hare and Jimmy Garrett collaborated to put together the first African-American studies program in the country.

African-American studies departments were created in a confrontational environment on American universities with the rejection of traditional curricula content. The curriculum preferred by these departments was to be an ordered arrangement of courses that progressed from introductory to advanced levels. Darlene Clark Hine (1990) contends that a sound African-American studies curriculum must include courses in African-American history,

literature, and literary criticism. These courses would be complemented by other courses that spoke to the black experience in sociology, political science, psychology, and economics. Furthermore, if resources would permit, courses in art, music, language, and on other geographical areas of the African diaspora should be available.

Mainstream university support for African-American studies emerged in the late 1960s. This was done in conjunction with the protests of the civil rights movement, the Black Power movement, and the admission of a massive influx of black students into predominantly white institutions. The preconditions for the growth of African-American studies were demographic, social, and political. Between 1945 and 1965, more than three million blacks left the South and migrated to northeast, north central and western states. The black freedom movement, in both the civil rights phase (1955–1965) and Black Power component (1966–1975), fostered the racial desegregation and the empowerment of black people within previously all-white institutions. The racial composition of U.S. colleges changed dramatically. In 1950 approximately 75,000 blacks were enrolled in colleges and universities. In the 1960s three quarters of all black students attended HBCUs. By 1970, approximately 700,000 blacks were enrolled in college, three quarters of whom were in predominantly white institutions.

Organization and Objectives

One must be careful not to use African-American studies programs, departments, and centers interchangeably; they are not synonymous. According to Hine, African-American studies departments are best described as a separate, autonomous unit possessing exclusive rights and privileges to hire and terminate, grant tenure to their faculty, certify students, confer degrees, and administer a budget. Programs may offer majors and minors, but rarely do they confer degrees. Furthermore, faculty appointments in programs are usually joint, adjunct, or associate positions. Centers, on the other hand, focus more on the production and dissemination of scholarship and the professional development of teachers and scholars in the field than on undergraduate teaching. The difference in the structure and mission between centers, departments, and programs tend to complicate the attempt to assess and identify African-American studies accurately.

TABLE 1

Basic objectives of African-American studies

- To teach what is called the black experience in its historical and current unfolding.

- To assemble and create a body of knowledge that contributes to intellectual and political emancipation.

- To create a body of black intellectuals who are dedicated to community service and development rather than vulgar careerism.

- To advocate the cultivation, maintenance, and continuous expansion of a mutually beneficial relationship between the campus and the community.

- To establish African-American studies as a legitimate, respected, and permanent discipline.

SOURCE: Based on Karenga, Maulana. 1993. *Introduction to Black Studies*, 2nd edition. Los Angeles: University of Sankore Press. Pages 13–15.

However, Maulana Karenga outlines several objectives that African-American studies seeks to achieve. These basic goals are listed in Table 1.

These objectives have served as the backdrop for the discipline since its evolvement in the 1970s. However, the discipline has been under great scrutiny and has been challenged by many academics about its objectives and its relevance. Karenga argues that there are fundamental and undeniable grounds of relevance of African-American studies that clearly define the field's academic and social contributions and purpose. These are outlined in Table 2.

From 1968 to 1971, hundreds of African-American studies departments and programs were developed. Approximately 500 colleges and universities provided full scale African-American studies programs by 1971. Up to 1,300 institutions offered at least one course in African-American studies as of 1974. Some estimates place the number of African-American studies programs reaching its peak at 800 in the early 1970s and declining to about 375, due to the lack of resources and support, by the mid-1990s.

African-American studies has been evolving as a result of a radical social movement opposed to institutional racism in U.S. higher education. Considering the conventional roles of American education and its institutionalized racism, African Americans in many sectors view education as oppressive and/or liberating. In result, many African Americans began to consider African-American studies and black education as having a special assignment to challenge white mainstream knowledge for its deficiencies and corruption.

The development of African-American studies from the very outset was marked by blacks being compelled to evaluate the largely racist nature of established education in America. Due to European cultural hegemony, blacks and Africans in the diaspora have found the issue of perspective to be perennially problematic. The disastrous experience of chattel slavery, the basis for cultural hegemony, produced historical discontinuity and preempted normative culture building through a decentering process. Although the experience of oppression and exploitation required movement away from an African center, it was this experience that produced the conditions for the emergence of an African-centered consciousness. Thus, the problem of perspective emerged as the black intellectual tradition.

See also: ACADEMIC MAJOR, THE; MULTICULTURALISM IN HIGHER EDUCATION; RACE, ETHNICITY, AND CULTURE, *subentry on* CULTURAL EXPECTATIONS AND STUDENT LEARNING; WOMEN'S STUDIES.

BIBLIOGRAPHY

ADAMS, RUSSELL L. 1977. "African-American Studies Perspectives." *Journal of Negro Education* 46(2):99–117.

ALKALIMAT, ABDUL. 1990. *Paradigms in Black Studies.* Chicago: Twenty-first Century Books and Publications.

ALLEN, RICHARD L. 1974. "Politics of the Attack on African-American Studies." *Black Scholar* 6.

BANKS, JAMES A. 1993. "The Canon Debate, Knowledge Construction, and Multicultural Education." *Educational Researcher* (June–July).

CROUCHETT, L. 1971. "Early Black Studies Movements." *Journal of Black Studies* 2(2):189–200.

FRANKLIN, JOHN HOPE. 1986. "On the Evolution of Scholarship in Afro-American History." In *The State of Afro-American History: Past, Present, and Future,* ed. Darlene Clark Hine. Baton Rouge: Louisiana State University Press.

GARRETT, JAMES P. 1998. "Black/Africana/Pan-African Studies: From Radical to Reaction to Reform? —Its Role and Relevance in the Era of Global Capitalism in the New Millennium." *Journal of Pan-African Studies* 1(1).

HINE, DARLENE CLARK. 1990. "Black Studies: An Overview." In *Black Studies in the United States:*

Three Essays, ed. Darlene Clark Hine, Robert L. Harris, and Nellie McKay. New York: The Ford Foundation.

KARENGA, MAULANA. 1993. *Introduction to Black Studies,* 2nd edition. Los Angeles: University of Sankore Press.

KERSHAW, TERRY. 1989. "The Emerging Paradigm in African-American Studies." *Western Journal of African-American Studies* 13(1):45–51.

MARABLE, MANNING. 2000. *Dispatches from the Ebony Tower.* New York: Columbia University Press.

MCCLENDON, WILLIAM H. 1974. "African-American Studies: Education for Liberation." *The Black Scholar* 6:15–25.

MOSS, ALFRED A. 1981. *The American Negro Academy: Voice of the Talented Tenth.* Baton Rouge: Louisiana State University Press.

SEMMES, CLOVIS E. 1981. "Foundations of an Afrocentric Social Science: Implications for Curriculum Building, Theory, and Research in African-American Studies." *Journal of African-American Studies* 12:3–17.

SEMMES, CLOVIS E. 1992. *Cultural Hegemony and African American Development.* Westport, CT: Praeger.

TURNER, JAMES, and MCGANN, C. STEVEN. 1980. "African-American Studies as an Integral Tradition in African American Intellectual History." *Journal of Negro Education* 49:52–59.

WOODSON, CARTER G. 1919. "Negro Life and History in Our Schools." *Journal of Negro History* 4.

WOODYARD, JEFFREY L. 1991. "Evolution of a Discipline: Intellectual Antecedents of African American Studies." *Journal of African-American Studies* 22(2): 239–251.

RODERIC R. LAND
M. CHRISTOPHER BROWN II

AFTER-SCHOOL JOBS

See: EMPLOYMENT, *subentry on* AFTER SCHOOL.

AFTER-SCHOOL PROGRAMS

See: RECREATION PROGRAMS IN THE SCHOOLS; STUDENT ACTIVITIES.

TABLE 2

Relevance of African-American studies

African-American studies contributes to:

- Humanity's understanding of self.
- U.S. society's understanding of itself.
- The university's realization of its claim and challenge to teach the whole truth, or something as close to it as humanly possible.
- The rescue and reconstruction of black history and humanity.
- A new social science and humanities which will not only benefit blacks, but also the United States and the world.
- The development of a black intelligentsia and professional stratum whose knowledge, social competence, and commitment translates as a vital contribution to the liberation and development of the black community and thus as a contribution to society as a whole.
- The critique, resistance, and reversal of a progressive Europeanization of human consciousness and culture.

SOURCE: Based on Karenga, Maulana. 1993. *Introduction to Black Studies,* 2nd edition. Los Angeles: University of Sankore Press.

AGGRESSIVE BEHAVIOR

Educational and psychological research conducted from the 1960s to the 1990s has established that academic underachievement in the elementary school years is associated with the failure to make adequate educational progress in adolescence and young adulthood. This research also demonstrates that in itself early problems with underachievement may not be the main cause of later-occurring educational problems. Rather, severely disruptive social behavior in early childhood, particularly aggression, has been implicated as a primary cause of both early and later-occurring academic underachievement, the need for special education, and problems with truancy and school dropout. With aggressive and disruptive behaviors showing sharp increases during the last three decades of the twentieth century and prevalence rates of elementary schoolchildren suffering from these behavior disorders estimated at about 20 percent in the 1990s, the negative impact of aggressive/disruptive behavior on children's educational progress has become a serious concern for American society. Accordingly, the purpose here is to review recent findings on the nature and causes of these behavior problems and their relation to children's failure to make educational progress, and to examine promising information regarding preventive measures and treatments.

Aggression and Related Behavior Problems: The Disruptive Behavior Disorders

Narrowly defined, the aggressive child is one who purposely harms others either physically (e.g., fighting) or socially (e.g., spreading malicious rumors). Though this seems a straightforward definition, it does not adequately describe the great majority of aggressive children who are sometimes aggressive but who are more often oppositional (refusing to comply with adult requests), hyperactive, or inattentive. It is now known that this broader range of behavior problems provides a more reliable description of children who experience educational problems throughout their school careers. In fact very few children show severe forms of aggression, oppositionality, hyperactivity, or inattention alone. The great majority show some combination. An important outgrowth of this is that these children are diagnosed by psychologists, psychiatrists, and pediatricians as suffering from one or more of the disruptive behavior disorders, that is, attention deficit hyperactivity disorder (ADHD), oppositional defiant disorder (ODD), or, when older, conduct disorder (CD). Thus, these children are best described as suffering from some form of a disruptive behavior disorder (also called externalizing, acting out, or emotionally disturbed disorder) rather than focusing more narrowly on aggression alone.

Impact of Disruptive Behavior on Educational Progress

There are three types of studies used to assess whether or not a particular aspect of children's lives–in this case disruptive behavior–has a negative impact on children's educational progress: (1) concurrent, correlational studies (also called observational studies) that document the co-occurrence of both disruptive behavior and various forms of academic failure; (2) longitudinal, correlational studies that document academic problems at a later time (poor achievement, placement in special education, truancy, etc.) based on disruptive behaviors occurring at an earlier time; and (3) experiments (also called clinical trials) in which disruptive behavior is allowed to develop in a control group but is decreased in a treatment group (usually by replacement with positive behaviors), and it is later observed that the treatment group experiences educational success but the control group does not.

Experiments can be evaluated after a short or long follow-up period after treatment. Given that the study of children's social and academic development requires a long-term perspective, only long-term outcomes (follow-ups of at least three months) are considered here. There are two types of experiments: *prevention* trials begun in early childhood for children at risk of developing disruptive behavior but before symptoms have appeared and *intervention* trials begun after children have become symptomatic (i.e., have received a diagnosis of ADHD, ODD, CD, or are classified as severely behaviorally or emotionally disturbed). There are two types of preventions, those focusing exclusively on children and those focusing on children and their parents. There are also two types of interventions, those using medications such as methylphenidate (Ritalin) and those using educational and behavioral means to decrease disruptive behaviors. Because it most clearly establishes that the disruptive behavior targeted for prevention is an actual cause of academic problems and not just a co-occurring problem, by far the most important of these study types is the prevention experiment.

Concurrent and longitudinal correlational studies have clearly established a relation between early occurring disruptive behavior and both early and later-occurring school problems. However, child-focused intervention experiments using both behavioral/educational and medication treatments aimed at replacing disruptive behaviors with cooperative and attentive behaviors have not demonstrated positive educational gains for children. Nor have child-focused prevention experiments had good results. Realizing that the exclusion of parents in these experiments could explain their failure to demonstrate a causal role for disruptive behaviors in children's educational problems, family-based experiments have also been conducted. These studies, both intervention and prevention trials, have been successful, providing evidence that children's disruptive behavior does interfere with children's academic progress. They also provide a useful basis for planning large-scale preventive and interventive efforts.

Successful Prevention and Intervention

In a 1998 paper, Steven McFadyen-Ketchum and Kenneth Dodge reviewed eight long-term, family-based experimental studies (four preventions and four interventions), which successfully decreased children's disruptive behavior and produced improved educational outcomes. In all of these studies disruptive behavior was reduced, and cooperative attentive behavior was increased for periods ranging from one to fourteen years. Educational gains included higher grades, higher achievement scores, higher IQ scores, improved use of expressive language, decreased participation in special education, and decreased truancy and dropout rates. It is important to emphasize that these gains occurred only when parents as well as children were participants in the prevention and intervention programs. This means that in addition to replacing disruptive behavior with more cooperative/attentive behavior in children, it was also necessary to replace negative (e.g., nagging) and ineffective (e.g., failing to set clear limits) behaviors in parents with behaviors that were firm and friendly as well as with a parental willingness to consistently attend to children's cooperative efforts instead of taking them for granted.

Contribution to Theory

It has long been known that children's cognitive and intellectual deficits interfere with early academic achievement and long-term educational success. The studies discussed here clearly identify an additional source of dysfunction that also seriously interferes with educational progress: aggression and other forms of disruptive social behavior. These studies also clearly demonstrate that preventive/interventive efforts can be successfully applied to these behavior problems with positive educational results. In addition, they achieve a third, though less obvious, goal, that is the clarification of theory regarding the causes of children's disruptive behavior disorders.

As mentioned above, prevention and intervention experiments whose goal was to decrease disruptive behavior in children, but without also addressing the contribution of parents, consistently failed to show positive gains in treatment when compared with control groups of children. In contrast, those experiments that included parents consistently succeeded. Children in these successful treatment groups showed both behavioral and educational gains compared to control-group children. The clear implication is that in addition to whatever genetic or other environmental factors may be at work (e.g., lead poisoning), the parents' support of their children's positive behavioral efforts is necessary if children are to experience educational success. Because some of these experiments were preventions conducted before disruptive behavior problems had developed, these findings demonstrate that positive

parental behavior toward young children plays a causal role in children's behavioral and educational success.

These findings may appear to be in sharp contrast to the often-reported finding that genetics play a primary causal role in the kinds of behavioral and educational problems being discussed here, especially for children diagnosed with ADHD. What these findings demonstrate, and what has also been argued by geneticists who study childhood behavior problems, is that genes are not destiny. Children can be helped to perform well in school if it is recognized that their parents play a causal role in producing cooperative, attentive behavior, and are included in the educational process.

See also: AFFECT AND EMOTIONAL DEVELOPMENT; CLASSROOM MANAGEMENT; STRESS AND DEPRESSION.

BIBLIOGRAPHY

ACHENBACH, THOMAS, and HOWELL, CATHERINE T. 1993. "Are America's Children's Problems Getting Worse? A Thirteen-Year Comparison." *Journal of the American Academy of Child and Adolescent Psychiatry* 32:1145–1154.

AMERICAN PSYCHIATRIC ASSOCIATION. 2000. *Diagnostic and Statistical Manual of Mental Disorders (DSM-IV-TR),* 4th edition, text revision. Washington, DC: American Psychiatric Association.

CARLSON, CARYN L.; TAMM, LEANNE; and GAUB, MIRANDA. 1997. "Gender Differences in Children with ADHD, ODD, and Co-Occurring ADHD/ODD Identified in a School Population." *American Academy of Child and Adolescent Psychiatry* 36:1706–1714.

COIE, JOHN D., and DODGE, KENNETH A. 1998. "Aggression and Antisocial Behavior." In *Handbook of Child Psychology,* Vol. 3: *Social, Emotional and Personality Development,* ed. Nancy Eisenberg and William Damon. New York: Wiley.

HINSHAW, STEPHEN P. 1992. "Academic Underachievement, Attention Deficits, and Aggression: Comorbidity and Implications for Intervention." *Journal of Consulting and Clinical Psychology* 60:893–903.

HINSHAW, STEPHEN P. 1992. "Externalizing Behavior Problems and Academic Underachievement in Childhood and Adolescence: Causal Relationships and Underlying Mechanisms." *Psychological Bulletin* 111:127–155.

McFadyen-Ketchum, Steven A., and Dodge, Kenneth A. 1998. "Problems in Social Relationships." In *Treatment of Childhood Disorders,* 2nd edition, ed. Eric J. Mash and Russell A. Barkley. New York: Guilford.

Plomin, Robert; DeFries, John C.; McClearn, Gerald E.; and Rutter, Michael. 1997. *Behavioral Genetics,* 3rd edition. New York: Freeman.

Schachar, Russell, and Tannock, Rosemary. 1993. "Childhood Hyperactivity and Psychostimulants: A Review of Extended Studies." *Journal of Child and Adolescent Psychopharmacology* 3:81–97.

Yoshikawa, Hirokazu. 1994. "Prevention As Cumulative Protection: Effects of Early Family Support and Education on Chronic Delinquency and Its Risks." *Psychological Bulletin* 115:28–54.

Steven A. McFadyen-Ketchum

AGRICULTURAL EDUCATION

Agricultural education encompasses the study of applied sciences (e.g., biology, chemistry, physics), and business management principles. One of the major purposes of agricultural education is to apply the knowledge and skills learned in several different disciplines to agricultural education.

Agricultural education goes beyond knowledge and skills development in that students are able to develop an understanding of: 1) the significance of agriculture in a global society, and the U.S. society in particular, through the application of scientific and business principles and problem solving strategies; and 2) the interdependency and relationships between the agricultural industry and other significant business interwoven with the entire economic and social structure of the community, state, nation, and world. This program places an emphasis on food systems, environmental issues, and development of life skills.

The study of agricultural education focuses on the needs of individuals and groups and in developing individually satisfying and socially responsible knowledge, skills, and occupational values. Such a focus recognizes the value of, and relies heavily on, experiences as the context in which knowledge and skills are learned.

Agricultural education focuses on, but is not limited to, study in horticulture, forestry, conservation, natural resources, agricultural products and processing, production of food and fiber, aquaculture and other agricultural products, mechanics, sales and service, economics, marketing, and leadership development. Of relevance to a general audience (K–adult), agricultural education programs assist with providing lifelong learning opportunities in and about agriculture. Agricultural education provides opportunities to learn basic agricultural skills and knowledge, occupation training and retraining, and professional growth and development.

Formal programs in agricultural education are conducted at secondary schools, community colleges, and universities. As a vocational education program, agricultural education focuses on three major components: formal classroom instruction, career experience programs, and leadership development. These components are delivered through a competency-based curriculum in the context of agriculture.

Agricultural education is an old and well-established area of study in the United States. The Philadelphia Society for Promoting Agriculture, one of the first organizations in the United States designed to deal with agricultural education, was founded in 1780. R. F. Johnstone, writing in 1854, attributed many early American ideas about agricultural practices and agricultural education to the British:

> One of the first efforts made to arouse the minds of farmers of this country . . . was that of the . . . men who organized the New York State Agricultural Society in 1835. Those men had observed the good effects of the Royal Agricultural Society of England and resolved to awaken in their own State and country a spirit of inquiry similar to that which had been aroused by their English prototype. (16)

Early Congressional Efforts

In 1862 citizens and politicians throughout the United States joined forces to further advance the lives of farmers and rural people through the creation of the land-grant college system, enacted as part of the Morrill Act. According to Kandel, "the major thrust of Morrill's arguments in 1857 and 1862 was to deplore the decline of American agriculture due to a lack of scientific knowledge. [Morrill] said, 'that this bill would lift up the intellectual and moral standard of the young and industrial classes of our country'"(Moreland and Goldenstein, p. 117).

Morrill also claimed that it was wrong to call the proposed colleges *agricultural colleges,* since he was interested in a broad education. Clearly, philosophical debates were already taking place over just what the role of education should be. According to Moreland and Goldenstein, there was "great debate whether their chief purpose was to provide vocational education only or a liberal education combined with some vocational applications" (p. 120).

The original plan of the land-grant colleges was to have young people who grew up on farms attend the colleges. This did not work as well as expected, however, so other programs were developed. The first of these was the establishment of agricultural experiment stations by the Hatch Act of 1887. The second was the creation of the state extension services by the Smith-Lever Act of 1914. The third was the creation of vocational agriculture programs for high schools, which were eventually funded through the Smith-Hughes Act of 1917.

The National Society for the Promotion of Industrial Education, formed in 1906, was instrumental in stimulating the states to pass vocational training acts. The philosophy of this and similar societies was to create "incentive aid," which encouraged local school boards to establish vocational education programs while maintaining local control. In 1907 President Theodore Roosevelt observed, "We of the United States must develop a system under which each citizen shall be trained so as to be effective individually as an economic unit and fit to be organized with his fellows so that he and they can work in efficient fashion together" (Soretire, p. 18). Clearly, Roosevelt saw vocational education as both an economic necessity and as a socializing process.

Smith-Hughes Act of 1917. The culmination of the actions by these different organizations and state agencies was the passage of the Smith-Hughes Act of 1917. The purposes of this act were:

- To provide for the promotion of vocational education.

- To provide for cooperation with the states in the promotion of vocational education in agriculture and industry.

- To provide for cooperation with the states in the preparation of teachers of vocational subjects.

- To appropriate money and regulate its expenditure.

According to the Smith-Hughes Act, the main purpose of vocational education was to make young people fit for employment on the farm or in the farm home. The bill also stated that all secondary schools with agricultural education needed to provide directed or supervised practice in agriculture.

The Smith-Hughes Act allocated federal funds to the states for the purpose of agricultural education. These funds were to be matched by state and local funds, and were to be used for the training and salaries of teachers, supervisors, and directors of agriculture, and for programs in home economics, agricultural economics, and industrial subjects. The act also provided for a Federal Board for Vocational Education. To receive these monies, each state had to submit a plan detailing how they would spend it.

The act also required that all students were to participate in a work experience focusing on livestock and crop projects outside of the regular school day. This was certainly not a new idea. Rousseau and Pestalozzi had advocated supervised educational practice in Europe as early as the eighteenth century. More recently this practice has been discussed by Froebel, Dewey, Warmbrod, Lamar, and others.

Not all educators, however, agreed that vocational agriculture education was a good use of money, and there was both public and political debate regarding the value of vocational agricultural education. In fact, the balance between purely academic and vocational education remains a continuing debate.

The National Vocational Education Act, passed in 1963, broadened the scope of the original Smith-Hughes Act by adding flexibility, providing for career counseling and employment training, expanding the age groups covered, and providing for the needs of people with special educational needs. The objectives of this new act were:

1. To develop agricultural competencies needed by individuals engaged in or preparing to engage in production agriculture.

2. To develop agricultural competencies needed by individuals engaged in or preparing to engage in agricultural occupations other than production agriculture.

3. To develop an understanding of, and appreciation for, career opportunities in

agriculture and the preparation needed to enter and progress in agricultural occupations.

4. To develop the ability to secure satisfactory placement and advance in an agricultural occupation through a program of continuing education.

5. To develop those abilities in human relations that are essential in agricultural occupations.

6. To develop the abilities needed to exercise and follow effective leadership in carrying out occupational, social, and civic responsibilities.

It is difficult to get a precise sense of what philosophy was at the root of these various Congressional acts. The role that the federal government played seems to have been one of providing money for the training of farmers and farm wives in practical skills, and for training teachers in agricultural and home economics education. Little mention was made of socializing skills until the later congressional acts. To gain a deeper understanding of exactly what the philosophy of agricultural education was during those times, writings of a different sort must be examined, specifically, writings by people involved directly, as educators, with agricultural education.

An Early Philosophy of Agricultural Education

At its onset agricultural education was part of a broad-based approach to rural education. The idea of making rural improvement a national issue was brought before President Roosevelt in 1906. As a result, the Country Life Commission was appointed in August 1908. The commission listed several factors that negatively affected rural families. Chief among them was the need for education.

As early as 1906 the importance of relevant education was being discussed, as was the idea of rural-life development. For example, Liberty Hyde Bailey began his book *The Training of Farmers* (1909) with the lines: "The so-called rural problem is one of the great public questions of the day. It is the problem of how to develop a rural civilization that is permanently satisfying and worthy of the best desires" (p. 3). In the preface to Aretas Nolan's *The Teaching of Agriculture* (1918), an author named Davenport wrote "That measure [success] is found in the performance of those who actually go to the land, live there, and succeed; for, after all, the fundamental purpose of our great system of agricultural education is to insure a better agriculture and make a country life as nearly perfect as possible" (p. vii).

Bailey was fairly articulate about the role of education. He believed that education should "assist the farmer to rely on himself and to be resourceful, and to encourage him to work with other farmers for the purpose of increasing the profitableness of farming and of developing a good social life in rural communities." Further, "all citizenship must rest ultimately on occupation, for all good citizens must be workers of one kind or another." A good citizen "must be actively interested in the public welfare, and be willing to put himself under the guidance of a good local leader" (Bailey, pp. 10–12).

According to Bailey, proper education is needed for this to happen; education, which must start at the elementary level. He felt that education began "with the child's world and not with the teacher's world, and we must use the common objects, phenomena and activities as means of education." Thus, "agriculture becomes a means of education" (p. 150).

Nolan, writing nine years after Bailey, added that the aims of vocational agricultural education should be to give the student "preparation for wholesome and successful farming and country life" (p. 2), as well as the skills needed to be a successful farmer. He also explained that agricultural education should be part of a larger educational picture that would produce "an educated country gentleman who works with his hands and gathers about him all the best things which civilization afford."

Good education depends on good teaching, which depends, in turn, on good teachers. The well-educated vocational agricultural teacher, according to Nolan, must be a thorough scientist and a technically trained agriculturalist. He should also have studied rural sociology, agricultural economics, public speaking and "other work to liberalize his general training" (p. 163), as well as having a thorough understanding of educational principles, psychology, and management. This is because the teacher's "influence and activities extend outside of the school to the rural life of the community" (p. 163).

Nolan devoted an entire chapter of his book to nature study, because it was his belief that studying nature in the field teaches observation and helps students understand the conservation of natural resources. Nolan believed the teaching of agriculture must result in the wise use and conservation of these natural resources.

However Theodore Eaton's *Vocational Education in Farming Occupations: The Part of the Public*

High School (1923) showed that the philosophy of agricultural education was beginning to change. Eaton agreed on the importance of "a philosophy of social purpose in organization, and an organization contributing to the achievement of that purpose" (p. 7), but his approach was a little more sophisticated than that of his predecessors. For example, his book includes a discussion of socialism versus democracy. He also connects Bailey's idea of environment and conservation to John Dewey's environment ideal, writing that the "environment is, perhaps, as Dewey tells us, best defined as consisting in those situations which affect the conduct, thoughts, emotions and attitudes of men" (p. 31–32).

Eaton goes on to outline four general purposes for education: (1) the adjustment of the individual to his environment, (2) social efficiency, (3) self-realization, and (4) individual growth. He believed that there were three fundamental principles that governed education. These were: (1) education is modification—all education consists in changes in the mode of action, thought, and feelings of human beings; (2) the business of the educator is the making of stimulus-response bonds in the "educand" (student)—the main problem for the educator is deciding which bonds the student should make; and (3) education is about being able to transfer newly acquired skills.

Philosophically, Eaton saw education in a dualistic and hierarchical manner. This view reflected the philosophy of Watson, Thorndike, and the other behavioralists. He thus defined education as "the formal process of interaction between the conscious and purposeful manipulator of environment, the 'educator,' at one pole, and the conscious, but so far as the aim of education is concerned, not purposeful 'educand' at the other pole" (p. 45).

By the time of Eaton's writing in 1923, the philosophy of agricultural education was becoming complex, drawing elements from several different sources. The importance of socialization was carried over from earlier times, and a humanistic focus on the development of the individual was also stressed. Elements from Dewey's pragmatic education theory were included, such as the ideas of education as change and transfer. Finally, aspects of behavioral theory were being added, which stressed the dualistic and hierarchic nature of education.

Eaton also discussed the importance of both supervised work on farms and supervised employment in agricultural education. In his discussion Eaton claimed that supervised work needed to be complimented with classroom work that was balanced between academic and vocational classes.

From the above writings, one can begin to get a sense of the philosophy of the founders of agricultural education. Farm settlers were an individualistic lot, separated by significant distances and bad roads. But the nation was growing, and agricultural production needed to catch up with the rest of the country. For this to happen, the infrastructure of rural life needed to be improved, along with agricultural production methods. A change in philosophy was beginning at this time, as the writings of Thorndike and the early behavioralists began to influence the psychology of education.

Agricultural Education from the 1930s to the 1970s

Agricultural education during the first third of the twentieth century was, for the most part, seated in the humanistic and pragmatic philosophy of John Dewey. It was therefore focused on training men and women in the practical skills needed to run a successful farm, on the development of a more proficient agriculture system, and on the development of rural communities. During the second third of the century, more emphasis was placed on the *science* of education, as educators came more under the influence of the positivistic philosophy that arose during that time and held sway as the predominant philosophy in mainstream education until the 1960s.

Glen Cook, for example, writing in 1936, continued the emphasis on both classroom work and supervised farm experience. He claimed that the ultimate purpose of agricultural education was to "train the individual to think in order that he may solve the problems, both social and economic, which he may meet, and to prepare him for complete living" (p. 13). He then added to that list the "worthy use of leisure time" and ethical character.

R. M. Stewart, in his 1938 essay "Teacher Education," explained that more emphasis was being placed on developing better teachers. He felt that "the newer trends of teacher education today tend rather to relate themselves to the more specific practices of teachers and to the improvement of their programs" (p. 56). He maintained, however, that the local farms "constitute the natural educational settings in which problems of farming are discerned and attacked" (p. 57). As such, he supported on-farm experience.

What became important within the institutions of teacher training was the improvement of the teacher education programs themselves. An important aspect of this improvement was the development of job placement for the graduates, for those graduating from production agricultural programs knew they would have jobs. In order to attract good people, teacher training programs needed to be able to do the same.

Another area of importance was the development of effective and up-to-date teaching materials. According to Stewart, "A forward-looking program of agricultural education always involves recognition of changing social and economic needs, and of the contributions of scientific and technical knowledge to the new problems arising" (p. 57). Farmer training originally involved teaching "scientific agriculture," or the practice of applying scientific principles to agricultural problems. Then came technical science teaching, then social and economic training. From these came the "professional" aspects of agriculture. As a profession, Stewart explained, specific materials had to be developed, sorted, and evaluated in order to train teachers. What was needed were "more and better materials and methods and more focusing of attention upon what is to be done in the education of the people on the land" (p. 58).

Stewart also emphasized the importance of supervised training: "Supervised participation is rapidly becoming the core of agricultural education. . . . If the best way to learn is by doing, then the principle holds as true of the student teacher as of the student farmer. This places directed observation and directed teaching—under supervision—as the *central emphasis* on the professional side of a teacher's preparation. The prospective teacher must have *representative experiences,* which include such things as administration, getting to know the people of the community, supervising pupil's farming programs, and making commercial contracts" (p. 58).

In his 1940 essay Omer Aderhold echoes the philosophy of John Dewey, writing that "the schools, like the nation, are in need of a central purpose which will verify and guide all intellectual plans" (p. 2). To Aderhold, a nation's education system must contribute to the "ends of the society in which it lives." This means that education should be grounded in democratic action, which requires an understanding, by the population at large, of the problems faced by the citizens.

Aderhold claimed that the major objectives of education should be to promote reflective thinking for the individual and to promote group living on an intelligent basis of cooperation for the group. This could be accomplished at both the individual and group levels, by encouraging the use of the scientific method of thought, that is, by drawing inferences and formulating hypotheses about problems, by testing those inferences, and then drawing sound conclusions. In this way vocational education could help farmers attain a higher standard of living.

During the 1940s and 1950s agricultural education maintained its status quo. The nation's economy was doing well, the country was growing in status and power, and agriculture was becoming more efficient and effective as a result of agricultural chemical and mechanical advances. Farmers were entering the middle class and moving into the economic mainstream. Agricultural educators acted to support the scientific revolution, while at the same time keeping their own profession basically unchanged.

In a 1966 essay Robert Warmbrod and Lloyd Phipps summarized changes in the focus of agricultural education from its inception until the 1960s. They explained that, prior to 1917, agriculture was taught as an informational or general education subject. Following Smith-Hughes, there was an increase in the number of classes focusing on vocational agricultural and a reduction of classes oriented towards general education. This trend reflected the objectives of federal financial assistance.

Herbert Hamlin believed that this "specialization" led to an "over-simplification of public school education," while Phipps claimed that the curricula needed to be expanded and that more emphasis needed to be placed on preparation for employment in agriculture-related industries. He also argued for occupational guidance and job counseling. A survey by the Research Committee of the Southern Region also found strong support for training to help people be good citizens, intelligent consumers, and efficient producers.

According to Warmbrod and Phipps the general public saw agricultural education as being of a vocational nature only. Experts in the field disagreed however, and believed that was too strict a definition. In addition, Warmbrod and Phipps stated that agricultural education should include training not only in vocational agriculture, but in those skills needed to be successful in any occupation, including preparation for advanced education.

In 1963 Congress passed the Vocational Training Act of 1963, which provided funding "for vocational education in any occupation involving knowledge and skills in agricultural subjects" (Warmbrod and Phipps, p. 7).

Philosophical Writings after 1970

Since the 1970s agricultural educators have attempted to more directly define the philosophy of agricultural education. For example, Phipps claimed that agricultural educators are pragmatists; emphasize learning by doing; emphasize individual self-awareness, work-awareness, and career decision-making; believe in the importance of leadership and citizenship development; learn how to work with people who are disadvantaged and handicapped; advocate the use of problem solving as a way of encouraging thinking; and believe in community and community service.

A. Kahler and colleagues also set about defining the philosophy of agricultural education for *Project 2000*. They listed three functions of agricultural and agribusiness education: (1) educating individuals for employment in the fields of agriculture and agribusiness, (2) avocational agricultural course work, and (3) issues having to do with the "food crisis." The authors went on to explain that agricultural education is based on decision making through problem solving; is centered on experience; addresses both individual and community needs; is related to resource management; and perceives agriculture as an integrated part of a dynamic world system.

This provides some insight into how agricultural educators see their world, which is, in the spirit of Dewey, as a place that is both experiential and that requires consciousness for problem solving. It is, therefore, neither a realist-based philosophy, nor a strictly empirical one. It retains the humanist's view of the importance of the individual learner, but also points towards the importance of community at both the human and social level, as well as the environmental level. And finally, it is similar to a postpositivist philosophy in its recognition of diversity and process.

In a 1978 article G. M. Love compared agricultural education and general education. He described

agricultural educators as being pragmatists and experientially oriented. Metaphysically, agricultural educators see the world analytically and prescriptively. Furthermore, they believe that the "real" world is that which can be experienced with the senses. Meaning is not predetermined, it is determined by the individual within the context of his or her experiences and that of his or her community. Therefore, learning to solve current, life-like problems is the best way to equip a person to effectively solve problems in the future.

Epistemologically, agricultural educators believe that both knowledge and truth stem from empirical investigation. They also believe that both of these are temporary. A high value is placed on self-activity, association, and effect. For this reason vocational agriculture makes use of both work experiences and activities in student organizations. In addition, the improvement of social behavior through participation in the democratic process is an important aspect in the philosophy of agricultural education.

Educationally, agricultural educators see themselves as research project directors and their students as discoverers. Love wrote that teachers in agricultural education regard students as experience organisms who deserve individual attention and who work in a "life-oriented environment." Thus, a flexible curricula is needed.

Love explained however, that while agricultural education is based on a realist philosophy, reality is based on the individual's relationship to a larger community, and is therefore relativistic (and changeable).

Philosophically, agricultural educators see education as a process of problem solving. As teachers, agricultural educators see students as *experience organisms* and believe education is hierarchical, in that they see themselves as directors and their students as discoverers. Axiologically, therefore, they value their own experiences over those of their students. It is their job to direct the student towards that particular vision, which often includes the concept of democracy. In other words, although education is about discovery, it is a prescribed discovery, with political overtones.

Another recent attempt to articulate a philosophy for agricultural education was the one done by the National Summit on Agricultural Education. In 1989 agricultural educators at the university, community college, and secondary school levels held a series of meetings to again look at where agricultural education is and where it needs to go. In their mission statement, this group explained that the mission of agricultural education was to provide a total dynamic educational system, to aspire to excellence, to serve people, and to inform the public about agriculture's needs, opportunities, and challenges. In attempting to accomplish this, the consortium listed the following objectives:

- To provide instruction in and about agriculture.
- To serve all populations.
- To develop the whole person.
- To respond to the needs of the market place.
- To advocate free enterprise.
- To function as a part of the total education system.
- To utilize a proven educational process, one which includes formal instruction, experiential learning, leadership, and personal development.

This list, while not really philosophical in nature, does suggest a view that is somewhat different than Love's. Specifically, its emphasis on the whole person suggests a move away from viewing the learner simply as a "sense organism," and away from a strict empirical view of reality. Also, by including all populations, the marketplace, and free enterprise, it takes a more overt political stand than did Love.

Agricultural education has had to change to meet the changing demands of its clientele. R. Kirby Barrick listed several points that he claimed were essential for a true discipline of agricultural education, including that it must be based on sound theory. Barrick understood that agricultural education has to look deeper into both theory and philosophy. Philosophically, this again suggests a movement away from a realist and empirically grounded philosophy.

To David Williams the discipline of agricultural education is only as strong as its means for verifying existing knowledge, for creating new knowledge, and for disseminating and applying that knowledge. This is done through research, which "must be the strongest component of a discipline, serving as a foundation for teaching and extension" (Williams, p. 5). Williams found several weakness in agricultural education research, including that it is often piecemeal (i.e., not cumulative); that it lacks a sound theoretical framework; and that it lacks depth.

Finally, according to R. A. Martin (1991), agricultural education is based on three critical compo-

nents: technical agriculture, experiential learning, and human development. For Martin the purpose of teaching agricultural knowledge and skills is to prepare students to be able to use that knowledge and those skills in meaningful ways in their lives. He claimed that one of the best ways of ensuring student understanding is through the use of experiential learning, both in and out of school. More importantly, according to Martin, "the heart and soul of the program is the student" (p. 21–22). As such, agricultural education is committed to the growth of the individual student in all three learning domains. But more importantly, from a philosophical basis, he points to a move away from a strictly empirical philosophy, and toward one which was both humanistic and idealistic.

Current Status

Even though the philosophy of agricultural education has not continually been developing, principles that form the foundation for agricultural education have not changed. These principles are: providing up-to-date technical skills and knowledge in agriculture; conducting experiential learning activities in the real world or agricultural careers; and involving students in leadership and personal development activities at the local, state, and national levels.

In the early twenty-first century, there are more than 8,000 secondary school agricultural programs across the United States. More than 500,000 students are involved in these programs focused on career educational in agriculture.

Over the years the curriculum has changed dramatically. The original curricular focus was on production agriculture (farming). The expansion of careers in other areas of the agriculture industry (horticulture, food science, products and processing, biotechnology, entrepreneurship, forestry, and natural resources) has had a significant impact on the curriculum. The enrollment of students in these programs continues to grow.

Beyond the secondary school agriculture programs, community colleges and universities provide excellent opportunities for students to specialize and gain skills and knowledge in agriculture. University programs in agricultural education focus on teaching and learning processes that prepare students for professional positions in education, agri-industry, and public service agencies.

The future of agriculture education is bright. Although less than 2 percent of the U.S. population is involved in production agriculture, the food, fiber, and natural resource system requires the services of people well educated in the agricultural sciences. These people need experiential learning and personal leadership development training in the context of agriculture. Agricultural education programs can provide the education and training needed to serve the needs of the vast industry called agriculture.

See also: SECONDARY EDUCATION; VOCATIONAL AND TECHNICAL EDUCATION; YOUTH ORGANIZATIONS, *subentry on* NATIONAL FUTURE FARMERS OF AMERICA.

BIBLIOGRAPHY

ADERHOLD, OMER CLYDE. 1940. "A Philosophy of Vocational Education in Agriculture." *Bulletin of the University of Georgia* 10:5b.

BAILEY, JOSEPH CANNON. 1945. *Seaman A. Knapp: Schoolmaster of American Agriculture.* New York: Columbia University Press.

BAILEY, LIBERTY HYDE. 1909. *The Training of the Farmer.* New York: The Century Company.

BARRICK, R. KIRBY. 1989. "Agricultural Education: Building Upon Our Roots." *Journal of Agricultural Education* 30 (4):24–29.

COOK, GLEN CHARLES. 1936. *Handbook on Teaching Vocational Agriculture,* 3rd edition. Danville, IL: Interstate Printers.

DEWEY, JOHN. 1931. "Some Aspects of Modern Education." *School and Society* October.

EATON, THEODORE H. 1923. *Vocational Education in Farming Occupations.* Philadelphia: J.P. Lippincott.

HAMLIN, HERBERT M. 1962. *Public School Education in Agriculture.* Danville, IL: Interstate Publishing.

JOHNSTON, PAUL F. 1968. "Looking Ahead in Vocational Agriculture." *State of Iowa Department of Public Instruction Bulletin,* Bulletin No. 16-710-406.

JOHNSTONE, R. F. 1854. *Agricultural Education, An Individual, State and National Necessity: Suggestions for the Establishment and Endowment of an Agricultural College in Michigan.* Detroit, MI: Calhoun County Agricultural Society.

KAHLER, A. 1967. "Factors Related to the Occupations of Nebraska Farm Male High School Graduates." Ph.D. diss., Iowa State University.

KAHLER, A.; LEINGIN, J.; ARCHER, T.; and MAGILL, J. 1976. *Project 2000: Basic Principles for Agriculture and Agribusiness Education.* Ames, IA: Iowa State University, Department of Agricultural Education.

LAMAR, CARL F. 1971. "Work Experience Programs." *Agricultural Education* 43:164–165.

LEISING, J. G. 1976. "Perceptions of Selected Groups Towards the Philosophic Principle of Experience in Agriculture and Agribusiness Education in Iowa." Ph.D. diss., Iowa State University.

LOVE, G. M. 1978. "An Introduction to the Philosophy of Agricultural Education." *Journal of the American Association of Teacher Educators in Agriculture* 19(1):2–10.

MARTIN, R. A. 1991. "The Essence of Agricultural Education." *Agricultural Education* 63(8):21–22.

MCCRAKEN, J. DAVID. 1983. "A Profession in Need of Academicians." *Journal of the American Association of Teacher Educators in Agriculture* 24(1):2–12.

MORELAND, WILLIS D., and GOLDENSTEIN, ERWIN H. 1985. *Pioneers in Adult Education.* Chicago: Nelson-Hall.

NOLAN, ARETAS WILBUR. 1918. *The Teaching of Agriculture.* Boston: Houghton Mifflin.

PHIPPS, LLOYD J. 1956. "Agricultural Education." *Review of Educational Research* 26:359–369.

PHIPPS, LLOYD J., and OSBORNE, EDWARD W. 1988. *Handbook on Agricultural Education in Public Schools.* Danville, IL: Interstate Printers.

SORETIRE, E. O. 1968. "History of Vocational Education in Agriculture in Iowa." Master's thesis, Iowa State University.

STEWART, R. M. 1938. "Teacher Education." In *Whither Agricultural Education,* ed. Roy A. Olney. Des Moines, IA: Meredith.

TRUE, ALFRED CHARLES. 1929. *A History of Agricultural Education in the United States, 1785–1925.* Washington, D.C.: U.S. Department of Agriculture.

WARMBROD, J. ROBERT, and PHIPPS, LLOYD J. 1966. *Review and Synthesis of Research in Agricultural Education.* Columbus, OH: Center for Vocational and Technical Education.

WILLIAMS, DAVID L. 1991. "Focusing Agricultural Education Research, Strategies for the Discipline." Journal of Agricultural Education 32(1):7–12.

STEPHEN MICHAEL CAMPBELL
ROBERT ALLEN MARTIN

AIDS

See: RISK BEHAVIORS, *subentry on* HIV/AIDS AND ITS IMPACT ON ADOLESCENTS.

ALBERTY, H. B. (1890–1971)

Harold Bernard Alberty, professor of education at The Ohio State University, was a pioneer in the field of curriculum. Born in Lockport, New York, Alberty attended rural schools in northeastern Ohio. In 1912 he graduated from Baldwin University (now Baldwin-Wallace College) in Berea, Ohio. He began teaching the eighth grade during his senior year of college. In 1913 he graduated from Cleveland Law School and was admitted to the Ohio bar. Alberty was promised a position in the law firm of one of his teachers, but that teacher died suddenly. Alberty was unable to find another position in law and continued to teach. He found teaching fascinating and promotions came quickly. Although still determined to practice law, Alberty realized he needed additional education in school administration and entered graduate school at the Ohio State University in the summer of 1920. The final summer of his master's degree program he enrolled in a course taught by Boyd H. Bode, "Modern Educational Theories," that forcefully challenged Alberty's educational beliefs. Although their views differed on a number of accounts, Bode recognized Alberty's talent and offered him an assistantship in the department to continue his studies. Alberty was later appointed to the faculty.

Heavily influenced by Bode's thinking, Alberty began to explore the educational implications of experimentalism. School administration, teacher education, and the relatively new field of curriculum engaged his interest. In 1931 he published *Supervision in the Secondary School* with Vivian T. Thayer. In this publication the authors argued that school supervisors should be curriculum leaders and that, contrary to established patterns, leadership in the schools ought to be democratic. They asserted that "the ultimate criterion of a supervisor's success [is]

that the school in its organization within and without the classroom shall contribute towards the preparation of boys and girls for an intelligent participation in democratic citizenship" (p. 94). The implications of democracy for school practice became a central theme running throughout Alberty's thirty-five-year career at Ohio State.

One aspect of Alberty's work focused on the kind of general education needed for effective citizenship—education, as he wrote, that would "facilitate building, on the part of each pupil, of an independent social outlook on life" (1933, p. 273). He contrasted general education, required of all citizens, with specialized education, designed to develop individual talents and interests, and sought to create balance between these two types. Alberty assisted in the Eight-Year Study sponsored by the Progressive Education Association. In 1937 and 1938 he served as a member of the study's curriculum staff, aiding participating school faculties in clarifying their aims, helping them, in the words of Wilford Aikin, director of the study, "[to see] the social significance of their work and to give it direction" (p. 190). He worked with faculty in all the participating schools, including the Ohio State University School.

In addition, Alberty served on a committee associated with the Eight-Year Study that explored the place of science in general education. The committee's report, *Science in General Education* (1939), written by Alberty, reflected a conception of general education that Alberty described earlier in these words: "It must . . . be based upon the interests and needs of adolescents in our culture to the extent that they can be discovered; and . . . it must meet these needs and cultivate these interests in such a way as to contribute to the understanding, reconstruction, and refinement of the democratic way of life" (1937, p. 388). Alberty's work on the curriculum staff and in general education influenced his decision to accept the directorship of the Ohio State University School, a position he held from 1938 to 1941. As director, Alberty was provided the opportunity to further develop his curricular ideas and to assist the faculty to produce a guiding philosophy statement, one that helped teachers to understand the place of the disciplines in general education.

In 1941 Alberty chaired a committee charged with the task of writing a guiding philosophy for the Progressive Education Association. The document that was produced drew heavily on Alberty's prior experience with the faculties associated with the

Eight-Year Study. It presented a moderate position between two extreme factions of the PEA, the child-centered and social-reformist positions. Alberty's compromise pleased no one. Association members failed to agree to a platform; this, over time, contributed to its decline.

As director of the Ohio State University School and in his work with the faculties of the Eight-Year Study schools, Alberty sought to make sense of the range of curriculum work being done in general education. There were no specific guidelines to participation in the study; the hope was that school faculties would experiment with the curriculum. Considering the diversity of the schools and seeking a model that would be useful for curriculum development, Alberty generated a conceptual framework, called *core*, that included five types, or approaches, to general education. These types were generated from his study of school curricula but were formulated logically to reflect degrees of subject matter integration. Over time the model evolved. Type 1 was a separate subject design, where academic subjects were taught individually and the content was unrelated to the other subjects. In Type 2, correlated curriculum, formal connections were made among the disciplines but they were taught separately. Type 3, fusion, unified subject areas and organized the curriculum around themes or perhaps time periods. Alberty's preference was for Type 4, which was developed at the Ohio State University School, where the subject matter was organized around broad units, often chosen in consultation with students, and reflecting an understanding of the shared interests, common problems, and social issues facing young people. Type 5 was entirely driven by teacher-student planned activities without reference to formal structure. The work of the Eight-Year Study proved that a significant departure from the traditional subject-centered curriculum for general education, particularly Types 1, 2, and 3, had a positive effect on student learning. Unfortunately, this lesson was lost in post-*Sputnik* America, where a math- and science-focused curriculum was seen as the key to competing with the Soviet Union.

With the exception of Type 1, each of the approaches presented serious challenges to teachers. Alberty pioneered the resource unit as a means for replacing textbooks that dominated the curriculum and stifled innovation. Generated by teachers for teachers, the resource unit presented and organized instructional materials in ways that supported content integration. He worked tirelessly to further the cause of the core curriculum, believing that Type 4, usually taught in a block of time, was the best approach to secondary general education. His full argument is presented in *Reorganizing the High School Curriculum,* which went through three editions (1947, 1953, 1962), each of which was recognized by the National Education Association as a "Best Book." Despite the passage of time, the framework remains a useful departure point for thinking about curriculum reform, particularly cross-disciplinary or interdisciplinary curriculum design. The books themselves are unique in a number of respects, including how each presents the results of Alberty's ongoing engagement with curriculum issues with his students and in consultation with practitioners and his struggle to strengthen the link between democracy, democratic citizenship, and public education.

See also: BODE, BOYD H.; CURRICULUM, SCHOOL; EIGHT-YEAR STUDY; PROGRESSIVE EDUCATION.

BIBLIOGRAPHY

AIKIN, WILFORD. "Division of High-School and College Relations." 1936. *Educational Research Bulletin* October 14, p. 190. Columbus: Ohio State University.

ALBERTY, HAROLD B. Papers. Columbus: The Ohio State University Archives.

ALBERTY, HAROLD B. 1933. "Supervision as a Means of Integrating the Total Secondary Program." *Schoolman's Week Proceedings* 20:273.

ALBERTY, HAROLD B. 1937. "Philosophy of General Education with Some Implications for Science Teaching." *Journal of Educational Method* 16:237.

ALBERTY, HAROLD B. 1947. *Reorganizing the High School Curriculum.* New York: Macmillan.

ALBERTY, HAROLD B., and THAYER, VIVIAN T. 1931. *Supervision in the Secondary School.* Boston: D. C. Heath.

BULLOUGH, ROBERT V., JR. 1976. "Harold B. Alberty and Boyd H. Bode: Pioneers in Curriculum Theory." Ph.D. diss., Ohio State University.

LAWHEAD, VICTOR. 1996. "Harold Alberty, Teacher and Guide." In *Teachers and Mentors: Profiles of Distinguished Twentieth-Century Professors of Education,* ed. Craig Kridel, Robert V. Bullough,

Jr., and Paul Shaker, pp. 151–162. New York: Garland.

ROBERT V. BULLOUGH JR.

ALCOHOL ABUSE AND DRINKING

See: DRUG AND ALCOHOL ABUSE; FAMILY COMPOSITION AND CIRCUMSTANCE, *subentry on* ALCOHOL, TOBACCO, AND OTHER DRUGS; PERSONAL AND PSYCHOLOGICAL COUNSELING AT COLLEGES AND UNIVERSITIES; PERSONAL AND PSYCHOLOGICAL PROBLEMS OF COLLEGE STUDENTS.

ALTERNATIVE SCHOOLING

The term *alternative schooling* has always referred to nontraditional public and private educational approaches available by choice to parents and students. These programs, ranging from actual schools to programs within schools to single classrooms, began to evolve during the late 1960s and grew from a few isolated innovations in local communities into an educational reform involving millions of students. By the year 2000 it was estimated that over 15 percent of the students enrolled in public education in the United States were attending a public school of choice.

Since the late 1500s there have been private schools, parochial schools, or home schooling alternatives for those who could afford them or whose beliefs dictated a particular approach to education. Yet until the latter part of the twentieth century, public education in the United States was characterized by an unusual uniformity. With the exception of vocational/technical schools and a few selective programs for at-risk or gifted and talented students, almost all school districts had traditionally assigned families to schools based on residence addresses and geographic boundaries. Since students were assigned to a particular school, public education worked to assure that all schools had uniform programs. By the mid- to late 1960s, this emphasis on public school uniformity began to change. Beginning with a few highly innovative experimental schools and dropout and continuation programs, alternative schooling emerged as a grassroots revolution, which has grown

to include a variety of different types of educational options in the private and public sectors. These include religious and private not-for-profit schools, technological educational options, and thousands of distinctive public alternative, magnet, and charter schools. The concept of alternative schooling, which first emerged as a radical idea on the fringe of public education, evolved to a mainstream approach found in almost every community in the United States and increasingly throughout the world. This mosaic of distinctive educational programs is referred to as *public schools of choice.*

Alternative schools represent one of the most significant educational movements ever to occur in the United States. According to a 1999 study from the Policy Analysis for California Education (PACE) of Stanford University and the University of California, Berkeley, between 1993 and 1996 the number of students attending public schools of choice rose from 11 percent to 13 percent. PACE projected that the number of students attending a public school of choice would increase another 15 percent by 2000. Career-theme magnet schools, the most widely used type of educational option in public education, have likewise experienced dramatic growth. From 1991 to 1992 school districts across the United States operated 2,400 magnet schools and 3,200 magnet programs involving more than a million students. By 1996 the number of students attending magnet schools had grown to 1.5 million students, with over 120,000 students on waiting lists. In 2001 magnet schools were expected to enroll more than two million students in over 5,000 schools and programs. Charter schools also have experienced rapid growth, following the opening of the nation's first two schools in Minnesota in 1992, to an estimated 2,500 charters as of 2001, serving 1 to 2 percent of all public school students.

Two states in particular have experienced significant growth in alternative schooling within public education. In Minnesota, the numbers of students enrolled in some type of alternative schooling has grown from 4,000 students in 1990 to more than 112,000 students in the year 2000. In Arizona, as of 2000, there were 359 charter schools serving about fifty thousand students—about 6 percent of the states' 800,000 students.

National statistics regarding school choice often do not include the number of parents choosing nonpublic options (those choosing private schools, home schooling, participating in for-pay, online learning) or who are influenced in selecting their home residence by where their children will go to school. The number of K–12 home-schooled students grew from approximately 800,000 in 1990 to 1.7 million in 1998; by 1999 it was estimated that there were approximately two million children and youth being home schooled. In 1993 the National Center for Education Statistics (NCES) estimated that 20 percent of the students in grades 3 to 12 were enrolled in public and private schools chosen by their parents. PACE estimated that the number would rise to 25 percent by the year 2000. In addition, 39 percent of the parents interviewed by NCES reported that the public school their children would attend influenced their choice of residence. Even more striking, they reported that 72 percent of parents earning more than $50,000 responded that they had first chosen some type of school of choice—private schools, public school optional programs, or public schools—and then selected their residence.

For a concept that has had such a revolutionary impact on public education, the idea of alternative schooling and public schools of choice is really quite simple. It involves little more than diversifying public education by creating distinctive educational programs designed to meet the needs and interests of specific groups of students and providing these programs to parents, students, and teachers through voluntary choice. More recently, as charter schools have developed, the concept of school choice has also come to mean the opportunity for an individual school to exchange many state and locally mandated rules, regulations, and requirements for contractually specified student performance outcomes.

Since the first alternative public schools were identified and studied in the late 1960s, the underlying definition and characteristics of schools of choice have remained relatively unchanged. They include:

- **Voluntary participation:** Students, parents, and teachers voluntarily participate in a school of their choice.

- **Small school size:** Schools of choice (alternative, magnet, and charter schools) have sought to humanize and personalize learning by creating small educational options. The average enrollment for a school of choice has remained at approximately 250 students for more than twenty years.

- **Caring teachers with high expectations:** Since teachers voluntarily participate in schools of choice, they become highly invested in the

school. This investment translates into a strong motivation for both student achievement and school success.

- **Customized curriculum/personalized instruction:** Schools of choice offer students, parents, and teachers opportunities to participate in a highly focused curriculum with value-added enhancements. Students in public schools of choice meet state requirements for high school graduation through participating in a curriculum designed to both motivate student learning and provide experiences that relate to individual needs, interests, and career aspirations.

- **Safe learning environment:** Research has documented a remarkable lack of violence, vandalism, and disruptive behavior in schools of choice. Students and families consistently report feeling both physically and emotionally safe to participate and learn.

While these five critical components can be found in alternative, magnet, and charter schools, research during the latter 1990s further developed these core characteristics into a complex of essential components, which represent the current spectrum of different types of established school models.

Types of Alternative Schools

By the year 2000 alternative schooling had expanded to include a dozen distinctive opportunities to participate in schools of choice.

- **Alternative or optional schools:** A wide variety of established alternative schools serve all levels and kinds of students. These schools range from programs for at-risk, expelled, and violent students to schools for the exceptionally gifted and talented. Many alternative or optional schools serve heterogeneous student bodies with average achievement and behavior characteristics.

- **Career-theme or technical magnet schools:** Originally popularized as part of court-ordered desegregation efforts, magnet schools emerged over time into specialized programs employing career themes. Students complete high school graduation requirements while they focus on and apply curriculum to a career theme, academic discipline, or area of emphasis, and by participating in relevant work and service experiences.

- **Charter schools:** As of 2001 these schools had been approved by legislatures in thirty-eight states, the District of Columbia, and Puerto Rico. Charter schools exchange many of the rules and regulations of public education for the opportunity to operate with autonomy to demonstrate student achievement.

- **Contract schools:** School districts "contract" with an organization or group (usually private) to provide public education services. Examples of these schools include schools to teach disruptive and/or suspended students, programs to supplement reading services, and in some cases actually contracting out the entire administrative and/or educational operation of a school district.

- **Open enrollment programs:** Parents and their children may choose to attend any public school in their district or in another district to which their state education funds would follow. Transportation is usually provided if the students' home residence district and school district share a common physical boundary.

- **Residential alternatives:** A number of states, including North Carolina, Maine, Louisiana, and Texas have established academic-focused residential science/mathematics high schools for gifted and talented students in cooperation with state universities.

- **Voucher programs:** Three states, Wisconsin, Ohio, and Florida, have attempted to establish voucher programs to provide publicly funded vouchers to poor students "trapped" in low-performing public schools. These vouchers may be applied to the tuition costs of attending private or parochial schools. Publicly funded voucher programs, as of 2001, continue to be involved in litigation regarding the issue of expending public funds for private or parochial education.

- **Home schools:** Since the 1970s there has been a dramatic growth in the home schooling of K–12 students. Most states require public schools to offer a variety of services, courses, and programs to home-schooled students.

- **Internet courses and programs:** During the late 1990s a growing number of courses, programs, and schools available through the Internet emerged. These learning opportunities are offered by community colleges, universities, private educational organizations, and an increasing number of public school districts.

- **Blending high school with college:** A number of states encourage high school students to begin taking college courses during the eleventh and twelfth grades. Some states have created "middle colleges" within community colleges and universities to better serve high school students. A number of states permit students to double-list mutually approved courses so that they meet both high school and college requirements.

- **Area learning centers:** Established first in Minnesota, area learning centers are open from early morning to late evening year-round (some are open twenty-four hours a day), serving K–12 students and adults. The centers offer both General Educational Development (GED) and regular diplomas as well as child care and are available to students on a full- or part-time basis.

Each of these school/program types are represented by established, successful working models. These programs serve as the benchmarks of effective practice in alternative schooling.

Alternative School Models

Thousands of schools of choice offering alternative schooling have been developed, successfully evaluated, and replicated. Within these schools exist a wide array of approaches to implementing curriculum, instruction, and school governance and management. These established models reflect a truly worldwide educational revolution and include:

- **Schools that focus on unique curricular and instructional approaches:** These alternative schools include: Montessori schools, based on the ideas of the Italian physician and educator Maria Montessori; open schools, outgrowths of the British infant school design; Waldorf schools, inspired by the philosophy of the German educator Rudolf Steiner; multiple intelligence schools, founded on the theories of the Harvard University psychologist Howard Gardner; Paideia schools, established by the philosopher Mortimer Adler; free schools and self-directed education based on the concepts of the Scottish educator Alexander S. Neill; as well as continuous progress schools, schools without walls, and traditional "back-to-basics" schools.

- **Schools that focus on the needs and interests of students:** The vast majority of alternative schools were developed to address the specific needs of children. These alternatives include: teen parent schools, dropout and dropout-prevention schools, schools for expelled or incarcerated students, and schools for the gifted and talented.

- **Schools that focus on career themes and professional relevance:** Career-theme magnet schools complement academic studies with intensive experience in workplace/career settings. These schools, which operate primarily at the secondary level, include: performing arts schools, radio and television broadcasting schools, health professional schools, law/legal schools, science/technology schools, teaching career schools, and dozens of other career-focused educational options as well as academic, disciplinary-focused programs in international studies, multicultural issues, environmental studies, and most of the traditional academic disciplines.

- **Alternatives that focus on experiential learning:** Based on the ideas of the American philosopher John Dewey, many alternative schools in the United States emphasize learning by doing. Examples of these programs include Schools Without Walls, where students learn in banks, businesses, courtrooms, museums, and government agencies rather than in typical school classrooms; Foxfire, where students learn by collecting and publishing the folklore of their region; and Outward Bound/Expeditionary Learning, where students learn through expeditions and experiences in their communities.

- **Alternatives that focus on organization, administration, governance, and funding:** There are also a number of established models for organizing, administering, governing, and funding alternative schooling. These include the stand-alone alternative schools, schools within schools, clusters of alternative schools, complex systems of alternatives, such as those found in Louisville, Kentucky; Houston, Texas; Los Angeles, California; and Vancouver, Washington. In many of these districts, as high as 30 percent of the total student enrollment participate in schools of choice. The most recent type of alternative school, the charter school, which may represent any of the described alternative models, receives a state charter and public funding to operate in a highly autonomous manner.

These models represent the landscape of alternative schools successfully operating as of 2001. No two are exactly alike, as a primal characteristic of these programs is their unique identity. While these schools share the common concepts of alternative programs, their actual operations often vary considerably.

International Alternative Schools

As alternative schools began to appear in the late 1960s in the United States, similar development was occurring around the globe. Jerry Mintz's 1996 book *The Handbook of Alternative Education* identified alternative schooling in twenty-three nations representing the Americas, Europe, the Middle East, Russia, Asia, Australia, Micronesia, and the West Indies. Canada, with 114 programs reported throughout its provinces, clearly held the largest number, as most other countries reported five or fewer programs. Most of the programs identified represented the categories of independent, Montessori, Waldorf, open/choice programs, and schools for at-risk students. While the handbook represents the most recent source for documenting the existence of international alternative schools, many schools undoubtedly were not identified. Denmark, for example, has hundreds of Tvind alternative public schools, and other nations, such as Hong Kong, Brazil, Japan, Russia, and Australia have multiple examples of alternative schools. Charter schools have also begun to appear in other nations, particularly in Canada.

As most countries provide public education through national systems of organization and governance, it is important to note that local control, as is practiced in the United States, clearly appears to foster dramatically higher numbers and types of alternative schools. Yet, as of 2001, interest in and growth of alternative programs and schools in other nations is clearly on the increase. The public demand for choice in schooling appears to be significantly impacting educational systems throughout the world.

Conclusion

Alternative schooling has become an integral component of public education in the United States and is also gaining increasing popularity in many other nations. These developments have evolved from a grassroots effort by parents and educators, experimenting to locate better ways to educate their school-age children and integrate educational ideas from some of the world's most recognized educational leaders. Federal support in the United States of schools of choice has also contributed to the growth of choice programs. Nationally elected officials of the United States, representing their public constituencies, have clearly identified schools of choice as a valued priority. As of 2001 it is clear that alternative schooling, with three decades of development and success, is not only effective in teaching all types of students but is also highly desired by parents and students. It is also obvious that the practices developed in the early schools of choice are contributing to local, state, and national efforts to improve public education in the United States. Based on these realities, the continued growth and expansion of schools of choice is likely to continue.

See also: HOME SCHOOLING; MAGNET SCHOOLS; PRIVATE SCHOOLING; SCHOOL REFORM.

BIBLIOGRAPHY

BARR, ROBERT D., and PARRETT, WILLIAM H. 1997. *How to Create Alternative, Magnet and Charter Schools that Work.* Bloomington, IN: National Education Service.

BARR, ROBERT D., and PARRETT, WILLIAM H. 2001. *Hope Fulfilled for At-Risk and Violent Youth.* Needham Heights, MA: Allyn and Bacon.

COOKSON, PETER W. 1994. *Schools of Choice: The Struggle for the Soul of American Education.* New Haven, CT: Yale University Press.

FINN, CHESTER E., JR.; MANNO, B. V.; and VANOUREIC, G. 2000. *Charter Schools in Action.* Princeton, NJ: Princeton University Press.

FULLER, BRUCE, et al. 1999. *School Choice: Abundant Hopes, Scarce Evidence of Results.* Berkeley: University of California; Stanford, CA: Stanford University, Policy Analysis for California Education (PACE).

GLENN, CHARLES L. 1998. "Public School of Choice: Searching for Direction."*Principal* 77(5):10–12.

HARDY, LAWRENCE. 2000. "Public Schools of Choice," *American School Boards Journal* 187(2):22–26.

MINTZ, JERRY. 1996. *The Handbook of Alternative Education.* New York: Macmillan.

NATHAN, JOE. 1996. *Charter Schools.* San Francisco: Jossey-Bass.

NATHAN, JOE. 2000. "Students Excel in Alternative Learning Settings," *St. Paul (Minnesota) Free Press,* February 28.

RAYWID, MARY ANN. 1983. "Schools of Choice: Their Current Nature and Prospects." *Phi Delta Kappan* 64:684–688.

SMITH, VERNON H.; BARR, ROBERT; and BURKE, D. 1986. *Alternatives in Education.* Bloomington, IN: Phi Delta Kappa.

WEHLAGE, GARY G., et al. 1989. *Reducing the Risk: Schools as Communities of Support.* Philadelphia: Faliner Press.

WILL, GEORGE. 2000. "Straight Talk from Arizona." *Newsweek* 135(76).

INTERNET RESOURCE

ERIC CLEARINGHOUSE ON EDUCATIONAL MANAGEMENT. 1999. "Trends and Issues: School Choice." <http://eric.uoregon.edu/trends_issues/choice/index.html>.

ROBERT D. BARR
WILLIAM H. PARRETT

AMERICAN ACADEMY OF ARTS AND SCIENCES

The American Academy of Arts and Sciences is an international learned society dedicated to the promotion of critical analysis of the important social and intellectual issues of the day through the free exchange of ideas and perspectives. Through its publication, *Daedalus,* as well as its meetings, conferences, and symposia, it strives to develop useful policy initiatives while encouraging the development of new generations of scholars committed to improving the level of social discourse and creating a truly civil society.

Program

The academy brings multidisciplinary, collaborative attention to bear on three major areas of interest: science, technology, and global security; social policy and education; and the humanities and culture. Within these broad areas of interest, a wide range of topics are explored with the goal of achieving practical improvements that will benefit society as a whole.

Organization

The academy is governed by a council consisting of seventeen voting members and six nonvoting, advisory members. The council meets three times annually to set policy and plan initiatives. Although its base of operations remains in Massachusetts, it has two regional centers, one at the University of Chicago and another at the University of California at Irvine. In addition, it maintains affiliations with many of the nation's public and private universities.

Members

From its initial sixty-one members, the academy has grown dramatically. At the end of the twentieth century it had a membership of 3,700 American fellows and 600 international (honorary) fellows. Among these were 160 Nobel laureates and 50 Pulitzer Prize winners. Membership is divided into classes, defined by the intellectual disciplines represented. There are five classes: mathematics and physical sciences; biological sciences; social sciences; humanities and the arts; and public affairs, business, and administration. To become a member, an individual must be nominated by a current member and elected by the academy as a whole. Once exclusively male, the academy inducted its first female member in 1848.

Financial Support

The academy is a private, nonpartisan organization that maintains its independence in order to encourage the free and unfettered exchange of ideas. It receives its funding from individual charitable contributions as well as from grants provided by foundations and public agencies. In addition it receives revenues from the sale of *Daedalus,* a highly respected journal of opinion and policy. Most of its budget is devoted to covering the costs of individual research projects, as well as sponsoring seminars and symposia.

History

During the American Revolution, a group of gentleman scholars gathered together in the city of Cambridge, Massachusetts, to form a scholarly society: the American Academy of Arts and Sciences. Numbering such leaders as John and Samuel Adams, James Bowdoin, and John Hancock among them, the first academy's membership shared the belief that, as "men of genius," they had a duty to their country and their fellow citizens to cultivate the arts and sciences and to spread knowledge of them throughout the populace.

The founders did not believe that a true scholar should remain aloof from the mundane world. Rather, they were convinced that the arts and sciences were fundamental to success in all aspects of life, from agriculture to commerce, architecture to industry. Further, they believed that these pursuits were vital to the happiness, dignity, and advancement of the populace.

Their goal was to create a forum in which intellectuals of all sorts would share their learned insights in order to come up with practical solutions to problems as wide ranging as international affairs, farming and animal husbandry, medicine, and meteorology. Drawing on the example of learned societies in Europe, they foresaw an important role for the "citizen scholar" in the new nation. Through their writings, speeches, and other activities, the early members of the academy were highly successful in spreading new ideas throughout New England's educated class and creating a culture that celebrated the practical application of scholarly knowledge.

At the outset, the academy took special interest in antiquities (archaeology), natural history, mathematics and philosophy, astronomy, meteorology, geography, and advances in medicine. Over time, however, the disciplinary focus of the organization changed, and by the twentieth century the emphasis was placed more squarely on the public service and policymaking aspect of the original charter. Nonetheless, the academy continues to take seriously its goal of mentoring new generations of scholars and honoring scholarly achievement.

Throughout its history, the academy has fulfilled its purpose by facilitating discourse among educated and interested people both in the United States and abroad. The present academy still holds tightly to the founders' conviction that knowledge is best shared, and as a matter of principle insists on the swift publication and wide dissemination of any findings, reports, or data it generates. It remains committed to the belief that the advancement of knowledge can only enhance the strength, welfare, and security of a healthy nation.

INTERNET RESOURCE

AMERICAN ACADEMY OF ARTS AND SCIENCES. 2002. <www.amacad.org>.

JOHN VOSS
Revised by
NANCY E. GRATTON

AMERICAN ALLIANCE FOR HEALTH, PHYSICAL EDUCATION, RECREATION, AND DANCE

The American Alliance for Health, Physical Education, Recreation, and Dance (AAHPERD) is the only voluntary professional organization in the world that brings together teachers, students, administrators, and practitioners in these related fields. AAHPERD's mission is to promote healthy lifestyles by supporting quality programs in health, physical education, recreation, dance, and sports. AAHPERD also strives to provide members with professional development opportunities that improve skills and encourage sound professional practices. Members come from elementary and secondary schools, colleges and universities, dance and sports training centers, health care institutions, and various government and voluntary agencies.

Program

The central concern of AAHPERD is motivating people of all ages to achieve and maintain physical fitness, health, and well-being. Most alliance programs are responses to this concern. Through clinics conducted by master teachers, educators learn new ways of instructing large groups, improvising in the use of inexpensive equipment, and using available space creatively and effectively. AAHPERD programs demonstrate that when young people have opportunities to learn individual sports, as opposed to traditional team sports, they are more likely to build sports activity into their daily regimens and continue it throughout their lives.

The alliance is deeply concerned with the health problems of the day and especially with the way in which teachers may deal more effectively with such problems as accidents, smoking, drug and alcohol abuse, diet and obesity, and sexually transmitted diseases. AAHPERD encourages teachers, parents, and adult leaders to take greater responsibility for educating children and youth about the hazards of smoking, drinking, drug abuse, overeating, and other unhealthy behaviors.

Aware of the need for increased recreation opportunities for urban populations, the alliance has involved its members in planning for recreational facilities and programming sports and physical activities for children and youth in American cities.

Health educators in the alliance are involved with service programs in the inner city, as well as in isolated rural areas.

AAHPERD is particularly concerned with promoting physical fitness and health education in American elementary, middle, and high schools. The alliance supports efforts to improve teacher salaries and to have a greater share of the national income apportioned for school needs. AAHPERD has also taken up such issues as the scheduling of physical education activities, particularly in light of the pressures of academic requirements. Other issues of importance to AAHPERD are the age at which social values can best be taught and the school's responsibility for teaching sex education to students. Another major concern of the alliance is the extent to which the school should be open for activity beyond the traditional school day, week, and year, and the place of sports and athletics in the extended school schedules.

Programs for young people include Jump Rope for Hearts and Hoops for Hearts, which are popular educational fund-raising events sponsored jointly by AAHPERD and the American Heart Association and held in thousands of American elementary and middle schools. These events help raise funds for educational programs that teach students the benefits of physical activity and for medical research and programs that help prevent heart disease and stroke.

AAHPERD also organizes conferences, workshops, and other professional meetings; develops standards for health and physical fitness education; interprets problems and issues to the public; and maintains relationships with organizations and agencies that have similar agendas. The alliance awards scholarships and recognition awards for distinctive contributions to the profession of health and physical fitness education. Through their journals, newsletters, and other publications, AAHPERD facilitates professional exchange and helps disseminate research findings. Publications include the monthly *Journal of Health, Physical Education, Recreation, and Dance;* the monthly *Physical Activity Today,* which offers important research findings about sports, health, and physical fitness; the bimonthly *Strategies* magazine; the *American Journal of Health Education,* a refereed journal for professional health educators and researchers; the *Research Quarterly for Exercise and Sport,* which publishes articles about research in the science of human movement; and *Update,* the alliance's member newsletter.

AAHPERD holds an annual national convention, which includes workshops, conferences, sessions, and activities covering such topics as recreation, lifestyles and fitness, aging, physical education, and dance technology. The convention includes a major exposition where fitness, sporting goods, and publishing companies can exhibit products and services related to the interests of the alliance and its members.

Organizational Structure

AAHPERD is an alliance of six national associations, six geographic district associations, and a research consortium. The district associations are central, eastern, midwestern, northwestern, southern, and southwestern. Each district elects it own officers, including a representative to the national board of directors. There are fifty-three state associations, including those for Puerto Rico, Guam, and the District of Columbia.

The six national associations each represent a special interest area. The National Dance Association (NDA) promotes sound professional practices in dance education. The American Association for Leisure and Recreation (AALR) supports professional recreation practitioners, educators, and students who advance the profession through creative recreation experiences. The American Association for Health Education (AAHE) helps health care professionals promote good health through education. The National Association for Sports and Physical Education (NASPE) promotes professional practices in sports and physical activity through research and dissemination of information to the public. The National Association for Girls and Women in Sports (NAGWS) recommends guidelines and standards for women's athletic programs in colleges and schools and works for gender equity by fighting for equal funding, equal quality, and respect for girls' and women's sports programs. The American Association for Active Lifestyles and Fitness (AAALF) helps educators conduct programs concerning physical activity and fitness. Members of AAHPERD's six national associations who are interested in research can also join the Research Consortium, which provides services and publications in support of alliance research.

A sixteen-member board of governors is the executive arm of the alliance, and as such it initiates and transacts alliance business. Members of the board meet twice a year—in the fall and in the spring. The board is made up of a president, past president, president-elect, and one representative from each of the six associations and six districts.

Committees carry on a large share of the alliance's work and serve as a means by which members throughout the nation assist in planning, recommending policy, and giving direction to alliance programs. AAHPERD maintains twelve standing committees and organizes special committees as the need arises. Each committee is charged with responsibility for some part of the alliance's work.

In addition, some of the AAHPERD headquarters staff are specialists in various aspects of health education and recreation and offer consultation services to members and to national groups. They serve as liaisons with divisions and committees and act as directors of special projects.

Membership and Financial Support

Membership in the alliance is open to all who are professionally engaged in health education, school nursing, safety education, physical education, athletics, recreation, and dance. Students in programs of professional preparation may become members and are entitled to special students rates. Others interested in supporting the alliance's activities may become associate or contributing members. In 2001 AAHPERD served over 26,000 members.

Most of the alliance's funds come from grants for special projects, the sale of professional publications, and membership fees, with a small amount coming from advertising and other miscellaneous sources.

History and Development

The history of the alliance closely parallels the development of physical education as a part of the curriculum in U.S. schools and colleges. In 1885 William Gilbert Anderson, a physical fitness instructor in Brooklyn, New York, invited a group of gymnastics trainers to gather and discuss their profession; this group became the American Association for the Advancement of Physical Education. In 1893 the organization had its first contact with the National Education Association (NEA), when the latter sponsored the International Congress on Education and included physical education and hygiene as a program topic.

In 1903 the organization changed its name to the American Physical Education Association. A committee on women's athletics was formed in 1917, beginning one of the most influential interest groups within the association. In 1937 the association became a department of the NEA, when it merged with the NEA's Department of School Health and Physical Education. A Division of Recreation was established, and in 1938 the name was changed to include this interest area. The National Dance Association became an official AAHPERD association in 1974, and the name changed again to reflect the status of dance in the organization.

INTERNET RESOURCE

American Alliance for Health, Physical Education, Recreation, and Dance. 2002. <www.aahperd.org>.

Carl A. Troester Jr.
Revised by
Judith J. Culligan

AMERICAN ASSOCIATION FOR HIGHER EDUCATION

The American Association for Higher Education (AAHE) is an independent professional membership organization that promotes change and reform in higher education, fosters quality teaching and learning at the college and university level, and promotes public awareness of the value of higher education in the United States. The AAHE's objectives include identifying and analyzing critical problems, trends, and developments in higher education and seeking constructive solutions; helping to coordinate the efforts of educational institutions and agencies at all levels; encouraging the improvement of professional work in all areas of higher education; and developing a better understanding by the general public of higher education and of college teaching as a profession. In pursuing these goals, the AAHE provides a forum for the expression of ideas relating to higher education and public policy.

Program

The AAHE National Conference on Higher Education is the best-known regular activity of the association. Held annually in March, the conference has established itself as a central forum for addressing the most pressing issues facing postsecondary educa-

tion in the United States. Other annual AAHE conferences include the Assessment Conference and the Conference on Faculty Roles and Rewards. The first is sponsored by the AAHE's Assessment Forum, which promotes the development of new and effective approaches to faculty, student, and institutional assessment. The second conference is sponsored by the AAHE Forum on Faculty Roles and Rewards, which was inaugurated in 1991 with the mission of reexamining methods of communicating faculty expectations and evaluating faculty rewards and remuneration.

Since 1993 the AAHE Quality Initiatives program has explored the application of continuous quality improvement principles to postsecondary education. In 1996 the Quality Initiatives program began holding an annual Summer Academy at which teams of six to ten people from up to thirty-five institutions gather to discuss and develop programs to enhance the quality of undergraduate education.

In early 2001 the AAHE launched a major diversity initiative aimed at studying and addressing the impact of race and ethnicity on student choice and learning in higher education. One of the goals of the initiative was to develop strategies for increasing the success of minority college students. In particular, the diversity initiative promoted the importance of including diversity issues in college curriculums and the removal of barriers to the success of minority students.

Other AAHE programs include the Service Learning Project, a two-part initiative that promotes the integration of service learning in all disciplines; the project includes the preparation and publication of an eighteen-volume series addressing community-based learning. The AAHE's Teaching Initiatives program helps institutions improve the effectiveness and status of college-level teaching. AAHE members involved in this initiative work to promote the view that postsecondary teaching is important scholarly work and to generate dialogue about the value and effectiveness of teaching in institutions of higher education.

AAHE publications include the bimonthly *Journal of Higher Education,* a scholarly journal published since 1930, and the bimonthly magazine *Change,* published in conjunction with the Helen Dwight Reid Education Foundation. *Change* features articles on new trends in higher education and analyzes the implications of new educational practices.

The *AAHE Bulletin,* published every month from September through June, is a newsletter for members that features interviews, reports, practical articles, and news about AAHE activities.

In 1991 the AAHE's National Teaching and Learning Forum began a major joint venture with the Educational Resources Information Center (ERIC) Clearinghouse on Higher Education to publish and disseminate important research literature on various topics in higher education. The AAHE also publishes numerous books, monographs, and papers on topics of concern to the higher education community, many in collaboration with other publishers and organizations. In addition to these, special publications are produced in conjunction with current AAHE projects or in areas where a need for additional information has been determined. All AAHE publications are available to the association's members free or at a reduced cost. Some are available electronically via the AAHE website.

Special projects consistent with the AAHE's goals are undertaken with funds from outside sources and through partnerships. Notable among these projects is the Urban Universities Portfolio Project: Assuring Quality for Multiple Publics, a three-year effort begun in 2000 in partnership with Indiana University–Purdue University Indianapolis (IUPUI) and the Pew Charitable Trusts. The Portfolio Project aims at helping urban institutions of higher education create institutional portfolios and innovative auditing processes that can be effectively communicated to the public. Such projects underscore the AAHE's concern for the teaching-learning process as the center toward which a major part of its activities are oriented.

Organizational Structure

The AAHE is governed by a twenty-member board of directors, which is headed by a chair and a chair-elect. Board members are chosen by AAHE members by mail ballot each year. The board establishes policy, determines programs, and appoints committees as needed. The day-to-day operations of the AAHE are overseen by a staff of approximately twenty-five individuals under the direction of an appointed president.

Membership

The AAHE is the only national higher education organization open to faculty, administrators, and students alike, regardless of rank, discipline, or type or size of institution. Its membership is a cross section of the American academic community, including college and university presidents, deans, faculty, counselors, and registrars, as well as representatives from government, business, the media, educational foundations, accrediting agencies, and other organizations concerned with higher education. In 2001 the AAHE had approximately 10,000 members.

History and Development

Founded in 1870, the AAHE was one of four original departments of the National Education Association (NEA). It was then known as the Department of Higher Education. In 1952 the name was changed to the Association for Higher Education, and in 1967 to the American Association for Higher Education. A major turning point in the history of the AAHE occurred in 1968, when it elected to move from a departmental relationship with the NEA to the status of independent organization.

INTERNET RESOURCE

American Association for Higher Education. 2002. <www.aahe.org>.

G. Kerry Smith
Revised by
Judith J. Culligan

AMERICAN ASSOCIATION FOR THE ADVANCEMENT OF SCIENCE

The American Association for the Advancement of Science (AAAS, pronounced *triple-A-S*) is the largest general scientific organization in the world. Its objectives are to further the work of scientists and promote cooperation among them, to foster academic freedom and responsibility, to improve and reform science education, and to encourage and facilitate better understanding about the nature of science, scientific research, and technology.

Programs

From its early years, the AAAS has promoted quality science education for children and adults, and many AAAS programs promote science literacy in schools and in communities. Project 2061, begun in 1985, is a major long-term initiative aimed at helping all

Americans learn more about science, mathematics, and technology. One of Project 2061's main goals is the reformation of the American kindergarten through twelfth grade science, mathematics, and technology curriculum. In 1989 Project 2061 released its influential publication *Science for All Americans,* which established guidelines for what American students need to know about science, mathematics, and technology by the time they graduate from high school.

The AAAS's Directorate for Education and Human Resources also works for science education reform through fifty programs and a wide variety of publications. Among its many programs, the directorate produces a weekly half-hour radio program called *Kinetic City Super Crew.* The program features a team of resourceful children chasing adventures and solving problems using science. Other radio programs, including *Science Update* and *Why Is It?* draw young people into science with interesting jargon-free science stories.

At the adult level the AAAS produces or sponsors a number of radio and television programs about science. In 1992 the AAAS and the National Institute on Drug Abuse launched the Science Plus Literacy for Health Drug Education Project to create materials for use in adult science literacy programs and community-based adult substance abuse and mental health education programs.

The AAAS's Directorate for International Programs promotes international scientific cooperation and fosters the potential of science and technology to solve many challenges facing the global community, especially those involving health and the environment. The Directorate for International Programs also works to strengthen the role and status of engineers and scientists in developing countries.

Among scientists, AAAS is best known for its large annual scientific meeting, which is devoted to the discussion of research topics and problems in all branches of science. The organization is also known for its weekly magazine, *Science,* an international journal that offers rapid publication of new research findings, as well as analyses of social, governmental, and educational policies and trends of interest to scientists and science teachers. The journal is popular with members and nonmembers alike.

The AAAS annually makes awards for excellent science writing in newspapers and magazines of general circulation. Other annual AAAS awards include the Philip Hauge Abelson Prize, the Scientific Freedom and Responsibility Award, the Award for International Scientific Cooperation, the Award for Public Understanding of Science and Technology, the Newcomb Cleveland Prize, and the Mentor Prize. All awards are presented at the annual national meeting.

Organizational Structure

The AAAS is divided into twenty-four sections, each organized in an area of special interest, including agriculture, astronomy, biology, chemistry, engineering, linguistics, mathematics, medicine, psychology, physics, and zoology. The AAAS also includes sections covering the history and philosophy of science and the economic, social, and political sciences. Four regional divisions (Arctic, Caribbean, Pacific and Southwestern, and Rocky Mountain) each hold annual meetings, manage their own affairs independently, elect their own officers, and carry out other regional activities.

Affiliated with AAAS are 273 national and regional organizations in pure and applied science, including 226 scientific societies and forty-seven academies of science. Affiliates include such diverse organizations as the American Ethnological Society, the American Chemical Society, the American Ornithologists Union, the Institute of Food Technologists, the National Marine Educators Association, the Linguistic Society of America, the American Nuclear Society, and the Poultry Science Association. Each affiliate is entirely responsible for managing its own affairs. The AAAS maintains a special relationship with its forty-seven affiliate academies, because they, like the AAAS, cover many fields of science and in this sense take on the role of AAAS local branches.

The AAAS board of directors, elected annually by members for one-year terms, conducts association affairs. The board is headed by a chairperson, a president, and a president-elect. An eighty-three-member council meets annually to discuss and establish the association's general governing policies.

Membership and Financial Support

Membership is open to any interested persons, especially working scientists, engineers, science educators, policymakers, and undergraduate and post-doctoral students in any scientific field. The activities of the association are financed by dues, advertising, nonmember subscriptions to *Science,* the sale of other association publications, and registration fees at the annual meeting. Additional activities, such as the development of materials for teaching science in the elementary grades, are supported by grants from private foundations or government agencies interested in science and science education.

History and Development

The AAAS was founded at the library of the Academy of Natural Sciences in Philadelphia, Pennsylvania, on September 20, 1848. The eighty-seven scientists who gathered that day were members of the Association of American Geologists and Naturalists who wished to form a new organization called the American Association for the Advancement of Science. In its wide coverage and membership and in its interest in science education and the public understanding of science, as well as in scientific research, the new AAAS was to a large extent patterned after the British Association for the Advancement of Science. Most early members were scientists or engineers, but some, notably U.S. President Millard Fillmore and author Henry David Thoreau, were laypeople who were interested in science. The first woman to become a member was astronomer Maria Mitchell, who joined in 1850. The AAAS began publishing the journal *Science* (first published by Thomas Edison beginning in 1880) in 1883, and many leading scientists of the following decades, including Edmund B. Wilson, Thomas Hunt Morgan, Albert Einstein, and Edwin Hubble published articles in the journal.

In the years since 1848, the association has grown to include some 138,000 members worldwide. The AAAS has attracted to membership most of the leading scientists of the day. Among the distinguished men and women who have served as presidents have been zoologist and geologist Louis Agassiz, botanist Asa Gray, astronomer Simon Newcomb, geologist John Wesley Powell, mathematician Mina Rees, anthropologist Margaret Mead, physicist Leon Lederman, paleontologist Stephen Jay Gould, and chemist Mary L. Good. The association has always included scientists of great distinction, but it has also maintained its basic and original character of a general scientific society open to any person interested in science.

BIBLIOGRAPHY

KOHLSTEDT, SALLY GREGORY; LEWENSTEIN, BRUCE; and SOKAL, MICHAEL, eds. 1999. *Establishment of Science in America: 150 Years of the American Association for the Advancement of Science.* New Brunswick, NJ: Rutgers University Press.

WOLFLE, DAEL LEE. 1989. *Renewing a Scientific Society: The American Association for the Advancement of Science from World War II to 1970.* Washington, DC: American Association for the Advancement of Science.

INTERNET RESOURCE

AMERICAN ASSOCIATION FOR THE ADVANCEMENT OF SCIENCE. 2002. <www.aaas.org>.

DAEL WOLFLE
Revised by
JUDITH J. CULLIGAN

AMERICAN ASSOCIATION OF COLLEGES FOR TEACHER EDUCATION

The American Association of Colleges for Teacher Education (AACTE), formally established in 1948, exists to enhance the condition and improve the quality of education schools in the nation's colleges and universities.

Program

With offices in Washington, D.C., AACTE serves as the voice for its members at the national and federal level. Always seeking to strengthen teacher and principal preparation programs, AACTE works with its members to help them strengthen their offerings, build partnerships with their local pre-K–12 schools, find leadership for their programs, influence their state legislatures, work with the media, and carry out research and many other tasks.

AACTE's Governmental Relations unit seeks to influence federal policy regarding teacher education issues and also spends time tracking and analyzing federal and state education legislation for AACTE member institutions.

AACTE's Professional Development unit operates a busy schedule of conferences, workshops, and institutes throughout the year to help member institutions become better preparers of school professionals. The AACTE Annual Meeting attracts over twenty-five hundred participants who share the latest teacher education research, policy, and practices and build contacts with other members. This department also oversees the association's publications, producing several books, monographs, and articles each year as well as a biweekly newsletter. The department also coordinates contracts and communications with the member-editors and publisher of the *Journal of Teacher Education,* the field's premier journal.

The Professional Issues unit serves as the association's liaison to groups involved with accreditation, academic standards, service learning, and many other issues affecting teacher education. This department offers both professional development and technical assistance to member institutions in many of these areas.

The Research and Information unit conducts an array of research and activities, and runs several grant-funded projects on issues such as culturally responsive practice and HIV/AIDS prevention education. It administers the Professional Education Data System, an annual survey of member institutions conducted jointly by AACTE and the National Council for Accreditation of Teacher Education. This department also houses the ERIC Clearinghouse on Teaching and Teacher Education.

These four programmatic departments at AACTE are supported by Finance and Administration and Executive Office functions. In addition to its staff, the association has several standing committees, special study groups, and focus councils comprising individuals from member institutions. These groups delve into issues such as special education, multicultural issues, reading, and technology to inform the board, staff, and membership of the specific concerns and topics facing teacher education.

Organizational Structure

AACTE is governed by a twenty-two person board of directors, drawn from member institutions and is run by a staff of nearly fifty professionals and managers. The president and CEO of AACTE works closely with the chair of the board of directors to carry out the association's agenda. Each member institution is allotted a certain number of institutional representatives, based on the size of its education program, to receive member benefits and to vote on issues brought before the membership at the annual business meeting. There is also a chapter of AACTE in almost every state that works on education issues

specific to the region. State chapters also inform the national discussion through an annual meeting of their elected leaders.

Membership and Financial Support

Comprising over 760 colleges and universities, AACTE's members are accredited four-year colleges and universities with education programs. In the first years of the twenty-first century, the association is seeking to expand its membership to include nontraditional providers of teacher preparation, such as for-profit, online, and other organizations. The association's activities are supported by the dues its members pay, based on the size of their education programs, and the grants it receives for special projects.

INTERNET RESOURCE

AMERICAN ASSOCIATION OF COLLEGES FOR TEACHER EDUCATION. 2002. <www.aacte.org>.

DAVID G. IMIG

AMERICAN ASSOCIATION OF COLLEGES OF PHARMACY

The American Association of Colleges of Pharmacy (AACP) is a nonprofit, national organization representing pharmaceutical education in the United States. Its mission is to serve its member colleges and schools and their respective faculties by acting as their advocate and spokesperson at the national level, by providing forums for interaction and exchange of information among its members, by recognizing outstanding performance among its member educators, and by assisting member colleges and schools in meeting their mission of educating and training pharmacists and pharmaceutical scientists.

The association was established in 1900 with twenty-one member colleges. At that time, the typical pharmacy program was a two-year course of study, and most schools admitted students with only a grammar or elementary school education. As of 2001 the association comprised eighty-two colleges and schools with pharmacy degree programs accredited by the American Council on Pharmaceutical Education. The doctor of pharmacy degree (Pharm.D.), a four-year professional degree program following a minimum of two years of pre-professional college study, is the predominant degree granted and is consistent with the profession's support of a single professional degree program. Students who successfully complete the requirements for a professional degree must also pass a state licensing examination in order to engage in professional practice.

All accredited U.S. colleges and schools of pharmacy are regular institutional members of AACP. Each regular member has two votes in the AACP House of Delegates (one representing the school's faculty voting in the Council of Faculties and the other representing the school's administration voting in the Council of Deans). Faculty may also be individual members of AACP, entitling them to receive a number of services and to participate in the various activities of the association. Nearly two-thirds of all full-time faculty choose to become members of AACP, a high percentage of individual membership for a national organization. The AACP enjoys the widespread support of the community it represents, and there is a high degree of faculty participation in association committees, academic sections, and special-interest groups. Several publications and reports are among the benefits of membership in AACP. The *American Journal of Pharmaceutical Education* is an internationally distributed quarterly publication devoted to communication among pharmaceutical educators. The *AACP News,* a monthly publication, provides current information on issues, events, and employment opportunities in pharmaceutical education. The annual *Roster of Faculty and Professional Staff* is a tool for locating and communicating with fellow educators in pharmacy schools across the country. The *Profile of Pharmacy Faculty* is an annual report that provides a summary of demographics, teaching discipline, rank, highest degree earned, tenure status, type of appointment, and compensation. Other annual research reports, such as the *Profile of Pharmacy Students* and the *Pharmacy College Admission Requirements,* are available for purchase by individual members of AACP.

The association is structured as a democratic organization with decision-making vested in a house of delegates, a board of directors, and the executive vice president. The house of delegates meets annually and generally considers issues of major policy. The board of directors consists of three presidential officers, three representatives of school administrations,

three representatives of school faculties, one representative of academic disciplines, and the executive vice president. The board generally meets three times per year to authorize policy and program implementation and to consider significant matters related to the operational and financial affairs of the association. The executive vice president is selected and employed by the board of directors as the chief executive officer of the association, with overall responsibility for the administration of the policies and programs adopted by the house of delegates and the board of directors. The executive vice president, who is responsible for all actions taken by staff members on the association's behalf, appoints the association's staff.

BIBLIOGRAPHY

BUERKI, ROBERT A. 1999. *In Search of Excellence—The First Century of the American Association of Colleges of Pharmacy.* Durham, NC: Litho Industries.

INTERNET RESOURCE

AMERICAN ASSOCIATION OF COLLEGES OF PHARMACY. 2002. <www.aacp.org>.

RICHARD P. PENNA

AMERICAN ASSOCIATION OF COMMUNITY COLLEGES

The American Association of Community Colleges (AACC), a nonprofit, advocacy organization, represents more than 1,100 two-year, associate degree-granting, public and private, community, junior, and technical institutions with more than 10 million students from diverse age groups and a variety of socioeconomic, racial, and ethnic backgrounds. The AACC serves as the national voice for its member institutions and works with other higher education associations, the federal government, and national organizations to promote the goals of community colleges in particular and higher education in general. The association cites its mission as "providing a national focus agenda that promotes, supports, and advances the cause of its member colleges." Its leadership is exercised through involvement in federal policy initiatives, advocating its national agenda externally and internally, doing research on community college issues, supporting educational services that promote professional growth, and building coordination with related-interest groups.

History of the Association

The founding of the association was a critical event in the early history of the two-year college movement. The American Association of Junior Colleges (AAJC) was founded in 1920 when Philander Claxton, U.S. commissioner of education, and George Zook, higher education specialist, brought together thirty-four junior college representatives in St. Louis, Missouri. As Michael Brick noted in his 1964 study, these represented the fledging but rapidly expanding and unique American junior college system, which emerged at the turn of the century to offer the first two years of university course work and later added occupational courses. Although it was expected that the AAJC would function as an accrediting body for the increasing number of junior colleges, be a forum for addressing issues, and serve as a source of mutual support among institutions, it did lead to the forging of a common identity and provided a forum for discussing the proper role and organization of junior colleges within higher education.

The association has grown significantly since 1920. In the early twenty-first century it is governed by a thirty-two-member board of directors, has twenty-one affiliate councils, and seven commissions. There have been seven chief executives, beginning with the appointment in 1922 of Doak S. Campbell, a former professor at George Peabody College and a junior college president, as executive secretary. The AAJC acquired greater national stature with the selection in 1938 of Walter Crosby Eells, a Stanford professor, who assumed the full-time position and relocated the organization to Washington, D.C. Succeeding Eells were former junior and community college presidents Jesse Bogue in 1946; Edmund J. Gleazer Jr., as executive director, in 1958; Dale Parnell, as president, in 1981; David Pierce in 1991; and George R. Boggs in 2000.

In 1930 the association began its own journal, with Eells as editor, which evolved into the *Community College Journal*. In the 1980s it established its own Community College Press and began the *Community College Times,* a biweekly newspaper, and the legislative brief *AACC Letter*. With the creation of an Internet site in the mid-1990s, book publications, reports, press releases, policy briefs, national and state

enrollment, and other data became available via that medium. Continued since the 1920s, the annual conference has evolved to focus on seminars for aspiring and new presidents, session presentations by researchers and practitioners, recognition of current and noted former outstanding community college students, and meetings of affiliated councils. In April 2001, at its annual meeting in Chicago, Illinois, the AACC celebrated 100 years of the existence of American community colleges by honoring the oldest continuous two-year college, Joliet Junior College, founded in 1901 in Joliet, Illinois.

As the number of two-year colleges grew and membership increased, the association underwent several name changes. These occurred after two phenomenal growth periods. One growth period occurred after World War II due to the combined effects of the return of thousands of military personnel, the enactment of the Servicemen's Readjustment Act in 1944 (G.I. Bill of Rights), and the release of President Truman's Commission on Higher Education Report in 1947, *Higher Education for American Democracy*. The Truman Report, as it became known, called for expanding educational opportunity to veterans, women, and low-income individuals; preparing students for lives of citizenship and work through a series of terminal degree programs; and renaming these institutions community colleges to reflect their responsiveness to their local communities. The latter suggestion, however, did not become popular until the 1960s.

Leland Medsker and Dale Tillery, in a 1971 study, described how the next enormous growth period followed the civil rights movement in the 1960s, when community colleges with their open access admissions policies grew more rapidly than any other segment of higher education. The creation of financial aid under the Higher Education Act of 1965, supported by the association, greatly accelerated educational access. Community college enrollments more than tripled between 1960 and 1970, as older people, women, people of diverse racial and ethnic backgrounds, veterans, people with disabilities, and low-income individuals went to college for the first time. As the U.S. Bureau of the Census's statistics show, this growth occurred almost entirely in the two-year public sector, enrolling 95 percent of all college students.

After more than fifty years as the American Association of Junior Colleges, the organization became the American Association of Junior and

Community Colleges (AACJC) in 1972 to reflect the increasing name shift to community colleges and the highly expanded mission of technical and vocational education. In 1992 the AACJC became the American Association of Community Colleges, recognizing that its member institutions now referred to themselves almost exclusively as community colleges.

The Twenty-First-Century Community College

After a century of evolution of the junior college into the community college and over eighty years as an association, the AACC has gone from representing thirty-four institutions to more than 1,100 public and independent, comprehensive, and technical institutions in the twenty-first century. These institutions promote educational opportunity and access to college; offer lower, affordable tuition; and provide varied curricula for students of all ages. Curricular offerings include articulated transfer courses leading to the bachelor's degree; state-of-the-art technical and vocational certificate and associate degree programs leading directly to employment; contracted special skills courses for business and industry; noncredit adult education courses in basic literacy skills, General Educational Development (GED), English as a second language (ESL), and citizenship; concurrent enrollment courses for high school students; service-learning and school-to-work internship opportunities; innovative distance-learning options; continuing education programs; community development service programs; and partnership programs with four-year institutions, such as teacher preparation.

Community colleges also provide professional academic and career guidance; a range of financial assistance; many academic and student support services; flexible day, evening, off-campus, and weekend class meeting times; and distance-learning courses to accommodate diverse scheduling needs. Located in urban, suburban, and rural areas to serve local constituents, community colleges vary widely in their size, type, organization, and governance, from affiliation with state universities to multicampus districts and single institutions with locally elected governing boards. As of 2000, approximately one-third of all higher education institutions were community colleges, nearly half of all undergraduates were community college students, and almost two-thirds of them were from diverse racial and ethnic backgrounds. Thus, the AACC represents a highly diversified and still-changing constituency.

See also: COMMUNITY COLLEGES; STUDENT SERVICES, *subentry on* COMMUNITY COLLEGES.

BIBLIOGRAPHY

BRICK, MICHAEL. 1964. *Forum and Focus for the Junior College Movement.* New York: Bureau of Publications, Teachers College, Columbia University.

BRINT, STEVEN, and KARABEL, JEROME. 1989. *The Diverted Dream: Community Colleges and the Promise of Educational Opportunity in America, 1900–1985.* New York: Oxford University Press.

DIENER, THOMAS. 1986. *Growth of An American Invention: A Documentary History of the Junior and Community College Movement.* New York: Greenwood Press.

GOODWIN, GREGORY. 1971. "The Historical Development of the Community-Junior College Ideology." Ph.D. diss., University of Illinois.

MEDSKER, LELAND, and TILLERY, DALE. 1971. *Breaking the Access Barrier.* New York: McGraw-Hill.

U.S. BUREAU OF THE CENSUS. 1975. *Historical Statistics of the United States: Colonial Times to 1970.* Washington, DC: U.S. Government Printing Office.

VAUGHAN, GEORGE B. 2000. *The Community College Story.* Washington, DC: Community College Press.

WILDS, DEBORAH J. 2000. *Minorities in Higher Education 1999–2000. Seventeenth Annual Status Report.* Washington, DC: American Council on Education.

INTERNET RESOURCE

AMERICAN ASSOCIATION OF COMMUNITY COLLEGES. 2002. <www.aacc.nche.edu>.

BERTA VIGIL LADEN

AMERICAN ASSOCIATION OF PHYSICS TEACHERS

The fundamental objectives of the American Association of Physics Teachers (AAPT) are the advancement of the teaching of physics and the furtherance of the role of physics in our culture. The association serves as the spokesperson for physics teachers at all levels of education and welcomes to membership all physicists who are interested in education.

Program

The AAPT is one of the founding-member societies of the American Institute of Physics (AIP) and elects five members to the AIP government board. The AAPT also works closely with the American Physical Society (APS). There is close cooperation among the three organizations in educational programs. Some projects, such as the Physics Teacher Education Coalition (PhysTEC) and the National Task Force on Undergraduate Physics, are conducted jointly by the AAPT, the AIP, and the APS.

The AAPT publishes two journals, *The Physics Teacher,* published nine times per year, and the monthly *American Journal of Physics.* The AAPT also publishes the quarterly *Announcer,* which addresses association news and issues. In addition, the AAPT maintains the "Physical Sciences Resource Center," a website that provides resources and materials useful for teaching physics and astronomy in elementary, middle, and high schools.

The AAPT also gives several awards. The annual Oersted Medal, which recognizes notable contributions to the teaching of physics, is the association's most prestigious award. The annual Millikan Medal is awarded to a man or woman who has made creative contributions to the teaching of physics; the recipient of this medal gives the Robert A. Millikan Lectures at the AAPT's summer meeting. At the winter meeting another lecture, the Richtmeyer Memorial Lecture, is given by a selected member of the physics community. Other AAPT awards include the Klopsteg Memorial Lecture, the Excellence in Undergraduate Physics Teaching Award, the Excellence in Pre-College Physics Teaching Award, and the AAPT Distinguished Service Citation. The citation is given to four to six people each year. Past AAPT award winners have included Carl Sagan, Shirley Anne Jackson, Murray Gell-Mann, Enrico Fermi, and Richard P. Feynman.

The AAPT also awards numerous grants, endowments, and scholarships, and sponsors various workshops, conferences, task forces, competitions, and contests related to the study of physics.

Organizational Structure

The AAPT is made up of forty-six sections representing parts of the United States, Canada, and Puerto Rico. Each section elects its own president and board of officers. The national association is governed by a president and a president-elect, who serve one-year terms, and a secretary and a treasurer, who serve two-year terms.

Membership

The AAPT offers the following categories of individual membership: regular, junior (students), emeritus, and honorary. Members of AAPT include physics teachers in universities, colleges, and high schools; graduate and undergraduate students enrolled full-time in accredited degree-granting programs; and scientists in industrial and government laboratories. Industrial organizations interested in improving the teaching of physics join the association as sustaining members.

History and Development

The AAPT was organized in December 1930 by a vigorous and influential group of physicists. In 1958 the association was incorporated under the laws of the state of New York, and in 1959 it was granted tax-free status. Starting with forty-two members in 1930, the organization has now grown to a membership of thousands.

BIBLIOGRAPHY

FRENCH, A. P., and GREENSLADE, THOMAS B., eds. 1995. *Physics History from AAPT Journals II.* College Park, MD: American Association of Physics Teachers.

NEWELL-PHILLIPS, MELBA, ed. 1985. *Physics History from AAPT Journals.* College Park, MD: American Association of Physics Teachers.

INTERNET RESOURCE

AMERICAN ASSOCIATION OF PHYSICS TEACHERS. 2002. <www.aapt.org>.

MARK W. ZEMANSKY
Revised by
JUDITH J. CULLIGAN

AMERICAN ASSOCIATION OF SCHOOL ADMINISTRATORS

The American Association of School Administrators (AASA) was founded in 1865. AASA is the professional organization for more than 14,000 educational leaders across America and in many other countries. Its members are superintendents of public school systems, assistant and associate superintendents, principals, graduate students, and professors of educational administration, as well as others interested in educational leadership.

Purpose

AASA's mission is to support and develop effective school system leaders who are dedicated to the highest quality public education for all children. The four major focus areas for AASA are:

- Improving the condition of children and youth
- Preparing schools and school systems for the twenty-first century
- Connecting schools and communities
- Enhancing the quality and effectiveness of school leaders

The organization, with a staff of fifty, is one of elementary and secondary education's long-standing professional organizations.

Publications and Programs

AASA publishes a monthly magazine, *The School Administrator,* featuring articles and interviews on leadership, technology, and educational trends and issues. AASA's president, executive director, and guest columnist offer commentary in monthly columns. Its Internet site is a resource for administrators, graduate students, teachers, and members of the public seeking information about education in the news, policy and practice, legislation, and AASA activities.

Other publications include *School Governance and Leadership,* published for superintendents and school boards; the *AASA Bulletin,* a supplement to *The School Administrator;* and a variety of titles published in cooperation with Scarecrow Education.

The National Conference on Education, held annually, attracts more than 10,000 school system leaders, school board members, professors, and more than 350 exhibitors to its program sessions and exposition. Other conferences and seminars are held throughout the year for rural and suburban school system leaders, women administrators, and the officers and staff of AASA's chartered affiliates.

Governance

AASA is governed by an elected executive committee of twelve members, elected by the membership for three-year terms. The president appoints one member to the executive committee. The membership annually elects a president-elect, who serves a three-year sequence of one year as president-elect, then president, and immediate past president. The delegate assembly, comprising members from every state, meets annually to adopt resolutions that help determine the policy and action agendas for the association.

Membership

Active membership in AASA is open to anyone employed in school district administration; associate, college professor, graduate student, and retired memberships are also available. As of 2001 the total membership exceeded 14,000. Financial support comes from membership dues, publication sales, conference registrations and exhibits, sponsorships, and federal and private foundation funding for specific programs.

Influence

AASA maintains an active presence on Capitol Hill, effectively lobbying the U.S. House of Representatives and Senate on behalf of its members. The association has been active in advocating for increased funding and resources for schools serving large numbers of poor children; for additional funding for small, rural schools; and for full funding for special education provisions. The Legislative Corps, a grassroots-based communications network of AASA members who agree to respond to e-mail alerts by contacting their legislators, extends the influence of the government relations effort through messages from local administrators to their representatives in Washington, D.C.

AASA seeks to improve the preparation and skills of school system leaders through reform of educational-leadership preparation programs and improvement of the conditions surrounding the superintendency. Through leadership of the National Policy Board of Educational Administration and other programs, the association works to ensure that preparation programs are redesigned to meet the current needs of school systems and their leaders. AASA collaborates with other professional organizations to better inform the public about the accomplishments of public school systems and to build support for improved educational opportunity for all students.

History

AASA is a nonprofit association that was organized in 1865 by state and city school superintendents attending a meeting of the National Teachers' Association in Pennsylvania. At its first meeting in 1866 the group adopted the name National Association of School Superintendents. In 1870 the association became the Department of School Superintendence within the National Education Association. The association was part of the National Education Association until 1973, when it became an autonomous organization.

See also: EDUCATIONAL LEADERSHIP.

INTERNET RESOURCE

AMERICAN ASSOCIATION OF SCHOOL ADMINISTRATORS. 2002. <www.aasa.org>.

PAUL D. HOUSTON

AMERICAN ASSOCIATION OF STATE COLLEGES AND UNIVERSITIES

The American Association of State Colleges and Universities (AASCU) is a Washington, D.C.-based organization whose more than 430 members include U.S. public colleges, universities, and thirty systems of higher education. More than half of the students in public four-year institutions in America are enrolled in colleges and universities that belong to AASCU. According to the AASCU website, as of 2001 more than one-third of the bachelor's degrees, more than one-quarter of the master's degrees, and almost 10 percent of the doctorates in the United States have been awarded by AASCU members.

AASCU's basic aims are to increase knowledge of the importance of public higher education in the United States and to identify the distinctive contributions of AASCU institutions. The association operates through a series of commissions, committees, and task forces in which the membership's chancellors and presidents participate in discussions and take action on the major issues in higher education. AASCU aids its members in building academic quality, intellectual diversity, and academic freedom. The mission of AASCU is supported by a structure of operating divisions. For example, the association's Division of Government Relations and Policy Analysis monitors and analyzes public policy relating to higher education and acts as an advocate for its members in policy matters at the national, state, and campus levels. Within the division, Federal Relations and Policy Analysis lobbies for AASCU members, keeps the membership informed on current legislative proposals, and arranges for presidents and chancellors to testify before congressional committees. State Relations and Policy Analysis looks at affairs at the state level and keeps the membership informed through "EdLines," a weekly online news service; the annual *State Issues Digest;* and the *State Issues Network.* The subdivision of State Relations is cosponsor of an annual State Relations conference. AASCU has an Office of Urban and Metropolitan Programs, which maintains an information clearinghouse and acts as an advocate for urban institutions. The association has an Office of Rural Programs, which represents the interests of rural institutions of higher education and aids these institutions in revitalizing rural America.

The Division of Academic Leadership and Change deals with academic program issues. Its Office of Teacher Education seeks, through collaborative efforts, to improve teacher preparation. An International Education Office promotes AASCU members' participation in international education. There is also an Office for the Advancement of Public Black Colleges (OAPBC), cosponsored with the National Association of State Universities and Land Grant Colleges (NASULGC), which advocates the advancement of historically black public colleges and universities.

AASCU has two national conferences each year—a summer council, held in July, which brings together college and university presidents and their families for professional development, and an annual meeting in November for discussions of national higher education policy issues. The organization makes available professional development and support for member chief executive officers and their spouses. The spouse program provides an opportunity for presidents' spouses to meet during the national meetings. A spouse-mentoring program assists the spouses of new presidents and chancellors.

The association has a history of advocating low tuition and equal opportunity. It aids its institutions in finding ways to increase access to higher education for historically underrepresented and financially disadvantaged students, and it helps colleges and universities promote diversity. AASCU's president is a member of the small group of higher education associations that meets informally once a week to discuss issues of common interest, particularly in relation to federal legislation that affects their members. This group, often identified as the Big Six, represents the major types of higher education institutions in the United States. AASCU's membership overlaps with the NASULGC and the American Association of Community Colleges (AACC), and these three often find common ground for cooperation on federal policy, promoting low tuition, and exploring state and urban issues.

One of the major associations representing public higher education, AASCU was created in response to the rapid expansion of a higher education sector in the 1960s and 1970s that was underrepresented nationally: comprehensive state universities, many of which had been teachers' colleges; municipal universities; agricultural schools; institutes of technology; and four-year institutions that had been community colleges.

See also: AMERICAN ASSOCIATION OF COMMUNITY COLLEGES; AMERICAN COUNCIL ON EDUCATION; ASSOCIATION OF AMERICAN COLLEGES AND UNIVERSITIES; NATIONAL ASSOCIATION OF STATE UNIVERSITIES AND LAND-GRANT COLLEGES.

BIBLIOGRAPHY

AMERICAN ASSOCIATION OF STATE COLLEGES AND UNIVERSITIES. *File No. 994.* Washington, DC: AASCU Division of Academic Leadership and Change.

BLOLAND, HARLAND G. 1985. "Associations in Action: The Washington, D.C. Higher Education Community." *ASHE-ERIC Higher Education Report No. 2.* Washington, DC: Association for the Study of Higher Education.

COOK, CONSTANCE EWING. 1998. *Lobbying for Higher Education: How Colleges and Universities Influence Federal Policy.* Nashville, TN: Vanderbilt University Press.

INTERNET RESOURCE

AMERICAN ASSOCIATION OF STATE COLLEGES AND UNIVERSITIES. 2002. <www.aascu.org>.

HARLAND G. BLOLAND

AMERICAN ASSOCIATION OF UNIVERSITY PROFESSORS

The American Association of University Professors (AAUP) held its first meeting in 1915, in response to a 1914 call by a committee of full professors at Johns Hopkins university to organize a national association of professors. Concerned about the faculty role in college and university decision-making, the committee members made clear that the new organization was to serve university professors in ways parallel to the ways that the American Medical Association served doctors and the American Bar Association served lawyers, and the AAUP addressed many professorial concerns in its early years. The most pressing concern was academic freedom; although, according to the association's first president, John Dewey, academic freedom issues were thrust upon the organization.

The first academic freedom investigations, at the University of Utah and the University of Colorado, where the presidents had dismissed faculty members, set the precedent for future AAUP investigations, focusing on the reform of institutional practices and procedures. The association representatives negotiated with all of the parties involved (including dismissed professors not qualified for AAUP membership, administrators, and trustees) and the association published all of the evidence. The first AAUP report on the principles of academic freedom and academic tenure was the 1915 *General Declaration of Principles and Practical Proposals.* The report served as the basis for a 1925 conference on academic freedom that resulted in a code of academic freedom, the 1925 *Conference Statement on Academic Freedom and Tenure.* By 1930 the association recognized that it needed a method to inform professors, administrators, trustees, students, and even the general public when colleges and universities failed to meet the standards of academic freedom and tenure. In 1931 association members agreed to publish a list of such institutions, institutions that in 1938 became known as *censured* colleges and universities. The

AAUP still uses this method of highlighting the most intransigent administrations and governing boards.

The AAUP appointed its first full-time general secretary, Ralph E. Himstead, in 1935. Himstead was influential in the negotiations between the AAUP and the Association of American Colleges (AAC) dealing with a revision of the 1925 *Conference Statement,* insisting upon implementation of a maximum acceptable probationary period of seven years for professors in tenure-track positions. These negotiations resulted in the 1940 *Statement of Principles on Academic Freedom and Tenure,* which the AAUP continues to use, and the association has secured endorsement of the statement by a wide range of education associations.

AAUP Committees

From its beginning the AAUP has designated its standing committees by letter—including Committee A for academic freedom, Committee T for governance issues, and Committee Z for salary concerns. Association concerns about professors' economic conditions began in 1916 when it negotiated with representatives of the Carnegie Foundation for the Advancement of Teaching to determine the future of a rapidly decreasing pension fund for professors. In 1920 Committee T presented the results of the first AAUP survey of faculty participation in institutional governance, concluding that extensive faculty participation was rare. Subsequent Committee T reports in the 1920s and 1930s reiterated that finding.

Post–World War II Activities

In the decade following the end of World War II, the AAUP began a period of inaction, especially in the area of investigations of alleged violations of academic freedom. The association did not publish any investigations of alleged violations of academic freedom and tenure from the summer of 1949 until the spring of 1956, even though professors were under attack. Senator Joseph P. McCarthy was the primary force in these attacks, but requirements such as loyalty oaths for faculties and trustees' condemnations of irreligious professors went far beyond McCarthy's work in the United States Senate. The AAUP leadership feared the consequences of investigating the attacks, and the association offered no defense of beleaguered professors.

General Secretary Himstead died in 1955, and he was replaced by Ralph F. Fuchs. Fuchs accelerated the removal of the backlog of Committee A cases by appointing a special committee to report on academic freedom cases arising since 1948. The committee exercised considerable caution in its 1956 report in response to still powerful anti-Communist sentiments; the report also signaled, however, a renewed AAUP commitment to academic freedom principles. William P. Fidler became the AAUP's general secretary in 1958, a position he would hold until 1967. The AAUP enjoyed considerable success while Fidler was general secretary, expanding its programs in a variety of areas.

In 1958 Committee Z began a remarkable program to address members' concerns about their low salaries and benefits. The committee began not only to survey colleges and universities to determine institutions' salary scales for professors, it also began grading the salary scales. This program continued until the 1980s, and the AAUP continues to publish an annual report of professors' salaries at most U.S. colleges and universities.

Also in 1958 Committee T began to develop a revision of a statement of principles on faculty-administration relationships that had first been presented in 1937. In the early 1960s the committee began negotiating with representatives of the AAC and the American Council on Education in order to develop a statement on governance. In 1966 the AAUP approved its *Statement on College and University Government,* a statement soon endorsed by the AAC, the American Council on Education, and the Association of Governing Boards of Universities and Colleges. The statement espoused a cooperative approach to governance, arguing that governing boards and administrations, faculties, and students all had important responsibilities in the operations and policies of colleges and universities.

The association initially expressed an interest in legal proceedings with the 1958 decision to file an *amicus curiae* brief in a United States Supreme Court case (*Barenblatt v. United States,* 360 U.S. 109, June 8, 1959) on academic freedom. In 1954 Professor Barenblatt refused to answer some questions, on the basis of the First Amendment, at a hearing of a subcommittee of the House Un-American Activities Committee. Although the Court used AAUP arguments to sustain a decision contrary to the association's arguments (the Court upheld Barenblatt's conviction for contempt of the United States Congress), the association had developed another means of addressing faculty concerns. Since then the AAUP has often filed briefs in court cases, typically in support of professors' grievances.

By 1964 the AAUP leadership recognized that the faculty union movement was developing and began to raise questions about the association's role in collective bargaining. Despite the organizers' intent to create a professional association, the AAUP had often faced claims that it was a trade union, and association leaders had consistently denied any affiliation with unions and based association programs on negotiations with administrators and trustees. When the AAUP first approved collective bargaining in 1966, it did so as a tentative organizational commitment, declaring faculty unionization to be appropriate under only the most extreme conditions of administrative intransigence. In 1972 the AAUP established a firm commitment to faculty collective bargaining, although a substantial number of leaders and members were not convinced of the wisdom of such activity. For several years the association struggled with its new role, on the one hand continuing its work to reform practices in higher education, while on the other assisting local faculties in their efforts to unionize, an activity that at times led the AAUP into direct conflict with college and university administrations.

Since the mid-1970s the AAUP has attempted to address faculty concerns on a wide range of issues— in addition to academic freedom, tenure, and faculty unions. The association has offered policy statements on such matters as hate speech, the relationship of gender and race to academic freedom, and the rapid increase of part-time faculty members. It also continues to provide assistance to college and university faculties considering unionization. Most importantly, however, it remains the primary voice for professors on issues relating to academic freedom and tenure, supporting professors' unique opportunity to offer reasoned, even critical, assessments of the world at large.

See also: ACADEMIC FREEDOM AND TENURE; FACULTY ROLES AND RESPONSIBILITIES; HIGHER EDUCATION IN THE UNITED STATES, *subentry on* HISTORICAL DEVELOPMENT.

BIBLIOGRAPHY

GRUBER, CAROL. 1975. *Mars and Minerva: World War I and the Uses of Higher Learning.* Baton Rouge: Louisiana State University Press.

HOFSTADTER, RICHARD, and METZGER, WALTER P. 1955. *The Development of Academic Freedom in the United States.* New York: Columbia University Press.

HUTCHESON, PHILO A. 2000. *A Professional Professoriate: Unionization, Bureacratizion, and the AAUP.* Nashville, TN: Vanderbilt University Press.

METZGER, LOYA. 1978. "Professors in Trouble: A Quantitative Analysis of Academic Freedom and Tenure Cases." Ph.D. diss., Columbia University.

SCHRECKER, ELLEN W. 1986. *No Ivory Tower: McCarthyism and the Universities.* New York: Oxford University Press.

PHILO HUTCHESON

AMERICAN ASSOCIATION OF UNIVERSITY WOMEN

The American Association of University Women (AAUW) is an education organization open to women who hold baccalaureate or higher degrees from a college or university on the AAUW list of qualified institutions or from foreign institutions recognized by the International Federation of University Women. In keeping with its purpose of practical educational work, the association develops programs that enable college women to continue their intellectual growth and to further the advancement of women in universities and colleges around the world. The AAUW also supports gender-discrimination lawsuits and works to promote legislation concerning issues of importance to women, such as equity in education, family and medical leave, child day care for working parents, reproductive rights, equal pay for equal work, affirmative action, and access to adequate health care.

Program

For more than a century the AAUW has endeavored to improve the quality and effectiveness of education for women and girls at all levels. AAUW branches across America work to discourage discrimination and promote gender-fair practices in the classroom. Members develop mentoring programs and encourage girls and women to study mathematics, science, and technology. Its members also initiate community-action projects and lobby local, state, and national legislators on women's issues. Analyzing their individual community needs, local branch members throughout the country have launched a variety of volunteer service projects embracing such activities as career guidance and scholastic counseling; working for school bond issues; cooperating with Head Start officials; and publishing valuable education information, such as lists of preschools and local compilations of scholarships and loans for prospective college students. Continuing interests of AAUW branches include mental health, aging, family-life studies, and the American judicial system. The AAUW also supports the United Nations, United Nations Children's Fund (UNICEF), and United Nations Educational, Scientific and Cultural Organization (UNESCO).

Basic to the AAUW's educational activities has been a drive for adequate financing and staffing of public schools by federal, state, and local governments. A standing committee on legislation assists branches in following the progress of pertinent bills at all levels, with emphasis on aid to education, foreign assistance, international cooperation and trade agreements, assistance for the disadvantaged, consumer education, urban problems, and protection of the physical environment.

In 1958 the AAUW established the AAUW Educational Foundation, which awards nearly $3.5 million annually in fellowships and grants, making it the world's largest source of funding exclusively for women scholars. Over 7,800 awards have been made to women in 120 countries since the AAUW was founded. Notable AAUW awardees have included Marie Curie, Barbara McClintock, and Judith Resnik. Between 2001 and 2002 a total of 287 women received funding from the AAUW Education Foundation. The Education Foundation also supports numerous community-action projects and symposia, round tables, and forums that promote education and equity for women and girls.

The Education Foundation fellowship and grant programs include American Fellowships of up to $30,000 for doctoral candidates and postdoctoral researchers; Career Development Grants of up to $8,000 for college graduates who wish to advance their careers; Community Action Grants of up to $7,000 for individual or organizational research programs that promote education and equity for women; Eleanor Roosevelt Teacher Fellowships of up to $5,000 for women teachers in public schools;

and International Fellowships of up to $30,000 to help women who are not U.S. citizens pursue university-level research. AAUW's Selected Professions Fellowships offer up to $20,000 to U.S. citizens who follow certain designated degree programs where women have traditionally been underrepresented, particularly architecture, computer sciences, engineering, and mathematics. In 1969 the foundation established the Coretta Scott King Fund, which gives educational grants to talented but economically disadvantaged African-American women studying in specific fields. The Education Foundation also makes one annual University Scholar-in-Residence Award of up to $50,000 to support a woman scholar doing research on gender-equity issues.

In addition, the Education Foundation makes three annual national awards to recognize outstanding achievement by women scholars; these are the AAUW Recognition Award for Emerging Scholars, the Founders Distinguished Senior Scholar Award, and the Annie Jump Cannon Award in Astronomy. The Eleanor Roosevelt Fund Award, presented biennially, honors an individual or institution for outstanding contributions to women's equity and education.

In 1981 the AAUW established the Legal Advocacy Fund to help women students and educators fight sex discrimination at colleges and universities. The fund accomplishes this goal through campus education and outreach programs, which draw attention to the problem of gender inequity at educational institutions. The fund also provides financial support for sex discrimination lawsuits and enlists volunteer attorneys and social scientists to serve as legal consultants. The Legal Advocacy Fund makes an annual $10,000 Progress in Equity Award to recognize efforts to improve the climate for women on campus.Publications from the AAUW national office include *Action Alert*—a monthly public policy newsletter, *Outlook*—a magazine with articles discussing women's rights issues and describing leaders in the movement for women's rights, such as Ruth Bader Ginsburg, Shirley Chisholm, and Donna Shalala; and *Get the Facts*—e-mail and fax alerts that provide members with information about important legislation and congressional proposals that affect women and families. The AAUW also publishes numerous bibliographies, study guides, and legislative guides.

Organizational Structure, Membership, and Funding

The AAUW is made up of three units: the association, a 150,000-member organization with more than 1,500 branches in fifty states, the District of Columbia, Guam, and Puerto Rico; the Education Foundation, which funds community action projects and offers fellowships and grants to outstanding women scholars; and the Legal Advocacy Fund, which supports women seeking judicial redress for sex discrimination at colleges and universities.

National AAUW officers are women distinguished in academic and civic life. The principal officers are elected at biennial conventions and serve four-year terms. The organization is composed of members-at-large and branch members, the branch being the basic unit through which the association functions in a community to promote its purposes and policies. All branches are members of their respective state divisions, which are organized into ten geographical regions. Each region has a vice president who is on the national board of directors.

All AAUW members are automatically affiliated with the International Federation of University Women, which unites the association in various countries. Dues are the main source of funds. The fellowships program is voluntarily supported by contributions from AAUW members, fund-raising projects in branch associations, bequests, and corporate and institutional sponsors. Endowment funds are used for fellowships, research, and publications.

History and Development

The forerunner of the AAUW was the Association of Collegiate Alumnae, organized by 65 young women graduates in Boston, Massachusetts, in 1882. It was joined by the Western Association of Collegiate Alumnae (ACA) in 1889. In 1921 the ACA and the Southern Association of College Women combined to form the American Association of University Women.

BIBLIOGRAPHY

AMERICAN ASSOCIATION OF UNIVERSITY WOMEN. 1998. *Gender Gaps: Where Schools Still Fail Our Children.* Washington, DC: American Association of University Women.

AMERICAN ASSOCIATION OF UNIVERSITY WOMEN. 1999. *Gaining a Foothold: Women's Transitions through Work and College.* Washington, DC: American Association of University Women.

LEVINE, SUSAN. 1995. *Degrees of Equality: The American Association of University Women and the Challenge of Twentieth-Century Feminism.* Philadelphia: Temple University Press.

INTERNET RESOURCE

AMERICAN ASSOCIATION OF UNIVERSITY WOMEN. 2002. <www.aauw.org>.

BETTY WILLIAMS
Revised by
JUDITH J. CULLIGAN

AMERICAN COUNCIL OF LEARNED SOCIETIES

The American Council of Learned Societies (ACLS) is a private, nonprofit federation of sixty-six national scholarly organizations in the humanities and social sciences. The object of the council, as set forth in its constitution, is the "advancement of humanistic studies in all fields of learning and the maintenance and strengthening of relations among the national societies devoted to such studies." The council funds humanities scholarships, convenes meetings and conferences that identify and address issues of concern to the academic humanities and its constituent learned societies, and advocates on behalf of the academic humanities.

Purpose

ACLS is best known as a funder of humanities research through fellowships and grants awarded to individuals and, on occasion, to groups and institutions. The centerpiece of this work is the ACLS Fellowship Program. ACLS Fellowships are designed to permit recipients to devote six to nine months of research and writing in such fields as literatures and languages, history, anthropology, political and social theory, philosophy, classics, religion, the history of art, linguistics, musicology, and the study of diverse world civilizations and cultures. The intensive peer-review process that results in the selection of these fellows is an opportunity for distinguished scholars to reach broad consensus on standards of quality in humanistic research.

An endowment provides the funds that the ACLS Fellowship Program awards to individual scholars, but the council also funds scholarly research through regranting funds awarded to it by foundations, the U.S. government, and foreign organizations. Some of these programs are focused on particular fields, such as the Henry Luce Foundation/ACLS Dissertation Fellowship in American Art that supports Ph.D. candidates working on the history of the visual arts of the United States. With the support from the Andrew W. Mellon foundation, the ACLS has begun a program of Frederick Burkhardt Residential Fellowships for Recently Tenured Scholars, designed to allow a small number of younger scholars in the humanities to undertake long-term, ambitious scholarly projects. The Charles A. Ryskamp Fellowship Program, also supported by the Andrew W. Mellon Foundation, provides sizeable fellowships to advanced assistant professors who have advanced their fields and who have well-designed and carefully developed plans for new research.

The ACLS has long engaged in international studies by providing opportunities for American scholars to advance scholarly projects on an international basis and by developing contacts with overseas academic communities. The development of area studies in this country owes much to the impetus provided by the ACLS. In the 1920s the ACLS became one of the first American scholarly organizations to promote studies of East Asia. The original concept of organizing scholarly expertise around an area or cultural region grew out of the council's early work in Oriental studies and language training, and its ability to bring a wide variety of humanists and social scientists together in interdisciplinary work. ACLS made it possible to launch area studies and sustain them over an extended period. After World War II, when the practical need for such competence was evident, ACLS and the Social Science Research Council joined to organize and develop African, Asian, Latin American, Near and Middle Eastern, Slavic, and East and West European studies. For more than forty years, the council has cooperated with the Social Science Research Council in organizing research and area studies on global issues. The ACLS Committee on East European Studies has expanded and consolidated scholarship on that region; it publishes *East European Politics and Societies,* the only significant peer-reviewed scholarly journal dedicated to that field. With funding from the Carnegie Corporation of New York, ACLS has begun a program proving grants to sustain individuals in Belarus, Russia, and Ukraine who are doing exemplary

work in a time of crisis and contraction, so as to assure continued future leadership in the humanities.

Among the council's publication ventures, the most ambitious and substantial is the *American National Biography* (*ANB*), which was published in print in 1999 and in an online version in 2000. The *ANB* is, in print, a twenty-five volume collection of approximately 18,000 biographies of significant individuals in American history, written by more than 7,000 expert authors. It is a successor to the *Dictionary of American Biography,* first published in 1928 and also sponsored by ACLS. Also important is the *Dictionary of Scientific Biography,* with articles on significant scientists from antiquity to modern times. A third major reference work, the *Dictionary of the Middle Ages,* was completed in 1989. In addition to these reference works, other publications of importance to scholarship sponsored by ACLS include the ongoing publication of the *Correspondence of Charles Darwin* in a thirty volume edition. The ACLS also published a critical and definitive edition of the *Works of William James* in nineteen volumes and supports the ongoing preparation and publication of the *Correspondence of William James* in twelve volumes. In 1999 ACLS, together with five of its constituent learned societies and ten university presses, launched the History E-Book Project, which will publish, in electronic format, both new and time-tested works of history.

The ACLS, as the most broadly based organization representing scholars as scholars rather than as specialists in particular fields, is well-positioned to serve as advocate on behalf of the scholarly humanities in public forums and policy arenas. The council's critical role in helping to establish (in 1964) and to reauthorize (in 1985) the National Endowment for the Humanities (NEH) is perhaps the most notable example of its exercise of this function.

ACLS draws together learned societies and affiliates for consideration of shared concerns, particularly those related to maintaining and improving conditions for scholarship, education, and communication among scholars in the humanities. Each member society appoints a delegate, who serves as its representative. The delegates gather each year at the ACLS annual meeting. The principal staff members of the constituent societies comprise the conference of administrative officers, which meets in the fall and again in the spring.

Through its committees ACLS has encouraged the development of research in many fields, set criteria and professional standards, planned and accumulated bibliographical and reference materials, and helped to establish scholarly journals. Several national societies of scholars had their beginnings in ACLS committees. Among these are the Medieval Academy of America, the Renaissance Society of America, the Far Eastern Association (now the Association for Asian Studies), the American Studies Association, the American Association for the Advancement of Slavic Studies, and the Middle East Studies Association.

Organization

The council consists of a fifteen-member board of directors and one delegate from each constituent society. An elected board of directors establishes and reviews policies, sets strategic directions, oversees the investment of endowed funds, and reports on all major decisions to the constituent societies. The council holds an annual meeting, elects officers and members of the board of directors, provides general and fiscal oversight, and assisted by the executive committee of the delegates, admits new members. Membership in the ACLS is restricted to organizations. There are three types of membership. The constituent learned societies of the American Council of Learned Societies are national or international organizations in the humanities and related social sciences. Associate members are a group of more than 200 colleges, universities, research libraries, and other scholarly institutions that each year signal their commitment to the work of the council through their financial contributions. Affiliate members are organizations and institutions (such as the Association of Research Libraries and the Federation of State Humanities Councils) whose goals and purposes are closely linked to those of ACLS.

The ACLS is supported by income from endowment, dues from constituent societies and affiliates, contributions from college and university associates, private and public grants, government contracts, and private gifts.

BIBLIOGRAPHY

BLOLAND, HARLAND G., and BLOLAND, SUE M. 1974. *American Learned Societies in Transition.* New York: McGraw-Hill.

KIGER, JOSEPH C. 1963. *American Learned Societies.* Washington, DC: Public Affairs Press.

KIGER, JOSEPH C. 1982. *Research Institutions and Learned Societies.* Westport, CT: Greenwood.

VOSS, JOHN, and WARD, PAUL L., eds. 1970. *Confrontation and Learned Societies.* New York: New York University Press.

INTERNET RESOURCE

AMERICAN COUNCIL OF LEARNED SOCIETIES. 2002. <www.acls.org>.

STEVEN C. WHEATLEY

AMERICAN COUNCIL ON EDUCATION

The American Council on Education (ACE) is a national association of accredited, degree-granting colleges and universities, higher education associations, and other educational organizations. ACE is the premier public voice for higher and adult education, a definer of issues, and a leader in coordinating higher education policies and in representing higher education to government. The chief executives of the 1,800 member organizations are generally the representatives to ACE.

The council seeks to create consensus on policy issues among the associations in the Washington, D.C., higher education community. One of its most important tasks is to lobby Congress and the federal agencies, presenting a coherent, unified voice for higher education on particular issues. ACE has commitments to support increases in federal aid to students and to limit the federal regulatory burdens on colleges and universities. The council promotes diversity in higher education and has engaged the issue of how to strengthen teacher education.

The council maintains an extensive research program on higher and adult education, and it offers advice to institutions on such matters as minority and women's issues and college and university administration. ACE initiated a higher education/business forum, which brings together corporate leaders and higher education executives for discussions of mutual interest, and the organization administers the General Educational Development (GED) tests for adult learners. ACE publishes a semimonthly newsletter, *Higher Education and National Affairs;* a triennial magazine, *The Presidency;* and a number of special reports; and is involved in book and guide publishing with Greenwood Publishing Group's ACE/Oryx Series on Higher Education.

The council is the leader and convener of a series of informal and formal groups, which meet to discuss issues and coordinate activities, particularly in the federal relations area. At the center of coordination and policy is the group often called the Six or the Big Six. The Six include ACE's president, as the convener, and the chief executive officers of five other Washington, D.C., associations: the Association of American Universities (AAU), the National Association of State Universities and Land-Grant Colleges (NASULGC), the National Association of Independent Colleges and Universities (NAICU), the American Association of State Colleges and Universities (AASCU), and the American Association of Community Colleges (AACC). These represent the major sectors of accredited higher education institutions in the United States. As part of its coordinating responsibilities, ACE convenes the Washington Higher Education Secretariat, a group of more than forty-five higher education associations whose representatives meet monthly to discuss higher education issues and affairs.

The American Council on Education was founded in March 1918 as the Emergency Council on Education, a federation of fourteen national educational associations, to coordinate higher education's resources to meet national wartime needs. The presidents of colleges and universities were concerned with the unpredictability of federal government decisions that affected higher education, and they worried that wartime conditions would sharply curtail the number of students who would attend colleges and universities. In July 1918 the Emergency Council on Education changed its name to the American Council on Education. It set up a permanent Washington, D.C., office and named a director, Samuel Capen, who had been head of the federal Bureau of Education. One of his early acts was to establish the *Educational Record,* a quarterly journal that published articles on higher education.

From the beginning, ACE viewed itself as an umbrella organization, a vehicle that would speak for all of higher education on general education questions. Initially its members were associations of colleges and universities. ACE argued that because its membership covered all of higher education, and thus did not speak for any particular group in higher education, the council could speak for all of higher education. However, even as an association of associations, ACE offered to give financial and curricular advice to individual institutions. During the 1920s, ACE expanded its interests to include international education, attempting to give some order to a confusing field by incorporating several international education associations.

In 1919 ACE defined its membership to include colleges and universities as well as associations. This gave the association a stronger financial base, provided a means for broadening its activities, and protected it from the charge that its purposes and activities were too far removed from the problems of individual institutions. However, the decision immediately engendered charges of duplication and overlap. Institutions were now members of ACE as well as members of the other presidential associations, such as the Association of American Universities (AAU). If a university was represented to the council through its national association, for example AAU, why did the institution need to also be a member of ACE? The issue of the relationship of institution and association membership in the council was to plague ACE for many years.

In the 1930s membership in ACE brought in representatives from lower education, including state departments of education and city school systems. They were later joined by some private secondary schools and, by 1940, town school systems. Then some trade associations and business corporations became members of ACE, and the council entered into some business arrangements. These activities added to the complexity of developing coherent coordinative policies.

In 1950 ACE purchased a building on Massachusetts Avenue large enough to accommodate its growing needs and to house fifteen other major higher education associations. Another move came in 1968, when the Kellogg Foundation funded the building of the National Center for Higher Education at One Dupont Circle. More than forty associations occupied the offices, managed by the council.

Representing higher education to the federal government has always been one of the most important but difficult activities of ACE. The various sectors of higher education have regularly presented different and sometimes opposing interests they wished to foster and protect. Public and private institutions at times have been divided on the question of how federal student aid should be distributed. The interests of research-dominated, graduate institutions and the perspectives of institutions emphasizing undergraduate education have not always coincided. These and other conflicting interests reflected in the policies of the Washington, D.C., associations have made it difficult to find common ground among its members on which to present a unified position to Congress and the significant government agencies. Nevertheless, when the associations are in agreement, they can act swiftly and effectively.

For many years, the Washington, D.C., higher education associations were reluctant to enter the political arena with sustained, coordinated efforts. They and their constituents thought lobbying was unseemly for higher education, and they felt constrained by laws that restricted lobbying among nonprofit organizations to a minor part of their activities. ACE tended not to act until it had some agreement among its association and institutional members. As a result the council was often accused of reacting slowly to events and practices of great concern to its members.

The American Council on Education, in 1962, restructured the council's board to virtually eliminate association representatives and replace them with institutional representation. Also in 1962, the Secretariat, a group of higher education association members of ACE, was created, partly as a result of the lack of association representation on the ACE board.

In the 1960s ACE and the other major associations entered into intensified relations with the federal government. Congress was in the process of passing major legislation to provide aid for higher education, including the Higher Education Act of 1965. The issue was whether the legislation would emphasize aid to institutions or directly to students. ACE took the lead in lobbying for aid to institutions of higher education. However, the 1972 amendments clearly emphasized direct aid. ACE's reaction to this defeat was to strengthen its governmental relations division and establish a policy analysis service. Also, in 1972 the ACE board was restructured to include six elected association representatives. In 1978 representation on the ACE board increased to thirteen associations.

In the 1980s major objectives for ACE and the other associations were to increase federal funding for student assistance programs, reduce the imbalance between federal student loans and grants, and increase the federal government's commitment to academic research. Through the 1990s ACE continued to emphasize coordination among the Big Six associations, increased federal support for student financial aid, improved policy analysis and research capacity, and reduced negative consequences for colleges and universities from the proliferation of federal regulations. The first Republican Congress in many years encouraged ACE and the other associations to seek a more bipartisan relationship than they had under Democratic majorities. The Big Six faced challenges in the 1990s that included major attacks on higher education for the rising cost of tuition, misconduct charges in university research, high levels of student loan defaults, overemphasis on rewarding research over teaching, and not paying enough attention to undergraduate education. The associations confronted the issues of academic earmarking and the creation of State Postsecondary Review Entities (SPREs), which threatened to sharply increase federal and state accountability controls over institutions of higher education. The Council for Postsecondary Accreditation (COPA), the national umbrella organization on accrediting, disintegrated, and the Big Six associations became deeply involved in creating a new national organization on accrediting.

ACE and the other members of the Big Six remain a cohesive voice for higher education, and despite having been joined by a large number of other groups interested in lobbying Congress on issues related to higher education, ACE and the other presidential associations are still the major voices representing higher education to the federal government.

See also: AMERICAN ASSOCIATION OF COMMUNITY COLLEGES; AMERICAN ASSOCIATION OF STATE COLLEGES AND UNIVERSITIES; ASSOCIATION OF AMERICAN UNIVERSITIES; NATIONAL ASSOCIATION OF INDEPENDENT COLLEGES AND UNIVERSITIES; NATIONAL ASSOCIATION OF STATE UNIVERSITIES AND LAND-GRANT COLLEGES.

BIBLIOGRAPHY

BLOLAND, HARLAND G. 1985. "Associations in Action: The Washington D.C. Higher Education Community." *ASHE-ERIC Higher Education Report No. 2*. Washington, DC: Association for the Study of Higher Education.

BLOLAND, HARLAND G. 2001. *Creating the Council for Higher Education Accreditation*. Phoenix, AZ:

American Council on Education and Oryx Press.

COOK, CONSTANCE EWING. 1998. *Lobbying for Higher Education: How Colleges and Universities Influence Federal Policy.* Nashville, TN: Vanderbilt University Press.

HAWKINS, HUGH. 1992. *Banding Together: The Rise of National Associations in American Higher Education.* Baltimore: Johns Hopkins University Press.

INTERNET RESOURCE

AMERICAN COUNCIL ON EDUCATION. 2002. <www.acenet.edu>.

HARLAND G. BLOLAND

AMERICAN FEDERATION OF TEACHERS

The American Federation of Teachers (AFT) is a nationwide union of more than one million public school teachers, higher education faculty and staff, public employees, nurses and health care professionals, and paraprofessionals and other school-related personnel. The AFT is affiliated with the American Federation of Labor and the Congress of Industrial Organizations (AFL-CIO), a federation of trade and industrial unions representing more than thirteen million people. According to the AFT Futures II Report, adopted July 5, 2000, the union works "to improve the lives of our members and their families, to give voice to their legitimate professional, economic and social aspirations, to strengthen the institutions in which we work, to improve the quality of the services we provide, to bring together all members to assist and support one another and to promote democracy, human rights and freedom in our union, in our nation and throughout the world."

Program

Like other labor unions, the AFT works for higher pay and better benefits and working conditions for its members. The union also offers numerous benefits and services to its members, including low-cost insurance, retirement savings plans, credit union services, legal representation, and consumer discounts. The AFT, along with the AFL-CIO, strongly advocates continued access to free public education and affordable health care. The AFT also negotiates contract provisions relating specifically to the teaching profession, such as class size, student discipline codes, adequate textbooks and teaching materials, and professional development and evaluation.

In the past the AFT has worked to desegregate public schools, eliminate child labor, establish collective bargaining rights for teachers, and address the educational needs of disadvantaged and disabled children. Among the AFT's major educational reform initiatives during the 1990s and early 2000s was the *Lesson for Life: Responsibility, Respect, Results* campaign. Launched in 1995, this initiative promotes high academic standards, stronger curricula, and more safe and orderly classrooms. The AFT's annual *Making Students Matter* report examines and evaluates academic standards in all fifty states. The *Educational Research and Dissemination Program* is a professional development program that uses a "train-the-trainer" approach in which subject matter experts help teachers improve their teaching of core subjects. The AFT's *Zero Tolerance* initiative works toward implementing stricter policies for violent and disruptive behavior in schools so that teachers can teach and students can learn in a safe environment. The *Support for the National Board for Professional Teaching Standards* initiative promotes higher standards for teacher certification, including National Board certification, and salary increases for teachers who pass the board exam. Other AFT programs and initiatives address such issues as merit pay, distance learning, whistle blower protection, charter schools, and low performing schools. The AFT asserts that such reforms would be more effective in improving the quality of education than voucher systems of tuition payment or privatization of public schools.

The AFT also addresses issues of specific concern to the various branches of its membership. For members involved in higher education, the union tackles such issues as tenure, the role of part-time faculty, and the high cost of secondary education. For AFT members who are public employees, the union works to improve labor-management relations, job security, and the public perception of the value of government employees. The AFT must take on a wide range of issues, including professional certification and occupational safety, for the diverse body of workers called paraprofessionals and other school-related personnel. For nurses and health care professionals, the AFT's *Health Care Quality First* campaign fights to protect the quality of patient care and preserve safe staffing levels for nurses and other health care professionals in the face of profit-driven managed health care and restructuring in hospitals and clinics.

The AFT holds a large annual convention every summer, and sponsors numerous meetings and conferences throughout the year on a variety of topics. The AFT also sponsors scholarships and educational grants for members and their children. Since 1992 the Robert G. Porter Scholars Program has awarded $1,000 grants to AFT members who want to pursue courses in labor relations and related fields, and $8,000 four-year college scholarships for dependents of AFT members who wish to study labor, education, health care, or government service.

ATF periodical publications include the weekly e-mail newsletter *Inside AFT,* the monthly journal *American Teacher,* the semimonthly newsletter *Health Wire* for nurses and health care professionals, the quarterly newsletter *PSRP Reporter* for paraprofessionals and other school-related personnel, and the monthly magazine *On Campus* for higher education teachers and staff.

Organization

The national AFT is headed by a president, executive vice president, and a secretary treasurer who are elected by members. Local affiliates elect their own officers. The union is made up of five divisions: Pre-K–12 Teachers, Higher Education Teachers, Healthcare-Federation of Nurses and Health Professionals, the Federation of Public Employees, and Paraprofessional and School-Related Personnel. The Pre-K–12 Teachers division represents public school kindergarten, elementary, middle, and high school teachers, counselors, and librarians. The Higher Education Division represents more than 120,000 faculty, graduate employees, and professional staff at over two hundred two-year and four-year colleges around the country. The Healthcare-Federation of Nurses and Health Professionals division represent about 60,000 nurses and other health professionals working in hospitals, clinics, home health agencies, and schools in nineteen states. The AFT Paraprofessional and School-Related Personnel Division represents approximately 200,000 support staff in schools from kindergarten through college, including custodians, bus drivers, food service workers, groundskeepers, secretaries, bookkeepers, mechanics, and a

variety of other jobs. The Federation of Public Employees represents more than 100,000 city, county, and state employees in a variety of jobs in twenty-one states.

The AFT's various departments include the Financial Services Department, which assists treasurers and other officers of local AFT affiliates with financial and administrative duties. The Human Rights and Community Relations Department keeps local and state affiliates informed of current trends, publications, and laws related to civil, human, and women's rights. The International Affairs Department provides information to members on important international issues, particularly human and trade union rights for teachers and other professionals around the world. The Union Leadership Institute helps develop the leadership skills of local AFT officers, trains AFT members in activism, and educates members about the union and its activities. The Legislative Action Center keeps track of how the U.S. Congress and state legislatures vote on issues of concern to the union, communicates official AFT positions to elected officials, and enables members to send faxes or e-mails directly to elected leaders on key issues. The Pre-K–12 Educational Issues Department works to educate the public and institute reforms related to such issues as school standards, class size, early education, school choice, safety and discipline, and teacher quality.

History

The AFT was founded in Winnetka, Illinois, in 1916 by a small group of teachers from three Chicago unions and one Gary, Indiana, union who believed that their profession needed a national organization to speak for teachers and represent their interests. They called their new union the Teachers International Union of America, and named Charles B. Stillman as president. They were joined by other teacher unions in Pennsylvania, Oklahoma, New York, and Washington, D.C. Within days of its establishment, the new union contacted the powerful AFL and requested affiliation. AFL president Samuel Gompers supported the affiliation, but suggested changing the union's name to American Federation of Teachers. The AFL issued a charter to the AFT on May 9, 1916.

Since its early years, the AFT has been on the forefront of the fight for civil rights and was one of the first unions to extend full membership to African Americans. As early as 1918, the AFT called for equal pay for African-American teachers and, in subsequent years, for the election of African-Americans to local school boards and equal educational opportunities for African-American children. In 1954 the AFT filed a brief before the U.S. Supreme Court in support of the plaintiffs in *Brown v. Board of Education of Topeka, Kansas.* During the 1960s the AFT was actively involved in the civil rights movement and lobbied extensively for passage of civil rights legislation.

The AFT had included paraprofessional and other school-related staff since its early years, but an increasing number joined in the last two decades of the twentieth century. After the 1960s the union's membership grew more diverse as nurses, health care workers, and public employees joined as constituent groups.

See also: SHANKER, ALBERT; TEACHERS UNION.

BIBLIOGRAPHY

EATON, WILLIAM EDWARD. 1975. *The American Federation of Teachers, 1916–1961: A History of the Movement.* Carbondale: Southern Illinois University Press.

MURPHY, MARJORIE. 1990. *Blackboard Unions: The AFT and the NEA, 1900–1980.* Ithaca, NY: Cornell University Press.

MUNGAZI, DICKSON A. 1995. *Where He Stands: Albert Shanker of the American Federation of Teachers.* Westport, CT: Praeger.

DAVID SELDEN
Revised by
JUDITH J. CULLIGAN

AMERICAN OVERSEAS SCHOOLS

American overseas schools are kindergarten through twelfth grade institutions that have U.S. sponsorship through private businesses, churches, parent groups and/or government agencies and serve eligible U.S. students in foreign nations. In Latin American nations, however, such schools are not classified as *overseas.*

These schools typically have a basic American curriculum. Instruction is in English, although other languages—especially that of the host nation—may be emphasized as well. Attendance by students from the host nation and from other countries is encouraged. Wherever appropriate and applicable, schools attempt to honor host-country rules related to education, so that school years and holidays can vary widely. Many schools in the Southern Hemisphere are in session only from March to December, and church-supported schools often observe special holidays of the sponsoring sect. Most of the schools observe holidays of the host nation—especially in Muslim nations—and some observe holidays of developing countries that have many students in attendance.

Not addressed in this discussion are college programs; special international programs in elementary and secondary schools, such as the International Baccalaureate; schools sponsored by foreign governments and international schools that operate in the United States (such as the United Nations school); and church mission schools in foreign lands, which are aimed primarily at host-nation children.

Two major classifications of American overseas schools exist: (1) dependent schools, operated by the U.S. Department of Defense (DoD); and (2) independent schools, some of which are sponsored by the U.S. Department of State (DoS). Either type of school can accept students from private and military sectors. In instances where there are not enough students to operate a DoD school, tuition is paid by the U.S. military to independent schools. Similar arrangements exist where private-sector dependents are located on or adjacent to a U.S. military site. In 2000 approximately 250,000 U.S. school-age children were overseas; most were enrolled in DoD schools, but these enrollments are dropping and independent schools' enrollments are increasing, a cycle that occurs when cold-war tensions ease.

Department of Defense Dependent Schools (DoDDS)

Military schools officially started on American frontier posts in 1821, often under the leadership of a chaplain who doubled as the schoolmaster. These schools fluctuated in the recognition and support they received until schools were established in Germany, Japan, and Austria in 1946. DoDDS enrollment then grew rapidly, and by the end of the 1946–1947 school year enrollment had reached 2,992. By 1949 the U.S. Army, Navy, and Air Force were independently operating approximately 100 such units around the world, and by the late 1960s more than

300 schools were operated abroad. Then, in 1964, the Secretary of Defense combined the three separate school systems within the department, and by 1969 more than 300 DoD schools existed.

During the 1960s and 1970s, worldwide K–12 enrollment averaged 160,000 students. In 1976, the Department of Defense assumed the direct management of all of the schools. In 1979, the name for the system became the Department of Defense Dependent Schools (DoDDS), the name still commonly used to identify the system. After the Cold War ended, DoDDS schools decreased in number. As of 2000 approximately 220 schools existed in fifteen foreign countries and Puerto Rico, with about 68 percent of the students enrolled in elementary schools, 15 percent in middle schools, and 17 percent in high schools. All DoD programs are accredited by the North Central Association of Schools and Colleges.

Independent Schools

Originally, independent schools, at least those sponsored by U.S. government agencies prior to World War II, were limited in number. The Office of Overseas Schools' records list eighteen such schools that existed in the early 1940s, mostly located in Latin America to combat the influence of German-sponsored schools. Before then, few employees took their families overseas. During World War II, the U.S. Department of State did provide some support via grants through the American Council on Education to a small number of schools. Nelson Rockefeller, a presidential adviser at the time, is credited with initiating this effort. During this period, American students either attended a DoD school, a corporate school, a mission school, a boarding school, or they stayed at home in the United States.

By the beginning of President John F. Kennedy's tenure in 1961, many government agencies and private businesses were expanding overseas. Groups of parents started their own schools, but without the benefit of federal aid. In 1961, the Fulbright-Hays Act established the Bureau of Educational and Cultural Affairs, and the Foreign Assistance Act created the United States Agency for International Development (USAID), both of which could give limited grants-in-aid to K–12 efforts. A 1963 Foreign Service Act provision allowed aid for dependents of persons carrying out U.S. government activities overseas. The U.S. Department of State established its Office of Overseas Schools (OOS) in 1964.

State Department Schools

The major purpose of Department of State (DoS)-supported schools, other than educating American dependents, has been to provide a foreign showcase of democracy through high-quality education programs that are open to both host- and third-nation students. Curricula often are binational for acculturation purposes—and to meet host-nation regulations along with U.S. accreditation standards. In 1998 Congress strengthened U.S. educational activities overseas by returning the U.S. Information Agency to the Department of State. Overseas schools continued to expand and flourish.

In 2000 the State Department supported 181 schools in 131 nations. There is great variety among these schools, ranging from tiny schools such as the American Independent School in Sierra Leone and the American Embassy School in Reykjavik, Iceland, with about a dozen students each, to the Singapore American School, which has more than 2,500 students. Facilities for the schools range from rented homes and American Embassy rooms to multimillion-dollar campuses in such cities as London, Singapore, Madrid, and Manila. A few even have boarding facilities.

Types of Schools

Independent schools fall into five major categories:

1. *Community schools,* which are nonprofit units supported by governmental and business interests and are established through parents in the area. These schools are the most common type supported by the DoS.

2. *Embassy schools* operate within an embassy or consulate, often for security purposes, and have small enrollments. As the American presence grows in the areas where these schools exist, community schools are often formed and ultimately replace the embassy schools.

3. *Corporate schools,* such as those operated by oil companies, primarily provide private education for children of company employees, whether they are from the United States or other nations. These schools are usually in nations where other U.S. schools do not exist. More than one language track is often involved, and nonemployees' children generally are accepted into the school.

4. *Proprietary schools,* as the name indicates, are

established as a business, with a definite profit motive in mind, or at least with the expectation that sufficient income will be generated to remain solvent as a not-for-profit corporation. Such schools are often started in developing nations, or as exclusive private schools in established areas.

5. *Church schools* with varied curricula and open admissions policies often can meet the American student enrollment needs in a community, and they can also receive tuition aid or special grants for secular purposes to assist with operating costs. These schools, however, are not to be confused with church mission schools, which have a completely different, and definitely religious, purpose.

Governance systems for American independent overseas schools vary. Although local control of public schools in the United States is a well-established feature, such control is often tempered by state and federal regulations. Independent schools overseas attempt to offer opportunities for more direct input from parents because of the insular nature of the enterprise. The bylaws of these schools usually mandate the direct participation of all stakeholders in governance decisions, usually to a much larger extent than would be experienced in American public schools.

Most American overseas schools, however, end up looking very much like schools in the United States. Curricula have common elements, pupil-teacher ratios are similar, texts are standard and represent those usually found in stateside schools; extracurricular activities, including athletics, are numerous and resemble those found in U.S. schools. Part of the reason for this similarity is that the American schooling model is a familiar one; but this also happens because parents are eager for their children to have the same, or at least a similar, school experience as those children "back home." In many ways, this desire is also prompted by the knowledge that, at some point, children from the overseas school will have to transition back into the stateside school system.

As much as the American overseas schools may wish to mirror those in the United States, the schools are subject to local (foreign) governmental regulation. Schools must follow the laws of the host nation, even if they conflict with the stated mission of the school. Some nations, for example, require instruction in the official national language. Others control who can become a teacher, using requirements quite different from the licensing standards associated with American teacher preparation. However, if a school wants stateside accreditation, it has to meet the American licensing standards. American overseas schools may also have to incorporate under local law if they wish to conduct business activities in the host country, such as hiring employees, purchasing supplies, maintaining bank accounts, and building or renting facilities. Without such legal status in a country, a school could not operate. The U.S. Embassy in most areas has a legal attaché, provided by the U.S. Department of Labor, who can assist schools in personnel matters.

Factors Affecting Overseas Schools

American overseas schools are not immune to changes in world policy. The number of DoD schools overseas decreases along with the number of U.S. military personnel located overseas during peaceful times. However, all other types of American overseas schools increase and become more multiethnic in the constituency of their governing boards, their staffs, and their students. In fact, in most independent schools in the early twenty-first century, U.S. children were in a minority—although the curriculum had to still meet American criteria and accreditation standards.

All of the schools try to keep up with the latest developments in schooling. Technology, for example, is important, and distance education is a popular means of instruction. However, incorporating the latest innovations is not always easy. For example, at the Karl C. Parrish School in Barranquilla, Columbia, the administrative team made a commitment to build a computer lab. The construction began and all the necessary wiring and furnishings were put into place; even air conditioning was installed. Then the country had a drought and the government declared that there would be daily twelve-hour blackouts because of the shortage of hydroelectric power.

Attracting and retaining qualified teachers and administrative staff can also be a challenge. As attractive as the idea of teaching abroad may be to educators, particularly the notion of travel and new experiences, there are some potential disadvantages to consider. Moving overseas to teach is not a good way to escape problems at home, whether those problems are personal or professional. Such problems can be magnified in new surroundings, and without well-established support networks in place a newcomer can be at a distinct disadvantage. Foreign environments have a way of testing people; often the greatest test is unpredictability. Therefore, flexibility is one of the most helpful traits a person who wants to embark on an overseas assignment can have. Other attributes that prove helpful are patience and tolerance. There also needs to be an understanding that teachers or administrators who move abroad to accept positions in American overseas schools will become foreigners themselves. And, as foreigners, American teachers abroad may face indifference, intolerance, or outright hostility—just as foreigners in the United States sometimes encounter these attitudes among Americans.

Living and working overseas is often easier on a military base, where the people, customs, and routines are familiar, than it is for educators who choose to work in independent schools. Yet the amount of cultural experience and travel is primarily the choice of the individual teacher, and the opportunities are obvious and unlimited for those who relish exploring new cultures and expanding their global awareness.

Resources

A number of resources exist that provide information about American overseas schools. The Association for the Advancement of International Education (AAIE) has served primarily the independent sector since 1966. One of AAIE's earliest efforts was to establish school-to-school partnerships between overseas units and stateside counterparts. The mission of AAIE is to be the "preeminent forum for the exchange of ideas promoting intercultural, international education and to be proactive in providing services which meet the needs of American/International schools worldwide" (Simpson and Duke, p. 8).

Another useful resource is the American Overseas Schools Historical Society (AOSHS), founded in 1995 to collect and secure the stories and data relating to U.S. educational efforts overseas. Membership consists primarily of current and former employees and students of DoDDS. The main source of program and personnel information for DoD is the United States Department of Defense Dependents Schools (DoDDS).

Some information about teaching opportunities in overseas schools can be obtained from the International Schools Services (ISS). Its annual *ISS Directory of Overseas Schools* is a comprehensive guide to American and international schools worldwide.

See also: FEDERAL EDUCATION ACTIVITIES; SECONDARY EDUCATION, ***subentry on*** INTERNATIONAL ISSUES.

BIBLIOGRAPHY

SIMPSON, ROBERT J., and DUKE, CHARLES R., eds. 2000. *American Overseas Schools.* Bloomington, IN: Phi Delta Kappa Foundation.

INTERNET RESOURCES

AMERICAN OVERSEAS SCHOOLS HISTORICAL SOCIETY. 2002. <http://aoshs.wichita.edu>.

ASSOCIATION FOR THE ADVANCEMENT OF INTERNATIONAL EDUCATION. 2002. <www.aaie.org>.

INTERNATIONAL SCHOOLS SERVICES. 2002. <www.iss.edu>.

U.S. DEPARTMENT OF DEFENSE EDUCATIONAL ACTIVITIES. 2002. <www.odedodea.edu>.

CHARLES R. DUKE
ROBERT J. SIMPSON

ARISTOTLE (384–322 B.C.E.)

Aristotle, the Greek philosopher and scientist, was born in Stagira, a town in Chalcidice. At the age of seventeen he became a member of the Greek philosopher Plato's school, where he stayed for twenty years. After Plato's death in 348 B.C.E. Aristotle taught philosophy, first at Atarneus in Asia Minor, then in Mytilene on the island of Lesbos. Then he became tutor of Alexander the Great at the court of Macedonia. In 335 or 334 B.C.E. he returned to Athens and founded a school called the Lyceum.

Aristotle's first writings were dialogues modeled on Plato's examples; a few have survived in fragmentary form. The main body of writings that have come down to us consists of treatises on a wide range of subjects; these were probably presented as lectures, and some may be notes on lectures taken by students. These treatises lay unused in Western Europe after the collapse of the Roman Empire in the sixth century C.E., until they were recovered in the Middle Ages and studied by Muslim, Jewish, and Christian thinkers. The large scope of the treatises, together with the extraordinary intellect of their author, gained for Aristotle the title, "the master of those who know."

The treatises are investigative reports, describing a method of inquiry and the results reached. Each treatise includes: (1) a statement of the aim of the subject matter; (2) a consideration of other thinkers' ideas; (3) an examination of proposed principles with the aim of determining the one that has the best prospect of explaining the subject matter; (4) a search for the facts that illustrate the proposed principle; and (5) an explanation of the subject matter by showing how the proposed principle explains the observed facts. The treatises were essential to the work of the Lyceum, which was a school, a research institution, a library, and a museum. Aristotle and his students compiled a *List of Pythian Winners*; researched the records of dramatic performances at Athens; collected 158 constitutions, of which only *The Constitution of Athens* has survived; prepared a literary and philological study called *Homeric Problems;* and put together a collection of maps and a museum of objects to serve as illustrations for lectures.

Aristotle's writings on logic worked out an art of discourse, a tool for finding out the structure of the world. The other subject matters of Aristotle's treatises are of three kinds: (1) the theoretical sciences—metaphysics, mathematics, and physics—aim to know for the sake of knowing; (2) the productive sciences—such as poetics and rhetoric—aim to know for the sake of making useful or beautiful things; and (3) the practical sciences—ethics and politics—aim to know for the sake of doing, or for conduct. Aristotle said that the theoretical sciences are capable of being understood by principles which are certain and cannot be other than they are; as objects of study their subject matters are necessary and eternal. The productive sciences and the practical sciences are capable of being understood by principles that are less than certain; as objects of study their subject matters are contingent.

Thus Aristotle's idea was that distinct sciences exist, the nature of each to be determined by principles found in the midst of the subject matter that is peculiarly its own. A plurality of subject matters exists, and there is a corresponding plurality of principles explaining sets of facts belonging to each subject matter. What is learned in any subject matter may be useful in studying others; yet there is no hierarchy of subject matters in which the principles of the highest in the order of Being explain the principles of all the others.

Education for a Common End

Unlike Plato's *Republic* and *Laws,* Aristotle's treatises do not contain lengthy discussions of education. His most explicit discussion of education, in Books 7 and 8 of the *Politics,* ends without being completed. Yet, like Plato, Aristotle's educational thinking was inseparable from his account of pursuing the highest good for human beings in the life of a community. The science of politics takes into account the conduct of the individual as inseparable from the conduct of the community. Thus Aristotle holds that ethics is a part of politics; and equally, politics is a part of ethics. This leads him to argue that the end of individuals and states is the same. Inasmuch as human beings cannot realize their potentiality apart from the social life that is necessary for shaping their mind and character, an investigation into the nature of society is a necessary companion to an investigation into the nature of ethics. The good life is inescapably a social life—a life of conduct in a community. For Aristotle, "the Good of man must be the end of the science of Politics" (1975, 1.2.1094b 7–8). In community life, the activity of doing cannot bring into existence something apart from doing; it can only "end" in further doing. And education, as one of the activities of doing, does not "produce" anything apart from education, but must be a continuing process that has no end except further education.

In Aristotle's explicit remarks about the aims of education, it is clear that, like all activities in pursuit of the good life, education is "practical" in that it is a way of conduct, of taking action. At the same time, in pursuing the good life, the aim is to know the nature of the best state and the highest virtues of which human beings are capable. Such knowledge enables us to have a sense of what is possible in education. Educational activity is also a "craft" in the sense that determining the means appropriate for pursuing that which we think is possible is a kind of making as well as a kind of doing. It is commonplace to say that, in doing, we try to "make things happen." Education is an attempt to find the kind of unity of doing and making that enables individuals to grow, ethically and socially.

The *Politics* ends by citing three aims of education: the possible, the appropriate, and the "happy mean." The idea of a happy mean is developed in the *Nicomachean Ethics.* There human conduct is held to consist of two kinds of virtues, moral and intellectual; moral virtues are learned by habit, while intellectual virtues are learned through teaching. As examples, while humans are not temperate or courageous by nature, they have the potentiality to become temperate and courageous. By taking on appropriate habits, their potentialities can be actualized; by conducting themselves appropriately they can learn to actualize their moral virtues. Thus children learn the moral virtues before they know what they are doing or why they are doing it. Just because young children cannot control their conduct by intellectual principles, Aristotle emphasizes habit in training them. First, children must learn the moral virtues; later, when their intellectual powers have matured, they may learn to conduct themselves according to reason by exercising the intellectual virtues.

Arguing that the state is a plurality that should be made into a community by education, Aristotle insisted that states should be responsible for educating their citizens. In the *Politics,* Book 8, he makes four arguments for public education: (1) from constitutional requirements; (2) from the origins of virtue; (3) from a common end to be sought by all citizens; and (4) from the inseparability of the individual and the community. In most states in the Greek world before Aristotle's time, private education had prevailed.

Finally, Aristotle's enduring legacy in education may be characterized as threefold. First is his conception of distinct subject matters, the particular nature and conclusions reached in each to be determined as the facts of its subject matter take their places in the thinking and conduct of the investigator. Second is his insistence on the conjoint activities of ethics and politics, aiming to gain the practical wisdom that can be realized only insofar as citizens strive for the highest good in the context of a community of shared ends. This means that the end of ethics and politics is an educational end. And, third, the education that states need is public education.

Although thinkers may know in a preliminary way what the highest good is—that which is required by reason—they will not actually find out what it is until they learn to live in cooperation with the highest principles of reason. The highest good is never completely known because the pursuit of it leads to further action, which has no end but more and more action. The contingent nature of social existence makes it necessary to find out what is good for us in what we do; we cannot truly learn what it is apart from conduct. While reason is a part of conduct, alone it is not sufficient for realizing the highest good. Only by our conduct can we find out what our possibilities are; and only by further conduct can we strive to make those possibilities actual.

See also: PHILOSOPHY OF EDUCATION.

BIBLIOGRAPHY

ARISTOTLE. 1944. *Politics,* trans. Harris Rackham. Cambridge, MA: Harvard University Press.

ARISTOTLE. 1975. *Nicomachean Ethics,* trans. Harris Rackham. Cambridge, MA: Harvard University Press.

ARISTOTLE. 1984. *Complete Works of Aristotle: The Revised Oxford Translation,* 2 vols., ed. Jonathan Barnes. Princeton, NJ: Princeton University Press.

CURREN, RANDALL R. 2000. *Aristotle on the Necessity of Public Education.* Lanham, MD: Rowman and Littlefield.

EDEL, ABRAHAM. 1982. *Aristotle and His Philosophy.* Chapel Hill: University of North Carolina Press.

RANDALL, JOHN HERMAN, JR. 1960. *Aristotle.* New York: Columbia University Press.

ROSS, WILLIAM D. 1959. *Aristotle: A Complete Exposition of His Works and Thought.* Cleveland, OH: World Publishing.

J. J. CHAMBLISS

ART EDUCATION

SCHOOL
  Donovan R. Walling
PREPARATION OF TEACHERS
  D. Jack Davis

SCHOOL

Art is more than creative expression, which has been the dominant theme of art education for much of the twentieth century. Expression is important, but researchers are also finding connections between learning in the visual arts and the acquisition of knowledge and skills in other areas. According to a 1993 Arts Education Partnership Working Group study, the benefits of a strong art program include intensified student motivation to learn, better school attendance, increased graduation rates, improved multicultural understanding, and the development of higher-order thinking skills, creativity, and problem-solving abilities.

Curriculum Developments

Art education has its roots in drawing, which, with reading, writing, singing, and playing an instrument comprised the basic elementary school curriculum in the seventeenth century. Drawing continued to be a basic component of the core curriculum throughout the eighteenth and nineteenth centuries, when educators saw drawing as important in teaching handwork, nature study, geography, and other subjects. Art education later expanded to include painting, design, graphic arts, and the "plastic arts" (e.g., sculpture and ceramics), although art continued to be seen primarily as utilitarian.

In the twentieth century, with the advent of modernism, art education in the United States edged away from a utilitarian philosophy to one of creative expression, or art-making for personal development. Art continued to be valued, although less often as a core subject, during the early decades of the century and then declined in importance with the advent of World War II. In the postwar period, particularly after the launch of *Sputnik* in 1957, core-subject emphasis shifted dramatically to mathematics and science. Art education reached a low point in the 1970s, when a shrinking school-age population (the graduating baby boomer generation) and a serious national energy crisis brought about many school closings and program cuts. Art programs were among the first to be reduced or eliminated.

But the 1970s also ushered in a period of intense work by art educators to revive interest in art education. At the Getty Center for Education in the Arts, for example, work began on the implementation of a transformational theory: discipline-based art education (DBAE). This theory proposed that art making (or "studio art")—the thrust of creative expression—needed to be extended and informed by attention to the complementary disciplines of art history, aesthetics, and art criticism, even when teaching the youngest pupils. DBAE theory, most observers now agree, has been instrumental in rein-

vigorating art education and gaining a place for art in school reform.

Interest in the general quality of U.S. education rose during the 1980s, especially after the 1983 publication of *A Nation at Risk* by the National Commission on Excellence in Education. The commission's report spoke of "a rising tide of mediocrity" in K–12 schools and ushered in ongoing school reform efforts at all levels. National attention reached a peak in 1994 with the passage of the federal Goals 2000: Educate America Act. This act led to the formation of goal-setting groups, among them the National Coalition for Education in the Arts, which took up the task of ensuring that the arts, writ large, would assume their rightful place within the basic curriculum. This coalition included, among others, the American Alliance for Theatre and Education, the National Art Education Association, the Music Educators National Conference, and the National Dance Association. It defined arts education broadly as "the process of teaching and learning how to create and produce the visual and performing arts and how to understand and evaluate art forms created by others" (Arts Education Partnership Working Group, p. 5).

The National Art Education Association took a central role in defining the expectations for art education, which were written into the national standards: Students should understand and apply art media and processes; use visual arts structures and functions; choose and evaluate a range of subject matter, symbols, and ideas; understand art in relation to history and cultures; reflect upon and assess the merits of their own work and that of others; and make connections between art and other disciplines.

This view of art education coalesced with other theories, which became generally accepted during the last quarter of the twentieth century. Three are noteworthy. First, constructivism supplanted behaviorism as a guiding instructional theory, drawing on work by educators and researchers, such as Jerome Bruner (1960), Jean Piaget (1974), and Lev S. Vygotsky (1978). Constructivism posits that learners play a crucial role in "constructing" their own knowledge. Where behaviorism tends to see the teacher as a dispenser of knowledge, constructivism views the teacher as a facilitator who helps students acquire understandings and put them to individual use.

Second, postmodernism became the successor to modernism. First identified in architecture by

Charles Jencks (1977), the unifying feature of post-modern theory is the absence of cultural dominance. In art education this led to greater emphasis on multiculturalism and expansion of the traditional canon.

Third, the multiple intelligences theory, developed by Howard Gardner (1983), points out that children think and learn based on individual intellectual strengths. Gardner initially identified seven intelligences—musical, bodily-kinesthetic, logical-mathematical, linguistic, spatial, interpersonal, and intrapersonal—and later added others. Art education, particularly as viewed through the lens of DBAE theory, taps intelligences that are not typically used in other core subjects.

By implementing arts curricula based on these theories, many arts educators believe that "students can arrive at their own knowledge, beliefs, and values for making personal and artistic decisions. In other terms, they can arrive at a broad-based, well-grounded understanding of nature, value, and meaning of arts as a part of their own humanity" (Consortium of National Arts Education Associations, pp. 18–19).

Elementary and Middle Schools

Children are natural artists. From infancy, they delight in the interplay of light and shadow, shape and color. Objects dangling from a mobile and the elemental shapes of balls and blocks fascinate them. As children develop, they connect the visual and the tactile: playing in spilled cereal, sculpting sand on a beach, finger painting, and scribbling with crayons. They create shadows in patches of sunlight and lay out sticks to form patterns.

By the time most children enter formal schooling, they have moved from scribbling and stacking to more deliberate two- and three-dimensional representation. For younger children, first representations usually are of inner realities. When asked to describe their artworks, they tell detailed and imaginative stories. As time goes by, children's drawings and sculptures begin to reflect their observations of the world.

Nurturing the natural development of artistic sensitivities and creative responses is the universal thrust of elementary art education. Formalized study is introduced gradually, as children move through the elementary grades and into middle school, which begins in the United States at fifth, sixth, or seventh grade, depending on the school system.

Elementary art specialists in some schools function mainly as art teachers, working with classes in isolation and focusing almost exclusively on art making. While a classroom teacher's pupils work with a specialist (art, music, physical education, etc.), the teacher gains planning time. However, with increasing emphasis on DBAE and national standards, many art specialists and classroom teachers are now working as partners.

An art specialist may work directly with pupils for as little as forty or fifty minutes once each week, but ideally art is taught more often—daily in some schools. Art also is integral to language arts, social studies, mathematics, and science in many schools. The art specialist, in addition to teaching children, helps classroom teachers blend art with other subjects. Such collaboration also expands the subject matter of art, raising questions about aesthetics and the place of art in culture and society. When art is valued as a core subject in this way, children's artworks proliferate in classrooms and corridors. The artworks incorporate themes from other subjects and are creative and individualistic.

Ideally the collaboration and integration that distinguish elementary art education are carried into programs for young adolescents. Many U.S. middle schools use a team-teaching approach to organize classes and schedules, which facilitates an art-and-humanities framework and fosters the inclusion of art in the core curriculum. In middle schools that function more like high schools, art classes tend to be organized around media and art forms and are treated as electives.

Secondary Schools

Art education reform, which began in the 1980s and 1990s, focuses on moving art into the core curriculum, "where art is studied and created so that the students will gain insights into themselves, their world, human purposes, and values" (Wilson, p. 168). Some U.S. high schools are oriented in this manner, and most others are moving philosophically in this direction, even though many also continue to offer traditional art courses aimed, in part, at educating students as artists. Art is an elective subject in most secondary schools.

Course offerings, however, may be extensive. It is not unusual for larger high schools to offer thirty to forty separate art classes, including beginning, intermediate, and advanced levels. Subjects include drawing, painting, photography, commercial art, sculpture, ceramics, weaving and fiber art, jewelry, design, and art history. Where DBAE theory has been influential, classes in aesthetics and art criticism may be offered separately, but art topics also will be addressed in the context of classes in most subjects. Some schools pair art with other subjects in teamed classes, such as photography with journalism and film making with film study.

The influence of postmodernism is evident in broadening the art canon to include more multicultural imagery. Art reproductions used in Western classrooms portray images from African and Asian cultures along with those from European sources. Particular attention to including African-American art images can be seen in many U.S. schools.

Adolescent notions of art are shaped by many influences, ranging from popular culture to formal schooling. Thus the teenage years are a time of aesthetic questioning. Secondary school art programs should be about educating students to be consumers, as well as producers, of art. Situating art education in the core curriculum facilitates such study and helps students develop sound judgment of art.

Technology

The rapid advancement of computer technology has transformed art at all levels. Art-making, whether in the professional world or in schools, often is aided by computer programs that allow artists to create and manipulate images electronically. This new capability raises aesthetic questions about the nature of art. For example, must a finished artwork be frameable? When, for that matter, should a work be considered "finished"? In the commercial world, an illustrator's work may exist only as a computer file until it finally appears in a book or magazine. As an electronic file, the image also can be altered repeatedly by the artist or by a publisher's art director until the moment it is printed.

Computer technology also provides resources for art history and criticism. Images for classroom study are routinely available in electronic formats, such as CD-ROM, making it easy for a school to maintain an extensive collection of visual references. Electronic editions of encyclopedias and other texts offer "extras" not found in print, such as film footage and sound bites. These extras enliven and enlarge the resources so that students do not merely read the information, but experience it.

The number of "wired" classrooms continues to increase. Electronic connections between a classroom or laboratory computer and the Internet make virtual field trips increasingly available as instructional tools. If teachers cannot take their students physically to a museum, they may be able to take them electronically. Virtual tours of many of the world's art galleries and museums are expanding instructional horizons. Some institutional sites, such as the website of the Louvre Museum in Paris, also encourage cross-cultural studies by allowing electronic visitors to take the virtual tour in several languages and by providing links to other historical and cultural websites.

See also: ART EDUCATION, *subentry on* PREPARATION OF TEACHERS; CURRICULUM, SCHOOL; ELEMENTARY EDUCATION, *subentry on* CURRENT TRENDS; SECONDARY EDUCATION, *subentry on* CURRENT TRENDS.

BIBLIOGRAPHY

ARTS EDUCATION PARTNERSHIP WORKING GROUP. 1993. *The Power of the Arts to Transform Education.* Washington, DC: John F. Kennedy Center for the Arts.

BRUNER, JEROME. 1960. *The Process of Education.* New York: Vintage.

CONSORTIUM OF NATIONAL ARTS EDUCATION ASSOCIATIONS. 1994. *National Standards for Arts Education: What Every Young American Should Know and Be Able to Do in the Arts.* Reston, VA: Music Educators National Conference.

GARDNER, HOWARD. 1983. *Frames of Mind: The Theory of Multiple Intelligences.* New York: Basic.

GOOD, HARRY G. 1962. *A History of American Education,* 2nd edition. New York: Macmillan.

JENCKS, CHARLES. 1991. *The Language of Post-Modern Architecture,* 6th edition. New York: Rizzoli.

LARSON, GARY O. 1997. *American Canvas.* Washington, DC: National Endowment for the Arts.

NATIONAL ART EDUCATION ASSOCIATION. 1995. *A Vision for Art Education Reform.* Reston, VA: National Art Education Association.

PIAGET, JEAN. 1974. *To Understand Is to Invent: The Future of Education.* New York: Viking.

VYGOTSKY, LEV S. 1978. *Mind in Society.* Cambridge: Harvard University Press.

WALLING, DONOVAN R. 2000. *Rethinking How Art Is Taught: A Critical Convergence.* Thousand Oaks, CA: Corwin.

WILSON, BRENT. 1997. *The Quiet Evolution: Changing the Face of Arts Education.* Los Angeles: Getty Education Institute for the Arts.

DONOVAN R. WALLING

PREPARATION OF TEACHERS

Visual arts teacher education includes the preparation of art specialist teachers as well as general classroom teachers. At the beginning of the twenty-first century, there are several issues that teacher education in the visual arts must address, including: (a) changes in approaches to determining the art content (art history, criticism, aesthetics, and production) and pedagogical knowledge base for teachers; (b) the challenges of alternative licensure options; (c) the administration of programs of teacher preparation; and (d) conceptions of quality in teacher education in the visual arts.

Teacher Education and Visual Arts Education

Teacher education in the visual arts is unique because of the need to prepare two types of teachers at the elementary level (specialist and general classroom teachers), and because of the broad possibilities that exist for the preparation of the secondary teacher of the visual arts. The preparation of specialist teachers varies greatly, ranging from a professional degree in art, in which a substantial portion of the degree is devoted to courses in the visual arts, to a professional degree in education, in which there are fewer courses in art and more in professional education and general education. The preparation of general classroom teachers almost always occurs within an education program. Courses, when required, are usually taught by a professional art educator, who may be a member of either an art faculty or an education faculty.

Current Structure and Organization

While most teacher education in the visual arts in the United States occurs at the undergraduate level, programs exist in a variety of types of institutions, ranging from large research institutions to small liberal arts colleges. A small number of programs are fifth-year, postbaccalaureate programs. The administration of programs for the preparation of visual arts teachers also varies greatly. Some are administered as a subdiscipline within a visual arts program, while others are administered through a professional education unit. Regardless of the home base of the program, effective administration requires collaboration between the visual arts unit and the professional education unit on a campus. Neither the research nor the theoretical literature suggests a clear position about where such programs of instruction are most effectively administered.

National Efforts to Improve Teacher Education in the Arts

Between 1996 and 2001 several major national efforts were initiated related to the preparation of visual arts teachers. The National Art Education Association (NAEA) published a new set of standards for art teacher preparation in 1999; the International Council of Fine Arts Deans (ICFAD) adopted an agenda for teacher education in 1998—and they published *To Move Forward* in collaboration with the Consortium of National Arts Education Associations and the Council of Arts Accrediting Associations in 2001. The purpose of this publication is an affirmation of a continuing commitment to arts education; the statement identifies accomplishments in a number of areas and suggests a reasonable number of next steps to advance student learning. The Council of Chief State School Officers, through its Interstate New Teacher Assessment and Support Consortium (INTASC), initiated an effort in 1998 to establish standards for teacher preparation in the arts, including the visual arts, for elementary classroom teachers and elementary arts specialists. The Arts Education Partnership has also addressed the issue of teacher education in the arts through the establishment of a national task force and by holding several meetings devoted to the topic. The Institute for Education Inquiry's (IEI) National Network for Educational Renewal launched a national arts and teacher education initiative in 1999 that is focused on including a comprehensive approach to teaching and learning in and through the arts in the preparation of elementary classroom teachers.

The five-point agenda adopted by the International Council of Fine Arts Deans in 1998 consists of: (1) defining the nature of teaching and learning in the arts for all students; (2) reviewing and revising the curriculum of undergraduate teacher education programs to insure that prospective arts specialists, working with classroom teachers, are prepared to deliver a balanced curriculum (production and performance, history, criticism, and aesthetics) that addresses multicultural issues and the use of technology in the arts; (3) insuring that prospective arts specialist and classroom teachers are prepared to engage in meaningful collaborations with classroom teachers; (4) addressing and incorporating the national standards in the arts into the preparation of prospective arts specialist and classroom teachers; and (5) insuring that prospective arts specialist and classroom teachers understand the role of the arts in the real world by recognizing the necessity for effective advocacy and meaningful partnerships. Paramount in moving this agenda forward is the recognition that art teacher educators must be provided with opportunities for professional development. Four of the seven major sections of *To Move Forward* address teacher education issues—outlining accomplishments and identifying necessary steps to move forward.

Both the National Art Education Association (NAEA) and the Council of Chief State School Officers (CCSSO) have initiated efforts to establish performance-based standards for the preparation of specialist and classroom teachers in the arts. The NAEA standards deal with the visual arts specialist teacher only, while the INTASC standards deal with all of the arts, for the elementary arts specialist teacher and the classroom teacher. Both efforts herald a new direction for teacher education, in that both are based on performance standards for the prospective teacher as opposed to program standards that are often based on increments of time.

The NAEA standards support a comprehensive approach to teaching and learning in the arts and outline standards and skills for the art teacher candidates in the content of art, knowledge of the students, curriculum development, instruction, and assessment of student learning outcomes, teacher effectiveness, and program effectiveness. The INTASC standards are designed to promote standards-based reform of teacher preparation, licensing, and professional development. The standards are built around ten core principles related to: (1) "the central concepts, tools of inquiry, and structures of the discipline(s)," and the creation of learning experiences that make these aspects of subject matter meaningful for students; (2) "how children learn and develop," and being able to provide "learning opportunities that support their intellectual, social, physical, and

personal development;" (3) "how students differ in their approaches to learning," and creating "instructional opportunities that are adapted to diverse learners;" (4) using "a variety of instructional strategies to encourage students' development of critical thinking, problem solving, and performance skills;" (5) "individual and group motivation and behavior to create a learning environment that encourages positive social interaction, active engagement in learning, and self-motivation;" (6) "effective verbal, nonverbal, and media communication techniques to foster active inquiry, collaboration, and supportive interaction in the classroom;" (7) "planning instruction based upon knowledge of subject matter, students, the community, and curriculum goals;" (8) using "formal and informal assessment strategies to evaluate and ensure the continuous intellectual, social, and physical development of the learner;" (9) insuring that the teacher "is a reflective practitioner who continually evaluates the effects of his/her choices and actions on others (students, parents, and other professionals in the learning community), and who actively seeks out opportunities to grow professionally;" and (10) fostering "relationships with school colleagues, parents, and agencies in the larger community to support students' learning and well-being."

While the IEI project and the Arts Education Partnership efforts have not produced any documents to date, both have strong potential for making significant contributions to the improvement of teacher preparation in the visual arts. The IEI project is planned to: (1) design a component in the teacher education curriculum to help prospective elementary education teachers understand and acquire literacy in the arts through a comprehensive approach to learning and teaching in and through the arts; (2) foster and enhance partner schools where prospective elementary teachers are mentored by experienced teachers demonstrating success in engaging students deeply in a comprehensive approach to teaching and learning in and through the arts in their classroom activity; (3) foster and enhance partnerships with local and regional arts organizations that can have a positive impact upon teacher education programs and upon teaching and learning in partner schools; and (4) work with faculty in arts departments and colleges, schools, and departments of education, as well as with appropriate campus administrators, to ensure that general education requirements include a comprehensive approach to learning and teaching in and through the arts. The Arts Education Partnership has addressed the issue by establishing a task force that is examining how the partnership's constituent organizations can become involved in both pre-service and in-service teacher education.

All of these national efforts are focused on improving the quality of teacher education in the arts, and they emphasize a comprehensive approach to teaching and learning in and through the arts. Among the concerns raised through these efforts are: (a) relationships and responsibilities of the art educator, the professional artist, and the professional general educator in teaching and teacher preparation in the visual arts; (b) appropriate entry levels into practice for the art educator; and (c) validation of the basic preparation for teachers.

ART EDUCATION, *subentry on* SCHOOL; CURRICULUM, SCHOOL; ELEMENTARY EDUCATION, *subentry on* CURRENT TRENDS; SECONDARY EDUCATION, *subentry on* CURRENT TRENDS.

BIBLIOGRAPHY

COUNCIL OF CHIEF STATE SCHOOL OFFICERS. 1992. *Model Standards for Beginning Teacher Licensing and Development: A Resource for State Dialogue.* Washington, DC: Council of Chief State School Officers.

DAY, MICHAEL D., ed. 1997. *Preparing Teachers of Art.* Reston, VA: National Art Education Association.

DARLING-HAMMOND, LINDA, and COBB, VELMA L. 1996. "The Changing Context of Teacher Education." In *The Teacher Educator's Handbook: Building a Knowledge Base for the Preparation of Teachers,* ed. Frank B. Murray. San Francisco: Jossey-Bass.

GAILBRAITH, LYNN. 1993. "Familiar, Interactive, and Collaborative Pedagogy: Changing Practices in Preservice Art Education." *Art Education* 46(5):6–11.

GAILBRAITH, LYNN, ed. 1995. *Preservice Art Education: Issues and Practice.* Reston, VA: National Art Education Association.

GORE, JENNIFER M. 2001. "Beyond Our Differences: A Reassembling of What Matters in Teacher Education." *Journal of Teacher Education* 52(2):124–135.

HENRY, CAROL. 1999. "The Role of Reflection in Student Teachers's Perceptions of Their Professional Development." *Art Education* 52(2):14–20.

KOWALCHUK, ELIZABETH A. 1999. "Perceptions of Practice: What Art Student Teachers Say They Learn and Need to Know." *Studies in Art Education* 41(1):71–90.

NATIONAL ART EDUCATION ASSOCIATION. 1999. *Standards for Art Teacher Preparation.* Reston, VA: National Art Education Association.

ZIMMERMAN, ENID. 1994. "Current Research and Practice about Pre-service Visual Art Specialist Teacher Education." *Studies in Art Education* 35(2):79–89.

ZIMMERMAN, ENID. 1994. "Concerns of Pre-service Art Teachers and Those Who Prepare Them to Teach." *Art Education* 47(5):59–67.

INTERNET RESOURCES

CONSORTIUM OF NATIONAL ARTS EDUCATION ASSOCIATIONS; INTERNATIONAL COUNCIL OF FINE ARTS DEANS; and COUNCIL OF ARTS ACCREDITING ASSOCIATIONS. 2001. *To Move Forward.* <www.naea-reston.org/ToMove.pdf>.

INTERNATIONAL COUNCIL OF FINE ARTS DEANS. 1998. "Teacher Education in the Arts for the Twenty-First Century." <www.rowan.edu/icfad>.

D. JACK DAVIS

ASSESSMENT

CLASSROOM ASSESSMENT
Richard Stiggins
DYNAMIC ASSESSMENT
David Tzuriel
NATIONAL ASSESSMENT OF EDUCATIONAL
PROGRESS
James W. Pellegrino
PERFORMANCE ASSESSMENT
Edward A. Silver
PORTFOLIO ASSESSMENT
Joan L. Herman
Stephen A. Zuniga

CLASSROOM ASSESSMENT

Classroom assessments are those developed or selected by teachers for use during their day-to-day instruction. They are different from the standardized tests that are conducted annually to gauge student achievement, and are most frequently used to serve formative purposes, that is, to help students learn. However, classroom assessments also can be used summatively to determine a student's report card grade. Standardized tests, on the other hand, tend to be considered summative assessments, as they are used to judge student progress over an extended period of time.

As the research summarized below reveals, assessment used during instruction can have a profound impact on student achievement. But to do so, the assessments must provide accurate information and they must be used in appropriate ways.

Research on Impact

In 1984, Benjamin Bloom published a summary of research on the impact of mastery learning models, comparing standard whole-class instruction (the control condition) with two experimental interventions—a mastery learning environment (where students aspire to achieving specific learning standards) and one-on-one tutoring of individual students. One hallmark of both experimental conditions was extensive use of formative classroom assessment during the learning process. Analysis of summative results revealed unprecedented gains in achievement for students in the experimental treatments—when compared to the control groups. To be sure, the entire effect cannot be attributed to the effective use of classroom assessment. But, according to Bloom, a major portion can.

Based on his 1988 compilation of available research, Terry Crooks concluded that classroom assessment can have a major impact on student learning when it:

- Places great emphasis on understanding, not just recognition or recall of knowledge; as well as on the ability to transfer learning to new situations and other patterns of reasoning

- Is used formatively to help students learn, and not just summatively for the assignment of a grade

- Yields feedback that helps students see their growth or progress while they are learning, thereby maintaining the value of the feedback for students

- Relies on student interaction in ways that enhance the development of self-evaluation skills

- Reflects carefully articulated achievement expectations that are set high, but attainable, so as to maximize students' confidence that they can succeed if they try and to prevent them from giving up in hopelessness

- Consolidates learning by providing regular opportunities for practice with descriptive, not judgmental, feedback

- Relies on a broad range of modes of assessment aligned appropriately with the diversity of achievement expectations valued in most classrooms

- Covers all valued achievement expectations and does not reduce the classroom to focus only on that which is easily assessed

A decade later, Paul Black and Dylan Wiliam examined the measurement research literature worldwide in search of answers to three questions: (1) Is there evidence that improving the quality and effectiveness of use of formative (classroom) assessments raises student achievement as reflected in summative assessments? (2) Is there research evidence that formative assessments are in need of improvement? (3) Is there evidence about the kinds of improvements that are most likely to enhance student achievement? They uncovered forty articles that addressed the first question with sufficiently rigorous research designs to permit an estimation of the effects of improved classroom assessment on subsequent standardized test scores. They also uncovered profoundly large effects, including score gains that, if realized in the international math and science tests of the 1990s, would have raised the United States and England from the middle of the pack in the rank order of forty-two participating nations to the top five. Black and Wiliam go on to reveal that "improved formative assessment helps low achievers more than other students, and so reduces the range of achievement while raising achievement overall" (p. 141). They contend that this result has direct implications for districts having difficulty reducing achievement gaps between minorities and other students. The answer to their second question is equally definitive. Citing a litany of research similar to that referenced above, they describe the almost complete international neglect in assessment training for teachers.

Their answer to the third question, asking what specific improvements in classroom assessment are likely to have the greatest impact, is the most interesting of all. They describe the positive effects on student learning of (a) increasing the accuracy of classroom assessments, (b) providing students with frequent informative feedback, rather than infrequent judgmental feedback, and (c) involving students deeply in the classroom assessment, record keeping, and communication processes. They conclude that "self-assessment by pupils, therefore, far from being a luxury, is in fact an essential component of formative assessment. When anyone is trying to learn, feedback about the effort has three elements: redefinition of the desired goal, evidence about present position, and some understanding of a way to close the gap between the two. All three must be understood to some degree by anyone before he or she can take action to improve learning" (p. 143).

Standards of Quality

To have such positive effects, classroom assessments must be carefully developed to yield dependable evidence of student achievement. If they meet the five standards of quality described below, they will, in all probability, produce accurate results.

These standards can take the form of the five questions that the developer can ask about the assessment: (1) Am I clear about what I want to assess? (2) Do I know why I am assessing? (3) Am I sure about how to gather the evidence that I need? (4) Have I gathered enough evidence? (5) Have I eliminated all relevant sources of bias in results? Answers to these questions help judge the quality of classroom assessments. Each is considered in greater detail below.

Standard 1. In any classroom assessment context, one must begin the assessment development process by defining the precise vision of what it means to succeed. Proper assessment methods can be selected only when one knows what kind of achievement needs to be assessed. Are students expected to master subject-matter content—meaning to *know* and *understand*? If so, does this mean they must know it outright, or does it mean they must know where and how to find it using reference sources? Are they expected to use their knowledge to reason and solve problems? Should they be able to demonstrate mastery of specific performance skills, where it's the doing that is important, or to use their knowledge, reasoning, and skills to create products that meet standards of quality?

Because there is no single assessment method capable of assessing all these various forms of achievement, one cannot select a proper method without a sharp focus on which of these expectations is to be assessed. The main quality-control challenge is to be sure the target is clear before one begins to devise assessment tasks and scoring procedures to measure it.

Standard 2. The second quality standard is to build each assessment in light of specific information about its intended users. It must be clear what purposes a particular assessment will serve. One cannot design sound assessments without asking who will use the results, and how they will use them. To provide quality information that will meet people's needs, one must analyze their needs. For instance, if students are to use assessment results to make important decisions about their own learning, it is important to conduct the assessment and provide the results in a manner that will meet their needs, which might be distinctly different from the information needs of a teacher, parent, or principal. Thus, the developer of any assessment should be able to provide evidence of having investigated the needs of the intended user of that assessment, and of having conducted that assessment in a manner consistent with that purpose. Otherwise the assessment is without purpose. The quality-control challenge is to develop and administer an assessment only after it has been determined precisely who will use its results, and how they will use them.

Within this standard of quality, the impact research cited above suggests that special emphasis be given to one particular assessment user, the student. While there has been a tendency to think of the student as the subject (or victim) of the assessment, the fact is that the decisions students make that are based on teacher assessments of their success drive their ultimate success in school. Thus, it is essential that they remain in touch with and feel in control of their own improvement over time.

Standard 3. Since there are several different kinds of achievement to assess, and since no single assessment method can reflect them all, educators must rely on a variety of methods. The options available to the classroom teacher include selected response (multiple choice, true/false, matching, and fill-in), essays, performance assessments (based on observation and judgment), and direct personal communication with the student. The assessment task is to match a method with an intended target, as depicted

TABLE 1

Aligning achievement targets to assessment methods

Target To Be Assessed	Assessment Method			
	Selected Response	Essay	Performance Assessment	Personal Communication
Knowledge Mastery	Multiple-choice, true/false, matching, and fill-in questions can sample mastery of elements of knowledge	Essay exercises can tap understanding of relationships among elements of knowledge	Not a good choice for this target	Can ask questions, evaluate answers and infer mastery—but a time-consuming option
Reasoning Proficiency	Can assess understanding of basic patterns of reasoning	Written descriptions of complex problem solutions can provide a window into reasoning proficiency	Can watch students solve some problems and infer about reasoning proficiency	Can ask student to "think aloud" or can ask follow-up questions to probe reasoning
Performance Skills	Can assess mastery of the prerequisites of skillful performance, but cannot tap the skill itself—not a good choice for this target	Can assess mastery of the prerequisites of skillful performance, but cannot tap the skill itself—not a good choice for this target	Can observe and evaluate skills as they are being performed	Strong match when skill is oral communication proficiency; also can assess mastery of knowledge prerequisite to skillful performance
Ability To Create Products	Can assess mastery of knowledge prerequisite to the ability to create quality products, but cannot assess the quality of products themselves—not a good choice	Can assess mastery of knowledge prerequisite to the ability to create quality products, but cannot assess the quality of products themselves—not a good choice	A strong match—can assess: (a) proficiency in carrying out steps in product development, as well as (b) attributes of the product itself	Can probe procedural knowledge and knowledge of attributes of quality products—but not product quality

SOURCE: Adapted from Stiggins, Richard J. 2001. *Student-Involved Classroom Assessment,* 3rd edition. Columbus, OH: Merrill.

in Table 1. The quality-control challenge is to be sure that everyone concerned with quality assessment knows and understands how the various pieces of this puzzle fit together.

Standard 4. All assessments rely on a relatively small number of exercises to permit the user to draw inferences about a student's mastery of larger domains of achievement. A sound assessment offers a representative sample of all those possibilities that is large enough to yield dependable inferences about how the respondent would perform if given all possible exercises. Each assessment context places its own special constraints on sampling procedures, and the quality-control challenge is to know how to adjust the sampling strategies to produce results of maximum quality at minimum cost in time and effort.

Standard 5. Even if one devises clear achievement targets, transforms them into proper assessment methods, and samples student performance appropriately, there are still factors that can cause a student's score on a test to misrepresent his or her real achievement. Problems can arise from the test, from the student, or from the environment where the test is administered.

For example, tests can consist of poorly worded questions; they can place reading or writing demands on respondents that are confounded with mastery of the material being tested; or they can have more than one correct response, be incorrectly scored, or contain racial or ethnic bias. The student can experience extreme evaluation anxiety or interpret test items differently from the author's intent, and students may cheat, guess, or lack motivation. In addition, the assessment environment could be uncomfortable, poorly lighted, noisy, or otherwise distracting. Any of these factors could give rise to inaccurate assessment results. Part of the quality-control challenge is to be aware of the potential sources of bias and to know how to devise assessments, prepare students, and plan assessment environments to deflect these problems before they ever have an impact on results.

See also: ASSESSMENT, *subentries on* DYNAMIC ASSESSMENT, NATIONAL ASSESSMENT OF EDUCATIONAL PROGRESS, PERFORMANCE ASSESSMENT; ASSESSMENT TOOLS, *subentries on* PSYCHOMETRIC AND STATISTICAL, TECHNOLOGY BASED; STANDARDS FOR

STUDENT LEARNING; TESTING, *subentry on* STANDARDIZED TESTS AND HIGH-STAKES ASSESSMENT.

BIBLIOGRAPHY

BLACK, PAUL, and WILIAM, DYLAN. 1998. "Assessment and Classroom Learning." *Assessment in Education* 5(1):7–74.

BLACK, PAUL, and WILIAM, DYLAN. 1998. "Inside the Black Box: Raising Standards through Classroom Assessment." *Phi Delta Kappan* 80 (2):139–148.

BLOOM, BENJAMIN. 1984. "The Search for Methods of Group Instruction as Effective as One-to-One Tutoring." *Educational Leadership* 41:4–17.

CROOKS, TERRY J. 1988. "The Impact of Classroom Evaluation on Students." *Review of Educational Research* 58(4):438–481.

STIGGINS, RICHARD J. 2001. *Student-Involved Classroom Assessment,* 3rd edition. Columbus, OH: Merrill.

RICHARD STIGGINS

DYNAMIC ASSESSMENT

The term *dynamic assessment* (DA) refers to an assessment, by an active teaching process, of a child's perception, learning, thinking, and problem solving. The process is aimed at modifying an individual's cognitive functioning and observing subsequent changes in learning and problem-solving patterns within the testing situation. The goals of the DA are to: (a) assess the capacity of the child to grasp the principle underlying an initial problem and to solve it, (b) assess the nature and amount of investment (teaching) that is required to teach a child a given rule or principle, and (c) identify the specific deficient cognitive functions (i.e., systematic exploratory behavior) and non-intellective factors (i.e., need for mastery) that are responsible for failure in performance and how modifiable they are as a result of teaching. In contrast, the term *static test* (ST) generally refers to a standardized testing procedure in which an examiner presents items to an examinee without any attempt to intervene to change, guide, or improve the child's performance. A static test usually has graduated levels of difficulty, with the tester merely recording and scoring the responses.

DA is usually administered to children who demonstrate some learning disability, low scores on standardized tests, or some emotional or personality disturbance. Very frequently it is given to children coming from a low socioeconomic or culturally different background. The differences between the ST and DA approaches derive from different philosophical perspectives: ST is related to *passive acceptance* (acceptance of a child's disability and accommodation of the environment to fit these disabilities), while DA is based on *active modification* (active efforts to modify the child's disabilities by intensive mediation and the establishment of relatively high cognitive goals).

DA development has been motivated by the inadequacy of standardized tests. The inadequacy can be summarized in the following points: (1) Static tests do not provide crucial information about learning processes, deficient cognitive functions that are responsible for learning difficulties, and mediational strategies that facilitate learning. (2) The manifested low performance level of many children, as revealed in ST, very frequently falls short of revealing their learning potential, especially of those identified as coming from disadvantaged social backgrounds, or as having some sort of learning difficulty. Many children fail in static tests because of lack of opportunities for learning experiences, cultural differences, specific learning difficulties, or traumatic life experiences. (3) In many static tests children are described in general terms, mostly in relation to their relative position of their peer group, but they do not provide clear descriptions of the processes involved in learning and recommendations for prescriptive teaching and remedial learning strategies. (4) Static tests do not relate to non-intellective factors that can influence individuals' cognitive performance, sometimes more than the "pure" cognitive factors. Non-intellective factors (i.e., intrinsic motivation, need for mastery, locus of control, anxiety, frustration, tolerance, self-confidence, and accessibility to mediation) are no less important in determining children's intellectual achievements than are the "pure" cognitive factors. This is especially true with individuals whose emotional or motivational problems interfere with their cognitive performance.

In comparison with ST, DA is designed to provide accurate information about: (a) an individual's current learning ability and learning processes; (b) specific cognitive factors (i.e., impulsivity, planning behavior) responsible for problem-solving ability and academic success or failure; (c) efficient teaching strategies for the child being studied; and (d) motivational, emotional, and personality factors that affect cognitive processes.

Lev Vygotsky's concept of a *zone of proximal development* (ZPD) and Reuben Feuerstein's theory of mediated learning experience (MLE) served as the main conceptual bases for most of the DA elaboration. The ZPD is defined as the difference between a child's "actual developmental level as determined by independent problem solving" and the higher level of "potential development as determined through problem solving under adult guidance or in collaboration with more capable peers" (Vygotsky, p. 86). MLE interactions are defined as a process in which parents or experienced adults interpose themselves between a set of stimuli and a child and modify the stimuli for the developing child. In a DA context, the examiner mediates the rules and strategies for solving specific problems on an individual basis, and assesses the level of internalization (i.e., deep understanding) of these rules and strategies as well as their transfer value to other problems of increased level of complexity, novelty, and abstraction.

The Nature of Dynamic Assessment

DA is meant to be a complement to standardized testing, not a substitute for it. It is presented as a broad approach, not as a particular test. Different criteria of change are used in DA: pre- to post-teaching gains, amount and type of teaching required, and the degree of transfer of learning. The choice to use change criteria to predict future cognitive performance (as well as predicted outcome of intervention programs) is based on the belief that measures of change are more closely related to teaching processes (by which the child is taught how to process information), than they are to conventional measures of intelligence. The major differences between DA and conventional tests in regard to goals, testing processes, types of instruments, test situations, and interpretation of results, are presented in Table 1.

Using DA. Clinical experience has shown that it is most useful to use DA when standardized tests yield low scores; when standardized tests hover around margins of adequacy in cognitive functioning; when there are serious discrepancies between a child's test scores and academic performance; when a child comes from a low socioeconomic or culturally or linguistically different background; or when a child shows some emotional disturbance, personality disorder, or learning disability.

Reliability of DA. One of the objectives of DA is to change an individual's cognitive functioning within the testing context so as to produce *unreliability* among test items (i.e., lack of consistency between repeated responses). DA reliability is usually assessed by interrater agreement (two or more observers rate the child's behavior) regarding the child's cognitive performance, mediation (teaching) strategies required to change the child's functioning, cognitive functions (i.e., level of impulsivity, planning behavior) that affect performance, and motivational-emotional factors. Such test reliability has been demonstrated with learning disabled and educable mentally retarded (EMR) children. Overall interrater agreement for the type of intervention (mediation) required to change a child's performance for deficient cognitive functions, such as impulsivity, lack of planning, and lack of systematic behavior, has been shown to be about 89 percent. For different cognitive tasks, different profiles of deficient cognitive functions have been observed and different types of teaching can be applied.

Current Research

Educational perspectives. Previous research has shown that standardized IQ tests underestimate the cognitive ability of children from low socioeconomic settings, from minority groups, and children having learning difficulties. Criteria of change (i.e., pre- to post-teaching gains on a test), as measured by DA, have been found to be more powerful in predicting academic performance, more accurate in prescribing individualized educational plans and specific cognitive interventions, and better able to distinguish between different clinical groups than ST scores. David Tzuriel and Pnina Klein, using the Children's Analogical Thinking Modifiability (CATM) test, showed that the highest pre- to post-teaching gains were found among children identified either as disadvantaged or advantaged, compared with children with special education needs and mentally retarded children. Higher levels of functioning, for all groups, were found on the CATM than on the Raven's Colored Progressive Matrices (RCPM)—when the latter was given as a standardized test—especially when comparing performance on analogy items of the RCPM versus problems on the CATM. The advantaged and disadvantaged children scored 69 percent and 64 percent, respectively, on the CATM, compared with 39 percent and 44 percent on the RCPM. The effects of teaching were more articulated in difficult tasks than in easy ones.

TABLE 1

Major differences between dynamic assessment and standardized testing		
Dimensions of comparison	Dynamic assessment	Standardized testing
Testing goals	Assessment of change Assessment of mediation Assessment of deficient cognitive functions Assessment of nonintellective factors	Evaluation of static performance Comparison with peers Prediction of future success
Orientation	Processes of learning Metacognitive processes Understanding mistakes	End products (static) Objective scores Score profiles
Context of testing	Dynamic, open, and interactive Guidance, help, and feedback Feelings of competence Parents and teachers may observe	Standardized Structured Formal Parents and teachers are not allowed to observe
Interpretation of results	Subjective (mainly) Peak performance Cognitive modifiability Deficient cognitive functions Response to mediation	Objective (mainly) Average performance
Nature of tasks	Constructed for learning Graduated for teaching Guaranteed for success	Based on psychometric properties Termination after failures

SOURCE: Tzuriel, David. 2001. *Dynamic Assessment of Young Children*. New York: Kluwer Academic/Plenum. Reprinted with permission.

Findings with the Children's Inferential Thinking Modifiability (CITM) and the Children's Seriational Thinking Modifiability (CSTM) tests indicate that children from minority groups or disadvantaged background have an initial lower level of functioning than children from mainstream groups or an advantaged background. After a teaching phase, however, they showed higher levels of gain and narrowed the gap. The gap between the two groups was also narrower in a transfer phase consisting of more difficult problems. The degree of improvement was higher in high-complexity problems than in low-complexity problems.

In several studies DA was found to verify the distinction between *cultural deprivation* and *cultural difference*. Tzuriel, following Feuerstein, differentiated between those who function poorly as a result of cultural differences and those who have experienced cultural deprivation. The DA approach, in this respect, offers a solution not only for its differential diagnostic value, but also for its potential prescriptive remediation of deficiencies and its enhancement of learning processes.

For certain DA measures, significant positive correlations have been found between the level of difficulty of an item and the level of improvement on that item, and DA post-teaching scores have been shown to be better predictors of academic achievement than static scores. In addition, a higher prediction value was found among children with high learning potential than among children with average learning potential. Findings of many studies raise heavy doubts, especially with low functioning groups, about the ability of ST scores to represent accurately an individual's ability and to serve as indicators for future intervention and change.

Evaluation of Cognitive Education Programs

Dynamic assessment has also been used to evaluate cognitive education programs designed to develop learning and thinking skills. Given that one of the major goals of these programs is advancing *learning to learn* skills, it is essential that the change criteria in DA be assessed several studies have shown that experimental groups who received any one of a number of cognitive education programs (e.g., Bright Start, Instrumental Enrichment, Peer-Mediation with Young Children) attained higher pre- to post-teaching gains on DA tests than did control groups. The DA scores depicted the effects of the intervention better than ST scores did.

Developmental Perspective

Developmental research using DA has focused on predicting learning ability by assessing the quality of parent–child interactions, specifically mother–child mediated learning experience (MLE). MLE interactions are defined as an interactional process in which parents, or substitute adults, interpose themselves between a set of stimuli and the child and modify the stimuli for the developing child. The mediator modifies the stimuli by focusing the child on their characteristics, by arousing curiosity, vigilance, and perceptual acuity in the child, and by trying to improve and/or create in the child the cognitive functions required for temporal, spatial, and cause-effect relationships. Major findings have been that children's post-teaching scores are more accurately predicted by MLE mother–child interactions than by ST scores and that mediation for transcendence (expanding an experience by making a rule or principle, generalizing an event beyond the concrete experience) has emerged as the most powerful predictor of children's ability to change following teaching. These findings support the hypothesis that mother–child mediation strategies arc internalized and used later in other learning contexts. Children whose mothers used a high level of mediation for transcendence internalized the mechanism and used it in other learning contexts where they needed this type of mediation. Findings of several studies confirm the hypothesis that MLE interactions, conceptualized as the proximal factor of cognitive development (i.e., directly explaining cognitive functioning), predicted children's cognitive change, whereas distal factors (i.e., SES, mothers' IQ, child's personality orientation, mother's emotional attitudes toward the child) did not predict cognitive change in children.

Future Research

In spite of the efficacy of DA, some problems exist. First, DA takes more time to administer and requires more skill, better training, more experience, and greater effort than ST. A cost-effectiveness issue is raised by psychologists, educators, and policymakers who are not convinced that the information derived from DA is worth the investment required to get it, and that the information acquired will then be used efficiently to enhance specific learning strategies and academic achievements.

Second, the extent to which cognitive modifiability is generalized across domains needs further investigation. This issue has practical implications for the designing of tests and mediational procedures. Third, validation of DA is much more complex than validation of ST because it has a broader scope of goals (assessing initial performance, deficient cognitive functions, type and amount of mediation, nonintellective factors, and certain parameters of change). In validating DA one needs to develop criteria variables that measure changes that are due to a cognitive intervention.

Finally, the literature is replete with evidence showing a strong relation between IQ (an ST measure) and school achievement (r = .71). This means that nearly 50 percent of the variance in learning outcomes for students can be explained by differences in psychometric IQ. However, three extremely important questions remain: (1) What causes the other 50 percent of achievement variance? (2) When IQ predicts low achievement, what is necessary to defeat that prediction? and (3) What factors influencing the unexplained variance can help to defeat the prediction in the explained variance?

See also: ASSESSMENT, *subentry on* CLASSROOM ASSESSMENT; TESTING, *subentry on* STANDARDIZED TESTS AND HIGH-STAKES TESTING.

BIBLIOGRAPHY

FEUERSTEIN, REUVEN; RAND, YA'COV; and HOFFMAN, MILDRED B. 1979. *The Dynamic Assessment of Retarded Performers: The Learning Potential Assessment Device: Theory, Instruments, and Techniques.* Baltimore: University Park Press.

HAYWOOD, H. CARL. 1997. "Interactive Assessment." In *Assessment of Individuals with Mental Retardation,* ed. Ronald L. Taylor. San Diego, CA: Singular.

HAYWOOD, H. CARL, and TZURIEL, DAVID, eds. 1992. *Interactive Assessment.* Berlin: Springer-Verlag.

LIDZ, CAROL S., ed. 1987. *Dynamic Assessment.* New York: Guilford.

TZURIEL, DAVID. 1999. "Parent-Child Mediated Learning Transactions as Determinants of Cognitive Modifiability: Recent Research and Future Directions." *Genetic, Social, and General Psychology Monographs* 125:109–156.

TZURIEL, DAVID. 2001. *Dynamic Assessment of Young Children.* New York: Kluwer Academic/Plenum.

TZURIEL, DAVID, and HAYWOOD, H. CARL. 1992. "The Development of Interactive-Dynamic Approaches for Assessment of Learning Potential." In *Interactive Assessment,* ed. H. Carl Haywood and David Tzuriel. New York: Springer-Verlag.

TZURIEL, DAVID, and KLEIN, PNINA S. 1985. "Analogical Thinking Modifiability in Disadvantaged, Regular, Special Education, and Mentally Retarded Children." *Journal of Abnormal Child Psychology* 13:539–552.

TZURIEL, DAVID, and SAMUELS, MARILYN T. 2000. "Dynamic Assessment of Learning Potential: Inter-Rater Reliability of Deficient Cognitive Functions, Type of Mediation, and Non-Intellective Factors." *Journal of Cognitive Education and Psychology* 1:41–64.

VYGOTSKY, LEV. S. 1978. *Mind in Society.* Cambridge, MA: Harvard University Press.

DAVID TZURIEL

NATIONAL ASSESSMENT OF EDUCATIONAL PROGRESS

The primary means to monitor the status and development of American education, the National Assessment of Education Progress (NAEP), was conceived in 1963 when Francis Keppel, U.S. Commissioner of Education, appointed a committee to explore options for assessing the condition of education in the United States. The committee, chaired by Ralph Tyler, recommended that an information system be developed based on a battery of psychometric tests.

NAEP's Original Purpose and Design

A number of key features were recommended in the original design of NAEP, several of which were intended to make it substantially different than typical standardized tests of academic achievement. Many, but not all, of these features were incorporated into the first assessments and have persisted throughout NAEP's history. Others have changed in response to policy needs.

With respect to matters of content, each assessment cycle was supposed to target one or more broadly defined subject areas that corresponded to familiar components of school curricula, such as mathematics. For each subject area, panels of citizens would be asked to form consensus groups about appropriate learning objectives at each target age. Test questions or items were to be developed bearing a one-to-one correspondence to particular learning objectives. Thus, from NAEP's beginning, there have been heavy demands for content validity as part of the assessment development process.

Several interesting technical design features were proposed for the assessment program. Of special note was the use of matrix-sampling, a design that distributes large numbers of items broadly across school buildings, districts, and states but limits the number of items given to individual examinees. In essence, the assessment was designed to glean information from hundreds of items, several related to each of many testing objectives, while restricting the amount of time that any student has to spend responding to the assessment. The target period proposed was approximately fifty minutes per examinee. All test items were to be presented by trained personnel rather than by local school personnel in order to maintain uniformly high standards of administration.

The populations of interest for NAEP were to be all U.S. residents at ages 9, 13, and 17, as well as young adults. This would require the selection of private and public schools into the testing sample, as well as selection of examinees at each target age who were not in school. Results would be tabulated and presented by age and by demographic groups within age—but never by state, state subunit, school district, school, or individual. Assessment results would be reported to show the estimated percentage of the population or subpopulation that answered each item and task correctly. And finally, only a subset of the items would be released with each NAEP report. The unreleased items would remain secure, to be administered at a later testing for determining performance changes over time, thereby providing the basis for determining trends in achievement.

The agenda and design laid out for NAEP in the mid-1960s reflected the political and social realities of the time. Prominent among these was the resistance of state and local policymakers to a national curriculum; state and local leaders feared federal erosion of their autonomy and voiced concern about pressure for accountability. Several of NAEP's features thwarted perceptions of the program as a federal testing initiative addressing a nationally prescribed curriculum. Indeed, NAEP's design provided nationally and regionally representative data on the educational condition of American schools, while avoiding any implicit federal standards or state, district, and school comparisons. NAEP was coined the "nation's educational barometer." It became operational in 1969 and 1970 and the first assessments were in science, citizenship, and writing.

Pressures for Redesign of NAEP

As federal initiatives during the 1960s and 1970s expanded educational opportunities, they fostered an administrative imperative for assessment data to help gauge the effect on the nation's education system. NAEP's original design could not accommodate the increasing demands for data about educationally important populations and issues. Age-level (rather than grade-level) testing made it difficult to link NAEP results to state and local education policies and school practices. Furthermore, its reporting scheme allowed for measurement of change on individual items, but not on the broad subject areas; monitoring the educational experiences of students in varied racial and ethnic, language, and economic groups was difficult without summary scores. Increasingly, NAEP was asked to provide more information so that government and education officials would have a stronger basis for making judgments about the adequacy of education services; NAEP's constituents were seeking information that, in many respects, conflicted with the basic design of the program.

The first major redesign of NAEP took place in 1984, when responsibility for its development and administration was moved from the Education Commission of the States to the Educational Testing Service. The design for NAEP's second generation changed the procedures for sampling, objective-setting, item development, data collection, and analysis. Tests were administered by age and grade groupings. Summary scores were provided for each subject area; scale scores were introduced for reporting purposes. These and other changes afforded the program much greater flexibility in responding to policy demands as they evolved.

Almost concurrently, however, the report *A Nation at Risk* was issued in 1983. It warned that America's schools and students were performing poorly and spawned a wave of state-level education reforms. As states invested more and more in their education systems, they sought information about the effectiveness of their efforts. State-level policymakers looked to NAEP for guidance on the effectiveness of alternative practices. The National Governors' Association issued a call for state-comparable achieve-

ment data, and a new report, *The Nation's Report Card*, recommended that NAEP be expanded to provide state-level results.

As the program retooled to accommodate this change, participants in a 1989 education summit in Charlottesville, Virginia, set out to expand NAEP even further. President George Bush and the nation's governors challenged the prevailing assumptions about national expectations for achievement in American schools. They established six national goals for education and specified the subjects and grades in which progress should be measured with respect to national and international frames of reference. By design, these subjects and grades paralleled NAEP's structure. The governors called on educators to hold students to "world-class" standards of knowledge and skill. The governors' commitment to high academic standards included a call for the reporting of NAEP results in relation to rigorous performance standards. They challenged NAEP to describe not only what students currently know and can do, but also what young people should know and be able to do as participants in an education system that holds its students to high standards.

NAEP in the Early Twenty-First Century

The program that took shape during the 1990s is the large and complex NAEP that exists in the early twenty-first century. The NAEP program continues to evolve in response to both policy challenges and results from federally mandated external evaluations. NAEP includes two distinct assessment programs with different instrumentation, sampling, administration, and reporting practices. The two assessments are referred to as trend NAEP and main NAEP.

Trend NAEP is a collection of test items in reading, writing, mathematics, and science that have been administered many times since the 1970s. As the name implies, trend NAEP is designed to document changes in academic performance over time. During the 1990s, trend NAEP was administered in 1990, 1992, 1994, 1996, and 1999. Trend NAEP is administered to nationally representative samples of students aged 9, 13, and 17 following the original NAEP design.

Main NAEP consists of test items that reflect current thinking about what students should know and be able to do in the NAEP subject areas. They are based on contemporary content and skill outlines developed by consensus panels for reading, writing, mathematics, science, U.S. history, world history, geography, civics, the arts, and foreign languages. These content frameworks are periodically reviewed and revised.

Main NAEP is further complicated by having two components, national NAEP and state NAEP. The former assesses nationally representative samples of students in grades 4, 8, and 12. In most but not all subjects, national NAEP is supposed to be administered two, three, or four times during a twelve-year period, to make it possible to examine short term trends in performance over a decade. State NAEP assessments are administered to state representative samples of students in states that voluntarily elect to participate in the program. State NAEP uses the same large-scale assessment materials as those used in national NAEP, but is only administered in grades four and eight in reading, writing, mathematics, and science. In contrast to national NAEP, the tests are administered by local school personnel rather than an independent contractor.

One of the most substantial changes in the main NAEP program is the reporting of results relative to performance standards. In each content area, performance standards are defined for three levels of achievement: basic, proficient, and advanced. The percentage of students at a given grade level whose performance is at or above an achievement level standard is reported, as are trends in the percentages over successive administrations of NAEP in a content area. Achievement level reporting is done for both main NAEP and state NAEP and has become one of the most controversial aspects of the NAEP program.

NAEP's complex design is mirrored by a complex governance structure. The program is governed by the National Assessment Governing Board (NAGB), appointed by the secretary of education but independent of the department. The board, authorized to set policy for NAEP, is designed to be broadly representative of NAEP's varied audiences. It selects the subject areas to be assessed and ensures that the content and skill frameworks that specify goals for assessment are produced through a national consensus process. In addition, NAGB establishes performance standards for each subject and grade tested, in consultation with its contractor for this task. NAGB also develops guidelines for NAEP reporting. The commissioner of education statistics, who leads the National Center for Education Statistics (NCES) in the U.S. Department of Education, retains responsibility for NAEP operations and technical quality control. NCES procures test development and administration services from cooperating private companies.

Evaluations of NAEP

As part of the process of transforming and expanding NAEP during the 1990s, Congress mandated periodic, independent evaluations of the NAEP program. Two such multiyear evaluations were conducted, the first by the National Academy of Education and the second by the National Academy of Sciences. Both evaluations examined several features of the NAEP program design including development of the assessment frameworks, the technical quality of the assessments, the validity of the achievement level reporting, and initiation of the state NAEP assessments. The evaluations concluded that there are many laudatory aspects of NAEP supporting its label as the "gold standard" for assessment of academic achievement. Among the positives is NAEP's attempt to develop broad, consensus-based content area frameworks, incorporate constructed response tasks and item formats that tap more complex forms of knowledge, use matrix sampling to cover a wide range of curriculum content area topics, and employ powerful statistical methods to analyze the results and develop summary scores. These evaluations also concluded that state NAEP, which had developmental status at the start of the 1990s, served a valuable purpose and should become a regular part of the NAEP program, which it did.

The two evaluations also saw considerable room for improvement in NAEP, in many of the areas mentioned above where strength already existed. Two areas of concern were of particular note. The first was the need to broaden the range of knowledge and cognitive skills that should be incorporated into NAEP's assessment frameworks and included as part of the assessment design. Both evaluations argued that NAEP was not fully taking advantage of advances in the cognitive sciences regarding the nature of knowledge and expertise and that future assessments needed to measure aspects of knowledge that were now deemed to be critical parts of the definition of academic competence and achievement. Suggestions were made for how NAEP might do this by developing a portfolio of assessment methods and approaches.

The second major area of concern was the validity of the achievement level analysis and reporting process. Both evaluations, as well as others that preceded them, were extremely critical of both the process that NAEP was using to determine achievement levels and the outcomes that were reported. It was judged that the entire achievement level approach lacked validity and needed a major conceptual and operational overhaul. As might be expected, this critique met with less than resounding approval by the National Assessment Governing Board, which is responsible for the achievement level–setting process.

Many of the concerns raised in the two major evaluations of NAEP, along with many other reviews of various aspects of the NAEP program, have served as stimuli in an ongoing process of refining, improving, and transforming NAEP. One of NAEP's hallmarks as an assessment program is its capacity to evolve, engage in cutting edge assessment development work, and provide results of value to many constituencies. It continues to serve its role as "The Nation's Report Card."

See also: ASSESSMENT TOOLS, *subentries on* PSYCHOMETRIC AND STATISTICAL, TECHNOLOGY BASED.

BIBLIOGRAPHY

ALEXANDER, LAMAR. 1991. *America 2000.* Washington, DC: U.S. Department of Education.

ALEXANDER, LAMAR, and JAMES, H. THOMAS. 1987. *The Nation's Report Card: Improving the Assessment of Student Achievement.* Stanford, CA: National Academy of Education.

GLASER, ROBERT; LINN, ROBERT; and BOHRNSTEDT, GEORGE. 1992. *Assessing Student Achievement in the States.* Stanford, CA: National Academy of Education.

GLASER, ROBERT; LINN, ROBERT; and BOHRNSTEDT, GEORGE. 1993. *The Trial State Assessment: Prospects and Realities.* Stanford, CA: National Academy of Education.

GLASER, ROBERT; LINN, ROBERT; and BOHRNSTEDT, GEORGE. 1996. *Quality and Utility: The 1994 Trial State Assessment in Reading.* Stanford, CA: National Academy of Education.

GLASER, ROBERT; LINN, ROBERT; and BOHRNSTEDT, GEORGE. 1997. *Assessment in Transition: Monitoring the Nation's Educational Progress.* Stanford, CA: National Academy of Education.

JONES, LYLE V. 1996. "A History of the National Assessment of Educational Progress and Some Questions about Its Future." *Educational Researcher* 25(6):1–8.

MESSICK, SAMUEL; BEATON, ALBERT; and LORD, FREDERICK. 1983. *National Assessment of Educational Progress Reconsidered: A New Design for a New Era.* Princeton, NJ: Educational Testing Service.

NATIONAL CENTER FOR EDUCATION STATISTICS. 1974. *NAEP General Information Yearbook.* Washington, DC: U.S. Department of Education.

NATIONAL COMMISSION ON EXCELLENCE IN EDUCATION. 1983. *A Nation at Risk: The Imperative for Educational Reform.* Washington, DC: U.S. Government Printing Office.

OFFICE OF TECHNOLOGY ASSESSMENT. 1992. *Testing in America's Schools: Asking the Right Questions.* Washington, DC: U.S. Government Printing Office.

PELLEGRINO, JAMES W.; JONES, LEE R.; and MITCHELL, KAREN J. 1999. *Grading the Nation's Report Card: Evaluating NAEP and Transforming the Assessment of Educational Progress.* Washington, DC: National Academy Press.

JAMES W. PELLEGRINO

PERFORMANCE ASSESSMENT

The term *performance assessment* (PA) is typically used to refer to a class of assessments that is based on observation and judgment. That is, in PA an assessor usually observes a performance or the product of a performance and judges its quality. For example, to judge one's competence to operate an automobile, it is normally required that one pass a road test, during which actual driving is observed and evaluated. Similarly, Olympic athletes are judged on the basis of observed performances. PA has long been used to judge proficiency in industrial, military, and artistic settings, and interest in its application to educational settings has grown at the start of the twenty-first century.

Educators' interest in PA can be attributed to several factors. It has been argued that performance measures offer a potential advantage of increased validity over other forms of testing that rely on indirect indicators of a desired competence or proficiency. That is, to assess ability to spell one might prefer to have direct evidence that a person can spell words correctly rather than inferring the ability from tasks that involve identifying misspelled words in a list. Proponents of performance assessment have identified many possible benefits, such as allowing a broad range of learning outcomes to be assessed and preserving the complex nature of disciplinary knowledge and inquiry, including conceptual understanding, problem-solving skills, and the application of knowledge and understanding to unique situations. Of particular interest is the potential of PA to capture aspects of higher-order thinking and reasoning, which are difficult to test in other ways.

Moreover, because some research has reported that teachers tend to adapt their instructional practice to reflect the form and content of external assessments, and because performance assessments tend to be better than conventional forms of testing at capturing more complex instructional goals and intentions, it has been argued that "teaching to the test" might be a positive consequence if PA were used to evaluate student achievement. Finally, some proponents have argued that PA could be more equitable than other forms of assessment because PA can engage students in "authentic," contextualized performance, closely related to important instructional goals, thus avoiding the sources of bias associated with testing rapid recall of decontextualized information.

Educational Uses of Performance Assessment

Although performance assessment has been employed in many educational settings, including the assessment of teachers, a primary use in education has been to assess student learning outcomes. PA has long been used in classrooms by teachers to determine what has been learned and by whom. PA may be applied in the classroom in informal ways (as when a teacher observes a student as she solves a problem during seat work) or in more formal ways (as when a teacher collects and scores students' written essays). Within the classroom PA can serve as a means of assigning course grades, communicating expectations, providing feedback to students, and guiding instructional decisions. When PA is used for internal classroom assessment, both the form and content of the assessment can be closely aligned with a teacher's instructional goals. Therefore, the use of performance assessment in the classroom has been seen by some as a promising means of accomplishing a long-standing, elusive goal—namely, the integration of instruction and assessment.

Performance assessment has also been employed in the external assessment of student learning outcomes. PA received significant attention from educators and assessment specialists during the latter part of the 1980s and throughout the 1990s. This increased interest in PA occurred as subject matter standards were established and corresponding changes in instructional practice were envisioned. A growing dissatisfaction with selected-response testing (e.g., true/false questions and multiple-choice items) and an awareness of advances in research in cognition and instruction also spawned interest in PA. Constructed-response tasks (e.g., tasks calling for brief or extended explanations or justifications) became increasingly popular as a means of capturing much of what is valued instructionally in a form that could be included in an external assessment of student achievement. In addition, for subjects such as science and mathematics, tasks that involve hands-on use of materials and tools have been developed. The net result of approximately fifteen years of research and development effort is the inclusion of written essays and constructed-response tasks in tests intended to assess achievement in various subject areas, including writing, history, mathematics, and science. A survey of state assessment practices in the mid-1990s found that thirty-four states required writing samples, and ten states incorporated constructed-response tasks into their assessments.

Performance Assessment: Challenges and Opportunities

A variety of technical and feasibility issues have plagued attempts to employ PA on a large scale. Among the technical issues that await satisfactory resolution are concerns about ensuring generalizability and comparability of performance across tasks and concerns about the scoring of complex tasks and the appropriate interpretation of performances. Efforts to use PA have also been limited due to concerns about the relatively high costs of development, administration, and scoring, when compared to more conventional testing. Finally, despite the hopes of advocates of PA regarding the likely benefits of its widespread adoption, some analyses have raised concerns about equity issues and the limited positive impact on classroom teaching of using PA in external testing.

Despite the problems that have prevented widespread adoption of performance assessment, many educators and assessment experts remain enthusiastic about the potential of PA to address many limitations of other forms of assessment. In particular, advances in the cognitive sciences and technology, along with the increasing availability of sophisticated technological tools in educational settings, may provide new opportunities to resolve many of these issues. For example, the costs of development, administration, and scoring may be decreased through the use of new technologies. And generalizability across tasks may be increased through the use of intelligent systems that offer ongoing assessment well integrated with instruction and sensitive to changes in students' understanding and performance, with performance data collected over a long period of time as opposed to one-time, on-demand testing.

See also: ASSESSMENT, *subentry on* CLASSROOM ASSESSMENT; STANDARDS FOR STUDENT LEARNING.

BIBLIOGRAPHY

AIRASIAN, PETER W. 1991. *Classroom Assessment.* New York: McGraw-Hill.

BAXTER, GAIL P., and GLASER, ROBERT. 1998. "Investigating the Cognitive Complexity of Science Assessments." *Educational Measurement: Issues and Practice* 17(3):37–45.

BENNETT, RANDY E., and WARD, WILLIAM C., eds. 1993. *Construction Versus Choice in Cognitive Measurement.* Hillsdale, NJ: Lawrence Erlbaum Associates.

BOND, LLOYD A. 1995. "Unintended Consequences of Performance Assessment: Issues of Bias and Fairness." *Educational Measurement: Issues and Practice* 14(4):21–24.

BOND, LLOYD A.; BRASKAMP, DAVID; and ROEBER, EDWARD. 1996. *The Status Report of the Assessment Programs in the United States.* Oak Brook, IL: North Central Regional Educational Laboratory.

BRENNAN, ROBERT L., and JOHNSON, EUGENE G. 1995. "Generalizability of Performance Assessments." *Educational Measurement: Issues and Practice* 14(4):9–12, 27.

COLE, NANCY S. 1988. "A Realist's Appraisal of the Prospects for Unifying Instruction and Assessment." *Assessment in the Service of Learning: Proceedings of the 1987 ETS Invitational Conference.* Princeton, NJ: Educational Testing Service.

DARLING-HAMMOND, LINDA. 1995. "Equity Issues in Performance-Based Assessment." In *Equity and Excellence in Educational Testing and Assessment,* ed. Michael T. Nettles and Arie L. Nettles. Boston: Kluwer.

FREDERIKSEN, JOHN R., and COLLINS, ALLAN. 1989. "A Systems Approach to Educational Testing." *Educational Researcher* 18(9):27–32.

GAO, X. JAMES; SHAVELSON, RICHARD J.; and BAXTER, GAIL P. 1994. "Generalizability of Large-Scale Performance Assessments in Science: Promises and Problems." *Applied Measurement in Education* 7:323–342.

GLASER, ROBERT, and SILVER, EDWARD A. 1994. "Assessment, Testing, and Instruction: Retrospect and Prospect." In *Review of Research in Education,* Vol. 20, ed. Linda Darling-Hammond. Washington, DC: American Educational Research Association.

GREEN, BERT F. 1995. "Comparability of Scores from Performance Assessments." *Educational Measurement: Issues and Practice* 14(4):13–15, 24.

HEUBERT, JAY, and HAUSER, ROBERT. 1999. *High Stakes: Testing for Tracking, Promotion, and Graduation.* Washington, DC: National Academy Press.

MESSICK, SAMUEL. 1994. "The Interplay of Evidence and Consequences in the Validation of Performance Assessments." *Educational Researcher* 23(1):13–23.

MESSICK, SAMUEL, ed. 1995. "Special Issue: Values and Standards in Performance Assessment: Issues, Findings, and Viewpoints." *Educational Measurement: Issues and Practice* 14(4).

PELLEGRINO, JAMES; CHUDOWSKY, NAOMI; and GLASER, ROBERT. 2001. *Knowing What Students Know: The Science and Design of Educational Assessment.* Washington, DC: National Academy Press.

RECKASE, MARK, ed. 1993. "Special Issue: Performance Assessment." *Journal of Educational Measurement* 30(3).

RESNICK, LAUREN B., and RESNICK, DANIEL P. 1992. "Assessing the Thinking Curriculum: New Tools for Educational Reform." In *Changing Assessments: Alternative Views of Aptitude, Achievement, and Instruction,* ed. Bernard R. Gifford and Mary C. O'Connor. Boston: Kluwer.

SHAVELSON, RICHARD J.; BAXTER, GAIL P.; and GAO, X. JAMES. 1993. "Sampling Variability of Performance Assessments." *Journal of Educational Measurement* 30:215–232.

SHAVELSON, RICHARD J.; BAXTER, GAIL P.; and PINE, JERRY. 1992. "Performance Assessments: Political Rhetoric and Measurement Reality." *Educational Researcher* 21(4):22–27.

SILVER, EDWARD A.; ALACACI, CENGIZ; and STYLIANOU, DESPINA. 2000. "Students' Performance on Extended Constructed-Response Tasks." In *Results from the Seventh Mathematics Assessment of the National Assessment of Educational Progress,* ed. Edward A. Silver and Patricia A. Kenney. Reston, VA: National Council of Teachers of Mathematics.

SMITH, MARY L. 1991. "Put to the Test: The Effects of External Testing on Teachers." *Educational Researcher* 20(5):8–11.

WIGGINS, GRANT. 1989a. "Teaching to the (Authentic) Test." *Educational Leadership* 46(7):41–47.

WIGGINS, GRANT. 1989b. "A True Test: Toward More Authentic and Equitable Assessment." *Phi Delta Kappan* 70:703–713.

WIGGINS, GRANT. 1992. "Creating Tests Worth Taking." *Educational Leadership* 49(8):26–33.

WOLF, DENNIE; BIXBY, JANET; GLENN, JOHN, III; and GARDNER, HOWARD. 1991. "To Use Their Minds Well: Investigating New Forms of Student Assessment." In *Review of Research in Education,* Vol. 17, ed. Gerald Grant. Washington, DC: American Educational Research Association.

EDWARD A. SILVER

PORTFOLIO ASSESSMENT

Portfolio assessment is a term with many meanings, and it is a process that can serve a variety of purposes. A portfolio is a collection of student work that can exhibit a student's efforts, progress, and achievements in various areas of the curriculum. A portfolio assessment can be an examination of student-selected samples of work experiences and documents related to outcomes being assessed, and it can address and support progress toward achieving academic goals, including student efficacy. Portfolio assessments have been used for large-scale assessment and accountability purposes (e.g., the Vermont and Kentucky statewide assessment systems), for purposes of school-to-work transitions, and for

purposes of certification. For example, portfolio assessments are used as part of the National Board for Professional Teaching Standards assessment of expert teachers.

The Development of Portfolio Assessment

Portfolio assessments grew in popularity in the United States in the 1990s as part of a widespread interest in alternative assessment. Because of high-stakes accountability, the 1980s saw an increase in norm-referenced, multiple-choice tests designed to measure academic achievement. By the end of the decade, however, there were increased criticisms over the reliance on these tests, which opponents believed assessed only a very limited range of knowledge and encouraged a "drill and kill" multiple-choice curriculum. Advocates of alternative assessment argued that teachers and schools modeled their curriculum to match the limited norm-referenced tests to try to assure that their students did well, "teaching to the test" rather than teaching content relevant to the subject matter. Therefore, it was important that assessments were worth teaching to and modeled the types of significant teaching and learning activities that were worthwhile educational experiences and would prepare students for future, real-world success.

Involving a wide variety of learning products and artifacts, such assessments would also enable teachers and researchers to examine the wide array of complex thinking and problem-solving skills required for subject-matter accomplishment. More likely than traditional assessments to be multidimensional, these assessments also could reveal various aspects of the learning process, including the development of cognitive skills, strategies, and decision-making processes. By providing feedback to schools and districts about the strengths and weaknesses of their performance, and influencing what and how teachers teach, it was thought portfolio assessment could support the goals of school reform. By engaging students more deeply in the instructional and assessment process, furthermore, portfolios could also benefit student learning.

Types of Portfolios

While portfolios have broad potential and can be useful for the assessments of students' performance for a variety of purposes in core curriculum areas, the contents and criteria used to assess portfolios must be designed to serve those purposes. For example, *showcase portfolios* exhibit the best of student performance, while *working portfolios* may contain drafts that students and teachers use to reflect on process. *Progress portfolios* contain multiple examples of the same type of work done over time and are used to assess progress. If cognitive processes are intended for assessment, content and rubrics must be designed to capture those processes.

Portfolio assessments can provide both formative and summative opportunities for monitoring progress toward reaching identified outcomes. By setting criteria for content and outcomes, portfolios can communicate concrete information about what is expected of students in terms of the content and quality of performance in specific curriculum areas, while also providing a way of assessing their progress along the way. Depending on content and criteria, portfolios can provide teachers and researchers with information relevant to the cognitive processes that students use to achieve academic outcomes.

Uses of Portfolios

Much of the literature on portfolio assessment has focused on portfolios as a way to integrate assessment and instruction and to promote meaningful classroom learning. Many advocates of this function believe that a successful portfolio assessment program requires the ongoing involvement of students in the creation and assessment process. Portfolio design should provide students with the opportunities to become more reflective about their own work, while demonstrating their abilities to learn and achieve in academics.

For example, some feel it is important for teachers and students to work together to prioritize the criteria that will be used as a basis for assessing and evaluating student progress. During the instructional process, students and teachers work together to identify significant pieces of work and the processes required for the portfolio. As students develop their portfolio, they are able to receive feedback from peers and teachers about their work. Because of the greater amount of time required for portfolio projects, there is a greater opportunity for introspection and collaborative reflection. This allows students to reflect and report about their own thinking processes as they monitor their own comprehension and observe their emerging understanding of subjects and skills. The portfolio process is dynamic and is affected by the interaction between students and teachers.

Portfolio assessments can also serve summative assessment purposes in the classroom, serving as the basis for letter grades. Student conferences at key points during the year can also be part of the summative process. Such conferences involve the student and teacher (and perhaps the parent) in joint review of the completion of the portfolio components, in querying the cognitive processes related to artifact selection, and in dealing with other relevant issues, such as students' perceptions of individual progress in reaching academic outcomes.

The use of portfolios for large-scale assessment and accountability purposes pose vexing measurement challenges. Portfolios typically require complex production and writing, tasks that can be costly to score and for which reliability problems have occurred. Generalizability and comparability can also be an issue in portfolio assessment, as portfolio tasks are unique and can vary in topic and difficulty from one classroom to the next. For example, Maryl Gearhart and Joan Herman have raised the question of comparability of scores because of differences in the help students may receive from their teachers, parents, and peers within and across classrooms. To the extent student choice is involved, contents may even be different from one student to the next. Conditions of, and opportunities for, performance thus vary from one student to another.

These measurement issues take portfolio assessment outside of the domain of conventional psychometrics. The qualities of the most useful portfolios for instructional purposes—deeply embedded in instruction, involving student choice, and unique to each classroom and student—seem to contradict the requirements of sound psychometrics. However, this does not mean that psychometric methodology should be ignored, but rather that new ways should be created to further develop measurement theory to address reliability, validity, and generalizability.

See also: ASSESSMENT, *subentries on* CLASSROOM ASSESSMENT, DYNAMIC ASSESSMENT.

BIBLIOGRAPHY

CAMP, ROBERTA. 1993. "The Place of Portfolios in Our Changing Views." In *Construction versus Choice in Cognitive Measurement: Issues in Constructed Response, Performance Testing, and Portfolio Assessment,* ed. Randy E. Bennett and William C. Ward. Hillsdale, NJ: Erlbaum.

CHEN, YIH-FEN, and MARTIN, MICHAEL A. 2000. "Using Performance Assessment and Portfolio Assessment Together in the Elementary Classroom." *Reading Improvement* 37(1):32–37.

COLE, DONNA H.; RYAN, CHARLES W.; and KICK, FRAN. 1995. *Portfolios Across the Curriculum and Beyond.* Thousand Oaks, CA: Corwin.

GEARHART, MARYL, and HERMAN, JOAN L. 1995. "Portfolio Assessment: Whose Work Is It? Issues in the Use of Classroom Assignments for Accountability." *Evaluation Comment.* Los Angeles: University of California, Center for the Study of Evaluation.

GRAVES, DONALD H. 1992. "Portfolios: Keep a Good Idea Growing." In *Portfolio Portraits,* ed. Donald H. Graves and Bonnie S. Sunstein. Portsmouth, NH: Heinemann Educational Books.

HERMAN, JOAN L.; GEARHART, MARYL; and ASCHBACHER, PAMELA. 1996. "Portfolios for Classroom Assessment: Design and Implementation Issues." In *Writing Portfolios in the Classroom,* ed. Robert Calfee and Pamela Perfumo. Mahwah, NJ: Erlbaum.

HEWITT, GEOF. 2001. "The Writing Portfolio: Assessment Starts with A." *Clearing House* 74(4):187.

LOCKLEDGE, ANN. 1997. "Portfolio Assessment in Middle-School and High-School Social Studies Classrooms." *Social Studies* 88(2):65–70.

MEADOWS, ROBERT B., and DYAL, ALLEN B. 1999. "Implementing Portfolio Assessment in the Development of School Administrators: Improving Preparation for Educational Leadership." *Education* 120(2):304.

MURPHY, SANDRA M. 1997. "Who Should Taste the Soup and When? Designing Portfolio Assessment Programs to Enhance Learning." *Clearing House* 71(2):81–85.

STECHER, BRIAN, and HERMAN, JOAN L. 1997. "Using Portfolios for Large Scale Assessment." In *Handbook of Classroom Assessment,* ed. Gary Phye. San Diego, CA: Academic Press.

WENZLAFF, TERRI L. 1998. "Dispositions and Portfolio Development: Is There a Connection?" *Education* 118(4):564–573.

WOLF, DENNIE P. 1989. "Portfolio Assessment: Sampling Student Work." *Educational Leadership* 46:35–39.

JOAN L. HERMAN
STEPHEN A. ZUNIGA

ASSESSMENT TOOLS

PSYCHOMETRIC AND STATISTICAL
Mark Wilson
TECHNOLOGY BASED
Sean Brophy

PSYCHOMETRIC AND STATISTICAL

The place of psychometric and statistical tools in assessment must be understood in terms of their use within a process of evidence gathering and interpretation. To see this, consider the assessment triangle featured in a recent National Research Council Report and shown in Figure 1. The central problem in assessment is making inferences about cognition from limited observations. Psychometric and statistical tools are located at the interpretation vertex of the triangle, where their role is to negotiate between the other two vertices. To appreciate the way these tools work, one must first understand the other two vertices. Hence, each vertex is described below. Robert Mislevy and Mark Wilson describe similar and more elaborated approaches. The triangle should be seen as a process that is repeated multiple times in both assessment development and in the application of assessment in education.

The Assessment Triangle

Ideally, all assessment design should begin with a theory of student cognition, or set of beliefs about how students represent knowledge and develop competence in a particular area. This theory should be the basis for a construct: the cognitive characteristic to be measured. Constructs are based on what the "assessment designers" know from foundational research in psychology and instruction and on experts' judgments about how students develop in a particular area. The construct distinguishes expert performance from other levels of performance in the area and considers those levels from the perspective of a developmental process. Furthermore, educational outcomes are not as straightforward as measuring

FIGURE 1

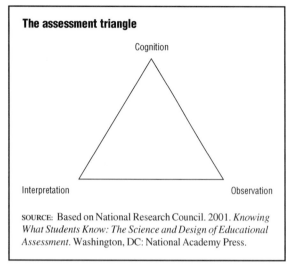

The assessment triangle

Cognition

Interpretation   Observation

SOURCE: Based on National Research Council. 2001. *Knowing What Students Know: The Science and Design of Educational Assessment.* Washington, DC: National Academy Press.

height or weight—the attributes to be measured are often mental activities that are not directly observable.

Having delineated the nature of the construct, one then has to determine what kinds of observations of behavior, products, and actions can provide evidence for making inferences concerning the construct, at the same time avoiding data that hold little value as evidence for the construct. In the classroom context, observations of learning activity are the relevant things that learners say and do (such as their words, actions, gestures, products, and performances) that can be observed and recorded. Teachers make assessments of student learning based on a wide range of student activity, ranging from observation and discussion in the classroom, written work done at home or in class, quizzes, final exams, and so forth. In large-scale assessment, standardized assessment tasks are designed to elicit evidence of student learning. These may range across a similar variation of types of performances as classroom-based assessments, but are often drawn from a much narrower range.

At the interpretation vertex is located the chain of reasoning from the observations to the construct. In classroom assessment, the teacher usually interprets student activity using an intuitive or qualitative model of reasoning, comparing what she sees with what she would expect competent performance to look like. In large-scale assessment, given a mass of complex data with little background information about the students' ongoing learning activities to aid in interpretation, the interpretation model is usually

a psychometric or statistical model, which amounts to a characterization or summarization of patterns that one would expect to see in the data at different levels of competence.

Standard Psychometric Models

Probably the most common form that the cognition vertex takes in educational assessment is that of a continuous latent variable—cognition is seen as being describable as a single progression from less to more or lower to higher. This is the basis for all three of the dominant current approaches to educational measurement: Classical test theory (CTT), which was thoroughly summarized by Frederick Lord and Melvin Novick; generalizability theory (GT), which was surveyed by Robert Brennan, and item response theory (IRT), which was surveyed in the volume by Wim van der Linden and Ronald Hambleton. In CTT, the continuous variable is termed the true score, and is thought of as the long-run mean of the observed total score. In GT, the effects of various measurement design factors on this variable are analyzed using an approach that analyzes the variance. In IRT, the focus shifts to modeling individual item responses: The probability of an item response is seen as a function of the underlying latent variable representing student competence (often denoted by θ), and parameters representing the item and the measurement context.

The most fundamental item parameter is the item *difficulty*, but others are also used where they are thought to be useful to represent the characteristics of the assessment situation. The difficulty parameter can usually be seen as relating the item responses to the construct (i.e, the θ variable). Other parameters may relate to characteristics of the observations. For example, differing item *slopes* can be interpreted as indicating when item responses are also possibly dependent on other (unmodeled) dimensions besides the θ variable (these are sometimes called discrimination parameters, although that can lead to confusion with the classical discrimination index). Parameters for lower-item and upper-item asymptotes can be interpreted as indicating where item responses have "floor" and "ceiling" rates (where the lower asymptote is often called a guessing parameter). There is a debate in the literature about whether to include parameters beyond the basic difficulty parameters in the response model in order to make the model flexible, or whether to see them as indicating deviations from a regularity condition (specific objectivity) that sees them as threatening the interpretability of the results.

A second possible form for the construct is as a set of discrete classes, ordered or unordered depending on the theory. The equivalent psychometric models are termed *latent class* (LC) models, because they attempt to classify the students on the basis of their responses as in the work of Edward Haertel. In these models, the form of cognition, such as problem-solving strategy, is thought of as being only possible within certain classes. An example might be strategy usage, where a latent class approach would be seen as useful when students could be adequately described using only a certain number of different classes. These classes could be ordered by some criterion, say, cognitive sophistication, or they could have more complex relations to one another.

There are other complexities of the assessment context that can be added to these models. First, the construct can be seen as being composed of more than a single attribute. In the continuous construct approach, this possibility is generally termed the *factor analysis* model when a classical approach is taken, and a *multidimensional item response model* (MIRM) when starting from the continuum approach as in the work by Mark Reckase and Raymond Adams and his colleagues. In contrast to the account above, where parameters were added to the models of the item to make it more complex, here the model of the student is what is being enhanced. These models allow one to incorporate evidence about different constructs into the assessment situation.

There are other ways that complexities of the assessment situation can be built into the measurement models. For example, authors such as Susan Embretson, Bengt Muthen, and Khoo Siek-Toon have shown how repeated assessments over time can be seen as indicators of a new construct: a construct related to patterns of change in the original construct. In another type of example, authors such as Gerhard Fischer have added linear effect parameters, similar to those available in GT, to model observational effects such as rater characteristics and item design factors, and also to model complexities of the construct (e.g., components of the construct that influence item difficulty, such as classes of cognitive strategies).

Incorporating Cognitive Elements in Standard Psychometric Models

An approach called developmental assessment has been developed, by Geoffrey Masters and colleagues, building on the seminal work of Benjamin Wright and using the Rasch model, to enhance the interpretability of measures by displaying the variable graphically as a *progress map* or *construct map*. Mark Wilson and Kathryn Sloane have discussed an example shown in Figure 2, where the levels, called Criterion Zones in the figure, are defined in Figure 3. The idea is that many important features of assessments can be displayed in a technically accurate way by using the strength of the idea of a map to convey complicated measurement techniques and ideas. For example, one central idea is that the meaning of the construct can be conveyed by examining the order of item locations along the map, and the same technique has been used by Wilson as the basis for gathering validity evidence. In Figure 2, one can see how an individual student's assessments over time can be displayed in a meaningful way in terms of the Criterion Zones. The same approach can be adapted for reporting group results of assessments, and even large national surveys (e.g., that of Australia's Department of Employment, Education and Youth Affairs in 1997).

One can also examine the patterns of results of individual students to help diagnose individual differences. An example from the GradeMap software developed by Wilson and his colleagues is shown in Figure 4. Here, an overall index of "fit" was used to flag the responses of subject Amy Brown that needed extra attention. In the figure, the expected result for each item for Amy Brown is shown using the gray band across the middle, while the observed results are shown by the black shading. Clearly Amy has responded in surprising ways to several items, and a content analysis of those items may prove interesting. An analogous technique has been developed by Kikumi Tatsuoka (1990, 1995) with the advantage of focusing attention on specific cognitive diagnoses.

Adding Cognitive Structure to Psychometric Models

One can go a step further than the previous strategy of incorporating interpretative techniques into the assessment reporting—elements of the construct can be directly represented as parameters of the psychometric model. From a statistical point of view, this would most often be the preferred tactic, but in

FIGURE 2

A student's progress chart produced using the GradeMap software

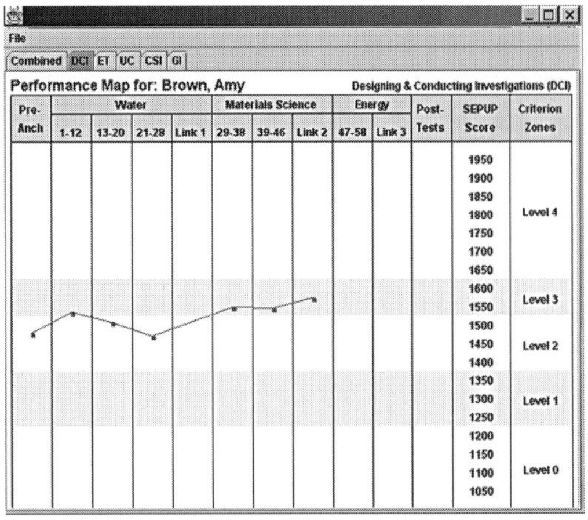

SOURCE: Wilson, Mark; Draney, Karen; and Kennedy, Cathleen. 2001. *GradeMap*. Berkeley: BEAR Center, University of California, Berkeley. Reprinted with permission.

practice, it may add to the complexity of interpretation, so the merits should be considered for each application. A relatively straightforward example of this is the incorporation of differential item functioning (DIF) parameters into the psychometric model. Such parameters adjust other parameters (usually item difficulty parameters) for different effects between (known) groups of respondents. Most often it has been seen as an item flaw, needing to be corrected. But in this context, such parameters could be used to allow for different construct effects, such as using different solution strategies or linguistic differences.

Another general strategy is the delineation of hierarchical classes of observation that group together the original observations to make them more interpretable. This can be seen as acting on either the student or the item aspects of the psychometric model. This could be seen as a way to split up the students into latent groups for diagnostic purposes as in the work of Edward Haertel and David Wiley. Or it could be seen as a way to split up the items into classes, allowing interpretation of student results at the level of, say, classes of skills rather than at the individual item level, as in the work of Rianne Janssen and her colleagues. Wilson has combined the continuum and latent class approaches, thus allowing

constructs that are partly continuous and partly discontinuous. For example, the Saltus Model is designed to incorporate stage-like developmental changes along with more standard incremental increases in skill, as illustrated in the work of Mislevy and Wilson.

Generalized Approaches to Psychometric Modeling of Cognitive Structures

Several generalist approaches have been proposed. One is the Unified Model, developed by Louis de Bello and his colleagues, which is based on the assumption that task analyses can classify students' performances into distinct latent classes. A second general approach, Peter Pirolli and Mark Wilson's M2RCML, has been put forward and is based on a distinction between knowledge level learning, as manifested by variations in solution strategies, and symbol-level learning, as manifested by variations in the success of application of those strategies. In work by Karen Draney and her colleagues, this approach has been applied to data related to both learning on a Lisp tutor and a rule assessment analysis of reasoning involving the balance scale.

A very general approach to modeling such structures called Bayes Nets has been developed by statisticians working in other fields. Two kinds of variables appear in a Bayes Net for educational assessment: those that concern aspects of students' knowledge and skill, and others that concern aspects of the things they say, do, or make. All the psychometric models discussed in this entry reflect this kind of reasoning, and all can be expressed as particular implementations of Bayes Nets. The models described above each evolved in their own special niches; researchers in each gain experience in use of the model, write computer programs, and develop a catalog of exemplars. Bayes Nets have been used as the statistical model underlying such complex assessment contexts as intelligent tutoring systems as in the example by Mislevy and Drew Gitomer.

Appraisal of Psychometric Models and Future Directions

The psychometric models discussed above provide explicit, formal rules for integrating the many pieces of information that may be relevant to specific inferences drawn from observation of assessment tasks. Certain kinds of assessment applications require the capabilities of formal statistical models for the interpretation element of the assessment triangle. The psychometric models available in the early twenty-first century can support many of the kinds of inferences that curriculum theory and cognitive science suggest are important to pursue. In particular, it is possible to characterize students in terms of multiple aspects of proficiency, rather than a single score; chart students' progress over time, instead of simply measuring performance at a particular point in time; deal with multiple paths or alternative methods of valued performance; model, monitor, and improve judgments based on informed evaluations; and model performance not only at the level of students, but also at the levels of groups, classes, schools, and states.

Unfortunately, many of the newer models and methods are not widely used because they are not easily understood or are not packaged in accessible ways for those without a strong technical background. Much hard work remains to focus psychometric model building on the critical features of models of cognition and learning and on observations that reveal meaningful cognitive processes in a particular domain. If anything, the task has become more difficult because an additional step is now required—determining simultaneously the inferences that must be drawn, the observations needed, the tasks that will provide them, and the statistical models that will express the necessary patterns most efficiently. Therefore, having a broad array of models available does not mean that the measurement model problem is solved. More work is needed on relating the characteristics of measurement models to the specifics of theoretical constructs and types of observations. The longstanding tradition of leaving scientists, educators, task designers, and psychometricians each to their own realms represents perhaps the most serious barrier to the necessary progress.

See also: ASSESSMENT, *subentries on* CLASSROOM ASSESSMENT, NATIONAL ASSESSMENT OF EDUCATIONAL PROGRESS; TESTING, *subentry on* STANDARDIZED TESTS AND HIGH-STAKES ASSESSMENT.

BIBLIOGRAPHY

ADAMS, RAYMOND J.; WILSON, MARK; and WANG, WEN-CHUNG. 1997. "The Multidimensional Random Coefficient Multinomial Logit Model." *Applied Psychological Measurement* 21(1):1–23.

BRENNAN, ROBERT L. 2002. *Generalizability Theory.* New York: Springer-Verlag.

FIGURE 3

The evidence and tradeoffs scoring guide

Category	Score	Using Evidence: Response uses objective reason(s) based on relevant evidence to support choice.
Beyond correct	4	Response accomplishes Level 3 and goes beyond in some significant way, such as questioning or justifying the source, validity, and/or quantity of evidence.
Correct	3	Response provides major objective reasons and supports each with relevant and accurate evidence.
Partially complete (ii) —some objective reasons and some evidence	2	Response provides some objective reasons and some supporting evidence, but at least one reason is missing and/or part of the evidence is incomplete.
Partially complete (i) —subjective and/or inaccurate reasons	1	Response provides only subjective reasons (opinions) for choice and/or uses inaccurate or irrelevant evidence from the activity.
Missing or irrelevant	0	No response; illegible response; response offers no reasons and no evidence to support choice made.
No opportunity	X	Student had no opportunity to respond.

SOURCE: Adapted from Wilson, Mark, and Sloane, Kathryn. 2000. "From Principles to Practice: An Embedded Assessment System." *Applied Measurement in Education* 13(2):181–208.

BRYK, ANTHONY S., and RAUDENBUSH, STEPHEN. 1992. *Hierarchical Linear Models: Applications and Data Analysis Methods.* Newbury Park: Sage.

DEPARTMENT OF EMPLOYMENT, EDUCATION, AND YOUTH AFFAIRS (DEETYA). 1997. *National School English Literacy Survey.* Canberra, Australia: Department of Employment, Education, and Youth Affairs.

DiBELLO, LOUIS V.; STOUT, WILLIAM F.; and ROUSSOS, LOUIS A. 1995. "Unified Cognitive/ Psychometric Diagnostic Assessment Likelihood-Based Classification Techniques." In *Cognitively Diagnostic Assessment,* ed. Paul D. Nichols, Susan F. Chipman, and Robert L. Brennan. Hillsdale, NJ: Erlbaum.

DRANEY, KAREN L.; PIROLLI, PETER; and WILSON, MARK. 1995. "A Measurement Model for a Complex Cognitive Skill." In *Cognitively Diag-*

FIGURE 4

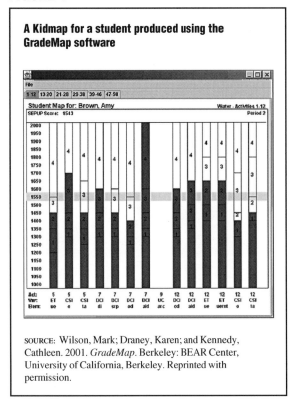

A Kidmap for a student produced using the GradeMap software

SOURCE: Wilson, Mark; Draney, Karen; and Kennedy, Cathleen. 2001. *GradeMap*. Berkeley: BEAR Center, University of California, Berkeley. Reprinted with permission.

nostic Assessment, ed. Paul D. Nichols, Susan F. Chipman, and Robert L. Brennan. Hillsdale, NJ: Erlbaum.

EMBRETSON, SUSAN E. 1996. "Multicomponent Response Models." In *Handbook of Modern Item Response Theory*, ed. Win J. van der Linden and Ronald K. Hambleton. New York: Springer.

FISCHER, GERHARD. 1977. "Linear Logistic Test Models: Theory and Application." In *Structural Models of Thinking and Learning*, ed. Hans Spada and Willem Kempf. Bern, Germany: Huber.

HAERTEL, EDWARD H. 1990. "Continuous and Discrete Latent Structure Models for Item Response Data." *Psychometrika* 55:477–494.

HAERTEL, EDWARD H., and WILEY, DAVID E. 1993. "Representations of Ability Structures: Implications for Testing." In *Test Theory for a New Generation of Tests*, ed. Norman Frederiksen, Robert J. Mislevy, and Isaac I. Bejar. Hillsdale, NJ: Erlbaum.

HAMBLETON, RONALD K.; SWAMINATHAN, HARIHAN; and ROGERS, H. JANE. 1991. *Fundamentals of Item Response Theory*. Newbury Park: Sage.

JANSSEN, RIANNE; TUERLINCKX, FRANCES; MEULDERS, MICHEL; and DE BOECK, PAUL. 2000. "An Hierarchical IRT Model for Mastery Classification." *Journal of Educational and Behavioral Statistics* 25(3):285–306.

LORD, FREDERICK M., and NOVICK, MELVIN R. 1968. *Statistical Theories of Mental Test Scores*. Reading, MA: Addison-Wesley.

MISLEVY, ROBERT J. 1996. "Test Theory Reconceived." *Journal of Educational Measurement* 33(4):379–416.

MISLEVY, ROBERT J., and GITOMER, DREW H. 1996. "The Role of Probability-Based Inference in an Intelligent Tutoring System." *User Modeling and User-Adapted Interaction* 5:253–282.

MISLEVY, ROBERT J., and WILSON, MARK. 1996. "Marginal Maximum Likelihood Estimation for a Psychometric Model of Discontinuous Development." *Psychometrika* 61:41–71.

MUTHEN, BENGT O., and KHOO, SIEK-TOON. 1998. "Longitudinal Studies of Achievement Growth Using Latent Variable Modeling." *Learning and Individual Differences* 10:73–101.

NATIONAL RESEARCH COUNCIL. 2001. *Knowing What Students Know: The Science and Design of Educational Assessment*. Washington, DC: National Academy Press.

PIROLLI, PETER, and WILSON, MARK. 1998. "A Theory of the Measurement of Knowledge Content, Access, and Learning." *Psychological Review* 105(1):58–82.

RECKASE, MARK D. 1972. "Development and Application of a Multivariate Logistic Latent Trait Model." Ph.D. diss., Syracuse University, Syracuse, NY.

TATSUOKA, KIKUMI K. 1995. "Architecture of Knowledge Structures and Cognitive Diagnosis: A Statistical Pattern Recognition and Classification Approach." In *Cognitively Diagnostic Assessment*, ed. Paul D. Nichols, Susan F. Chipman, and Robert L. Brennan. Hillsdale, NJ: Erlbaum.

VAN DER LINDEN, WIM J., and HAMBLETON, RONALD K., eds. 1996. *Handbook of Modern Item Response Theory*. New York: Springer.

WILSON, MARK. 2002. *Measurement: A Constructive Approach*. Berkeley: BEAR Center, University of California, Berkeley.

Wilson, Mark; Draney, Karen; and Kennedy, Cathleen. 2001. *GradeMap.* Berkeley: BEAR Center, University of California, Berkeley.

Wilson, Mark, and Sloane, Kathryn. 2000. "From Principles to Practice: An Embedded Assessment System." *Applied Measurement in Education* 13(2):181–208.

Wright, Benjamin D. 1977. "Solving Measurement Problems with the Rasch Model." *Journal of Educational Measurement* 14:97–116.

Mark Wilson

TECHNOLOGY BASED

Assessment methods can be learning opportunities for students, though identifying methods to accomplish this can be challenging. Some new instructional methods may target learning outcomes that traditional assessment methods fail to measure. Automated assessment methods, such as multiple-choice and short-answer questions, work well for testing the retrieval of facts, the manipulation of rote procedures, solving multiple-step problems, and processing textual information. With carefully designed multiple-test items it is possible to have students demonstrate their ability to perform causal reasoning and solve multi-step problems. However, students' participation in these kinds of traditional assessment activities do not necessarily help them "learn" and develop complex skills.

What students and teachers need are multiple opportunities to apply new information to complex situations and receive feedback on how well they are progressing toward developing the ability to synthesize and communicate ideas and to systematically approach and solve problems. Technologies are emerging that can assess students' ability to gather, synthesize, and communicate information in a way that helps improve their understanding and that informs teachers how they can improve their instruction. Several instructional techniques and technologies have been designed to help students develop complex skills and help teachers develop students' causal reasoning, diagnose problem-solving abilities, and facilitate writing.

Developing Causal Reasoning

Volumes of information can be shared efficiently by using a graphical image. The potential for students to learn from integrating ideas into graphical information can be very powerful and can demonstrate what they know and understand. One example of how information is portrayed in graphical form is a common street map. Expert mapmakers communicate a wealth of information about the complicated network of roads and transportation routes that connect the various locations in a city. Mapmakers use colored lines to indicate which roads have the higher speed limits, such as expressways and highways. Therefore, people can use the map as a tool to make decisions about a trip by using a map to plan out the fastest route, rather than taking the shortest distance—which may include city roads that have a lower speed limit or are potentially congested. A road map efficiently illustrates the relative location of one place and its relation to another, as well as information about the roads that connect these locations.

Learners can share what they know about a complex topic by creating a concept map, which illustrates the major factors of a topic and descriptive links detailing the relationships between these factors. For example, a river is a complex ecosystem containing a variety of elements, such as fish, macroinvertebrates, plants, bacteria, and oxygen, which are highly dependent on one another. Changes in any of these elements can have a ripple effect that is difficult to determine without some method to represent the links between the elements. Scientists often create a concept map of a system to help keep track of these interdependencies in a complex system. A concept map such as Figure 1 can help students notice when their intuitions are not enough to make sense of a complex situation. Therefore, creating a concept map can be a very authentic activity for students to do as they explore the intricacies of science.

Concept mapping activities also provide an excellent opportunity for assessment. Students can demonstrate their current conceptions of a system at various stages of their inquiry. A simple method to evaluate concept maps is to compare what the learners create relative to what an expert creates. A point can be given for each relevant element and links identified by the students. A second point can be added for correctly labeling the link (e.g., *produce* as in "plants *produce* oxygen"). A common observation is that as students begin exploring a topic area like ecosystems, their concept maps contain only a few elements, many of which are irrelevant, and they use very few links or labels of links. If they include

FIGURE 1

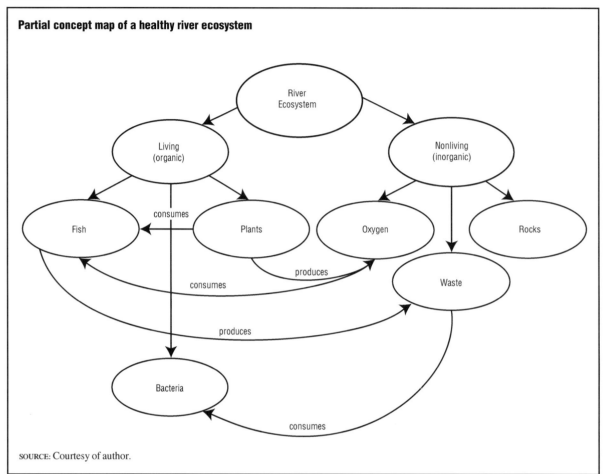

Partial concept map of a healthy river ecosystem

SOURCE: Courtesy of author.

links, they are unable to describe what the links are, though they know there is some dependency between factors. As students begin to investigate more about a system and how it works, they are often able to redraw their maps to include the relevant element links and labels to illustrate the interdependence of the elements of a system. However, grading these maps multiple times can be very time-consuming for a teacher.

New computer software has been developed to provide students with a simple interface to create hierarchical concept maps. The software can also score students' performance on these concept maps, depending on the goals of the instruction. For example, students' concept maps can be compared with those of experts for completeness and accuracy. An expert's model of a system would include a complete list of factors and named links. Comparing a student's map to an expert's map provides a method of identifying if students know what factors are relevant, as well as the relationships between factors.

Causal maps are similar to concept maps and include information about how one factor influences another factor. For example, the relationship "fish consume plants" in Figure 1 could also be expressed as "fish decrease plants" and "plants increase oxygen." The visual representation—with qualitative information about the relationship between factors—gives students an illustration they can use to make predictions about what will happen to the system when one of the factors changes. They can use the causal map as a tool to answer the question "What happens if we add a larger number of fish into a river?" Then, students can follow the *increase* and *decrease* links to derive a hypothesis of what they think might happen to the other factors.

Causal maps also provide a method to use technology as both an instructional tool and an assessment tool to measure students' understanding of a complex system. A research group at the Learning Sciences Institute at Vanderbilt University (formerly the Learning Technology Center) has created a computer system, called *teachable agents,* that provides students with a method to articulate what they know and to test their ideas by helping a *virtual agent* use their knowledge to answer questions. Students teach this agent how a particular system works by creating a causal map of a system, which becomes the agent's representation of its knowledge. Testing how well the agent has learned is accomplished by asking the agent questions about the relationships in the system. The agent reasons through questions using the causal map the students have provided them.

As the agent reasons through a question, the factors and links are highlighted to illustrate what information it is using to make a decision on how to answer the question. If the causal map is incomplete or has contradictory information, then the computer agent will explain that it doesn't know, or is confused about what to do next. The feedback from watching the computer agent "think" about the problem can help students identify what knowledge is missing or incorrectly illustrated in their causal map. Therefore, students learn by having to debug how their agent thinks about the world. This kind of computer tool tests a student's understanding of the processes associated with a system and provides an automatic method for self-assessment.

Diagnosing Problem-Solving Abilities

Problem solving is a process that incorporates a wide range of knowledge and skills, including identifying problems, defining the source of a problem, and exploring potential solutions to a problem. Many challenging problems, such as designing a house, creating a business plan, diagnosing a disease, troubleshooting a circuit, or analyzing how something works, involve a range of activities. Such situations require the ability to make decisions using available information—and the inquiry process necessary to locate new information. This process can also include making reasonable assumptions that help constrain a problem, thus making it easier to identify a potential solution. Novices often don't have enough background knowledge to make these decisions, relying instead on a trial-and-error method to search for solutions. If a teacher could watch each student solve problems and ask questions about why they made certain decisions, the teacher could learn more about what the students understand and monitor

their progress toward developing good problem-solving skills.

The IMMEX system, created by Ron Stevens at UCLA, is a web-based problem-solving simulation environment that tracks many of the decisions a person makes while attempting to solve a problem. Stevens initially created IMMEX to help young immunologists practice their clinical skills. These interns are given a case study detailing a patient's symptoms, and they must make a range of decisions to efficiently and conclusively decide what is wrong with the patient. They must choose from a range of resources—including lab tests, experts' comments, and patient's answers to questions—to help gather evidence to support a specific diagnosis. Each decision that is made can have a cost associated with it in terms of both time and money. The young internists must use their current medical knowledge to make good decisions about what resources to use and when to use them. The IMMEX system tracks these decisions and reports them in the form of a node and link graph (visually similar to a concept map) that indicates the order in which the resources were accessed. In addition, a neural network can compare the decision path the intern makes with the decision path of an expert doctor to identify where the interns are making bad decisions. Students can use these traces to help them evaluate the strategies they use to solve a problem and learn about more optimal strategies. Also, an instructor can use these decision traces to evaluate common errors made by the students. The result is a system that provides students with the opportunity to solve complex problems and receive automated feedback they can use to improve their performance, while professors can use it to refine their instruction to better meet the needs of the students. IMMEX now has programs created for K–12 education.

Facilitating Writing

Writing is a fundamental skill that requires careful use of language to communicate ideas. Learning to write well takes practice and feedback on content, form, style, grammar, and spelling. Essay and report writing are therefore critical assessment tools used to capture students' ability to bring together ideas related to a course of study. However, a teacher can only provide a limited amount of feedback on each draft of a student's essay. Therefore, the teacher's feedback may consist of short comments in the margin, punctuation and grammar correction, or a brief note at the end summarizing what content is missing or what ideas are still unclear. Realistically, a teacher can only give this feedback on a single draft before students hand in a final version of their essays. Most word processors can help students check their spelling and some mechanical grammar errors, which can help reduce the load on the teacher. What students need is a method for reflecting on the content they've written.

Latent semantic analysis (LSA) has great potential for assisting students in evaluating the content of their essay. LSA can correlate the content of a student's essay with the content of experts' writings (from textbooks and other authoritative sources). The program uses a statistical technique to evaluate the language experts use to communicate ideas in their published writings on a specific topic area. Students' essays are evaluated with the same statistical technique. LSA can compare each student's writing with the writing of experts and create a report indicating how well the paper correlates in content on a scale from 1 to 5. The numerical output does not give students specific feedback on what content needs to change, but it helps them identify when more work needs to be done. Students can rewrite and submit their papers to the LSA system as many times as necessary to improve the ranking. The result should be that students' final essays have a much higher quality of content when they hand them in to the teacher. In addition, the students must take on a larger role in evaluating their own work before handing in the final project, allowing the teacher to spend more time evaluating the content, creativity, and synthesis of ideas.

Summary

Assessment of abilities such as problem solving, written communication, and reasoning can be a difficult and time-consuming task for teachers. Performance assessment methods such as class projects and presentations are important final assessments of students' ability to demonstrate what research they have done, as well as their ability to synthesize and communicate their ideas. Unfortunately, teachers often do not have enough time to give students multiple opportunities to engage in these kinds of activities, or to give them sufficient feedback before they perform these final demonstrations of what they have learned. Systems like teachable agents, IMMEX, and LSA provide a method for students to test what they know in a very authentic way as they progress

toward their final objectives. These technologies provide a level of feedback that requires the students to reflect on their performance and define their own learning goals to increase their performance. In addition, teachers can use an aggregate of this feedback to evaluate where a class may need assistance. Technology can provide assessment methods that inform students on where they need assistance and that require the learners to define their own learning outcomes.

See also: ASSESSMENT, *subentries on* CLASSROOM ASSESSMENT, DYNAMIC ASSESSMENT; ASSESSMENT TOOLS, *subentry on* PSYCHOMETRIC AND STATISTICAL.

BIBLIOGRAPHY

BISWAS, GAUTAM; SCHWARTZ, DANIEL L.; BRANSFORD, JOHN D.; and TEACHABLE AGENTS GROUP AT VANDERBILT. 2001. "Technology Support for Complex Problem Solving: From SAD Environments to AI." In *Smart Machines in Education: The Coming Revolution in Educational Technology*, ed. Kenneth D. Forbus and Paul J. Feltovich. Menlo Park, CA: AAAI Press.

LANDAUER, THOMAS K., and DUMAIS, SUSAN T. 1997. "A Solution to Plato's Problem: The Latent Semantic Analysis Theory of the Acquisition, Induction, and Representation of Knowledge." *Psychological Review* 104:211–240.

INTERNET RESOURCES

CHEN, EVA J.; CHUNG, GREGORY K. W. K.; KLEIN, DAVINA C.; DE VRIES, LINDA F.; and BURNAM, BRUCE. 2001. *How Teachers Use IMMEX in the Classroom. Report from National Center for Research on Evaluation Standards and Student Testing.* <www.immex.ucla.edu/TopMenu/Whats New/EvaluationForTeachers.pdf>.

COLORADO UNIVERSITY, BOULDER. 2001. *Latent Semantic Analysis at Colorado University, Boulder.* <http://lsa.colorado.edu>.

IMMEX. 2001. <www.immex.ucla.edu>.

TEACHABLE AGENTS GROUP AT VANDERBILT. 2001. <www.vuse.vanderbilt.edu/~vxx>.

SEAN BROPHY

ASSISTIVE TECHNOLOGY

Assistive technology is a relatively new term used to describe devices and services that lessen or remove barriers faced by persons with disabilities. Although the term is contemporary, the use of assistive technology is not new. For centuries, individuals with disabilities have used a variety of assistive devices to help them overcome demands in the environment. For example, years ago individuals with a hearing loss realized that placing a horn to their ear amplified sounds and consequently created a primitive version of today's hearing aid. Unfortunately, until the 1970s it was up to individuals to find appropriate devices to help them ameliorate their disabilities. In 2002, with support from federal legislation, schools and businesses are required to help individuals with disabilities identify and use appropriate assistive technologies and services. The first piece of such legislation was Section 504 of the Rehabilitation Act of 1973 (Pub. L. 99-506). This law prohibits discrimination of persons with disabilities in places of federal employment. Section 504 mandates that federal employees with disabilities must have the necessary accommodations to enable them to access databases, telecommunications systems, and other software programs, to contribute to work-related tasks, and to communicate with others in their system.

Subsequent to Section 504 of the Rehabilitation Act, the Technology-Related Assistance for Individuals with Disabilities Act of 1988 (Pub. L. 100-407), better known as the Tech Act, was passed into law. This piece of legislation provided financial assistance for states to plan and implement a consumer-responsive system of assistive-technology services for individuals of all ages with disabilities. The provisions of the Tech Act required states to identify existing assistive-technology services and ensure that persons with disabilities acquired access to assistive-technology services, including assessment, funding for devices, training, and technical assistance.

Following on the heels of the Tech Act was the Americans with Disabilities Act (ADA) of 1990 (Pub. L. 101-336). This legislation is designed to prevent discrimination against persons with disabilities in four major areas: employment, public facilities, transportation, and telecommunications. Many of these accommodations are made through the use of assistive technologies, such as modified workstations, ramps at the entrances to buildings, and telecommunications devices for persons who are deaf.

The Education of the Handicapped Act (EHA) Amendments of 1990 (Pub. L. 101-476) officially changed EHA to the Individuals with Disabilities Education Act (IDEA). At this time, assistive technology was added to the list of special education services that must be included in a student's Individualized Education Program (IEP). IDEA defines assistive-technology services as "any service that directly assists a child with a disability in the selection, acquisition, or use of an assistive technology device."

Under IDEA, assistive-technology services include:

- the evaluation of the needs of a child identified with a disability, including a functional evaluation of the child in the child's customary environment;

- purchasing, leasing, or otherwise providing for the acquisition of assistive-technology devices;

- selecting, designing, fitting, customizing, adapting, applying, maintaining, repairing, or replacing of assistive-technology devices;

- coordinating and using other therapies, interventions, or services with assistive-technology devices, such as those associated with existing education and rehabilitation plans and programs;

- training or technical assistance for a child or, where appropriate, the family of the child; and

- training or technical assistance for professionals (including individuals providing education and rehabilitation services), employers, or other individuals who provide services to, employ, or are otherwise substantially involved in the major life functions of a child with an identified disability.

IDEA defined an assistive-technology device as "any item, piece of equipment or product system, whether acquired commercially off the shelf, modified, or customized, that is used to increase, maintain, or improve the functional capabilities of children with disabilities."

The use of assistive-technology devices and services by students with disabilities is further supported in the amendments to IDEA (Pub. L. 105-17). The law mandates that, beginning in July 1998, assistive technology must be considered for all students eligible for special education services. Although the regulations do not elaborate on how assistive technology must be considered, the law states that the IEP team must be involved in the decision-making process. It further states that outside evaluators must be used when the IEP team lacks the expertise to conduct an evaluation and make an informed decision regarding assistive technology. In addition, it is the responsibility of the school system to secure funding for the device and to provide training to school personnel, family members, and the student as educationally appropriate.

Assistive Technology and Human Functions

As of 2001, thousands of different assistive technologies have been developed to provide a broad array of support to individuals with disabilities. These assistive technologies have been categorized into seven functional areas: (1) existence; (2) communication; (3) body support, protection, and positioning; (4) travel and mobility; (5) environmental interaction; (6) education and transition; and (7) sports, fitness, and recreation. Following is a short description of each of the seven functional areas, with examples of assistive-technology devices and services available to support individuals with disabilities.

Problems in the existence area are associated with the functions needed to sustain life, including eating, grooming, dressing, elimination, and hygiene. Some assistive technologies in this area are adapted utensils, dressing aids, adapted toilet seats, toilet training, and occupational therapy services.

Students with communication needs have difficulties associated with the functions needed to receive, internalize, and express information, and to interact socially, including oral and written expression and visual and auditory reception. Solutions may include hearing amplifiers, magnifiers, pointers, alternate computer input, augmentative communication devices and services, social skills training, and speech/language therapy services.

Body support, protection and positioning issues are associated with the functions needed to stabilize support or protect a portion of the body while sitting, standing, or reclining. Assistive technologies may include prone standers, furniture adaptations, support harnesses, stabilizers, head gear, and physical therapy services.

Travel and mobility needs are associated with the necessity to move horizontally or vertically, including crawling, walking, navigating, stair climbing, and transferring either laterally or vertically. Tech-

nologies to assist with travel and mobility include wheelchairs, scooters, hoists, cycles, walkers, crutches, and orientation- and mobility-training services.

Difficulties in environmental interaction are associated with the functions needed to perform activities across environments, including operating computer equipment and accessing facilities. Assistive-technology solutions may include the use of switches to control computers, remote-control devices, adapted appliances, ramps, automatic door openers, modified furniture, driving aids, and rehabilitation services.

Problems in education and transition are associated with the functions needed to participate in learning activities and to prepare for new school settings or postschool environments. Assistive technologies may include educational software, computer adaptations, community-based instruction, and services from an assistive technologist.

Persons needing assistive technology for sports, fitness, and recreation require assistance with individual or group sports, play, and hobbies and craft activities. Those individuals may benefit from modified rules and equipment, adapted aquatics, switch-activated cameras, and braille playing cards, and may participate in adapted physical education services.

Employing Assistive Technology

Federal law mandates that assistive technology must be considered for all individuals served under IDEA. When assistive technologies are being considered, it is important to remember that the consideration must be based on the needs of the individual rather than on the type of disability. Factors of human function must guide any decision as to the appropriateness of assistive technology. Every individual with a disability faces a unique set of challenges and demands, and the successful use of assistive technology means that these challenges and demands can be lessened or removed. The power and promise of assistive technology can be realized only when the needs of a person with a disability are identified and the assistive technology is designed to meet those needs. If this is not done, the potential power of assistive technology will not be realized.

See also: ADAPTED PHYSICAL EDUCATION; SPECIAL EDUCATION, *subentries on* CURRENT TRENDS, HISTORY OF, PREPARATION OF TEACHERS.

BIBLIOGRAPHY

ALLIANCE FOR TECHNOLOGY ACCESS. 2000. *Computers and Web Resources for Persons with Disabilities: A Guide to Exploring Today's Assistive Technology,* 3rd edition. Alameda, CA: Hunter House.

BLACKHURST, A. EDWARD, and LAHM, ELIZABETH A. 2000. "Technology and Exceptional Foundations." In *Technology and Exceptional Individuals,* ed. Jimmy D. Lindsey. Austin, TX: Pro-Ed.

CHAMBERS, ANTOINETTE C. 1997. *Has Technology Been Considered? A Guide for IEP Teams.* Reston, VA: Council of Administrators of Special Education and the Technology and Media Division of the Council for Exceptional Children.

COOK, ALBERT M., and HUSSEY, SUSAN M. 1995. *Assistive Technologies: Principles and Practice.* St. Louis, MO: Mosby.

FLIPPO, KAREN F.; INGE, KATHERINE J.; and BARCUS, J. MICHAEL, eds. 1995. *Assistive Technology: A Resource for School, Work, and Community.* Baltimore: Brookes.

GALVIN, JAN C., and SCHERER, MARCIA J. 1996. *Evaluating, Selecting and Using Appropriate Assistive Technology.* Gaithersburg, MD: Aspen.

GOLDEN, DIANE. 1998. *Assistive Technology in Special Education: Policy and Practice.* Reston, VA: Council of Administrators of Special Education and the Technology and Media Division of the Council for Exceptional Children.

Individuals with Disabilities Education Act of 1997. U.S. Public Law 105-17. *U.S. Code.* Vol. 20, secs. 1400 et seq.

INTERNET RESOURCE

NATIONAL ASSISTIVE TECHNOLOGY RESEARCH INSTITUTE. 2001. "Assistive Technology Fundamentals." <http://natri.uky.edu>.

TED S. HASSELBRING
MARGARET E. BAUSCH

ASSOCIATION OF AMERICAN COLLEGES AND UNIVERSITIES

The Association of American Colleges and Universities (AAC&U) is the national association that works to advance and strengthen undergraduate liberal education for all college students, regardless of their academic specialization or intended career. Since its founding in 1915, AAC&U's membership as of 2001 included more than 735 accredited public and private colleges and universities of every type and size.

AAC&U functions as a catalyst and facilitator, forging links among presidents, administrators, and faculty members who are engaged in institutional and curricular planning. Its mission is to reinforce the collective commitment to liberal education at both the national and local levels and to help individual institutions keep the quality of student learning at the core of their work as they evolve to meet new economic and social challenges.

In 1995 the AAC&U board of directors approved five priorities that guide AAC&U's work: (1) mobilizing collaborative leadership for educational and institutional effectiveness; (2) building faculty leadership in the context of institutional renewal; (3) strengthening curricula to serve student and societal needs; (4) establishing diversity as an educational and civic priority; and (5) fostering global engagement in a diverse but connected world.

Educational Vision

AAC&U advocates for excellence in liberal education as an equal opportunity commitment—to all students regardless of where they study, what they major in, or what their career goals are. Although liberal education has always set the standard for excellence in higher education, the content of a liberal education has changed markedly over time, and the educational vision and nature of AAC&U's programmatic work has changed accordingly. Since AAC&U's founding, however, liberal education at American colleges and universities has consistently fostered the development of intellectual capacities and ethical judgment and the attainment of a sophisticated understanding of nature, culture, and society. AAC&U believes that liberal education prepares graduates better for work and for civic leadership in their society.

As it has evolved over the last few decades of the twentieth century and the first years of the twenty-first century, liberal education has come to place new emphasis on diversity and pluralism. In a board statement approved in 1998, AAC&U asserted that, "by its nature, liberal education is globalistic and pluralistic. It embraces the diversity of ideas and experiences that characterize the social, natural, and intellectual world. To acknowledge such diversity in all its forms is both an intellectual commitment and a social responsibility, for nothing less will equip students to understand our world and to pursue fruitful lives."

In the twenty-first century AAC&U members are working together to reinvent liberal education and stress both its analytic and practical benefits. Liberal education now involves first-year seminars and programs, newly revitalized and developmental general education curricula, topically linked courses and learning communities, undergraduate research, community-based diversity projects, online scientific experimentation, and advanced interdisciplinary studies.

This contemporary liberal education is both conceptually rigorous and pragmatic. Ideally it will prepare graduates to use the knowledge they gain in college and across their working lives in thoughtful, ethical ways.

History and Development

AAC&U's mission has consistently focused on advancing liberal education and defining the aims of a college education in America. First named the Association of Colleges (AAC), the organization was established at a meeting of college presidents in 1915 in Chicago, Illinois. Robert L. Kelly, president of Earlham College, served as its first president. Although most of its founding-member schools were small liberal arts colleges, from the outset, AAC has been composed of colleges and universities from all sectors of higher education, including public or tax-supported institutions.

In 1923 the association voted to admit new members and amended its original charter to read "College of Liberal Arts of" in the case of universities or other institutions that had several departments or schools, beginning its long history of including many types of colleges and universities among its membership. This aspect of the association distinguishes it from most other higher education associations.

Throughout its history, AAC has also consistently engaged the challenges of diversity in American higher education. In 1969 AAC released a statement on "Racial Problems and Academic Programs" asserting, in part, that "The nation owes a debt of gratitude to its minorities for giving a fresh

and morally compelling impetus to the movement for restoring relevance to academic programs, not in any trivial or opportunistic sense but in the sense that the worth of an educational system is ultimately measured by the quality of the society it serves." AAC also launched its continuing Project on the Status and Education of Women, the first such office at a Washington-based association, in 1971. The project's first director, Bernice R. Sandler, coined the phrase "chilly climate" to describe the campus environment for many women and minority men.

Acting on recommendations of a blue-ribbon committee, AAC voted in 1976 to withdraw from all formal federal lobbying activities and dedicate itself solely to the mission of being the "voice for liberal learning" in the United States. At this time, AAC assisted in establishing the National Association of Independent Colleges and Universities to work on federal relations on behalf of private or independent institutions. In 1995 the organization formally changed its name to the Association of American Colleges and Universities to better reflect the diversity of its member institutions.

In 1985 AAC issued an influential report to the academic community on "Integrity in the College Curriculum." The conclusions of this report guided AAC's work from the mid-1980s into the 1990s. The organization continues to work on issues of curricular coherence in the undergraduate experience through a variety of programs and initiatives.

Programs and Organizational Activities

All of AAC&U's work connects goals for student learning with institutional planning and practice. Through a combination of continuing programs and grant-funded initiatives, AAC&U provides resources and direct practical assistance to campuses working on improving undergraduate education. It also works more broadly to shape the national dialogue on central educational issues.

During the 1980s and 1990s AAC&U programs and initiatives focused on curriculum transformation and general education reform, undergraduate learning outcomes, re-forming college majors, faculty development and preparing future faculty, building faculty leadership for educational and institutional change, campus diversity, and global learning. At any given time AAC&U generally runs about ten to fifteen funded projects. The organization also runs a variety of meetings and summer institutes, including the Asheville Institute on General Education (sponsored since 1991 in collaboration with the University of North Carolina, Asheville). It also publishes several quarterlies including *Peer Review, On Campus with Women, Diversity Digest,* and *Liberal Education,* its flagship journal, which it has published under this title since 1959.

Signature AAC&U initiatives have included Greater Expectations: The Commitment to Quality as a Nation Goes to College; American Commitments: Diversity, Democracy and Liberal Learning; Preparing Future Faculty; Shared Futures: Learning for a World Lived in Common; and Science Education for New Civic Engagements and Responsibilities.

Membership and Financial Support

Membership in AAC&U is institutional and open to all accredited colleges and universities in the United States. As of 2001 AAC&U comprised 700 member institutions. The association's general operating funds are furnished by membership dues and income from publication sales and meeting attendance. For major programs and initiatives, the association seeks grants from independent and corporate foundations and from the federal government. AAC&U has its headquarters in Washington, D.C.

BIBLIOGRAPHY

ASSOCIATION OF AMERICAN COLLEGES AND UNIVER- SITIES. 1985. *Integrity in the College Curriculum.* Washington, DC: Association of American Colleges and Universities.

ASSOCIATION OF AMERICAN COLLEGES AND UNIVER- SITIES. 1995. *The Drama of Diversity and Democracy: Higher Education and American Commitments.* Washington, DC: Association of American Colleges and Universities.

SCHNEIDER, CAROL, and SHOENBERG, ROBERT. 1998. *Contemporary Understandings of Liberal Education.* Washington, DC: Association of American Colleges and Universities.

INTERNET RESOURCE

ASSOCIATION OF AMERICAN COLLEGES AND UNIVER- SITIES. 2002. <www.aacu-edu.org>.

DEBRA HUMPHREYS

ASSOCIATION OF AMERICAN UNIVERSITIES

The Association of American Universities (AAU) is a Washington, D.C.-based organization representing sixty-one of the most prestigious North American higher education institutions, fifty-nine in the United States and two in Canada. Membership is by invitation only, with an approximately 50 percent split between public and private institutions. A majority of 75 percent of the current members must approve an institution before it can become a new member.

The member institutions have major interests in quality research and graduate and professional education. AAU represents those interests nationally and provides its members with a forum to discuss common institutional issues. Two AAU meetings are held annually, with one meeting taking place on a member's campus and one held in Washington, D.C.

AAU's internal structure includes an Executive Committee from the membership; a Council on Federal Relations, consisting of senior officers from the institutions whose responsibilities include federal relations for their own campuses; the Association of Graduate Schools, composed of the graduate deans of the AAU institutions; and a Public Affairs Network whose participants are public affairs officers of the AAU institutions.

Each year AAU institutions award about half of the doctorates given in the United States, one-fifth of the master's degrees, and one-sixth of the bachelor's degrees. According to the association's website, AAU member institutions contribute more than half of higher education's research and development performance and receive around 60 percent of the federal funds for academic research.

History

The AAU was formed in 1900, during a meeting at the University of Chicago of fourteen representatives of the major institutions of higher education granting doctoral degrees. The American system was fragmented, and standards for graduate study were low. Diploma mills abounded, and European institutions' opinion of American higher education was unflattering. The purposes of the Chicago meeting were to find means to raise the standards of higher education institutions, increase the value of American graduate degrees, protect the term *university* from indiscriminate use, and gain the respect of European universities. The result of the meeting was the creation of the Association of American Universities.

By 1914 the association was acting as an accrediting agency that provided European institutions with lists of approved colleges whose graduates were deemed capable of advanced graduate work. Graduate deans did site visits, and certified colleges were included in the "AAU Accepted List."

Although the AAU was essentially a presidents' organization, the focus on accreditation resulted in drastic losses of attendance by presidents. AAU had become a deans' forum. In 1949, in order to return the association to the presidents, and as a result of the deans' desire to expand the accreditation service, AAU dropped accreditation entirely. It split into two organizations, one a presidential organization keeping the name Association of American Universities, and the second taking on the name the Association of Graduate Schools in the AAU.

For a good part of its life, AAU's federal affairs activities were minimal. However, World War II brought AAU and its institutions into a closer relationship with the federal government, and in the postwar period the creation of the National Science Foundation (NSF), the Office of Naval Research (ONR), and National Institutes of Health (NIH) meant large sums of research funds were directed to AAU institutions. The relationship with the federal government became more complicated and demanding, and AAU established a permanent office in Washington, D.C. However, AAU's reluctance to participate in lobbying continued, and it was not until 1977 that the association named its own president for the Washington office. This was followed in 1978 with the naming of a director of federal relations and the development of a full-time staff that dealt with federal issues.

By the 1980s AAU had expanded its activities to include an interest in foreign languages and area studies, the organization of a clearinghouse on corporate–university research partnerships, and the collection of data on graduate education. AAU joined other Washington higher education associations in lobbying on such issues as student financial aid, federal support of the humanities, tax policies affecting higher education, and intercollegiate athletic activities.

As university–industry relationships became closer in the U.S. struggle to remain economically competitive, AAU became deeply involved in the problems that emerged. Three issues in particular concerned AAU: conflicts of interest and research misconduct, indirect research costs disagreements, and academic earmarking.

Robert M. Rosenzweig's 1998 study revealed how the increasing complexity of university–industry research relationships generated conflict-of-interest questions. For example, some commercial clients of universities required the institutions to prevent or postpone publication of research results—a violation of academic values. In response to this and other issues related to university–industry relations, AAU set up a clearinghouse to allow its members to share their policies. Several highly publicized cases of alleged misconduct in research in the late 1980s combined with the probability of more such cases led AAU to put together and distribute workable guidelines for institutions.

No issue was more contentious and difficult for AAU to deal with than that of earmarking—the practice by an institution of directly soliciting influential members of Congress for research dollars, thus avoiding the conventional practice of competitive peer review as a basis for being awarded federal funding. This issue seriously divided AAU's membership. Peer review was a well-established and legitimate method for determining who would receive federal research awards and reflected university values of rewarding merit. But earmarking proved attractive to some colleges, universities, and members of Congress, for it provided direct aid to individual institutions and perhaps to the local economies. The issue was deeply divisive, and the association was never able to reach a satisfactory solution. Earmarking increased greatly in the 1990s and into the 2000s.

AAU and its members have had a long history of contentious negotiations with the federal government concerning indirect costs, the reimbursement of facilities, and administrative costs of federally funded research. Indirect costs have been an issue since the 1930s. Determining indirect costs is complicated. The issue involves disputes in which government tends to see universities as demanding exorbitant reimbursement for overhead costs, while universities contend that the charges are reasonable and necessary to take account of administrative and facility costs to the institutions.

AAU is an association member of the American Council on Education (ACE) and participates in and coordinates activities with the informal group of Washington Associations, often called the Big Six. AAU also has affiliations with the Council of Graduate Schools (CGS), the Association of American Medical Schools (AAMS), and the Council on Government Relations (CGR).

See also: AMERICAN ASSOCIATION OF COMMUNITY COLLEGES; AMERICAN COUNCIL ON EDUCATION; ASSOCIATION OF AMERICAN COLLEGES AND UNIVERSITIES.

BIBLIOGRAPHY

HAWKINS, HUGH. 1992. *Banding Together: The Rise of National Associations in American Higher Education.* Baltimore: Johns Hopkins University Press.

ROSENZWEIG, ROBERT M. 1998. *The Political University.* Baltimore: Johns Hopkins University Press.

INTERNET RESOURCE

ASSOCIATION OF AMERICAN UNIVERSITIES. 2002. <www.aau.edu>.

HARLAND G. BLOLAND

ATTENDANCE POLICY
See: COMPULSORY SCHOOL ATTENDANCE.

ATTENTION

Because some forms of learning are critically dependent upon attention, it is important for educators to be familiar with modern developments in this field. The most widely known definition of attention extends back to the late 1800s. The psychologist and philosopher William James (1842–1910) defined it as "the taking possession of the mind, in clear and vivid form, of one out of what seem several simultaneously possible objects or trains of thought" (pp. 403–404).

This definition conveys intuitive feeling for the subject. However, it is common to break the subject down into two subdivisions: (1) arousal and (2) selection of information. The processes involved in *arousal* involve achieving and maintaining an alert state sufficient to remain in contact with environ-

mental stimuli. This sense of attention separates the waking state from conditions such as sleep or coma. *Selective attention* refers to the processes involved in selecting information for consciousness, for immediate response, or for storing information in memory. The conscious content of selective attention is only a small subset of the information that could be available at any given moment. Thus, the ability to switch or orient one's attention is critical to the successful use of attention in any environment.

Attention can also be considered in terms of its underlying anatomy. It is useful for educators to think about attention as an organ system, not unlike the familiar organ systems of respiration and circulation. Attention has a distinct anatomy that carries out basic psychological functions and that can be influenced by specific brain injuries and states. The network involved in achieving an alert state involves midbrain centers that are the source of the chemical norepinepherine. This network appears to be asymmetric at the cortical level, with greatest involvement of the right cerebral hemisphere, particularly in the frontal regions. Two networks are involved in the process of selection of information. One of these relates to orienting to sensory information, and involves areas of the parietal lobe, frontal eye fields, and superior colliculus, which are also part of the eye movement system. A second network is related to attention to internal thoughts. This network involves areas of the frontal midline (anterior cingulate), the left and right lateral prefrontal cortex, and the underlying basal ganglia.

The Study of Attention

The study of attention has greatly expanded as new methods have become available for its study. From the early beginnings of psychology in the late 1880s, studies of attention employed simple experimental tasks that required rapid responses to single targets—or to one of a small number of targets—in an effort to study limitations in people's speed and capacity for attending to input information. A good example of the type of tasks used is the *Stroop effect.* This effect occurs when subjects are asked to respond to the color of ink in which a conflicting word may be written (e.g., the word blue written in red ink). Performance on this task requires an act of selection to ignore the word and respond to the ink color. Another task used to explore selection is a *visual search task.* It has been shown that attention can be efficiently summoned to any part of a natural scene in which luminance or motion clearly signal a change, but even radical changes of content that occur outside the focus of attention are not reported. This indicates that the subjective impression of being fully aware of the world around one is largely an illusion. People have very poor knowledge about things they are not currently attending to, but a very good ability to orient toward an area of change.

In the 1950s functional models of information flow in the nervous system were developed in conjunction with an interest in computer simulation of cognitive processes. In the 1970s studies using microelectrodes on alert monkeys showed that the firing rate of cells in particular brain areas were enhanced when the monkey attended to a stimulus within the cells' receptive field. In the 1980s and 1990s human neuroimaging studies allowed examination of the whole brain during tasks involving attention. These newer methods of study also improved the utility of more traditional methods, such as: (1) the kinds of experimental tasks discussed above, (2) the use of patients with lesions of particular brain areas, and (3) the use of recordings of brain waves (EEG) from scalp electrodes. The ability to trace anatomical changes over time has provided methods for validating and improving pharmacological and other forms of therapy.

Attention in Infants

Infants as young as four months old can learn to anticipate the location of an event and demonstrate this by moving their eyes to a location where the event will occur. Thus, caregivers can teach important aspects of where a child should focus, and they can also use orienting to counteract an infant's distress well before the infant begins to speak. Infants also show preferences for novel objects in the first few months of life. In early childhood, more complex forms of attentional control begin to emerge as the frontal areas undergo considerable development. These networks allow children to make selections in the face of conflicting response tendencies. Late in the first year, infants first show the ability to reach away from the line of sight, and later the developing toddler and preschooler begin to develop the ability to choose among conflicting stimuli and courses of action.

Infants come into the world with a definite set of reactions to their environment, and even siblings can be very different in their reactions to various events. These individual differences, which include individual differences in orienting and effortful control of attention, constitute *temperament*. One infant, for example, is easily frustrated, has only a brief attention span, and becomes upset with even moderate levels of stimulating play. Another may tolerate very rough play and frequently seek out exciting events, focusing on each interest so strongly that it is difficult to get the child's attention. Thus, even early in life, when attention serves mainly orienting functions, children will differ in what captures their interest—and in how this interest is maintained. These functions will continue to serve the child during the school years, where interest accounts for about 10 percent of the variability in children's achievement. However, later-developing attention systems will prove to be even more important in schooling.

Effortful Control

Later in childhood, maturation of the frontal lobe produces more reliance on executive attention, allowing increased scope for methods of socialization. The strength and effectiveness of this later developing effortful control system is also an important source of temperamental differences. Among older children, some will be able to intentionally focus and switch attention easily, to use attention to inhibit actions they have been told not to perform, and to plan for upcoming activities. Other children will be less able to control their own attention and actions. These differences reflect effortful control and have been found to play an important role in the development of higher-level systems of morality and conscience as well as being generally important in the control and programming of action and emotion.

Intelligence

Children's abilities also differ in the cognitive domain, as is shown in tests of intelligence. Differences in cognitive ability rest in part on the frontal structures related to the development of the executive attention systems. Areas of the left and right ventral prefrontal cortex become active in questions that require general intelligence. A likely reason is that these areas are important for holding information in the mind, while other brain areas retrieve related knowledge that might be important in solving problems. The ability to solve problems like those present in intelligence tests requires both specific knowledge and the ability to retrieve information in response to the prompts present on the test. High-level attentional networks involving frontal areas are very important in this process.

The learning of new skills, such as reading and arithmetic, also requires attention so that relevant input can be stored. The storage of such information rests upon structures that lie deep within the temporal lobe. Attention appears to play an important role at several stages of acquisition of reading. It is important for subjects to be able to break visual and auditory words into their constituent letters or phonemes in order to gain knowledge of the alphabetic principle that allows visual letters to be related to word sounds. The role of frontal attentional networks also plays a key role in accessing word meanings.

Teachers are usually aware that maintaining an alert state in the school environment is dependent both upon factors that are intrinsic to the child—such as adequate rest, good nutrition, and high motivation—and those that can be controlled by the teacher, such as the use of novel and involving exercises at an appropriate level to challenge the student. Capturing the child's interest is important in fostering achievement, but effortful control allows the practice of skills that can lead to new interests, and the developing goal structures of children will allow the development of interest in activities or skills that will lead them to their chosen goals.

Teachers thus need to be aware of individual differences in the development of the mechanisms of selective attention important in the storage and retrieval of information relevant to various tasks. Assessment of attentional capacities may be very useful for this purpose. Children can then be encouraged by exercises appropriate to their level to sustain the effort necessary for effective problem solving. Assessment of the school environment may also be useful in considering children's attentional capacities. The application of effortful control can be tiring, and the opportunities for skill learning and for active play may be important in supporting its activity.

Finally, attention is also important in the development of children's social skills. When teachers point out aspects of other children's experiences and focus on the welfare of others, they can train the direction of a child's interest and concern. Again, this activity will be easier with some children than with others, but it can serve the goal of encouraging empathy and discouraging aggression in a child's development.

See also: LEARNING, *subentry on* PERCEPTUAL PROCESSES.

BIBLIOGRAPHY

JAMES, WILLIAM. 1890. *Principles of Psychology.* New York: Henry Holt.

POSNER, MICHAEL I., and RAICHLE, MARCUS E. 1994. *Images of Mind.* New York: Scientific American Books.

POSNER, MICHAEL I., and ROTHBART, MARY K. 2000. "Developing Mechanisms of Self-Regulation." *Development and Psychopathology* 12:427–441.

RUFF, HOLLY A., and ROTHBART, MARY K. 1996. *Attention in Early Development: Themes and Variations.* New York: Oxford University Press.

MICHAEL I. POSNER
MARY K. ROTHBART

ATTENTION DEFICIT HYPERACTIVITY DISORDER

The most common reason that children are referred to child-guidance clinics is for attention deficit hyperactivity disorder (ADHD). ADHD is a behavioral disorder with a strong hereditary component, which likely results from neurological dysfunction. According to the American Psychiatric Association's *Diagnostic and Statistical Manual of Mental Disorders, Text Revision (DSM-IV-TR)*, there are three diagnostic categories of ADHD: (1) ADHD, Predominantly Inattentive Type; (2) ADHD, Predominantly Hyperactive-Impulsive Type; and (3) ADHD, Combined Type. ADHD often occurs simultaneously with other behavioral and learning problems, such as learning disabilities, emotional or behavioral disabilities, or Tourette's syndrome.

A 1998 study by Russell A. Barkley stated that ADHD is a deficit in behavior inhibition, which sets the stage for problems in regulating behavior. Students with ADHD may experience problems in working memory (remembering things while performing other cognitive operations), delayed inner speech (self-talk that allows people to solve problems), problems controlling emotions and arousal, and difficulty analyzing problems and communicating solutions to others. Hence, students with ADHD may find it difficult to stay focused on tasks such as schoolwork—tasks that require sustained attention and concentration, yet are not intrinsically interesting. In addition, the majority of individuals with ADHD experience significant problems in peer relations and demonstrate a higher incidence of substance abuse than that of the general population.

Although professionals did not recognize ADHD as a diagnostic category until the 1980s, evidence of the disorder dates from the beginning of the twentieth century. The physician George F. Still is credited with being one of the first authors to bring those with "defective moral control" to the attention of the medical profession in 1902. In the 1930s and 1940s Heinz Werner and Alfred Strauss were able to identify children who were hyperactive and distractible—children who exhibited the Strauss syndrome. Later, in the middle of the twentieth century, the term *minimal brain injury* was used to refer to children of normal intelligence who were inattentive, impulsive, and/or hyperactive. This term fell out of favor and was replaced by *hyperactive child syndrome.* Professionals eventually rejected this term, as inattention, not hyperactivity, was recognized as the major behavior problem associated with the disorder.

Students with ADHD are eligible for special education services under the category "other health impaired (OHI)." This category has dramatically increased in size; however, the number of students served in this category remains well below the estimated prevalence rate of 3 to 5 percent of the school-age population. From discrepancies such as this, researchers have estimated that fewer than half of all students with ADHD are receiving special education services.

As Barkley noted in his 1998 study, the effective diagnosis of ADHD requires a medical exam, a clinical interview, and teacher and parent rating scales. During the medical exam the physician must rule out other possible causes of the behavior problem, and through the clinical interview, the clinician obtains information from both parents and child about the child's physical and psychological characteristics. Finally, parents, teachers, and in some cases children themselves, complete behavioral rating scales, such as the Connors scales and the ADHD Rating Scale–IV in order to quantify observed behavior patterns.

Frequently students with ADHD are treated with psychostimulants, such as methylphenidate (Ritalin), which stimulate areas of the brain responsible for inhibition. Despite some negative publicity in the media, most authorities in the area of ADHD are in favor of Ritalin's use. In addition to medication, students with ADHD also benefit from carefully designed educational programming. In the early 1960s William Cruickshank was one of the first to establish an educational program for students who would meet what has become the criteria for ADHD. This program, proposing a degree of classroom structure rarely seen in the early twenty-first century, advocated: (1) a reduction of stimuli irrelevant to learning and enhancement of material important for learning and (2) a structured program with a strong emphasis on teacher direction. In addition to educational programs that emphasize and provide structure, a 1997 study by Robert H. Horner and Edward G. Carr indicated that students with ADHD benefited from instructional approaches examining the consequences, antecedents, and setting events that maintain inappropriate behaviors. Other researchers' findings indicated that they also profited from behavior management systems in which the student with ADHD learns to monitor his or her own behavior. These strategies, although effective, are not generally powerful enough to completely remedy the symptoms of children with ADHD. The majority of children diagnosed with ADHD continue to demonstrate symptoms in adulthood.

See also: SPECIAL EDUCATION, **subentries on** CURRENT TRENDS, HISTORY OF.

BIBLIOGRAPHY

AMERICAN PSYCHIATRIC ASSOCIATION. 1994. *Diagnostic and Statistical Manual of Mental Disorders, Text Revision,* 4th edition. Washington, DC: American Psychiatric Association.

BARKLEY, RUSSELL. A. 1998. *Attention-Deficit Hyperactive Disorder: A Handbook for Diagnosis and Treatment.* New York: Guilford Press.

CONNORS, C. KEITH. 1989. *Connors Teacher Rating Scale-28.* Tonawanda, NY: Multi-Health Systems.

DUPAUL, GEORGE J.; POWER, THOMAS J.; ANASTOPOLOUS, ARTHUR D.; and REID, ROBERT. 1998. *ADHD Rating Scale–IV: Checklists, Norms, and Clinical Interpretations.* New York: Guilford Press.

HALLAHAN, DANIEL P., and COTTONE, E. A. 1997. "Attention Deficit Hyperactivity Disorder." In

Advances in Learning and Behavioral Disabilities, Vol. 11, ed. Thomas E. Scruggs and Margo A. Mastropieri. Greenwich, CT: JAI Press.

HORNER, ROBERT H., and CARR, EDWARD G. 1997. "Behavioral Support for Students with Severe Disabilities: Functional Assessment and Comprehensive Intervention." *Journal of Special Education* 31:1–11.

SHAPIRO, EDWARD S.; DUPAUL, GEORGE J.; and BRADLEY-KLUG, KATHY L. 1998. "Self-Management as a Strategy to Improve the Classroom Behavior of Adolescents with ADHD." *Journal of Learning Disabilities* 31:545–555.

DEVERY R. MOCK
DANIEL P. HALLAHAN

AUGUSTINE, ST. (354–430)

St. Augustine was bishop of Hippo, in North Africa, and his writings established the intellectual foundations of Christianity in the West. He was born in Thagaste, a town forty-five miles south of Hippo in the Roman province of Numidia, which is now Algeria. His father, Patricius, was a pagan, and his mother, Monica, a Christian. In his late teens he went to Carthage for further study, and through his reading of Cicero, he became enthused about philosophy. He became a teacher of rhetoric in Carthage and later in Rome and Milan. Augustine was a restless seeker rather than a systematic thinker, and after a brief flirtation with the dualistic philosophy of Manichaeanism, he immersed himself in the Neoplatonic philosophy of Plotinus. His whole life may be characterized as an intellectual and moral struggle with the problem of evil, a struggle that he worked out through synthesizing the ideas of the Neoplatonists with Christianity. He upheld the teachings of the Bible, but he realized that maintaining them in the intellectual and political climate of his age required a broad liberal education.

In his struggle against evil, Augustine believed in a hierarchy of being in which God was the Supreme Being on whom all other beings, that is, all other links in the great chain of being, were totally dependent. All beings were good because they tended back toward their creator who had made them from nothing. Humans, however, possess free will, and can only tend back to God by an act of the will.

Man's refusal to turn to God is, in this way of thinking, *nonbeing,* or evil, so although the whole of creation is good, evil comes into the world through man's rejection of the good, the true, and the beautiful, that is, God. The ultimate purpose of education, then, is turning toward God, and Augustine thought the way to God was to look into oneself. It is here one finds an essential distinction Augustine makes between knowing about something (*cogitare*), and understanding (*scire*). One can know about oneself, but it is through understanding the mystery of oneself that one can come to understand the mystery of God. Thus the restless pursuit of God is always a pursuit of a goal that recedes from the seeker. As humans are mysteries to themselves, God is understood as wholly mysterious.

Augustine and Teaching

To be a teacher in the context of this struggle was, for Augustine, an act of love. Indeed, he advised teachers to "Imitate the good, bear with the evil, love all" (1952, p. 87). This love was required, for he knew the hardships of study, and the active resistance of the young to learning. He also considered language to be as much a hindrance as a help to learning. The mind, he said, moves faster than the words the teacher utters, and the words do not adequately express what the teacher intends. Additionally, the student hears the words in his own way, and attends not only to the words, but also to the teacher's tone of voice and other nonverbal signs, thus often misunderstanding the meaning of the teacher. The teacher, thus, must welcome students' questions even when they interrupt his speech. He must listen to his students and converse with them, and question them on their motives as well as their understanding. He saw education as a process of posing problems and seeking answers through conversation. Further, he saw teaching as mere preparation for understanding, which he considered an illumination of the "the teacher within," who is Christ.

Augustine, then, thought teachers should adapt their teaching to their students, whom he distinguished into three kinds: those well educated in the liberal arts, those who had studied with inferior teachers of rhetoric and who thought they understood things they did not actually understand, and those who were uneducated. The teacher needs to begin with all students by questioning them about what they know. When teaching well-educated students, Augustine cautioned teachers not to repeat for them what they already knew, but to move them along quickly to material they had not yet mastered. When teaching the superficially educated student, the teacher needed to insist upon the difference between having words and having understanding. These students needed to learn docility and to develop the kind of humility that was not overly critical of minor errors in the speech of others. With regard to the uneducated student, Augustine encouraged the teacher to be simple, clear, direct, and patient. This kind of teaching required much repetition, and could induce boredom in the teacher, but Augustine thought this boredom would be overcome by a sympathy with the student according to which, "they, as it were, speak in us what they hear, while we, after a fashion, learn in them what we teach" (1952, p. 41). This kind of sympathy induces joy in the teacher and joy in the student.

All three of these kinds of teaching are to be done in what Augustine called the *restrained style.* This style requires the teacher not to overload the student with too much material, but to stay on one theme at a time, to reveal to the student what is hidden from him, to solve difficulties, and to anticipate other questions that might arise. Teachers also should be able from time to time to speak in what he called the *mixed style*—using elaborate yet well-balanced phrases and rhythms—for the purpose of delighting their students and attracting them to the beauty of the material. Teachers should also be able to speak in the *grand style,* which aims at moving students to action. What makes the grand style unique is not its verbal elaborations, but the fact that it comes from the heart—from emotion and passion—thus moving students to obey God and use his creation to arrive at full enjoyment of God. This hoped-for response is wholly consistent with what is probably the most famous quotation from Augustine's autobiography, *The Confessions:* "You arouse us so that praising you may bring us joy, because you have made us and drawn us to yourself, and our heart is unquiet until it rests in you" (1997b, p. 3).

Influence

Of the two great traditions in liberal education, the oratorical and the philosophical, Augustine is distinctly an orator. He believed more in imparting the truth to students than in supporting the individual student's quest for truth. He used the dialogical mode as one who knows the truth, unlike the Greek philosopher Socrates, who used dialogue as one who does not know anything. He thus established a Christian philosophy, which has influenced scholars and educators throughout the history of the West.

Augustine directly influenced the Roman statesman and writer Cassiodorus and the Spanish prelate and scholar Isidore of Seville who, in the sixth and seventh centuries, established the *seven liberal arts* as a way of enriching the study of the Scriptures. The Anglo-Saxon scholar and headmaster Alcuin, in the eighth century, used Augustine's works on Christian teaching as textbooks. The Italian philosopher and religious leader Thomas Aquinas's attempt in the thirteenth century at synthesizing Aristotle and Christian faith may be understood as an extension of the work of Augustine, as can the Christian humanism of the Dutch scholar Erasmus in the fifteenth and sixteenth centuries.

In the first decade of the new millennium, Augustine's use of psychological autobiography speaks directly to those educators who view introspection and empathy as critical features in the life of a teacher. His awareness of the centrality of personal and political struggle in human existence, and of the educative and healing power of human dialogue still speaks to the condition of many teachers and educators.

See also: PHILOSOPHY OF EDUCATION.

BIBLIOGRAPHY

AUGUSTINE, ST. 1952. *The First Catechetical Instruction* (400), trans. Joseph P. Christopher. Westminster, MD: Newman Press.

AUGUSTINE, ST. 1968. *The Teacher* (389), trans. Robert P. Russell. Washington, DC: Catholic University of America Press.

AUGUSTINE, ST. 1997a. *On Christian Teaching* (426), trans. R. P. H. Green. New York: Oxford University Press.

AUGUSTINE, ST. 1997b. *The Confessions* (400), trans. Maria Boulding. New York: Vintage Books.

BROWN, PETER. 1969. *Augustine of Hippo.* Berkeley: University of California Press.

CHADWICK, HENRY. 1996. *Augustine.* New York: Oxford University Press.

RIST, JOHN M. 1999. *Augustine.* New York: Cambridge University Press.

STOCK, BRIAN. 1996. *Augustine the Reader: Meditation, Self Knowledge, and the Ethics of Interpretation.* Cambridge, MA: Belknap Press.

TIMOTHY LEONARD

AUTISM, EDUCATION OF INDIVIDUALS WITH

Though *autism* is a familiar term in the early twenty-first century, it was only recognized in the 1940s as a severe disability. Since that time, there has been extensive interest in and professional activity concerning autism. Children with autism have difficulty communicating, playing, and establishing relationships with others. Autism, often referred to as a neurological disorder, is usually evident by age three, reported in all countries, and affects between 2 and 21 individuals per 10,000, with 4 to 5 times more males than females diagnosed. About 80 percent of children with autism also meet the criteria for mental retardation, with significant limitations in IQ and adaptive behavior scores.

History

In 1943 Leo Kanner described those with autism as being unable to relate to themselves or others, with the term *autism* derived from the root *auto* for *self.* Since then, autism had been defined by the *Diagnostic and Statistical Manual of Mental Disorders,* 4th edition, as a pervasive developmental disorder having three classic behavioral features for its diagnosis: "the presence of markedly abnormal or impaired development in social interaction and communication and a markedly restricted repertoire of activity and interests" (p. 66). Currently the term *autism spectrum disorders* is used to refer to a comprehensive though controversial classification, which includes individuals with some characteristics of typical autism, but who may not be diagnosed with autistic disorder. Autism spectrum disorders range along a continuum of severity, from less severe forms such as pervasive developmental disorder/not otherwise specified (PDD-NOS) and Asperger's syndrome, to more severe forms that also are distinct from autism, such as childhood disintegrative disorder and Rett syndrome. Currently there is no biological diagnostic test for autism; diagnosis is based on behavioral indices. A diagnosis typically qualifies a child for special education services under the Individuals with Disabilities Education Act (IDEA) during infancy and the preschool years. The current incidence figures for autism have varied through the 1990s and into the twenty-first century, leading many to believe that actual incidence is higher than previously calculated.

Schools' Responses and Methods of Teaching

Children with autism have extensive, long-term educational needs that require thorough planning by a multidisciplinary team, ongoing monitoring of progress, and a wide range of service options. Of the three treatment approaches under study for those with autism, many educational/behavioral approaches have the strongest research basis. Pharmacological approaches are not viewed as being appropriate or effective for all, and must be used cautiously and in combination with sound educational treatments. Biomedical-neuroscience approaches are experimental with no validated treatments existing currently. There have been no controlled comparisons of educational or combined interventions despite the fact that some interventions claim "recovery" or cure with little scientific data to support such claims.

Authorities agree that students with autism benefit from individualized and often intense educational services beginning early in life. The most promising educational interventions for these children have the following characteristics: (1) behaviorally based; (2) carefully planned and monitored instruction involving task analyses of skills, individualized incentives, goals embedded in routines and activities, and adequate intensity and quality; (3) ongoing, planned opportunities for interaction with typical peers; (4) need-based supports and intervention for families; (5) services delivered in many different settings to meet support needs and promote generalization; (6) broad curricular content that addresses all developmental needs; and (7) proactive use of positive behavior support for challenging behavior. Children with autism typically require the services of special educators, general educators, and speech and language pathologists; occupational or physical therapists often address children's movement and sensory limitations. A collaborative team approach is necessary to plan, problem-solve, implement, and monitor the individualized education programs (IEPs) of these students.

Goals and Purposes of Education

Educational goals for students with autism usually aim for skills in communication, social interaction, appropriate behavior, choice making, and functional academic abilities. As these students grow older they need to reduce their dependence on others and extend their abilities to include supported functioning in the home, school, and neighborhood, using the nearby community, building social relationships with peers, engaging in leisure activities, and learning to work (paid or voluntary) with the necessary supports. Given sound intervention that starts early, the educational outcomes for these students can be highly effective, though there is much heterogeneity in their improvement.

Relationship of Autism to IDEA

Students with any of the pervasive developmental disorders typically qualify for special education services. The U.S. Department of Education reports that in 1998 to 1999 there were 53,561 students between the ages of six and twenty-one with labels of autism enrolled in public schools in the United States —.09 percent of the school population. Of these, 18 percent spend 80 percent or more of their day in general education classrooms, while 65 percent are in special education classrooms most or all of the day, and 17 percent in separate settings. Many schools are unequipped to address the comprehensive educational needs of this population. Litigation, which has characterized recent special education services for these students, has often judged their IEPs to be inadequate for achieving reasonable educational benefits.

Educational Trends, Issues, and Controversies

There is consensus about the recommended educational practices for students with autism. Analyses of the empirical basis of educational interventions are available, along with guidelines for selecting treatments (e.g., causes no harm, developmentally appropriate, scientifically validated). Unfortunately, because most individuals with autism have lifelong, pervasive support needs, families and educators, out of a sense of urgency, may adopt interventions based on testimonials rather than empirical support. Critical aspects of intervention also remain unknown, including the impact of family factors on outcomes and the relationship between an individual with autism, the appropriate treatment protocol, and the expected outcomes. Finally, there is a vast discrepancy between what is known about effective educational interventions and what is available for children with autism across settings, cultures, and income levels.

See also: SPECIAL EDUCATION, *subentries on* CURRENT TRENDS, HISTORY OF.

BIBLIOGRAPHY

AMERICAN PSYCHIATRIC ASSOCIATION. 1994. *Diagnostic and Statistical Manual of Mental Disorders*, 4th edition. Washington, DC: American Psychiatric Association.

KOEGEL, LYNN K. 2000. "Interventions to Facilitate Communication in Autism." *Journal of Autism and Developmental Disorders* 30:383–391.

LORD, CATHERINE, and RISI, SUSAN. 2000. "Diagnosis of Autism Spectrum Disorders in Young Children." In *Autism Spectrum Disorders: A Transactional Developmental Perspective*, ed. Ann M. Wetherby and Barry. M. Prizant. Baltimore: Brookes.

ROGERS, SALLY J. 2000. "Interventions that Facilitate Socialization in Children with Autism." *Journal of Autism and Developmental Disorders* 30:399–409.

SCHRIEBMAN, LAURA. 2000. "Intensive/Behavioral/ Psychoeducational Treatments for Autism: Research Needs and Future Directions." *Journal of Autism and Developmental Disorders* 30:373–378.

U.S. DEPARTMENT OF EDUCATION. 2000. *Twenty-Second Annual Report to Congress on the Implementation of the Individuals with Disabilities Education Act.* Washington, DC: U.S. Department of Education.

MARTHA E. SNELL

B

BAGLEY, WILLIAM C. (1874–1946)

Professor of education at Teachers College, Columbia University (1917–1940), William C. Bagley is commonly referred to as the founder of essentialist educational theory. Bagley was born in Detroit, Michigan, and after his family relocated to the east coast, he attended elementary school in Weymouth, Massachusetts. When his family moved back to Detroit in 1887, Bagley attended high school there and graduated from Detroit's Capitol High School in 1891 at the age of seventeen. Bagley entered Michigan Agricultural College (now Michigan State University), with the intention of preparing himself to become a farmer. Upon graduation in the spring of 1895, Bagley had no land and no money to begin farming. After a fruitless search for employment, he soon decided to teach, a decision that influenced the rest of his life. He accepted a teaching position in a rural one-room schoolhouse near Garth and Rapid River, Michigan.

Early Career

Bagley taught in Michigan for two years, during which time he dedicated his professional life to the improvement of teaching. He attended the University of Chicago in the summer of 1896, and then transferred to the University of Wisconsin in Madison. Working under Joseph Jastrow, he earned his master's degree in psychology, in the spring of 1898. Upon completion of this degree, he accepted a Sage Fellowship at Cornell University to study with well-known psychologist Edward Bradford Titchener. For four years, Bagley worked under Titchener and learned the structuralist psychology of his mentor. Bagley completed his Ph.D. in 1900 and spent the following academic year as an assistant in Titchener's laboratory. Still committed to the improvement of good teaching, Bagley accepted a position, beginning in the fall of 1901, as principal of Meramec Elementary School in St. Louis, Missouri. He worked in St. Louis for only one year, after which he accepted his first professorship as director of the Teacher Practice School and professor of psychology and pedagogy at the Montana State Normal School in Dillon, Montana. While in Montana, Bagley became active throughout the state by speaking at teachers institutes, by delivering commencement speeches, and by creating the first journal in the Rocky Mountain region dedicated specifically to education, *The Intermountain Educator.*

While working in Montana Bagley wrote his first major book, the *Educative Process* (1905). As a comprehensive portrayal of an early "science of education," the work became a popular textbook throughout the United States for courses on the introduction to educational psychology. The *Educative Process* was well received by professors as well as by the general public. With this book, Bagley's name received national, and even international, prominence.

Bagley received an offer to return to New York State to work at Oswego State Normal School in Oswego, New York. In the fall of 1906 he began his appointment there as superintendent of the Teacher Training Department. He also served as principal of the practice school and taught courses on educational methods. After only two short years he left Oswego to accept his first position at a state university, the University of Illinois.

At Illinois, Bagley helped to develop the Department of Education to the point that it became one of the most well known in the nation. In the nine years he was on the Illinois faculty, Bagley attracted to Illinois such prominent educational scholars as Guy M. Whipple, Lewis Flint Anderson, Lotus D. Coffman, and Charles H. Johnston. He also worked with several of his colleagues in 1910 to create the *Journal of Educational Psychology,* a scholarly publication that has remained significant for almost 100 years. Moreover, during this time, he helped to found Kappa Delta Pi, an honor society in education that has since opened chapters internationally.

As a professor at the University of Illinois, Bagley worked diligently to create a School of Education that was to differ remarkably from the Department of Education that he inherited. This transition ultimately required three main ingredients: an additional number of education faculty members, the construction of a building to house the school, and the creation of a program that permitted the School of Education to enroll its own students. Bagley had to prevail against the view, held by many professors of liberal arts, that future teachers needed no special preparation beyond a sound liberal arts education. Bagley certainly agreed that a sound liberal arts education was essential for future teachers. He also, however, believed that for people who planned to be teachers, a liberal arts curriculum should be accompanied by an equally sound sequence of professional education courses. Bagley eventually founded the University of Illinois' School of Education, although the construction of the building was not completed until 1918, one year after he left Illinois.

Teachers College

In the fall of 1917 Bagley began his final academic appointment at Teachers College, Columbia University, where he joined a stellar education faculty that included such prominent scholars as John Dewey, Edward L. Thorndike, William Heard Kilpatrick, and George D. Strayer. Bagley's official position was professor of normal school administration. This role allowed him to use his many years as a normal school professor, to work toward the improvement of normal school education across the nation—in effect becoming for more than twenty years the nation's dean of normal schools, or dean of teacher education.

While at Teachers College, Bagley entered into some of the most heated educational discussions of his career. Sometimes with, and often against, his colleague Kilpatrick, Bagley engaged in debates about the relative weight that should be given in ed-

ucational theory to academic subject matter, on the one hand, and to the interests and needs of students on the other. Bagley never denied the importance of designing a curriculum that met the interests and needs of students. He often argued, however, that the emphasis that theorists such as Kilpatrick placed on the individual needs of students often eclipsed the necessity for academic subject matter in the curriculum. Importantly, Bagley sought a reasonable view of professional education that balanced the needs of students with a rigorous academic curriculum.

While at Teachers College in the 1920s, Bagley also entered into educational discussions about the role of intelligence testing in the schools. In *Determinism in Education: A Series of Papers on the Relative Influence of Inherited and Acquired Traits,* Bagley argued against the determinist viewpoint, held by people such as Thorndike, that education played little or no role in the improvement of a person's intelligence. Instead, Bagley asserted that the recently created intelligence tests actually measured the educational opportunity experienced by students rather than their innate ability.

In 1934 Bagley published what he believed to be his most significant contribution to educational theory. In *Education and Emergent Man: A Theory of Education With Particular Application to Public Education in the United States,* Bagley applied Gestalt psychology to teaching, arguing against what he called mechanistic psychology, represented most prominently by Thorndike and what might be termed *extreme pragmatism,* advocated by Kilpatrick. This final book of Bagley's, however, received little attention from his colleagues. This lack of recognition likely played into the final major event of Bagley's career, the founding of essentialism in 1938.

In that year, Bagley joined with some of his colleagues to create an organization that would counteract some of the extreme tendencies of Progressive education. In the *Essentialist's Platform,* which Bagley published in April 1938, the essentialists offered several basic educational principles. First, they recognized the right of an immature student to the guidance of a well-educated, caring, and cultured teacher. Second, they proposed that an effective democracy demanded a democratic culture in which teachers impart the ideals of community to each succeeding generation of children. Third, they called for a specific program of studies that required thoroughness, accuracy, persistence, and good workmanship on the part of pupils. Bagley's basic point with his role in the founding of essentialism was that the currently dominant theories of education were feeble and insufficient. He wanted these dominant theories complemented, and perhaps replaced, with a philosophy that was strong, virile, and positive. He did not, however, want to destroy completely the dominant theories that he was critiquing. Throughout his life, he supported both the academic disciplines and certain basic tenets of Progressive education.

Soon after the founding of essentialism, Bagley retired from Teachers College. During retirement and until his death on July 1, 1946, in New York City, he served as editor of *School and Society*. He died while completing editorial work for this journal. Bagley can be remembered as an untiring fighter for professional education, a supporter of the academic disciplines, and both a critic and a supporter of different aspects of the complex movement known as Progressive education.

See also: CURRICULUM, SCHOOL; KILPATRICK, WILLIAM H.; PHILOSOPHY OF EDUCATION.

BIBLIOGRAPHY

BAGLEY, WILLIAM C. 1905. *The Educative Process.* New York: Macmillan.

BAGLEY, WILLIAM C. 1925. *Determinism in Education: A Series of Papers on the Relative Influence of Inherited and Acquired Traits.* Baltimore: Warwick and York.

BAGLEY, WILLIAM C. 1934. *Education and Emergent Man: A Theory of Education With Particular Application to Public Education in the United States.* New York: Nelson.

BAGLEY, WILLIAM C. 1938. "An Essentialist's Platform for the Advancement of American Education," *Educational Administration and Supervision* 24(April):241–256.

JOHANNINGMEIER, ERWIN V. 1967. "A Study of William Chandler Bagley's Educational Doctrines and His Program For Teacher Preparation." Ph.D. diss., University of Illinois.

KANDEL, I. L. 1961. *William Chandler Bagley: Stalwart Educator.* New York: Kappa Delta Pi and Teachers College, Columbia University.

NULL, JAMES WESLEY. 2001. "A Disciplined Progressive Educator: The Life and Career of William Chandler Bagley, 1874–1946." Ph.D. diss., The University of Texas at Austin.

J. WESLEY NULL

BARKAN, MANUEL (1913–1970)

"A visionary art educator at Ohio State University" who had "designed a model of art education that combined the teaching of art history and art criticism with art making activities" (J. Paul Getty Trust, p. 39), Manuel Barkan recognized the role of disciplinary structures of knowledge in guiding curriculum decisions but his views on curriculum reform embodied a synthesis of viewpoints, some reflecting the influence of social reconstructionism and Progressive education from the 1930s.

Barkan was born in Brooklyn, New York, in 1913; his parents were Orthodox Jews who had emigrated to the United States from Poland. He went to the New York public schools and entered New College at Teachers College, Columbia University in the 1930s. In this setting students went beyond mere academic discussion and were urged to participate in various social and political movements, in other words, "to have a special concern for reconstructing educational institutions in the light of the needs of a changing civilization." (*Teachers College Bulletin*, p. 7). Discussion seminars were organized around the pressing social issues of the day rather than around formal courses in abstract subject matter. The student's final step took the form of a period of internship in a public or private school.

In succeeding years Barkan taught art for the Rosslyn, Long Island, school district. He left New York to accept a position in the education department of the Toledo museum and, during the war years, worked as an industrial designer. In 1947 he was offered a position to teach design at the Ohio State University, a position which he had initially accepted. On arriving he realized that art education was his vocation of choice, and began work on his doctorate. While a graduate instructor, he taught undergraduate courses in art education and became head of the art education area after receiving his degree in 1951. He held this position until his death in 1970.

Barkan regarded the social environment as a place where the child learns through his or her interactions with others. This stood in marked contrast to the prevalent view in art education that favored creative self-expression and tended to view the social environment essentially as a corrupting influence that could thwart the unfolding of individual creativity. Barkan did not regard self-expression as the principle aim of art education as was common with his contemporaries. Rather, he saw it as a means through which children could be encouraged to interact with other human beings thereby to establish their sense of self. His first book, *A Foundation for Art Education* (1955), based on his doctoral dissertation, provided a reasoned account of what art education should attempt to accomplish, and drew heavily upon concepts from the transactional psychology of Ames and Cantril, the social theories of George Herbert Mead, and the philosophy of John Dewey.

Barkan's next book, *Through Art To Creativity* (1960), studied a series of art classrooms as social environments, documenting the interactions between teachers and children. Its point was to show how effective teachers stimulate the child's imaginative powers through their action, speech, and gestures. The book title reflected the widely held belief that through experiences in the arts a general creativeness could be cultivated that would transfer to other areas of human endeavor such as the sciences. However, Barkan later disavowed this claim.

By 1957 Soviet space achievements triggered a series of curriculum reforms in the United States grounded in the leading ideas of the disciplines, an idea clearly articulated by the cognitive psychologist Jerome Bruner. This was at variance with the socially oriented views of curriculum that Barkan acquired in his New College days. Still adhering to the belief that the curriculum should focus on problem-centered inquiries, he sought ways to integrate these with the structures of knowledge found in the disciplines. A problem-centered curriculum addressed problems in society or in daily living. Although this engaged students in authentic problem-solving activities, it did not lead them to an understanding of the underlying disciplines through which human understanding has been developed—disciplines that might ultimately assist in meeting the problems faced by society.

Arthur Foshay and David Ecker suggested to Barkan that a curriculum can be "both problem-centered and discipline-centered"—to enable students to confront problems centered in their lives, problems involving man's relation to man, man's re-

lation to himself, in his solitude and so forth, but that such inquiries had to be discipline centered as well. This synthesis rested upon the realization that problem-centered human meaning questions are also confronted by artists, critics, and historians when engaged in their work. They are problem centered and discipline centered at the same time, and hence, the artist, the critic, and the art historian are "models of inquiry" (Barkan 1966, p. 246). This synthesis of views was most clearly articulated in Barkan's address at the Penn State Seminar on Research and Curriculum Development that was held in 1965.

Basing curriculum reforms on the organized structures of knowledge was an innovative idea readily applicable in science and mathematics education, however, for art educators, it entailed a totally new way of thinking about curriculum since the teaching of art and the training of art teachers was almost wholly guided by developmental considerations and philosophies of creative expression. Thus, in the period following this seminar until his death in 1970, Barkan worked on several curriculum development projects that embodied aspects of these views. With Laura Chapman he prepared *Guidelines for Art Instruction through Television for the Elementary School* followed by a set of guidelines for aesthetic education, a program of the Central Midwestern Regional Educational Laboratory.

In the years since 1970 the concept of discipline-based art education has taken hold in art education. For Barkan art was indeed a discipline, but not one undertaken in academic isolation since the problems confronted within the visual arts come from life itself. Though Barkan's contribution was duly acknowledged by proponents of the discipline-based view, this movement tended to lose sight of the social vision that undergirded Barkan's integrated vision of the curriculum.

See also: ART EDUCATION.

BIBLIOGRAPHY

BARKAN, MANUEL. 1955. *A Foundation for Art Education.* New York: Ronald Press

BARKAN, MANUEL. 1960. *Through Art to Creativity.* Boston: Allyn and Bacon.

BARKAN, MANUEL. 1962. "Transition in Art Education: Changing Conceptions of Curriculum Content and Teaching." *Art Education* 15:12–18.

Barkan, Manuel. 1966. "Curriculum Problems in Art Education." In *A Seminar in Art Education for Research and Curriculum Development,* ed. Edward L. Mattil. U.S. Office of Education Cooperative Research Project No. V-002. University Park: Pennsylvania State University.

Barkan, Manuel, and Chapman, Laura. 1967. *Guidelines for Art Instruction through Television for the Elementary Schools.* Bloomington, IA: National Center for School and College Television.

Barkan, Manuel; Chapman, Laura; and Kern, E. 1970. *Guidelines: Curriculum Development for Aesthetic Education.* St. Louis, MO: Central Midwestern Regional Educational Laboratory.

Bruner, Jerome. 1960. *The Process of Education.* Cambridge, MA: Harvard University Press.

Ecker, David. 1963. "The Artistic Process as Qualitative Problem Solving." *Journal of Aesthetics and Art Criticism* 21(3):283–290.

Efland, Arthur. 1984. "Curriculum Concepts of the Penn State Seminar: An Evaluation in Retrospect." *Studies in Art Education* 25(4):205–211.

Foshay, Arthur. 1962. "Discipline Centered Curriculum." In *Curriculum Crossroads,* ed. Harry A. Passow. New York: Bureau of Publications, Teachers College, Columbia University.

J. Paul Getty Trust. 1985. *Beyond Creating: The Place for Art in America's Schools.* Malibu, CA: J. Paul Getty Trust.

Kilpatrick, Franklin P., ed. 1961. *Explorations in Transactional Psychology.* New York: New York University Press.

Mead, George Herbert. 1934. *Mind, Self, and Society.* Chicago: University of Chicago Press.

Teachers College Bulletin: New College (1936–1937). 1937. New York: Teachers College Columbia University.

Zahner, Mary. 1987. "Manuel Barkan: Twentieth Century Art Educator." Ph.D. diss., The Ohio State University.

Arthur D. Efland

BEACON EDUCATION MANAGEMENT, INC.

A participant in the field of public school management, Beacon Education Management managed twenty-five charter schools of approximately 7,500 students in Michigan, Missouri, Massachusetts, New York, North Carolina, and the District of Columbia as of April 2001.

Beacon was incorporated as a for-profit company in Delaware in December 1999, and is headquartered in Westborough, Massachusetts; its predecessor entities commenced operations in 1993, originally as Alternative Public Schools, Inc., in Nashville, Tennessee.

As the Alternative Public Schools, this company attracted notice as a pioneer in the public school management business when it assumed management of Turner Elementary School in Wilkinsburg, Pennsylvania, in 1995. That management arrangement generated national attention and considerable debate, including a court action by the Pennsylvania State Education Association to declare the contract invalid. Eventually, the Pennsylvania Supreme Court ruled that the Wilkinsburg School Board did not have the authority under state law to contract for the management of the school, and the arrangement ended after three years. The debate stimulated by the Wilkinsburg contract was an important part of the evolution of innovative public-school management arrangements that began to develop in the latter part of the 1990s.

By 1996 Beacon was also managing a charter school in Massachusetts, and had attracted an investment by the notice of William Hambrecht, a prominent California investment banker. Michael B. Ronan, formerly superintendent of the Uxbridge, Massachusetts, school district, joined Beacon in 1997, assuming the post of chief operating officer, and later chief executive officer. Ronan led the company's growth in the ensuing four years.

Beacon's philosophy is based on the concept that management of public schools should be a collaborative enterprise with parents, students, teachers, and the local community. Though Beacon is a growing national provider of education management services, the company strives to meet the local needs of its students, educators, administrators and parents, while at the same time capitalizing on economies of scale and maintaining systemwide quality. The Beacon School Design consists of a rigorous and comprehensive standards-based curriculum that emphasizes teacher-directed instruction and project-based learning, supported by Beacon's back office administrative and financial services.

As of May 2001 the company's principal business was the management and operation of charter schools. It was also planning, however, to expand into the contract management market as the other key category in which to leverage its core strengths.

Beacon's strategy focuses on the following competitive strengths:

- **Adaptability:** Its education management services model is flexible and can be tailored to specific community circumstances.

- **Revenue model:** Beacon charges a fixed fee based on a percentage of the school's revenues. Therefore, its incentive to make a profit from this fee does not conflict with the charter board's goal of maximizing services to students.

- **Controlled cost structure:** Beacon strives to maintain relatively low central office expenses, focus on geographic regions that are composed of cluster groups of three to six schools, and maintain a corporate culture that emphasizes and respects the careful use of public funds.

Beacon has had two primary influences on the education management arena. As a pioneer, it helped introduce the concept of contract management of public schools to educators as well as the general population. Later, Beacon's core strategies—local adaptation, fixed fee revenue model, and careful cost controls—influenced the evolution of school management practices as the industry has grown and developed.

In December 2001 Beacon merged with Chancellor Academies, Inc., to form Chancellor Beacon Academies, Inc., based in Coconut Grove, Florida. The combination created the second largest public school management system in the United States.

BIBLIOGRAPHY

HILL, PAUL T.; PIERCE, LAWRENCE C.; and GUTHRIE, JAMES. W. 1997. *Reinventing Public Education: How Contracting Can Transform America's Schools.* Chicago: University of Chicago Press.

NATHAN, JOE. 1996. *Charter Schools: Creating Hope and Opportunity for American Education.* San Francisco: Jossey-Bass.

INTERNET RESOURCE

EDUCATION COMMISSION OF THE STATES. 1999. "Governing America's Schools: Changing the Rules—Report of the National Commission on Governing America's Schools." <www.ecs.org/clearinghouse/11/72/1172.pdf>.

WILLIAM DeLOACHE JR.

BENJAMIN, H. R. W. (1893–1969)

Harold R. W. Benjamin was a professor of education and university administrator whose written work spoke to educational policy concerns. He was born in Gilmanton, Wisconsin and received degrees from Oregon Normal School, the University of Oregon, and Stanford University. Benjamin had a long and illustrious career in education as an elementary and secondary school teacher, a school administrator, a university professor (professor emeritus at Vanderbilt University), and dean of the College of Education at the universities of Colorado and Maryland. At the University of Maryland, where he was dean from 1947 until 1952, a campus building is dedicated to his name.

Benjamin is most well known for the 1939 publication of his satirical commentary on the nature of schooling and school reform, *The Saber Tooth Curriculum.* Written under the pseudonym J. Abner Peddiwell, *The Saber Tooth Curriculum* is considered a classic work that illustrates how unexamined traditions of schooling can result in resisting needed change. The book presents a series of lectures by Professor Peddiwell on the topic of stone-age education. Readers learn that in the Paleolithic curriculum, children were taught how to grab fish, club woolly horses, and scare saber tooth tigers. They needed these skills to sustain themselves—to get food and protect themselves from danger. In time, however, colder climatic conditions prevailed. The local waters grew muddier, making it impossible to see, let alone grab the fish, and the horses and tigers eventually died away. Yet the schools continued to teach fish grabbing, horse clubbing, and tiger scaring techniques, believing them to be fundamentals with inherent character-building and mind-training value. Progressive stone-age educators would argue that new skills needed to be taught, including fishnet making and ways to deal with a new menace, the glacier bear.

Through *The Saber Tooth Curriculum* Benjamin showed how schools often conduct themselves in ways that are unresponsive to the emerging needs of the life experience. The book was also a criticism of the mentalistic methods of teaching touted by traditional humanists in the liberal arts at the time. J. Abner Peddiwell periodically reappeared in Benjamin's speeches and in 1965, Benjamin wrote Peddiwell's autobiography, highlighting the story of his formal education, in a book titled *The Sage of Petaluma.*

Benjamin was also a noted authority in the field of comparative international education and was known for his facility with languages. He conducted studies and acted as a consultant in countries across Europe, Asia, Africa, and most extensively, Latin and South America. Benjamin's penultimate work in comparative education, *Higher Education in the American Republics* (1965), is a examination of the history, governance, financing, and curriculum programs of higher education in Central American, South American, and Caribbean nations (excluding Cuba), as well as in the United States. Benjamin catalogued important differences between the nations, focusing on boards of control, administrative offices, financial support, degree programs, selection and admissions processes, methods of instruction, and characteristics in the student and faculty populations.

As a writer with a clear progressive agenda, Benjamin authored several other books, including *Under Their Own Command* (1947), and the 1949 Inglis lecture, given at Harvard University and published as *The Cultivation of Idiosyncrasy.* Throughout his work, Benjamin highlighted his concerns for the preservation of democratic processes in American schooling and for an awakening of instructional consciousness toward individual differences.

See also: EDUCATIONAL POLICY; PHILOSOPHY OF EDUCATION.

BIBLIOGRAPHY

BENJAMIN, HAROLD R. W. [J. ABNER PEDDIWELL, PSEUD.] 1939. *The Saber Tooth Curriculum.* New York: McGraw-Hill.

BENJAMIN, HAROLD R. W. 1947. *Under Their Own Command: Observations on the Nature of a People's Education for War and Peace.* New York: Macmillan.

BENJAMIN, HAROLD R. W. 1949. *The Cultivation of Idiosyncrasy.* Cambridge, MA: Harvard University Press.

BENJAMIN, HAROLD R. W. 1965. *Higher Education in the American Republics.* New York: McGraw-Hill.

BENJAMIN, HAROLD R. W. 1965. *The Sage of Petaluma.* New York: McGraw-Hill.

PETER HLEBOWITSH

BENNE, KENNETH D. (1908–1992)

Kenneth D. Benne is well remembered as both an influential philosopher of education and a theorist of organizational change. The thematic link between these two domains was, for Benne, theorizing the practices of democratic life.

Contribution

Born in 1908, Benne began his early career as an elementary and secondary school teacher in rural Kansas and went on to become a cofounder of three major scholarly organizations: the Philosophy of Education Society, the National Training Laboratories Institute of Behavioral Science, and the International Association of Applied Social Scientists. His breadth of interests and influence is further illustrated in his professional association presidencies: the Philosophy of Education Society, the American Education Fellowship, and the Adult Education Association of the United States.

Benne completed his B.S. degree in 1930 at Kansas State University with a double major in science and English literature. He completed an M.A. in philosophy at the University of Michigan and a Ph.D. at Teachers College, Columbia University, in 1944. His doctoral dissertation, "A Conception of Authority," was published by Teachers College Bureau of Publications. It was republished in 1971 in response to that later era's challenges to authority in education and in the wider society. For a period of five decades and through professorships at Teachers College, Columbia; University of Illinois at Urbana-Champaign; and Boston University, Benne continued to write, teach, and practice in the field of democratic educational and social change. His authorship includes more than 200 articles and books in philosophy, adult education, social science, and organizational change. He defied academic convention by publishing his poetry within his writings, and late in life self-published a volume of poems, *Teach*

Me to Sing of Winter (1988), many of which he had sent to his friends over a fifty-year period.

Concept of Democratic Authority

For fifty years following his dissertation, Benne continued to search for how authority could be constituted in democratic life, and how people could develop the capacities to engage in democratic authority relations in their efforts to solve shared problems. Benne's original insights included a working conception of authority that distinguished it as a human relationship distinct from the more varied phenomena of power. In addition, he analyzed that relationship as triadic in nature, including a bearer of authority, a willing subject, and an agreed-on "field" of interaction that marks the limits of legitimate authority. Finally, he presented criteria for distinguishing nonauthoritarian from authoritarian authority relationships. Benne's concept of democratic authority depended heavily on dialogue among the participants in authority relations so that coercive influences could be detected and addressed. His commitment to dialogic authority prefigured German theorist Jurgen Habermas's conception of uncoerced speech communities, as well as Brazilian educator Paulo Freire's dialogic pedagogy.

Social Foundations of Education

While Benne was working out his conception of authority in democratic life at Teachers College, he was also a part of the Kilpatrick discussion group there, named after the influential philosopher of education William Heard Kilpatrick and including R. Freeman Butts, Harold Rugg, George Counts, Bruce Raup, and other educational theorists with disciplinary roots in the social sciences and humanities. Over a period of fifteen years, this group founded and developed the field of social foundations of education, the interdisciplinary, critical analysis of the relationships between education and social contexts. Several Teachers College graduates, including Benne, migrated to University of Illinois at Urbana-Champaign, which became a site for the further development of the social foundations enterprise.

At Urbana, Benne teamed up with other social-foundations-trained scholars to create a social foundations division in the College of Education. There Benne coedited, with his University of Illinois colleagues B. O. Smith, Ralph Stanley, and Archibald Anderson, the *Social Foundations of Education* (1956), the leading social foundations of education book of its era.

Benne's interest in democratic authority relations took him beyond philosophy of education to conceptualize learning in organizations other than in schools. During the Columbia and Illinois years, Benne had been active in cofounding the concept of the training group, or T-group, with Kurt Lewin and other social and behavioral scientists at National Training Laboratories in Bethel, Maine. Later, after Benne left Urbana for Boston University, he relied on his organizational change background when he teamed with Warren Bennis and Robert Chin to coedit and author *Planning of Change* (1961), an influential book that has remained in print for more than forty years. Bennis, who soon became a leader in the organizational change and development field, wrote an "intellectual memoir" in 2001 that recalled *Planning of Change* as "an attempt to encompass in one volume the most seminal and original essays in the yet unborn field of organizational change"(Bennis, Spreitzer, and Cummings, p. 261). Bennis credits Benne with coining the phrase "change agent" in that volume.

A Benne contribution that has received much less attention was his coauthorship in 1943 of the *Discipline of Practical Judgment in a Democratic Society* with Raup, Smith, and George Axtelle. This book, which came out during the war years and was scarcely noticed, was re-released in 1950 as the *Improvement of Practical Intelligence: The Central Task of Education*. It again caused hardly a stir in the midst of the postwar era that feared threats to democracy from external ideologies rather than from within. This volume sought to address what the authors framed as the basic problem confronting contemporary civilization, namely "the development of methods of public deliberation and institutions that will create and clarify common perspectives and will promote decisions and policies in which all interested parties participate" (Raup et al., p. 41). They saw this as an educational and political challenge to which educational philosophers had a contribution to make. It was a belief that Benne never abandoned, as is demonstrated in his last book, *The Task of Post-Contemporary Education: Essays in Behalf of a Human Future.*

See also: EDUCATIONAL PSYCHOLOGY.

BIBLIOGRAPHY

BENNE, KENNETH D. 1971. *A Conception of Authority* (1943). New York: Russell and Russell.

BENNE, KENNETH D. 1990. *The Task of Post-Contemporary Education: Essays in Behalf of a Human Future.* New York: Teachers College Press, Columbia University.

BENNIS, WARREN; BENNE, KENNETH D.; and CHIN, ROBERT. 1984. *The Planning of Change,* 4th edition. New York: Holt, Rinehart and Winston.

BENNIS, WARREN; SPREITZER, GRETCHEN M.; and CUMMINGS, THOMAS G., eds. 2001. *The Future of Leadership.* San Francisco: Jossey-Bass.

BURNETT, JOE R. 1979. "Response to Kenneth D. Benne's 'Diagnosis of Our Time.'" *Studies in Philosophy and Education* 4(4):299–312.

BUTTS, R. FREEMAN. 1993. "Kenneth Benne: The Compleat Teacher, or the Philosopher's Practice of Civic Virtue." *Educational Theory* 43(2):223–228.

GREENE, MAXINE. 1993. "Kenneth Benne, Poet of the Limits, Poet of Possibility." *Educational Theory* 43(2):219–221.

RAUP, R. BRUCE; AXTELLE, GEORGE E.; BENNE, KENNETH D.; and SMITH, B. OTHANEL. 1950. *The Improvement of Practical Intelligence: The Central Task of Education.* New York: Harper.

SMITH, B. OTHANEL; BENNE, KENNETH D.; STANLEY, RALPH; and ANDERSON, ARCHIBALD. 1956. *The Social Foundations of Education.* New York: Dryden.

STEVE TOZER

BEREA COLLEGE

Known for its unique approach to service learning, Berea College provides an education to those traditionally denied access because of race or poverty. Founded in 1855, the college was fully incorporated on April 5, 1866, with the first bachelor's degrees granted in 1873. Berea began as a one-room school in Berea, Kentucky, under the direction of the abolitionist Reverend John G. Fee. Edward H. Fairchild was the first Berea president (1869–1889), followed by William B. Stewart (1890–1892) and William G. Frost (1892–1920). Reverend Fee was never an official president, but served as the president of the board of trustees from 1858–1892. Articles of incorporation for the college were adopted in 1859 in the midst of increasing hostility to abolitionists.

Fee advocated an education built on Christian character, excellence, and equality for all, including African Americans. Teachers for Berea were recruited from Oberlin, an Ohio institution known for its antislavery stance. Following the Civil War, Berea began to enroll African-American and white students. The admission of African-American students was not without controversy and influenced policy from 1875 through 1890; the debate continued through the tenure of William Frost. Frost sought to strengthen the financial endowment of Berea, and gained support from notables such as Theodore Roosevelt, Julia Ward Howe, Charles Eliot, and Woodrow Wilson.

Concern for the education of African Americans in the era of Jim Crow was undermined when the Kentucky legislature passed the Day Law in 1904, which forbade the education of African Americans and whites together. In 1901 Berea was the only interracial institution in the South. Although Berea officials challenged the law, the Kentucky Court of Appeals and the U.S. Supreme Court upheld segregation. The enforced segregation led Berea to establish the Lincoln Institute near Louisville, Kentucky, for the education of African-American students.

The effects of the Day Law and the influence of Frost led Berea to stress the education of the white mountain people of Appalachia, whom Frost believed were of pure Anglo-Saxon stock. Part of the new mission was to train teachers to teach in the remote areas of Appalachia. Frost also advocated a form of manual training that integrated intellectual and vocational labor as a form of social and economic support. This emphasis on labor was continued during the term of President William James Hutchins, who served Berea from 1920 to 1939. Building on its commitment to the region, Berea committed itself to remedial education through an nongraded high school, continuing to serve students needing financial assistance. Guided by Berea's motto, "To Promote the Cause of Christ," Hutchins sought to prepare mountain leaders for Christian citizenship and service to others. Following the end of World War II and the repeal of the Day Law in 1950, Berea once again slowly began to educate African Americans. During the 1960s changes were made in the curriculum to place more emphasis on student freedom, flexibility, and responsibility. This resulted in strengthening the liberals arts and the professional programs, and included a growing interest in African-American studies and civil rights.

In the early twenty-first century, Berea's mission emphasizes a commitment to equality of opportunity for students from Appalachia, including all people of color. This commitment is grounded in a strong focus on the Christian ethic through study of the liberal arts; an understanding and appreciation of labor; a sense of democratic community; and an obligation of service to Appalachia. Students are admitted to Berea on need and pay no tuition except through their labor.

See also: SERVICE LEARNING, *subentries on* HIGHER EDUCATION, SCHOOLS.

BIBLIOGRAPHY

FROST, WILLIAM G. 1937. *For the Mountains: An Autobiography by William Goodell Frost.* New York: Fleming Revell.

PECK, ELISABETH S. 1982. *Berea's First 125 Years, 1855–1980.* Lexington: University of Kentucky Press.

WOOD, GERALD E. 1998. "Organizational Culture and Leadership at Berea College." Ph.D diss., West Virginia University, Morgantown.

SAM STACK

BESTOR, A. E., JR. (1908–1994)

After establishing himself as an academic historian, Arthur Eugene Bestor Jr. achieved national renown during the 1950s as a critic of Progressive education. In the 1920s Bestor attended the Lincoln School at Teachers College, Columbia University. He received a Ph.B. and Ph.D. in history from Yale University in 1930 and 1938, respectively. In 1959 Bestor earned an LL.D. from Lincoln University. After serving as an instructor at Yale, Bestor taught at Teachers College, Columbia University (1936–1942); at Stanford University (1942–1946); at the University of Illinois (1947–1962); and at the University of Washington (1962–1986). Three phases characterize Bestor's academic career: historical scholarship; Progressive education criticism; constitutional scholarship.

During the 1930s and 1940s, Bestor investigated the history of eighteenth- and nineteenth-century utopian socialism in the United States. In his most important work on this topic, *Backwoods Utopias* (1950), Bestor traced the development of communitarian societies from their sectarian origins in the 1660s through their demise as secular experiments in social reform during the mid-nineteenth century. Bestor demonstrated that commitment to voluntarism, experimentalism, social harmony, faith in reform, and group procedures characterized this uniquely American brand of communitarian socialism. He contrasted the communitarian approach to reform with individualist, gradualist, and revolutionary approaches. Influenced by his father's political progressivism and activism, particularly manifest in his leadership capacities at Chautauqua, Bestor considered communitarian societies a model for social reform— "a method for social regeneration of mankind." (1950, p. 7)

Bestor won notoriety, however, not for his serious scholarship, but for his popular criticism of Progressive education. The teacher shortage that followed World War II resulted in an increase of enrollments in education courses and a corresponding decrease of enrollments in liberal arts courses. Tensions between the two faculties emerged at many institutions, including University of Illinois, where Bestor was teaching. Bestor aimed his initial attack on Progressive education for a lack of academic standards, and specifically, at advocates of "life adjustment" education on the faculty at the University of Illinois. Bestor eventually broadened his critique from life adjustment education in particular to Progressive education writ large.

In *Educational Wastelands* (1953), Bestor charged that professional educationists had "lowered the aims of the American public schools," particularly by "setting forth purposes for education so trivial as to forfeit the respect of thoughtful men, and by deliberately divorcing the schools from the disciplines of science and scholarship" (pp. 8, 10). For Bestor, the traditional liberal arts curriculum represented the only acceptable form of secondary education. He claimed that Progressive educators, "by misrepresenting and undervaluing liberal education, have contributed . . . to the growth of anti-intellectualist hysteria that threatens not merely the schools but freedom itself." (p. 11)

Bestor articulated his ideal high school curriculum in *The Restoration of Learning* (1956), where he prioritized, in order of decreasing importance, the functions of the secondary school as follows: (1) intellectual training in the fundamental disciplines, which should be geared to the serious student and targeted at the upper two-thirds of ability; (2) special opportunities for academically superior students; (3) balancing programs for the top third of students with programs for the bottom third; (4) physical education; and (5) vocational training. Of lowest priority, Bestor considered, were extracurricular activities; his priority was the further education of top students and retention in school of the least able. For Bestor, secondary education existed almost exclusively to serve the academically talented, even at the expense of nonacademic students.

Inspired by the experience of the communitarian utopians he had studied, Bestor discarded the protocols of academic discourse and employed rhetorical tactics and even methods of propaganda in his attack on Progressives. In *Educational Wastelands* (1953), for example, he assigned pejorative nicknames to Progressive educators, such as "curriculum doctors," "life adjusters," and "curriculum engineers" and dubbed Progressive education "regressive education." (p. 44). Although academic responses to his criticism appeared, Bestor refused to issue rejoinders. Faculty at the University of Illinois attempted to block publication of his criticism because of its lack of academic integrity, and even scholars sympathetic with his critique disapproved of his methods. Bestor published extensively in professional journals and popular periodicals, and his views garnered wide exposure. Despite his political liberalism, however, Bestor's criticism resonated with conservative opponents of Progressivism and public education. Over time, Bestor adjusted his views to accommodate his increasingly conservative audience.

As the *Sputnik* crisis brought an emphasis on science and mathematics to education reform, Bestor's advocacy of the liberal arts became obsolete. After earning a law degree in 1959, Bestor returned to serious scholarship and devoted the remainder of his career to the study of constitutional history. Bestor analyzed sweeping historic developments such as territorial expansion, slavery, and the Civil War, as well as their interrelationships, in terms of how they influenced and were influenced by constitutionalism. In contradistinction to his educational criticism, Bestor wrote his constitutional history in a dignified, scholarly tone.

In the midst of the "excellence" educational reform movement of the 1980s, a second edition of Bestor's *Educational Wastelands* was released. Its main text was unchanged from the first edition, but the second edition was notable for the retrospectives written by Clarence J. Karier and Foster McMurry, and, in a new preface and a supplementary statement, for Bestor's resolute commitment to the positions he struck thirty years earlier. To document "that educational standards are still endangered as they were in 1953, and that deterioration remains unchecked" (p. 227), Bestor uncritically presented a litany of purportedly damaging findings about American education, which had been alleged in the 1983 report, *Nation at Risk: The Imperative for Educational Reform.* Bestor had changed neither his stance on, nor his tactics for, criticizing the public schools.

See also: CURRICULUM, SCHOOL.

BIBLIOGRAPHY

BESTOR, ARTHUR E., JR. 1950. *Backwoods Utopias.* Philadelphia: University of Pennsylvania Press.

BESTOR, ARTHUR E., JR. 1953, revised 1985. *Educational Wastelands: The Retreat from Learning in Our Public Schools.* Urbana, IL: University of Illinois Press.

BESTOR, ARTHUR E., JR. 1956. *The Restoration of Learning.* New York: Knopf.

BESTOR, ARTHUR E., JR. 1964. "The American Civil War as a Constitutional Crisis." *The American Historical Review* 49:327–352.

WELTMAN, BURTON DAVID. 2000. "Reconsidering Arthur Bestor and the Cold War in Social Education." *Theory and Research in Social Education* 28:11–39.

WENTWORTH, MARLENE M. 1992. "From Chautauqua to Wastelands: The Bestors and American Education, 1905–1955." Ph.D. diss., University of Illinois at Urbana-Champaign.

WILLIAM G. WRAGA

BETHUNE, MARY MCLEOD
(1875–1955)

A leading African-American activist and educator, Mary McLeod Bethune was born in a log cabin near Mayesville, South Carolina. Bethune was the fifteenth of seventeen children born to Samuel and Patsy McLeod. Her parents and several of her older siblings had been born slaves, and the family was scattered as the children were sold to different owners. After the Civil War, the McLeods managed to reassemble their family and eventually bought five acres of land near Mayesville, where they made a living growing cotton and corn.

McLeod began working in the fields at an early age. She did not attend school because there were no schools for black children nearby. When Bethune was nine years old, however, the missionary board of the Presbyterian Church opened a one-room school for African-American children in Sumter County, about four miles from the family farm, and Bethune was invited to attend. She studied there for four years, and then won a scholarship to attend Scotia Seminary for girls (now Barber-Scotia College) in Concord, North Carolina, where she studied for the next five years. Wishing to become a missionary in Africa and supported by another scholarship, Bethune enrolled in 1894 in the Bible Institute for Home and Foreign Missions (now the Moody Bible Institute) in Chicago. After two years of training she applied to the Presbyterian Mission Board for a position in Africa, but was devastated to discover that the board would not send black missionaries to Africa.

Bethune returned to the South and taught for a brief time at her former elementary school in Sumter County. In 1897 she was appointed to a teaching post at Haines Normal and Industrial Institute in Augusta, Georgia. The school's founder was the pioneering black educator Lucy Craft Laney. Laney's determination, intelligence, and spirit of service greatly impressed Bethune and provided an early model for much of her later work as an educator and missionary. After one year at Haines, Bethune was transferred to the Kindell Institute in Sumter, South Carolina, where, in 1898, she met and married Albertus Bethune and moved with him to Savannah. Their son, Albert, was born the following year.

In 1899 Bethune moved with her husband and infant son to Palatka, Florida, where she established a Presbyterian mission school. The Bethunes remained in Palatka for five years, and then moved further south to Daytona Beach, where Mary felt that her services as a teacher and a missionary were greatly needed. In October 1904 she rented a small house for eleven dollars a month, made benches and desks out of discarded crates, obtained other supplies through charity and resourcefulness, and enrolled five young students in the Daytona Normal and Industrial Institute for Negro Girls. Bethune taught them reading, writing, and mathematics, along with religious, vocational, and home economics training.

The Daytona Institute struggled in the beginning, with Bethune selling baked goods and ice cream to raise funds. The school grew quickly, however, and within two years had more than two hundred students and a staff of five. In 1907 the institute was able to relocate to a larger, permanent facility, and in 1910 Bethune bought land to be used for agricultural instruction and the cultivation of food crops for the student cafeteria. Bethune was a talented and tireless fundraiser who solicited donations from individuals, churches, and clubs, and later from prominent business leaders and philanthropists. Over the next decade, the school expanded steadily: taking in more students, increasing its academic offerings, constructing more school buildings, and gradually gaining a national reputation. By 1922, Bethune's school had an enrollment of more than 300 girls and a faculty of 22. The Daytona Institute became coeducational in 1923 when it merged with the Cookman Institute in nearby Jacksonville. By 1929 it was known as Bethune-Cookman College, with Bethune herself serving as president until 1942. In 1941, Bethune-Cookman began awarding bachelor's degrees as a fully accredited college.

During her lengthy career as an educator and activist Bethune served in a variety of increasingly important positions. Notable among her many accomplishments was the founding in 1920 of the Southeastern Association of Colored Women and in 1935 of the National Council of Negro Women. She also served as president of the National Association of Colored Women from 1924 to 1928, took part in Calvin Coolidge's Child Welfare Conference in 1928, and participated in Herbert Hoover's 1930 White House Conference on Child Health. During the Great Depression, Bethune served as special adviser on minority affairs to Franklin D. Roosevelt, and she became the first African-American woman to head a federal agency when Roosevelt appointed her director of the Division of Negro Affairs of the National Youth Administration in 1936, a position she held until 1943. During the 1940s, Bethune was also a member of the council that selected the first female officers for America's new Women's Army Auxiliary Corps. In 1945 Bethune served with W. E. B. Du Bois and Walter White as an adviser on interracial affairs during the charter conference of the United Nations.

Before she died, Bethune wrote a "Last Will and Testament" that was published posthumously in August, 1955, in *Ebony*. In her will, Bethune bequeathed to subsequent generations her thirst for education, her sense of responsibility to young people, and her spirit of service.

See also: HIGHER EDUCATION IN THE UNITED STATES, *subentry on* HISTORICAL DEVELOPMENT; MULTICULTURAL EDUCATION.

BIBLIOGRAPHY

BETHUNE, MARY MCLEOD. 1999. *Mary McLeod Bethune: Building a Better World, Essays and Selected Documents,* ed. Audrey Thomas McCluskey and Elaine M. Smith. Bloomington: Indiana University Press.

FLEMMING, SHEILA Y. 1995. *Bethune-Cookman College, 1904–1994: The Answered Prayer to a Dream.* Virginia Beach, VA: Donning.

HOLT, RACKHAM. 1964. *Mary McLeod Bethune: A Biography.* Garden City, NY: Doubleday.

JUDITH J. CULLIGAN

BILINGUAL EDUCATION

Bilingual education is a broad term that refers to the presence of two languages in instructional settings. The term is, however, "a simple label for a complex phenomenon" (Cazden and Snow, p. 9) that depends upon many variables, including the native language of the students, the language of instruction, and the linguistic goal of the program, to determine which type of bilingual education is used. Students may be native speakers of the majority language or a minority language. The students' native language may or may not be used to teach content material. Bilingual education programs can be considered either *additive* or *subtractive* in terms of their linguistic goals, depending on whether students are encouraged to add to their linguistic repertoire or to replace their native language with the majority language (see Table 1 for a typology of bilingual education). *Bilingual education* is used here to refer to the use of two languages as media of instruction.

Need for Bilingual Education

At the beginning of the twenty-first century, proficiency in only one language is not enough for economic, societal, and educational success. Global interdependence and mass communication often re-quire the ability to function in more than one language. According to the 2000 U.S. Census, more than 9.7 million children ages five to seventeen—one of every six school-age children —spoke a language other than English at home. These *language-minority children* are the fastest-growing segment of the U.S. school-age population. Between 1990 and 2000, the population of language-minority children increased by 55 percent, while the population of children living in homes where only English is spoken grew by only 11 percent.

Language-minority students in U.S. schools speak virtually all of the world's languages, including more than a hundred that are indigenous to the United States. Language-minority students may be monolingual in their native language, bilingual in their native language and English, or monolingual in English but from a home where a language other than English is spoken. Those who have not yet developed sufficient proficiency in English to learn content material in all-English-medium classrooms are known as *limited English proficient* (LEP) or *English language learners* (ELLs). Reliable estimates place the number of LEP students in American schools at close to four million.

Benefits of Bilingualism and Theoretical Foundations of Bilingual Education

Bilingual education is grounded in common sense, experience, and research. Common sense says that children will not learn academic subject material if they can't understand the language of instruction. Experience documents that students from minority-language backgrounds historically have higher drop-out rates and lower achievement scores. Finally, there is a basis for bilingual education that draws upon research in language acquisition and education. Research done by Jim Cummins, of the Ontario Institute for Studies in Education at the University of Toronto, supports a basic tenet of bilingual education: children's first language skills must become well developed to ensure that their academic and linguistic performance in the second language is maximized. Cummins's *developmental interdependence theory* suggests that growth in a second language is dependent upon a well-developed first language, and his *thresholds theory* suggests that a child must attain a certain level of proficiency in both the native and second language in order for the beneficial aspects of bilingualism to accrue. Cummins also introduced the concept of the *common underlying proficiency*

TABLE 1

A typology of bilingual education

WEAK FORMS OF EDUCATION FOR BILINGUALISM

Type of Program	Typical Type of Child	Language of the Classroom	Societal and Educational Aim	Aim in Language Outcome
Submersion (structured immersion)	Language-minority	Majority language	Assimilation	Monolingualism
Submersion (withdrawal classes/sheltered English)	Language-minority	Majority language with "pull-out" L2 lessons	Assimilation	Monolingualism
Segregationist	Language-minority	Minority language (forced, no choice)	Apartheid	Monolingualism
Transitional (early exit bilingual education)	Language-minority	Moves from minority to majority language	Assimilation	Relative monolingualism
Mainstream with foreign language teaching	Language-majority	Majority language with L2/FL lessons	Limited enrichment	Limited bilingualism
Separatist	Language-minority	Minority language (out of choice)	Detachment/ autonomy	Limited bilingualism

STRONG FORMS OF EDUCATION FOR BILINGUALISM AND BILITERACY

Type of Program	Typical Type of Child	Language of the Classroom	Societal and Educational Aim	Aim in Language Outcome
Immersion (foreign language immersion/ Canadian immersion)	Language-majority	Bilingual with initial emphasis on L2	Pluralism and enrichment	Bilingualism and biliteracy
Maintenance/Heritage Language/Developmental Bilingual Education	Language-minority	Bilingual with emphasis on L1	Maintenance, pluralism, and enrichment	Bilingualism and biliteracy
Two-Way Bilingual Education/Dual Language/Two-Way Immersion/Dual Immersion	Mixed language-minority and language-majority	Minority and majority	Maintenance, pluralism, and enrichment	Bilingualism and biliteracy
Mainstream Bilingual	Language-majority	Two majority languages	Maintenance, pluralism, and enrichment	Bilingualism and biliteracy

Notes:
L2 = Second language; L1 = First language; FL = Foreign language

SOURCE: Based on Baker, Colin. 1996. *Foundations of Bilingual Education*, 2nd edition. Clevedon, Eng.: Multilingual Matters.

model of bilingualism, which explains how concepts learned in one language can be transferred to another. Cummins is best known for his distinction between *basic interpersonal communication skills* (BICS) and *cognitive academic language proficiency* (CALP). BICS, or everyday conversational skills, are quickly acquired, whereas CALP, the highly decontextualized, abstract language skills used in classrooms, may take seven years or more to acquire.

Stephen Krashen, of the School of Education at the University of Southern California, developed an overall theory of second language acquisition known as the *monitor model*. The core of this theory is the distinction between acquisition and learning—acquisition being a subconscious process occurring in authentic communicative situations and learning being the conscious process of knowing about a language. The monitor model also includes the natural order hypothesis, the input hypothesis, the monitor hypothesis, and the affective filter hypothesis. Together, these five hypotheses provide a structure for, and an understanding of how to best design and implement, educational programs for language-minority students. Krashen put his theory into practice with the creation of the *natural approach* and the *gradual exit model,* which are based on a second tenet of bilingual education—the concept of comprehensible input. In other words, language teaching must be designed so that language can be acquired easily, and this is done by using delivery methods and levels of language that can be understood by the student.

Bilingual Education around the World

It is estimated that between 60 and 75 percent of the world is bilingual, and bilingual education is a common educational approach used throughout the world. It may be implemented in different ways for majority and/or minority language populations, and there may be different educational and linguistic goals in different countries. In Canada, immersion education programs are designed for native speakers of the majority language (English) to become proficient in a minority language (French), whereas heritage-language programs are implemented to assist native speakers of indigenous and immigrant languages become proficient in English.

In Israel, bilingual education programs not only help both the Arabic- and Hebrew-speaking populations become bilingual, they also teach Hebrew to immigrants from around the world. In Ireland, bilingual education is being implemented to restore the native language. In many South American countries, such as Peru and Ecuador, there are large populations of indigenous peoples who speak languages other than Spanish. Bilingual education programs there have the goal of bilingualism. Throughout Europe, bilingual education programs are serving immigrant children as well as promoting bilingualism for speakers of majority languages.

Bilingual Education in the United States

Since the first colonists arrived on American shores, education has been provided through languages other than English. As early as 1694, German-speaking Americans were operating schools in their mother tongue. As the country expanded, wherever language-minority groups had power, bilingual education was common. By the mid-1800s, there were schools throughout the country using German, Dutch, Czech, Spanish, Norwegian, French, and other languages, and many states had laws officially authorizing bilingual education. In the late 1800s,

however, there was a rise in nativism, accompanied by a large wave of new immigrants at the turn of the century. As World War I began, the language restrictionist movement gained momentum, and schools were given the responsibility of replacing immigrant languages and cultures with those of the United States.

Despite myths to the contrary, non-native English speakers neither learned English very quickly nor succeeded in all-English schools. A comparison of the high-school entry rates based on a 1908 survey of public schools shows, for example, that in Boston, while 70 percent of the children of native whites entered high school, only 32 percent of the children of non-native English-speaking immigrants did so. However, at the beginning of the twentieth century one could easily find a good job that did not require proficiency in English.

By 1923, thirty-four states had passed laws mandating English as the language of instruction in public schools. For the next two decades, with significantly reduced immigration levels, bilingual education was virtually nonexistent in the public schools, although parochial and private schools continued to teach in languages other than English.

In the post–World War II period, however, a series of events—including increased immigration, the *Brown vs. Board of Education* Supreme Court decision, the civil rights movement, the Soviet launch of the *Sputnik* satellite, the National Defense Education Act, the War on Poverty, and the Elementary and Secondary Education Act of 1965—led to a rebirth of bilingual education in the United States. In 1963, in response to the educational needs of the large influx of Cuban refugees in Miami, Coral Way Elementary School began a two-way bilingual education program for English-speaking and Spanish-speaking students. In 1967, U.S. Senator Ralph Yarborough introduced a bill, the *Bilingual Education Act,* as Title VII of the *Elementary and Secondary Education Act,* noting that children who enter schools not speaking English cannot understand instruction that is conducted in English. By the mid-1970s, states were funding bilingual education programs, and many passed laws mandating or permitting instruction though languages other than English.

In 1974, the Supreme Court heard the case of *Lau v. Nichols,* a class-action suit brought on behalf of Chinese students in the San Francisco schools, most of whom were receiving no special instruction despite the fact that they did not speak English. The Court decided that these students were not receiving equal educational opportunity because they did not understand the language of instruction and the schools were not doing anything to assist them. The Court noted that "imposition of a requirement that, before a child can effectively participate in the educational program, he must already have acquired those basic [English] skills is to make a mockery of public education."

While there has never been a federal mandate requiring bilingual education, the courts and federal legislation—including Title VI of the Civil Rights Act of 1964, which prohibits discrimination on the basis of race, color, or national origin in federally-assisted programs and activities, and the Equal Educational Opportunities Act of 1974, which defines a denial of educational opportunity as the failure of an educational agency to take appropriate action to overcome language barriers that impede equal participation by its students in its instructional programs—have attempted to guarantee that LEP students are provided with comprehensible instruction.

The population of the United States became more and more diverse as immigration levels reached record levels between the 1970s and the turn of the century, and bilingual education programs were implemented throughout the country. The Bilingual Education Act was reauthorized in 1974, 1978, 1984, 1988, 1994, and 2001, each time improving and expanding upon the opportunities for school districts and institutions of higher education to receive assistance from this discretionary, competitive grant program. The 2001 reauthorization significantly changed the program, replacing all references to bilingual education with the phrase "language instruction educational program" and turning it into a state-administered formula-grant program.

Characteristics of Good Bilingual Education Programs

Good bilingual education programs recognize and build upon the knowledge and skills children bring to school. They are designed to be linguistically, culturally, and developmentally appropriate for the students and have the following characteristics:

1. High expectations for students and clear programmatic goals.

2. A curriculum that is comparable to the material covered in the English-only classroom.

3. Instruction through the native language for subject matter.

4. An English-language development component.

5. Multicultural instruction that recognizes and incorporates students' home cultures.

6. Administrative and instructional staff, and community support for the program.

7. Appropriately trained personnel.

8. Adequate resources and linguistically, culturally, and developmentally appropriate materials.

9. Frequent and appropriate monitoring of student performance.

10. Parental and family involvement.

Debate over Bilingual Education

The debate over bilingual education has two sources. Part of it is a reflection of societal attitudes towards immigrants. Since language is one of the most obvious identifiers of an immigrant, restrictions on the use of languages other than English have been imposed throughout the history of the United States, particularly in times of war and economic uncertainty. Despite claims that the English language is in danger, figures from the 2000 Census show that 96 percent of those over the age of five speak English well or very well. Rolf Kjolseth concluded that language is also closely associated with national identity, and Americans often display a double standard with regard to bilingualism. On the one hand, they applaud a native English-speaking student studying a foreign language and becoming bilingual, while on the other hand they insist that non-native English speakers give up their native languages and become monolingual in English.

Much of the debate over bilingual education stems from an unrealistic expectation of immediate results. Many people expect LEP students to accomplish a task that they themselves have been unable to do—become fully proficient in a new language. Furthermore, they expect these students to do so while also learning academic subjects like mathematics, science, and social studies at the same rate as their English-speaking peers in a language they do not yet fully command. While students in bilingual education programs maintain their academic progress by receiving content-matter instruction in their native language, they may initially lag behind students in all-English programs on measures of English language proficiency. But longitudinal studies show that not only do these students catch up, but they also often surpass their peers both academically and linguistically.

Proposition 227, a ballot initiative mandating instruction only in English for students who did not speak English, and passed by 63 percent of the 30 percent of the people in California who voted in 1998, is both a reflection of the public debate over bilingual education and an example of the impact of public opinion on education policy. Although only 30 percent of the LEP students in California were enrolled in bilingual education programs at the time (the other 70 percent were in all-English programs), bilingual education was identified as the cause of academic failure on the part of Hispanic students (many of whom were monolingual in English), and the public voted to prohibit bilingual education. Instead, LEP students were to be educated through sheltered English immersion during a temporary transition period not normally to exceed one year. Three years after the implementation of Proposition 227, the scores of LEP students on state tests were beginning to decline rather than increase.

Research Evidence on the Effectiveness of Bilingual Education

There are numerous studies that document the effectiveness of bilingual education. One of the most notable was the eight-year (1984-1991) Longitudinal Study of Structured English Immersion Strategy, Early-Exit and Late-Exit Programs for Language-Minority Children. The findings of this study were later validated by the National Academy of Sciences. The study compared three different approaches to educating LEP students where the language of instruction was radically different in grades one and two. One approach was *structured immersion,* where almost all instruction was provided in English. A second approach was *early-exit transitional bilingual education,* in which there is some initial instruction in the child's primary language (thirty to sixty minutes per day), and all other instruction in English, with the child's primary language used only as a support, for clarification. However, instruction in the primary language is phased out so that by grade two, virtually all instruction is in English. The third approach was *late-exit transitional bilingual education,*

where students received 40 percent of their instruction in the primary language and would continue to do so through sixth grade, regardless of whether they were reclassified as fluent-English-proficient.

Although the outcomes were not significantly different for the three groups at the end of grade three, by the sixth grade late-exit transitional bilingual education students were performing higher on mathematics, English language, and English reading than students in the other two programs. The study concluded that those students who received more native language instruction for a longer period not only performed better academically, but also acquired English language skills at the same rate as those students who were taught only in English. Furthermore, by sixth grade, the late-exit transitional bilingual education students were the only group catching up academically, in all content areas, to their English-speaking peers; the other two groups were falling further behind.

Virginia Collier and Wayne Thomas, professors in the Graduate School of Education at George Mason University, have conducted one of the largest longitudinal studies ever, with more than 700,000 student records. Their findings document that when students who have had no schooling in their native language are taught exclusively in English, it takes from seven to ten years to reach the age and grade-level norms of their native English-speaking peers. Students who have been taught through both their native language and English, however, reach and surpass the performance of native English-speakers across all subject areas after only four to seven years when tested in English. Furthermore, when tested in their native language, these bilingual education students typically score at or above grade level in all subject areas.

Ninety-eight percent of the children entering kindergarten in California's Calexico School District are LEP. In the early 1990s, the school district shifted the focus of its instructional program from student limitations to student strengths—from remedial programs emphasizing English language development to enriched programs emphasizing total academic development; from narrow English-as-a-second-language programs to comprehensive developmental bilingual education programs that provide dual-language instruction. In Calexico schools, LEP students receive as much as 80 percent of their early elementary instruction in their native language. After students achieve full English proficiency, they continue to have opportunities to study in, and further develop, their Spanish language skills. By the late 1990s, Calexico's dropout rate was half the state average for Hispanic students, and more than 90 percent of their graduates were continuing on to junior or four-year colleges and universities.

The evidence on the effectiveness of dual immersion (or two-way) bilingual education programs is even more compelling. In dual immersion programs, half of the students are native speakers of English and half are native speakers of another language. Instruction is provided through both languages and the goal of these programs is for all students to become proficient in both languages. In her research, Kathryn Lindholm-Leary, a professor of child development in the College of Education at San Jose State University, found that in developing proficiency in the English language, both English and Spanish speakers benefit equally from dual-language programs. Whether they spend 10 to 20 percent or 50 percent of their instructional day in English, students in such programs are equally proficient in English. Mathematics achievement was also found to be highly related across the two languages, demonstrating that content learned in one language is available in the other language. Despite limited English instruction and little or no mathematics instruction in English, students receiving 90 percent of their instruction in Spanish score at or close to grade level on mathematics achievement tests in English.

Bilingual education offers great opportunities to both language-majority and language-minority populations. It is an educational approach that not only allows students to master academic content material, but also become proficient in two languages—an increasingly valuable skill in the early twenty-first century.

See also: BILINGUALISM, SECOND LANGUAGE LEARNING, AND ENGLISH AS A SECOND LANGUAGE; FOREIGN LANGUAGE EDUCATION.

BIBLIOGRAPHY

BAKER, COLIN. 1995. *A Parents' and Teachers' Guide to Bilingualism.* Clevedon, Eng.: Multilingual Matters.

BAKER, COLIN. 1996. *Foundations of Bilingual Education and Bilingualism,* 2nd edition. Clevedon, Eng.: Multilingual Matters.

BAKER, COLIN. 2000. *The Care and Education of Young Bilinguals: An Introduction for Professionals.* Clevedon, Eng.: Multilingual Matters.

BAKER, COLIN, and HORNBERGER, NANCY H., eds. 2001. *An Introductory Reader to the Writings of Jim Cummins.* Clevedon, Eng.: Multilingual Matters.

CAZDEN, COURTNEY B., and SNOW, CATHERINE E., eds. 1990. "English Plus: Issues in Bilingual Education." *Annals of the American Academy of Political and Social Science,* Volume 508. London: Sage.

COLLIER, VIRGINIA P. 1992. "A Synthesis of Studies Examining Long-Term Language Minority Student Data on Academic Achievement." *Bilingual Research Journal* 16(1&2) 187–212.

COLLIER, VIRGINIA P., and THOMAS, WAYNE P. 1997. *School Effectiveness for Language Minority Students,* NCBE Resource Collection Number 9. Washington, DC: National Clearinghouse for Bilingual Education.

COLLIER, VIRGINIA P., and THOMAS, WAYNE P. 2002. *A National Survey of School Effectiveness for Language Minority Students' Long-Term Academic Achievement: Executive Summary.* Santa Cruz, CA: Crede.

CRAWFORD, JAMES. 1991. *Bilingual Education: History, Politics, Theory and Practice,* 2nd edition. Los Angeles: Bilingual Educational Services.

CRAWFORD, JAMES. 1997. *Best Evidence: Research Foundations of the Bilingual Education Act.* Washington, DC: National Clearinghouse for Bilingual Education.

CUMMINS, JAMES. 1979. "Linguistic Interdependence and the Educational Development of Bilingual Children." *Review of Educational Research* 49:222–251.

CUMMINS, JAMES. 1980. "The Entry and Exit Fallacy in Bilingual Education." *NABE Journal* 4:25–60.

CUMMINS, JAMES. 2000. *Language, Power, and Pedagogy: Bilingual Children in the Crossfire.* Clevedon, Eng., and Buffalo, NY: Multilingual Matters.

KJOLSETH, ROLF. 1983. "Cultural Politics of Bilingualism." *Society* 20(May/June):40–48.

KRASHEN, STEPHEN D. 1999. *Condemned Without a Trial: Bogus Arguments Against Bilingual Education.* Portsmouth, NH: Heinemann.

LINDHOLM-LEARY, KATHRYN. 2000. *Biliteracy for a Global Society: An Idea Book on Dual Language*

Education. Washington, DC: National Clearinghouse for Bilingual Education.

LINDHOLM-LEARY, KATHRYN. 2001. *Dual Language Education*. Clevedon, Eng., and Buffalo, NY: Multilingual Matters.

NATIONAL CLEARINGHOUSE FOR BILINGUAL EDUCATION. 2000. *The Growing Number of Limited English Proficient Students*. Washington, DC: National Clearinghouse for Bilingual Education.

RAMÍREZ, J. DAVID; YUEN, SANDRA D.; and RAMEY, DENA R. 1991. *Final Report: Longitudinal Study of Structured English Immersion Strategy, Early-Exit and Late-Exit Programs for Language-Minority Children*. Report Submitted to the U.S. Department of Education. San Mateo, CA: Aguirre International.

SKUTNABB-KANGAS, TOVE. 1981. *Bilingualism or Not: The Education of Minorities*. Clevedon, Eng.: Multilingual Matters.

UNITED STATES GOVERNMENT ACCOUNTING OFFICE. 2001. *Meeting the Needs of Students with Limited English Proficiency*. Washington, DC: Government Accounting Office.

ZELASKO, NANCY FABER. 1991. *The Bilingual Double Standard: Mainstream Americans' Attitudes Towards Bilingualism*. Ph.D. diss., Georgetown University.

NANCY F. ZELASKO

BILINGUALISM, SECOND LANGUAGE LEARNING, AND ENGLISH AS A SECOND LANGUAGE

The term *bilingual* refers to individuals who can function in more than one language. The category of bilinguals is very broad—encompassing individuals who are sophisticated speakers, readers, and writers of two or more languages, as well as those who use a limited knowledge of a second language (L2) for purposes such as work or schooling, and who may be literate in only one language (or even completely illiterate). Because of the consequences of colonization, migration, nation-formation, traditions of exogamy, and modernization, some degree of bilingualism is typical of most people in the world.

Bilingualism is a feature not just of individuals, but also of societies. Societies in which two languages are used regularly, or in which more than one language has official status or a recurrent function, can be called bilingual. For example, Canada is a bilingual country because French and English are both official languages, even though many citizens of Canada are monolingual English speakers. Saudi Arabia is also a bilingual society, as most Saudis speak both Arabic and English, though English has no official status. The nature of individual bilingualism is quite different in different communities—there are those where bilingualism is the norm for all educated citizens (as it is, for example, in relatively small language communities like Scandinavia and The Netherlands); those where bilingualism is the norm for the minority language speakers but not those with the greatest political or economic power in the society (e.g., for Quechua speakers in Peru, for Turkish speakers in the Netherlands, for Spanish speakers in the United States); and those where bilingualism is the norm for the upper classes and better educated but not the relatively powerless (e.g., Colombia). It must be noted that the United States and other traditionally English-speaking countries observe a norm of monolingualism (low expectations for second/foreign language proficiency, low value placed on immigrant languages, universal emphasis on the need to speak English) that is possible only for speakers of a 'language of wider communication' living in an economy that is globally highly influential.

Bilingualism is often the product of second language (L2) learning after the first language (L1) has been acquired—either through nontutored exposure or through instruction. Individuals can become bilingual at any age, depending on when the need to learn the L2 emerges or when instruction becomes available. In some cases, though, bilingualism is a characteristic of a child's earliest language system. For example, children growing up in bilingual households—where both parents speak two languages regularly, or where each parent speaks a different language—are typically bilingual from the very beginning of language acquisition. Children growing up with parents who speak a minority language (within the larger societal context) may also be natively bilingual, if visitors, neighbors, television, regular caretakers, and other sources make the majority language available.

English as a second language (ESL) refers to the process of producing bilinguals by teaching English as an L2 to learners in an English-speaking context. ESL is distinguished from English as a foreign language (EFL), which is instruction delivered in a context where English is not used regularly outside the classroom, using the instructional techniques and the intensity of instruction required to achieve success. The term ESOL (English for speakers of other languages) is meant to encompass both ESL and EFL. Given the importance of English in the modern, globalized economy, ESOL is a large field of practice buttressed by considerable bodies of research and many curricular resources.

ESL instruction also needs to be distinguished, in the American schooling context, from instruction referred to as *bilingual education,* in which some instructional content is delivered in the learner's L1 while English is being acquired. Bilingual programs range from those that use the native language briefly (and primarily for emotional support), to programs that seek to develop L1 literacy as a source of transfer to English literacy, to those that continue to teach L1 oral and literacy skills at least through the elementary grades. Some districts also offer *two-way bilingual,* or *double immersion* programs, in which half the students are L1 speakers of English and half are L1 speakers of another language, and instruction is given to all children in both languages, with the goal of producing high-level bilinguals from both English- and other-language backgrounds.

Bilingual education programs, which were first supported by federal funding as a result of the Federal Bilingual Education Act of 1968, are offered in districts where sufficient numbers of students from a single L1 background exist; such programs came under attack as ineffective in 1998 in California, where they were severely curtailed as a result of ballot proposition 227. Since then, political action to eliminate the bilingual schooling option has spread to other states. The difficulty of carrying out well-designed evaluations of bilingual education has frustrated its supporters because there is, as a result, no unambiguous demonstration that bilingual education generates achievement advantages. Nonetheless, both theory and meta-analyses suggest that bilingual education is the best approach to ensuring educational achievement and reducing the risk of reading failure for many language-minority children.

The major challenge of education for language minority children in the U.S. is to ensure adequate literacy development; scores from the National Assessment of Educational Progress (NAEP) continue to show serious deficits in literacy for non-native speakers of English, even after several years of U.S. schooling. Thus, focusing on educational treatments that promote literacy is a high priority in research and practice innovations.

Early Literacy Development of English Language Learners (ELLs)

The central role of language in the emergence of key literacy-related skills raises important questions about the nature of literacy development among bilingual children, and, about the impact of bilingual or second language instructional settings on children's emerging literacy-related abilities. There is surprisingly little systematic research on these issues. It is known, however, that Spanish-speaking children (the most widely studied group) just beginning kindergarten in the United States show wide variation in both their Spanish literacy skills and in their level of oral English proficiency. Since children's abilities in both of these areas have been shown to independently predict English reading performance in middle school, both must be considered critical to children's future academic success.

There is also considerable evidence that many key literacy-related skills, including phonological awareness, print concepts, decoding skills, and extended discourse, are transferable from an L1 to an L2. Low-income ELLs, like other children of low socioeconomic status, tend to begin school with relatively few literacy-related skills in general, and they may have vocabularies in each of their two languages that are more restricted even than those of their low-income, monolingual peers—possibly because they have had fewer resources and opportunities to acquire at home the language and literacy skills that have been linked to school success.

Language-of-Instruction Studies

One critical question is how effective literacy instruction is linguistically organized in bilingual or second language (ESL) classroom settings—and with what effect. Non-English-speaking or bilingual preschool children in the United States typically find themselves in one of three types of classroom language settings: first-language classrooms in which all interaction occurs in the children's primary language; bilingual classrooms in which interaction is split between the primary language and English; and

English-language classrooms in which English is the exclusive language of communication. Studies of the education offered to L2 learners tend to focus on language use, rather than on the quality of children's learning opportunities. These studies, nevertheless, converge on two important sets of findings.

First, studies that have compared preschool program types by language have found certain academic and linguistic advantages for children in bilingual, as opposed to English-only, classrooms at both the preschool and the K–6 level. One longitudinal evaluation of the Carpinteria Preschool Program in California found Spanish-language classrooms to be associated with higher levels of language and early literacy attainment in both Spanish and English through grade five. Unfortunately, these studies have not examined what, specifically, goes on in preschool classrooms to produce such results.

Second, studies that have explored the language proficiencies of Spanish-speaking children who attended preschool versus those who stayed home have found that the main effect of preschool attendance, even in bilingual programs, is improved English proficiency. There is contradictory evidence, however, as to whether acquiring English in preschool necessarily endangers children's home language development.

Systematic studies focused on investigating the predictors of English literacy development for ELLs were launched in 2000, when the National Institute of Child Health and Human Development (NICHD) and the Office of Educational Research and Improvement (OERI) initiated collaborative funding focused on bilingual reading. Questions about both the design and quality of schooling for ELLs are of practical as well as theoretical importance, especially since the majority of ELL preschoolers and school-age children in the United States find themselves in predominantly English-language classroom settings. Expressing concern for the additional risk that such settings may pose, the National Research Council report *Preventing Reading Difficulties in Young Children* recommended the need for additional research to examine "whether high-quality preschool experiences are equally beneficial to Spanish-speaking children when offered in English as when offered in Spanish" (Snow, Burns, and Griffin, p. 157).

Consequences of Bilingualism

There has been much discussion of the consequences of early bilingualism. Historically, early bilingualism was seen as dangerous, leading to confusion and exacerbating language disorders and language delay. Research has made clear that early bilingualism may well bring cognitive advantages, particularly in domains such as helping children understand the arbitrary nature of language systems and literacy systems. Nonetheless, such advantages are also small—few months' precocity on tasks that monolingual children also typically come to accomplish without difficulty.

Obviously, the major positive consequence of bilingualism is knowing two languages—and thus being able to converse with a larger array of individuals, as well as having access to two cultures, two bodies of literature, and two worldviews. For children in language-minority communities, maintaining their ancestral language preserves ties to their grandparents and keeps open the option of experiences that build ethnic identification and pride, as well as cultural continuity. Speaking other languages also has economic advantages, as bilinguals are in demand in the new global economy.

Despite these advantages, the most typical trajectory for immigrant families in the United States is that only first-generation children (or the *one-and-a-half* generation—those born in the U.S. shortly after their parents' arrival) are bilingual, and that the second and later generations are likely to be absorbed into the norms of the larger monolingual society. Given the relatively poor outcomes of foreign language teaching in the United States, this trajectory reflects the forfeiture of linguistic resources that might well be conserved with educational policies more focused on maintaining and developing immigrants' language skills in L1 as well as L2.

Factors Influencing Second Language Learning

Forces that impinge on the likelihood of successful L2 learning include cognitive influences (e.g., knowledge of L1, linguistic analysis capacity, memory), motivational influences (e.g., interest in the L2, value of the L2 to the learner, positive affect toward speakers of the L2), social influences (e.g., opportunities to interact with L2 speakers, access to useful feedback from L2 speakers), and instruction (e.g., quantity, quality, design). These influences all tend to covary with age, with the social status of the learner, and with other factors, such as reasons for learning the L2.

Although the myth of a critical period for L2 acquisition dominates public understanding, there are, in fact, no biological data supporting the existence of a critical period for second language learning. Older learners can achieve high, even native-like levels of proficiency in an L2 under the right conditions, and younger learners sometimes do not achieve this level of proficiency. Very young learners in an immigrant situation are also much more likely to lose their first language in the process of acquiring the second, thus ending up monolingual rather than bilingual as a result of L2 acquisition.

Summary

Questions about individuals' second language learning cannot be understood without simultaneous attention to the larger sociocultural and sociolinguistic framework within which learning a second language is occurring. Certainly there are cognitive challenges associated with L2 acquisition—learning new phonological, grammatical, semantic, and interactional rules is hard. But the cognitive challenge associated with learning Spanish, for example, is quite different for the Aymara speaker in Peru, who sees it simultaneously as the language of economic advancement and of oppression, than it is for the English speaker in Kansas, who sees it as the language of underpaid immigrant workers, or for the third-generation Mexican American in California, who sees it as the language of history and extended family. Until it is understood how the larger sociocultural and sociolinguistic factors interact with the cognitive and psycholinguistic factors influencing acquisition and maintenance of a second language, it will be difficult to design optimal educational programs for either language-minority children or English speakers learning foreign languages.

See also: BILINGUAL EDUCATION; INDIVIDUAL DIFFERENCES, *subentry on* ETHNICITY; LANGUAGE AND EDUCATION; LITERACY AND CULTURE.

BIBLIOGRAPHY

AUGUST, DIANE, and HAKUTA, KENJI, eds. 1997. *Improving Schooling for Language-Minority Children: A Research Agenda.* Washington, DC: National Academy Press.

BIALYSTOK, ELLEN. 1997. "Effects of Lingualism and Biliteracy on Children's Emerging Concepts of Print." *Developmental Psychology* 33(3):429–440.

CAMPOS, S. JIM. 1995. "The Carpinteria Preschool Program: A Long-Term Effects Study. In *Meeting the Challenge of Linguistic and Cultural Diversity in Early Childhood Education,* ed. Eugene Garcia and Barry McLaughlin. New York: Teachers College Press.

CAMPOS S. JIM, and KEATINGS, H. ROBERT. 1988. "The Carpinteria Language-Minority Student Experience: From Theory to Practice, to Success." In *Minority Education: From Shame to Struggle,* ed. Tove Skutnabb-Kangas and Jim Cummins. Clevedon, Eng.: Multilingual Matters.

CISERO, CHERYL, and ROYER, JAMES. 1995. "The Development and Cross-Language Transfer of Phonological Awareness." *Contemporary Educational Psychology* 20:275–303.

CUMMINS, JIM. 1979. "Linguistic Interdependence and the Educational Development of Bilingual Children." *Review of Educational Research* 49(2):222–251.

DURGUNOGLU, AYDIN Y.; NAGY, WILLIAM E.; and HANCIN-BHATT, BARBARA J. 1993. "Cross-Language Transfer of Phonological Awareness." *Journal of Educational Psychology* 85:453–465.

GOLDENBERG, CLAUDE. 2001. "Making Schools Work for Low-Income Families in the 21st Century." In *Handbook of Early Literacy Research,* ed. Susan Neuman and David Dickinson. New York: Guilford Press.

GOLDENBERG, CLAUDE; REESE, LESLIE; and GALLIMORE, RONALD. 1992. "Effects of School Literacy Materials on Latino Children's Home Experiences and Early Literacy Achievement." *American Journal of Education* 100:497–536.

GREENE, JAY. 1998. *A Meta-analysis of the Effectiveness of Bilingual Education.* Austin, TX: The Tomas Rivera Policy Institute.

MARINOVA-TODD, STEFKA; MARSHALL, D. BRADFORD; and SNOW, CATHERINE E. 2000. "Three Misconceptions about Age and Second-Language Learning." *TESOL Quarterly* 34(1):9–34.

MEYER, MICHAEL M., and FIENBERG, STEVEN E., eds. 1992. *Assessing Evaluation Studies: The Case of Bilingual Education Strategies.* Washington, DC: National Academy Press.

NATIONAL ASSESSMENT OF EDUCATIONAL PROGRESS. 2000. *NAEP 1999 Trends in Academic Progress: Three Decades of Student Performance.* Washington, DC: National Center for Education Statistics.

NATIONAL CENTER FOR EDUCATION STATISTICS. 1996. *Quick Tables and Figures: Family Literacy Activities.* Washington, DC: U.S. Department of Education.

REESE, LESLIE; GARNIER, HELEN; GALLIMORE, RONALD; and GOLDENBERG, CLAUDE. 2000. "Longitudinal Analysis of the Antecedents of Emergent Spanish Literacy and Middle-School English Reading Achievement of Spanish-Speaking Students." *American Educational Research Journal* 37(3):633–662.

RODRIGUEZ, JAMES L.; DIAZ, RAFAEL M.; DURAN, D.; and ESPINOSA, LINDA. 1995. "The Impact of Bilingual Preschool Education on the Language Development of Spanish-Speaking Children." *Early Childhood Research Quarterly* 10(4):475–490.

SANDOVAL-MARTINEZ, STEVEN. 1982. "Findings from the Head Start Bilingual Curriculum Development and Evaluation Effort." *NABE Journal* 7(1):1–12.

SNOW, CATHERINE; BURNS, M. SUSAN; and GRIFFIN, PEG. 1998. *Preventing Reading Difficulties in Young Children.* Washington DC: National Academy Press.

TABORS, PATTON, and SNOW, CATHERINE. 2001. "Young Bilingual Children and Early Literacy Development." In *Handbook of Early Literacy Research,* ed. Susan Neuman and David Dickinson. New York: Guilford Press.

VERHOEVEN, LUDO. 1994. "Transfer in Bilingual Development." *Language Learning* 14:381–415.

WILLIG, ANNE. 1985. "A Meta-Analysis of Selected Studies of the Effectiveness of Bilingual Education." *Review of Educational Research* 55:269–317.

WONG-FILLMORE, LILY. 1991. "When Learning a Second Language Means Losing the First." *Early Childhood Research Quarterly* 6:323–346.

INTERNET RESOURCE

CENTER FOR APPLIED LINGUISTICS. "Two-Way Immersion." <www.cal.org/twi>.

CATHERINE E. SNOW
MARGARET FREEDSON-GONZALEZ

BINET, ALFRED (1857–1911)

Best known for his development with Théodore Simon of the first standardized intelligence test, Alfred Binet can be considered one of the few "renaissance" psychologists of the twentieth century. His research included the measurement of individual differences in reaction times, association of auditory times with specific colors, auditory and visual imagery, and children's memory capabilities. In his early research, Binet also investigated children's fears. Using questionnaires, he studied creative artists of his time, such as Alexandre Dumas, in an attempt to provide insight into their methods of work and the sources of their creativity. As Theta Wolf notes, Binet also was known for his severe criticism of the methods of experimental psychology for its "sterile laboratory conditions" (pp. 90–91). His work on individual differences described in a 1896 article with Victor Henri initiated his work on measuring individual differences and took into account both the quantitative and qualitative aspects of individuals' responses. Binet was also a leader in providing programs for children with mental disabilities and establishing a pedagogical institute to provide appropriate instructional methods.

Background

Binet's choice of a career as a psychologist matured outside of any formal educational study. He first entered law school earning his license at age twenty-one and then began study for the doctorate. However, he lost interest in that field and began medical studies, but did not complete them. Soon after, he began reading books in psychology. For the next six years he worked in the laboratory of Jean-Martin Charcot, a well-known neurologist, with mental patients and also developed an interest in hypnosis. At age thirty Binet completed a paper that stressed the importance of studying the normal individual before studying persons with serious emotional problems. The paper, which received a substantial monetary award from the Academy of Moral and Political Sciences, was cited for the demonstration of Binet's competence as an observer and his knowledge of the experimental method. The award committee concluded that Binet had a "gifted and uncommon mind" (Wolf, p. 6).

Research

In 1890 Binet published papers that dealt with the observational study of his two daughters. Wolf suggests that these studies preceded those of Piaget's and possibly influenced Piaget in his research. Between 1888 and 1894 Binet studied in his father-in-law's laboratory at the College de France and took courses in botany and zoology. Wolf also noted that he became interested in comparative psychology, and researched the behavior and physiology of insects, earning a doctorate in 1894.

At the same time Binet and Henri Beaumis began the first French psychological journal. In 1894 Binet published four original papers, eighty-five reviews, and was appointed to the board of associates of the *American Psychological Review*. He also published two books: one on experimental psychology and other "on the psychology of master calculators and chess players" (Wolf, p. 9).

Binet's wide range of interests in a number of different academic areas was demonstrated by his authorship of several articles for biology journals and his review of research findings from the field of histology, anatomy, and physiology. In 1895 Binet was invited to give a series of lectures at the University of Bucharest. Though offered a professorship, Binet declined the appointment to return to Paris. Although Binet was now considered to be the "foremost, if not the only French experimental psychologist," he never received an appointment at a French institution of higher learning (Wolf, p. 22). Raymond Fancher believes this was due in part to Binet's lack of official credentials resulting from his self-trained status and lack of personal support from his instructors.

Measurement of Children's Abilities

In the 1890s, Binet became associated with Théodore Simon, who had earned a medical degree and was an intern at an institution for retarded children. He became Binet's collaborator in the development of the first intelligence scale.

In 1899 Binet was invited to become a member of the new Society for the Study of the Child because of his interest in children's intellectual development. Wolf mentions that under Binet's leadership, members of the society aggressively pushed the French Ministry of Instruction to offer suitable instructional programs for children with mental disabilities. Binet's leadership also led to an appointment to a government commission to study the needs of these children in the public schools. He became convinced of the need to ascertain how to differentiate children with learning problems from those who could not learn adequately.

Wolf considers that Binet's greatest productivity was between 1901 to 1911. After his appointment to the government commission on the retarded in 1904, Binet noted that educational officials were primarily interested in administrative problems of the schools. There was no interest in how to differentiate objectively retarded children from normal children or to provide appropriate instruction for them. In 1905 Binet and his colleagues recommended special classes and schools for the retarded, which up to that time did not exist. A bill for such provisions was introduced in 1907 and in 1909 a law passed establishing classes for educational improvement. Binet and Simon were provided the criteria for entry and aided in the selection of students for the first special classes in the Paris schools. In 1905 Binet along with Simon published the first standardized scale of intelligence for which he is best known. The scale was composed of thirty items and was the product of more than fifteen years of careful investigations and experimental research with children. Subsequent revisions of the scale appeared in 1908 and 1911. A number of these items are still included in the latest (1960 and 1986) revisions of their test. During this period Binet also helped to establish the first pedagogical laboratory in France. Wolf noted that in the same time period he worked on the psychology of court testimony and, in 1909, published a popular book for teachers and parents about children, which contained many of his ideas about intelligence. In 1906 Binet and Simon published a paper that addressed "new methods for diagnosing idiocy, imbecility, and moronity," an important contribution because, for the first time, criteria were specified that allowed professionals to agree on different levels of retardation (Wolf, pp. 142–143).

Contribution

Alfred Binet remains an important figure in modern psychology. He was among the first to emphasize that no child suspected of retardation should be removed from the regular classroom without undergoing a psychological and medical assessment that would help confirm the retardation. Binet and Simon emphasized that diagnostic errors could be due to lack of "attitude" on the part of the examiner; variability in the meaning of the terms used, or lack of precision in the examination of the child.

Binet and Simon stated that test items used in assessment of children needed to be graded in difficulty and be age appropriate. In their discussion of new methods for the diagnosis of retarded children, Binet and Simon emphasized the properties inherent in the assessment of intelligence. These included the need to separate natural intelligence from lack of performance due to inadequate instruction. Attempting to reduce the effects of instruction, Binet and Simon did not require the child to read or write any material. For them the heart of the meaning of intelligence was judgment, to comprehend well, and to reason well.

Binet's sophisticated comments written in 1911 on how to proceed with an examination of the child could easily be repeated word-for-word for early-twenty-first-century psychology students. He stressed the importance of the observation of children and their activities, and outlined with Simon the normal development of intelligence in children from three to twelve years of age in an article published in 1916 (b). These comments were the result of detailed presentation of many test items and careful observations of the responses of the subjects. This article also contained a revision of the 1905 scale. Their monograph could also be read in the early twenty-first century by psychologists for its observational insights in the assessment of children's abilities. Binet and Simon's discussion of the different attitudes and motivations of school personnel concerning retarded children also remains relevant. The intelligence scale of 1908 was changed from one that assessed lack of intelligence into one that classified the intelligence of the retarded, the normal child, and those of superior intelligence. Of the thirty items that composed the 1905 scale, Binet and Simon retained only fourteen without any change.

Binet established the Laboratory of Experimental Pedagogy in Paris in 1905, the first such laboratory established in a school in Europe. The purpose of the laboratory was to provide a continuing source for experimental work with children and provide consultative help to teachers who wished to teach re-tarded children. Because of the work in these areas of psychology and education Binet can be considered the first school psychologist in the Western world.

One result of this lab-school collaboration was a study by Binet and Simon that focused on vision problems of school children. They noted that children might be labeled slow only because of difficulty in seeing the blackboard. Their concern resulted in the development of a standardized test of vision that teachers could use without the involvement of physicians. Binet was also interested in criteria for a good school, evaluation of teacher competence, the influence of environmental factors on intelligence, such as socioeconomic status, and the provision of classes for those of superior intelligence.

See also: ASSESSMENT; INTELLIGENCE.

BIBLIOGRAPHY

BINET, ALFRED. 1916. "New Investigations upon the Measure of the Intellectual Level among School Children" (1911). In *The Development of Intelligence in Children.* Baltimore: Williams and Wilkins.

BINET, ALFRED, and SIMON, THÉODORE. 1916a. "Applications of the New Methods to the Diagnosis of the Intellectual Level among Normal and Subnormal Children in Institutions and in Primary Schools" (1908). In *The Development of Intelligence in Children,* ed. Henry H. Goddard. Baltimore: Williams and Wilkins.

BINET, ALFRED, and SIMON, THÉODORE. 1916b. "The Development of Intelligence in the Child" (1908). In *The Development of Intelligence in Children.* Baltimore: Williams and Wilkins.

BINET, ALFRED, and SIMON, THÉODORE. 1916c. "New Methods for the Diagnosis of the Intellectual Level of Subnormals" (1905). In *The Development of Intelligence in Children,* ed. Henry H. Goddard. Baltimore: Williams and Wilkins.

FANCHER, RAYMOND E. 1998. "Alfred Binet, General Psychologist." In *Portraits of Pioneers in Psychology.* Vol. 3, ed. Gregory A. Kimble and Michael Wertheimer. Hillsdale, NJ: Erlbaum.

WOLF, THETA H. 1973. *Alfred Binet.* Chicago: University of Chicago Press.

GILBERT R. GREDLER

BLIND STUDENTS

See: Visual Impairments, Education of Individuals with.

BLOOM, B. S. (1913–1999)

Renowned as the architect of the taxonomy of educational objectives and famous for his work on mastery learning, Benjamin S. Bloom was a true educational researcher, who thrived on questions to guide his inquiry. His research revolved around the following queries.

- What is the variety of educational objectives that can (and perhaps should) be taught in school?

- To what extent are human characteristics such as intelligence and motivation fixed at birth and to what extent can they be modified by experience?

- How can one teach entire classrooms of students so that the results approximate what can be achieved in one-to-one tutoring?

- How is it that certain individuals reach the highest level of accomplishment in their chosen fields?

These are but some of the questions that Bloom asked, and answered, during a career that spanned five decades, the vast majority of which was spent on the faculty of the University of Chicago.

Bloom was born in Lansford, Pennsylvania, of Russian immigrant parents. His father was a picture framer and his mother a housewife. Bloom attended public schools in Lansford, graduating in 1931 as class valedictorian. In the fall of 1931 he enrolled at the Pennsylvania State University, completing his B.A. and M.A. degrees in psychology in four years.

Following college graduation, he was employed for a year as a research worker with the Pennsylvania State Relief Organization. He then moved to Washington, D.C., where he took a similar position with the American Youth Commission. It was while working at the commission that he met Ralph W. Tyler. Bloom was so impressed with Tyler that he decided to study with him. He began his doctoral studies at Chicago in the summer of 1939. That summer he met his future wife, Sophie, and they were married a year later.

While completing his doctoral program, Bloom was a research assistant in the Office of the Universi-

ty's Board of Examinations under Tyler's supervision. He received his Ph.D. in 1942, and remained with the Board of Examinations until 1959. In 1948, Bloom convened a meeting of college and university examiners throughout the country to discuss the possibility of designing a common framework for classifying the wide variety of intended learning outcomes that the examiners routinely encountered. Eight years later *The Taxonomy of Educational Objectives, The Classification of Educational Goals,* Handbook I: *The Cognitive Domain* was published. By the late 1960s, it became known simply as Bloom's taxonomy.

The majority of Bloom's writings during his years with the board (and concurrently as a junior faculty member in the Department of Education) focused on testing, measurement, and evaluation. Then, in 1959 to 1960, he left his position with the board and spent a year at the Center for Advanced Study in Behavioral Sciences at Stanford University in Palo Alto, California.

During his stay at the center, Bloom began work on what was to become his work *Stability and Change in Human Characteristics.* The book consisted primarily of an extensive review of research in several areas (e.g., intelligence, achievement, and personality). Based on this review, Bloom suggested that the ability of environmental factors to influence change in human characteristics decreases over time, as the characteristics become more stable. He discussed his findings with U.S. President Lyndon B. Johnson, and his testimony before Congress played a large part in the federal Head Start program in 1965. The program became an important part of Johnson's Great Society, and has enjoyed bipartisan congressional support since then.

In 1968 Bloom published a small paper titled "Learning for Mastery," which had great significance in the field. His central thesis was that most students (perhaps more than 90%) could master what they were expected to learn in school, and it was the task of teachers to provide the quality of instruction that would produce these results. Critical elements of this quality of instruction were (1) clearly communicating the learning expectations; (2) giving students specific feedback as to their progress in achieving them; and (3) providing additional time and help as needed by students.

During the 1970s Bloom worked at incorporating this thesis into a full-blown theory of school learning and challenging educators to solve what he termed in 1984 the "two sigma problem." Based on available data, Bloom argued that the average student who received tutoring scored two standard deviations higher on standardized achievement tests than average student who received traditional group-based instruction. Because the Greek symbol sigma is used to denote the standard deviation of a population, the problem of finding ways to design and deliver group-based instruction that was as effective as one-to-one tutoring was known as the two sigma problem.

In 1984 Bloom published his last major study, in which he identified and described the processes by which those individuals who reached the highest levels of accomplishment in their chosen fields (e.g., concert pianists, research mathematicians, Olympic swimmers) were able to develop their capabilities so fully. The results suggested that the initial characteristics (or gifts) of the individuals would not by themselves enable extraordinary levels of accomplishment unless there is a long and intensive process of encouragement, nurturing, and training.

Bloom will be remembered for introducing educators to the world of possibilities: There are educational objectives that lie beyond rote memorization. All students, not just a select group, can learn and learn well. Talent is not something to be found in the few; it is to be developed in the many. His unflagging belief in the power of education, both for the welfare of individuals and for the betterment of society; the frameworks he developed for thinking about and talking about educational issues and problems; the *Taxonomy;* his theory of school learning; and his stages of talent development are his enduring legacy to education.

See also: EDUCATIONAL PSYCHOLOGY; INSTRUCTIONAL DESIGN; INSTRUCTIONAL OBJECTIVES; INSTRUCTIONAL STRATEGIES; TAXONOMIES OF EDUCATIONAL OBJECTIVES.

BIBLIOGRAPHY

BLOOM, BENJAMIN S. 1956. *Taxonomy of Educational Objectives,* Handbook 1: *The Cognitive Domain.* New York: Longman.

BLOOM, BENJAMIN S. 1964. *Stability and Change in Human Characteristics.* New York: Wiley.

BLOOM, BENJAMIN S. 1968. "Learning for Mastery." *UCLA Evaluation Comment* 1(2):1–8.

BLOOM, BENJAMIN S. 1976. *Human Characteristics and School Learning.* New York: McGraw-Hill.

BLOOM, BENJAMIN S. 1984. "The 2 Sigma Problem: The Search for Methods of Group Instruction as Effective as One-to-One Tutoring." *Educational Researcher* 13(6):4–16.

BLOOM, BENJAMIN S. 1985. *Developing Talent in Young People.* New York: Ballentine.

LORIN W. ANDERSON

BLOW, SUSAN (1843–1916)

A defender of Friedrich Froebel's original German methods, Susan Blow was an influential educator who helped start public kindergartens in St. Louis and trained many younger kindergarten directors. She was the daughter of a wealthy St. Louis businessman and Republican politician, Henry Taylor Blow, who served two terms as a U.S. Congressman and as minister to Brazil. Her mother, Minerva Grimsley, from an affluent St. Louis family, was a devout Presbyterian, as was Blow's father. Educated at home by private tutors until she was sixteen, Blow then attended Henrietta Haines's private girls' school in New York City. Blow led the faction of the American kindergarten movement that interpreted Froebel's pedagogy symbolically and resisted Progressives' attempts to make kindergarten practice more child-centered and psychologically based.

Blow was particularly attracted to philosophical and spiritual aspects of Froebel's ideas, which she encountered while traveling in Europe with her family in 1870. When she returned to St. Louis in 1871, she met with William Torrey Harris, the superintendent of the St. Louis schools, who was a Hegelian and already a kindergarten supporter. While substitute teaching in St. Louis, Blow began experimenting with Froebel's methods. With Harris's encouragement, she went to New York City in 1872 to study under Maria Kraus Boelte, one of the German kindergarten experts who had brought the movement to the United States. Blow immersed herself in the specificities of Froebel's carefully prescribed "gifts" and "occupations," the series of blocks and other educational materials and handwork activities, which formed the core of his pedagogy. When she returned, she convinced Harris to pay for a teacher and provide space for a kindergarten class, which opened in the Des Peres School in 1873. Other than a short-lived experiment in Boston in 1870, this was the first public kindergarten in the United States.

In 1874, Blow started a kindergarten training school, which soon became a center for the diffusion of Froebelian methods. Numerous kindergarten directors and leaders, including Elizabeth Harrison and Laura Fisher, trained under Blow, who visited Germany again in 1876 to learn more from German kindergarten educators. A charismatic public speaker, Blow began a series of popular lectures for mothers and others interested in kindergartens. Her fame spread. By 1877, her classes, which she expanded to include other educational and philosophical topics, attracted more than 200 participants.

Under the influence of William Torrey Harris, with whom she collaborated closely for many years, Blow became deeply interested in Hegelian philosophy and its application to education. Like Harris, Blow was committed to the kindergarten more for its intellectual and academic benefits than for its potential as a means of Progressive educational and social reform. This tension within American education generally, between promoting school achievement and promoting schools as agents of social change, fractured the kindergarten movement. Blow and Harris saw the kindergarten as a mentally stimulating rather than emotionally nurturing environment. Younger kindergarten teachers began challenging Blow, especially Alice Putnam in Chicago, and Anna Bryan in Louisville, who adapted symbolic kindergarten activities to the realities of urban children's daily lives, and encouraged open-ended free play over teacher-directed replication of Froebel's stylized forms.

In the later part of her career, Blow became an increasingly dogmatic adherent to Froebelianism. Because of mental and physical health problems, she withdrew from direct kindergarten work in 1884, and in 1889, moved to Cazenovia, New York. She entered into a long period of treatment with the Boston neurologist James Jackson Putnam, with whom she corresponded extensively. In 1894, she began writing five volumes on the kindergarten, published under the auspices of her mentor, William Torrey Harris. These books, which included a translation of Froebel's *Mother Play,* a book of songs and games for use by parents and kindergarten teachers, propounded Blow's abstract interpretation of Froebel's work. She was a lecturer at Columbia University's Teachers College from 1905 to 1909, where she

taught a kindergarten course. Obstinately orthodox and rather abstruse, her lectures were not a success, and Blow was eventually replaced by Patty Smith Hill, the leader of the Progressive wing of the kindergarten movement.

In the twentieth century, the merging of Progressive education and the new science of child psychology widened the division between didactic, teacher-directed kindergarten pedagogy and more developmental, child-centered approaches. Blow was a member of the International Kindergarten Union's Committee of Nineteen, which attempted to mediate these differences that had become highly contentious. The divide proved irreconcilable. Blow authored the conservative report, which, along with a moderate and progressive report, was published in 1913 in *The Kindergarten.* Although Blow's personal dynamism and determination delayed the decline of traditionalist orthodoxy in the face of changing educational views, she was unable to sustain Froebelianism. The loss of Froebel's aesthetically sophisticated symbol system, which some are trying to revive in the early twenty-first century, should be balanced against the increased attention to socioemotional well-being and individual creativity, which are the hallmarks of modern early childhood education. Susan Blow was a firm advocate for the more formalistic vision of preschool education. Her force of character and intellect helped bring kindergarten philosophy into the mainstream of educational thought, and into the consciousness of the American public.

See also: EARLY CHILDHOOD EDUCATION, *subentries on* OVERVIEW, PREPARATION OF TEACHERS.

BIBLIOGRAPHY

BLOW, SUSAN E. 1894. *Symbolic Education.* New York: D. Appleton and Company.

BLOW, SUSAN E. 1895. *The Mottoes and Commentaries of Friedrich Froebel's Mother Play.* New York: D. Appleton and Company.

BLOW, SUSAN E. 1899. *Letters to a Mother on the Philosophy of Froebel.* New York: D. Appleton and Company.

BLOW, SUSAN E. 1908. *Educational Issues in the Kindergarten.* New York: D. Appleton and Company.

BEATTY, BARBARA. 1995. *Preschool Education in America: The Culture of Young Children from the*

Colonial Era to the Present. New Haven, CT: Yale University Press.

BROSTERMAN, NORMAN. 1997. *Inventing Kindergarten.* New York: Abrams.

SHAPIRO, MICHAEL STEVEN. 1983. *Child's Garden: The Kindergarten Movement from Froebel to Dewey.* University Park: Pennsylvania State University Press.

TROEN, SELWYN K. 1975. *The Public and the Schools: Shaping the St. Louis School System, 1838–1920.* Columbia: University of Missouri Press.

WEBER, EVELYN. 1969. *The Kindergarten: Its Encounter with Educational Thought in America.* New York: Teachers College Press, Columbia University.

BARBARA BEATTY

BOARD OF TRUSTEES, COLLEGE AND UNIVERSITY

Independent, nonprofit, and public colleges and universities utilize a board format for their governing structure. These boards are often referred to as a *board of trustees* (similar terms include *board of regents* or *board of visitors*), and they act as the legal agent or "owner" of the institution. As a collective body, the trustees hold the authority and responsibility to ensure the fulfillment of an institution's mission. They are also ultimately responsible for the fiscal health of the college or university. The board of trustees' governing role is typically limited to selection of the president and policy approval, with the daily operations and management of the institution vested in the president.

Structure and Composition

An institution's charter and bylaws dictate its board size. These governing documents are informed by history, tradition, and needs of the institution. A board can range from a small handful of individuals to more than fifty people. Trustees are elected or appointed to the board for a specific term, which may be renewable. Most trustees come from the forprofit corporate world. Many institutions work diligently to assemble a diverse representation of community leaders on their board in an effort to broaden support for the institution. For some state

and religiously affiliated institutions the board itself may not select all of the trustees. In the case of public institutions, the governor will usually make the appointments. For religious colleges and universities, the affiliated organization (i.e., a church governing council) will either select or approve the trustees. On occasion, independent colleges and universities will make an individual a life trustee. Life trustees typically have demonstrated an exceptional level of commitment to the institution. Other constituents who may receive a trustee position in an ex officio capacity include alumni, faculty, staff, and students. In some cases these ex officio trustees have full voting rights, while in other cases they are only a representative voice.

Governance

By law, the board of trustees is the governing body for an institution. Many states have established coordinating or consolidated boards that oversee institutional boards of public colleges and universities. A coordinating board may function in an advisory or regulatory capacity. The role of an advisory board is limited to review and recommendation, with no legal authority to approve or disapprove institutional actions, while a regulatory-type coordinating board would have program approval. Consolidated boards within a state usually take the form of one single board for all postsecondary institutions, though they may take the form of multiple boards, with each board responsible for one institutional type (e.g., two-year institutions, four-year institutions). It is not uncommon for states to utilize both coordinating and consolidated boards. On most campuses, tradition and higher-education culture dictate some level of shared governance with faculty. On some campuses, shared governance even extends to staff and students.

Authority

The authority of a board of trustees is derived from the institution's charter. The charter lays out the initial structure and composition of the board. Once the board is in place, it has the power to modify its own structure and composition as it believes necessary. Authority is given to the board as a whole rather than to individual trustees, and individual trustees have little authority and no ownership of an institution. It is the board, in its entirety, that is recognized as the legal owner of an institution's assets. For some public and religiously affiliated institutions, there may be another board (i.e., a consolidated board) or parent organization (i.e., the church denomination) to which the institutional board is beholden. This will impact, and potentially limit, the board's range of autonomy and authority.

Responsibilities

Typically, the board chair is responsible for setting the agenda of the board. Most often this agenda is established in collaboration with the college president. Other board officers, such as the secretary or treasurer, usually have their associated roles completed by institutional staff. The board, as a group, has several basic responsibilities, including setting or reaffirming the institution's mission, acting as the legal owner of the institution, selecting a president, evaluating and supporting the president, setting board policies, and reviewing institutional performance.

Beyond these responsibilities, most boards are involved with institutional fundraising, strategic planning, and ensuring sensible management. The selection of a president can be the greatest influence a board has on an institution. Boards typically relinquish significant amounts of their power and authority to the president. The president usually takes the lead in setting an agenda for the board, and, therefore, for the institution. As an individual, a trustee is typically expected to support the institution financially, either personally or through influence. Trustees also act as ambassadors in their home community to build support for the institution.

Board Committees

Each board determines the number and type of committees they believe will serve the institution best. The following types of committees are typically found at colleges and universities: *Academic Affairs* oversees curriculum, new educational programs, and approves graduates; *Audit* is responsible for ensuring institutional financial records are appropriately reviewed by a third party; *Buildings and Grounds* reviews and recommends capital improvements and maintenance plans for the campus; the *Committee on Trustees* is charged with developing a list of potential trustees and reviewing the commitment of current trustees; *Executive* acts on issues of urgency that arise between full board meetings and sets the board agenda in concert with the president; *Finance* reviews and recommends institutional budgets; *Institutional Advancement* ensures appropriate

plans are in place for alumni relations, fundraising, and public perception of the institution; *Investment* oversees the long-term assets of the institution, as well as determining how the endowment funds are invested; and *Student Affairs* is charged with issues concerning the out-of-classroom experience of students—this may include health centers, recreation facilities, residence halls, and student activities.

See also: Colleges and Universities, Organizational Structure of; Faculty Senates, College and University; Governance and Decision-Making in Colleges and Universities; Presidency, College and University.

BIBLIOGRAPHY

Fisher, James L., and Koch, James V. 1996. "Governing Boards and the President." In *Presidential Leadership: Making a Difference*, ed. James L. Fisher and James V. Koch. Phoenix, AZ: Oryx Press.

Heilbron, Louis H. 1973. *The College and University Trustee*. San Francisco: Jossey-Bass.

Ingram, Richard T. 1996. *Effective Trusteeship: A Guide for Board Members of Public Colleges and Universities*. Washington, DC: Association of Governing Boards of Universities and Colleges.

Ingram, Richard T. 1997. *Trustee Responsibilities: A Basic Guide for Governing Boards of Independent (or Public) Institutions*. Washington, DC: Association of Governing Boards of Universities and Colleges.

INTERNET RESOURCE

Association of Governing Boards of Universities and Colleges. 2002. <www.agb.org>.

Alan P. Duesterhaus

BOBBITT, FRANKLIN (1876–1956)

Professor of educational administration at the University of Chicago, Franklin Bobbitt played a leading role during the first three decades of the twentieth century in establishing curriculum as a field of specialization within the discipline of education. Born in English, Indiana, a community of less than 1,000 people in the southeast part of the state, Bobbitt earned his undergraduate degree at Indiana University and then went on to teach, first in several rural schools in Indiana and later at the Philippine Normal School in Manila. After receiving his doctorate at Clark University in 1909, he joined the faculty of the University of Chicago, where he remained until his retirement in 1941. As part of his university duties Bobbitt periodically undertook surveys of local school systems in which he assessed the districts' operations, particularly the adequacy of their curricula. His most famous surveys were a 1914 evaluation of the San Antonio Public Schools and a 1922 study of the Los Angeles City Schools' curriculum.

Scientific Curriculum Making

Bobbitt is best known for two books, *The Curriculum* (1918) and *How to Make a Curriculum* (1924). In these volumes and in his other writings, he developed a theory of curriculum development borrowed from the principles of scientific management, which the engineer Frederick Winslow Taylor had articulated earlier in the century in his efforts to render American industry more efficient.

The key principal for Taylor was the task idea, the notion that each worker should be given a narrowly defined production assignment that he was to perform at a specific rate using certain predefined procedures. It was the responsibility of an emerging profession of efficiency experts to identify these precise steps. The procedures for curriculum planning, which Bobbitt referred to as job analysis, were adapted from Taylor's work and began with the identification of the specific activities that adults undertook in fulfilling their various occupational, citizenship, family, and other social roles. The resulting activities were to be the objectives of the curriculum. The curriculum itself, Bobbitt noted, was comprised of the school experiences that educators constructed to enable children to attain these objectives.

Some of these objectives, according to Bobbitt, were general in nature and represented the knowledge that all children needed to prepare for their responsibilities as adult citizens. Such an education, he maintained, would provide students with the large group consciousness necessary for them to act together for the common good. Other objectives, however, were more specific and constituted the skills that youth needed to prepare for the array of specialized occupations that adults held in modern society. The curriculum that Bobbitt advocated included elements of general education for all youth, but was for

the most part differentiated into a number of very specialized vocational tracks. Influenced no doubt by the then-popular mental testing movement, Bobbitt believed that schools should assign children to these specialized curricular tracks, on the basis of assessments of their intellectual abilities, which foretold their ultimate destinies in life.

Social Efficiency Movement

Bobbitt along with a handful of other early-twentieth-century educators, including W. W. Charters, Ross L. Finney, Charles C. Peters, and David Snedden, gave life to what has come to be called the social efficiency movement in education. The schools, for these individuals, were a key institution in dealing with the disruptions and dislocations in American life that they associated with the nation's late-nineteenth- and early-twentieth-century transformation into an urban, industrial society. The purpose of education, they argued, was to prepare youth for the specific work and citizenship roles, which they would hold when they reached adulthood, and in so doing render society more orderly and stable. The test for the schools and its program, as these thinkers saw it, was its utility in fulfilling this social purpose.

Bobbitt's Contribution

Bobbitt's legacy falls into four areas. First, he was one of the first American educators to advance the case for the identification of objectives as the starting point for curriculum making. He, along with the authors of the National Education Association's *Cardinal Principles of Secondary Education,* argued that the content of the curriculum was not self-evident in the traditional disciplines of knowledge, but had to be derived from objectives that addressed the functions of adult work and citizenship. Education was not important in its own right for Bobbitt. Its value lay in the preparation it offered children for their lives as adults. Second, his so-called scientific approach to curriculum making served as a precedent for the work of numerous educators during the next half-century in spelling out the procedures for designing the course of study. It was a method that became and has remained the conventional wisdom among American educators concerning the process of curriculum development.

Third, Bobbitt along with other early-twentieth-century efficiency-oriented school reformers made the case that the curriculum ought to be differentiated into numerous programs, some academic and preparatory and others vocational and terminal, and that students ought to be channeled to these tracks on the basis their abilities. His work lent credence to efforts to vocationalize the curriculum, and provided legitimacy to what has become one of the most questionable features of the modern school curriculum, the practices of tracking and ability grouping. Finally, Bobbitt was one of the first American educators to define the curriculum as an instrument of social control or regulation for addressing the problems of modern society. True to the ideals of social efficiency, he saw the task of the schools as that of instilling in youth the skills, knowledge, and beliefs that they required to function in the urban, industrial, and increasingly heterogeneous society that America was becoming during the early years of the twentieth century.

See also: CURRICULUM, SCHOOL.

BIBLIOGRAPHY

BOBBITT, FRANKLIN. 1918. *The Curriculum.* Boston: Houghton Mifflin.

BOBBITT, FRANKLIN. 1922. *Curriculum Making in Los Angeles.* Chicago: University of Chicago Press.

BOBBITT, FRANKLIN. 1924. *How to Make a Curriculum.* Boston: Houghton Mifflin.

FRANKLIN, BARRY M. 1986. *Building the American Community: The School Curriculum and the Search for Social Control.* London: Falmer.

NATIONAL EDUCATION ASSOCIATION. 1918. *Cardinal Principles of Secondary Education: A Report of the Commission of the Reorganization of Secondary Education.* Washington, DC: U.S. Government Printing Office.

BARRY M. FRANKLIN

BODE, BOYD H. (1873–1953)

A leading spokesperson of Progressive education and a founder of American pragmatism, Boyd H. Bode was born Boyo Hendrik Bode in Ridott, Illinois. Bode was the eldest son in a family of eight children of Dutch parents, Hendrik and Gertrude Weinenga Bode. His father, both a farmer and minister in the Christian Reformed Church, fully expected Bode to follow him into the ministry. To this end, Boyd was allowed to pursue an education. He received an bachelor's degree in 1896 from William Penn College (affiliated with the Quakers) and from the University of Michigan in 1897. He completed his Ph.D. in philosophy at Cornell University in 1900. While away at school Bode decided not to enter the ministry, and wrote to his father: "Your letter gave me the impression that you still have the fear that I—after all—will still lapse into unbelief. Let me again put your mind at ease that here is little danger for that . . . . It appears to me that morals without religion does not mean much."

During the 1890s American higher education developed in directions that made a career in academics, separate from the ministry, possible. Upon graduating from Cornell, Bode assumed a position at the University of Wisconsin, Madison, as an instructor and later assistant professor of philosophy and psychology. In 1909 he took a position at the University of Illinois, where he served as professor of philosophy until 1921. Although he left Wisconsin a firm idealist, among his supporters in Madison were the pragmatists John Dewey and William James, whose positions Bode had challenged in publication. At the time Bode found the pragmatist position inadequate to account for the nature of the mind or of knowing, and a weak foundation for morality.

Despite his professional success at the University of Illinois, Bode became increasingly dissatisfied with the role of idealism in solving pressing human problems. By 1909 he wrote of his work in philosophy to friend and fellow philosopher Max Otto: "A good deal of the work is mere drill and I don't find that I am getting anything out of it any more." Gradually he began to reevaluate idealism; and his views about both Dewey and James' positions changed. The pragmatist challenge to idealism demanded attention, and as Bode struggled to respond he gradually thought himself out of idealism and into pragmatism. He sought a philosophy that made a difference, as he put it, a philosophy "brought to earth." He concluded that Dewey was correct: Human experience was sufficient to explain questions of truth and morality.

At Illinois, partly because of the influence of his Cornell classmate William Chandler Bagley, Bode became increasingly interested in educational issues. In particular, he recognized the profound educational differences that follow differing conceptions of mind, a concern fully explored a few years later in his classic *Conflicting Psychologies of Learning* (1929). In 1917 he joined Dewey and other pragmatists in coauthoring *Creative Intelligence,* in which Bode developed a pragmatic conception of consciousness as action. At Illinois he began to teach a graduate seminar on educational theory, and soon he was teaching regularly in the department of education. In 1916 Dewey published *Democracy and Education,* which offered a definition for philosophy that was consistent with Bode's developing thinking. Bode began to publish on educational issues, including entering the debate over the question of transfer of training. In 1921 *Fundamentals of Education* was published, and he assumed the position as head of the department of principles and practice of education at The Ohio State University. His departure from the University of Illinois caused quite a stir. Bagley asserted that he was "a remarkable teacher—by far the most effective, I am sure, at the University of Illinois." Students protested that he was being pushed out from the university because he was seen as "Socrates [who] corrupted the young men of Athens" and held a "too liberal attitude in intellectual matters" for the time.

At Ohio State Bode came to be perhaps the most articulate spokesmen for pragmatism in education. Acknowledging his influence, *Time* magazine declared Bode to be "Progressive education's No. 1 present-day philosopher." Bode was at the center of what came to be known as the "Ohio School of Democracy" in education. In numerous publications he sought to clarify the educational meaning of democracy as a way of life. In articulating his position, which centered on the ideals of faith in the common person's ability to make wise decisions and in the "method of intelligence" as a means of establishing truth (with a small "t"), he took issue with those, including John L. Childs and George Counts, who would impose a social vision on the public schools. His hope was grounded in a profound faith in the process of democratic decision making, the "free play of intelligence" in pursuit of social goods, and in the goodness of people, the "common man," rather than in the foresight of a few to anticipate the future. In *Democracy as a Way of Life* (1937) he presented his social and educational vision. On another front he challenged the extreme wings of educational progressivism, pointing out that it is not possible to build a school program on needs and interests without a clear social philosophy. He chastised progressive educators who ignored the importance of social philosophy in *Progressive Education at the Crossroads* (1938). He asserted that needs and interests are assigned, they do not inhere in individuals. Moreover, he forcefully argued that the disciplines of knowledge have a central role in education, and that to ignore their power and place in human progress as some progressives did was to invite educational disaster. Thus, he stood in a middle position between child-centered progressives on one side and those who were committed to reconstructing the society through a predetermined social program on the other. Both sides took issue with him.

In addition, Bode wrote about the dangers inherent in what he called the "cleavage" in American culture, that fundamental tension between the demands of democracy and the tendency to look outside of experience for ideals. America could not have it both ways: Democracy was an evolving experiment that drew its aims and means from human experience—the struggle to learn how to live together in order to maximize human development in its various forms. This issue increasingly demanded his attention in his later years particularly in response to the growing attack on progressivism and public education from the right.

Bode argued his position from the pulpit and through publication. As a speaker he was forceful and funny. One attendee at his session during the 1937 Progressive Education Association conference wrote that "To have heard Dr. Boyd Bode of Ohio poke linguistic rapiers, sheathed in salving humor, into every sacred tradition of society, democracy, and theology, was to have experienced an awakening. Shocking it was at times—challenging every minute—and disturbingly logical."

Bode is not well remembered. When recalled, usually he is dismissed as a disciple of his colleague and friend John Dewey. But Bode was not a disciple. He differed with Dewey on a number of fronts, not the least being his dissatisfaction with Dewey's concept of "growth" as an educational ideal. More properly, he ought to be considered one of the founders of educational American pragmatism. Even today the clarity of his prose and quality of his thinking distinguish him from other philosophers of education; his works remain one of the surest and most pleasant roads to understanding of pragmatism and education.

See also: DEWEY, JOHN; PHILOSOPHY OF EDUCATION; PROGRESSIVE EDUCATION.

BIBLIOGRAPHY

BODE, BOYD H. 1921. *Fundamentals of Education.* New York: Macmillan.

BODE, BOYD H. 1927. *Modern Educational Theories.* New York: Macmillan.

BODE, BOYD H. 1929. *Conflicting Psychologies of Learning.* Boston: Heath.

BODE, BOYD H. 1937. *Democracy as a Way of Life.* New York: Macmillan.

BULLOUGH, ROBERT V., JR. 1981. *Democracy in Education: Boyd H. Bode.* Bayside, NY: General Hall.

CHAMBLISS, JOSEPH J. 1964. *Boyd H. Bode's Philosophy of Education.* Columbus: Ohio State University Press.

CHILDS, JOHN L. 1956. *American Pragmatism and Education.* New York: Holt.

DEWEY, JOHN. 1916. *Democracy and Education.* New York: Macmillan.

ROBERT V. BULLOUGH JR.

BOND, HORACE MANN
(1904–1972)

President of two historically black colleges from 1939 to 1957, and dean of the School of Education at Atlanta University from 1957 until shortly before his death in 1972, Horace Mann Bond was also a historian and social scientific observer of the condition of African Americans. He was born on November 8, 1904, in Nashville, Tennessee, the sixth of seven children of a Congregationalist minister and a teacher, both of whom had attended Oberlin College. Bond grew up as his father pastored various churches and took other ministerial positions in Tennessee, Kentucky, Alabama, and Atlanta, Georgia. He attended schools in Alabama and Georgia and graduated from the Lincoln (Kentucky) Institute, a high school for African Americans indirectly tied to Berea College. His collegiate career began at Lincoln University in Pennsylvania, from where he graduated, and continued with postbaccalaureate study at the Pennsylvania State College (now University). He did his graduate work at the University of Chicago, from which he earned a master's degree and a Ph.D. in education, with an emphasis on the history and sociology of education. He finished his doctorate in 1936. Among his teachers were Newton Edwards in history of education, Frank S. Freeman in tests and measurements, and Robert Park in sociology. His family valued education enormously, encouraging all their children to achieve to their utmost. Horace's closest sibling, J. Max Bond, also earned his doctorate in education and had a rewarding academic career.

Career

Bond worked at a variety of academic institutions before finishing his doctorate, including Langston University in Langston, Oklahoma; Fisk University in Nashville, Tennessee; and Dillard University in New Orleans, Louisiana. He also worked as a researcher for a time for the Julius Rosenwald Fund, a philanthropic organization with which he would maintain a close, working relationship for approximately two decades, lasting until its dissolution in 1948. He worked his way up in the hierarchy of black colleges, becoming a dean at Dillard in 1934, chairman of the education department at Fisk University later in that decade, and president of the Fort Valley State College in Georgia in 1939. In 1945 he was chosen as president of his alma mater, Lincoln University, in Chester County, Pennsylvania, where he served until 1957. While at Lincoln, he pointed the attention of the college and its students and faculty toward Africa and Africans, building relationships with famous African Lincoln alumni, such as Kwame Nkrumah of Ghana and Nnamdi Azikiwe of Nigeria. He made several trips to Africa in these years and was an officer of the American Society for African Culture (AMSAC). After leaving Lincoln, he became dean of the School of Education at Atlanta University. He worked at Atlanta until his death in 1972.

Publications and Scholarly Pursuits

Bond's publications in the 1920s included two articles critical of the racial bias in the intelligence testing movement. He continued to publish numerous articles in the 1930s, a decade in which he also published a textbook for education courses in historically black colleges, *The Education of the Negro in the American Social Order* (1934), and *Negro Education in Alabama: A Study in Cotton and Steel* (1939), which was based on his doctoral dissertation. While at the rural Fort Valley State College in the 1940s, Bond published *Education for Production: A Text-*

book on *How to Be Healthy, Wealthy, and Wise* (1944). In the 1950s, after leaving Lincoln, he gave several lectures at Harvard University, which were subsequently published as *The Search for Talent* (1959). The theme of black academic excellence, which had animated Bond's own life and much of his early work, as well as his Harvard lectures, was explored again in *Black American Scholars: A Study of Their Beginnings* (1969). Finally, Bond's *Education for Freedom: A History of Lincoln University,* was published posthumously in 1976. His scholarship was mainly in the areas of educational tests and measurements, educational history, and educational sociology. Much of his early and middle career was devoted to teacher training, and issues involved in its pursuit in black colleges. His later years were devoted to the pursuit of positive relations between Africans and African Americans, as well as expansions of his earlier scholarly interests.

Bond was an accomplished student, and his early scholarly career was one of great promise. His detour into academic administration, encouraged by the Rosenwald interests, took him away from his scholarly pursuits until late in his life. By that time, his absence from the scholarly arena for several years hampered his efforts, though it did not stop his productivity. His accomplishments as a college president were considerable at Fort Valley, where he pioneered the collegiate development of one of the three black colleges in the Georgia State University System. His tenure at Lincoln, however, was marred by acrimonious relationships with some faculty and alumni, which eventually culminated in his dismissal as president, an outcome which he considered, with some bitterness, to be totally unjust. At Atlanta he was reasonably successful as a dean but exhibited little enthusiasm for the work. He was more interested in research on black educational history and black academic achievement and pursued these interests after being named head of the School of Education's Bureau of Educational Research.

Family Life

Bond married Julia Agnes Washington, a student he met while on the Fisk faculty in the 1920s, in 1929. Julia Washington was from an economically successful and prominent African-American family in Nashville, Tennessee, and she and Horace had three children: Jane Marguerite, born in 1939; Horace Julian, born in 1940; and James, born in 1945. He had high academic expectations for all of his children,

expectations which were met initially only by his daughter. His son, Horace Julian, became a leader in the black college student wing of the civil rights movement in the 1960s, went on to become a state legislator in Georgia, and in his political activism achieved a fame that had eluded his father. In the early twenty-first century he serves as president of the National Association for the Advancement of Colored People (NAACP) and teaches history at the University of Virginia.

See also: MULTICULTURAL EDUCATION.

BIBLIOGRAPHY

BOND, HORACE MANN. 1934. *The Education of the Negro in the American Social Order.* New York: Prentice Hall.

BOND, HORACE MANN. 1939. *Negro Education in Alabama: A Study in Cotton and Steel.* Washington, DC: Associated Publishers.

BOND, HORACE MANN. 1969. *Black American Scholars: A Study of Their Beginnings.* Detroit, MI: Balamp.

BOND, HORACE MANN. 1976. *Education for Freedom: A History of Lincoln University.* Princeton, NJ: Princeton University Press for Lincoln University.

URBAN, WAYNE J. 1992. *Black Scholar: Horace Mann Bond, 1904–1972.* Athens: University of Georgia Press.

WILLIAMS, ROGER. 1971. *The Bonds: An American Family.* New York: Atheneum.

WAYNE J. URBAN

BOWEN, HOWARD (1908–1989)

Economist Howard Bowen was a notable figure in university administration and the author of several classic works on the economics of higher education. Born in Spokane, Washington, he married Lois B. Schilling of Green Bay, Wisconsin, in 1935; they had two sons. Bowen earned his B.A. in 1929 and his M.A. in 1933 from Washington State University. He earned his Ph.D. at the University of Iowa in 1935 and pursued postdoctoral study at the University of Cambridge, England, and the London School of Economics from 1937 to 1939.

After teaching economics at the University of Iowa from 1935 to 1942, Bowen took a position as the chief economist at Irving Trust Company from 1942 to 1945, and then held the position of chief economist, Joint Committee on Internal Revenue Taxation, U.S. Congress (1945 to 1947). Yet he recalled his experience at the University of Iowa with the most pleasure, and he decided to return to university teaching and research. He accepted an appointment as dean of the College of Commerce in 1947 at the University of Illinois. There he was instrumental in substantially improving the programs in the college, although at considerable political cost. Senior professors resisted the curricular and faculty changes that Bowen implemented, and he had to resign his position in 1952.

Unwilling to leave higher education, he took a position as a professor of economics at Williams College in Massachusetts. Bowen found the life there to be enriching, with well-prepared students and well-qualified faculty members. Yet he preferred administration to teaching, and in 1955 he accepted the presidency of Grinnell College in Iowa, where he was able to increase enrollment, the quality of students and of the faculty, and the endowment, helping to elevate the college to national stature. Bowen remained there until 1964 when he became president of State University of Iowa, a position he held until 1969. While president he convinced the legislature and governor to change the institution's name to the University of Iowa. The late 1960s was a turbulent period in United States higher education, with many student demonstrations over such issues as the war in Vietnam and racism. Bowen made the decision to use local and state police officers to quell demonstrations, a decision he later reflected upon as difficult but necessary. He also tried to maintain a dialogue with protesting students, even inviting them into his home for discussion.

Bowen oversaw a great deal of growth in enrollment, facilities, and the budget in his years as president of the University of Iowa. Nevertheless, approaching the end of his career, he realized that he did not want to spend more than five years in the position. He and his wife moved to California, where he returned to teaching and research, as professor of economics at Claremont Graduate School, a position which he held, however, for only one year (1969–1970).

In the spring of 1970 the president of Claremont University Center resigned, and the governing board asked Bowen to serve as acting president for one year. Discussions about the reorganization of Clare-

mont University Center, a very decentralized group of institutions, led to his appointment as chancellor of the center from 1971 to 1974. In 1973, frustrated by the challenges of a decentralized university, he requested and received a half-time release from his duties as chancellor, and returned to full-time faculty status in 1974.

Bowen finished his career as the R. Stanton Avery Professor of Economics and Education, Claremont Graduate School, holding that position from 1974 to 1984. He decided that his experience in education combined with his administrative expertise offered an important vantage point, and he published three important works, *Investment in Learning,* the *Costs of Higher Education,* and *American Professors: A National Resource Imperiled* (coauthored with Jack Schuster).

Bowen argued in his works that the economics of higher education centered not on profit motives, but rather on prestige and increasing the quality of students' educational experience. He also stressed that society and individuals benefited from higher education far more in terms of non-monetary issues such as emotional development, citizenship, and equality than in financial returns. As a result, Bowen contended, higher education ought to be based on social and individual considerations and not simply on the basis of efficiency and accountability.

Bowen held membership in several economics, finance, and education associations, including the National Academy of Education and the American Economic Association. He was president of the American Finance Association (1950), the American Association for Higher Education (1975), the Western Economic Association (1977), and the Association for the Study of Higher Education (1980). He was also the recipient of awards from the National Council of Independent Colleges and Universities, the National Association of Student Personnel Administrators, the Council of Independent Colleges, the Council for the Advancement and Support of Education, the Association for Institutional Research, and the Association for the Study of Higher Education. His works on the economics of higher education, assessing both the financial and nonfinancial returns on higher education for individuals and the society at large, remain classics. He also identified how colleges and universities sought to raise more money in order to spend more money, rather than seeking ways of efficiently using their income. His coauthored work on the professoriate, although highly controversial for its prediction that there would be a shortage of well-qualified professors by the mid-1990s, nevertheless captured a deep sense of unease within the academic profession.

See also: ACCOUNTING SYSTEMS IN HIGHER EDUCATION; FACULTY RESEARCH AND SCHOLARSHIP, ASSESSMENT OF; FACULTY PERFORMANCE OF RESEARCH AND SCHOLARSHIP; TEACHING AND RESEARCH, THE RELATIONSHIP BETWEEN.

BIBLIOGRAPHY

BOWEN, HOWARD. 1977. *Investment in Learning: The Individual and Social Value of American Higher Education.* San Francisco: Jossey-Bass.

BOWEN, HOWARD. 1980. *The Costs of Higher Education: How Much Do Colleges and Universities Spend Per Student and How Much Should They Spend?* San Francisco: Jossey-Bass.

BOWEN, HOWARD. 1988. *Academic Recollections.* Washington, DC: American Association for Higher Education.

BOWEN, HOWARD, and SCHUSTER, JACK. 1986. *American Professors: A National Resource Imperiled.* New York: Oxford University Press.

PHILO HUTCHESON

BOYER, ERNEST (1928–1995)

An innovator of secondary and postsecondary education, Dr. Ernest L. Boyer served as U.S. Commissioner of Education from 1977 to 1979 and president of the Carnegie Foundation for the Advancement of Teaching from 1979 to 1995. Born in Dayton, Ohio, Boyer finished high school early to study at Messiah Academy in Grantham, Pennsylvania. He completed his studies in Illinois at Greenville College in 1950, and received master's and doctoral degrees in speech pathology and audiology at the University of Southern California, in 1955 and 1957, respectively. He began his teaching career at Loyola University in California while a graduate student, and then served as a professor of speech pathology and audiology at Upland College in California.

In 1960 Ernest Boyer moved from teaching to administration and leadership. He accepted a position with the Western College Association, as director of the Commission to Improve the Education of Teachers. Two years later he became the director of the Center for Coordinated Education at the University of California, Santa Barbara. In this position Boyer was free to administer projects for the improvement of the California education system, from kindergarten to college.

In 1965, eight years after earning his doctorate, Boyer moved to Albany, New York, and joined the new State University of New York (SUNY) system as its first executive dean. Three years later he was named vice president and, two years after that, chancellor. He was intent on creating new connections in the system between the many independent colleges.

One of his most significant accomplishments as chancellor was the creation of the Empire State College in Saratoga Springs, New York. This college allows adult students to earn degrees without attending classes on campus. The students earn degrees via workshops, reading, television, and hands-on experience. Boyer also created the rank of "Distinguished Teaching Professor" to emphasize the importance of teaching and learning, not merely research. He established an experimental three-year degree program for the brightest students so that they could move quickly toward graduate work. While chancellor of SUNY, Dr. Boyer unified sixty-two campuses. He established a dialogue between the campuses and called for cooperation and community. He initiated a statewide art program and equal opportunity centers for the minority students. Boyer remained with the SUNY system until 1977, when President Jimmy Carter invited him to become the U.S. Commissioner of Education.

Washington, D.C.

As Commissioner of Education, Boyer vowed to give priority to basic education, skills, and educational reform. During his tenure, Boyer created a service-learning program enabling students to get hands-on experience in their communities. He also became increasingly aware of the troubles of Native American education systems, and set up programs and conducted studies on the improvement of the Native American school system. In addition to helping the nation's less-privileged students, Dr. Boyer also managed to increase federal funds for education by 40 percent over three years.

Regarding the challenges of working in Washington, Boyer remarked: "I became informed about the issues of public education, got involved in the discussions about excellence and quality, and confronted more directly the crisis that may overwhelm us in the end: the gap between the haves and the have-nots" (Goldberg, p. 47). His mission in Washington focused on the government's obligation to bridge the gap that separates those who are challenged by economic disadvantage and prejudice. Toward the end of his term as commissioner of education, Boyer was offered the position of president of the Carnegie Foundation for the Advancement of Teaching, a post he assumed at the end of 1979.

Carnegie Foundation for the Advancement of Teaching

Boyer moved the foundation center to Princeton, New Jersey. He did, however, keep an office in Washington to maintain his connections to political agendas related to education. He expanded the Carnegie Foundation to include public education: "My top priority at Carnegie will be efforts to reshape the American high school and its relationship with higher education . . . . I'm convinced that the high school is the nation's most urgent education problem." Dr. Boyer's main goal as president was not to create programs but to initiate dialogue concerning education issues. His speeches and writings conveyed ideas on education, and are a testimony to the impact that he had on the nation's education system.

Reports and Publications

One of Boyer's major accomplishments was creating a dialogue between teachers and administrators about teaching methods and programs. While at the Carnegie Foundation, he wrote several reports that changed the face of education. By addressing certain issues including secondary and primary education, Boyer was able to generate discussions about issues facing education reform.

High School: A Report on Secondary Education in America (1983) was the result of a fifteen-month study of the nation's high schools. Here Boyer recommended adopting a "core curriculum" for all students and tougher foreign language and English requirements; he also called for community service before graduation, and stressed excellence for all students and teachers.

Boyer's next report, published in 1987, *College: The Undergraduate Experience in America,* found that many faculty members of undergraduate insti-

tutions placed more emphasis on research than teaching. Boyer claimed that the students were not getting the full attention of their instructors, contending that the nation must put more resources into undergraduate education, expand orientation and faculty mentoring for new students, and create community service programs for students. With both *High School* and *College,* Boyer connected students with their teachers and professors and the worlds outside the institutions. The development of community service programs in many high schools and colleges around the nation has benefited all involved.

Boyer persisted in his commitment to stimulate the debate about education practices. In 1990 the Carnegie Foundation published *Campus Life: In Search of Community.* Boyer realized that the old ideas of campus communities were disappearing due to the diverse backgrounds of many students, writing "if a balance can be struck between individual interests and shared concerns, a strong learning community will result" (Perrone, pp. 22–23). Many colleges and universities have since created programs to rebuild their campus community using Boyer's ideas.

Also published in 1990, *Scholarship Reconsidered: Priorities of the Professoriate* challenged the current views of faculty priorities and the true meaning of scholarship. Calling for a new approach to teaching, Boyer categorized four kinds of scholarship: discovery, integration, application, and teaching. This report has fueled debates in many circles around the country and has influenced many colleges and universities to assess their faculty differently. In 1997 Charles E. Glassick, Mary Taylor Huber, and Gene I. Maeroff wrote a response, *Scholarship Assessed: Evaluation of the Professoriate.* Their preface stated, "the effort to broaden the meaning of scholarship simply cannot succeed until the academy has clear standards for evaluating this wider range of scholarly work."

In *Ready to Learn: A Mandate for the Nation* (1991) Boyer emphasized the importance of preparing young children for school. Education of the parents of preschoolers was essential so that they might know "all of the forces that have such a profound impact on the children's lives and shape their readiness to learn." This study led to educational television programs such as *Sesame Street,* and landmark legislation such as the Ready to Learn Act of 1994.

In 1995 the Carnegie Foundation published a groundbreaking report, *The Basic School: A Community for Learning.* This report emphasized the importance of the first years of formal learning. Boyer wanted the general public to understand that the school is a community with a vision, "teachers as leaders and parents as partners." He also called for a "powerful voice for the arts in education." This report led to the Basic School Network, as outlined by Boyer himself in the report. A trial program consisted of sixteen schools, public and private, including the Tiospa Zina tribal school in North Dakota. Boyer worked closely with school administrators and staff on the tenets of the Basic School, including new ways to create a curriculum, the importance of language and the arts, and the involvement of parents. Unfortunately, Boyer did not live to see his dream come true. However, the Basic School Network now boasts centers and affiliates around the country and is a successful tool for improving elementary education.

International Achievements

Boyer spent a great deal of time examining the U.S. education system, and his interest extended outside our nation as well. He set up a learning program with the Soviet Union in the 1970s, an unheard of accomplishment due to the consequences of the cold war. He also set up a similar agreement with Israel. Boyer established a partnership with the National Center for Education Development Research (NCEDR) in Beijing, China. This partnership has created a discourse between the People's Republic of China and the United States on all levels of education. He worked on various international committees under Presidents Nixon, Ford, Carter, and Reagan. Under President Ronald Reagan he was appointed chair of the U.S. Department of State's Overseas Schools Advisory Council.

Awards

Dr. Boyer has received honorary degrees from colleges and universities around the world, including the University of Beijing and Tel Aviv University. He served as senior fellow at the Woodrow Wilson School of Public and International Affairs at Princeton University, where he also taught public policy courses. He was awarded the Distinguished Service Medal, Columbia University–Teachers College; the Horatio Alger Award; The Harold W. McGraw Jr. Prize in Education; and countless other awards.

Values and Principles

Boyer's focus was on the people who were involved in all aspects of education. He saw education not as the policy behind it or buildings that house it, but he saw it as the students, parents, faculty, and staff. Boyer's main idea and philosophy of life centered on unity and cooperation. All the analyses and studies that he conducted promoted cooperation within the education system.

Dr. Boyer was a man with a heart and head for public speaking. People describe him as charismatic and persuasive but never overbearing. His main principles were simple yet profound: schools are a community; focus on the children; serve others; and knowledge and learning are a continuous journey. As Boyer once wrote, "In the end, our goal must not be only to prepare students for careers, but also to enable them to live with dignity and purpose; not only to give knowledge to the student, but also to channel knowledge to humane ends. Educating a new generation of Americans to their full potential is still our most compelling obligation."

As Dr. Doug Jacobsen discusses in his article, "Theology as Public Performance: Reflections on the Christian Convictions of Ernest L. Boyer," "a small act of care or kindness could transform a life from despair to hope. Boyer's personal faith was journey towards holiness, but that journey was never solitary. The straightest path to heaven was the path that took the most detours to serve others" (p. 9).

After a three-year battle with cancer, Ernest Boyer died in 1995. In 1997, the Boyer Center at Messiah College, Grantham, Pennsylvania, was established. This center houses Boyer's letters, papers, and speeches, in addition to photographs, awards, and other memorabilia. The Boyer Center fosters the enrichment of learning for students and teacher through implementation of the educational vision of Ernest Boyer.

See also: FACULTY ROLES AND RESPONSIBILITIES; NONGOVERNMENTAL ORGANIZATIONS AND FOUNDATIONS.

BIBLIOGRAPHY

BOYER, ERNEST. 1983. *High School: A Report on Secondary Education in America.* New York: Harper and Row.

BOYER, ERNEST. 1987. *College: The Undergraduate Experience in America.* New York: Harper and Row.

BOYER, ERNEST. 1990. *Campus Life: In Search of Community. A Special Report.* Princeton, NJ: The Carnegie Foundation for the Advancement of Teaching.

BOYER, ERNEST. 1990. *Scholarship Reconsidered: Priorities of the Professoriate.* Princeton, NJ: The Carnegie Foundation for the Advancement of Teaching.

BOYER, ERNEST. 1991. *Ready to Learn: A Mandate for the Nation.* Princeton, NJ: The Carnegie Foundation for the Advancement of Teaching.

BOYER, ERNEST. 1995. *The Basic School: A Community for Learning.* Princeton, NJ: The Carnegie Foundation for the Advancement of Teaching.

GOLDBERG, MARK F. 1995. "A Portrait of Ernest Boyer." *Educational Leadership* 52(5):46–48.

PERRONE, VITO. 1996. "Ernest L. Boyer: A Leader of Educators, An Educator of Leaders, 1928–1995." *The Ninety-First Annual Report of the Carnegie Foundation for the Advancement of Teaching.* Princeton, NJ: The Carnegie Foundation for the Advancement of Teaching.

PERRONE, VITO. 1996. "The Life and Career of Ernest Boyer (1928–1995)." *Educational Leadership* 53(6):80–82.

INTERNET RESOURCES

BOYER, ERNEST L. Papers. <www.boyercenter.org>.

JACOBSEN, DOUGLAS. 2000. "Theology as Public Performance: Reflections on the Christian Convictions of Ernest L. Boyer." *Messiah College-Presidential Scholar's Lecture, February 17, 2000.* <www.boyercenter.org>.

GLENN R. BUCHER
AMBER M. WILLIAMS

BRAIN-BASED EDUCATION

The overall goal of brain-based education is to attempt to bring insights from brain research into the arena of education to enhance teaching and learning. The area of science often referred to as "brain research" typically includes neuroscience studies that probe the patterns of cellular development in various brain areas; and brain imaging techniques, with the latter including functional MRI (fMRI) scans and positron-emission tomography (PET) scans that allow scientists to examine patterns of activity in the awake, thinking, human brain. These brain imaging techniques allow scientists to examine activity within various areas of the brain as a person engages in mental actions such as attending, learning, and remembering. Proponents of brain-based education espouse a diverse group of educational practices and approaches, and they generally attempt to ground claims about effective practice in recently discovered facts about the human brain. They argue that there has been an unprecedented explosion of new findings related to the development and organization of the human brain and that the current state of this work can inform educational practice in meaningful ways. Indeed, advances in brain science led brain-based educator David A. Sousa to proclaim that "no longer is teaching just an art form, it is a science" (1998, p. 35).

Summary Principles of Brain-Based Research

Although brain-based education has no seminal source or centrally recognized leader, examples of commonly cited works include special issues of education journals and popular books such as *How the Brain Learns: A Classroom Teacher's Guide,* by Sousa; *Teaching with the Brain and Mind,* by Eric Jensen; *Making Connections: Teaching and the Human Brain,* by Renate Nummela Caine and Geoffrey Caine; *A Celebration of Neurons: An Educator's Guide to the Human Brain,* by Robert Sylwester; and *Teaching for the Two-Sided Mind: A Guide to Right Brain/Left Brain Education,* by Linda VerLee Williams. Such works, invariably written by education writers rather than brain researchers, claim to help teachers turn research on brain function into practical lessons and activities that will enhance student learning. A common step in many brain-based education efforts involves disseminating findings from brain science in the form of basic summary principles that are designed to be accessible to educators. For example, Caine and Caine (1994) claim to have deduced twelve principles from brain science that hold strong implications for education and that can be linked to specific educational practices:

- "The brain is a complex adaptive system."
- "The brain is a social brain."
- "The search for meaning is innate."
- "The search for meaning occurs through patterning."
- "Emotions are critical to patterning."

- "The brain processes parts and wholes simultaneously."
- "Learning involves both focused attention and peripheral perception."
- "Learning always involves conscious and unconscious processes."
- "We have at least two different types of memory: a spatial memory system and a set of systems for rote learning."
- "We understand and remember best when facts and skills are embedded in natural, spatial memory."
- "Learning is enhanced by challenge and inhibited by threat." (pp. 88–95)

There are three problems with such summary principles. First, they are not necessarily endorsed by brain scientists as appropriate summaries of the research. Second, they are exceedingly global statements that could potentially encompass a wide variety of educational practices that are not necessarily compatible with one another. Third, few of the practices that are deemed "brain based" have been evaluated for their relative effectiveness. These problems make it difficult to evaluate the merits and usefulness of the kind of global claims offered by brain-based education writers, as exemplified by Caine and Caine.

Nevertheless, brain-based education proponents typically argue that a particular educational approach or practice *is* warranted by these kinds of basic summary principles and the related supporting evidence from brain research. Given that such links between brain research and education practice are initially speculative in nature and are often not subjected to evaluations that demonstrate their effectiveness, the label of "brain-based education" does not necessarily imply that the recommended educational approach or practice is "evidence based." The brain science evidence merely provides a rationale for speculating about potentially useful educational practices.

Often proponents of brain-based education use collections of claims (as above) to promote a rationale for doing away with traditional forms of education in favor of educational reforms based on constructivist learning principles and more active engagement in individualized learning and group problem solving. For example, Susan Kovalik, developer of the Integrated Thematic Instruction model,

argued "disciplines have to go; the textbooks have to go; the worksheets have to go—because they have nothing to do with how the brain works" (Cohen, p. 1). Along these lines, brain-based education is often cited as a mandate for "orchestrated immersion," such as having children work through problems in curriculum by engaging in activities that simulate real-world problem solving or by engaging in group cooperative learning.

Are such broad claims warranted by the evidence provided by brain science? In 1996, seventy-four brain scientists and education professionals gathered at a meeting held by the Education Commission of the States and the Charles A. Dana Foundation to explore the extent to which neuroscience had uncovered facts about the brain that educators might apply in the classroom. At the conclusion of this meeting, which was called "Bridging the Gap between Neuroscience and Education," neuroscientists warned educators that many brain research findings might be too narrow and isolated to ever provide a detailed plan of action for restructuring schools. Furthermore, some scientists "cautioned educators to resist the temptation to . . . use neuroscience as a propaganda tool to promote a pet program" (Taher, p. 5). At this same meeting Joseph LeDoux, a prominent psychologist and neuroscientist, warned that "these ideas are very easy to sell to the public, but it's too easy to take them beyond their actual basis in science" (Taher, p. 5).

The specific claims made within brain-based research vary widely but typically take the form of two interrelated assertions: (1) assertions of basic summary principles that are held to be broadly supported by neuroscience research and (2) assertions that particular educational approaches or practices should be promoted on the basis of the stated principles of brain science. Critics of contemporary brain-based education literature, such as John T. Bruer and Paul Grobstein, have raised questions about whether the basic summary principles delivered to teachers might be too overly simplified to capture the most useful information in brain research and have raised concerns about the validity of the inferential leap that takes place between accepting a basic summary principle from brain research and creating a particular recommendation for educational practice. The remainder of this article summarizes the major points raised in critiques of brain-based education in light of evidence available in the early twenty-first century and discusses promising directions for future research that might help the fields of brain science and education to mutually inform one another in productive ways.

Critiques of Brain-Based Education

In some cases, summary principles can oversimplify research to the extent that the most useful level of detail for educational implications is lost. For example, in a 1999 article, Bruer pointed to Sousa's summary claiming that brain research had established that the left hemisphere of the brain is responsible for language processes (including logical processes, coding information verbally, reading, and writing) and the right hemisphere is responsible for spatial processing (and also creativity, intuition, and encoding information via pictures). Sousa had furthermore argued that, based on this insight, teachers should provide time for both left and right hemisphere activities so that children receive a balance of left and right hemisphere activity. Bruer, however, pointed to more recent brain research that demonstrated that the left and right hemispheres do not strictly divide the labor of thought between processing information about space on the right and language on the left, with this research finding instead that both spatial and language processes draw upon the left and right hemispheres and that subcomponents within each of these skills draw differentially on left and right hemispheres. In light of these findings, the related brain-based education claims appear to be invalid. This discussion underscores the dangers of relying on outdated notions of brain organization and function and the importance of making rigorous and detailed links between educational practice and the best available brain science data.

In other cases of brain-based research, summary statements appear to be general enough to have broad appeal to educators, but they are perhaps so broad that they have little or no meaningful connection to brain research and have only vague or perhaps misleading implications for educational practice. To take one example, in 1994 Caine and Caine stated that one basic principle of brain research (already mentioned above) was that wholes and parts are perceived simultaneously. Bruer pointed out that although this is statement is likely to be true, the statement is framed in such a way that it cannot be used to identify any particular brain system, nor can it provide direct and compelling implications for educational practice. Furthermore, Bruer directly challenged the validity of the inference that

the Caines made in using this principle to argue that whole-language instruction and cooperative learning are warranted by brain research because such programs encourage students to think about both parts and wholes.

Another challenge Bruer posed for many basic summary statements relating to brain science is that the evidence that best supports many such summary statements does not actually come from neuroscience or brain scans but comes, rather, from other disciplines that have been around for decades. For example, in his 1998 article "Is the Fuss about Brain Research Justified?" Sousa listed several claims about how current "brain research" can influence educational practice. On the topic of memory, he wrote about insights into how previous knowledge and judgments of meaningfulness influence people's ability to store new information. On the topic of timing and learning, he wrote about insights into how breaking learning time up into twenty-minute segments that are spaced over time might be an advantage over massing all that same study time together into one long stretch. One problem with these claims is that these insights were achieved with little or no direct support from brain studies. Instead, these claims are well supported by existing evidence in cognitive psychology, in the form of compelling information-processing studies on the influence of prior knowledge on memory recall and on the benefits of spaced versus massed practice in recall. In this sense, referring to these claims as brain based can be misleading; after all, existing bodies of cognitive psychology may have a great deal more to contribute to educational practice than the currently available brain studies.

Directions for Future Research

This literature on brain-based education that makes summary claims about brain processes and their implications is augmented by a literature that makes much closer ties to emerging research in brain science and that cautiously explores possibilities for enhancing research. For example, Pat Wolfe (2001) made several recommendations to educators related to taking a proactive stance as consumers and users of insights from brain science. These recommendations are for educators to learn the general structures and functions of the brain, to gain some skills in assessing the validity of a study, to exercise caution and restraint when attempting to employ insights from research studies in a classroom, and to intelligently combine insights from brain science with knowledge from cognitive psychology and educational research. To achieve these goals, Sousa argued in 1998, there is a need for professional development opportunities for prospective and current teachers to get firsthand contact with scientists involved in cognitive neuroscience—the field of combing cognitive psychology with brain-imaging techniques. Such programs are beginning to become available at a national level and involve some of the nation's top scientists, as evidenced by advanced courses offered by the National Institute of Mental Health, Harvard University, and the University of Washington.

Other brain-based education literature that makes closer ties with brain research focuses on brain imaging of particular learning disabilities. Sousa wrote "we are gaining a deeper understanding of learning disabilities, such as autism and dyslexia. Scanning technology is revealing which parts of the brain are involved in these problems, giving hope that new therapies . . . will stimulate their brains and help them learn" (p. 54). Such direct ties between investigations of brain mechanisms associated with learning problems and intervention attempts provide a promising direction for brain-based educational research. Understanding how brain mechanisms of basic visual and language processes work together in typically and atypically developing readers is of central interest to many brain scientists and educators. Several studies centered on these issues were underway in fMRI laboratories in the early twenty-first century, with many of the studies involving brain scans collected before a particular educational intervention. Such direct interplay between educational intervention and brain-based measurements provides a means of assessing the degree to which a particular educational program impacts brain mechanisms associated with learning within a particular domain, such as reading.

Early mathematical abilities represent another very promising area of research that holds the potential for rigorous interaction between brain science investigation and educational practice. fMRI imaging work has provided insights into brain mechanisms of basic numerical abilities such as symbol recognition, digit naming ability, and estimation of magnitude. Future work that combines educational psychology and cognitive neuroscience may examine how educational programs help to train up these brain mechanisms and how remediation programs might help children with atypically developing mathematical abilities improve the operation and integration of these brain mechanisms for number symbol identification, naming, and magnitude estimation.

The examples of early reading and early mathematics skills have several qualities in common that perhaps make them ideally suited for a new form of brain-based education. In both of these domains, multiple years of brain research have been invested in elucidating the specific brain mechanisms that underlie the particular skill; efforts have been made to map out differences in the brain activity patterns between typical and atypically developing learners; and each of these two content domains represent an educational challenge that many students and teachers struggle with.

As mentioned at the 1996 "Bridging the Gap" meeting, perhaps the best way to pursue this form of brain-based research will involve collaborations between educational researchers and brain science researchers. Such forms of collaboration hold the advantage of combining teachers' intervention ideas with techniques for imaging brain areas associated with particular cognitive skills, thereby allowing researchers to track the changes in brain activity patterns that occur over the course of learning. Perhaps by explicitly combining evidence-based investigations of specific educational practices with brain imaging and psychological studies of learning, future research might take a step closer toward the goals of brain-based education and provide empirically validated contributions to enhancing education based on scientific insights into learning.

See also: LEARNING, *subentry on* NEUROLOGICAL FOUNDATION.

BIBLIOGRAPHY

BRUER, JOHN T. 1997. "Education and the Brain: A Bridge Too Far." *Educational Researcher* 26(8):4–16.

CAINE, RENATE NUMMELA, and CAINE, GEOFFREY. 1994. *Making Connections: Teaching and the Human Brain.* New York: Addison-Wesley.

CHABRIS, CHRISTOPHER F., and KOSSLYN, STEPHEN M. 1998. "How Do the Cerebral Hemispheres Contribute to Encoding Spatial Relations?" *Current Directions in Psychology* 7:8–14.

COHEN, PHILLIP. 1995. "Understanding the Brain: Educators Seek to Apply Brain Based Research." *Education Update* 37:1–2.

DEHAENE, STANISLAUS. 1996. "The Organization of Brain Activations in Number Comparison." *Journal of Cognitive Neuroscience* 8:47–68.

DEHAENE, STANISLAUS. 1997. *The Number Sense.* Oxford: Oxford University Press, Getty Center for Education and the Arts.

DEHAENE, STANISLAUS; SPELKE, ELIZABETH; PINEL, PHILIPPE; STANESCU, RUXANDRA; and TSIVLIN, SANNA. 1999. "Sources of Mathematical Thinking: Behavioral and Brain Imaging Evidence." *Science* 284:970–974.

JENSEN, ERIC. 1998. *Teaching with the Brain in Mind.* Alexandria, VA: Association for Supervision and Curriculum Development.

MCCANDLISS, BRUCE D.; MARITNEZ, ANTIGONA; SANDAK, REBECCA; BECK, ISABEL; PERFETTI, CHARLES; and SCHNIEDER, WALTER S. 2001. "A Cognitive Intervention for Reading Impaired Children Produces Increased Recruitment of Left Peri-sylvian Regions during Word Reading: An fMRI Study." *Neuroscience Abstracts* 27:961–964.

MCCANDLISS, BRUCE D.; SANDAK, REBECCA; MARTINEZ, ANTIGONA; BECK, ISABEL; PERFETTI, CHARLES; and SCHNIEDER, WALTER S. 2001. "Imaging the Impact of Reading Intervention in Children." *Journal of Cognitive Neuroscience* 13(supplement):66.

POSNER, MICHAEL I., and RAICHLE, MARK E. 1994. *Images of Mind.* New York: Scientific American Library.

SOUSA, DAVID A. 1995. *How the Brain Learns: A Classroom Teacher's Guide.* Reston, VA: National Association of Secondary School Principals.

SOUSA, DAVID A. 1998. "Is the Fuss about Brain Research Justified?" *Education Week* 18(16):35.

SYLWESTER, ROBERT. 1995. *A Celebration of Neurons: An Educator's Guide to the Human Brain.* Alexandria, VA: Association for Supervision and Curriculum Development.

WILLIAMS, LINDA VERLEE. 1986. *Teaching for the Two-Sided Mind: A Guide to Right Brain/Left Brain Education.* New York: Simon and Schuster.

WOLFE, PAT. 2001. "Applying Brain Research to Classroom Practice." *Education Update* 43 (4):1–2.

INTERNET RESOURCE

TAHER, BONNIE. 1996. *Bridging the Gap between Neuroscience and Education: Summary of a Workshop Cosponsored by the Education Commission of the States and the Charles A. Dana Foundation.* Denver, CO: Education Commission of the States, pp. 1–17. <www.ecs.org/clearinghouse/11/98/1198.htm>.

BRUCE MCCANDLISS

BRAMELD, THEODORE (1904–1987)

A philosopher and visionary educator who developed the reconstructionist philosophy of education, Theodore Brameld spent a lifetime working for personal and cultural transformation through education. Influenced by John Dewey's educational philosophy, Brameld urged that schools become a powerful force for social and political change. He welcomed reasoned argument and debate both inside and outside the classroom. After completing a doctorate in philosophy at the University of Chicago in 1931, Brameld taught at Long Island University and spent much of his career at New York University and Boston University.

In the 1930s Brameld was drawn to a social activist group of scholars at Teachers College, Columbia University, including George Counts, Harold Rugg, Merle Curti, and William Heard Kilpatrick. Counts especially influenced him profoundly. Writing in *The Social Frontier,* a journal of educational and political critique, Brameld argued for a radical philosophy that focused analysis on weaknesses in the social, economic, and political structure. From this analysis came constructive blueprints for a new social order that challenged social inequities like prejudice, discrimination, and economic exploitation. These issues were addressed in *Minority Problems in Public Schools,* published in 1945.

Placing abundant faith in the common person, Brameld considered democracy the core of his educational philosophy. In 1950 he asserted in *Ends and Means in Education: A Midcentury Appraisal* that education needed a reconstructed perspective and suggested reconstructionism as an appropriate label to distinguish this philosophy. Many of Brameld's ideas grew out of his experience in applying his philosophical beliefs to a school setting in Floodwood, Minnesota. There he worked with students and teachers to develop democratic objectives. Insisting that controversial issues and problems ought to play a central role in education, he considered no issue out of bounds for discussion and critical analysis.

Brameld never wavered in his conviction that philosophy must be related to real-life issues. Philosophers as well as educators must act decisively on their values, he affirmed. Throughout the 1940s and 1950s he remained defiant and courageous in the face of intimidation and harassment by the forces of McCarthyism that tried to muffle his resolute voice.

Starting in 1950 with the publication of *Patterns of Educational Philosophy: A Democratic Interpretation,* Brameld developed his cultural interpretation of four philosophies of education: essentialism, perennialism, progressivism, and reconstructionism. He viewed essentialism as an educational philosophy concerned mainly with the conservation of culture; perennialism as centering on the classical thought of ancient Greece and medieval Europe; progressivism as the philosophy of liberal, experimental education; and reconstructionism as a radical philosophy of education responding to the contemporary crisis. In his writings throughout the 1950s, Brameld maintained that reconstructionists—like progressivists—opposed any theory that viewed values as absolute or unchanging. Values must be tested by evidence and grounded in social consensus.

Brameld continued to refine his philosophy in his many publications. In 1965 a small but influential book, *Education as Power,* appeared in English, Spanish, Portuguese, Japanese, and Korean editions (and was reissued in 2000). *Education as Power* clearly and concisely outlines many of the major tenets of reconstructionism.

Education has two major roles: to transmit culture and to modify culture. When American culture is in a state of crisis, the second of these roles—that of modifying and innovating—becomes more important. Reconstructionism, Brameld affirmed, is a crisis philosophy; the reconstructionist is "very clear as to which road mankind should take, but he [or she] is not at all clear as to which road it will take" (2000, p. 75).

Above all, reconstructionism is a philosophy of values, ends, and purposes, with a democratically empowered world civilization as the central goal of education. Social self-realization, "the realization of the capacity of the self to measure up to its fullest, most satisfying powers in cooperative relationship with other selves" (2000, p. 93), is the capstone of reconstructionist theory and practice, but Brameld also pays attention to politics, human relations, religion, and the arts in his philosophy. A commitment to existential humanism remains constant. Defensible partiality, a central concept in reconstructionism, suggests a search for answers to human problems by exploring alternative approaches and then defending the partialities that emerge from a dialectic of opposition.

Brameld's abiding interest in the concept of culture led him to write a scholarly volume, *Cultural Foundations of Education: An Interdisciplinary Exploration* (1957), that demonstrated his debt to influential anthropologists. Following this came application of his theoretical framework to Puerto Rican culture and education in *The Remaking of a Culture* (1959), and application to a study of a Japanese fishing village and a segregated community in *Japan: Culture, Education, and Change in Two Communities* (1968).

One of Brameld's last books, *The Teacher As World Citizen: A Scenario of the 21st Century* (1976), provides a visionary outline and culmination of many of his lifelong hopes and beliefs. Written as if looking back from the eve of the year 2001, the teacher-narrator recalls global transformations of the preceding quarter century. Radical changes have occurred, especially establishment of a World Community of Nations based on a global Declaration of Interdependence.

Brameld's conception of the utopian spirit as a realizable vision of what could and should be achieved was influenced greatly by scholars like Lewis Mumford whose comprehensive organic, ecological, and humanistic philosophy had a profound influence on Brameld's reconstructionism. Some critics found Brameld's educational philosophy too goal-centered and utopian while others were disturbed by his advocacy of teachers as social change activists. Still others criticized his early interest in Marx, as well as his ongoing critique of the capitalist value system. Brameld's unpopular commitment in intercultural education and education for a world community in the 1950s was more widely embraced as multicultural and global education a half century later.

After becoming professor emeritus at Boston University in 1969, Brameld taught at Springfield

College in Massachusetts and at the University of Hawaii where he continued to write, conduct research, and become involved in community change initiatives. As he did throughout his professional life, Brameld wrote letters to the editors of newspapers and worked on articles for scholarly journals. Brameld participated in demonstrations against nuclear power and enjoyed spending time at his home in Lyme Center, New Hampshire and traveling around the world as an instructor with World Campus Afloat (a study-abroad program now known as the Semester at Sea).

Theodore Brameld died in October 1987 in Durham, North Carolina, at the age of eighty-three. The Society for Educational Reconstruction (SER), founded in the late 1960s by Brameld's former doctoral students and others inspired by his ideas, continues to sponsor conferences and symposia focusing on various dimensions of the reconstructionist philosophy of education.

See also: PHILOSOPHY OF EDUCATION; PROGRESSIVE EDUCATION.

BIBLIOGRAPHY

BRAMELD, THEODORE. 1971. *Patterns of Educational Philosophy: Divergence and Convergence in Culturological Perspective.* New York: Holt, Rinehart, and Winston.

BRAMELD, THEODORE. 1976. *The Teacher as World Citizen: A Scenario of the 21st Century.* Palm Springs, CA: ETC Publications.

BRAMELD, THEODORE. Archival Papers. Special Collections of the Bailey/Howe Library, University of Vermont, Burlington.

BRAMELD, THEODORE. 2000. *Education as Power* (1965). San Francisco: Caddo Gap Press.

CONRAD, DAVID R. 1976. *Education for Transformation: Implications in Lewis Mumford's Ecohumanism.* Palm Springs, CA: ETC Publications.

ROBERTS, SUSAN, and BUSSLER, DARROL, eds. 1997. *Introducing Educational Reconstruction: The Philosophy and Practice of Transforming Society Through Education.* San Francisco: Caddo Gap Press.

SHIMAHARA, NOBUO, and CONRAD, DAVID R. 1991. "Theodore Brameld's Culturological Vision: Profile of a Reconstructionist." *Qualitative Studies in Education* 4:247–259.

STANLEY, WILLIAM B. 1992. *Curriculum for Utopia: Social Reconstructionism and Critical Pedagogy in the Postmodern Era.* Albany: State University of New York Press.

DAVID R. CONRAD

BROOKINGS INSTITUTION

The Brookings Institution is a private, independent, and nonpartisan research institution dedicated to the study of policy issues of U.S. national interest. It conducts research and disseminates its findings to the nation's leadership as well as to the general public, in the hope of offering practical solutions to problems in the areas of government, economics, and foreign policy. It prides itself on the caliber of its research fellows, the timeliness of its research, and the jargon-free accessibility of its publications on complex issues.

Program

The Brookings Institution provides an institutional base for scholars drawn from within academia as well as from the fields of government, business, and the professions. Although the institution does not exercise control over the results of the research, its president and board of directors do set the general research agenda. Having identified the problems that need to be addressed, the institution then invites specialists in relevant fields to conduct the necessary research and, when the work is done, provides a publishing venue to disseminate the results to the public.

In addition to serving this research function, the institution conducts graduate programs in economics, foreign and domestic policy, and urban issues, among other subjects. It provides facilities for visiting scholars engaged in private research relevant to the institution's own areas of interest. In addition it awards postdoctoral research fellowships to qualified individuals and sponsors advanced study seminar programs, which are open to government officials, business executives, labor leaders, and others.

Research at the institution falls under three general areas of specialization: economics, foreign policy, and government. Within each of these general disciplinary areas, there are a number of individual policy centers devoted to specific topics. Thus the economics policy center is comprised of the Urban Center, which focuses on urban development and the resolution of problems facing the nation's cities, and the Center on Social and Economic Dynamics, which studies such things as demographic change. In foreign policy there is the Center for Northeast Asian Policy Studies and the Center on the U.S. and France. Under government, there is the Brookings Center on Educational Policy and the Center for Public Service.

One important division in the government studies area is the Presidential Appointee Initiative. This center, established in the 1960s, provides guidance, advice, and training for individuals joining government service during the transition from one presidential administration to the next. The goal here is to guarantee the smooth continuity of governmental services and programs.

The institution also operates the Brookings Institution Press, which publishes the results of recent and ongoing research. In addition to books, the press also publishes the highly respected *Brookings Review,* a quarterly newsletter that features articles, written by the staff, dealing with the important policy issues of the day. It also produces several annual papers on educational policy, trade issues, economic activity, financial services, and urban affairs. The Latin American and Caribbean Economic Association, a research center at the institution, publishes *Economia,* a semiannual review of economic policy issues of importance in that region of the world.

Financial Support

The institution supports its activities with an endowment, supplemented by grants from foundations, corporations, and private individuals. In addition, it contracts to undertake research for the government and collects fees for some of its educational programs. It does not accept direct government funding, however, and maintains its independence from governmental control by asserting its right to independently publish its findings, even when the research is done in service to a government contract.

Organization

The institution is run by a board of trustees, which approves research projects and is charged with maintaining the independence of the organization. Heading the board is the institution's president, who acts as chief administrative officer and serves the important roles of fund-raiser and organizational

spokesperson. The actual research is conducted by a professional staff of residential scholars, assisted in their efforts by the contributions of academics and professionals whenever the need arises.

History

In 1916 a group of civic-minded business executives and educators came together to discuss their perception that the day-to-day operation of the government was woefully in need of modernization. They formed the Institute for Government Research (IGR), the first private organization dedicated to research in the field of public policy. The IGR set as its first task the reorganization of the accounting and operational practices used by various government agencies. Their success in this effort earned them the role of adviser to Congress as it drafted accounting and budgeting legislation in the early 1920s.

Over the next few years other groups were formed that shared the IGR's concerns, notably the Institute of Economics (founded in 1922) and the Robert Brookings Graduate School (founded in 1924). In 1927 these two organizations joined forces with IGR to form the Brookings Institution, named for the St. Louis businessman who provided much of the inspiration for the enterprise. Robert Somers Brookings was named first chairperson of the new institution.

Robert Brookings provided more than inspiration and leadership during the institution's early years. Over his lifetime he personally contributed more than $1 million to the enterprise. On his death in 1932, however, his financial support ended, and the institution had to find new funding sources. It began to accept contract work from the government and private organizations, and for the next several years these provided the bulk of its income. Institute research contributed to much of the important legislation and administrative and policy initiatives of the 1930s and 1940s, including the development of the accounting procedures that supported the Social Security Administration, researching the problems of mobilization and manpower needs before the United States' entry into World War II, and the development of the Marshall Plan for European postwar recovery.

In 1952 the institution underwent significant reorganization, during which the three-field division of research into centers for economic, government, and foreign policy studies was developed. Academic specialists were actively recruited, and the institution gained broader public recognition. Throughout the next two decades the institution enjoyed the respect and support of the nation's political leadership, but this relationship broke down during the Nixon administration.

During this time the government began developing its own policy analysis capabilities and the Congressional Office of the Budget was formed, thus eliminating many of the contract opportunities on which the institution had long depended for funding. The institution shifted focus to reflect these changes, expanding its outreach to the general population and increasing its educational programs. By 1995 the Brookings Institution had once again redefined its role, nearly eliminating its contract work with the government and placing greatest emphasis on independent research and educational programs. It remains, however, one of the most highly respected and influential policy think tanks in the nation's capital.

INTERNET RESOURCE

BROOKINGS INSTITUTION. 2002. <www.brookings. edu>.

CHARLES B. SAUNDERS
Revised by
NANCY E. GRATTON

BROUDY, HARRY S. (1905–1998)

Relatively late in a career that spanned seven decades of academic writing and public speaking, Harry S. Broudy became in his time a prominent philosopher of education in the United States. He achieved this status in part by writing and speaking to many audiences about popular educational debates of the day, including the purposes and practices of general education, teacher education, aesthetic education, and democratic education in a post–World War II society.

Broudy was born in Filipowa, Poland, in 1905 and in 1912 came to the United States with his family, settling in Milford, Massachusetts. Broudy attended Massachusetts Institute of Technology before graduating from Boston University in 1929 with a bachelor's degree in Germanic literature and philosophy. At Harvard, where he completed his master's

and doctorate of philosophy degrees, Broudy read Heidegger and Kierkegaard in German and Bergson in French. Studying with William E. Hocking, C. I. Lewis, Alfred North Whitehead, and John Wild, among others, Broudy completed his Ph.D. dissertation, "The Metaphysical Presuppositions of Existence," in 1935.

After a brief period working in the Massachusetts Commonwealth Department of Education, Broudy began his academic career in 1937, teaching the philosophy of education at North Adams State Teachers College. From there he moved to Framingham State Teachers College in 1949, then on to the University of Illinois at Urbana-Champaign in 1957. Although he had already achieved national stature in philosophy of education circles and had become president of the Philosophy of Education Society in 1953, his move to Illinois marked the beginning of a three-decade period in which Broudy's work was embraced by many audiences with a range of educational concerns.

Though he formally retired from the University of Illinois in 1974, Broudy continued teaching, advising students, serving on university committees, and writing. By the time of his last book, *The Uses of Schooling* (1988), Broudy had accepted many invitations to speak on various subjects in education, received three honorary doctoral degrees, had become a member of the National Academy of Education and a fellow of the Center for Advanced Study in Behavioral Sciences at Stanford University, and served as advisory board member and senior faculty member of the Getty Institute for Educators on the Visual Arts. In 1992, the *Journal of Aesthetic Education* devoted an entire issue to Broudy's contributions.

One remarkable feature of this extraordinary record of achievement and prominence is that Broudy accomplished it without aligning himself with successive trends in education or philosophy. When he completed his dissertation on existentialism in 1935, most philosophers of education were engaged in one or another brand of pragmatism. In the 1940s and 1950s, when early-twentieth-century ideas of differentiated curriculum were being solidified into a three-track schooling system that prepared children and youth for different places in American society, Broudy tried to articulate a democratic logic and practice of a common curriculum that was based on a general education for all students. When analytic philosophy began to dominate the fields of philosophy and philosophy of education in the 1960s and

1970s, Broudy's research program remained grounded in a classical realist epistemology and an appeal to what he saw as the logic of democracy.

Democracy demanded, he believed, a common general education for all, based on the academic disciplines, which required different ways of knowing the world and of verifying that knowledge. As Donald Vandenberg put it, "Broudy consistently distinguished between two questions, What is good knowledge? And what is knowledge good for? He relegated the first to specialists in the various disciplines and the second to define his own research program" (p. 7). Broudy's concerns about a common education in a democratic society were reflected throughout his career, beginning with *Building a Philosophy of Education* (1954) and extending through *Democracy and Excellence in American Secondary Education* (with B. Othanel Smith and Joe R. Burnett) (1964), *The Real World of the Public Schools* (1972), *Truth and Credibility: The Citizen's Dilemma* (1981) and *The Uses of Schooling* (1988). *The Uses of Schooling* is a concise, eloquent summation of Broudy's educational thought. It contends that the criteria used in determining and justifying general or liberal studies in schooling are misconceived and misapplied because the full range of the purpose of education in democratic life is not well understood. Understanding the uses of schooling requires attention to not only the usual "replicative" and "applicative" criteria of use, which attend to whether students can replicate and apply what they have learned; but also the "associative" and "interpretive" uses of knowledge as well. These uses require an "allusionary base" of information, understanding, and values, derived from the disciplines that inform experience with ideas that help each person represent predicaments and problems symbolically. Equipping each person with these symbolic tools, Broudy believed, should be an essential aim of schools in a democratic society.

Broudy's regard for the associative and interpretive functions of schooling is also related to other bodies of his considerable authorship. For example, *Aesthetic Education in a Technological Society* (1962) and *Enlightened Cherishing: An Essay in Aesthetic Education* (1972) illustrate how aesthetic studies, like general studies, tend to fall into the "nice, but not necessary" category of curriculum policy formation. Broudy pointed out that aesthetic studies provide the student with associative and interpretive experiences and develop the capacities for interpretation

and informed criticism, as well as a richer vocabulary for self-expression.

Similarly, beginning with *Case Studies for the Foundations of American Education* (1960) and ending with "Case Studies—How and Why," Broudy for much of his career infused his extensive writing on teacher education with a vision of the use of cases in professional preparation. The cases Broudy described were designed for stimulating association, interpretation, and criticism, not simply for replication and application. Broudy believed that, compared to other professions, the absence of widely used case studies in teacher preparation was a considerable limitation on the profession.

It is likely that Broudy would be regarded in the early twenty-first century as a "public intellectual": one who sought to inform the social and educational debates of his day from a scholarly perspective, framed in language accessible to the nonspecialist.

See also: ART EDUCATION, *subentries on* PREPARATION OF TEACHERS, SCHOOL; PHILOSOPHY OF EDUCATION.

BIBLIOGRAPHY

BROUDY, HARRY S. 1961. *Building a Philosophy of Education* (1954), 2nd edition. Englewood Cliffs: Prentice-Hall.

BROUDY, HARRY S. 1988. *The Uses of Schooling.* New York: Routledge.

BROUDY, HARRY S.; PARSONS, MICHAEL J.; SNOOK, IVAN A.; and SZOKE, RONALD D. 1967. *Philosophy of Education: An Organization of Topics and Selected Sources.* Urbana: University of Illinois Press.

BROUDY, HARRY S.; SMITH, B. OTHANEL; and BURNETT, JOE R. 1964. *Democracy and Excellence in American Secondary Education.* Chicago: Rand McNally.

JOURNAL OF AESTHETIC EDUCATION (Special Issue). 1992. "Essays in Honor of Harry S. Broudy." *Journal of Aesthetic Education* 26(4).

MARGONIS, FRANK. 1986. "Harry Broudy's Defense of General Education." M.A. thesis, University of Illinois.

SYKES, GARY, and BIRD, TOM. 1992. "Teacher Education and the Case Idea." In *Review of Research in Education,* ed. Gerald Grant. Washington, DC: American Educational Research Association.

VANDENBERG, DONALD. 1992. "Harry Broudy and Education for a Democratic Society." *Journal of Aesthetic Education* 26(4):5–20.

STEVE TOZER

BUCHANAN, SCOTT (1895–1968)

Scott Milross Buchanan shaped the Great Books program in American higher education as it developed at the People's Institute (New York City), the University of Chicago, and St. John's College (Annapolis, Maryland). A philosopher, critic, author, and educator, Buchanan promoted and experimented with the pursuit of the liberal arts through discussion of classic texts in philosophy, literature, mathematics, physics, astronomy, political science, history, economics, and languages.

Buchanan was born in Sprague, Washington, to William Duncan Buchanan, a medical doctor, and Lillian Bagg Buchanan. Their only child, he moved with his family to Jeffersonville, Vermont, where he spent his boyhood years. His father died in 1902.

Soon after he entered Amherst College in 1912, Buchanan became a devoted follower of its president, Alexander Meiklejohn, an educator nationally noted for his defense of liberal education and his masterful use of Socratic seminar methods. Buchanan's custom-tailored undergraduate curriculum amounted to a triple major in Greek, French, and mathematics. After graduating with a B.A. in 1916, he spent two years as an administrator and an instructor at Amherst before attending Oxford as a Rhodes scholar from 1919 to 1921. There, he met Stringfellow Barr, a Rhodes scholar from Virginia who would become his lifelong friend and his partner in innovative academic endeavors.

Upon returning to the United States, Buchanan married Miriam Damon Thomas, a teacher and social worker. The couple had one child, Douglas Buchanan. Determined to seek further academic study, particularly in philosophy, Buchanan entered Harvard University, where the English mathematician and philosopher Alfred North Whitehead offered him intellectual encouragement. He received his doctorate at Harvard in 1925. His dissertation, a philosophical inquiry into imaginative and scientific possibility, was published in 1927 as *Possibility*.

From 1925 to 1929 Buchanan served as assistant director of the People's Institute, an educational outreach endeavor affiliated with Cooper Union College in New York City. The intent of the institute, founded in 1895 by Columbia University professor Charles Sprague Smith, was to deliver academic and literary lectures that would attract and invigorate a community of both recent immigrants and privileged intellectuals. With Buchanan's help, this popular approach to adult education soon included smaller discussions after and between the lectures and a series of seminars at public library branches. On the advice of Columbia University professor Mortimer Adler, Buchanan incorporated elements of the Columbia Honors Course in Great Books for the library seminar series. The original list of books was adopted from British intellectual Sir John Lubbock who devised it in the 1880s for publication and use in the Workers' and Mechanics' Institute in London.

While lecturing at the People's Institute, Buchanan explored the elements of poetry and mathematics and determined that relationships among the words of poetry and the ratios of mathematics deserved further inquiry. That inquiry became his book *Poetry and Mathematics,* published in 1929, the same year Buchanan accepted a faculty appointment in the philosophy department at the University of Virginia. There, he renewed his friendship with Stringfellow Barr, a professor of history, and worked with a committee on honors courses that pushed unsuccessfully for an emphasis on Great Books during the first two years of honors study. During a year-long leave of absence in England in 1931 through 1932, he studied the work of George and Mary Boole and other mathematicians, publishing his findings about symbols in literature and measurement in *Symbolic Distance in Relation to Analogy and Fiction* (1932).

In 1936 Buchanan and Barr left the University of Virginia at the invitation of Robert Maynard Hutchins, president of the University of Chicago, who was attempting to strengthen the liberal arts program against the wishes of many on his faculty. Buchanan and Barr joined Mortimer Adler and Richard McKeon, who had come to Chicago from Columbia University, and together they formed a Committee on Liberal Arts chaired by Buchanan. Although all four were instrumental in crafting the Great Books program at the University of Chicago, Buchanan worried about some of their philosophical differences. Within a year, he and Barr accepted the challenge of trustees of the barely surviving St.

John's College, Annapolis, Maryland, to revive it as a prominent liberal arts college.

With Buchanan in the position of dean and Barr in the position of president, St. John's quickly became known as an intellectually exciting and innovative institution. Firmly defending the liberal arts, it required all students to read and discuss approximately 100 enduring classic texts of the Western intellectual tradition, from ancient Greece to the twentieth century. Tutors and Socratic seminars were the means to dialogue that illuminated the learning from these texts. The program areas covered included languages, mathematics, science, political science, philosophy, literature, music, and history.

Buchanan quickly became known as a brilliant thinker and teacher, as well as an ardent defender of the liberal arts during a time of increasing vocational education and a proponent of the required curriculum during a time of elective coursework. For him the aim of a liberal education was to spark insight, understanding, and imagination that would result in a disciplined and vibrant intellect prepared for lifelong learning. During his stay at St. John's, Buchanan joined with friends and associates Mark Van Doren, Mortimer Adler, Robert Maynard Hutchins, and others who sought to infuse liberal arts into the public debate about the ends and means of higher education. While at St. John's, he authored *The Doctrine of Signatures: A Defense of Theory in Medicine* (1938).

Buchanan left St. John's in 1947 to pursue a series of endeavors that were personally important to him. For two years, he directed Liberal Arts, Incorporated, in Pittsfield, Massachusetts. From 1948 to 1958, he served as a consultant, trustee, and secretary of the Foundation for World Government; and, during that time, he spent a year as chairman of the Department of Religion and Philosophy at Fisk University, Nashville, Tennessee. He became a founder and senior fellow of the Center for the Study of Democratic Institutions in Santa Barbara, California.

A final manuscript, *Truth in the Sciences*, remained unpublished when Buchanan died in 1968. It was published in 1972.

See also: Higher Education in the United States, **subentry on** Historical Development; St. John's College.

BIBLIOGRAPHY

American Council of Learned Societies. 1988. "Scott Milross Buchanan." In *Dictionary of American Biography,* Sup. 8. New York: Scribners.

Buchanan, Scott. 1975. *Possibility* (1927). Chicago: University of Chicago Press.

Buchanan, Scott. 1975. *Poetry and Mathematics* (1929). Chicago: University of Chicago Press.

Nelson, Charles A., ed. 1995. *Scott Buchanan: A Centennial Appreciation of His Life and Work.* Annapolis, MD: St. John's College Press.

Wofford, Harris, Jr., ed. 1969. *Embers of the World: Scott Buchanan's Conversations with Harris Wofford Jr.* Santa Barbara, CA: Center for the Study of Democratic Institutions.

Katherine C. Reynolds

BUDGETING, PUBLIC SCHOOL

See: Public School Budgeting, Accounting, and Auditing.

BUROS, OSCAR KRISEN (1905–1978)

Founder of the Institute of Mental Measurements, Oscar Krisen Buros produced the first major source of evaluative information on tests and test products. Born at Lake Nebagamon, Wisconsin, he was the fourth oldest of the nine children of Herman and Tone (Tillie) Buros (both immigrants to the United States from Norway). In 1925 he graduated with a B.S. with distinction from the University of Minnesota (Educational Administration and Supervision). He received his M.A. from Teachers College, Columbia University, in 1928. He was a professor of education at Rutgers University from 1929 through 1965. During his tenure at Rutgers University he taught courses in testing and statistical methods in the Department of Educational Psychology.

When he retired from Rutgers University in 1965 he held the title of professor of education and director of the Institute of Mental Measurements. During his career, he was active in several important projects and programs in the field of educational measurement, including the Eight-Year Study, Educational Testing Service Invitational Conference on Testing Problems, and the beginnings of the testing program for the military, where he served as academic examinations officer from 1942 to 1945. He also served as an educational consultant in Africa. From 1956 to 1957 he was a Senior Fulbright Lecturer in Statistics at Makere College, Kampala, Uganda. Then in 1965 to 1967 he held the position of visiting professor at the University College of the University of East Africa, Nairobi, Kenya.

The creation of the Institute of Mental Measurements was Buros's primary contribution to education. Under the auspices of the Institute of Mental Measurements, Buros published, beginning in 1938, critical reviews of commercially available tests. Concerned about the proliferation of tests, and the unsubstantiated claims by their developers about the potential uses of tests in education, psychology, and business, Buros initiated a movement to examine the testing industry and its products. These reviews were published in a series created by Buros called the Mental Measurements Yearbook (MMY). The 1938 yearbook contained reviews of more than 200 tests; over the years, multiple yearbooks have been published (the Fourteenth Mental Measurements Yearbook contains reviews of more than 400 tests). Each yearbook limits its scope to only new or revised, commercially available tests.

Over the history of the Mental Measurements Yearbook series, more than 6,300 tests have been reviewed. These reviews provide essential information to test users about the strengths and weaknesses of testing products, aiding in informed consumer decisions about test products. Buros published a total of eight Mental Measurements Yearbooks during his lifetime. In addition, a new series, called Tests in Print, was started in 1961. Because each Mental Measurements Yearbook only evaluated new and revised commercially available tests, Buros realized that a volume that provided an inventory of all in-print commercially available tests would be useful to test consumers as it would provide a starting place for examining the quality of test products.

In addition, Tests in Print identified which yearbook contained the relevant test reviews. Therefore, a consumer could first refer to the most recent volume in the Tests in Print series (Tests in Print V was published in 1999) to identify possible tests for their use and then refer to the relevant test reviews in the Mental Measurements Yearbook series to gain additional insights into the appropriateness of these tests for their use. The Institute of Mental Measurements started another series in the mid-1960s that collected test reviews by content category, such as personality or reading. Several of these volumes were published by the Institute of Mental Measurements.

Buros received many recognitions and awards for his work in educational testing. These include an award from the Psychometric Society in 1953 for his twenty years of service to users of psychometric techniques; a citation from the American Educational Research Association and the American Psychological Association, also in 1953, for his contributions to measurement; the Educational Testing Services Award for Distinguished Service (1973); and in 1980 a posthumous tribute from the American Educational Research Association and the National Council on Measurement in Education for his high principles of quality and integrity represented in his work and in his life.

A biographical entry of Buros would not be complete without mention of the contributions of his devoted wife, Luella Gubrud Buros. Upon their marriage in 1925, she abandoned a promising career as an artist to become her husband's partner in his crusade to provide candidly critical information about tests and test products. The Institute of Mental Measurements was always strapped for financial resources, and so Luella Buros provided support as typist, administrative assistant, and advertisement consultation; plus, borrowing from her artistic talent, she added an element of elegance to the products through her aesthetic sense of style and design. Upon the death of her husband in 1978, Luella Buros continued her personal and financial support of the Buros Institute of Mental Measurements as the work of Oscar Buros was transferred to the University of Nebraska—Lincoln. In 1994 the Oscar and Luella Buros Center for Testing broadened its focus to finally achieve Buros's dream of extending the critical evaluations of tests beyond commercially available instruments.

See also: TESTING.

BIBLIOGRAPHY

BUROS, OSCAR KRISEN. 1938. *The Nineteen Thirty Eight Mental Measurements Yearbook.* New Brunswick, NJ: Rutgers University Press.

BUROS, OSCAR KRISEN. 1961. *Tests in Print: A Comprehensive Bibliography of Tests In Use In Educa-*

tion, Psychology, and Industry. Highland Park, NJ: Gryphon Press.

PLAKE, BARBARA S.; CONOLEY, JANE C.; KRAMER, JACK J.; and MURPHY, LINDA U. 1991. "The Buros Institute of Mental Measurements: Commitment to the Tradition of Excellence." *Journal of Counseling and Development* 69:449–455.

PLAKE, BARBARA S., and IMPARA, JAMES C., eds. 2001. *The Fourteenth Mental Measurements Yearbook.* Lincoln, NE: Buros Institute of Mental Measurements.

BARBARA S. PLAKE
LINDA L. MURPHY

BUSINESS EDUCATION

SCHOOL
  Tena B. Crews
  Wanda L. Stitt-Gohdes
COLLEGE AND GRADUATE STUDY
  Kwabena Dei Ofori-Attah
PREPARATION OF TEACHERS
  Judith J. Lambrecht

SCHOOL

For many years, *business education* has been defined as the courses at the secondary level that prepare students for the business world. While that definition continued to have validity at the beginning of the twenty-first century, by then the range of the courses had expanded to include preparation for additional study at postsecondary institutions. As business education courses changed over the years, so did the level at which the classes are taught. For example, computer applications courses are often taken at the middle school level and keyboarding may be introduced in the third grade. Secondary level courses include accounting and management, but also branch into technology-based courses such as desktop publishing, multimedia, computerized accounting, and web page design.

The advent of business education in America occurred when the Plymouth Colony hired a school teacher to teach reading, writing, and casting accounts. Casting accounts, the predecessor to accounting, was a subject taught in business arithmetic. Signs of early school-to-work initiatives were evident as students who wanted a commerce or business career left school to work as an apprentice. It should not be surprising, then, that bookkeeping was the earliest business course taught in public schools, being offered in Boston in 1709, in New York City in 1731, and in Philadelphia in 1733.

The founding of Benjamin Franklin's Academy in 1749 was a significant event for business education. The Academy had three departments: the Latin School, the English School, and the Mathematical School. Business subjects offered included "accounts, French, German, and Spanish for merchants; history of commerce; rise of manufacturers; progress and changing seats of trade" (Hosler, p. 3). By 1827 Massachusetts passed legislation requiring municipalities with 500 or more families to establish a high school; Bookkeeping was one of the specific courses that had to be offered. During this time private business colleges opened to meet the increasing demand for well-educated business workers.

Several occurrences in the 1860s hastened the development of business education as an area of study. In 1862 the Morrill Act, more commonly referred to as the land-grant act, gave every state 30,000 acres of land for every congressional representative to establish a college for agricultural, mechanical arts, and business instruction. Also in 1862 shorthand was first offered in public high schools; the first comprehensive high school, which offered both college preparatory and vocational programs of study, was established. Educators generally accept this as the most important contribution to education. Finally, in 1868 Christopher Sholes invented the first practical typewriter. Historically, typewriting and subsequently keyboarding courses frequently encouraged students to enroll in additional business education courses. In the late 1800s John Robert Gregg brought his shorthand system to the United States from Great Britain and "by 1935 it was offered in 96 percent of public high schools teaching shorthand in this country" (Hosler, p. 10).

A turning point regarding business education curriculum occurred in 1946 with the invention of the first electronic computer, ENIAC (Electronic Numerical Integrator and Calculator). As might be expected, the 1960s brought significant change in business education. IBM introduced the first Selectric typewriter in 1961 and the Magnetic Tape Selectric typewriter in 1964. In 1962 the United Business Education Association (UBEA) changed its name to the National Business Education Association (NBEA). In 1963 the Joint Council on Economic Education brought together "over 60 collegiate and secondary school business educators . . . to discuss how economics could be implemented in business courses" (Hosler, p. 23). That same year the National Business Education Association published the first *NBEA Yearbook*. The year 1965 saw the first minicomputer invented and word processing was then offered as a part of the business education curriculum. This marked the beginning of dramatic curricular change in business education.

The 1980s saw an era of standards development and the need for increased accountability. In 1983 the U.S. Department of Education accepted the Standards for Excellence in Business Education, developed by Calfrey C. Calhoun. This was followed in 1985 by *The Unfinished Agenda, The Role of Vocational Education in the High School,* and in 1987 by the *Database of Competencies for Business Curriculum Development, K–14* and the *Business Teacher Education Curriculum Guide.* The National Association of Business Teacher Educators (NABTE) published *Standards for Business Teacher Education* in 1988. All these efforts affected business education curriculum and standards from kindergarten through graduate school.

The Secretary's Commission on Achieving Necessary Skills (SCANS) report, *Learning a Living: A Blueprint for High Performance,* was published in 1992. It provided clear guidelines regarding foundational skills needed for workplace success. This was followed in 1994 by the Goals 2000: Educate America Act. The Goals 2000 Act, as it is often called, codified into law the six original education goals:

1. School readiness
2. School completion
3. Student academic achievement
4. Leadership in math and science
5. Adult literacy
6. Safe and drug-free school

Two new goals were also added to encourage teacher professional development and parental participation. This act also established the National Skills Standards Board to develop voluntary national skill standards.

Federal Legislation

As the nation grew and developed, and the economy changed from agrarian to industrial to technological, a number of factors consistently have influenced funding for educational endeavors. A few of these influences include the economy, society, demographics, and technological advances. Beginning in 1862 with the passage of the Morrill Act, the U.S. government supported vocational education. However, it took nearly one hundred years after the Morrill Act for business education to be brought under the vocational education umbrella. And yet, at the beginning of the twenty-first century, some continue to hold the opinion that business education is not vocational education. However, the following definition of vocational education provided by the 1990 Carl D. Perkins Vocational and Applied Technology Education Act, challenges that perspective: "organized educational programs offering a sequence of courses which are directly related to the preparation of individuals in paid or unpaid employment in current or emerging occupations requiring other than a baccalaureate or advanced degree" (Scott and Sarkees-Wircenski, p. 3). Clearly, business education at both the middle and high school levels falls under this definition. The value and merit of secondary business education programs is their ability to enable a student to pursue a program of study, graduate, and successfully move into the workforce or postsecondary education.

The Smith-Hughes Act of 1917, also known as the Vocational Act of 1917, promoted the vocational education programs of agriculture, trade and industry, and home economics. Key elements of this legislation defined vocational education as "less than college grade, for persons over 14 years of age who desire day time training, and for persons over 16 years of age who seek evening class training" (Scott and Sarkees-Wircenski, p. 122). This legislation also provided funding for teachers' salaries for the three program areas.

With the Vocational Act of 1963, the definition of vocational education was broadened to include "any program designed to fit individuals for gainful employment in business and office occupations" (Scott and Sarkees-Wircenski, p. 130). This was the first piece of federal legislation to specifically include business education. Vocational education funding was amended several times in the 1970s; however, the passage of the Carl D. Perkins Vocational Education Act of 1984 brought with it a stronger emphasis on local control. "The act had two interrelated goals, one economic and one social. The economic goal was to improve the skills of the labor force and prepare adults for job opportunities—a long-standing goal traceable to the Smith-Hughes Act. The social goal was to provide equal opportunities for adults in vocational education" (Scott and Sarkees-Wircenski, p. 145). The 1984 Perkins Act was amended in 1990 and renamed the Carl D. Perkins Vocational and Applied Technology Education Act. This act was significant for two reasons: first, a major goal was increased vocational opportunities for the disadvantaged; and second, funds were authorized for technical preparation (tech-prep) programs. Tech-prep programs are often referred to as 2+2+2, which refers to the articulated agreements between two years of concentrated vocational coursework at the high school level plus two years of advanced technical education at the postsecondary level and the potential for an additional two years of education leading to the baccalaureate degree. An important part of the Perkins legislation was the requirement of implementing state councils on vocational education and the development of long-term state plans for vocational education.

The Goals 2000: Educate America Act of 1994 had as its goal the development of national goals and standards and assistance to states in helping students reach these goals and, in turn, helping them succeed in a technology-based economy and society. A key part of this legislation was the creation of a National Skills Standards Board "to stimulate the development of a voluntary national system of occupation standards and certification" (Scott and Sarkees-Wircenski, p. 156).

"The School-to-Work Opportunities Act (1994) was passed to address the national skills shortage by providing a framework to build a high skilled workforce for our nation's economy through partnerships between educators and employers" (Scott and Sarkees-Wircenski, p. 157). It was hoped the School-to-Work Opportunities Act (STWOA) would encourage the integration of academic and vocational courses, improve career guidance, and include work-based learning, many times in the form of apprenticeships.

In 1998 the Carl D. Perkins Vocational-Technical Education Act was amended. The amendments included more funding at the local level and required an equity coordinator in every state. While business education is specifically included in little federal legislation, the impact of federal legislation is felt in every business education program today. Not only does the funding provide computers for classrooms, more importantly it provides for exploratory courses at the middle school level and career guidance, which helps students imagine opportunities available to them in the world of work and for which business education is a key factor.

Certification

Certification is the process by which an individual becomes licensed to teach in a particular subject area or grade level. All fifty states have various routes to certification; however, common elements include a baccalaureate degree and some competency test. Typical baccalaureate degree programs include a liberal arts core and upper division courses in business education subject matter and professional education, including a teaching internship. In recent years a number of states have moved to using the Praxis II subject-area test in Business Education as the competency test. The advantage of this test for teachers is its mobility, allowing a person to earn a degree in one state and meet certification requirements there, and move to another state and already have met its certification requirements.

Teaching certification is not a lifelong certification. Certificates must be renewed over a period of time, such as every five years. States require a varying number of either graduate credit hours or continuing education units over a specified period of time for teachers to retain for their certification. Typically, colleges and universities use certification guidelines in planning their pre-service teacher preparation programs. These programs are reviewed periodically by the associations that accredit them.

Curriculum

The primary mission of business education is to provide instruction for and about business. In the past, courses such as accounting, data processing, economics, shorthand, typing, basic business, business law, business math, office procedures, and business communication were taught as a part of the business education curriculum. Many of these courses continue to be taught, but the content and technology aspect has changed drastically. Common business education courses now include computerized accounting, business management, business law, economics, entrepreneurship, international business, word processing, desktop publishing, multimedia computer programming, and web page design. Keyboarding is still taught in some business education programs as a separate course or as a four- to six-week part of a semester course in computer applications, but there is a push to teach keyboarding at a much earlier stage in education. Many schools teach keyboarding at the middle school level and some offer keyboarding as early as the third grade.

Historically, curriculum was developed on a course-by-course basis; and the courses were seen as separate entities. Today a much more integrated approach is taken to ensure business skills at many levels throughout the curriculum. National standards have been incorporated into business education in the United States. In 1995 the National Business Education Association revised existing standards that were developed around specific courses offered. The revised standards centered around twelve topical areas: accounting, business law, career development, communications, computations, economics, personal finance, entrepreneurship, information systems, international business, management, marketing, and interrelationships of business. In 1995 the NBEA determined the following standards that exemplify what America's students should know and be able to do in business:

1. Function as economically literate citizens through the development of personal consumer economic skills, a knowledge of social and government responsibility, and an understanding of business operations.

2. Demonstrate interpersonal, teamwork, and leadership skills necessary to function in multicultural business settings.

3. Develop career awareness and related skills to enable them to make viable career choices and become employable in a variety of business careers.

4. Select and apply the tools of technology as they relate to personal and business decision making.

5. Communicate effectively as writers, listeners, and speakers in social and business settings.

6. Use accounting procedures to make decisions about planning, organizing, and allocating resources.

7. Apply the principles of law in personal and business settings.

8. Prepare to become entrepreneurs by drawing from their general understanding of all aspects of business.

9. Understand the interrelationships of different functional areas of business and the impact of one component on another.

10. Develop the ability to participate in business transactions in both the domestic and international arenas.

11. Develop the ability to market the assets each individual has whether they be in the labor market or in the consumer goods market.

12. Manage data from all of the functional areas of business needed to make wise management decisions.

13. Utilize analytical tools needed to understand and make reasoned decisions about economic issues—both personal and societal.

The NBEA standards were developed by business educators at every level and are revised periodically. They were also developed with the belief that business education courses are designed for all students who need a general understanding of the role of business and its role in the economy.

The curriculum has developed into a critical-thinking curriculum with software applications combined. The students create real-world projects and are being taught about the "business of business" and not just simply how to create an accounting spreadsheet or use a word-processing software package. Topics such as ethics, diversity in today's society, global society, online learning, and emerging technology are also incorporated into the curriculum.

Work-experience programs are also a viable part of the business education curriculum. States have implemented different regulations, but many states have Cooperative Business Education (CBE) and/or apprenticeship programs associated with business education. Normally a course or courses are associated with the work-experience program, and students are given a specific amount of release time from school to work.

The connection between school and work has always been an important part of business education. These programs give the students the opportunity to gain hands-on experience in a real-world setting. It also gives them the opportunity to increase necessary business skills and connect their classroom knowledge to the business environment.

Student Organizations

Business education students have two student organizations from which to choose: Future Business Leaders of America (FBLA) and Business Professionals of America. In 1942 the National Council for Business Education sponsored the first FBLA chapter in Johnson City, Tennessee. Four years later the sponsorship was transferred to the then UBEA, now NBEA. In 1969 FBLA became an independent association. In 1958 Phi Beta Lambda, a collegiate division of FBLA was organized. Scott and Sarkees-Wircenski stated the purpose of FBLA-PBL is "to provide . . . opportunities for students in business and office education to develop vocational and career supportive competencies, and to promote civic and personal responsibilities" (p. 188).

International Business Education

The International Society for Business Education (ISBE) is an organization for anyone interested in international business education. Membership includes teachers, trainers, and administrators; however, collective memberships are also available to organizations, such as educational institutions, governmental and other agencies, industry, trade unions, and employers' associations. ISBE was founded in 1901 in Zurich, Switzerland. Approximately twenty countries worldwide have membership in ISBE. Groups from Eastern Europe, the Far East, Central and South America, and Africa are expected to join in the near future.

Trends

Educational environments experience continuous change and business education is no exception. Although it is clear that technology is an integral part of business education in the early twenty-first century at every level, a continuing question revolves around the appropriate use of technology: Does it drive the curriculum or should it be viewed as one tool in the curriculum toolbox? Distance learning and online learning are trends in the delivery systems. Providing educational excellence in a multifaceted technological environment is a huge challenge. Accountability for the education of students results in a careful approach to many areas in education and technological applications are no exception. As business changes, business education must continue to change to keep up with the needs of business.

Certification in many areas such as Microsoft Office User Specialist (MOUS), A++ (the name of the certification for networking), Certified Novell Administrator (CNA), and many others are also being considered at the secondary level. Some

courses are being designed so that the students will either become certified by the end of the course or be given the information to obtain certification on their own at the end of the course. Certification is obtained from an accrediting organization and may involve taking a test, depending on the type of certification.

Challenges

The shortage of business education teachers is definitely an additional challenge. Alternative certification processes are being developed in many areas of the country to address this shortage. Incentives such as scholarships or grants are also being allocated to encourage adults to choose business education as a major at the postsecondary level.

The ever-changing role of technology continues to be a challenge for all educators, but especially business educators. Business education teachers are constantly required to update their software and hardware skills as well as learn new technologically-based information. The incorporation of this new knowledge and the constant maintenance and updating of hardware is a real challenge for business educators.

Future Directions

Students may choose to take business education courses for a variety of reasons, such as learning about business, updating technology skills, and exploring career options. No matter what their reason, it is necessary for the business educators to provide those students with the skills to become productive and active members of society.

See also: EXPERIENTIAL EDUCATION; VOCATIONAL AND TECHNICAL EDUCATION, *subentries on* HISTORY OF, TRENDS.

BIBLIOGRAPHY

HOSLER, MARY MARGARET, ed. 2000. *A Chronology of Business Education in the United States 1635—2000.* Reston, VA: National Business Education Association.

LYNCH, RICHARD L. 1996. "Principles of Vocational and Technical Teacher Education." In *Beyond Tradition: Preparing the Teachers of Tomorrow's Workforce,* eds. Nancy K. Hartley and Tim L. Wentling. Columbia, MO: University Council for Vocational Education.

Nanassy, Louis C.; Malsbary, Dean R.; and Tonne, Herbert A. 1977. *Principles and Trends in Business Education.* Indianapolis: Bobbs-Merrill.

National Business Education Association. 1995. *National Business Education Standards.* Reston, VA: National Business Education Association.

National Business Education Association. 1999. *The Twenty-First Century: Meeting The Challenges to Business Education.* Reston, VA: National Business Education Association

Schrag, Adele F., and Poland, Robert P. 1987. *A System for Teaching Business Education,* 2nd edition. New York: McGraw-Hill.

Scott, John L., and Sarkees-Wircenski, Michele. 1996. *Overview of Vocational and Applied Technology Education.* Homewood, IL: American Technical.

INTERNET RESOURCE

International Society for Business Education. 2002. <www.siec-isbe.org>.

Tena B. Crews
Wanda L. Stitt-Gohdes

COLLEGE AND GRADUATE STUDY

More than 4,000 educational institutions in the United States offer undergraduate and graduate degrees in business. These institutions include two-year private and public colleges, four-year colleges, and graduate schools. A business school may be set up as a college or school within a university; in other cases, it may be a department within a two-year or a four-year educational institution such as a polytechnic. A degree in business is very popular in the United States because it gives the holder a specialized skill highly valued by the commercial, business, and industrial world. The types of degrees offered by business schools in the United States include associate, bachelors, certificate, diploma, masters, and doctoral degrees.

Degrees

A diploma degree usually is awarded after completion of a short-term course, lasting anywhere from eight to twelve months, and is designed for students who need basic or advanced skills for employment in business administration, management, or accounting. A diploma degree may also be an essential step for students who may later choose advanced studies in business. Business schools award diplomat degrees in areas such as marketing, accounting, management, finance, or office practice.

The associate in science (A.S.) or associate in arts (A.A.) in business administration degrees are generally two-year programs offered by for-profit schools or two-year community colleges in the United States. Most students who plan to enter the business job market soon after their studies enroll in associate degree programs. These programs also prepare students for their bachelor's degree in business. In many cases, the only requirement for a student who holds the associate degree in business studies and wishes to obtain the baccalaureate or bachelor's degree is to complete two years of further studies in a preferred area in business such as accounting, finance, or marketing. Many institutions such as Kaplan College, Hickey College, Allentown Business School, and Gibbs College also offer associate, certificate, or diploma degrees in business.

In the United States, as elsewhere in the world, business schools offer programs leading to the award of a bachelor of science (B.S.) and bachelor of arts (B.A.) degrees. A student working on the baccalaureate degree in business may obtain a B.S. degree in several areas including accounting, economics, finance and investments, management, and marketing. A student pursuing the B.A. degree in business may complete concentrated courses in business administration such as marketing, management, or accounting and study several areas in the social sciences. The baccalaureate program in business prepares students to work in several areas in business. It also prepares students for further studies in business at the graduate level.

Business schools in the United States also offer degrees in graduate studies. These degrees include master of science (M.S.) or master of accountancy (M.Acc.), executive master of business administration (E.M.B.A.), doctoral (Ph.D.) programs, and other professional certificate programs such as certified public accountant (C.P.A.). The master of accountancy (M.Acc.) is a program that attracts students who want to be corporate accountants. The M.S. degree is conferred on students who focus their studies on a particular subject area in business such as accounting, marketing, finance, banking, international business, or taxation.

The master of business administration (M.B.A.) is generally a two-year program, although it may be shorter in some business schools. Part-time students may take as many as six years to complete it. Students pursuing the M.B.A. degree may specialize in one of several specialized business areas: accounting, economics, finance, banking, computer information systems, marketing, management information systems, international business, health care administration, taxation, and e-commerce.

The master of business administration degree is very popular and in high demand all over the United States and the rest of the world because of the high prestige it confers on people who successfully complete it. It is often perceived as an avenue toward achieving an executive position in business, industry, education, and government. The financial rewards are in most cases very lucrative. These, and other factors like job satisfaction, make the M.B.A. a terminal or the highest degree required for a top position in the field of business for many people.

Several business schools in the United States offer joint degree programs. These degrees are offered in conjunction with other departments within the college or university system or a different educational institution elsewhere. Students pursue these degrees by simultaneously enrolling in the two programs that are of interest to them. A student may pursue a joint graduate degree in one of the following combinations: law and business (J.D./M.B.A.), medicine and business (M.D./M.B.A.), public policy studies and business (M.P.P./M.B.A.), social services administration and business (A.M./M.B.A.), master of science in accounting and business administration (M.S/M.B.A.), master of engineering management and business administration (M.Eng. Mgt./M.B.A.).

Business schools in the United States have designed several executive educational programs for people who do not want to quit their job for full-time studies in business. These programs are designed to be equivalent to a master's degree. These degrees are awarded in several areas after several credit hours of college work in business. The executive programs may lead to the award of the executive master of science in finance (E.M.S.F.), executive master of business administration (E.M.B.A.), international executive of master of business administration (I.E.M.B.A.), global executive master of business administration (G.E.M.B.A), and executive master of international business (E.M.I.B). Students who enroll in these programs usually work inten-

sively on weekends to complete the program within two years.

A certificate of advanced graduate studies (C.A.G.S.) or post–master's certificate (P.M.C.) in business administration is designed for graduate students who want to acquire special skills or update their business skills. A student may obtain a business certificate in financial planning, business management, business administration, business microcomputing, accounting, or marketing.

The Chicago School of Business within the University of Chicago in 1920 set up the first doctoral program (Ph.D.) in business administration in the United States. The doctor of business administration (D.B.A.) is the highest degree in business studies. Because a master's degree in business is often the only degree needed for gainful employment, few business schools offer doctoral programs in business studies. These include Baruch College, City University of New York; The Carroll School of Management, Boston College; Graduate School of Business and Behavioral Science, Clemson University; Columbia Business School, Columbia University; and John Molson School of Business, Concordia University. Other educational institutions that have doctoral programs in business include Johnson Graduate School of Management, Cornell University; College of Business, Florida State University; Fisher College of Business, Ohio State University; DuPree School of Management, Georgia Institute of Technology; Pamplin College of Business, Virginia Tech University; and Stanford Graduate School of Business, Stanford University.

Students pursuing the Ph.D. in business generally study for about five years after a master's degree program. Areas of specialization for the Ph.D. program in business include finance, marketing, accounting, business economics, organizational behavior, and human management, or business administration. Many people who hold Ph.D.s in business become college or university professors, business consultants, or research fellows.

Admission to Business School

Admission requirements for business studies vary from program to program and from institution to institution. Students seeking a certificate, diploma, or associate degree have few requirements to meet. The requirements may include a high school transcript, General Educational Development (G.E.D.)

test scores, ability to speak and write English, completion of self-assessment form, and a personal interview. For a certificate of advanced graduate studies (C.A.G.S), a graduate degree in the area of interest or a closely related area is required. Many of the two-year community colleges have an open door policy for admission, which makes it possible for a student who is eighteen years old or older to gain an admission. Under this policy, college and university students who have good academic records but decide to enroll in a community college for business education may have not find their A.A. degree a complement to their education.

Students who want to get an undergraduate degree in business have to meet the same admission requirements as other students enrolling for a baccalaureate degree. However, students who desire a B.S. or B.A. degree in business may apply to the business school after completing twenty or more credit hours of college work. In some cases, such students would be expected to have successfully completed several business courses at this time of their college work.

Generally, graduate schools and colleges have higher admission requirements. For the master of business administration (M.B.A.) program, business schools require students to have a baccalaureate degree, and an acceptable score on the Graduate Management Admission Test (GMAT). Indeed, very few business schools do not require a GMAT score. Other admission requirements include college transcripts showing acceptable grade point average (GPA), recommendation letters, resume, essays, and interview. Students applying for the executive master's degree in business such as executive master of business administration (E.M.B.A.) must also have seven or more years of professional work experience. Students applying for admission to complete a joint degree program must meet the admission requirements of all the departments or schools concerned. For instance, a student who wants a joint degree in law (J.D.) and business (M.B.A.) must meet the admission requirements of both the law school and business school. This means the student must obtain appropriate test scores on both the GMAT and the Law School Admission Test (LSAT).

The admission requirements for doctoral studies in business are similar to the requirements for a graduate degree. Emphasis is however, placed on essays written by the student, academic background and performance, research interest and potential, prior exposure to academic research, and the strength of recommendation letters.

See also: CURRICULUM, HIGHER EDUCATION; GRADUATE SCHOOL TRAINING.

BIBLIOGRAPHY

ETHERIDGE, HARLAN L.; HSU, KATHY H. Y.; and WILSON, THOMAS E., JR. 2001. "E-Business Education at AACSB-Affiliated Business Schools: A Survey of Programs and Curricula." *Journal of Education for Business* 76(6):328–331.

GILBERT, NIDDA. 2001. *Complete Book of Business Schools.* New York: Random House.

MERRIT, JENNIFER. 2001. "MBAs for Executives: The Top 25 Schools." *Business Week* October 15: 77–81.

PETERSON'S GUIDE INC. 2001. *Graduate Programs in Business, Education, Health, Information Studies, Law, and Social Work.* Princeton, NJ: Peterson's Guide Inc.

SNYDER, THOMAS D., and HOFFMAN, CHARLENE M. 2002. *Digest of Education Statistics, 2001.* NCES 2002-130. Washington, DC: National Center for Education Statistics.

ZOLLINGER, RICHARD, K., and PATTERSON, JUDITH F. 1991. "The International Business Education Program at Central Piedmont Community College." In *A Global Look at Business Education,* ed. Lonnie Echternacht. Reston, VA. National Business Education Association.

KWABENA DEI OFORI-ATTAH

PREPARATION OF TEACHERS

A person planning to teach business subjects in the twenty-first century faces a wide array of possibilities regarding the students, subject areas, school levels, and sites at which business subjects are taught. The routes to certification and licensure are equally diverse. The challenge in business teacher education is to provide viable paths for professional development and growth in settings that often require diverse technical skills and teaching competencies.

Business education as a field is part of two worlds that are sometimes viewed separately because of funding and licensing requirements. Business education is provided to meet both general education, and career and technical education needs. General education can further be divided between personal-use business skills and preparation for advanced study in business—two different types of goals. Calhoun and Robinson summarized these goals in 1995:

- Specialized instruction to prepare students for careers in business.

- Fundamental instruction to help students to assume their economic roles as consumers, workers, and citizens.

- Background instruction to assist students in preparing for professional careers requiring advanced study.

Several statements from the Policies Commission for Business and Economic Education (1997, 1998, 1999) note that business education represents a broad and diverse discipline (perhaps *field of study* is a better term) that is included in all types of educational delivery systems: elementary and secondary schools, one- and two-year schools and community colleges, and four-year colleges and universities. For many business teachers, a new and growing site for work is providing training or human resource development services in industry. Business education can begin at any level; it can be interrupted for varying periods of time; and it will very likely be continued throughout the life of an individual. Business education includes education for administrative support occupations, marketing and sales occupations, information technology occupations, business teaching, business administration, and economic understandings. At the secondary level of education, business courses are generally electives for students.

History of Business Teacher Education

The earliest teaching of business subjects in public grammar and secondary school dates back to the 1700s with the study of bookkeeping. Programs in private academies soon became popular in public high schools, especially for students who were not preparing for college. In the 1800s private business schools were also a large source of business preparation, and commercial teachers, as they were called, often were recruited from business colleges. The first collegiate institute to offer a program of preparation for business teachers was Drexel Institute in Philadelphia in 1898. One- and two-year normal schools came into existence in the early 1900s. From these informal to more formal preparation programs, two requirements were essential to ensure professional

competency in business teacher education: on-the-job experience and attendance at a university or teacher's college. These two prevailing requirements continue in the early twenty-first century.

The purposes of business teacher education coincide with the general breadth of the field and the dual objectives of employment-related and general education. Sources of funding for education have affected how business teachers are licensed. Since passage of federal vocational legislation in the early 1900s, such as the Smith-Hughes Act in 1917, the George-Deen Act of 1937, and the George-Barden Act of 1946, up through the Vocational Education Act of 1963 and the Tech-Prep and School-to-Work legislation of 1990, 1994, and 1998, teaching licensure, as provided by the various states, is generally of two types: (1) standard licensure for teaching in the secondary schools; and (2) career and technical licensure for teaching in programs reimbursed by state and federal career and technical education funds. Career and technical education programs and their corresponding licensing requirements can exist at either the secondary or postsecondary levels. Initial standard licensing in the past has generally required the completion of an undergraduate program. This is changing for those programs that have moved or are now moving to a postbaccalaureate degree requirement for standard, initial licensure. Postbaccalaureate- or graduate-level licensing is particularly attractive to persons who already possess a bachelor's degree in business and then decide they would like to enter teaching.

Work experience has been considered an essential part of business teacher preparation. It is frequently required for a career and technical education license. However, work experience is not generally required for graduation from business teacher education programs. Opinions about the value of work experience are mixed. Teachers value their business work experience and believe it gives them confidence in their teaching, but John Burrow and Nancy Groneman found in 1976 that the amount or frequency of related work experience of business teachers has not been shown to result in greater teaching effectiveness.

Professional Development for Business Teachers

In addition to initial licensing, business teacher education has been a provider of in-service teacher education and graduate coursework for the completion of advanced degrees. Provision of professional development opportunities is the responsibility not only of colleges and universities that provide formal coursework, but also of professional organizations in the field. Although business teachers participate in a wide variety of business professional groups, three can be said to have a key interest in teacher preparation: National Business Education Association (NBEA, founded in 1878), National Association for Business Teacher Education (NABTE, founded in 1927), and Delta Pi Epsilon, the graduate research-focused society of the profession (DPE, founded in 1936). NBEA and NABTE, respectively, are responsible for developing the *National Standards for Business Education,* which have directed curriculum development in the field at the K–14 grade levels, and *Business Teacher Education Curriculum Guide and Program Standards* for programs that prepare business teachers.

Trends in Business Teacher Education

There was a gradual and consistent increase in the number of business teacher education programs from the 1940s through the 1970s. Augmented funding from federal and state vocational legislation may have contributed to this. However, since 1980 several trends have been a source of concern: the shrinkage in the number of programs preparing business teachers in a time of teacher shortages; program responses to technological change; maintaining balance in business program offerings; and the use of technology as a form of distance learning.

In 2001 NABTE found that there were 124 institutions in the United States providing business teacher preparation by offering at least a bachelor's degree that meets the requirements of a "comprehensive" teaching license, or a license to teach the broadest range of business courses at the secondary level. This total of 124 programs compares to a high of 305 programs in 1980, an almost 60 percent loss of programs. A critical issue has been to understand reasons for program eliminations. Perhaps, when funds are being retrenched, teacher preparation program for courses that are generally electives at the secondary level are easier to eliminate than others. Retrenchment has been common as states have reduced or failed to increase funding to public universities.

This downward trend in program availability might justify the continued expectation of a business teacher shortage in the early 2000s. Because the demand for business teachers, in particular, parallels the demand for entry-level business employees, and the information technology area continues to be one of growth, a shortage of business teachers is a reasonable projection. Several states and professional organizations have implemented or are discussing alternative ways for teachers to become licensed more quickly than a four-year degree generally allows.

A major preoccupation of all business teachers is maintaining up-to-date programs with regard to information-processing technology. Demand in the workplace for employees in information technology jobs has made the provision of technical courses increasingly popular among students. Courses range from personal-use applications of personal computers through the preparation of employees to manage telecommunication networks.

As the demand for information technology courses increases, questions are also being raised about the too-early specialization of high school students for rapidly changing employment expectations. Further, interest in technical courses and technical certifications at either the secondary or postsecondary levels tends to reduce student time for other business courses and nonbusiness general education course work. Lack of more breadth may not only limited students' ability to understand business operations and the place of technology for meeting business needs, but it may also prevent broader understanding about the world and the diversity of options available for many life choices. Maintaining balanced curriculum choices for students is a challenge.

Not only must teachers be prepared to teach using current information-processing technology, programs themselves may be offered using telecommunications technology. Distance learning—the offering of selected courses or complete teacher-preparation programs over the Internet—is being viewed as one way to address a variety of challenges: the need to take full advantage of technology capabilities to serve the profession, the need to provide professional development opportunities for current teachers, and a way to counter the shrinkage of available teacher preparation programs for students across the country.

The ability to use technology to give students access to resources and allow communication with multiple groups of people makes telecommunications capabilities the new fad of the early twenty-first century. Too little is known about the outcomes of programs offered in part or in total by distance learning to be able to judge their quality. It is not known whether such new ventures broaden educational opportunities for under-served groups of people, or whether learning at a distance compromises learners' chances to actually become part of professional communities of teachers. Business teachers are not alone in experimenting with these new possibilities and their associated costs and risks.

Future Directions

Business teacher preparation continues to maintain a historical commitment to preparing teachers who have two basic goals: preparing students both for employment and for economic citizenship. They teach from the elementary, middle, and secondary school levels through the collegiate level in both public education and private training settings. Over the past two centuries, teacher preparation has progressed from informal on-the-job learning through four-year-degree and graduate-level licensing programs. Forces moving toward higher licensing standards are currently being countered by a shortage of teachers, which tends to create pressure to reduce licensing requirements. Nevertheless, changing technological capabilities require all business teachers to become responsible for doing more in the classroom as they teach about technology as a business tool as well as consider using technology as a teaching aid. Technology appears to be both part of a problem and part of the solution. It continually makes new demands on teachers' time and capabilities at the same time that, in the form of distance learning, it makes business teacher education opportunities available to more people when the number of traditional, campus-bound programs has been shrinking.

See also: NATIONAL BUSINESS EDUCATION ASSOCIATION; VOCATIONAL AND TECHNICAL EDUCATION, *subentries on* HISTORY OF, PREPARATION OF TEACHERS, CURRENT TRENDS.

BIBLIOGRAPHY

ANDERSON, MARCIA A., and SINHA, RATNA. 1999. "Business Teaching as a Career in the United States." *NABTE Review* 26:28–33.

BURROW, JOHN, and GRONEMAN, NANCY. 1976. *The Purposes of and Competencies Developed Through Occupational Experience for Vocational Education Teachers.* Lincoln: University of Nebraska.

BARTHOLOME, LLOYD W. 1997. "Historical Perspectives: Basis for Change in Business Education." In *The Changing Dimensions of Business Education,* eds. Clarice P. Brantley and Bobbye J. Davis. Reston, VA: National Business Education Association.

CALHOUN, CALFREY C., and ROBINSON, BETTY W. 1995. *Managing the Learning Process in Business Education.* Birmingham, AL: Colonial Press.

CURRAN, MICHAEL G., JR. 1996. "Business Education in the United States: 1993–1994 NABTE Survey Results." *NABTE Review* 23:3–7.

HOPKINS, CHARLES R. 1987. "Business Education in the United States: 1985–1986 NABTE Survey Results." *NABTE Review* 14:24–34.

HOSLER, RUSSELL J., and HOSLER, MARY MARGARET. 1993. *The History of the National Business Education Association.* Reston, VA: National Business Education Association.

LABONTY, DENNIS J. 1999. "Business Education in the United States: 1997–1998 NABTE Survey Results." *NABTE Review* 26:9–17.

MEGGISON, PETER F. 1989. "Business Education in Years Gone By." In *Asserting and Reasserting the Role of Business Education,* ed. Burton S. Kaliski. Reston, VA: National Business Education Association.

MCENTEE, ARTHUR L. 1997. "Business Education in the United States: 1995–1996 NABTE Survey Results." *NABTE Review* 24:4–7.

NATIONAL ASSOCIATION FOR BUSINESS TEACHER EDUCATION. 1997. *Business Teacher Education Curriculum Guide and Program Standards.* Reston, VA: National Association for Business Teacher Education.

NATIONAL BUSINESS EDUCATION ASSOCIATION. 1995. *National Standards for Business Education.* Reston, VA: National Business Education Association.

O'NEIL, SHARON LUND. 1993. "Business Education in the United States: 1991–1992 NABTE Survey Results." *NABTE Review* 20:5–15.

POLICIES COMMISSION FOR BUSINESS AND ECONOMIC EDUCATION. 1997. *Policy Statement 60: This We Believe About the Professional Development of Business Educators.* Reston, VA: Policies Commission for Business and Economic Education.

POLICIES COMMISSION FOR BUSINESS AND ECONOMIC EDUCATION. 1998. *Policy Statement 63: This*

We Believe About the Relationship Between Business Education and Students' Transition to Work. Reston, VA: Policies Commission for Business and Economic Education.

POLICIES COMMISSION FOR BUSINESS AND ECONOMIC EDUCATION. 1999. *Policy Statement 64: This We Believe About the Role of Business Education at All Educational Levels.* Reston, VA: Policies Commission for Business and Economic Education.

POLICIES COMMISSION FOR BUSINESS AND ECONOMIC EDUCATION. 1999. *Policy Statement 65: This We Believe About Distance Learning in Business Education.* Reston, VA: Policies Commission for Business and Economic Education.

REDMANN, DONNA H.; KOTRLIK, JOE W.; HARRISON, BETTY C.; and HANDLEY, CYNTHIA S. 1999. "Analysis of Secondary Business Teachers' Information Technology Needs with Implications for Teacher Education." *NABTE Review* 26:40–45.

JUDITH J. LAMBRECHT

BUSINESS INVOLVEMENT IN EDUCATION

The focus of this entry is on business involvement in influencing state and federal elementary and secondary education policy since 1983, the year the landmark report, *A Nation at Risk: The Imperative for Educational Reform,* was released.

A Nation at Risk

No education report in U.S. history has galvanized national attention like *A Nation at Risk* did when banner headlines in newspapers across the country declared that "a rising tide of mediocrity" threatened not only U.S. schools, but also its democratic institutions. In thirty-six short pages, it starkly declared, "If an unfriendly foreign power had attempted to impose on America the mediocre educational performance that exists today, we might well have viewed it as an act of war." The words rang true for many business leaders who not only were facing an economic downturn, but also growing international competition. They recognized that the U.S. economy demanded a fundamental transition to an emerging information age that relies on a workforce with ever-increasing skills and knowledge.

After the release of the report, governors and other state leaders established blue ribbon commissions in many states that included prominent business and civic leaders. The 1984 Perot Commission in Texas is one of the best-known examples of post-*Nation at Risk* models for business involvement in state education policy. However, in most states, these business-led commissions were short-lived; they disbanded after their recommendations were enacted into law.

Partnerships with Business

Through the 1980s, school-business partnerships formed the core of business involvement in education. By the end of the decade, many business leaders were expressing dissatisfaction with these local partnerships as little more than "feel good" projects that had few measurable or lasting results.

There was a marked shift in business involvement beginning in 1989 and continuing into the early twenty-first century. In 1989 President George Bush met with the chief executive officers of the Business Roundtable (BRT), an organization of chief executive officers from leading American companies that focuses on public policy issues that affect the economy. The president challenged the business leaders to commit personal time and company resources to improving elementary and secondary education in the United States. That same year, the president and state governors met in Charlottesville, Virginia, for the first National Education Summit and agreed to set National Education Goals to be achieved by the year 2000.

The Business Roundtable accepted the president's challenge. CEOs agreed that schools were preparing too few students to meet world standards in core academic subjects, and too many students were leaving school unprepared for productive work and effective citizenship. After considering different leverage points for change and assessing where CEOs of large U.S. corporations could most effectively improve U.S. education performance, members of the BRT decided to concentrate their efforts at the state level. Under the U.S. Constitution, states have primary responsibility for education.

State policy. In 1990 the CEOs made a ten-year commitment and adopted a state policy agenda to improve student achievement that was undergirded by the fundamental belief—revolutionary at the time—that all children can and must learn at higher levels. The changing economy demanded that all students obtain skills and knowledge once required only by those at the top. The policy agenda, refined over the decade, includes nine essential components of a successful education system: standards, assessments, accountability, professional development, school autonomy, technology, learning readiness, parent involvement, and safety and discipline. It was viewed as a coherent whole, with each of the essential elements aligned to high standards that articulate what all students need to know and be able to do to succeed in school, at work, and in life. It was not an a la carte menu.

State coalitions. In addition to adopting a state policy agenda, the BRT also asked business leaders to promote education reform in at least one state where the company had a significant employee presence. Companies were asked to join or create a state coalition to advocate these changes in the state capitol. The basic strategy was to encourage companies to shift from the "adopt-a-school" approach to an "adopt-a-state" model of partnership. The organizational structures and membership of these coalitions differ, and a variety of models have proven to be effective, depending on state-specific situations. In some states, CEOs turned to the state business roundtable of business council. In other states, CEOs created a new state business organization, an umbrella group of business organizations and companies, or a business–education coalition that includes business and education leaders. Some of these coalitions also include government and civic leaders. A few states have several state coalitions, each with a unique niche for business involvement. Today, forty-three states have state-level coalitions that provide a vehicle for business leaders to influence state education policy.

Standards-Based Reform

Throughout the 1990s this state policy agenda, which became known as standards-based reform, emerged as the leading reform strategy, with a primary focus on standards, assessment, and accountability. Other national business groups such as the National Alliance of Business and the Committee for Economic Development issued publications and policy statements that embraced this approach. It was complemented by a U.S. Department of Labor Commission, the Secretary's Commission on Achieving Necessary Skills (SCANS), that detailed the core competencies required in the modern work-

place. Business leaders were instrumental in sustaining this agenda as elected and appointed officials turned over in each state. With President Clinton's election in 1992, the business community backed two federal initiatives that were passed by Congress—Goals 2000: The Educate America Act, and the School to Work Opportunities Act—and one that failed to win support—the call for a voluntary national test.

At the state level, the standards movement hit a rocky period in the mid-1990s as opposition to outcomes-based education and national standards spread like wildfire across the country, largely fueled by conservative groups, but also striking a nerve with many parents who were concerned that many states' standards were "fuzzy," value-laden, and not measurable. Concerned that this opposition might sink the standards movement, governors and CEOs joined together in 1996 to create Achieve, an independent, bipartisan, nonprofit organization to help states benchmark standards and assessment systems, to build partnerships for states to work together, and to serve as a clearinghouse on standards and school reform.

By the end of the 1990s it was clear that the business community's initial ten-year commitment was insufficient. Despite the fact that forty-nine states had developed and strengthened their standards in core academic subjects, and promising progress could be seen in some of the states that had benefited from strong business involvement, far too many students still were not proficient in reading and mathematics, according to the National Assessment of Educational Progress (NAEP). The business community would have to stay the course and remain involved as a permanent partner with educators and policymakers. The need for ongoing business involvement was reinforced by a study of two states that made significant gains on NAEP and other measures during the 1990s—North Carolina and Texas. In both states, researchers found that one of the key factors explaining the gains was the business community's role in developing and sustaining reform. In both states, the business community provided a stable, persistent, and long-term influence on the state's education reform agenda.

Federal Education Policy

With President George W. Bush's election in 2000, a new phase of business involvement emerged. He had seen firsthand the importance of a close working partnership with business leaders on education reform issues as governor of Texas. In January 2001 the president introduced a basic framework for reform, known as *No Child Left Behind,* and asked CEOs to work with him and the Congress to get it passed. Companies and business organizations formed a coalition, the Business Coalition for Excellence in Education (BCEE), and put together a sophisticated lobbying effort that contributed to passage of a strong bill with overwhelming bipartisan support in December 2001.

The business community recognizes that the federal role in education in the United States is limited, with the lion's share of the resources at the state and local levels. However, perhaps more than any other group concerned about public schools, the business community recognizes the national and international context in which education operates. National leadership is needed to address the disturbing achievement gaps between poor students and their more affluent peers, as well as between African-American and Hispanic students and white and Asian students. Business leaders frequently cite the continuing achievement gap between the United States and its international competitors in math and science. Particularly troubling was the finding from the 1996 Third International Mathematics and Science Study (TIMSS) that showed the performance of U.S. students compared to their international peers declines as students progress through school. It is hardly surprising that according to the 2002 results of an annual survey of employers and college professors conducted since 1998 by Public Agenda and *Education Week,* far too many high school graduates continue to be rated "poor" or "fair" on skills such as writing clearly, grammar and spelling, being organized and on time, and basic mathematics.

The No Child Left Behind Act of 2001 included principles for reform advocated by the business community based on experience in promoting higher student achievement at the state level. Business support for this federal legislation went far beyond any previous involvement on federal education issues. CEOs and national business organizations like the National Alliance of Business, National Association of Manufacturers, American Electronics Association, and The Business Roundtable were convinced that the time was right for federal legislation that linked resources and accountability. If properly implemented, it could help accelerate reforms at the state and local levels that were beginning to show results. In part because the legislation requires schools to disaggregate student achievement data by major student subgroups and holds schools accountable for achievement gains by each of these student groups, business leaders and civil rights organizations were among the most passionate advocates for the bill's passage.

Staying the Course

In 1950, 80 percent of all jobs were classified as "unskilled labor," but by 2000, 85 percent of all jobs were classified as "skilled labor." The twin forces of technology and globalization mean that an excellent K–12 education system for all students, the competitiveness of the U.S. workforce, the vibrancy of its communities, and the future of its democracy are connected in ways that have never been clearer. Since the publication of *A Nation at Risk* in 1983, the condition of the economy has fluctuated, causing some critics of business involvement in education to argue that business overstates the connection between the quality of education and the health of the economy. However, despite the ups and downs of the business cycle, there is compelling evidence that higher skilled workers have more opportunities to succeed in the changing workplace.

While other education interest groups may not always agree with the positions taken by the business community on education issues, business is recognized as an effective voice for better schools and respected by political leaders on both sides of the aisle. As governors and other state policymakers vie for companies to locate in their states, they know that the quality of education in the state is a competitive advantage. Business is viewed as a credible advocate for education reform policies because business has an enlightened self-interest in strengthening public education in the United States. Business leaders are a force to be reckoned with in state capitols, and business leaders have helped states stay the course on standards-based reform. After working hard to pass the No Child Left Behind Act of 2001, the business community announced its intention to work closely with states to implement the federal legislation. All evidence points to continued involvement by the business community in helping to shape education policy in the United States.

See also: No Child Left Behind Act of 2001; School Reform; Standards Movement in American Education.

BIBLIOGRAPHY

THE BUSINESS ROUNDTABLE. 1995. *Continuing Commitment: Essential Components of an Educational System.* Washington, DC: The Business Roundtable.

THE BUSINESS ROUNDTABLE. 1999. *Transforming Education Policy: Assessing 10 Years of Progress in the States.* Washington, DC: The Business Roundtable.

FOSLER, R. SCOTT. 1990. *The Business Role in State Education Reform.* Washington, DC: The Business Roundtable.

GOLDBERG, MILTON, and TRAIMAN, SUSAN L. 2001. "Why Business Backs Education Standards." In *Brookings Papers on Education Policy,* ed. Diane Ravitch. Washington, DC: Brookings Institution Press.

GRISSMER, DAVID, and FLANAGAN, ANN. 1998. *Exploring Rapid Achievement Gains in North Carolina and Texas.* Washington, DC: National Education Goals Panel.

HILL, PAUL T., and WARNER, KELLY E. 1994. *A New Architecture for Education Reform.* Washington, DC: The Business Roundtable.

KEARNS, DAVID T., and HARVEY, JAMES. 2000. *A Legacy of Learning: Your Stake in Standards and New Kinds of Public Schools.* Washington, DC: Brookings Institution Press.

NATIONAL COMMISSION ON EXCELLENCE IN EDUCATION. 1983. *A Nation At Risk: The Imperative for Educational Reform.* Washington, DC: U.S. Government Printing Office.

SMITH, NELSON. 1996. *Standards Mean Business.* Washington, DC: National Alliance of Business.

TIMPANE, P. MICHAEL, and McNEILL, LAURIE MILLER. 1990. *Business Impact on Education and Child Development Reform.* Washington, DC: Committee for Economic Development.

U.S. DEPARTMENT OF LABOR. 1992. *Learning a Living: A SCANS Report of America 2000.* Report of the Secretary's Commission on Achieving Necessary Skills. Washington, DC: U.S. Department of Labor.

WADDOCK, SANDRA. 1994. *Business and Education Reform: The Fourth Wave,* Report Number 1091-94-RR. New York: The Conference Board, Inc.

INTERNET RESOURCE

NATIONAL ALLIANCE OF BUSINESS. "Business Coalition for Excellence in Education." <www.nab.com/bcee.htm>.

SUSAN TRAIMAN

BUSING

See: TRANSPORTATION AND SCHOOL BUSING.

BUTLER, NICHOLAS M.
(1862–1947)

President of Columbia University from 1902 to 1945, Nicholas Murray Butler was a prominent figure in the development of the modern American university and of public secondary education.

Born into a religious and politically active middle-class family in Elizabeth, New Jersey, Butler valued public service from an early age. He graduated from Paterson High School in New Jersey at age thirteen. Following independent study, he entered Columbia College in 1878 and began a sixty-nine-year association with that institution.

Early Career

While an undergraduate, Butler gained the attention of Columbia president Frederick A. P. Barnard. Butler considered a political and legal career, however, Barnard convinced him that he could have more impact in the emerging field of professionally directed education. Butler earned an A.B (1882), M.A. (1883) and Ph.D. (1884), all in philosophy, at Columbia, specializing in the writings of the German philosopher Immanuel Kant. He studied for a year at the universities of Berlin and Paris.

In 1885 Butler returned to Columbia as an assistant professor of philosophy. He quickly joined a faculty contingent seeking to expand Columbia College into a European-style graduate university—a vision shared by Barnard and his successor, Seth Low. As Low assumed the presidency in 1890, he asked Butler to outline this proposal to the faculty in a general assembly. The presentation marked Butler as a rising star. Elected dean of the philosophy department, he played significant roles in establishing Columbia's summer school and relocating the university to Morningside Heights on the upper West Side of Manhattan.

During this stage of his career, Butler saw that a professionally guided public school system would be vital to industrial-age America. This system would require competent teacher-training institutions, a professional literature base, separation from politics, and organized associations. When Barnard's plans for a Columbia training school for teachers was thwarted, he persuaded Butler in 1887 to accept the presidency of the Industrial Education Association of New York, which promoted vocational training for working-class children. Butler refocused the aims of the association on teacher training and encouraged it to purchase land adjoining Columbia. By 1893 it had become Teachers College, affiliated with Columbia.

In 1891 Butler founded the *Educational Review,* a journal of educational philosophies and developments. Serving as editor until 1921, Butler invited national educational and political figures to contribute. He also helped transform the National Education Association from an intellectual association into an organization advocating Progressive educational policies. While its president (1894–1895), Butler formed committees to examine the transition of students from school to college. One notable result was the introduction of the College Entrance Examination Board (1900), which standardized college entrance tests and clarified the role of secondary education.

Butler's interest in politics helped to establish professional autonomy for education systems. From 1887 through 1895 he served on the New Jersey State Board of Education. He chaired the Paterson school board from 1892 through 1893. In these roles he led efforts to remove state political interference from local New Jersey school systems. In New York City, he did the same, spurring the creation of a citywide school board that emphasized professionalism and policy over political spoils (1895–1897). When New York City's consolidation was complete, New York State sought a similar reform with Butler's advice, completed in 1904. During this time, Butler established a friendship with Governor Theodore Roosevelt, who nicknamed him "Nicholas Miraculous."

Columbia University

When Low resigned as Columbia's president in 1901, Butler became acting president, and president a year later. During his forty-four-year tenure, Columbia experienced phenomenal growth in enrollment, resources, and prestige. In 1911 Columbia's 7,500 students made it the largest university in the world. By 1914 it had the largest university endowment in America. Adopting a "corporate" model, Butler centralized the administration and ended the faculty's power to make top administrative appointments. He believed faculty should do what they do best—teach and research. His greatest faculty challenge involved academic freedom. Butler believed a faculty member's academic freedom was limited to an area of expertise and extended only to what he termed "university freedom," defined as a university's right to reach its institutional potential. No individual was greater than the university or had the right to harm its reputation. This issue subsided somewhat following World War I, and Butler took pride in the diversity of faculty perspectives and talent. Columbia in this age was often referred to as the "American Acropolis."

Political Career

His friendship with Theodore Roosevelt placed him in the president's inner circle until they disagreed over Roosevelt's antitrust initiatives. In 1913 he opposed Theodore Roosevelt's presidential bid and received Republican electoral votes for the vice presidency. He ran for the presidency on the Republican ticket in 1920, receiving New York's convention votes as "favorite son." He opposed the party's embrace of prohibition, however, and lost clout. His interests shifted toward international issues as American diplomatic influence increased. From 1925 to 1945 he was president of the Carnegie Endowment for International Peace. In 1927 he assisted the U.S. State Department in developing the Kellogg-Briand Pact, which called for disarmament and conscientious objection to war. In 1931 he shared the Nobel Peace Prize with Jane Addams.

See also: HIGHER EDUCATION IN THE UNITED STATES, *subentry on* HISTORICAL DEVELOPMENT; RESEARCH UNIVERSITIES.

BIBLIOGRAPHY

BUTLER, NICHOLAS MURRAY. 1915. *The Meaning of Education.* New York: Scribners.

BUTLER, NICHOLAS MURRAY. 1921. *Scholarship and Service.* New York: Scribners.

BUTLER, NICHOLAS MURRAY. 1939. *Across the Busy Years,* Vols. 1 and 2. New York: Scribners.

MARRIN, ALBERT. 1976. *Nicholas Murray Butler.* Boston: Twayne.

WHITTEMORE, RICHARD. 1970. *Nicholas Murray Butler and Public Education 1862–1911.* New York: Teachers College Press, Columbia University.

BENNETT G. BOGGS

C

CAMPBELL, ROALD F.
(1905–1988)

Born in Ogden, Utah, Roald Fay Campbell was reared on a farm near Aberdeen, Idaho, and first attended Idaho Technical Institute (now Idaho State University) in Pocatello. He took several years off from college to serve as a Mormon missionary in Texas and to teach school, then resumed his undergraduate studies at Brigham Young University.

After graduating from Brigham Young at age twenty-four, Campbell returned to southern Idaho as superintendent of schools in the rural town of Moore and then took a similar post in larger Preston. After four years there, during which he spent his summers earning a master's degree at Brigham Young University, his native curiosity and ambitious instincts prompted him to seek a doctorate and pursue a scholarly career. Campbell was accepted into the doctoral program at Stanford University's School of Education. Over the next six years, he continued to serve as superintendent of schools in Preston while pursuing his studies each summer.

He took a leave of absence from his job during the 1939 to 1940 academic year and began his dissertation study, an inquiry into the relationship between school board members' socioeconomic status and their voting records on educational issues. Stanford awarded Campbell his doctorate in the autumn of 1942. At the same time, he left the Preston school superintendency, and launched his long and successful professorial career.

He accepted a three-faceted appointment at the University of Utah as assistant professor and chair of the Department of Elementary Education, and director of the Wm. M. Stewart School—a laboratory school associated with the teacher education program at the university. Over the next decade, Campbell advanced through the ranks of associate professor and professor, while continuing to dispatch his dual administrative duties. He became a specialist in the emerging scholarly field of educational administration and found his research increasingly gratifying. Wishing to work single-mindedly as a scholar, and to spread his wings beyond the Great Basin, he moved to The Ohio State University as professor of educational administration in 1952. Over the next five years his research and writing about educational leadership was recognized nationally and internationally.

Campbell moved to the University of Chicago in 1957, where he served variously over a thirteen-year period as William C. Reavis Professor of Educational Administration, director of the Midwest Administration Center, chair of the Department of Education, and dean of the Graduate School of Education. These years were clearly the apogee of his career. Under his leadership, the University of Chicago achieved international renown as one of several premier institutions for scholarship in education and school administration. During his Chicago years, Campbell became a charter member of the National Academy of Education and of the board of directors of the University Council for Educational Administration. He served as founding editor of the *Educational Administration Quarterly,* president of the American Educational Research Association (1969–1970), and received may honors and awards. He wrote or coauthored more than a dozen books, many of which were landmarks in his field.

Living in an era that seemed to reduce everything to its parts and every scholar to a specialist, Roald Campbell stood as an exception. His was a lifelong quest to understand, bring together, and refine knowledge that could improve education. He read widely in many fields, studied other cultures, questioned every proposition about education and leadership, and ultimately struck every idea against the touchstone of reality: Could it work to further improve what we know and how we act as educators? His passion to form and integrate ideas was matched by his desire to influence events and institutions. Teacher and mentor to dozens of distinguished scholars and educational leaders throughout North America and the world, Campbell was a professor's professor—admired as much for his humane instincts and reasoned personal qualities as for his enduring professional achievements. To paraphrase Matthew Arnold, he lived life steadily and he lived it whole.

Beginning a remarkable retracing of his life's journey, Campbell returned to Ohio State in 1970 as the first Novice G. Fawcett Professor of Educational Administration. There he launched a massive national study of state policymaking for public education. He also opened a new domain of scholarship for himself and his field—the history of thought and practice in educational leadership. This theme shaped his intellectual activity during the 1970s. He started by assaying the existing state of scholarship and graduate education in educational administration, coauthoring a comprehensive study of professors in his field. From this base, with a group of younger colleagues, he began to explore the historical roots and philosophical underpinnings of educational administration.

In 1974 Campbell retired from the Fawcett Professorship and moved with his wife back to Salt Lake City to be closer to their children and grandchildren. But retirement was not in the cards. The University of Utah named him a distinguished adjunct professor, the first appointment of its kind. Over the next fourteen years he taught a variety of courses in the Department of Educational Leadership, and continued to research and publish at a prolific rate. He devoted enormous time and energy in fostering the growth of younger colleagues. In 1988, while visiting his sister in Aberdeen, Idaho, Campbell died suddenly of heart failure. He was 82. His customary autumn graduate seminar was scheduled to convene a few days later, and he left the course syllabus as well as a complete book manuscript stacked neatly on his University of Utah desk. Roald Fay Campbell was arguably the twentieth century's most influential and respected figure in the scholarly field of educational leadership.

See also: DEWEY, JOHN; IMMIGRANT EDUCATION, *subentries on* INTERNATIONAL, UNITED STATES; MIGRANTS, EDUCATION OF.

BIBLIOGRAPHY

CAMPBELL, ROALD F.; CUNNINGHAM, LUVERN L.; and McPHEE, RODERICK F. 1980. *The Organization and Control of American Schools* (1960), 4th edition. Columbus, OH: Merrill.

CAMPBELL, ROALD F.; FLEMING, THOMAS L.; NEWELL, L. JACKSON; and BENNION, JOHN. 1987. *A History of Thought and Practice in Educational Administration.* New York: Teachers College Press, Columbia University.

CAMPBELL, ROALD F., and MAZZONI, TIM L., JR. 1976. *State Policy Making for Public Schools.* Berkeley: McCutchan.

L. JACKSON NEWELL

CANADA

As in all immigrant societies, the spread of formal education in Canada followed a predictable pattern as religious orders and missions attempted to "civilize" both the aboriginal and the settler communities. All levels of formal education from the seventeenth century onward had their roots in Catholicism, Anglicanism, and after 1763, when the British assumed control, a whole range of protestant denominations. Dramatic change occurred in 1867 with the enactment of the Constitution Act (formerly the British North American Act) when the principle of secular and separate systems of education funded by the state was accepted throughout Canada with a few significant exceptions. Section 98 of the act allocated exclusive jurisdiction for education to the provinces. This division of constitutional powers has remained in place and has been the basis for a degree of tension between the federal government and the ten provincial governments. The federal government is responsible for education in the three northern territories. With regard to public education, Canadians subscribe to three common social and educational values: equality of access, equality of opportunity, and cultural pluralism.

Influences on the Educational Systems

According to Rodney Clifton, Canada is the "only country without a national office of education: all other nations, including all other federated nations, have national offices of education that coordinate and/or administer various aspects of their educational system" (p. 7). While there are many similarities among Canada's systems of education, they have each developed in unique ways. These systems are profoundly influenced by the distribution of the population of 31 million across the vast country, which covers four and one-half time zones. More than 80 percent of Canadians live in urban centers within 100 miles of the border with the United States.

Canadian society has developed as a mosaic of peoples, beginning with aboriginal populations and then followed by French, British, and other European settlement. Canada has two official languages: English is the mother tongue of 61 percent of the population, and French is the mother tongue of 26 percent. Most French speakers live in Quebec, where they make up 82 percent of the population, but there are also many French speakers in New Brunswick, Ontario, and Manitoba. Education is available in both official languages, but to a greater or lesser degree, depending on the region. In the last two decades of the twentieth century, immigrants from all parts of the world were attracted to Canada, with the largest proportion coming from Asia.

The patterns of immigration have had an enormous impact on the structure and organization of educational systems. Although the systems of the western provinces of Manitoba, Saskatchewan, Alberta, and British Columbia followed the patterns laid down in Ontario, more emphasis was placed on meeting the needs of all people, not just Anglicans and Catholics. While "separate" (Catholic) publicly funded schools were resisted in Manitoba, by World War II only British Columbia, out of the ten provinces, maintained a secular system of education. This stance was modified in 1977, when the province began providing subsidy to private and independent schools. In 1998 Newfoundland abandoned denominational education and became the only province with a secular system.

The French tradition and language have dominated educational systems in Quebec and parts of New Brunswick and Manitoba. Since the "Quiet Revolution" in Quebec in the 1960s and the adoption of a bilingual and multicultural policy at the federal level in the 1970s, French culture has become part of all Canadian educational systems. The challenge has been to privilege the "founding" cultures while at the same time recognizing aboriginal peoples and the vast range of other cultures that form Canadian society. The complexities that come with geography, immigration, and settlement gave rise to socialization processes that placed great emphasis on the role of education in molding Canadian citizens.

Twentieth-Century Developments

The "Great Transformation" in Canadian society, as it was dubbed by Karl Polanyi in 1944, is very much a twentieth-century phenomena. Mass public education that was free and compulsory through high school had become the norm by the 1950s. Public education is provided free to all Canadian citizens and permanent residents until the end of secondary school, normally at eighteen. The ages for compulsory schooling vary from one jurisdiction to another, but generally it is required from age six or seven to age sixteen. As the federal government assumed more responsibility for funding university education from the mid-1950s and recognized the importance of human capital, so the systems of higher education expanded. Expansion of the university system and the development of parallel college systems changed the nature of higher education in Canada. By 1976 every province was operating a binary system of universities and colleges, and furthermore the number of universities offering graduate programs had risen to forty-seven from the 1960 level of twenty-eight.

As in other countries of the Organisation for Economic Co-operation and Development (OECD), the baby boom generation flooded into the higher education system in the 1960s and the early 1970s. Enrollment continued to expand into the 1990s, but over the next decade it reached a plateau and then began to decline. Between 1991–1992 and 1999–2000, university full-time enrollment decreased from approximately 580,000 to 540,000, while part-time enrollment fell from 280,000 to 240,000. Between 1992–1993 and 1999–2000, full-time community college enrollment increased from approximately 360,000 to 400,000. Part-time community college enrollment declined from approximately

180,000 to 90,000. Furthermore, the gender balance has been reversed so that women are in the majority at the undergraduate level in both community colleges and universities and at parity with men at the graduate level.

The federal government had, through the incremental development of a science and technology policy, created an elaborate structure for funding and supporting research. In addition to the three national funding councils, which were established in the late 1970s and cover all the disciplines and fields represented in the academy, the government created other programs, such as the Networks of Centres of Excellence, the Canada Foundation for Innovation, and the Canada Research Chairs.

Education in Canada has traditionally been a public enterprise. Private or independent schools educate approximately 5 percent of the school-age population. Although these schools do generally follow the curriculum and diploma requirements of their jurisdiction, they function independently of the public system and charge fees. Five provinces—Alberta, British Columbia, Manitoba, Quebec, and Saskatchewan—provide some form of financial assistance to these schools. Prior to the 1990s, higher education was almost totally a public enterprise. During that decade the number of private institutions offering vocational and degree programs increased dramatically. Four provinces—Alberta, British Columbia, Ontario, and New Brunswick—have passed legislation to allow for the establishment of private universities.

The Place of Education in the Society

As an institutional form, education occupies a unique place in Canadian society. By the late 1960s, education had become a central legitimating institution in the modern Canadian state. Between 1960 and 1995–1996, the cost of public education increased from $1.7 billion to almost $60 billion. One in fourteen employed Canadians work in education, and 25 percent of the total population is involved with education. Public education is a major industry involving approximately 16,000 elementary and secondary schools, 200 postsecondary colleges, 75 universities and university colleges, 300,000 teachers, and 60,000 instructors and professors.

Relative to other developed countries, Canada invests a substantial amount on education. At all levels of education, Canadian expenditure per student is second highest (after the United States) among the G-7 countries (the other G-7 members being France, Italy, Germany, Japan, and the United Kingdom) and is substantially above the OECD average. Canada's educational expenditure of 7 percent of gross domestic product is the highest level among the G-7 countries and is one of the highest in the OECD. Eighty percent of Canada's adult population has completed upper-secondary (referred to as high school in North America) or postsecondary education. This is much higher than the OECD average of 64 percent. Fifty-two percent of the adult population has completed postsecondary education. This rate is the highest in the OECD and double the OECD average. Yet it should be noted that this ranking is due to the very high proportion of the population that is enrolled in nonuniversity postsecondary education.

By the mid-1990s, Canadian governments had created a mass postsecondary system. With a participation rate of more than 40 percent for eighteen- to twenty-one-year-olds, Canada ranked first among OECD nations. The system can be characterized as soft federalism. While the federal government has since the 1950s shouldered a significant portion of the bill for universities, constitutionally the responsibility has remained with the provinces. The level of institutional autonomy enjoyed by universities is probably more pronounced in Canada than in any other OECD country. The public monopoly over the binary structure (colleges and universities) accounts for the limited competition and the perceived equivalence among credentials across the country. This state public system is relatively homogeneous and, as a vestige of its roots in the United Kingdom and France, is still committed to the ethos of liberal education rather than vocationalism.

Issues and Problems

The key issues and problems facing the Canadian education systems are as follows: deprofessionalization; the dominance of a political-economic imperative in the formulation of state educational policy (accountability, privatization, market, choice, and decentralization); multiculturalism and diversity; restructuring and retrenchment; and the demographic changes facing all industrialized nations.

As governments have limited the size of the "public space" in Canadian society, so necessarily the ideals of professionalism have come under attack. On the one hand, the creation of professional "colleges of teachers" in British Columbia (in 1986) and in Ontario (in 1996), as well as the current attempts for such undertakings in Quebec, are indicators of the professionalizing trend. Other such initiatives, also present in other provinces (namely, Alberta, New Brunswick, and Nova Scotia), aim at raising the standards in teacher training and at better controlling its quality through the definition of standards for training and practice. Yet the discourse of professionalism has in some respects been co-opted by the state and transformed into government by norms. The substitution of credentials for professional practice, while intended to support professionalization, serves instead to undermine it. Credentialism becomes the overriding trend and the substitute for the promotion of professionalism.

In the 1990s, accountability replaced autonomy in discussions of roles within the state. Accountability has also come to mean recognition of the dominance of market ideology. Governments press educational institutions and systems to be more responsive to the economy and to create alliances with the private sector. The accountability models are embedded within the broader, ideological mechanisms—variously characterized as public-sector reform, new public management, and the "evaluative state"—that have accompanied the political-economic transition from welfare state to the global economy.

The severe limitations on public expenditures are linked to the general suspicion of public institutions and a belief in the greater efficiency of free-market forces. The key policy terms that are the symbols of both market and accountability are "choice" and "privatization." The battle against federal and provincial deficits and the adoption of neoliberal assumptions concerning the role of the state has led governments to inflict considerable budget cuts on educational systems while looking to maximize their services. Yet while the position of the provinces got worse, by 2000 the federal government had moved into surplus. Efforts to decentralize responsibility and increase the autonomy of school boards and school staffs has translated into a more significant role for parents, the development of an "in-service training" culture, and the elaboration of school programs that promote the acquisition of competencies required in the new knowledge society. A parent council structure was created in British Columbia in 2002 and was already in place in six other provinces, including Ontario and Quebec.

For a majority of teachers in urban settings, the combination of immigration policy, the long-standing commitment to diversity and multiculturalism and the new emphasis on "inclusion" has created schools very different from the ones that existed in the 1980s. Schools can contain students who speak as many as eighty different languages, a high proportion of ESL (English as a second language) students, and many students with special needs. The increasing cultural and linguistic diversity has become most evident in the three major urban centers, Montreal, Toronto, and Vancouver. On the other hand, diversity and equality have been safeguarded and extended through the teaching of heritage languages, curriculum design, and the development of programs to combat racism. The development of French-language school boards across the country is a good indicator of this trend.

A major retrenchment and restructuring has occurred throughout Canada as provincial ministries have drastically reduced the number of school boards through amalgamation. These changes have been accompanied by a tightening of control over expenditures at the local level.

Skills and knowledge have become central elements in economic policy as human resource policy has become the modern equivalent of human capital theory in the 1960s. In postsecondary education there has been a growing emphasis on technical and professional programs. Universities are developing closer links with business and industry. Since the late 1980s, the shift has been toward more private and less public expenditure on postsecondary education. Part of this shift is related to the increase in tuition fees, which have more than doubled, but this trend also includes the rise in nongovernmental sources of funding for research.

The most pressing need in Canadian education systems and the society at large is the expected shortfall in the supply of professional personnel. By 2010, Canada will need to replace 50 percent of its teachers, instructors, and professors.

See also: IMMIGRANT EDUCATION; INTERNATIONAL EDUCATION; LANGUAGE AND CULTURE; MULTICULTURAL EDUCATION.

BIBLIOGRAPHY

AXELROD, PAUL. 1997. *The Promise of Schooling: Education in Canada, 1800–1914.* Toronto: University of Toronto Press.

AXELROD, PAUL. 2002. *Values in Conflict: The University, the Marketplace, and the Trials of Liberal Education*. Montreal: McGill-Queen's University Press.

CANADIAN ASSOCIATION OF UNIVERSITY TEACHERS. 2002. *Almanac of Post-Secondary Education in Canada*. Ottawa, Ontario: Canadian Association of University Teachers.

CLIFTON, RODNEY. 2000. "Post-Secondary Education in Canada, 1960–2000: The Best Years We Have Ever Had." Paper presented at the annual meeting of the Canadian Society for the Study of Education, Sherbrooke, Quebec, May 26.

COUNCIL OF MINISTERS OF EDUCATION, CANADA. 1996. *The Development of Education: Report of Canada*. Toronto: Council of Ministers of Education, Canada.

COUNCIL OF MINISTERS OF EDUCATION, CANADA, and STATISTICS CANADA. 2000. *Education Indicators in Canada: Report of the Pan-Canadian Education Indicators Program, 1999*. Toronto: Council of Ministers of Education, Canada; Ottawa, Ontario: Statistics Canada.

DUNNING, PAULA. 1997. *Education in Canada: An Overview*. Toronto: Canadian Education Association.

FISHER, DONALD. 1991. *The Social Sciences in Canada: Fifty Years of National Activity by the Social Science Federation of Canada*. Waterloo, Ontario: Wilfrid Laurier University Press.

FISHER, DONALD; ATKINSON-GROSJEAN, JANET; and HOUSE, DAWN. 2001. "Changes in Academy/Industry/State Relations in Canada: The Creation and Development of the Networks of Centres of Excellence." *Minerva* 39:54–73.

FISHER, DONALD, and EDWARDS, GAIL. 1999. "The Legitimation of Education in Canadian Universities: A Social History of the Canadian Society for the Study of Education/Société Canadienne pour l'étude de l'éducation." In *A Challenge Met: The Definition and Recognition of the Field of Education,* ed. Michel Allard, James Covert, Collette Dufresne-Tassé, Angela Hildyard, and Michael Jackson. Ottawa, Ontario: Canadian Society for the Study of Education and University of Toronto Press.

FLEMING, THOMAS. 1993. *Review and Commentary on Schooling in Canada, 1993*. A Report to the United Nations Educational, Scientific and Cultural Organization International Seminar on Curriculum and Decentralization, Santiago, Chile, November 3–5.

GHOSH, RATNA, and RAY, DOUGLAS, eds. 1995. *Social Change and Education in Canada*, 3rd edition. Toronto: Harcourt Brace.

HARRIS, ROBIN S. 1960. *A History of Higher Education in Canada, 1663 to 1960*. Toronto: University of Toronto Press.

HEALY, DENNIS. 1978. *Report of the Commission on Graduate Studies in the Humanities and Social Sciences*. Ottawa, Ontario: Social Sciences and Humanities Research Council of Canada.

HUMAN RESOURCES DEVELOPMENT CANADA. 1996. *Federal and Provincial Support to Post-Secondary Education in Canada: A Report to Parliament, 1994–1995*. Hull, Quebec: Human Resources Development Canada.

ORGANISATION FOR ECONOMIC CO-OPERATION AND DEVELOPMENT. 1996. *Education at a Glance: OECD Indicators*. Paris: Organisation for Economic Co-operation and Development.

ORGANISATION FOR ECONOMIC CO-OPERATION AND DEVELOPMENT. 2001. *Education at a Glance: OECD Indicators*. Paris: Organisation for Economic Co-operation and Development.

PAGLIARELLO, CLAUDIO. 1994. "Private Elementary and Secondary Schools." *Elementary Quarterly Review* 1(1):42–50.

POLANYI, KARL. 1944. *The Great Transformation*. New York and Toronto: Farrar and Rinehart.

SCOTT, PETER. 1995. *The Meanings of Mass Higher Education*. Buckingham, Eng.: Society for Research into Higher Education; Bristol, PA: Open University Press.

SEARS, ALAN, and HUGHES, ANDREW S. 1996. "Citizenship Education and Current Educational Reform." *Canadian Journal of Education* 21:123–142.

STATISTICS CANADA. 1997. *Education in Canada, 1996*. Ottawa, Ontario: Statistics Canada.

WOTHERSPOON, TERRY. 1998. *The Sociology of Education in Canada*. Oxford: Oxford University Press.

INTERNET RESOURCE

CENTRE OF EDUCATION RESEARCH INFORMATION SYSTEM. 2001. "Theme: Parents." <www.schoolnet.ca/ceris/e/Parents1.html>.

DONALD FISHER

CAPSTONE COURSES IN HIGHER EDUCATION

In higher education, capstone courses, also known as senior seminars, offer undergraduate students nearing graduation the opportunity to summarize, evaluate, and integrate some or all of their college experience. The First National Survey of Senior Seminars and Capstone Courses conducted in 1999 suggested that these courses place the highest priority on culminating learning in the academic major. Enrollments in sections of senior seminars and capstone courses are most often kept at fewer than thirty students. These courses are generally treated as academic major or core requirements, most are at least one academic term in length, and most require a major project or presentation.

The earliest capstones can be traced to the end of the eighteenth century when college presidents taught courses generally integrating philosophy and religion. One of the most famous was a class at Williams College in Massachusetts taught by President Mark Hopkins that inspired, among others, future U.S. President James A. Garfield. Since its inception, the senior seminar has appeared and disappeared in colleges and universities throughout the United States.

The goals and methods of senior seminars and capstone courses in American higher education have been studied at least four times. The first was a study conducted in the early 1970s and sponsored by the Carnegie Council on Policy Studies in Higher Education. For this research, 270 catalogs from colleges and universities in the United States for the year 1975 were examined for course type and structure. The study found that only 3 percent of participating institutions sponsored senior seminars. Arthur Levine, the study's author, later concluded that these courses are offered, at any given time and in various forms, at one in every twenty institutions nationwide.

In a second effort, Joseph Cuseo evaluated proceedings from four national Conferences on the Se-

nior Year Experience and two national Conferences on Students in Transition that convened in the 1990s. His work, centering on characterizing the types, goals, and forms of the senior year experience, including capstone courses, suggested the following goals for the senior year:

1. promotion of the coherence and relevance of general education;

2. promotion of integration and connections between general education and the academic major;

3. fostering of integration and synthesis within the academic major;

4. promotion of meaningful connections between the academic major and work and career experiences;

5. explicit and intentional development of important student skills, competencies, and perspectives that are tacitly or incidentally developed in the college curriculum;

6. enhanced awareness of and support for the key personal adjustments encountered by seniors during their transition from college to postcollege life;

7. improvement of seniors' career preparation and pre-professional development, that is, facilitation of the transition from the academic to the professional world;

8. enhancement of seniors' preparation and prospects for postgraduate education;

9. promotion of effective life planning and decision making with respect to practical issues likely to be encountered in adult life after college (for example, financial planning, marriage, family planning).

In August 2000 Jean Henscheid reviewed modern senior seminars and capstone courses in publication abstracts and presentations available on the Educational Resources Information Center (ERIC) database. The review suggested that these courses are most often associated with a specific academic discipline and coordinated through an academic department or unit. Also in 2000, the National Resource Center for the First-Year Experience and Students in Transition at the University of South Carolina reported results from a nationwide survey of colleges and universities. This survey, in addition to the findings reported above, revealed that coursework and other experiences students have before they enter the academic major are generally not topics covered, at least in the 864 senior capstones or seminars described by these respondents.

Types of Courses

In the early twenty-first century senior seminars and capstone courses in higher education generally fall into one of five types. Varying goals, instructional strategies, and topics separate these course types.

Discipline- and department-based courses. The overriding goal of discipline- and department-based courses is to summarize learning within the academic major. These types of classes are also likely to make connections between the academic learning and the professional world. Some institutions use these courses as a means to encourage seniors to pursue postgraduate study. This subset of courses makes up the majority of the capstone courses offered. These courses are typically offered through the academic department and may be required for graduation. Faculty members within the academic discipline typically teach these courses at the conclusion of the students' academic careers. The classes are taught either by a single faculty member or team-taught by faculty members or staff; three hours of semester credit are normally offered for a letter grade. As this type of class is normally offered as the final "piece" of a student's academic major, credit for these classes is typically a requirement of the major. Topics for discipline and department-based courses vary by the academic major; but include issues that are relevant to the professions related to that major. These courses often use a major project and or presentation as a means for communicating and summarizing the student's academic learning.

Interdisciplinary courses. Interdisciplinary courses, representing a smaller percentage of senior seminars and capstones, offer students an opportunity to synthesize general education, major classes, and cocurricular learning. These courses are more likely to be found at private institutions, taught by a single faculty member. Letter grades are prevalent, and students receive three to four semester hours of credit for completing these courses. Credit for interdisciplinary senior seminars and capstone courses is applied most often as a major requirement, core requirement, or a general education requirement. Presentations and major projects are most often employed as instructional components in these courses. Topics are broad, often involving philosophical issues such as ethics. These courses tend to stress the inter-

relatedness of different academic majors and their role within society.

Transition courses. Transition courses, the third most prevalent type of senior seminars and capstones, focus on preparation for work, graduate school, and life after college. Faculty or career-center professionals most often teach these courses, which typically award a letter grade, although they are less likely to do so than discipline- and department-based courses and interdisciplinary courses. These classes generally earn the participating students one semester of credit.

Topics for transition courses mainly consist of students' transition issues, and students enrolled in them are likely to engage in job search and life transition planning. Discussions center around self-assessment, financial planning, the job search and the first year on the job, relationships, and diversity. Presentations weigh heavily in evaluation of performance in these courses, but rather than major projects, students often develop a portfolio or use the career center.

Career-planning courses. Career-planning courses assist students as they engage in pre-professional development. In some cases career planning is the only goal of these courses. In the 1999 First National Survey of Senior Seminars and Capstone Courses, these courses were the least frequently reported major type. Career planning courses are likely to be taught by career-center professionals, but in some cases academic faculty might teach them. Although students typically receive grades for these courses, they are less likely to receive as many credit hours as students enrolled in other types of senior seminars or capstone courses. The classroom experience in these courses is evaluated most often by the creation of a portfolio, followed by a major project and a presentation. Classroom topics for career-planning courses include current trends in the field, procedures for licensure and job seeking, students' roles in the workplace, and development of a résumé, cover letter, and portfolio.

Other. There are also a small number of senior seminars and capstone courses that do not fit in these four types. These courses often span curricular and cocurricular boundaries and attempt to address institutional goals. These courses do share many of the characteristics of other courses. The primary goals (fostering integration and synthesis within the academic major and promoting integration and connections between the academic major and world of work) are similar to those of most types of the other senior courses. These courses do not generally focus on general education, and are almost always taught by a member of the academic faculty. They tend to be the smallest of the senior courses, often enrolling fewer than nine students. They are most often held for one academic term and students are usually assigned a letter grade.

The Future

As is true with many trends in higher education, senior seminars and capstone courses will likely continue to appear and disappear in various forms. Instructional technologies and the changing delivery of student services will affect the content and character of these courses in the future. This, along with changing student demographics and needs of the institutions offering them, will determine the future goals and structure of these courses.

See also: COLLEGE SEMINARS FOR FIRST-YEAR STUDENTS; CURRICULUM, HIGHER EDUCATION, *subentries on* NATIONAL REPORTS ON THE UNDERGRADUATE CURRICULUM, TRADITIONAL AND CONTEMPORARY PERSPECTIVES.

BIBLIOGRAPHY

CUSEO, JOSEPH B. 1998. "Objectives and Benefits of Senior Year Programs." In *The Senior Year Experience: Facilitating Reflection, Integration, Closure and Transition,* ed. John N. Gardner, Gretchen Van der Veer, and Associates. San Francisco: Jossey-Bass.

GARDNER, JOHN N.; VAN DER VEER, GRETCHEN; and ASSOCIATES. 1998. *The Senior Year Experience: Facilitating Reflection, Integration, Closure and Transition.* San Francisco: Jossey-Bass.

HENSCHEID, JEAN M. 2000. *Professing the Disciplines: An Analysis of Senior Seminars and Capstone Courses.* Columbia, SC: University of South Carolina, National Resource Center for The First Year Experience and Students in Transition.

LEVINE, ARTHUR. 1978. *Handbook of Undergraduate Curriculum.* San Francisco: Jossey-Bass.

LEVINE, ARTHUR. 1998. "A President's Personal and Historical Perspective." In *The Senior Year Experience: Facilitating Reflection, Integration, Closure and Transition,* ed. John N. Gardner, Gretchen Van der Veer, and Associates. San Francisco: Jossey-Bass.

JEAN M. HENSCHEID
LISA R. BARNICOAT

CAREER COUNSELING IN HIGHER EDUCATION

The career services office supports the educational mission of a college or university by helping students to develop, evaluate, and pursue career goals. In the process, students acquire the knowledge and skills necessary to make lifelong career decisions. Career services offices accomplish these goals through career counseling and a range of programs and services designed to help students make the connection between the academic program and the workplace.

Career Counseling

Ideally, the career services office assists students throughout their stay at the institution, providing appropriate assistance at each stage of the student's career development. This process often begins with career counseling designed to help students develop the self-knowledge and awareness of options needed to select an academic major or a tentative career direction. Students are guided in thinking about their interests, values, competencies, and personal characteristics. Through conversation and exercises, students often discover previously unidentified interests.

Career counseling is frequently offered on a one-on-one basis, but at times this service is provided through group workshops, classes, or computerized guidance systems. When a student is asked to begin the exploration on a computer, an individual follow-up session with a counselor is generally encouraged. Career counseling often includes the use of standardized assessment instruments such as the Strong Interest Inventory, the Self-Directed Search, or other instruments designed to clarify career interests, values, personality, or self-identified skills.

As part of the career counseling process, students may be asked to research careers through either reading or interviews with professionals. Thus, a career resource library is an essential component of the career services office. These libraries generally include books on a wide range of career options as well as job search manuals and information on employers. Some information formerly provided in book form, such as directories of employers, is increasingly being delivered through the Internet.

New Trends

In the last decades of the twentieth century, the career services field began to place an increasing emphasis on experiential learning, the mixed bag of ways that students can connect classroom learning with experience in the world around them. The forms of experiential learning that most commonly fall under the career services umbrella are internships and cooperative education. Cooperative education is a full-time, paid work experience that generally occurs during a regular semester. Students receive credit for the work and do not take classes during that time. Internships are usually served part-time, concurrent with classes or during the summer or other school breaks, and may or may not be paid. In some institutions, internships and cooperative education are part of the academic program and may be handled by faculty departments. However, career services offices are becoming increasingly involved at a variety of levels. Some simply provide resources such as internship directories or online databases of available experiences; others develop internships, place students at the sites, and monitor their progress.

Another trend in career services is for colleges to engage alumni as career resources for students, thereby teaching students the skill of networking. Many colleges make alumni career resource databases available to interested students. These databases include employment and contact information on alumni who have volunteered to serve as mentors or otherwise assist students with career-related questions. Some colleges also coordinate events designed to connect students with alumni. These can include panels of alumni who speak at student events, dinners at which students are seated with alumni in relevant fields, or field trips through which students spend time shadowing relevant alumni.

The Job Search

A traditional function that remains an essential part of the career services role is helping students to develop job search skills. Career services counselors critique students' résumés and letters, provide booklets on résumé and employment letter writing, and teach résumé writing, job interviewing skills, and job

search strategies in group sessions. In practice job interviews, students are videotaped so they can see themselves in action. Some career services offices involve alumni or employers in critiquing résumés, conducting practice interviews, or leading workshops. Many also offer sessions on related topics such as networking, professional dress, or the transition to the work place. Etiquette dinners, designed to train students in the etiquette needed for job interviews and professional dinners, have become popular events on many campuses.

Nearly all career services offices also help students connect with potential employers for postgraduate positions. This is handled through a variety of methods. In on-campus interview programs, employers are invited to spend a day or more on campus, interviewing student candidates. Students who make a positive impression are later invited to the employment site for more extensive interviews. Some campuses give students access to a large number of employers in one day by coordinating career fairs, at which employers are stationed at tables to screen candidates and give information about their job openings. A trend that became popular in the 1990s and continues to be widely used is the consortium job fair, in which a number of colleges collaborate to coordinate a large event for the students at all participating schools.

Additional strategies designed to connect students with employers are résumé mailing services, in which career services offices send batches of applicable résumés to requesting employers, and candidate matching databases, which do the same thing electronically. Some colleges disseminate booklets of student résumés or offer credential services, in which student's résumés, letters of recommendation, and other application documents are mailed to employers at the student's request. For students who choose to go to graduate school rather than enter the workforce, career services offices often offer services such as graduate school fairs and databases to assist students in identifying programs that meet their criteria.

The Impact of Technology

The career services field has been strongly affected by the rise of the Internet in the 1990s. By the beginning of the twenty-first century, most career services offices had websites through which they offered career information and links to outside sites applicable to their student populations. Many also provided students with the option of scheduling appointments or campus interviews via the World Wide Web. Web-based databases, including employer databases, candidate résumé databases, internship databases, and job listing databases, are becoming increasingly common. In many cases, career services offices are forming partnerships with outside vendors to offer these services.

Many of the services named above are made available to alumni as well as current students, sometimes for a fee and sometimes at no charge. Some offices also offer fee-based services to community members.

See also: ACADEMIC ADVISING IN HIGHER EDUCATION; ADJUSTMENT TO COLLEGE; COLLEGE STUDENT RETENTION; INTERNSHIPS IN HIGHER EDUCATION; STUDENT SERVICES, *subentries on* COLLEGES AND UNIVERSITIES, COMMUNITY COLLEGES.

BIBLIOGRAPHY

BOLES, RICHARD N., and FIGLER, HOWARD. 1999. *The Career Counselor's Handbook.* Berkeley: Ten Speed Press.

BROWN, DUANE, and BROOKS, LINDA. 1996. *Career Choice and Development.* San Francisco: Jossey-Bass.

HOEFLIN, NANCY M.; ANDERSON, THAD D.; and TIMMINS, SUSAN F., eds. 1998. *Choices and Challenges: Job Search Strategies for Liberal Arts Students.* Bloomington: Indiana University Custom Publishing and the Indiana University Career Development Center.

KUMMEROW, JEAN, ed. 2000. *New Directions in Career Planning and the Workplace.* Palo Alto, CA: Davies-Black Publishing.

LUZZO, DARRELL ANTHONY, ed. 2000. *Career-Counseling of College Students: An Empirical Guide to Strategies that Work.* Washington, DC: American Psychological Institute.

MCDANIELS, CARL, and GYSBERS, NORMAN C. 1992. *Counseling for Career Development: Theories, Resources and Practice.* San Francisco: Jossey-Bass.

NATIONAL ASSOCIATION OF COLLEGES AND EMPLOYERS. 1998. *Professional Standards for College and University Career Services, May 1998.* Bethlehem, PA: National Association of Colleges and Employers.

MELISSA K. BARNES

CARIBBEAN

See: LATIN AMERICA AND THE CARIBBEAN.

CARNEGIE CLASSIFICATION SYSTEM, THE

The Carnegie Classification (of Institutions of Higher Education) is a taxonomy of U.S. colleges and universities. The categories are based on information about the institutions, such as types of degrees conferred, academic disciplines offered, and specialization. The classification system shows the diversity of American colleges and universities. The purpose of the Carnegie Classification system is to assist in higher education research efforts; it is not intended to rank the quality of the institutions.

History and Updates

The Carnegie Classification system was developed in 1970 by the Carnegie Foundation for the Advancement of Teaching, an independent, nonprofit center for educational research and policy studies. The Classifications were first published in the Carnegie Commission on Higher Education's report, *New Students and New Places* (1971). Revisions to the classifications were published in 1976, 1987, 1994, and 2000. Reclassifications reflect changes in the U.S. institutions, such as new colleges, closings, and the developments in existing institutions. Data from the National Center for Educational Statistics (NCES) are used to update revised editions of the Carnegie Classification. An extensive revision planned for 2005 will offer a multiple-classification system that will allow for more types of comparisons among the variety of institutions.

Classification Categories in 2000

The Carnegie Classification system includes all U.S. colleges and universities that grant degrees and are accredited by the U.S. Secretary of Education. Based on the 2000 edition of the Carnegie Classification, there are ten categories of institutions. Each category is briefly described below, and examples of public, private not-for-profit, and private for-profit institutions in each category are shown in Table 1.

- Doctoral/Research Universities–Extensive: These institutions typically offer a wide variety of baccalaureate degrees and award fifty or more doctoral degrees per year across at least fifteen

TABLE 1

Carnegie Classification of institutions of higher education

Carnegie Classification	Total number/ percentage	Public institution example/number	Private not-for-profit example/number	Private for-profit example/number
Doctoral/Research Universities—Extensive	151; 3.8%	University of California, Berkeley; 102	Vanderbilt University; 49	None
Doctoral/Research Universities—Intesive	110; 2.8%	College of William and Mary; 64	Baylor University; 44	University of Sarasota; 2
Master's Colleges and Univerities I	496; 12.6%	Lincoln University; 249	Fairfield University; 246	Colorado Technical University; 1
Master's Colleges and Universities II	115; 2.9%	Mississippi University for Women; 23	Le Moyne College; 85	Huron University; 7
Baccalaureate Colleges— Liberal Arts	228; 5.8%	Coastal Carolina University; 26	Allegheny College; 202	None
Baccalaureate Colleges— General	321; 8.1%	Western Montana College; 50	Tri-State University; 226	DeVry Institute of Technology; 5
Baccalaureate/Associate's Colleges	57; 1.4%	Utah Valley State College; 15	Peace College; 31	Sullivan College; 11
Associate's Colleges	1,669; 42.3%	Sante Fe Community College; 1,025	Maryland College of Art and Design; 159	ITT Technical Institute; 485
Specialized Institutions	766; 19.4%	United States Naval Academy; 67	Hebrew Union Seminary; 593	University of Phoenix; 106
Tribal Colleges and Universities	28; 0.7%	Institute of American Indian and Alaska Native Culture and Arts Development; 22	Blackfeet Community College; 6	None
Total	**3,941; 100%**	**1,643; 41.7%**	**1,681; 42.6%**	**617; 15.7%**

SOURCE: Carnegie Foundation for the Advancement of Teaching website.

academic disciplines. Doctoral degrees include the Ph.D., Doctor of Education, Doctor of Juridical Science, and Doctor of Public Health, among others.

• Doctoral/Research Universities–Intensive: These institutions typically offer a wide variety of baccalaureate degrees and award at least ten doctoral degrees per year across at least three academic disciplines or at least twenty doctoral degrees per year overall.

• Master's Colleges and Universities I: These institutions typically offer a wide variety of baccalaureate degrees and award forty or more master's degrees per year across three or more academic disciplines.

• Master's Colleges and Universities II: These institutions typically offer a wide variety of baccalaureate degrees and award twenty or more master's degrees per year.

• Baccalaureate Colleges–Liberal Arts: These institutions award at least half of their baccalaureate degrees in liberal arts fields. Examples of liberal arts fields include English, foreign languages, biological sciences, mathematics, philosophy and religion, physical sciences, social sciences, and humanities.

• Baccalaureate Colleges–General: These institutions award less than half of their baccalaureate degrees in liberal arts fields.

• Baccalaureate/Associate's Colleges: In these institutions, the number of bachelor's degrees awarded represent at least ten percent but less than half of all undergraduate awards.

• Associate's Colleges: This is the largest category in the Carnegie Classification. In these institutions, the number of bachelor's degrees awarded represent less than ten percent of all undergraduate awards.

• Specialized Institutions: These institutions typically award degrees in a particular field. Examples include medical and law schools; religious institutions, such as seminaries and rabbinical schools; schools of business, engineering, art, and design; and military institutes.

• Tribal Colleges and Universities: These institutions are members of the American Indian Higher Education Consortium and are typically tribally controlled and located on reservations.

1994 Classifications

The 1994 edition of the Carnegie Classification comprised the following eleven categories, outlined below for comparison with the revisions that were made in 2000:

• Research Universities I typically offered a full range of baccalaureate programs, awarded fifty or more doctoral degrees, and received annually $40 million or more in federal support.

• Research Universities II also typically offered a full range of baccalaureate programs and awarded fifty or more doctorates, but they received between $15 million and $40 million per year in federal support.

• Doctoral Universities I offered a full range of baccalaureate programs and awarded at least forty doctoral degrees annually in five or more disciplines.

• Doctoral Universities II offered a full range of baccalaureate programs and awarded at least ten doctoral degrees in three or more disciplines or twenty or more doctorates per year total.

• Master's (Comprehensive) Colleges and Universities I offered a full range of baccalaureate programs and awarded forty or more master's degrees annually in three or more disciplines.

• Master's (Comprehensive) Colleges and Universities II also typically offered a full range of baccalaureate programs, but they awarded twenty or more master's degrees per year in one or more disciplines.

• Baccalaureate (Liberal Arts) Colleges I were primarily undergraduate colleges with a major emphasis on baccalaureate programs. They awarded forty percent or more of their degrees in liberal arts fields, and their admissions policies were selective.

• Baccalaureate (Liberal Arts) Colleges II were also primarily undergraduate colleges with a major emphasis on baccalaureate programs. They awarded less than forty percent of their degrees in liberal arts fields, and their admissions policies were less selective.

• Associate of Arts Colleges offered associate of arts certificate or degree programs.

• Specialized Institutions offered at least fifty percent of degrees in a particular field. Examples include medical and law schools; faith-related institutions, such as seminaries and rabbinical schools; schools of business, engineering, art, and design; and military institutes.

• Tribal Colleges and Universities were members of the American Indian Higher Education Consortium and were typically tribally controlled and located on reservations.

The Carnegie Foundation for the Advancement of Teaching

The Carnegie Foundation, the third oldest foundation in the United States, was founded by Andrew Carnegie in 1905 and chartered by an act of Congress the following year. Governed by an independent, national board of trustees, the Carnegie Foundation uses its endowment to support educational research and publications. In addition to establishing the Carnegie Classification of Institutions of Higher Education, the foundation developed the largest pension system in the United States (TIAA–CREF), founded the Educational Testing Service, developed the Graduate Record Exam, and published numerous influential studies on the American higher education system. The Carnegie Foundation is located in Menlo Park, California.

See also: HIGHER EDUCATION IN THE UNITED STATES, *subentry on* SYSTEM.

BIBLIOGRAPHY

CARNEGIE COMMISSION ON HIGHER EDUCATION. 1971. *New Students and New Places.* New York: McGraw-Hill.

INTERNET RESOURCE

CARNEGIE FOUNDATION FOR THE ADVANCEMENT OF TEACHING. 2001. "Carnegie Classification of Institutions of Higher Education." <www. carnegiefoundation.org>.

AMY HIRSCHY

CARNEGIE UNITS

Adopted in the early 1900s to both standardize and ensure the quality of high school education, the Carnegie unit is viewed almost a century later by critics as an impediment to flexibility. Yet, for all of its limitations, the Carnegie unit remains the putative guarantor that students have invested in each of their courses an amount of time that warrants the credit that so many colleges and employers presume represents learning.

In fact, the search for the answer to the elusive question of how much learning results from each course gave birth to the Carnegie unit, and keeps the approach alive as a surrogate for knowledge gained. In another era, college admissions officers—especially at selective colleges—concerned themselves mostly with applicants from private preparatory schools, believing that they needed to become familiar with the quality of only those few schools. Even at a state institution such as the University of Michigan, it was the responsibility of the faculty to oversee academic standards at the secondary level. Admissions officials and faculty everywhere, however, could not keep track of the standards at new public high schools that proliferated across the country during the first decades of the 1900s.

Thus, the Carnegie Foundation for the Advancement of Teaching encouraged the adoption of what came to be known as the Carnegie unit, which equates seat-time with learning. Each unit represented about 130 instructional hours. The Carnegie Foundation defined a unit as a course that met for a period each school day for about 50 to 55 minutes. The Carnegie unit continues to influence much that is crucial to teaching and learning in high schools—the length of the class period, the school day and the school year, as well as the time expended to receive a diploma. The unit affects the very way that knowledge is organized for instructional purposes, discouraging interdisciplinary teaching because of the difficult question of deciding how many units to attribute to each discipline. Those who would organize and convey knowledge differently inveigh against the "tyranny" of the Carnegie unit, asserting that seat-time is not a proxy for learning and that secondary schools must be flexible to engage students and to heighten learning. The following developments add to the challenge:

- Block scheduling
- Out-of-classroom field experiences
- Distance learning and independent study
- Portfolios and other performance-based assessments

Under block scheduling, a course meets for a specified number of hours; but, this number may vary from that of traditional courses because of the way the time is arranged. Out-of-class experiences involve time configurations that only remotely relate to seat-time. Distance learning made possible by technology, in combination with independent study, tends to free students to spend as little or as much time as they require to cover the material. Performance-based assessment may be used in conjunction with the Carnegie unit, or it may argue for an appraisal of learning without regard for seat-time. Aspects of school reform underscore the idea that secondary students might benefit from less reliance on Carnegie units. The Coalition of Essential Schools, for instance, advocated a more limited but more intense curriculum under the motto of "Less Is More." Furthermore, the move to integrate subject matter, especially at small alternative high schools, made it less clear how to satisfy the unit requirement. But no widely accepted alternative guarantor of quality emerged by the beginning of the twenty-first century.

In fact, demands for accountability helped preserve the Carnegie unit. Taxpayers wanted assurances that the $350 billion a year they bestowed on public schools was not squandered. Colleges sought methods to compare applicants and to gauge the extent of their preparation. David Tyack and Larry Cuban cited the "interlocking reasons" (p. 107) that defenders of the status quo gave for regarding the Carnegie unit as part of a system that could not withstand tampering. This system—the time devoted to each class and each course, the departmental organization, the lecture method of teaching—was likened by its guardians to the building blocks that support an entire structure. Remove one, they said, and the stability of the others, and of the high school itself, was imperiled. Colleges and universities, prodded by the Carnegie Foundation, forced the unit requirement on secondary schools. It may be that altering or altogether eliminating the Carnegie unit will ultimately depend on whether educators can agree on a more meaningful symbol for knowledge gained in secondary education.

See also: CURRICULUM, SCHOOL; NONGOVERNMENTAL ORGANIZATIONS AND FOUNDATIONS; SECOND-

ARY EDUCATION, *subentry on* HISTORY OF; SCHOOL REFORM.

BIBLIOGRAPHY

LAGEMANN, ELLEN CONDLIFFE. 2000. *An Elusive Science: The Troubling History of Education Research.* Chicago: University of Chicago Press.

MAEROFF, GENE I. 1993. "The Assault on the Carnegie Unit." *Education Week* October 13, p. 36.

TYACK, DAVID, and CUBAN, LARRY. 1995. *Tinkering toward Utopia: A Century of Public School Reform.* Cambridge, MA: Harvard University Press.

GENE I. MAEROFF

CATEGORIZATION AND CONCEPT LEARNING

Education in every form entails the acquisition and modification of conventional categories and labels, as well as processes for inferring category membership. Consider these statements: "Fractions are numbers between two integers"; "Plants get energy through photosynthesis"; and "A noun is a person, place, or thing." The first claims a formal relation between well-defined number concepts. The second explains a biological concept by analogy. The third specifies (erroneously) a linguistic category. Teachers frequently make statements like these to elementary and secondary students. How, in fact, are the named concepts learned? How do concepts change with age, experience, and particularly education?

Form and Format of Conceptual Knowledge

A common misconception is that concepts are well defined, like dictionary entries. Though hundreds of concepts, particularly scientific ones, are well defined within a community of experts, most are "fuzzy" and metaphorical. Even patently well-defined categories like "odd number" are treated as if some examples are better than others.

Adults' concepts fall into a wide variety of abstract representations, such as taxonomic hierarchies, kinship systems, and legal definitions. Some representations mirror the structure of the physical environment, whereas others are rather arbitrary products of their cultural and linguistic environ-

ments. Most are a synthesis (e.g., biological categories reflect real patterns among organisms, yet are shaped by culturally specified theories). Children's concepts also reveal abstract representations, but these are generally less elaborate and less well-defined than those of adults.

Conceptual knowledge, as symbolic as it seems, is encoded as patterns of electrochemical activation within powerful neural networks in the neocortex. These concept patterns are derived from repeated experience. Experience trains massively interconnected systems of neural units (analogous to groups of neurons) by changing connection strengths. Over time, associated input patterns (e.g., sights and sounds of a cat) will activate a characteristic response pattern. This response is a concept (cat). Critical features of these concept patterns are graded activation (i.e., some inputs activate the response more strongly than others) and learning algorithms that specify how connection strengths change with experience. This pre-symbolic view of conceptual representation, though unintuitive, is dominant among cognitive scientists, and work in the mid-1980s through 1990s has answered some early criticisms. Still, questions remain about how conceptual thinking emerges from in neural networks. For example, it is not clear how current theoretical models can capture intricacies of conceptual knowledge (e.g., nonliteral usage of concepts, as in the ironic use of *award* in the "Golden Turkey Awards" for the year's worst movies).

A comprehensive proposal by Lawrence W. Barsalou in 1999 holds that concepts are inherently perceptual and experiential. So-called abstract conceptual knowledge is in fact the productive activation of remembered aspects of perceptual and internal experiences. As experiences are retained in memory, the associations among them permit new mental simulations that support a variety of functions. These functions include conceptual redescription, inference, imagination, and productive combination of concepts. These functions are traditionally ascribed to symbolic, completely abstract concepts, but Barsalou argues that they can more simply be attributed to a powerful system for manipulating stored perceptual knowledge. The power of the system rests on selective simulation: when the concept *cat* is activated, one does not recall every cat experience, but the experiences evoked by current contextual demands and recently activated information. Thus, the word *skunk* might normally activate the property *smelly,* but after watching a documentary showing footage of skunks foraging at night, the property *nocturnal* might be activated as well.

Educators should judiciously use definitions to teach new concepts. Students will not typically use definitions to judge category membership. Exposing students to multiple examples that highlight the distinctive properties of the category of interest, or comparing contrastive categories, is more effective. A common misunderstanding of concept learning can be seen in the traditional western approach to mathematics education that emphasizes abstract or "content-free" knowledge. There is no evidence of such decontextualized knowledge, and it should be assumed that mathematical concepts are derived from organized experience with concepts of quantity (e.g., cardinality, equivalence) and operations on quantities (e.g., concatenation; transformation), in a variety of familiar materials. Although it is trivially apparent that diverse, rich experiences eventually increase knowledge of mathematical and scientific concepts, the general, powerful principles for optimizing the presentation of multiple examples in classrooms, so that students' conceptual knowledge is effectively and efficiently enriched, have not yet been derived.

Theories of Category Learning

How do experiences give rise to new categories? Presumably individuals are exposed to various members, and sometimes told about category membership. Parents use various strategies for teaching children new categories, category labels, and associated properties. But how does experience generate new categories?

In the 1994 model of Robert M. Nosofsky and his colleagues, people distinguish contrasting categories by gradually modifying the degree of attention allocated to various features of possible category members, until the simplest and most diagnostic decision rule (i.e., set of attention "weights" focusing on the fewest possible features) is attained. Atypical category members (e.g., ostriches, which differ from typical North American birds in many regards) are represented separately, as exceptions. Current controversy focuses on the information retained from multiple experiences, exact algorithms for describing changes in represented categories with experience, and the uniformity of category learning across domains. For example, there is evidence that people treat atypical examples differently across the domains of natural, object, and social categories.

How do children learn categories? Little research addresses changes in category learning processes during and after childhood. Research on children's categories often confounds their conceptual knowledge with their comprehension of category labels. A current debate concerns what categories children acquire first. Though prelinguistic infants differentiate related categories (e.g., *cats* vs. *lions*), their knowledge might not transcend surface similarity. Knowledge of the dynamic or hidden properties of categories becomes evident after the first six months, but two-year-olds still sometimes fail to differentiate related categories (e.g., calling any water fowl *duckie*) or categorize different-looking entities. In such cases parents can shape children's naming. Children, however, select and organize social input about categories and labels. For example, parents predominantly use basic-level labels when talking to children. Basic-level categories (e.g., *car, bird*) capture a useful intermediate level of generality, compared to very broad (e.g., *animal*) or narrow (e.g., *parakeet*) categories. Compared to parents, however, preschool children use a much higher proportion of basic level labels, suggesting that children's inductive dispositions (or limitations) shape their acquisition and use of category labels.

Adults can help children focus on similarities of, and variability between, category members. Both social input and selection and tailoring of available examples can facilitate category learning. An unresolved question is how analog (i.e., rich, realistic), versus digital (i.e., reduced, electronic), examples can facilitate children's concept learning. This is a practical question, given the growing availability of computer technology for young children. A problem is that children sometimes mistake which features define a category (e.g., rejecting a barren island but accepting a tropical peninsula as examples of island). Predicting children's misconceptions about categories is therefore crucial for teachers. Verbal instruction about critical features can be ineffective or misleading, so teachers must orchestrate creative experiences and instruction to advance children's grasp of conventional categories.

Conceptual Change in Children

Children, adolescents, and adults enter classrooms with naive preconceptions about the world. Shifting these preconceptions can be onerous. In 1985 Susan

Carey documented children's changing biological concepts and related inferences about biological properties. For example, a child who conceptualizes people as prototypes of animals will extend traits of humans (e.g., respiring, sleeping) to similar creatures (e.g., gorillas), but not dissimilar ones (e.g., worms). In contrast, adults often generalize biological properties in a less anthropocentric manner.

The process of conceptual change is mysterious, and frustrates educators' desires to facilitate it. Researchers have suggested many procedures to promote conceptual change, but naive concepts can be extraordinarily intractable. For example, even after formal physics instruction, older students make pervasive errors about concepts like force. One approach to teaching stipulates having students articulate their concepts, setting up a demonstration that would yield different results under the naive and the conventional belief system, having students predict an outcome, and then conducting the demonstration. Apparently articulating and confronting the discrepancy between own and others' beliefs, and seeing relevant evidence, can provide a powerful springboard for conceptual change. Note, however, that this approach is effective with older students revising well-defined concepts in a mature science. Its effectiveness for young children, whose capacity to recognize disconfirming evidence is limited, has not been established.

The Functions of Categorization in Children's Thinking

The content of children's categories changes with age, but what of the uses of categorization and concepts? Concepts constrain perception, language, social interaction, and problem solving—every aspect of cognition. Categories permit economic thinking, inferring properties of novel instances, organizing memories, making analogies, and solving problems with flexibility. It is not known how education, informal learning, and maturation separately alter these functions. In short, there is a lack of a developmental theory of the ecology of categorization that takes into account development and schooling. Outlining this theory is a major task for developmental and educational psychology in the twenty-first century.

See also: LANGUAGE ACQUISITION; LEARNING, *subentry on* CONCEPTUAL CHANGE.

BIBLIOGRAPHY

BARSALOU, LAWRENCE W. 1999. "Perceptual Symbol Systems." *Behavioral and Brain Sciences* 22:577–660.

BRANSFORD, JOHN D.; FRANKS, JEFFERY J.; VYE, NANCY. J.; and SHERWOOD, ROBERT D. 1989. "New Approaches to Instruction: Because Wisdom Can't Be Told." In *Similarity and Analogical Reasoning,* ed. Stella Vosnaidou and Andrew Ortony. Cambridge, Eng.: Cambridge University Press.

CAREY, SUSAN. 1985. *Conceptual Change in Childhood.* Cambridge, MA: MIT Press.

CHI, MICHELINE T. H.; HUTCHINSON, JEAN E.; and ROBIN, ANNE F. 1989. "How Inferences about Novel Domain-Related Concepts Can Be Constrained by Structured Knowledge." *Merrill-Palmer Quarterly* 35:27–62.

DEÁK, GEDEON O. 2000. "Chasing the Fox of Word Learning: Why 'Constraints' Fail to Capture It." *Developmental Review* 20:29–80.

GELMAN, SUSAN A., et al. 1998. *Beyond Labeling: The Role of Maternal Input in the Acquisition of Richly Structured Categories.* Monographs of the Society for Research in Child Development 63(1). Chicago: University of Chicago Press.

HUNT, EARL, and MINSTRELL, JIM. 1994. "A Cognitive Approach to the Teaching of Physics." In *Classroom Lessons: Integrating Cognitive Theory and Classroom Practices,* ed. Kate McGilly. Cambridge, MA: MIT Press.

KEIL, FRANK C., and BATTERMAN, NANCY. 1984. "A Characteristic-to-Defining Shift in the Development of Word Meaning." *Journal of Verbal Learning and Verbal Behavior* 23:221–236.

LAKOFF, GEORGE. 1987. *Women, Fire, and Dangerous Things: What Categories Reveal about the Mind.* Chicago: University of Chicago Press.

LIVINGSTON, KENNETH R., and ANDREWS, JANET K. 1995. "On the Interaction of Prior Knowledge and Stimulus Structure in Category Learning." *Quarterly Journal of Experimental Psychology: Human Experimental Psychology* 48:208–236.

MANDLER, JEAN M. 2000. "Perceptual and Conceptual Processes in Infancy." *Journal of Cognition and Development* 1:3–36.

MEDIN, DOUGLAS L.; LYNCH, ELIZABETH B.; and SOLOMON, KAREN O. 2000. "Are There Kinds of Concepts?" *Annual Review of Psychology* 51:121–147.

MERVIS, CAROLYN B. 1987. "Child-Basic Object Categories and Early Lexical Development." In *Concepts and Conceptual Development,* ed. Ulric Neisser. Cambridge, MA: Cambridge University Press.

MURPHY, GEORGE L., and MEDIN, DOUGLAS L. 1985. "The Role of Theories in Conceptual Coherence." *Psychological Review* 92:289–316.

NOSOFSKY, ROBERT M.; PALMERI, THOMAS J.; and MCKINLEY, STEPHEN C. 1994. "Rule-Plus-Exception Model of Classification Learning." *Psychological Review* 101:53–79.

ROSCH, ELEANOR. 1978. "Principles of Categorization." In *Cognition and Categorization,* ed. Eleanor Rosch and Barbara Lloyd. Hillsdale, NJ: Erlbaum.

RUMELHART, DAVID E., and MCCLELLAND, JAMES L. 1989. *Parallel Distributed Processing: Explorations in the Microstructure of Cognition,* Vol. 1. Cambridge, MA: MIT Press.

GEDEON O. DEÁK

CATHOLIC SCHOOLS

In 1783 Philadelphia Catholics established the first Catholic parish school in the United States, and over the next two centuries, Catholic parochial schools would educate tens of millions of American citizens. By the middle of the 1960s, when the Catholic parochial school movement had reached its high point, there were more than 5.7 million children in parish elementary schools—12 percent of all of the children enrolled in schools in the United States at that time. The challenges of providing parish-based education have changed from one generation to the next, but Catholics schools have survived in spite of substantial obstacles.

Foundations

During the sixteenth, seventeenth, and eighteen centuries, colonial Catholics struggled merely to survive in that vast territory that would become the United States of America. In fact, the progress of the church in all of the colonies of the New World (Spanish, French, and English) was due largely to the personal sacrifices and skills of a cadre of great priests. Their willingness to give their all, including their lives, left a Catholic imprint on virtually every region of the country.

That is not to say that Catholic schools emerged because of these missionary efforts. It would take many generations for American Catholics to feel secure enough to establish their own schools. In fact, the very survival of Catholicism as a religion in America was in doubt until the late eighteenth century. Those Catholic schools that did emerge in the early decades of the American Republic were the direct result of a collaboration of interested parents, determined pastors, and compassionate sister teachers. Of special note was the persistence of Elizabeth Seton, who recruited and trained the sister teachers who were the backbone of the parish school system for nearly 125 years.

Yet the most important ingredient in the eventual spread of Catholic education in the nineteenth century was parental support. Beginning in the early 1800s, many American Catholic parents were willing to build and support parish schools. These parents believed that the future of Catholicism in the new nation was tied to educating the next generation in the ways of the faith.

Rapid social change and population growth, accompanied by misunderstanding, hostility, and resistance, were important ingredients in the process of Catholic educational development in the years before the Civil War. Civic leaders argued in favor of common schools that would transform a diverse population of children into a homogeneous, deferential, and very American citizenry. Catholics resisted these common schools because of their distinct Protestant overtone, and they built their own schools.

The tensions between public and Catholic schoolmen forced the two sides to modify the content of their curricula. After a decade of violence in the 1840s, both sides sought other ways of winning the hearts and minds of the Catholic population. Public schoolmen took measures to make their schools less sectarian. Catholic schoolmen countered with measures to make their schools more secular. Both sides were competing for the attention and loyalty of Catholic parents and their children. It was a competition that would continue well into the twentieth century.

Educational Choices

In the later decades of the nineteenth century, Catholics shifted their attention to controlling the growth and development of Catholic education from within the denomination. Catholic schoolmen realized that it was not enough to promulgate decrees requiring Catholics to send their children to parish schools. Catholic parents faced a variety of educational choices and their responses were determined largely by their perceptions of the values and dangers of common schooling. A significant percentage of Catholic parents—perhaps a majority—had relatively few qualms about public education. In fact, these parents saw the public school as the best means of insuring the future prosperity of their children in American society.

A second group of parents could not quite accept the idea of a curriculum totally devoid of religious instruction, but they were not willing to abandon the goals of public education. Their choice was to build formal working relationships with local school boards that provided for publicly supported secular institutions taught by Catholic teachers in parish-owned classrooms; religion was an after-school activity.

A third group of parents spurned formal relationships with public school boards, but nevertheless adapted many of the fundamental elements of the public school curriculum for use in parish classrooms. The result was the prototype for the Catholic parochial school that came to dominate the educational landscape in the twentieth century.

A fourth group of parents, most of whom were immigrants from Europe, not only spurned the public schools, but also established parish schools that emphasized native culture, language, and religion. The ethnic Catholic school was a powerful force within the Catholic Church well into the twentieth century. The movement ended abruptly, however, with the animosity toward all things foreign during World War I.

The style and substance of Catholic parochial education varied from region to region, diocese to diocese, and even from parish to parish across the United States during the last half of the nineteenth century and even into the first decade of the twentieth century. Bishops and pastors could not force Catholic parents to send their children to parish schools. State legislatures could not mandate public control over parochial institutions. Both sides learned that decisions on the education of Catholic children would be a family affair.

A Search for Order

At the turn of the twentieth century, American Catholic education remained a chaotic patchwork of school experiments held together by a common belief in the value of daily Catholic moral instruction as part of the educational process. Out of this chaos came a search for order during the years from 1900 to 1950. This search was evident in the movement within individual dioceses to establish school boards and appoint superintendents to provide greater uniformity in Catholic schooling from one parish to the next. The search was also evident in the establishment of the Catholic Educational Association in 1903 and the National Catholic Welfare Conference in 1918, two organizations that brought order to Catholic education on the national level.

The Catholic response to teacher preparation was a case study of the pressures on parochial education in the twentieth century. If parochial education was to survive, it had to compete with public education on its own terms. To do so meant that Catholic leaders had to better prepare women religious and other teachers for the classroom. Nevertheless, women religious never received all the teacher training they needed. At its core, Catholic teacher preparation was a combination of on-the-job training and summer school instruction.

The leadership role played by women religious in parochial education should not be underestimated. In fact, it would not be difficult to make the case that sister-teachers were the single most important element in the Catholic educational establishment both in the nineteenth and the twentieth centuries. Training was only a small part of their commitment to Catholic children.

A Generation of Crisis

The years from 1950 to 1990 were a generation of crisis in Catholic education. First, there was the crisis of growth in the 1950s when demand for parochial education (due to the increase in the school-age population during the Baby Boom) far outstripped the available space. Then came the crisis of confidence during the social upheaval of the 1960s when Catholic parents asked themselves if parochial schools were necessary. Self-doubt in the 1960s was followed by the crisis of decline in the 1970s when devoted pastors and parents asked themselves if Catholic schools would survive. Although the answer by the end of the decade was an unequivocal yes, it was unclear who would pay the high cost of sustaining these schools. In fact, the economic burden of parochial education would be the predominant issue of parochial schooling in the 1980s.

The 1980s were years of uncertainty. Once a haven of white immigrant children who were making the transition from Europe to America, the Catholic schools of the 1980s had become visible symbols of the commitment of some parents—both Catholic and non-Catholic—to the education of their children. To be sure, many Catholic parishes had closed their schools in the previous three decades and other parishes were unwilling to open new schools. But just as important were the many parishes in the inner cities as well as in the affluent suburbs that made great sacrifices to sustain their schools.

An Uncertain Future

The future of American Catholic parochial education is uncertain. In the 1960s, there were more than 5.7 million children enrolled in Catholic elementary schools, but by 2001 the enrollment had slipped to less than 2.6 million, a plunge of 54 percent. Even though the rate of decline had abated, it is not likely that Catholic education will ever see the strength of numbers it had at the middle of the twentieth century.

Why did Catholic parents abandon their schools over the last thirty years of the twentieth century? The answer is complex, intermingled with changing social values, changes in family structure, changes in the forms and content of public education, and the rising cost of private education relative to other living expenses. All these factors contributed to the decline of parochial education during the years from 1970 to 2000.

The beginning of the decline of Catholic parochial education can be traced to the drastic drop in religious vocations in the late 1960s. For more than a century, orders of priests and nuns staffed Catholic classrooms at minimal cost. However, in the years after the end of the Second Vatican Council in 1965, tens of thousands of these men and women abandoned their religious vows, and many others shifted to different ministries, forcing parish pastors and principals to hire lay teachers and pay them a living wage. Many school administrators found this task to be economically unfeasible and closed their schools.

A second factor was the changing structure of the American family. Where once the typical Ameri-

can Catholic family consisted of two parents and a gaggle of kids, the new American Catholic family was often a single parent with one or two children. Even in two-parent households, both parents worked and were in need of day-care facilities and after-school programs. Catholic families no longer had the time or energy to contribute to the operation and maintenance of a private parish school.

Related to the change in the structure of the typical Catholic family over the past thirty years has been a correlate change in American values. In such a consumer-oriented culture, Catholic parents found that they have no money left to pay parochial school tuition, let alone the resources needed to build a new school.

Another factor was the changing nature of public education. As late as the 1950s, public schools taught a form of nonsectarian Protestantism as part of the curriculum. Catholics in those areas and even in the big cities did not always feel welcome. But a 1961 decision by the Supreme Court stripped all public schools of any references to religion. Students of all faiths were treated equally.

Catholic parents were also attracted to public schools by the quality of the facilities, teachers, and courses. The principal concern of many parents—Catholic as well as non-Catholic—was the future careers and economic security of their children. Unlike their parents and grandparents, Catholic parents in the late twentieth century did not tend to value the spiritual development of their children as highly as their career development.

Catholic Schools and the Courts

There are also a sizable number of parents and educators—both Catholic and non-Catholic—who believe that they are being deprived of the right to fairly choose between public and private schools. At the turn of the twenty-first century, these "school choice" advocates have petitioned states legislatures and even the U.S. Congress to provide tuition tax credits and vouchers that would allow parents to make a fair choice between public and private schools. Legislatures in Wisconsin, Arizona, Ohio, and Vermont did establish school voucher programs, but these programs quickly became entangled in court litigation. Other school aid programs have been proposed in Michigan, California, Texas, and Florida.

Not surprisingly, Catholic school advocates have been active supporters of the school choice and tax voucher movements. If found to be constitutional, such aid could be an important source of financial support for many parents who struggle to pay thousands of dollars in parish school tuition each year. In 2000 the U.S. Supreme Court ruled in favor of providing tax-supported computers and remedial instruction in Catholic schools and in June 2002 upheld the use of public money for religious school tuition. Whatever the decision, however, Catholic school advocates do not believe that the voucher issue will affect the future of Catholic education.

Catholic Schools as Models

Many of the parish schools that have survived are worthy of emulation. In a 1993 study, *Catholic Schools and the Common Good,* three social scientists outlined the successful hallmarks of Catholic education, qualities that have been adapted by many public schools.

Foremost among the qualities of parish-based education is decentralization. For the most part, parish schools are administered at the local level. Funding for the schools comes from the community and teachers are hired by principals without interference from school superintendents or other educational bureaucrats. Parents have a greater involvement and effectiveness in the education process because they are working single institutions in their own neighborhoods rather than a centralized bureaucracy. A second quality related to the first is the fact that parents, students, and faculty share a broad set of beliefs that give each school a moral purpose. Shared values are possible if parents, students, and faculty care about education.

Another hallmark of parochial schools worthy of emulation is size. The small size of most parish schools promotes interaction between students, parents, and staff. Because teachers serve in many different roles during the school day (disciplinarians, counselors, and friends as well as specialists in one or more academic disciplines) they become mentors and role models. The small size of most parish schools insures that parents and teachers know one another and their children well.

Finally, parish schools place a special emphasis on academics. Small size and limited resources necessarily requires administrators to concentrate on basics. The result is a student body well grounded in the mathematical and literary skills so necessary for success at future educational levels. Large schools

with cafeteria-style curricula may very well meet short-term demands for relevant instruction, but there is little evidence that courses in industrial management and family living are as valuable as literacy and mathematical skills in a constantly changing society.

The parents of the children who are educated in these schools will determine the future of Catholic parochial education in the United States. More than two centuries ago, the parents and pastor of St. Mary's Parish in Philadelphia established the first American parochial school. As long as there are parents and pastors interested in parochial education, these schools will survive. Even though American Catholic parochial education is unlikely to attain the position of influence it had in the mid-twentieth century, parish schools will remain important education laboratories for some time to come.

See also: ELEMENTARY EDUCATION, *subentry on* HISTORY OF; JEWISH EDUCATION, UNITED STATES; NATIONAL CATHOLIC EDUCATIONAL ASSOCIATION; PRIVATE SCHOOLING; PROTESTANT SCHOOL SYSTEMS; SECONDARY EDUCATION, *subentry on* HISTORY OF.

BIBLIOGRAPHY

BUETOW, HAROLD A. 1988. *The Catholic School: Its Roots, Identity, and Future.* New York: Crossroad.

BRYK, ANTHONY S.; LEE, VALERIE E.; and HOLLAND, PETER B. 1993. *Catholic Schools and the Common Good.* Cambridge, MA: Harvard University Press.

DOLAN, JAY P. 1985. *The American Catholic Experience: From Colonial Times to the Present.* Garden City, NY: Doubleday.

DOLAN, JAY P., et al. 1989. *Transforming Parish Ministry: The Changing Roles of Catholic Clergy, Laity, and Women Religious.* New York: Crossroad.

PERKO, MICHAEL F., ed. 1988. *Enlightening the Next Generation: Catholics and their Schools, 1830–1980.* New York: Garland.

WALCH, TIMOTHY. 1996. *Parish School: American Catholic Parochial Education from Colonial Times to the Present.* New York: Crossroad.

YOUNISS, JAMES; CONVEY, JOHN; and MCLELLAN, JEFFREY, eds. 2000. *The Catholic Character of Catholic Schools.* Notre Dame, IN: University of Notre Dame Press.

YOUNISS, JAMES, and CONVEY, JOHN, eds. 2000. *Catholic Schools at the Crossroads.* New York: Teachers College Press.

TIMOTHY WALCH

CENTERS FOR TEACHING IMPROVEMENT IN COLLEGES AND UNIVERSITIES

Although teaching has been at the core of faculty life from the beginning of the modern university, emphasis on teaching improvement is a more recent phenomenon. Centers and programs that support excellence in college and university teaching have grown substantially since the mid-twentieth century, and offer a broad range of services and resources to various constituencies.

Terms

Teaching-improvement support is typically offered either through programs (run by individual faculty members or faculty committees) or centers (centrally located and funded units), and is categorized in a variety of ways—most typically as *faculty development* (or, in the case of graduate students, *teaching assistant development*). While some resist this term and its implications that instructors need to "be developed" (Gaff, p. 175), it is nonetheless commonly used to refer to a large range of activities focusing on the professional work of faculty and graduate students as teachers (and, to a lesser extent, as researchers).

Other terms often associated with teaching-improvement centers are *educational* or *instructional development,* which emphasizes the design of a course, the curriculum, and student learning activities. Organizational development, which focuses on the organizational structure of an institution and its subcomponents, is another form of support sometimes blended into teaching centers or programs.

History

Only in the late 1950s and early 1960s did significant cracks appear in the foundational assumption in higher education that content competence equated with teaching competence. According to Wilbert J. McKeachie, a pioneering researcher on college teaching, the first centers for the improvement of college teaching developed in the early 1960s at the University of Michigan and Michigan State University. Behaviorist psychology shaped the mission of these centers. Faculty developed instructional materials that reinforced student progress through a series of carefully designed learning steps. Early centers tended to focus on teaching in disciplines that responded best to such programmed learning, including foreign languages, statistics, and anatomy.

The social revolutions of the 1960s profoundly reshaped American colleges and universities. Students demanded, and often received, a larger voice in campus life. One manifestation of this change came with students evaluating classroom teaching, a rarity before the 1960s and the norm by the late 1970s. Despite the many flaws in these evaluations, university administrators soon began making personnel decisions in response, in part, to student commentary about teaching. Some faculty called for new support to improve teaching, both to enhance their own practice and to meet higher performance standards being advocated by students and administrators. In the late 1960s, only forty to fifty faculty development programs existed at colleges and universities nationwide; by the middle of the 1970s that number had exploded to more than 1,000. Private funds (from groups including the Danforth Foundation and the Lilly Endowment) and federal grants (from sources such as the Fund for the Improvement of Postsecondary Education) helped establish many of these new programs. Although this seed money allowed teaching centers to blossom quickly across the nation, over the next decade many programs struggled to survive when their initial grants expired.

These new teaching programs varied widely in their mission and structure. Typically a teaching-improvement program developed to meet an individual campus's needs, rather than in response to a larger national trend. Depending on the resources and interest involved, colleges developed formal or informal teaching-improvement programs; only the most well-funded universities tended to establish formal teaching centers that coordinated and enhanced improvement programs campus-wide. Centers at research universities often focused initially on training graduate students to teach. At comprehensive universities and community colleges, less well-funded programs usually concentrated on improving faculty teaching techniques.

As the number of teaching programs and centers expanded, college teachers and faculty developers created professional organizations to share best practices. The American Association for Higher Education (AAHE) spun off the National Education Association (NEA) in 1969. In 1976 a group of faculty developers founded the Professional and Organizational Development Network for Higher Education (POD), and in 1978 private and public grants helped establish the National Institute for Staff and Organizational Development (NISOD). Publications, conferences, and other activities by these three groups helped advance both the practice of faculty development and the visibility of teaching in higher education.

The assessment movement that took center stage in the 1980s reshaped both perceptions of teaching and the work of teaching-improvement programs. Advocates of assessment, from inside and outside the academy, asked pointedly, "Are students learning anything in college?" (B. Wright, pp. 299–300). As attention shifted from teaching to learning, faculty development work also changed its focus. Improving teaching techniques remained an important component of most programs, but more and more developers encouraged faculty to think about student learning. "Classroom assessment techniques" (CATs), pioneered by Thomas A. Angelo and K. Patricia Cross, emerged as a new and powerful way for faculty to regularly and informally monitor learning. Besides promoting the use of CATs, many teaching programs also emphasized topics such as cognitive processes, motivational strategies, and learning styles.

In the early 1990s Ernest L. Boyer of the Carnegie Foundation for the Advancement of Teaching, along with allies from the AAHE and other groups, proposed a significant reconsideration of faculty roles and responsibilities, including teaching. These proposals responded both to the assessment movement and demands for more public accountability in higher education, and to advances in learning sciences. A core component of Boyer's vision involved "the scholarship of teaching." Boyer argued that, like other forms of scholarship, to be scholarly the act of teaching must be public, open to critical evaluation by peers, and usable by others in the discipline.

The intellectual energy created by Boyer's proposal coincided with other trends to produce another period of growth and expansion for teaching-improvement programs. By 1994 roughly one-third of colleges and universities had a formal center for teaching improvement, and another third was con-

sidering the creation of a center. These centers existed at many (61%) research universities, and at some (41%) doctorate-granting institutions; such centers were relatively rare at liberal arts colleges and community colleges, although nearly all institutions had some sort of faculty development program, often focusing on teaching and learning.

Teaching centers populated many research universities by the 1990s due, in part, to increased emphasis on graduate student teaching assistant training. In 1986 the Ohio State University hosted the first national conference on teaching assistant development; seven years later a consortium of universities and private foundations launched Preparing Future Faculty, a major national initiative to train graduate students to be effective teachers and scholars. Preparing Future Faculty programs, and variations on that model, spread quickly, becoming a significant component of teaching center work at many research universities by the end of the decade.

Teaching centers also became assets to colleges and universities that struggled to deal with technological revolutions, changing student demographics, and increased competition in higher education. As computers and networked technology became ubiquitous, new ways of teaching and learning enticed many colleges and universities to explore distance and asynchronous education. These changes challenged teaching centers to help faculty and institutions focus on learning rather than on gadgets and gimmicks. Changing student demographics also confronted college teachers, leading to increased work for teaching centers to address the needs of adult learners in more culturally diverse classrooms. The quality of teaching and learning also became an issue as the growth of for-profit higher education and the proliferation of distance-learning programs gave students new opportunities to choose where, when, and how to pursue their education.

Resources and Services

Although the breadth of content and scope of teaching-improvement programs and centers can vary substantially from institution to institution, most offer some combination of the following services.

Consultation services. These services enable individual faculty and graduate students, as well as departments and schools, to better observe, assess, improve, and enhance their teaching practices. Such consultations may include instructional or curriculum design assistance, creation of models for evaluating teaching, videotaping of classes for review, classroom observation, or interviewing students to gather anonymous feedback for the instructor.

Programs on teaching. These programs include a broad range of offerings across such categories as audience (from a guest speaker on effective lecturing for all university faculty, to a workshop on active learning for physics teaching assistants), length (from a semester-long credit-granting graduate course on teaching sociology, to a one-hour lunch discussion about diversity in the classroom), and incentives for participation (from a required orientation for all new teaching assistants to a voluntary discussion group on teaching with cases, to a stipend-funded fellows program on service learning).

Grants, awards, and other incentives. Incentives are offered to motivate improvement in teaching or to reward excellence in teaching. These incentives can take a variety of forms, such as grants or release time for course redesign or other curricular innovations; fellows programs to build teaching-improvement support between peers; or financial support for attending professional conferences.

Print and electronic resources. These resources typically include libraries of books, videotapes, and articles on a variety of issues pertaining to teaching and learning in higher education. Some centers or programs publish their own newsletters or develop websites to further highlight research, principles of good practice, or other explorations on teaching.

Leadership and Constituencies

The people who lead teaching-support efforts likewise represent a broad range of backgrounds and institutional status. A 1996 survey of POD members (with a 46% response rate) revealed that of the 517 respondents, 53 percent were women; 90 percent were white; 77 percent had a doctorate as the highest degree earned; 26 percent had their graduate degree in education (versus 12% in psychology, and 11% in English); 44 percent had a faculty job classification (versus 36% with administrative or staff status); 44 percent had part-time appointments in faculty development (versus 30% with full-time); and 59 percent worked in programs or centers that report to a provost or other chief academic officer (versus 16% to a dean).

Teaching-improvement programs and centers often serve faculty and graduate students from across the entire institution, while others are dedicated to a particular school or division. The distinct mission and curricular changes of many professional schools, in particular, has motivated the creation of separate support units, such as Harvard Medical School's Office of Educational Development, established in 1985.

In a similar vein, participants vary in their level of motivation and reasons for using the resources and services offered: some are strongly encouraged or even required to participate by administrators, while others are more intrinsically motivated to examine their teaching or to learn innovative practices. In order to create an open environment for its constituency, most centers have a policy of confidentiality, and distance themselves from the formal review processes at the institution.

Assumptions and Impact

Some core assumptions infuse most teaching-improvement programs or centers: (1) that teaching practices can be learned and developed (versus the view that good teachers are born, not made); (2) that knowledge of a subject does not necessarily translate into effective teaching of that subject; (3) that the educational research literature can offer models and strategies for improving teaching; and (4) that great teaching, like all scholarly activity, is a constant process of inquiry, experimentation, and reflection.

Assessing the impact of teaching-improvement centers and programs is a complicated and sometimes elusive process: John P. Murray describes how in some programs, "faculty participation is often low," and those "most in need of development are the least likely to participate," making it difficult to judge whether or not these initiatives "cause any substantial or lasting changes in the classroom" (pp. 59–60). On the other hand, Arlene Bakutes claims that "research data indicate that faculty development centers and their counterparts are successful," citing a University of Delaware survey showing that 73 percent of faculty respondents made changes to their teaching due to their work at that university's Center for Teaching Effectiveness (p. 170). Jerry G. Gaff asserts that "faculty development has moved slowly from a fragmented, often misunderstood, and peripheral position to an integrated, better understood, and more centrally located position of importance" and is "on the verge of becoming fully institutionalized in American higher education" (p. 173).

See also: COLLEGE TEACHING; TEACHING AND LEARNING, *subentry on* HIGHER EDUCATION.

BIBLIOGRAPHY

ANGELO, THOMAS A., and CROSS, K. PATRICIA. 1993. *Classroom Assessment Techniques: A Handbook for College Teachers,* 2nd edition. San Francisco: Jossey-Bass.

BAKUTES, ARLENE PICKETT. 1998. "An Examination of Faculty Development Centers." *Contemporary Education* 69:168.

BOYER, ERNEST L. 1990. *Scholarship Reconsidered: Priorities of the Professoriate.* Princeton, NJ: Carnegie Foundation for the Advancement of Teaching.

CHISM, NANCY VAN NOTE. 1998. "Preparing Graduate Students to Teach: Past, Present, and Future." In *The Professional Development of Graduate Teaching Assistants,* ed. Michele Marincovich, Jack Prostko, and Frederic Stout. Bolton, MA: Anker.

DEZURE, DEBORAH, ed. 2000. *Learning from "Change": Landmarks in Teaching and Learning in Higher Education from "Change" Magazine 1969–1999.* Sterling, VA: Stylus.

ERICKSON, GLENN. 1986. "A Survey of Faculty Development Practices." In *To Improve the Academy,* Vol. 5. Joint publication of Professional and Organizational Development Network in Higher Education and National Council for Staff, Program and Organizational Development. Stillwater, OK: New Forums.

GAFF, JERRY G., and SIMPSON, RONALD D. 1994. "Faculty Development in the United States." *Innovative Higher Education* 18:167–176.

GLASSICK, CHARLES E.; HUBER, MARY TAYLOR; and MAEROFF, GENE I. 1993. *Scholarship Assessed: Evaluation of the Professoriate.* San Francisco: Jossey-Bass.

GRAF, DAVID L.; ALBRIGHT, MICHAEL J.; and WHEELER, DANIEL W. 1992. "Faculty Development's Role in Improving Undergraduate Education." In *Teaching in the Information Age: The Role of Educational Technology,* ed. Michael J. Albright and David L. Graf. San Francisco: Jossey-Bass.

LEWIS, KARRON G. 1996. "Faculty Development in the United Sates: A Brief History." *International Journal for Academic Development* 1(2):26–33.

MCKEACHIE, WILBERT J. 1991. "What Theories Underlie the Practice of Faculty Development?" In *To Improve the Academy,* Vol. 10, ed. Kenneth A. Zahorski. Stillwater, OK: New Forums.

MURRAY, JOHN P. 1999. "Faculty Development in a National Sample of Community Colleges." *Community College Review* 27(3):47–65.

TICE, STACY LANE; GAFF, JERRY G; and PRUITT-LOGAN, ANNE S. 1998. "Preparing Future Faculty Programs: Beyond TA Development." In *The Professional Development of Graduate Teaching Assistants,* ed. Michele Marincovich, Jack Prostko, and Frederic Stout. Bolton, MA: Anker.

WRIGHT, BARBARA D. 2000. "Assessing Student Learning." In *Learning from "Change": Landmarks in Teaching and Learning in Higher Education from "Change" Magazine 1969–1999.* Sterling, VA: Stylus.

WRIGHT, DELIVEE L. 2000. "Faculty Development Centers in Research Universities: A Study of Resources and Programs." In *To Improve the Academy,* Vol. 19, ed. Matthew Kaplan. Bolton, MA: Anker.

PETER FELTEN
ALLISON PINGREE

CENTRAL ASIA

See: EASTERN EUROPE AND CENTRAL ASIA.

CHALL, JEANNE (1921–1999)

Leading teacher, researcher, and writer in the field of reading, Jeanne S. Chall held views on the importance of direct, systematic instruction in reading that were slighted in the 1980s but justified in the late 1990s. She was deeply committed to teaching; to the importance of children's successful reading acquisition and the need to address failing readers; to the power of research to answer practical questions; and to the merit of understanding the historical background of research questions.

Born in Poland, Chall emigrated as a girl to New York City with her family. She graduated from the City College of New York in 1941 with a B.A. (cum laude). She became an assistant to Irving Lorge, who directed educational research at Teachers College, Columbia University. She then served as research assistant to Edgar Dale at the Bureau of Educational

Research at Ohio State University, where she received an A.M. in 1947 and a Ph.D. in 1952. Her review for Dale of the existing research on readability led to her *Readability: An Appraisal of Research and Application* (1958) and a keen appreciation of the value of historical synthesis. Dale's and Chall's collaboration culminated in their *Dale-Chall Formula for Predicting Readability* (1948), which combined vocabulary complexity with sentence length to evaluate text readability. (Chall updated it in 1995.) Between 1950 and 1965 Chall rose from lecturer to professor at City College. These years brought a lifelong collaboration with Florence Roswell on the diagnosis and treatment of reading difficulties, and led Chall to question whether some methods were superior to others in preventing reading failure.

In 1965 Chall moved to Harvard University to create and direct graduate programs in reading for master's and doctoral candidates. An excellent clinician herself, she founded the Harvard Reading Laboratory in 1967 (now named after her), directing it until her retirement in 1991. She was a member of numerous scholarly organizations, editorial boards, policymaking committees, and state and national commissions. She served on the board of directors of the International Reading Association, 1961 to 1964, and on the National Academy of Education's Commission on Reading that resulted in the report *Becoming a Nation of Readers* (1985). She received many professional awards, the last given by the International Dyslexia Association in 1996.

Chall was engaged in both practice and research, often at the same time. For more than fifty years she taught students of all ages, including remedial ones, and advised schools. She was a consultant for children's encyclopedias, an educational comic book, educational software, and educational television, including the children's literacy programs *Sesame Street, The Electric Company,* and *Between the Lions.*

Chall's most important professional contribution was a byproduct of the professional furor over Rudolf Flesch's *Why Johnny Can't Read—and What You Can Do About It* (1955). Flesch attacked the prevailing sight word methodology of teaching reading, claiming that reading professionals had ignored their own research. With beginning reading instruction now on the national agenda, the Carnegie Corporation funded a study that Chall conducted from 1962 to 1965. She reviewed the existing research, described methods of instruction, interviewed leading proponents of various methods, and analyzed two

leading reading series of the late 1950s and early 1960s. The results appeared in her *Learning to Read: The Great Debate* (1967).

Chall identified what she called "the conventional wisdom" of reading instruction: that children should read for meaning from the start, use context and picture clues to identify words after learning about fifty words as sight words, and induce letter–sound correspondences from these words. Like Flesch, she concluded that this conventional wisdom was not supported by the research, which found phonics superior to whole word instruction and "systematic" phonics superior to "intrinsic" phonics instruction. She also found that beginning reading was different in kind from mature reading—a conclusion that she reaffirmed in her *Stages of Reading Development* (1983), which found that children first learn to read and then read to learn. She recommended in 1967 that publishers switch to a code-emphasis approach in children's readers, which would lead to better results without compromising children's comprehension.

Chall's *Learning to Read* quickly became a classic. Major textbook publishers reacted by emphasizing more phonics earlier in their series, although no publisher already committed to initial whole word instruction switched to systematic phonics. Chall's book was updated in 1983 (and 1996) with even stronger research findings to support its conclusions, but by 1983 textbooks of all kinds were under attack from the Whole Language movement, which condemned textbooks as a genre. The climate was an unsympathetic one for Chall's coauthored study *Should Textbooks Challenge Students: The Case for Easier or Harder Textbooks* (1991), which explored the relationship between the decline in difficulty of textbooks between 1945 and 1975 and lower SAT scores. Chall's coauthored study of thirty low-income urban children, *The Reading Crisis: Why Poor Children Fall Behind* (1990), was also not universally well received. Whole Language proponents criticized it for relying on outdated tests; social scientists complained that it did not adequately explain its ethnographic techniques.

Chall showed her regard for the reading instruction of the past by reissuing, largely for home schooling use, stories from school readers of the 1880s to 1910s, titling them the *Classic American Readers* (1994). She had already given her own collection of over 9,500 imprints related to the history of reading research and the teaching of reading, spanning more than two centuries, to the Harvard Graduate School of Education's Monroe C. Gutman Library.

Chall's last work, published posthumously, was *The Academic Challenge: What Really Works in the Classroom* (2000). In it, she divided American instruction into "child-centered" and "teacher-centered" approaches, suggesting that the twentieth century was dominated by the former (discovery approaches) in spite of research that supported the superiority of the latter (explicit teaching). Earlier, Helen Popp had persuaded her to coauthor a contribution to explicit teaching: a handbook for teachers, *Teaching and Assessing Phonics* (1996). The Chall-Popp Phonics program was completed after her death (2000).

Written in a climate in which many members of her own profession still disdained explications of the English writing system, the 1996 handbook is true to many of Chall's core concerns: teaching reading, particularly to at-risk children, and research-validated explicit instruction.

See also: READING, *subentries on* BEGINNING READING, COMPREHENSION, TEACHING OF.

BIBLIOGRAPHY

ADAMS, MARILYN JAGER, and RATH, LINDA K., eds. 2000. "Jeanne Sternlicht Chall: The Difference One Life Can Make." *Perspectives* [issue devoted to memorial tributes of Jeanne Sternlicht Chall] 26(4):1, 4.

CHALL, JEANNE S. 1983. *Stages of Reading Development.* New York: McGraw-Hill.

CHALL, JEANNE S. 1993, 1994. "Fascination with Psychology and Teaching of Reading." *History of Reading News* 17(1):1–2; 17(2):2.

CHALL, JEANNE S. 1996. *Learning to Read: The Great Debate* (1967). New York: McGraw Hill.

CHALL, JEANNE S. 2000. *The Academic Achievement Challenge: What Really Works in the Classroom.* New York: Guilford.

CHALL, JEANNE S., and POPP, HELEN. 1996. *Teaching and Assessing Phonics: A Guide for Teachers.* Cambridge, MA: Educators Publishing Service.

RAVITCH, DIANE, et al. 2001. "A Tribute to Jeanne Chall." *American Educator* 25(1):16–23.

INTERNET RESOURCE

JEANNE CHALL READING LAB. 2002. "About Jeanne Chall." <www.gse.harvard.edu/~litlab/about chall.html>.

E. JENNIFER MONAGHAN

CHARACTER DEVELOPMENT

When a person is said to have character, it usually implies they have distinguishing moral qualities, moral virtues, and moral reasoning abilities. Less frequently used terms include *morality, virtue,* and *ethics.* A moral person understands right and wrong and willfully chooses what is right; a virtuous person engages in good behavior intentionally, predictably, and habitually; an ethical person figures out what is right or good when this is not obvious. At the beginning of the twenty-first century, there appears to be a desire to reconsider earlier goals of American education by taking character building more seriously. Most people share the view that schools should be formally and strategically involved in building moral character, virtues, and ethical behavior and should work in concert with parents and the community.

Looking Back

From the beginning of written history, the importance of building moral character has been recognized by parents, educators, and concerned citizens in every culture and society. Between 1640 and 1940, educators in the United States were as concerned about moral education as academic education. Throughout this 300-year period, the dominant pedagogical method was inculcation (repetitive direct instruction combined with reinforced practice), and the goals were inspiration, commitment, and habituation. During the early 1900s the American philosopher, psychologist, and educator John Dewey and other progressive educators expanded those goals to include critical thinking and reflection about values and morals; they stressed the value of experiential learning for building character. In 1951 the National Education Association (NEA) recommended combining these traditional and progressive approaches. This was not accomplished because concerns about academic competence and teaching specific values caused character education to be put aside as a formal undertaking. Public schools abandoned the dual focus on moral character and academic success and adopted a singular focus on academics. Character education continued informally through the hidden curriculum of Western democratic values and the independent efforts of teachers.

Between 1940 and 1970 cognitive-developmental psychologists generated some renewed interest in character by identifying levels of moral reasoning and trying to accelerate moral development. The more widely adopted values clarification movement was a response to the nation's preoccupation with individual freedom and self-improvement and the nationalistic push for better science and mathematics education. A third influence was built on the work of Erik Erikson and Robert James Havighurst, who identified processes and stages of socioemotional development. Affective-developmental psychologists and moral philosophers concerned with conscience and emotion began to expand the understanding of affective moral development.

Public concern about a moral decline in society and the disintegration of families and communities led to the reemergence of character education in the 1980s. By 1995 it had become a social movement with thousands of schools and communities involved. Throughout the 1980s and 1990s, proponents of traditional and progressive approaches engaged in a friendly dialogue, which energized the movement and accelerated the synthesis of ideas. Schools drew strategies from both approaches with little regard for the theoretical foundation for this synthesis. They taught and trained students using stories, moral exemplars, reinforcement, and lists of virtues as recommended by traditionalists; they provided active student experiences within caring communities through class meetings, cooperative learning, and service learning as recommended by progressives.

Many important contributions to character education occurred during the final two decades of the twentieth century. In 1992 representatives from many organizations devoted to building the civic virtue and moral character of students formed the Character Education Partnership (CEP). According to CEP's eleven principles, effective character education schools:

1. promote core ethical values as the basis of good character;

2. define character comprehensively to include thinking, feeling, and behavior;

3. promote core values intentionally and proactively through all parts of school life;

4. are caring communities;

5. give students opportunities for moral action;

6. have meaningful and challenging academic curriculums that respect learners;

7. develop students' intrinsic motivation;

8. have professionals who exemplify core values and maintain a moral community;

9. require moral leadership from educators and students;

10. recruit parents and community members as full partners;

11. evaluate school character, student character, and adults as character educators.

The Eclectic Ideal

Research and practice suggest that the most effective character education schools combine direct instruction, modeling, reinforcement, and various community-building strategies (class meetings, service learning, cooperative learning, intercultural exchange, social-skills training, and caring interpersonal support) to promote the development of moral virtues, moral reasoning, and other assets that make the will and ability to do what is right and good probable. They are concerned with all aspects of development, including social, emotional, moral, intellectual, and academic. They are child-need-centered without abandoning the responsibility to transmit core ethical values to youth. They endorse Robert D. Heslep's view that character education includes civic education (learning about laws, government, and citizenship), social education (learning social roles, responsibilities, and skills), prudential education (learning how to take care of oneself), cultural education (becoming historically and culturally literate), and moral education—the latter providing a context of principles that guide civic, social, prudential, and cultural education.

Good character educators are aware of the overlapping and interconnected parts of the moral person: knowledge, understanding, reasoning, autonomy, values, beliefs, standards, principles, perspective taking, conscience, empathy, emotion, virtues, intentions, will, commitment, motivation, duty, behavior, and habits. Marvin Berkowitz's 1995 model of the complete moral person includes moral values (beliefs and attitudes with an affective component), moral behavior (intentional moral acts), moral emotion (energizing feelings), moral character (a personality characteristic), moral identity (being or trying to be moral), and meta-moral characteristics such as self-discipline. Thomas Lickona's moral feeling, thinking, and action, and Kevin Ryan's knowing, loving, and doing the good are perhaps easier to remember and use. William G. Huitt's 2000 model treats moral will or volition as a part distinguishable from moral emotion, moral thought, and moral behavior.

Thomas F. Green (1999) connects the thinking and feeling parts of the moral person by describing five voices of conscience (craft, membership, responsibility, memory, and imagination). Jerome Kagan explains how several specific moral emotions compel adherence to standards of right and wrong beginning in early childhood. Many define moral behavior in terms of specific virtues or habits of conduct from which inner parts of the moral person can be inferred. Gordon G. Vessels distinguishes between primary virtues that reflect personal integrity (e.g., kindness, courage, ability, and effort) and primary virtues that reflect social integrity (e.g., friendship, teamwork, and citizenship). He incorporates elaborations of these virtues and theoretical propositions about moral-developmental processes into behavioral objectives for various age groups.

Early Twenty-First Century

At the beginning of the twenty-first century, the time devoted to character education in many schools is decreasing due to the popular focus on academic standards, accountability, standardized testing, and whole-school reform. The well-researched whole-school reform models that include character education are not among the most popular: Basic Schools, Child Development Project (CDP), Modern Red Schoolhouse, Positive Action, Responsive Classroom, School Development Program, and Expeditionary Learning Outward Bound. In general, American society may not be ready to think in terms of preventing social problems and improving schools by implementing a curriculum that balances character education and academic instruction, and the addition of nontraditional assessment measures that document products and processes reflecting good character and character growth such as Huitt's (2001) proposed use of cumulative electronic portfolios with scanned pictures and video clips.

Trends and concerns suggest that in order for character education to become a highly valued and fully integrated feature of education once again, character educators will have to focus on reducing societal problems and address concerns about the effectiveness of academic instruction in the schools. Barring a major shift in priorities, the future of character education appears to hinge on the evaluation of its potential for reducing school violence, drug use, teen pregnancy, disrespect, and prejudice; and improving school climate, student discipline, school safety, intercultural understanding, and academic achievement. Models for this type of program evaluation research are available. Leaders in education are not likely to change course unless research results show that academic goals are achievable using a curriculum that addresses all aspects of development, thereby integrating academic and character goals, objectives, and methods.

See also: AFFECT AND EMOTIONAL DEVELOPMENT; AGGRESSIVE BEHAVIOR; MORAL DEVELOPMENT; STRESS AND DEPRESSION.

BIBLIOGRAPHY

BATTISTICH, VICTOR; SOLOMON, DAVID; DONG-IL, KIM; WATSON, MARILYN; and SCHAPS, ERIC. 1995. "Schools As Communities, Poverty Levels of Student Populations, and Students' Attitudes, Motives, and Performance: A Multilevel Analysis." *American Educational Research Journal* 32:627–658.

BATTISTICH, VICTOR; SOLOMON, DAVID; WATSON, MARILYN; SOLOMON, DANIEL; and SCHAPS, ERIC. 1989. "Effects of an Elementary School Program to Enhance Prosocial Behavior on Children's Cognitive-Social Problem-Solving Skills and Strategies." *Journal of Applied Developmental Psychology* 10:147–169.

BENNINGA, JACQUES S.; TRACZ, SUSAN M.; SPARKS, RICHARD; SOLOMON, DANIEL; BATTISTICH, VICTOR; DELUCCHI, KEVIN; and STANLEY, BEVERLY. 1991. "Effects of Two Contrasting School Task and Incentive Structures on Children's Social Development." *Elementary School Journal* 92:149–167.

BERKOWITZ, MARVIN. 1995. *The Education of the Complete Moral Person.* Aberdeen, Scotland: Gordon Cook Foundation.

BOYER, ERNEST. 1995. *The Basic School: A Community for Learning.* Princeton, NJ: Carnegie Foundation for the Advancement of Teaching.

COMER, JAMES. 1997. *Waiting for a Miracle: Why Schools Can't Solve Our Problems—and How We Can.* New York: Penguin Putnam, Plume.

COMER, JAMES. 2001. "Schools That Develop Children." *American Prospect* 12(7): 30–35.

DUNCAN, BARBARA J. 1997. "Character Education: Reclaiming the Social." *Education Theory* 47(1):119–131.

ELAM, STANLEY; ROSE, LOWELL C.; and GALLUP, ALEC M. 1993. "The 25th Annual Phi Delta Kappa/Gallup Poll of the Public's Attitudes toward the Public Schools." *Phi Delta Kappan* 75(2):137–154.

ELLIOTT, STEPHEN N. 1995. *The Responsive Classroom Approach.* Washington, DC: District of Columbia Public Schools.

ERIKSON, ERIK. 1961. "The Roots of Virtue." In *The Humanist Frame: The Modern Humanist Vision of Life,* ed. Julian Huxley. New York: Harper.

ERIKSON, ERIK. 1980. *Identity and the Life Cycle.* New York: Norton.

ETZIONI, AMITAI. 1984. *Self-Discipline, Schools, and the Business Community.* Washington, DC: National Chamber Foundation.

GILLIGAN, CAROL. 1987. "Moral Orientation and Moral Development." In *Women and Moral Theory,* ed. Eva F. Kittay and Diana Meyers. Totowa, NJ: Rowman and Littlefield.

GINSBURG, ALAN L., and HANSON, SANDRA L. 1986. *Gaining Ground: Values and High School Success.* Washington, DC: U.S. Department of Education.

GREEN, THOMAS F. 1984. "The Formation of Conscience in an Age of Technology." *American Journal of Education* 94(1):1–32.

GREEN, THOMAS F. 1999. *Voices: The Educational Foundation of Conscience.* Notre Dame, IN: University of Notre Dame Press.

HAVIGHURST, ROBERT J. 1953. *Human Development and Education.* New York: Longmans, Green.

HAYES, B. GRANT, and HAGEDORN, W. BRYCE. 2000. "A Case for Character Education." *Journal of Humanistic Counseling, Education and Development* 39(1):2–4.

HESLEP, ROBERT D. 1995. *Moral Education for Americans.* Westport, CT: Praeger.

HINCK, SHELLY, and BRANDELL, MARY ELLEN. 1999. "Service Learning: Facilitating Academic Learning and Character Development." *NASSP Bulletin* 83(609):16–24.

HOFFMAN, MARTIN. 1982. "Development of Prosocial Motivation: Empathy and Guilt." In *The Development of Prosocial Behavior,* ed. Nancy Eisenberg. New York: Academic Press.

HOFFMAN, MARTIN. 1983. "Empathy, Guilt, and Social Cognition." In *The Relationship between Social and Cognitive Development,* ed. Willis Overton. Hillsdale, NJ: Erlbaum.

KAGAN, JEROME. 1984. *The Nature of the Child.* New York: Basic Books.

KOHLBERG, LAWRENCE. 1984. *The Psychology of Moral Development.* San Francisco: Harper and Row.

KRAJEWSKI, BOB, and BAILEY, ELSIE. 1999. Caring with Passion: The "Core" Value. *NASSP Bulletin* 83(609):33–39.

LEMING, JAMES S. 1997. "Research and Practice in Character Education: A Historical Perspective." In *The Construction of Children's Character,* ed. Alex Molnar. Chicago: National Society for the Study of Education; distributed by the University of Chicago Press.

LEMING, JAMES S.; HENDRICKS-SMITH, ASTRID; and ANTIS, J. 1997. "An Evaluation of the Heartwood Institutes: An Ethics Curriculum for Children." Paper presented at the annual meeting of the American Educational Research Association, Chicago.

LICKONA, THOMAS. 1993. *Educating for Character: How Our Schools Can Teach Respect and Responsibility.* New York: Bantam Books.

McCLELLAND, B. EDWARD. 1992. *Schools and the Shaping of Character: Moral Education in America, 1607–Present.* Bloomington, IN: ERIC Clearinghouse for Social Studies/Social Science Education and the Social Studies Development Center.

RYAN, KEVIN. 1996. *Character Education: Education's Latest Fad or Oldest Mission.* Keynote address presented at the Linking School and Community through Character Education conference at Emory University, March 7, planned and sponsored by the Georgia Humanities Council.

SCHAEFFER, ESTHER F. 1998. "Character Crisis and the Classroom." *Thrust for Educational Leadership* 28(1):14–17.

SCOTT, CHARLES L. 1992. "Shaping Character." *American School Board Journal* 179(12):28–30.

SIMON, SIDNEY B.; HOWE, LELAND W.; and KIRSCHENBAUM, HOWARD. 1972. *Values Clarification: A Handbook of Practical Strategies for Teachers and Students.* New York: Hart.

SOLOMON, DANIEL; SCHAPS, ERIC; WATSON, MARILYN; and BATTISTICH, VICTOR. 1992. "Creating Caring School and Classroom Communities for All Students." In *Restructuring for Caring and Effective Education: An Administrative Guide to Creating Heterogeneous Schools,* ed. Richard A. Villa, Jacqueline S. Thousand, William Stainback, and Susan Stainback. Baltimore: Brookes.

VESSELS, GORDON G. 1998. *Character and Community Development: A School Planning and Teacher Training Handbook.* Westport, CT: Greenwood.

WILLIAMS, MARY. 2000. "Models of Character Education: Perspectives and Developmental Issues." *Journal of Humanistic Counseling, Education and Development* 39:32–41.

INTERNET RESOURCES

DEVELOPMENTAL STUDIES CENTER. 2002. "Child Development Project." <www.devestu.org>.

EXPEDITIONARY LEARNING OUTWARD BOUND. 2002. <www.elob.org>.

GALLUP ORGANIZATION. 2001. "Gallup Poll Topics: Education." <www.gallup.com/poll/indicators/indeducation.asp>.

HUITT, WILLIAM G. 2000. "Moral and Character Development." *Educational Psychology Interactive.* Valdosta, GA: Valdosta State University. <http://chiron.valdosta.edu/whuitt/col/morchr/morchr.html>.

HUITT, WILLIAM G. 2001. "Becoming a Brilliant Star: Thought for the Day Activity." *Educational Psychology Interactive.* Valdosta, GA: Valdosta State University. <http://chiron.valdosta.edu/whuitt/brilstar/BrilStarThought.html>.

LICKONA, THOMAS; SCHAPS, ERIC; and LEWIS, CATHERINE. 2000. *Eleven Principles of Effective Character Education.* Washington, DC: Character Education Partnership. <www.character.org/principles/index.cgi>.

MODERN RED SCHOOLHOUSE INSTITUTE. 2002. <www.mrsh.org>.

NORTHEAST FOUNDATION FOR CHILDREN. 2002. "Responsive Classroom." <www.responsiveclassroom.org>.

POSITIVE ACTION. 2002. <www.positiveaction.net>.

SCHOOL DEVELOPMENT PROGRAM. 2001. <http://info.med.yale.edu/comer>.

WILLIAM G. HUITT
GORDON G. VESSELS

CHARTERS, W. W. (1875–1952)

Professor and director of the Bureau of Educational Research at Ohio State University, Werrett Wallace Charters contributed to the fields of curriculum development and audiovisual technology. Born in Hartford, Ontario (Canada), Charters earned his A.B. in 1898 from McMaster University, a teaching diploma from the Ontario Normal College in 1899, a B.Pd. from the University of Toronto, and his M.Ph. and Ph.D. from the University of Chicago, respectively in 1903 and 1904. After a three-year career in Canadian public schools as a teacher and principal, Charters spent the remainder of his career in the United States. Before joining Ohio State University in 1928, Charters served as a faculty member and/or dean at six institutions: the State Normal School in Winona, Minnesota, the University of Missouri, the University of Illinois, the Carnegie Institute for Technology, the University of Pittsburgh, and the University of Chicago. In 1923 Charters was awarded an honorary doctorate from McMaster University.

In his earliest scholarship, Charters attempted to develop what he called a "functional" theory of instruction derived from the ideas of the Progressive educator John Dewey (who, despite having discouraged Charters from pursuing doctoral study, had served as his doctoral adviser). In his first book, *Methods of Teaching,* Charters maintained that the function of school subject matter was "to satisfy needs and solve problems" faced by society (pp. 3, 31). A school's program of curriculum and instruction would put into practice this conception of subject matter by introducing subject matter when it addressed an actual or potential student need, enabling students to perceive its function. Charters discussed ways to organize subject matter and teaching to achieve such conditions, indicating, among other things, that students should not only be told about, but also should be allowed to "construct" functions of subject matter for themselves. Although he continued to embrace the notion of "functional" education, subsequently Charter's work departed significantly from Dewey's educational theory.

Charters's most significant contribution to the field of curriculum development came in the form of his activity-analysis approach to curriculum construction. Activity analysis essentially involved specification of the discrete tasks or activities involved in any social activity. For purposes of curriculum construction, the resulting specifications translated into program objectives. Activity analysis was considered a "scientific" approach to curriculum construction insofar as it represented a quantification of human activities as a basis for selecting educational objectives. Because activity analysis often amounted to little more than an accounting of tasks, critics of the approach characterized it as "scientism" in curriculum work and rejected it as overly mechanistic.

Charters's version of activity analysis differed from those of his contemporaries largely in terms of the emphasis that he placed on the inclusion of social ideals in the curriculum. In 1923 Charters articulated seven "rules" that governed curriculum construction.

1. Identify major educational aims through a study of contemporary social circumstances.

2. Classify the major aims into ideals and activities and reduce them to operational objectives.

3. Prioritize the aims and objectives.

4. Reprioritize the aims and objectives to lend greater importance to those relevant to children's experience than to those relevant to adults but remote from children.

5. Identify those aims and objectives achievable within the constraints of the school setting, relegating those best accomplished outside the school to extraschool experiences.

6. Identify materials and methods conducive to the achievement of the selected aims and objectives.

7. Order materials and methods consist with principles of child psychology.

Charters's approach to curriculum construction influenced a generation of curriculum scholars, including George S. Counts, Ralph W. Tyler, and Hilda Taba.

During the latter part of his career, Charters focused his attention on audiovisual education. In his book *Motion Pictures and Youth,* Charters summarized a series of twelve studies that he had directed that investigated the effects of motion pictures on children and youth. Among the earliest of their kind, these studies examined attendance at and content of movies and how they influenced children. In addition to ascertaining the retention of information from movies, the studies found that children and youth accepted movie content as true and that movies could exert a significant influence on attitudes. In his summary, Charters recognized not only that motion pictures were "a potent medium of education" (p.60), but also that films were potentially miseducative. Charters concluded that film clearly was a powerful source of information and attitudes, but that the extent of its influence on children and youth relative to other institutions, such as the home, church, and school, remained unclear.

Charters's contributions to scholarship were dwarfed, however, by his managerial and organizational accomplishments. In addition to directing the Bureau of Educational Research at Ohio State University from 1928 to 1942, Charters directly or indirectly managed numerous educational projects. These include codirecting the Commonwealth Teacher Training Study (1929), founding the Institute for Education by Radio (1930) and the *Journal of Higher Education,* serving on the United States Senate Committee on Racketeering (1933–1934), and conducting evaluations of pharmaceutical and library education programs and of the United States Armed Forces Institute (1942).

See also: CURRICULUM, SCHOOL.

BIBIOGRAPHY

CHARTERS, W. W. 1909. *Methods of Teaching, Developed From a Functional Standpoint.* Chicago: Row, Peterson.

CHARTERS, W. W. 1923. *Curriculum Construction.* New York: Macmillan.

CHARTERS, W. W. 1935. *Motion Pictures and Youth: A Summary.* New York: Macmillan.

PATTY, WILLIAM L. 1938. *A Study of Mechanism in Education.* New York: Teachers College, Columbia University.

ROSENSTOCK, SHELDON A. 1983. "The Educational Contributions of Werrett Wallace Charters." Ph.D. diss., Ohio State University.

WILLIAM G. WRAGA

CHIEF ACADEMIC AFFAIRS OFFICERS, COLLEGE AND UNIVERSITY

A college's chief academic affairs officer, often referred to as the chief academic officer (CAO), fulfills the essential role of ensuring that an institution's educational mission is achieved. Successful completion of this overarching goal involves work across multiple constituencies and the use of a number of measures, such as personnel and budgetary decisions, to influence educational outcomes. Despite the important role that the CAO plays in the educational endeavor, there is little empirical knowledge about the position. Current knowledge comes from a handful of empirical works and multiple personal reflections on what a chief academic officer should be engaged in doing, as well as how they should be doing it. Three main issues related to the CAO are examined: varying titles, typical career path, and the main roles of chief academic officers.

Various Titles

One of the difficulties in understanding the nature of the work of the CAO is the litany of various terms for the position. The two most common terms in current parlance are *provost* and *chief academic officer*. However, at least nine different terms have been used to refer to the position. One reason for the numerous titles is that CAOs are expected to complete many different roles within different institutions. Furthermore, as colleges and universities have grown, the way in which responsibility for the academic life of educational institutions is handled has also changed. This growth has coincided with a transformation in the titles applied to those in charge of academic affairs.

The role of the CAO evolved as colleges became more complex. Initially, colleges required little more administrative representation than that of a president. Until 1950 the role of chief academic officer was embodied within the presidency. But as institutions grew and diversified, it became necessary to establish the position of *dean*, then to create multiple deanships. These deans either oversaw individual colleges or were responsible for a specific dimension of institutional functioning, such as the dean of research or the dean of students. In this manner, the role of CAO became more clearly delineated, as deans of instruction or deans of faculties (two of the several terms used to refer to the CAO) presided over campus academic issues. Other terms include *academic dean,* the title most commonly found in small liberal arts colleges; *academic vice president, vice president for academic affairs,* and *vice president instructor* are used when an institution utilizes the *vice president* moniker for its administrative leaders. Otherwise, the title of provost is often used. In some instances, both the terms *provost* and *vice president of academic affairs* are incorporated to indicate the role of the individual as the second-in-command to the president as well as the head of institutional educational concerns. The title of *vice chancellor* is also sometimes used.

Typical Career Path

The typical career path of a CAO begins with a prolonged stint as a faculty member. During their time as faculty members, CAOs generally serve on many campus administrative committees, and often on the faculty senate. CAOs also tend to have prior experience as both chair and dean. In their current role, CAOs frequently serve as the second-in-command within their institutions, reporting directly to the president or chancellor.

The tenure of individuals in the role of CAO tends to be fairly abbreviated. A 1987 study by Gary Moden et al. found that the mean length of service of the CAO was 5.3 years. After serving in the CAO role, individual career paths go in varied directions. Moden and his colleagues found that 37 percent of CAOs aspired to a presidential position, while 35 percent viewed the CAO position as a final one, contemplating retirement at the end of their positional tenure or shifting to a similar position at another institution. Only 14 percent desired to return to teaching in their initial discipline. Women were underrepresented at the CAO level, with males making up 81 percent of the respondents in the Moden study; the report does not include the racial/ethnic composition of their sample.

Role of the Chief Academic Officer

While they support the president's needs, the central role of most CAOs is to maintain an inward vigilance toward the fulfillment of an institution's educational mission. The CAO therefore works closely with various constituencies on campus to enact that mission. By virtue of their position as second-in-command to the president, CAOs usually have jurisdiction over all academic deans, admissions, librarian, chief researcher, and all other academic officers. Therefore, the CAO generally has the power of approving all faculty appointments, as well as all college or departmental budgets and academic expenditures. CAOs are thus viewed as providing the internal focus of the administration, while the president provides the external vision and connection to community. While they may feel as if they are "on call" to the president, CAOs also have a great deal of power in their own right.

The CAO's internal focus may be conceived as having two elements: the development and implementation of academic goals for the institution and the allocation of resources to various departments and support services on campus to support those academic goals. As a result of this internal focus, CAOs frequently seek to balance competing needs across units within an institution to achieve the best outcomes for the institution as a whole. This often requires the CAO to act as negotiator and mediator, attempting to balance and accurately represent the interests of faculty and deans to the president and board of trustees—and vice versa.

In maintaining a focus on an institution's educational mission, the CAO is responsible for creating the principal connection between student progress and overall implementation of new programs. The CAO influences college values and outcomes, such as student progress through personnel, program, and budgetary decisions. Through a selective distribution of resources, the CAO may choose to reward or sanction programs that either meet or defy expectations. For instance, the CAO may provide increased funds for those departments with proven success or growing student enrollments, while paring down funds or faculty lines for those departments that show lower levels of educational outcomes or that no longer contribute strongly enough to the institutional mission. By hiring faculty who meet certain qualifications or supporting specific budget initiatives, the CAO may also seek to shape consensus or realize a vision for the institution's educational attainment.

The future of the CAO role is clouded in complexity. While CAOs may retain an inward focus and target the educational outcomes of an institution, the role of the CAO may be changing. As institutions continue to grow in complexity, the role of the CAO may shift from managing the academic enterprise directly to supervising and facilitating the actions of deans, who will begin to exercise greater control on the direction of academic issues within an institution.

See also: BOARD OF TRUSTEES, COLLEGE AND UNIVERSITY; COLLEGES AND UNIVERSITIES, ORGANIZATIONAL STRUCTURE OF; FACULTY SENATES, COLLEGE AND UNIVERSITY; GOVERNANCE AND DECISION-MAKING IN COLLEGES AND UNIVERSITIES; PRESIDENCY, COLLEGE AND UNIVERSITY.

BIBLIOGRAPHY

ASTIN, ALEXANDER W., and SCHERREI, RITA A. 1980. *Maximizing Leadership Effectiveness.* San Francisco: Jossey-Bass.

AUSTENSEN, ROY A. 1997. "Faculty Relations and Professional Development: Best Practices for the Chief Academic Officer." In *First Among Equals: The Role of the Chief Academic Officer,* ed. James Martin, James E. Samels, et al. Baltimore: Johns Hopkins University Press.

COFFMAN, JAMES R. 1997. "Leveraging Resources to Enhance Quality: Curriculum Development and Educational Technologies. In *First Among Equals: The Role of the Chief Academic Officer,* ed. James Martin, James E. Samels, et al. Baltimore: Johns Hopkins University Press.

EDELSTEIN, MARK G. 1997. "Academic Governance: The Art of Herding Cats." In *First Among Equals: The Role of the Chief Academic Officer,* ed. James Martin, James E. Samels, et al. Baltimore: Johns Hopkins.

EHRLE, ELWOOD B., and BENNETT, JOHN B. 1988. *Managing the Academic Enterprise: Case Studies for Deans and Provosts.* New York: Macmillan.

KNOWLES, ASA S. 1970. *Handbook of College and University Administration: Academic.* New York: McGraw-Hill.

MARTIN, JAMES, and SAMELS, JAMES E. 1997. "First Among Equals: The Current Roles of the Chief Academic Officer." In *First Among Equals: The Role of the Chief Academic Officer,* ed. James Martin, James E. Samels, et al. Baltimore: Johns Hopkins.

MODEN, GARY O.; MILLER, RICHARD I.; and WILLIFORD, A. M. 1987. *The Role, Scope, and Func-*

tions of the Chief Academic Officer. Paper presented at the Annual Forum of the Association of Institutional Research; ERIC Document Reproduction Service No. ED 293 441.

WEINGARTNER, RUDOLPH H. 1996. *Fitting Form to Function: A Primer on the Organization of Academic Institutions.* Phoenix, AZ: Oryx Press.

WOLVERTON, ROBERT E. 1984. "The Chief Academic Officer: Argus on Campus." In *Leadership Roles of Chief Academic Officers,* ed. David G. Brown. New Directions for Higher Education, no. 47, Vol. XII, No. 3, pp. 7–18. San Francisco: Jossey-Bass.

NATHANIEL J. BRAY

CHILD ABUSE AND NEGLECT

The concept of child abuse and neglect is relatively new to American society. Although children have been neglected, beaten, exploited, and even murdered by their parents and caregivers for hundreds of years, it is only since the mid–twentieth century that legislation requiring the reporting and prosecution of child abuse has been enacted. In 1974 Public Law 93-247, known as the Child Abuse Prevention and Treatment Act (CAPTA) was passed by Congress. Under this statue, only parents or caregivers can be perpetrators of child abuse or neglect. CAPTA provides minimum standards for the definition of child abuse and neglect for states that receive federal funds, and each state is left to define more specifically what constitutes maltreatment and to develop public policy that will guide courts, law enforcement, health care, and social services in the protection and care of children who are neglected or abused.

All fifty states and the District of Columbia have enacted laws that require that child abuse and maltreatment be reported to a designated agency or official. The purpose of these laws are to specify the conditions under which a state may intervene in family life; define abuse and neglect; encourage a therapeutic treatment approach to child abuse and neglect— rather than a punitive approach; and encourage coordination and cooperation among all disciplines that deal with abused and neglected children.

A number of terms are used to refer to the maltreatment of children, including the following:

- *Neglect.* An act of omission by a parent or caregiver that involves refusal or delay in providing health care, education, or basic needs such as food, clothes, shelter, affection, and attention. Neglect also includes inadequate supervision and abandonment.

- *Emotional abuse.* An act or omission by a parent or caregiver that involves rejecting, isolating, terrorizing, ignoring, or corrupting a child. Examples include, but are not limited to, verbal abuse; withholding food, sleep, or shelter; exposing a child to domestic violence; refusing to provide psychological care; and confinement. An important component of emotional abuse is that it must be sustained and repetitive.

- *Physical abuse.* An act of commission by a parent or caregiver that results in, or is likely to result in, physical harm to the child—including death. Examples include hitting, kicking, biting, shaking, burning, and punching the child. Spanking a child is usually considered a form of discipline, unless the child is bruised or injured.

- *Sexual abuse.* An act of commission by an parent or caregiver of sexual intrusion or penetration, molestation with genital contact, sodomy, rape, exhibitionism, or other forms of sexual acts in which the child is used to provide sexual gratification to the perpetrator. This type of abuse can also include child pornography.

Discussions of the number of children who are abused or neglected involve the use of two terms: *prevalence,* which describes the number of children who have suffered from a specific type of abuse at least once in their lifetime; and *incidence,* which describes the number of specific cases that are reported in a given time period. Obviously, incidents of physical abuse or extreme neglect are somewhat easier to identify and report than are other types of abuse. These are the cases that most frequently appear in child welfare offices and court cases. Actual reports of sexual abuse, emotional abuse, and neglect are generally thought to be grossly underrepresentative of the number of children affected by abuse.

Efforts to quantify the number of abuse cases in the United States include self-report surveys, in which parents are asked to report their own behavior toward their children; surveys of cases of abuse that were observed by someone outside the family and reported to community and public-agency professionals; and the collection of statistical information from child protective agencies. In 1990, the National Child Abuse and Neglect Data System was established. Information from this database indicates a growing trend in child abuse and neglect during the 1990s. In general, neglect is the most common form of child abuse reported, accounting for more than half of all reported cases. According to national statistics, approximately 2.8 million referrals for abuse and neglect are made annually. Less than half of these (approximately 1 million) are found to be substantiated cases. Of those that are substantiated, over half are for neglect, about 25 percent are for physical abuse, and slightly more than 10 percent are for sexual abuse. Approximately three children die each day of abuse or neglect in the United States.

Causes of Abuse and Neglect

According to the Child Welfare League of America, children whose parents abuse drugs and alcohol are almost three times more likely to be abused and four times more likely to be neglected than children of parents who are not substance abusers. Eighty-five percent of states that report statistics for child abuse and neglect cite parental substance abuse and poverty as the top two issues related to child abuse and neglect. Additionally, studies have shown that the most consistent finding in substantiated child abuse cases is that the abusive parents often report having been physically, sexually, or emotionally abused or neglected as children.

Certain children are at increased risk for abuse. Younger children are particularly vulnerable to certain types of abuse, such as *shaken baby syndrome* and *battered child syndrome.* Shaken baby syndrome is a severe form of head injury that occurs when a baby is shaken hard enough to cause the baby's brain to bounce against its skull. This causes bruising, swelling, and bleeding in the brain that can lead to permanent, severe brain damage or death. Even with immediate medical treatment, the prognosis for a victim of this syndrome is very poor. Most babies will be left with significant damage to their brain that can cause mental retardation or cerebral palsy. One of the difficulties in identifying this type of abuse is that there are usually no outward physical signs of trauma, which often creates a delay in the child receiving treatment.

Battered child syndrome is characterized by a group of physical and mental symptoms caused by long-term physical violence against the child. The abuse takes the form of cuts, bruises, broken bones,

burns, and internal injuries from hitting, punching, or kicking. Nearly half of the victims of this type of abuse are under the age of one. Parents who bring their abused children to an emergency room frequently offer complicated and vague explanations of the child's injuries. Medical personnel must be trained and knowledgeable of the causes of various types of injuries. For example, medical professionals have learned to recognize a spiral pattern on X-rays of broken bones, particularly in the arms and legs, that indicate an injury is the result of the twisting of a child's limb. Trained professionals also look for evidence of old injuries, such as a bruise that is several days old and bones that have broken and healed, in addition to the presenting injuries. Such a pattern of injuries helps constitute the diagnosis of battered child syndrome.

Effects of Abuse on Children

By its very nature, child abuse is threatening and disruptive to normal child development. The very persons charged with the care and nurturing of a child, and to whom the child turns for food, love, and safety, can cause the child pain and injury. The child then learns to distrust adults. Children who are neglected and abused exhibit a wide array of characteristics and behaviors. Most common among these are anger, acting out, depression, anxiety, aggression, social withdrawal, low self-esteem, and sleep difficulties. At the extreme end, abuse can cause a child to dissociate and develop disorders such as schizophrenia, amnesia, and personality disorder. Personality disorder is a mental disorder that affects a person's ability to function in everyday activities such as work, school, and interpersonal relationships. Borderline personality disorder is a frequent diagnosis for children who are victims of abuse or neglect. Symptoms can include paranoia, lack of impulse control, limited range of emotions, and inability to form close and lasting relationships.

Prevention of Child Abuse

Prevention is generally categorized as primary, secondary, or tertiary. Primary prevention includes the general distribution of information related to child abuse, including how to recognize and report abuse and what resources are available for the prevention, intervention, and treatment of child abuse. Secondary prevention combines information with services and interventions targeted to families identified at high risk for child abuse. Tertiary prevention is directed to families where abuse has already occurred, with the goal of decreasing the possibility of recurrence.

Health care–related prevention programs typically focus on encouraging pregnant women to receive prenatal care, teaching child care techniques, providing home health visits for newborns, and assisting parents of children with special needs in obtaining support and services. Community-based organizations such as YMCAs and YWCAs, Boys and Girls Clubs; community centers, food banks, shelter programs, and a wide array of advocacy and faith-based organizations target their efforts toward high-risk families and youth. These programs address the lack of resources such as adequate shelter, child care for working parents, appropriate nutrition, health and mental care, transportation, and education. Organizations providing tertiary prevention include crisis and emergency services, parent education, domestic violence shelters, and health and mental health treatment for victims.

In 1993 Public Law 103-66, also known as the Family Preservation and Support Initiative, was passed, providing federal funds for family support services and family preservation services with the intention of keeping families intact. This was followed by Public Law 105-89, also known as the Adoption and Safe Families Act of 1997. This second act clarified the congressional intent of Public Law 103-66 by changing the name of the funding program from *Family Support and Family Preservation Services* to *Promoting Safe and Stable Families.* This was a significant change in focus. Under the 1993 legislation, the goal of the program had been to keep families intact by providing services in the home. But service providers came to the realization that not every family can, or should be, kept together. Sometimes children must be removed for their own safety. Thus the 1997 legislation focused on two key outcomes for children and families: safety and stability. The Adoption and Safe Families Act recognizes the importance of timely, goal-directed, family-centered services within the larger context of assuring the safety of children and promoting their stability and permanence.

Schools play an important role in the identification, reporting, and treatment of child abuse. Neglect and abuse perpetrated on school-age children frequently first come to the attention of school officials in the form of truancy. Parents who neglect their children often fail to get their children to school, fail to provide the needed health screenings

and immunizations necessary for admission to school, and fail to provide school supplies. Children who are physically abused often show similar patterns of truancy because parents are reluctant to send children with obvious bruises or injuries to school. When children are at school, signs of neglect and abuse may include children in dirty clothing, children who appear very fatigued and fall asleep during class, and children who appear malnourished, depressed, withdrawn, aggressive, angry, or sad. Obviously, a child who is frequently absent from school, tired, hungry, angry, worried, depressed, and scared is not able to learn as effectively as other children. School personnel also need to be trained to look for signs of learning difficulties due to brain damage, hidden wounds or bruises (a child may be reluctant to dress for physical education class for fear of showing hidden injuries), hearing loss, untreated dental caries, and a wide variety of learning disabilities due to malnutrition, medical neglect, and physical abuse.

School personnel who are trained to observe these and other signs of abuse, and who know how and to whom to report abuse, can be very helpful to law enforcement and child protective services officials in providing documented patterns of neglect and abuse. Schools can also be helpful in cooperating with community-based agencies in the treatment plans for families, and in assuring that children are receiving school-based health, mental health, tutoring, food, and social services.

Child Protective Services (CPS) comprises a highly specialized set of laws, funding streams, agencies, lawyers, partnerships, and collaborations that together form the government's response to reports of child abuse and neglect. Criticisms of this system have led professionals to consider ways to reform the system to better identify, prevent, and treat child abuse. The criticisms include:

- *Overinclusion.* Many referrals for abuse and neglect are not substantiated. This exposes some families and their children to unnecessary investigations and intrusions and overburdens the system with investigations that cause delays in getting help to the families that really need it.

- *Capacity.* The number of referrals to the CPS system exceeds the system's ability to respond effectively. Both federal and state laws require CPS agencies to accept and respond to all reports of child abuse, but the resources dedicated to these activities have not kept pace with the demand. Most professionals agree that the system is significantly overloaded.

- *Underinclusion.* Some cases of abuse and neglect are not identified and reported. In both very rural areas and high-density cities, many cases of child abuse and neglect go unrecognized and unreported.
- *Service orientation.* The two basic service orientations of the CPS system are family preservation (keeping the child at home with services); and child safety and rescue (removing the child from the home for the protection of the child). These orientations are in direct conflict with each other and frequently do not serve families well.
- *Service Delivery.* Many suitable services are not always available, service delivery is unequal across communities and states, there is a shortage of culturally appropriate services, and services are often fragmented.

Those who propose to reform the CPS system see two changes as fundamental: (1) improvement of identification and reporting systems to focus on high-risk cases that need immediate intervention, and (2) the creation of community partnerships to provide services in more culturally appropriate ways. A third element is an emphasis on tailoring interventions to fit the needs of each family. Although these reforms do not necessarily cost additional dollars, they do require a significant shift in thinking and planning, and the reformers must develop new ways to track accountability. CPS is a very high-risk business, and by creating community partnerships the risk will be shared with other agencies. The challenge in reform is to create a system that manages the risk in a way that assures the safety of the children who depend upon it.

See also: CHILD PROTECTIVE SERVICES; VIOLENCE, CHILDREN'S EXPOSURE TO.

BIBLIOGRAPHY

ENGLISH, DIANA J. 1998. "The Extent and Consequences of Child Maltreatment." *The Future of Children* 8(1):35–53.

FINKELHOR, DAVID. 1994. "Current Information on the Scope and Nature of Child Sexual Abuse." *The Future of Children* 4(2):31–53.

MCCROSKEY, JACQUELIN, and MEEZAN, WILLIAM. 1998. "Family-Centered Services: Approaches and Effectiveness." *The Future of Children* 8(1):54–71.

WALDFOGEL, JANE. 1998. "Rethinking the Paradigm for Child Protection." *The Future of Children* 8(1):104–119.

INTERNET RESOURCES

CHILD WELFARE LEAGUE OF AMERICA. 2001. "Creating Connected Communities: Policy, Action, Commitment." <www.cwla.org/advocacy/nationalfactsheet01.htm>.

NATIONAL CLEARINGHOUSE ON CHILD ABUSE AND NEGLECT INFORMATION. 2001. <www.calib.com/nccanch/pubs/factsheets/canstats.cfm>.

NATIONAL INSTITUTE OF NEUROLOGICAL DISORDERS AND STROKE. 2001. "NINDS Shaken Baby Syndrome Information Page." <www.ninds.nih.gov/health_and_medical/disorders/shakenbaby.htm>.

WANG, CHING-TUNG. 1997. "Current Trends in Child Abuse Reporting and Fatalities: The Results of the 1997 Annual Fifty State Survey." <www.join-hands.com/welfare/1997castats.html>.

DEBBIE MILLER

CHILD CARE

AVAILABILITY AND QUALITY

Child care is a broad term used to describe any number of arrangements or settings where the primary responsibility is caring for young children. There are as many different settings as there are definitions of quality in child care. The number of young children under the age of five who are cared for during part of the day by adults other than their custodial parents has increased dramatically since 1980, due in large part to an increase in mothers joining the workforce.

According to the 2002 Quality Counts survey conducted by *Education Week*, approximately six out of every ten children, or almost 12 million children, age five and younger, are being jointly cared for by parents and early childhood educators, relatives, or other child-care providers.

While many parents may prefer to stay home with their infants or young children, this is not a financial option for most. The United States, unlike many other nations, does not have a paid parental leave plan for employees after the birth of a baby. This forces many families to return to work immediately and necessitates the need for weighing child-care options. Parents are forced to make child-care choices based on family financial resources, the availability or location of child care, hours of operation, or other factors not necessarily associated with quality. It is not uncommon to hear of a mother calling child-care centers to get on waiting lists before calling family members to share the joyful news that she is expecting. Waiting lists for quality programs can be years long, and some families may never gain entry despite all their prior planning. Many parents pay application fees at multiple centers in hopes of getting in somewhere. This can be costly, with application fees ranging from $25 to $150 or more annually.

Types of Care

There are several types of child care available to families of young children, and there are quality indicators associated with each. *In-home care* is one type of arrangement that allows the child or children to remain in their home environment. In this model of care, the provider either comes to the home or lives part- or full-time in the family's home. Frequently, a relative is the person providing the care, and in this situation it is not required that a child-care license be obtained. Families with low to moderate income levels often choose in-home care, with grandparents caring for multiple children of varying ages at one time.

Higher-income families may have the option of hiring an au pair or a nanny to provide in-home care. While there are no licensing requirements for being an au pair or a nanny, there are interview processes and agencies that can assist with this process. Typically, au pairs or nannies provide more than routine child care, often assisting with daily household activities, including running errands, shopping, doing laundry, fixing meals, and cleaning house.

The care of the child or children is the responsibility of the provider in much the same way as that of a parent. Quality-of-care indicators might include a child's overall development, health, and happiness, as defined and measured by the parent and provider. There are no overall standards related to fee structure, roles, and responsibilities, especially in the case of relative caregivers. Payment for services is dependant on factors such as whether the person providing care is receiving room and board and/or other benefits, and whether the person is a family member doing child care as a favor or as a family obligation.

Family day homes offer group care to young children in another person's home. This is often a choice families make based on either the desire to keep their child in a more typical family-friendly environment (compared to a child-care center), or on finances, since a family day home may not be as costly as a center-based program. The adult-to-child ratio may be the same, but the environment more closely resembles that of a family's home.

Each state has standards for family day homes and regulations regarding licensing. Unlike in-home care, which allows an unlimited number of related children, family care requires licensing if children from more than one family are present. Individual states set their own system for monitoring these day homes, and assessment scales are available for measuring quality of care and facilities. One commonly used tool is the Family Day Care Rating Scale, devised by Thelma Harms and Richard Clifford in 1989. This rating scale assesses the quality of care related to organization of space, interactions between adults and children (as well as adults with other adults, such as other professionals or parents), schedules for young children's activities, and provisions for children and adults.

Child-care centers offer another option for working parents or primary caregivers of young children. There is great disparity in child-care centers, ranging from where they are located to the fees they charge. Centers may be located in churches, at universities, in corporate settings, or in independent child-care buildings. These settings may be in urban, suburban, or rural communities. Fees are based on sliding scales determined by a family's income, and scholarships may be available if a family meets certain income criteria established by the agency providing care. Requirements vary from center to center in regard to the qualifications of staff and the program director.

Choosing Child Care

One of the greatest ways that centers differ is in their philosophies of child care. Many child-care centers follow what is considered developmentally appropriate practice for young children, or best practices, as established by the organizations and professionals in the field of early childhood, while some centers do not. While licensing standards are required for child-care centers, these standards are often minimal, and are generally focused on health and safety issues rather than good-quality practices with young children. These are only a few of the challenges a family encounters when seeking child-care services outside the home.

Families will weigh all the options for care when considering what works best for their individual child, children, or family. Every family seeking child care has its own unique set of circumstances and needs, priorities, and concerns regarding its children. Quality child care that is available everywhere and is standardly priced would serve a larger community, rather than being a luxury for only those who can afford it. Money does not necessarily translate into quality care. There are several high priced centers or child-care providers that provide less than high quality services for young children. So how does one determine quality standards of care when family situations are so unique, and when there is such disparity in need?

Indicators of Quality Care

The importance of the first three years of life in a child's development is clear. Brain research from the last decade of the twentieth century shows that children are learning from the moment of birth, and that the early years provide the essential building blocks for later learning. It is imperative that these early experiences are of high quality, and that children are given every opportunity to succeed. Early childhood specialists, organizations, and researchers have focused much attention on what constitutes quality care for infants and young children.

Defining high quality care is challenging, though there is a general consensus among early-childhood professional organizations and child-care licensing agencies regarding the categories to be included when evaluating quality. There are a multitude of child-care checklists available to assist families in seeking quality-care choices, as well as a multitude of provider checklists to assess the quality within their own programs.

The following issues may be considered when assessing quality of care: (1) the physical setting or environment; (2) learning activities or daily routines; (3) interactions; (4) staff, including ratios of adults to children, qualifications, and training; (5) health and safety issues; and (6) parental involvement. Quality is addressed here as it may be measured in a child-care center, as opposed to in-home or family group child-care settings.

Physical environment. The physical environment should be appealing, bright, and cheerful for young children. There should be plenty of space for children to move around, and areas should be designed to separate quiet play from active play, including in outdoor play areas. Inadequate space for the number of children creates difficulties for following the routines or does not allow enough open space for play. Child-care regulations stipulate the minimum space allowable based on the number of children enrolled. Space should be suitable for the activity or materials to be used. For example, if children are playing in a dramatic play center, there should be ample space available to carry out the activities or routines of the center, such as pretend shopping with counter space for a toy register, groceries on shelves, and room to move around and pretend shop without children bumping into each other. If space is not available to freely move about, the environment is not properly arranged to allow children to express themselves and play safely. It is important for materials to be available on a child's level, to promote independence in play. A variety of learning centers (i.e., home living, manipulative play, block area, book corner, and other age-appropriate centers) offer children opportunities to engage in a wide range of learning opportunities.

Daily activities and routines. Children learn to predict what comes next through consistent routines. Daily activities that allow children to be engaged in meaningful activities and to have some control over their environment will foster a child's choice-making and problem-solving skills. Adults should actively arrange the environment to allow for independence in young children, and activities should be designed to stimulate children in all areas of development, including social, emotional, physical, adaptive, cognitive, and communication domains.

Activities and routines must be appropriate for the age and developmental levels of the children being cared for, and individual needs of children should be considered in program and planning decisions. High quality child-care centers will employ adults that are respectful of children's interests and supportive, as well as actively involved in helping children resolve conflicts and problems without utilizing punitive behavior strategies.

Interactions. Positive interactions—those that indicate a healthy respect for children and adults—are another indicator of high quality in child care. Adults in a high-quality program listen to and talk to young children and their families. They are available and responsive to the children's wants and needs, and understand the importance of development and how it impacts children at different stages. It is important that they genuinely like young children and strive to help them learn skills such as cooperative play and to foster positive peer interactions. They also understand how relationships develop, and take responsibility for the part they play in making positive partnerships with families of children in their care.

Staff qualifications, training, adult-to-child ratios. State child-care licensing agencies offer minimum guidelines regarding appropriate ratios of child-care providers to children. National licensing organizations, such as the National Association for Education of Young Children (NAEYC), and professional organizations, such as Zero to Three, are generally more conservative in the numbers they recommend as best practice for group size and adult-to-child ratios, and offer good rationales for using smaller numbers. High-quality relationships between teachers and young children have been directly linked to better classroom social and thinking skills in subsequent grades.

The Cost, Quality, and Outcome research project, conducted by the University of North Carolina at Chapel Hill, the University of Colorado Health Sciences Center, the University of California, and Yale University, produced an executive summary in June 1999 that evaluated the effects of child care on a child's later performance in school. The overall results indicate that: (1) the quality of child care is an important element for preparing young children for school readiness; (2) high-quality care early in life continues to have an impact on children as they move on in school; (3) children who are traditionally considered at risk for developmental delays due to low income or other environments show more positive gains from quality child-care experiences than other children; and (4) early relationships with

teachers continue to influence children's social development as they move through elementary school.

Programs vary in the qualifications required for employing staff. Child-care providers have a variety of experiences and training related to working with young children. Quality indicators include individualized training or staff development for caregivers, support available for in-service training, benefits packages that support employees, CPR and first aid training requirements, formal and informal observations of adult caregivers, and caregivers knowledgeable in child development, both typical and atypical.

Health and safety. High-quality health and safety practices require ongoing evaluation and assessment. It is important to keep a facility or environment clean and free of hazards. Materials should be routinely cleaned and checked for safety. Safety precautions must be established, and policies regarding medication, hand washing, diapering or potty training, and storing cleaning materials out of reach must be adhered to. High-quality programs have emergency plans in place for any medical emergency, weather-related emergency, or unplanned for situations. Parents should be informed and knowledgeable about these plans.

Parent involvement. Parents are a child's first teachers, and generally, parents know their children best. High quality programs recognize the value of including parents, who are made to feel welcome and are encouraged to be involved on whatever level they are comfortable. Parents give input to the child-care program, and they are allowed to visit whenever they choose. Positive relationships between caregivers and parents are an indicator of quality in child care. Communication is open, respectful, and nondiscriminative. Parents feel comfortable sharing information because they understand they are in a partnership with the provider. Additionally, parents are linked to other service providers or programs in the community that may benefit their family.

A 1994 Carnegie Corporation report refers to the problems of the nation's youngest children and their families as "the quiet crisis." The report states that approximately half of America's young children start life at a disadvantage due to risk factors that include substandard child care. In the early twenty-first century, the well-being of many children is still in jeopardy due to inadequate child care.

See also: EARLY CHILDHOOD EDUCATION; LITERACY, *subentry on* EMERGENT LITERACY; PARENTAL INVOLVEMENT IN EDUCATION.

BIBLIOGRAPHY

BREDEKAMP, SUE. 1988. *Developmentally Appropriate Practice in Early Childhood Programs Serving Children From Birth Through Age 8,* expanded edition. Washington, DC: National Association of Education of Young Children.

FRANK PORTER GRAHAM CHILD DEVELOPMENT CENTER. 1999. *The Children of the Cost, Quality, and Outcomes Study Go to School.* Executive Summary. Chapel Hill: University of North Carolina, Frank Porter Graham Child Development Center.

HARMS, THELMA, and CLIFFORD, RICHARD. 1989. *Family Day Care Rating Scale.* New York: Teachers College Press.

LALLY, J. RONALD; GRIFFIN, ABBEY; FENICHEL, EMILY; SEGAL, MARILYN; SZANTON, ELEANOR; and WEISSBOURD, BERNICE. 1995. *Caring for Infants and Toddlers in Groups: Developmentally Appropriate Practice.* Washington, DC: Zero to Three.

QUALITY COUNTS. 2002. "In Early Childhood Education Care: Quality Counts." *Education Week* 17:8–9.

INTERNET RESOURCE

CARNEGIE CORPORATION OF NEW YORK. 1994. "The Quiet Crisis." <www.carnegie.org/starting_points/startpt1.html>.

AMY HARRIS-SOLOMON

COST AND FINANCING

The need for child care in the United States increased dramatically in the last two decades of the twentieth century—a direct result of a large increase in the percentage of mothers in the workforce. In 1965 only 17 percent of mothers who had children under the age of one were in the labor force. By 1991, however, 53 percent of this group were working outside the home.

The Quality Counts 2002 report, published in *Education Week,* estimated that 11.9 million children, or six in ten children under the age of five,

were enrolled in some form of child care during the previous year. In the United States, families are not offered extensive parental leave following the birth of a child, and often, due to financial constraints, mothers or both parents must return to work soon after a new baby is born, generally within six to eight weeks. More than half of all mothers return to work within the first year after a baby's birth.

The Cost of Care

Many of the families who need child care also require some financial assistance. Child care comes in many forms, and there is not a standard arrangement or fee based on the age of a child or a family's circumstance. The cost of care may be associated with the type of care provided, such as infant care, toddler care, preschool care, or care for children who have special needs or those who are considered at risk due to environmental or other factors.

Infant care and toddler care are usually more expensive than care for a preschooler or a school-age child, due to the number of adults required per child. In general, younger children require more adults to provide care. Rates may also vary from provider to provider based on location (rural or urban), reputation, hours of operation, population served, and requirements for teachers. However, there is no way to equate the quality of care a child receives with the costs associated with that care.

The expenses of child care can impact a budget significantly, regardless of who is paying for the service. A 1994 Carnegie Corporation report states that $120 billion to $240 billion are spent annually on goods and services devoted to the care and education of young children. The average cost for care for one child can range from $40 to $200 per week, not counting application fees, activity fees, transportation fees, late pickup fees, care for special holidays, or days a program is closed and alternate care must be arranged.

The Carnegie Corporation report further states that families who have incomes below $15,000 annually spend 23 percent of their income on child care, while families who have incomes of around $50,000 spend approximately 6 percent of their income on care. It is obvious that the lower-income family is affected more significantly when funding child care. In the United States, nearly one-quarter of the families who have children under the age of three live in poverty, and many are single-parent families. For these families, quality child care at an affordable cost is difficult to find.

The burden of the costs of child care is primarily the responsibility of families. Overall, families pay approximately 60 percent of child care, with the government paying 39 percent and the private sector 1 percent, according to statistics from the Quality Counts 2002 report.

Effects of Quality Child Care

There is ample research available in the field of early childhood education and child development that supports the importance of enriching and stimulating early experiences in promoting healthy development. The first three years of life are considered crucial, with brain development occurring most rapidly during this period. Parents are often left scrambling to make decisions on what environment is best for their child, and struggling to meet the high price of programs that claim to support these positive early developmental experiences. While there are a growing number of pre–K programs for preschoolers paid for by state dollars, most of the costs are funded by parents. It is not uncommon for a more elite academic preschool to cost between $3,000 and $10,000 annually.

Research from the Carolina Abecedarian Project underlines the need for high-quality preschool experiences for young children from low-income environments. Of the 100 children studied, half attended preschool and half did not. The children were studied until they reached the age of twenty-one. The children who attended preschool from infancy to age five scored higher on reading measures at age eight, and consistently until age twenty-one, than those children who did not attend preschool. The summary from a 1999 cost, quality, and outcome study conducted by researchers from four major universities confirms the benefits of high-quality early child care for children. In this study, high quality child care was directly linked to later school performance and success in social development throughout the early school years, especially for low-income children.

Funding Options

With more emphasis on quality child-care experiences coupled with the growing need for child care due to the increase in working mothers, options for funding child care are expanding, and creative ways to support the growing need are being explored. The Quality Counts 2002 report discusses how states are seeking new sources of funding for child-care initiatives, including taxing beer and cigarettes or utilizing proceeds from state lotteries.

Some businesses offer employees a form of corporate child care or a flexible work plan to accommodate child-care issues. Benefits are being extended for fathers of newborns, so leave is not exclusively for mothers. This allows families more flexibility in how they coordinate the first few months after a baby is born. Corporations are discovering that on-site child care gives employees peace of mind, allowing for more satisfaction in the work environment and more long-term retention of employees.

In 1996 welfare reform legislation was passed, providing almost $3 billion annually in the form of block grants to the states for low-income families. This money is designed to provide some financial support to single parents in the welfare-to-work program. Single parents (generally mothers) who are enrolled in a full-time work or school program are eligible to apply for these funds to help supplement their income for child-care costs.

Federal welfare funds distributed through the Child Care and Development Fund (CCDF) exceeded $4 billion in 2001. Additionally, $5 billion was utilized for child-care assistance through the Temporary Assistance for Needy Families program in 2000. As stated in the Quality Counts 2002 report, the subsidy from the federal welfare monies has had the biggest impact in the growth of state programs. Other programs supported through the federal government include Head Start, Title I, and the Individuals with Disabilities Education Act. These programs offer financial assistance for child care to children from low-income homes or to children who have special needs.

Many states are offering state-funded preschool programs in the early twenty-first century. While these programs are not accessible to every child, they are targeting the population that is most in need of state-funded school-based programs. Some states are moving toward the concept of universal preschool. Every state provides at least some funding for kindergarten.

States struggle to piece together systems of funding that will at least support the neediest populations—those who would not be able to afford preschool experiences without subsidies. Individual programs scramble to compete for available funding sources, often supplementing the cost of child care through grants from agencies (such as United Way), private corporations, or foundations.

Some agencies, due to budgetary constraints, are not capable of offering sliding fee scales or accepting state child-care certificates or scholarships for children who meet income eligibility. Many agencies work with the U.S. Department of Agriculture to procure reimbursement for children who meet income eligibility for free or reduced meals. At best, this is a patchwork system for parents, providers, government, and unfortunately all too often, for the children.

The benefits of high-quality care have been proven. In analyzing the system of child care and the funding associated with it, there is a need to further equate quality with expectations for qualified persons caring for young children. People who work in this field in the early twenty-first century are compensated at rates equivalent to people who work in fast-food restaurants and other nonprofessional positions. Teachers are responsible for helping shape the future and enhancing a child's early development. The quality of the environments young children are placed in, and the quality of the people caring for them, can influence their future. If quality is equated to dollars, quality care will only be accessible to the wealthy. Because child care is not locally accessible to all, some children will not receive the advantage of high-quality care. Families and other stakeholders that understand both the need and value of high-quality care will seek these programs for their children.

See also: EARLY CHILDHOOD EDUCATION; WELFARE REFORM.

INTERNET RESOURCES

CARNEGIE CORPORATION OF NEW YORK. 1994. "The Quiet Crisis." <www.carnegie.org/starting_points/startpt1.html>.

CARNEGIE CORPORATION OF NEW YORK. 2002. "Guarantee Quality Child Care Choices." <www.carnegie.org/starting_points/startpt1.html>.

EDUCATION WEEK. 2002. "Quality Counts 2002 Executive Summary—In Early Childhood Education Care: Quality Counts." *Education Week* 17:8–9. <www.edweek.org/sreports/qc02/>.

WELFARE INFORMATION NETWORK. 1998. "Financial Resources for Child Care." <www.welfareinfo.org/Issuechild.htm>.

AMY HARRIS-SOLOMON

CHILD DEVELOPMENT, STAGES OF GROWTH

Definitions of stages of growth in childhood come from many sources. Theorists such as Jean Piaget, Lev Vygotsky, Lawrence Kohlberg, and Erik Erikson have provided ways to understand development, and recent research has provided important information regarding the nature of development. In addition, stages of childhood are defined culturally by the social institutions, customs, and laws that make up a society. For example, while researchers and professionals usually define the period of early childhood as birth to eight years of age, others in the United States might consider age five a better end point because it coincides with entry into the cultural practice of formal schooling.

There are three broad stages of development: early childhood, middle childhood, and adolescence. The definitions of these stages are organized around the primary tasks of development in each stage, though the boundaries of these stages are malleable. Society's ideas about childhood shift over time, and research has led to new understandings of the development that takes place in each stage.

Early Childhood (Birth to Eight Years)

Early childhood is a time of tremendous growth across all areas of development. The dependent newborn grows into a young person who can take care of his or her own body and interact effectively with others. For these reasons, the primary developmental task of this stage is *skill development*.

Physically, between birth and age three a child typically doubles in height and quadruples in weight. Bodily proportions also shift, so that the infant, whose head accounts for almost one-fourth of total body length, becomes a toddler with a more balanced, adult-like appearance. Despite these rapid physical changes, the typical three-year-old has mastered many skills, including sitting, walking, toilet training, using a spoon, scribbling, and sufficient hand-eye coordination to catch and throw a ball.

Between three and five years of age, children continue to grow rapidly and begin to develop fine-motor skills. By age five most children demonstrate fairly good control of pencils, crayons, and scissors. Gross motor accomplishments may include the ability to skip and balance on one foot. Physical growth slows down between five and eight years of age, while body proportions and motor skills become more refined.

Physical changes in early childhood are accompanied by rapid changes in the child's cognitive and language development. From the moment they are born, children use all their senses to attend to their environment, and they begin to develop a sense of cause and effect from their actions and the responses of caregivers.

Over the first three years of life, children develop a spoken vocabulary of between 300 and 1,000 words, and they are able to use language to learn about and describe the world around them. By age five, a child's vocabulary will grow to approximately 1,500 words. Five-year-olds are also able to produce five- to seven-word sentences, learn to use the past tense, and tell familiar stories using pictures as cues.

Language is a powerful tool to enhance cognitive development. Using language allows the child to communicate with others and solve problems. By age eight, children are able to demonstrate some basic understanding of less concrete concepts, including time and money. However, the eight-year-old still reasons in concrete ways and has difficulty understanding abstract ideas.

A key moment in early childhood socioemotional development occurs around one year of age. This is the time when attachment formation becomes critical. Attachment theory suggests that individual differences in later life functioning and personality are shaped by a child's early experiences with their caregivers. The quality of emotional attachment, or lack of attachment, formed early in life may serve as a model for later relationships.

From ages three to five, growth in socioemotional skills includes the formation of peer relationships, gender identification, and the development of a sense of right and wrong. Taking the perspective of another individual is difficult for young children, and events are often interpreted in all-or-nothing terms, with the impact on the child being the foremost concern. For example, at age five a child may expect others to share their possessions freely but still be extremely possessive of a favorite toy. This creates no conflict of conscience, because *fairness* is determined relative to the child's own interests. Between ages five and eight, children enter into a broader peer context and develop enduring friendships. Social comparison is heightened at this time, and taking other people's perspective begins to play a role in how children relate to people, including peers.

Implications for in-school learning. The time from birth to eight years is a critical period in the development of many foundational skills in all areas of development. Increased awareness of, and ability to detect, developmental delays in very young children has led to the creation of early intervention services that can reduce the need for special education placements when children reach school age. For example, earlier detection of hearing deficits sometimes leads to correction of problems before serious language impairments occur. Also, developmental delays caused by premature birth can be addressed through appropriate therapies to help children function at the level of their typically developing peers before they begin school.

An increased emphasis on early learning has also created pressure to prepare young children to enter school with as many prerequisite skills as possible. In 1994 federal legislation was passed in the United States creating Goals 2000, the first of which states that "All children will enter school ready to learn" (U.S. Department of Education, 1998). While the validity of this goal has been debated, the consequences have already been felt. One consequence is the use of standardized readiness assessments to determine class placement or retention in kindergarten. Another is the creation of transition classes (an extra year of schooling before either kindergarten or first grade). Finally, the increased attention on early childhood has led to renewed interest in preschool programs as a means to narrow the readiness gap between children whose families can provide quality early learning environments for them and those whose families cannot.

Middle Childhood (Eight to Twelve Years)

Historically, middle childhood has not been considered an important stage in human development. Sigmund Freud's psychoanalytic theory labeled this period of life the *latency* stage, a time when sexual and aggressive urges are repressed. Freud suggested that no significant contributions to personality development were made during this period. However, more recent theorists have recognized the importance of middle childhood for the development of cognitive skills, personality, motivation, and interpersonal relationships. During middle childhood children learn the values of their societies. Thus, the primary developmental task of middle childhood could be called *integration,* both in terms of development within the individual and of the individual within the social context.

Perhaps supporting the image of middle childhood as a latency stage, physical development during middle childhood is less dramatic than in early childhood or adolescence. Growth is slow and steady until the onset of puberty, when individuals begin to develop at a much quicker pace. The age at which individuals enter puberty varies, but there is evidence of a secular trend—the age at which puberty begins has been decreasing over time. In some individuals, puberty may start as early as age eight or nine. Onset of puberty differs across gender and begins earlier in females.

As with physical development, the cognitive development of middle childhood is slow and steady. Children in this stage are building upon skills gained in early childhood and preparing for the next phase of their cognitive development. Children's reasoning is very rule based. Children are learning skills such as classification and forming hypotheses. While they are cognitively more mature now than a few years ago, children in this stage still require concrete, hands-on learning activities. Middle childhood is a time when children can gain enthusiasm for learning and work, for achievement can become a motivating factor as children work toward building competence and self-esteem.

Middle childhood is also a time when children develop competence in interpersonal and social relationships. Children have a growing peer orientation, yet they are strongly influenced by their family. The social skills learned through peer and family relationships, and children's increasing ability to participate in meaningful interpersonal communication, provide a necessary foundation for the challenges of adolescence. Best friends are important at this age, and the skills gained in these relationships may provide the building blocks for healthy adult relationships.

Implications for in-school learning. For many children, middle childhood is a joyful time of increased independence, broader friendships, and developing interests, such as sports, art, or music. However, a widely recognized shift in school performance begins for many children in third or fourth grade (age eight or nine). The skills required for academic success become more complex. Those students who successfully meet the academic challenges during this period go on to do well, while those who fail to build the necessary skills may fall further behind in later grades.

Recent social trends, including the increased prevalence of school violence, eating disorders, drug use, and depression, affect many upper elementary school students. Thus, there is more pressure on schools to recognize problems in eight- to eleven-year-olds, and to teach children the social and life skills that will help them continue to develop into healthy adolescents.

Adolescence (Twelve to Eighteen Years)

Adolescence can be defined in a variety of ways: physiologically, culturally, cognitively; each way suggests a slightly different definition. For the purpose of this discussion adolescence is defined as a culturally constructed period that generally begins as individuals reach sexual maturity and ends when the individual has established an identity as an adult within his or her social context. In many cultures adolescence may not exist, or may be very short, because the attainment of sexual maturity coincides with entry into the adult world. In the current culture of the United States, however, adolescence may last well into the early twenties. The primary developmental task of adolescence is *identity formation.*

The adolescent years are another period of accelerated growth. Individuals can grow up to four inches and gain eight to ten pounds per year. This growth spurt is most often characterized by two years of fast growth, followed by three or more years of slow, steady growth. By the end of adolescence, individuals may gain a total of seven to nine inches in height and as much as forty or fifty pounds in weight. The timing of this growth spurt is not highly predictable; it varies across both individuals and gender. In general, females begin to develop earlier than do males.

Sexual maturation is one of the most significant developments during this time. Like physical development, there is significant variability in the age at which individuals attain sexual maturity. Females tend to mature at about age thirteen, and males at about fifteen. Development during this period is governed by the pituitary gland through the release of the hormones testosterone (males) and estrogen (females). There has been increasing evidence of a trend toward earlier sexual development in developed countries—the average age at which females reach menarche dropped three to four months every ten years between 1900 and 2000.

Adolescence is an important period for cognitive development as well, as it marks a transition in the way in which individuals think and reason about problems and ideas. In early adolescence, individuals can classify and order objects, reverse processes, think logically about concrete objects, and consider more than one perspective at a time. However, at this level of development, adolescents benefit more from direct experiences than from abstract ideas and principles. As adolescents develop more complex cognitive skills, they gain the ability to solve more abstract and hypothetical problems. Elements of this type of thinking may include an increased ability to think in hypothetical ways about abstract ideas, the ability to generate and test hypotheses systematically, the ability to think and plan about the future, and meta-cognition (the ability to reflect on one's thoughts).

As individuals enter adolescence, they are confronted by a diverse number of changes all at one time. Not only are they undergoing significant physical and cognitive growth, but they are also encountering new situations, responsibilities, and people.

Entry into middle school and high school thrusts students into environments with many new people, responsibilities, and expectations. While this transition can be frightening, it also represents an exciting step toward independence. Adolescents are trying on new roles, new ways of thinking and behaving, and they are exploring different ideas and values. Erikson addresses the search for identity and independence in his framework of *life-span development.* Adolescence is characterized by a conflict between identity and role confusion. During this period, individuals evolve their own self-concepts within the peer context. In their attempts to become more independent adolescents often rely on their peer group for direction regarding what is normal and accepted. They begin to pull away from reliance on their family as a source of identity and may encounter conflicts between their family and their growing peer-group affiliation.

With so many intense experiences, adolescence is also an important time in emotional development. Mood swings are a characteristic of adolescence. While often attributed to hormones, mood swings can also be understood as a logical reaction to the social, physical, and cognitive changes facing adolescents, and there is often a struggle with issues of self-esteem. As individuals search for identity, they confront the challenge of matching who they want to become with what is socially desirable. In this context, adolescents often exhibit bizarre and/or contradictory behaviors. The search for identity, the concern adolescents have about whether they are normal, and variable moods and low self-esteem all work together to produce wildly fluctuating behavior.

The impact of the media and societal expectations on adolescent development has been far-reaching. Young people are bombarded by images of violence, sex, and unattainable standards of beauty. This exposure, combined with the social, emotional, and physical changes facing adolescents, has contributed to an increase in school violence, teen sexuality, and eating disorders. The onset of many psychological disorders, such as depression, other mood disorders, and schizophrenia, is also common at this time of life.

Implications for in-school learning. The implications of development during this period for education are numerous. Teachers must be aware of the shifts in cognitive development that are occurring and provide appropriate learning opportunities to support individual students and facilitate growth. Teachers must also be aware of the challenges facing their students in order to identify and help to correct problems if they arise. Teachers often play an important role in identifying behaviors that could become problematic, and they can be mentors to students in need.

Conclusion

The definitions of the three stages of development are based on both research and cultural influences. Implications for schooling are drawn from what is known about how children develop, but it should be emphasized that growth is influenced by context, and schooling is a primary context of childhood. Just as educators and others should be aware of the ways in which a five-year-old's reasoning is different from a fifteen-year-old's, it is also important to be aware that the structure and expectations of schooling influence the ways in which children grow and learn.

See also: DEVELOPMENTAL THEORY; ERIKSON, ERIK; KOHLBERG, LAWRENCE; PIAGET, JEAN; VYGOTSKY, LEV.

BIBLIOGRAPHY

ALLEN, K. EILEEN, and MAROTZ, LYNNE R. 1989. *Developmental Profiles: Birth to Six.* Albany, NY: Delmar.

BOWMAN, BARBARA T.; DONOVAN, M. SUZANNE; and BURNS, M. SUSAN, eds. 2001. *Eager To Learn: Educating Our Preschoolers.* Washington DC: National Academy Press.

BRANSFORD, JOHN D.; BROWN, ANN L.; and COCKING, RODNEY R., eds. 1999. *How People Learn: Brain, Mind, Experience, and School.* Washington DC: National Academy Press.

CHALL, JEANNE S.; JACOBS, VICKI A.; and BALDWIN, LUKE E. 1990. *The Reading Crisis: Why Poor Children Fall Behind.* Cambridge, MA: Harvard University Press.

COLLINS, W. ANDREW, ed. 1984. *Development During Middle Childhood: The Years From Six to Twelve.* Washington DC: National Academy Press.

GOLDBERG, SUSAN; MUIR, ROY; and KERR, JOHN, eds. 1995. *Attachment Theory: Social, Developmental, and Clinical Perspectives.* Hillsdale: Analytic Press.

GULLOTTA, THOMAS P.; ADAMS, GERALD R.; and MARKSTROM, CAROL A. 2000. *The Adolescent Experience,* 4th edition. San Diego: Academic Press.

KNOWLES, TRUDY, and BROWN, DAVE F. 2000. *What Every Middle School Teacher Should Know.* Portsmouth, NH: Heinemann.

NEWMAN, PHILLIP R., and NEWMAN, BARBARA M. 1997. *Childhood and Adolescence.* Pacific Grove, CA: Brooks/Cole.

ORENSTEIN, PEGGY. 1994. *School Girls: Young Women, Self-Esteem, and the Confidence Gap.* New York: Anchor Books.

PIPHER, MARY B. 1994. *Reviving Ophelia: Saving the Selves of Adolescent Girls.* New York: Putnam.

SHONKOFF, JACK P., and PHILLIPS, DEBORAH A., eds. 2001. *From Neurons to Neighborhoods: The Science of Early Childhood Development.* Washington, DC: National Academy Press.

WOLMAN, BENJAMIN B. 1998. *Adolescence: Biological and Psychosocial Perspectives.* Westport, CT: Greenwood Press.

INTERNET RESOURCE

U.S. DEPARTMENT OF EDUCATION. 1998. "Goals 2000: Reforming Education to Improve Student Achievement." <www.ed.gov/pubs/G2KReforming/>

RACHELLE FEILER
DANA TOMONARI

CHILD PROTECTIVE SERVICES

HISTORICAL OVERVIEW
William Wesley Patton
CURRENT SYSTEM
William Wesley Patton

HISTORICAL OVERVIEW

No ancient civilization considered child protection to be a governmental function. In ancient Rome, for instance, fathers were vested with an almost unlimited natural right to determine the welfare of their children. The welfare of minors was a family matter, not a governmental interest or obligation. Most other governments of the ancient world provided no limits to a father's right to inflict corporal punishment, including infanticide.

English Common Law

Experts disagree regarding the genesis of formalized state child protection under English common law. Litigation in England in the late fourteenth and early fifteenth centuries involved the king seeking vindication of his feudal incidents (powers and benefits of the King and Lords in relation to land and inheritance) regarding tenants' infant heirs. This governmental intervention indirectly protected children's estates from being depleted by opportunistic adults. By the late seventeenth century, the chancery court exercised its jurisdiction in determining the interest of minors subject to guardianships, though court jurisdiction was limited to issues of children's inheritance and real property interests. However, in *Corcellis v. Corcellis No. 1* (1673) and *Shaftsbury v. Hannam* (1677) the chancery court viewed the question of guardianship to be broad enough to include issues involving the proper education of wards. Legal historians disagree whether these early common-law inheritance cases were the basis for the government's general jurisdiction over the welfare of children through the doctrine of *parens patriae* ("father of the country," a term used in law to denote the government's power to protect its citizens).

In addition to the case-by-case determinations by the chancery court regarding children's property and guardianships, Parliament, in 1601, promulgated the Poor Law Act, which, among other provisions, provided the government jurisdiction to separate children from pauper parents and to place poor children in apprenticeships until the age of majority (21 for males and 16 for females). In 1660 Parliament passed the Tenures Abolition Act, which presaged the end of feudalism, including guardianships in chivalry that had formed the basis for the earlier Court of Wards and Court of Chancery over the guardianship of both children's and the Crown's inheritance and property interests. ("Guardianships in chivalry" provided that when a tenant on a lord's land died leaving an heir under the age of majority, the lord could control the minor heir's inheritance until the child became an adult.) The Tenures Abolition Act was revolutionary because it vested in the father the right to appoint a guardian for his child heir, which was previously forbidden under the feudal inheritance laws.

From 1660 until 1873 the Court of Chancery administered equity jurisdiction in conflicts between private parties over testamentary guardianships. It was during these equity determinations that the Court of Chancery expanded the substantive scope of child protection to include, in addition to inheritance and property, concerns over a ward's rights to marry, to a particular type of education or school, to the choice of religious training, and to child custody arrangements. In 1839 Parliament dramatically expanded the court's jurisdiction to determine the best interest of children through the Custody of Infants Act, which provided court jurisdiction to override a father's parental rights, including rights to custody and visitation. Most historians would agree that by the nineteenth century governmental concern in the child's best interest were perfected directly through the doctrine of *parens patriae,* rather than indirectly through legal contests over property and guardianships.

The American Colonies

The child protection policies of the early American colonists closely mirrored those of seventeenth- and eighteenth-century Britain. The colonists emphasized two aspects of English child protection theory: "the common law rules of family government; and the traditions and child-care practices of the Elizabethan Poor Laws of 1601" (Thomas, p. 299). Although colonial remedies of placing pauper children into involuntary apprenticeships or into poorhouses initially followed English legal customs, soon colonial theorists expanded court jurisdiction over juveniles to include contexts beyond poverty. For instance, in eighteenth-century Virginia, courts separated children not just from poor parents, but also from parents who were not providing "'good breeding,' neglecting their formal education, not teaching a trade, or were idle, dissolute, unchristian or 'uncapable'" (Rendleman, p. 210). Calvinist notions of poverty as idleness and sin permitted court expansion into the normative definitions of the "best interest" of children.

Until the mid-1800s, child protection laws did not differentiate among different classes of children; so that dependent children, status offenders, and juvenile delinquents were either housed together in poorhouses with adults or involuntarily apprenticed. However, by 1830, "an embryonic reform movement had begun," which removed dependent children from the teeming poorhouses and placed them in large orphan asylums. (Thomas, pp. 302–303). Due to the refuge movement (1824–1857), private corporations such as the New York House of Refuge (founded in 1824) received public funds and cared for both neglected and delinquent children in large institutions that separated juveniles from adult criminals and paupers. However, by the mid-1850s an anti-institution movement had developed, with the goal of placing poor city children in country foster placements rather than in large city institutions. Even though numerous state statutes were promulgated in the nineteenth century to care for abused and neglected children, government machinery was inadequate to implement sufficient protection.

In 1875 in New York, the first Society for the Prevention of Cruelty to Children (SPCC) was founded to help enforce child protection laws. However, since the SPCC was composed primarily of "wealthy, white men, almost all of them Protestant," who hired middle-class men as family investigators, the families that were targeted were largely poor immigrant families, who were judged by middle-class mores and vague standards such as "without proper parental guardianship" (Schiff, p. 413). The numerous competing reform movements and children's aid societies of the mid- to late 1800s focused on the child as a member of a family group, not as an autonomous individual, and most emphasized removing children from their own families and placing them into a different home environment. By 1879 the New York Children's Aid Society had sent 48,000 children out of New York to live with other families. After its first fourteen years, the New York Society for the Prevention of Cruelty to Children "investigated nearly 70,000 complaints of ill-treatment of 209,000 children. Prosecutions were pursued in 24,500 of these cases, resulting in almost 24,000 convictions and the removal of 36,300 children" (Schiff, pp. 413–414).

By the beginning of the twentieth century the tide had turned away from family separation and toward family preservation. At the 1909 White House Conference on the Care of Dependent Children, it was declared that "[h]ome life is the highest and finest product of civilization. It is the great molding force of mind and of character" (Tanenhaus, p. 550). The twentieth century ushered in a dramatic shift away from private child protective services in favor of governmental control by public agencies authorized under both federal and state child protection statutory schemes. In 1899 Illinois promulgated the first juvenile court, whose stated purpose was to provide for the care and custody of children in a manner that was an alternative equivalent to that of their parents. By 1920 all but three states had a juvenile court system.

But the goal of family reunification was rarely realized by the early juvenile courts, because few services were made available to assist poor uneducated parents in curing the conditions that led to state intervention. Instead, children remained in out-of-home placements for considerable periods of time. For instance, in Chicago, the city with the nation's first juvenile court, the rate of family reunification in 1921 was about the same as in 1912 (70%), but in 1921 more children were staying in institutions for longer periods than in 1912.

The Constitution and Child Protection Laws

Between 1875 and 1900 numerous challenges to the vague legal definitions of child dependency and the informal legal proceedings leading to the separation of parents and children were denied. Early court decisions did not speak in terms of parents' constitutional rights to rear their children, did not closely circumscribe the state's *parens patriae* power to protect children, rejected arguments based upon criminal law analogies, and failed to articulate procedural due process protections for families caught in the child protection legal maelstrom.

Although state and county juvenile courts continued to evolve and to provide different levels of due process in child protection proceedings, the modern child dependency court development was shaped by several decisions of the U.S. Supreme Court, which formalized the court process. In *Meyers v. Nebraska* (1923) the Court held that parents have a fundamental constitutional liberty interest in rearing their children. Based upon that liberty interest, the Court held in *Lassiter v. Department of Social Services* (1981) that, under certain circumstances, parents are entitled to court-appointed attorneys when they face involuntary termination of their parental rights in child protection proceedings. And in *Santosky v. Kramer* (1982) the Court held that the state has the burden of demonstrating, by clear and convincing evidence, that termination of parental rights is necessary to protect children. Local juvenile courts no longer had unbridled discretion to informally and permanently separate parents and children. However, the U.S. Constitution became the sounding board only in cases involving permanent severance of parental rights. States are still free to provide fewer due-process procedural rights in temporary child protection cases.

Federal Statutory Policy

In the 1980s and 1990s the autonomy of state child protection schemes was further compromised and homogenized by a series of federal statutes. In 1980, Congress passed the first comprehensive federal child protective services act, the Adoption Assistance and Child Welfare Act of 1980 (Pub. L. 96-272), which focused on state economic incentives to substantially decrease the length and number of foster care placements. This act also required specific family reunification services, reflecting the goals of the 1909 White House Conference. However, in 1997, in order to cure many of the defects in the 1980 act, Congress passed the Adoption and Safe Families Act, which shifted the focus from family reunification to expeditious permanency for children in adoptive placements. All state child protection systems adopted the federal guidelines as a requirement for receiving federal subsidies. Thus, because of constitutional and federal statutory requirements, the genesis of America's child protection system has led to great uniformity among state programs.

See also: CHILD ABUSE AND NEGLECT; CHILD PROTECTIVE SERVICES, *subentry on* CURRENT SYSTEM; VIOLENCE, CHILDREN'S EXPOSURE TO.

BIBLIOGRAPHY

ABRAMOWICZ, SARAH. 1999. "English Child Custody Law, 1660-1839: The Origins of Judicial Intervention in Paternal Custody." *Columbia Law Review* 90:1344–1391.

COGAN, NEIL HOWARD. 1970. "Juvenile Law, Before and After the Entrance of Parens Patriae." *South Carolina Law Review* 22:147–181.

COUPLET, SACHA M. 2000. "What to Do with the Sheep in Wolf's Clothing: The Role of Rhetoric and Reality about Youth Offenders in the Constructive Dismantling of the Juvenile Justice System." *University of Pennsylvania Law Review* 148:1303–1346.

ESPENOZA, CECELIA M. 1996. "Good Kids, Bad Kids: A Revelation about the Due Process Rights of Children." *Hastings Constitutional Law Quarterly* 23:407–545.

FOX, SANFORD J. 1970. "Juvenile Justice Reform: An Historical Perspective." *Stanford Law Review* 22:1187–1239.

LOKEN, GREGORY A. 1995. "'Thrownaway' Children and Throwaway Parenthood." *Temple Law Review* 68:1715–1762.

MACK, JULIAN W. 1909. "The Juvenile Court." *Harvard Law Review* 23:104–122.

RENDLEMAN, DOUGLAS R. 1971. "*Parens Patriae:* From Chancery to the Juvenile Court." *South Carolina Law Review* 23:205–259.

SCHIFF, CORINNE. 1997. "Child Custody and the Ideal of Motherhood in Late Nineteenth-Century New York." *Georgetown Journal on Fighting Poverty* 4:403–420.

SCHWARTZ, IRA M.; WEINER, NEIL ALAN; and ENOSH, GUY. 1998. "Nine Lives and Then Some: Why the Juvenile Court Does Not Roll Over and Die." *Wake Forest Law Review* 33:533–552.

SCHWARTZ, IRA M.; WEINER, NEIL ALAN; and ENOSH, GUY. 1999. "Myopic Justice? The Juvenile Court and Child Welfare Systems." *Annals of the American Academy of Political and Social Science* 564:126–141.

SCOTT, ELIZABETH S. 2000. "The Legal Construction of Adolescence." *Hofstra Law Review* 29:547–582.

TANENHAUS, DAVID S. 2001. "Growing Up Dependent: Family Preservation in Early Twentieth-Century Chicago." *Law and History Review* 19:547–582.

THOMAS, MASON P. 1972. "Child Abuse and Neglect Part I: Historical Overview, Legal Matrix, and Social Perceptions." *North Carolina Law Review* 50:293–349.

WILLIAM WESLEY PATTON

CURRENT SYSTEM

In the United States, methods for protecting abused and neglected children have progressed over the years. During the colonial era, the policy was to house pauper children in poorhouses or assign them to apprenticeships, while in the early nineteenth century the preference was to place these children in orphanages and industrial schools run by private societies. During the late nineteenth century and the twentieth century, state child-dependency statutory schemes became prominent, based upon the state's jurisdiction, through *parens patriae* ("father of the country," used in law to denote the government's power to protect its citizens), to intervene in family affairs for the protection of at-risk children. Contemporary children's services are characterized by a shift in power from state to federal policy control, with a resultant structural uniformity among state child-protection models.

Federal Policy

Federal child-protection policy has historically favored family preservation over the institutionalization of dependent minors. As early as 1909, through the White House Conference on the Care of Dependent Children, the federal government identified the importance of the home as the central forum for child development. Until recently, the history of child protection in America has reflected this presumption of family preservation being preferable to moving an at-risk child to a possibly better or safer environment. However, it was not until 1980 that Congress passed the first comprehensive federal child protective services act, the Adoption Assistance and Child Welfare Act (Pub. L. 96-272), which focused on state economic incentives to substantially decrease the length and number of foster care placements. This law also required specific family reunification services, reflecting the goals of the 1909 White House Conference.

In 1997, however, in order to cure many of the defects in the 1980 act, Congress passed the Adoption and Safe Families Act, which shifted the focus from family reunification to the best interests of children in expeditious permanency, which aims to rapidly finalize a permanent custodial home for minors rather than placing them temporarily in a series of different foster homes. Unlike the lengthy reunification services under the 1980 act, which often resulted in the termination of parental rights after two or three years of juvenile court intervention, the 1997 act required states to engage in "concurrent planning" at case intake. The federal goal of child protection had substantially shifted toward the child's individual needs, rather than primarily attempting family reunification through state services. In fact, in cases involving allegations of serious abuse, the 1997 act deleted the prior requirement of state reunification services and permitted states to immediately seek to sever parental rights and place children into the new preferred placement, adoption. The 1997 act created adoption subsidies and incentives to states. This federal adoption preference soon resulted in unprecedented increases in the number of dependent children being adopted.

Problems with the 1997 Act

Even though the 1997 act reduced the time within which dependent children placed outside the home would remain in temporary placements and increased the number of adoptions, it has also created new problems. First, the federal adoption subsidy program has convinced many potential foster parents to become adoptive parents, thus reducing the number of temporary placements for abused children. The adoption subsidy has also driven social service agencies toward decisions to sever parental rights in close cases, rather than continuing family reunification and temporary foster placements.

The greatest impact of this new rush to permanent adoption has been on sibling relationships. Most state statutory schemes do not recognize that significant sibling bonds are a sufficient reason to continue temporary placements, rather than split-ting siblings into different adoptive homes. Child welfare theorists argue that the speedy adoption permanency requirement of the 1997 act is having a significant deleterious cultural impact on poor and minority families. "Black families, who dominate foster care caseloads, are the main casualties of this shift away from a service provision toward coercive state intervention, which includes the requirement to relinquish custody of children as a condition of financial assistance" (Roberts, pp. 1641–1642).

Educational Implications

Prior to the 1997 act, dependent children often lived with many different foster families in different neighborhoods, and they therefore lacked any continuity in their formal education, either with teachers or with curricula. For instance, in 1993 California foster children "attend[ed] an average of 9 different schools by the age of 18 . . . [and] demonstrate[d] significantly lower achievement and lower performance in school" (Kelly, pp. 759–760).

This educational discontinuity results in a continuing introduction and departure of new and different friends and teachers, inadequate transfer of educational records, and lost academic credit. Even though "60% of children in foster care have measurable behavior or mental health problems . . . [and] [a]pproximately 35–45% . . . have developmental problems," most do not receive appropriate diagnosis for special education classes or psychological treatment (Practicing Law Institute, p. 115). It is clear that children with disabilities trapped in this legal maelstrom are not receiving the education promised by the Individuals with Disabilities Education Act, which established legal means "to ensure that all children with disabilities have available to them a free appropriate public education that emphasizes special education and related services designed to meet their unique needs and prepare them for employment and independent living."

The Decline in Child Dependency Cases

Child neglect and abuse reports increased an average of 6 percent annually from 1985 to 1991, when the number of reports reached 2.9 million. However, since 1991 there has been a continual decrease in the number sexual abuse reports, with a 26 percent decline from 1991 to 1998 in the number of reports and an average decline for all states of 37 percent in substantiated cases. In Los Angeles County, which has more foster children than any other county in

America, the number of foster care children dropped from 18.7 per thousand in 1997 to 13.1 per thousand in 2001, and the number of reported child abuse cases dropped from 71.2 reports per thousand in 1996 to 53.1 per thousand in 2000.

In 1990 the United States Advisory Board on Child Abuse and Neglect determined that the most significant factor in failing to provide dependent children with adequate services was the overload of cases. If the decline in the number of reported child abuse cases continues, and if social services agencies do not respond by a corresponding reduction of current staff, it may become possible to provide dependent children the social services and educational services commensurate with their needs.

See also: CHILD ABUSE AND NEGLECT; CHILD PROTECTIVE SERVICES, *subentry on* HISTORICAL OVERVIEW; VIOLENCE, CHILDREN'S EXPOSURE TO.

BIBLIOGRAPHY

BAKER, KATHERINE K. 2001. "Alternative Caretaking and Family Autonomy: Some Thoughts in Response to Dorothy Roberts." *Chicago-Kent Law Review* 76:1643–1650.

Individuals with Disabilities Education Act Amendments of 1997. U.S. Public Law 105-17. *U.S. Code.* Vol. 20, secs. 1400 et seq.

JONES, LISA, and FINKELHOR, DAVID. 2001. *The Decline in Child Sexual Abuse Cases.* Washington, DC: U.S. Department of Justice, Office of Juvenile Justice and Delinquency Prevention.

KELLEY, KATHLEEN. 2001. "The Education Crisis for Children in the California Juvenile Court System." *Hastings Constitutional Law Quarterly* 27:758–773.

MYERS, JOHN E. 1994. "Definition and Origins of the Backlash Against Child Protection." In *Excellence in Children's Law.* Denver, CO: National Association of Counsel for Children.

PRACTICING LAW INSTITUTE. 2000. "Early Intervention and Special Education Advocacy: A Missing Link in the Representation of Children in Foster Care." *Practicing Law Institute, Litigation and Administrative Practice Course Handbook Series, Criminal Law and Urban Problems* 185(C0-0016):103–166.

RIVERA, CARLA. 2001. "State's Children Facing Fewer Risks, Study Says." *Los Angeles Times* November 28:3.

ROBERTS, DOROTHY E. 2001. "Kinship Care and the Price of State Support for Children." *Chicago-Kent Law Review* 76:1619–1641.

SANDERS, DEBORAH. 2001. "Toward a Policy of Permanence for America's Disposable Children: A Survey of the Evolution of Federal Funding Statutes for Foster Care from 1961 to Present." In *Advocacy for Children and Families: Moving from Sympathy to Empathy.* Denver, CO: National Association of Counsel for Children.

TANENHAUS, DAVID S. 2001. "Growing Up Dependent: Family Preservation In Early Twentieth-Century Chicago." *Law and History Review* 19:547–582.

THOMAS, MASON P. 1972. "Child Abuse and Neglect, Part I: Historical Overview, Legal Matrix, and Social Perspectives." *North Carolina Law Review* 50:293–349.

WILLIAM WESLEY PATTON

CHILDREN'S LITERATURE

Children's literature is any literature that is enjoyed by children. More specifically, children's literature comprises those books written and published for young people who are not yet interested in adult literature or who may not possess the reading skills or developmental understandings necessary for its perusal. In addition to books, children's literature also includes magazines intended for pre-adult audiences.

The age range for children's literature is from infancy through the stage of early adolescence, which roughly coincides with the chronological ages of twelve through fourteen. Between that literature most appropriate for children and that most appropriate for adults lies young adult literature. Usually young adult literature is more mature in content and more complex in literary structure than children's literature.

Most of the literary genres of adult literature appear in children's literature as well. Fiction in its various forms—contemporary realism, fantasy and historical fiction, poetry, folk tales, legends, myths, and epics—all have their counterparts in children's literature. Nonfiction for children includes books about the arts and humanities; the social, physical, biological, and earth sciences; and biography and autobiography. In addition, children's books may take the form of picture books in which visual and verbal texts form an interconnected whole. Picture books for children include storybooks, alphabet books, counting books, wordless books, and concept books.

History

Literature written specifically for an audience of children began to be published on a wide scale in the seventeenth century. Most of the early books for children were didactic rather than artistic, meant to teach letter sounds and words or to improve the child's moral and spiritual life. In the mid-1700s, however, British publisher John Newbery (1713–1767), influenced by John Locke's ideas that children should enjoy reading, began publishing books for children's amusement. Since that time there has been a gradual transition from the deliberate use of purely didactic literature to inculcate moral, spiritual, and ethical values in children to the provision of literature to entertain and inform. This does not imply that suitable literature for children is either immoral or amoral. On the contrary, suitable literature for today's children is influenced by the cultural and ethical values of its authors. These values are frequently revealed as the literary work unfolds, but they are a means to an end, not an end in themselves. Authors assume a degree of intelligence on the part of their audience that was not assumed in the past. In this respect, children's literature has changed dramatically since its earliest days.

Another dramatic development in children's literature in the twentieth century has been the picture book. Presenting an idea or story in which pictures and words work together to create an aesthetic whole, the picture book traces its origin to the nineteenth century, when such outstanding artists as Randolph Caldecott, Kate Greenaway, and Walter Crane were at work. In the 1930s and 1940s such great illustrators as Wanda Gag, Marguerite de Angeli, James Daugherty, Robert Lawson, Dorothy Lathrop, Ludwig Bemelmans, Maud and Miska Petersham, and Ingri and Edgar Parin d'Aulaire began their work. Many of these and other equally illustrious artists helped to bring picture books to their present position of prominence. Since 1945 many highly talented illustrators have entered this field.

With the advent of computer-based reproduction techniques in the latter part of the twentieth century, the once tedious and expensive process of full color reproduction was revolutionized, and now almost any original media can be successfully translated into picture book form. Although many artists continue to work with traditional media such as printmaking, pen and ink, photography, and paint, they have been joined by artists who work with paper sculpture, mixed media constructions, and computer graphics.

The changes in literature for older children have been equally important. Among the early and lasting contributions to literature for children were works by Jack London, Mark Twain, Rudyard Kipling, Edgar Allan Poe, Robert Louis Stevenson, and Hans Christian Andersen. These writers, however, considered adults their major audience; therefore, they directed only some of their literary efforts toward young readers. Today, large numbers of highly talented authors have turned to younger readers for an audience and direct most, if not all, of their writings to them.

Another major change in publishing for children has been the rise in multicultural children's literature. Prior to the mid-twentieth century the world depicted in children's books was largely a white world. If characters from a nonwhite culture appeared in children's books they were almost always badly stereotyped. The civil rights movement alerted publishers and the reading public to the need for books that depicted the America of all children, not just a white majority. Although the percentage of children's books by and about people of color does not equate with their actual population numbers, authors of color such as Virginia Hamilton, Mildred Taylor, Alma Flor Ada, Walter Dean Myers, Gary Soto, and Laurence Yep, and illustrators such as Allen Say, Ed Young, John Steptoe, Jerry Pinkney, and Brian Pinkney have made major contributions to a more multiculturally balanced world of children's books.

Not only are there larger numbers of talented writers and artists from many cultures at work for children, but the range of subject matter discussed in children's fiction has also been extended remarkably. Topics that were considered taboo only a short time ago are being presented in good taste. Young readers from ten to fourteen can read well-written fiction that deals with death, child abuse, economic deprivation, alternative life styles, illegitimate pregnancy, juvenile gang warfare, and rejected children. By the early twenty-first century it had become more nearly true than ever before that children may explore life through literature.

Literature in the Lives of Children

Literature serves children in four major ways: it helps them to better understand themselves, others, their world, and the aesthetic values of written language. When children read fiction, narrative poetry, or biography, they often assume the role of one of the characters. Through that character's thoughts, words, and actions the child develops insight into his or her own character and values. Frequently, because of experiences with literature, the child's modes of behavior and value structures are changed, modified, or extended.

When children assume the role of a book's character as they read, they interact vicariously with the other characters portrayed in that particular selection. In the process they learn something about the nature of behavior and the consequences of personal interaction. In one sense they become aware of the similarities and differences among people.

Because literature is not subject to temporal or spatial limitations, books can figuratively transport readers across time and space. Other places in times past, present, or future invite children's exploration. Because of that exploration, children come to better understand the world in which they live and their own relationship to it.

Written language in its literary uses is an instrument of artistic expression. Through prose and poetry children explore the versatility of the written word and learn to master its depth of meaning. Through literature, too, children can move beyond the outer edges of reality and place themselves in worlds of make-believe, unfettered by the constraints of everyday life.

Environment

The three principal settings in which children's literature functions are the home, the public library, and the school. In each of these settings, the functions of literature are somewhat different, but each function supports the others and interacts with them.

Home. Irrefutable evidence indicates that those children who have had an early and continuing chance to interact with good literature are more apt to succeed in school than those who have not. Parents who begin to read aloud to their children, often from birth, are communicating the importance of litera-ture by providing an enjoyable experience. The young child makes a lasting connection between books, which provide pleasure, and the undisputed attention from the parent who takes time to do the reading. During the preschool years, books contribute to children's language structures and to their vocabulary. Children acquire a sense of language pattern and rhythm from the literary usage of language that is not found in everyday conversational speech. Then, too, children discover that print has meaning, and as they acquire the ability to read print as well as understand pictures, children find further pleasure in books. In finding that reading has its own intrinsic reward, children acquire the most important motivation for learning to master reading skills.

Public library. Public libraries have taken on an increasingly important role in serving children. Children's rooms, which were once the domain of a few select children, are inviting places for all children, whether or not they are inveterate readers. Libraries organize story hours, present films, and provide computers and quiet places to do homework as well as present special book-related events and sponsor book clubs and summer reading programs. Children's librarians guide the reading interests of children and act as consultants to parents. Full exploitation of the public library in the broader education of children has not yet been achieved, but growing acceptance by the public of the library as a community necessity rather than a luxury will help it to continue to play an increasingly important role in the lives of children.

School. Literature did not begin to make broad inroads into the reading curriculum until the 1950s. Before that time many schools had no library, and a good number of these schools did not even feel the need for one. Many schools relied almost exclusively on textbooks for instruction. By the end of the twentieth century, however, nearly every curriculum authority had come to recognize the importance of trade books (books other than textbooks) in the in-school education of children. In the early twenty-first century most schools have central libraries staffed by trained librarians and some schools provide financial support for classroom libraries as well. When this is not the case, teachers, recognizing the value of good literature, often reach into their own pockets to provide trade books for their classrooms. A 1998 survey of school library media programs by the Center of Education Statistics of the U.S. Department of Education found a mean of twenty-eight volumes per elementary school child in both public and private schools.

Function in the school curriculum. Literature plays an increasingly large role in the formal education of children in three related but rather discrete areas: the instructional reading program, the subject matter areas, and the literature program.

Most instructional reading programs recognize the importance of literature. Basal reading textbook programs generally recommend that trade books be used from the beginning of formal reading instruction in order to motivate readers through the long, and sometimes frustrating, efforts that learning to read usually demands. Through trade books the reader finds those efforts are rewarded by the pleasure gained from reading. In many schools the teaching of reading has been centered on trade books rather than textbooks. But in literature-based programs, teachers plan instruction around experiences with "real" books, experiences that include helping students make their own reading choices and giving children time to share responses to reading with their peer group. Schools with such literature-based programs recognize the importance of creating a classroom community of readers that will not only help children learn how to read but will also encourage them to become lifelong readers.

Subject matter areas, such as social studies and the sciences, have depended to a large extent upon textbooks to provide common learning for entire classes. However, there are limitations inherent in the nature of textbooks that require supplementation by trade books. Because textbooks survey broad areas of knowledge, space limitations prevent in-depth explorations of particular topics. Recent discoveries and events cannot always be included because textbook series require long periods of preparation. Content area textbooks are often subject to review by state committees that limit potentially controversial material. Trade books are widely used to offset these limitations. Nonfiction books provide opportunities for in-depth consideration of particular topics. Furthermore, the comparatively short time needed for the preparation and publication of trade books makes recent discoveries and occurrences available to the reader.

Elementary school literature programs vary widely. As state and national standards and testing drive curriculum some schools reflect the attitude that literature is a luxury, if not an undesirable frill.

In such schools little, if any, in-school time is devoted either to reading for pleasure or to the formal study of literature. Most schools, however, recognize children's need for some pleasurable experiences with literature that enable them to return to books to think more deeply about the characters, themes, and other literary elements. In such schools the study of literature is grounded in reader response theory that grew out of Louise Rosenblatt's contention in *Literature as Exploration* that "the literary work exists in a live circuit set up between reader and text" (p. 25). Thus the reader is seen as a co-constructor of meaning with the author. Any plan for the direct study of literary form, structure, and content as a means of heightening the pleasure of reading includes, at a minimum, teachers reading aloud from works of literature, and the formation of book circles where small groups of students regularly meet together to discuss books. In addition teachers should plan time for children to respond to books through writing, creative dramatics, and other art forms.

Awards

There are a number of awards made to authors and illustrators of children's books, and these awards frequently aid readers in the selection of books. The most prestigious American awards are the Newbery Medal and the Caldecott Medal. The Newbery Medal is presented each year to the author of the "most distinguished contribution to American literature for children" published in the previous year. To be eligible for the award, the author must be a U.S. citizen or a permanent resident of the United States. The winner is chosen by a committee of the Association of Library Services to Children (ALSC) of the American Library Association (ALA). The Caldecott Medal is given each year to "the artist of the most distinguished American picture book for children." The winner is selected by the same committee that chooses the Newbery winner. In addition to the Newbery and Caldecott medals, other prominent awards given under the auspices of the ALSC include the Laura Ingalls Wilder Award, which is given to an author or illustrator who has "made a substantial contribution to literature for children" over a period of years; the Robert F. Sibert Informational Book Award, which honors the author whose work of nonfiction has made a significant contribution to the field of children's literature in a given year; and the Batchelder Award, given to the publisher of the most outstanding book of the year that is a translation, published in the United States, of a book that was first published in another country. Other notable American book awards include the Coretta Scott King Awards given by the Social Responsibilities Round Table of the American Library Association to an African-American author and an African-American illustrator for outstanding inspirational and educational contributions to literature for children, and the Pura Belpré Award, which is sponsored by ALSC and REFORMA (the National Association to Promote Library Service to the Spanish Speaking). This award is presented annually to a Latino/Latina writer and illustrator whose work best portrays, affirms, and celebrates the Latino cultural experience in an outstanding book for children. The Hans Christian Andersen prize, the first international children's book award, was established in 1956 by the International Board on Books for Young People. Given every two years, the award was expanded in 1966 to honor an illustrator as well as an author. A committee composed of members from different countries judges the selections recommended by the board or library associations in each country.

The following list of outstanding children's books was selected from award winners of the twentieth century and is meant to mark important milestones in children's literature.

Aardema, Verna. 1975. *Why Mosquitos Buzz in People's Ears.* Illustrated by Leo Dillon and Diane Dillon. New York: Dial.

Alexander, Lloyd. 1968. *The High King.* New York: Holt, Rinehart and Winston.

Atwater, Richard, and Florence Atwater. 1938. *Mr. Popper's Penguins.* Boston: Little, Brown.

Bailey, Carolyn Sherwin. 1946. *Miss Hickory.* Illustrated by Ruth Gannett. New York: Viking.

Bang, Molly. 1999. *When Sophie Gets Angry— Really, Really Angry.* New York: Scholastic.

Bemelmans, Ludwig. 1939. *Madeline.* New York: Simon and Schuster.

Bontemps, Arna. 1948. *Story of the Negro.* New York: Knopf.

Brink, Carol Ryrie. 1935. *Caddie Woodlawn.* Illustrated by Kate Seredy. New York: Macmillan.

Brown, Marcia. 1947. *Stone Soup.* New York: Scribner's.

Brown, Marcia. 1961. *Once a Mouse.* New York: Scribner's.

Burton, Virginia Lee. 1942. *The Little House.* Boston: Houghton Mifflin.

Clark, Ann Nolan. 1952. *Secret of the Andes.* Illustrated by Jean Charlot. New York: Viking.

Cleary, Beverly. 1977. *Ramona and Her Father.* New York: Morrow.

Cleary, Beverly. 1984. *Dear Mr. Henshaw.* New York: Morrow.

Collier, James, and Collier, Christopher. 1974. *My Brother Sam Is Dead.* New York: Four Winds.

Cooney, Barbara, ed. and illus. 1958. *The Chanticleer and the Fox,* by Geoffrey Chaucer. New York: Crowell.

Cooper, Susan. 1973. *The Dark Is Rising.* New York: Atheneum.

Cooper, Susan. 1975. *The Grey King.* New York: Atheneum.

Creech, Sharon. 1994. *Walk Two Moons.* New York: HarperCollins.

Crews, Donald. 1978. *Freight Train.* New York: Greenwillow.

Curtis, Christopher Paul. 1999. *Bud, Not Budd.* New York: Delacorte.

Cushman, Karen. 1995. *The Midwife's Apprentice.* New York: Clarion.

de Angeli, Marguerite. 1949. *The Door in the Wall.* New York: Doubleday.

de Paola, Tomie. 1975. *Strega Nona.* New York: Simon and Schuster.

de Regniers, Beatrice Schenk. 1964. *May I Bring a Friend?* New York: Atheneum.

Emberley, Barbara. 1967. *Drummer Hoff.* Illustrated by Ed Emberley. New York: Prentice Hall.

Estes, Eleanor. 1944. *The Hundred Dresses.* San Diego, CA: Harcourt Brace.

Feelings, Muriel. 1971. *Moja Means One: A Swahili Counting Book.* Illustrated by Tom Feelings. New York: Dial.

Field, Rachel. 1929. *Hitty, Her First Hundred Years.* Illustrated by Dorothy P. Lathrop. New York: Macmillan.

Fleischman, Paul. 1988. *Joyful Noise: Poems for Two Voices.* New York: Harper and Row.

Forbes, Esther. 1943. *Johnny Tremain.* Illustrated by Lynd Ward. Boston: Houghton Mifflin.

Fox, Paula. 1973. *The Slave Dancer.* New York: Bradbury.

Freedman, Russell. 1987. *Lincoln: A Photobiography.* New York: Clarion.

Gág, Wanda. 1928. *Millions of Cats.* New York: Coward-McCann.

Gates, Doris. 1940. *Blue Willow.* New York: Viking.

Geisel, Theodor S. [Dr. Seuss]. 1951. *If I Ran the Zoo.* New York: Random House.

George, Jean. 1972. *Julie of the Wolves.* New York: Harper and Row.

Goble, Paul. 1978. *The Girl Who Loved Wild Horses.* New York: Bradbury.

Haley, Gail E. 1970. *A Story, A Story.* New York: Atheneum.

Hall, Donald. 1979. *Ox-Cart Man.* Illustrated by Barbara Cooney. New York: Viking.

Hamilton, Virginia. 1974. *M.C. Higgins the Great.* New York: Macmillan.

Henry, Marguerite. 1948. *King of the Wind.* Illustrated by Wesley Dennis. New York: Rand McNally.

Hesse, Karen. 1997. *Out of the Dust.* New York: Scholastic.

Hodges, Margaret. 1984. *Saint George and the Dragon.* Illustrated by Trina Schart Hyman. Boston: Little, Brown.

Hogrogian, Nonny. 1971. *One Fine Day.* New York: Macmillan.

Keats, Ezra Jack. 1962. *The Snowy Day.* New York: Viking.

Konigsburg, E. L. 1967. *From the Mixed-Up Files of Mrs. Basil E. Frankweiler.* New York: Atheneum.

Konigsburg, E. L. 1996. *The View from Saturday.* New York: Atheneum.

Langstaff, John. 1955. *Frog Went A-Courtin'.* Illustrated by Feodor Rojankovsky. San Diego, CA: Harcourt Brace.

Lawson, Robert. 1944. *Rabbit Hill.* New York: Viking.

L'Engle, Madeleine. 1962. *A Wrinkle in Time.* New York: Farrar, Straus.

Lenski, Lois. 1945. *Strawberry Girl.* New York: Lippincott.

Lester, Julius. 1968. *To Be a Slave.* New York: Dial.

Lionni, Leo. 1963. *Swimmy.* New York: Pantheon.

Lobel, Arnold. 1972. *Frog and Toad Together.* New York: Harper and Row.

Lobel, Arnold. 1980. *The Giver.* Boston: Houghton Mifflin.

Lowry, Lois. 1989. *Number the Stars.* Boston: Houghton Mifflin.

Macaulay, David. 1973. *Cathedral.* Boston: Houghton Mifflin.

Macaulay, David. 1990. *Black and White.* Boston: Houghton Mifflin.

MacDonald, Golden. 1946. *The Little Island.* Illustrated by Leonard Weisgard. New York: Doubleday.

MacLachlan, Patricia. 1985. *Sarah, Plain and Tall.* New York: Harper and Row.

Martin, Jacqueline Briggs. 1998. *Snowflake Bentley.* Illustrated by Mary Azarian. Boston: Houghton Mifflin.

Mathis, Sharon. *The Hundred Penny Box.* New York: Viking.

McCloskey, Robert. 1941. *Make Way for Ducklings.* New York: Viking.

McCloskey, Robert. 1948. *Blueberries for Sal.* New York: Viking.

McCully, Emily Arnold. 1992. *Mirette on the High Wire.* New York: Putnam.

McKissack, Patricia. 1988. *Mirandy and Brother Wind.* Illustrated by Jerry Pinkney. New York: Harper and Row.

Means, Florence Crannell. 1945. *The Moved-Outers.* Boston: Houghton Mifflin.

Milhous, Katherine. 1950. *The Egg Tree.* New York: Scribner's.

Minarik, Else. 1961. *Little Bear's Visit.* Illustrated by Maurice Sendak. New York: Harper and Row.

Murphy, Jim. 1995. *The Great Fire.* New York: Scholastic.

Musgrove, Margaret. 1976. *Ashanti to Zulu: African Traditions.* Illustrated by Leo Dillon and Diane Dillon. New York: Dial.

Myers, Walter Dean. 1988. *Scorpions*. New York: Harper and Row.

Myers, Walter Dean. 1997. *Harlem*. Illustrated by Christopher Myers. New York: Scholastic.

O'Dell, Scott. 1960. *Island of the Blue Dolphins*. Boston: Houghton Mifflin.

Paterson, Katherine. 1977. *Bridge to Terabithia*. New York: Crowell.

Paterson, Katherine. 1980. *Jacob Have I Loved*. New York: Crowell.

Peck, Richard. 2000. *A Year Down Yonder*. New York: Dial.

Perrault, Charles. 1954. *Cinderella*. Illustrated by Marcia Brown. New York: Harper and Row.

Pinkney, Andrea. 1997. *Duke Ellington: The Piano Prince and His Orchestra*. Illustrated by Brian Pinkney. New York: Hyperion.

Politi, Leo. 1949. *Song of the Swallows*. New York: Scribner's.

Ransome, Arthur. 1968. *The Fool of the World and the Flying Ship*. Illustrated by Uri Shulevitz. New York: Farrar, Straus.

Raschka, Chris. 1993. *Yo! Yes?* New York: Orchard.

Raskin, Ellen. 1978. *The Westing Game*. New York: Dutton.

Rathman, Peggy. 1995. *Officer Buckle and Gloria*. New York: Putnam.

Ringgold, Faith. 1991. *Tar Beach*. New York: Crown.

Rylant, Cynthia. 1992. *Missing May*. New York: Jackson/Orchard.

Sachar, Louis. 1998. *Holes*. New York: Delacorte.

San Souci, Robert D. 1989. *The Talking Eggs*. Illustrated by Jerry Pinkney. New York: Dial.

Sauer, Julia L. 1943. *Fog Magic*. New York: Viking.

Sawyer, Ruth. 1936. *Roller Skates*. Illustrated by Valenti Angelo. New York: Viking.

Sawyer, Ruth. 1953. *Journey Cake, Ho!* Illustrated by Robert McClosky. New York: Viking.

Say, Allen. 1993. *Grandfather's Journey*. Boston: Houghton Mifflin.

Scieszka, Jon. 1992. *The Stinky Cheese Man and Other Fairly Stupid Tales*. Illustrated by Lane Smith. New York: Viking.

Sendak, Maurice. 1963. *Where the Wild Things Are*. New York: Harper and Row.

Singer, Isaac Bashevis. 1968. *When Shlemiel Went to Warsaw and Other Stories*. New York: Farrar, Straus.

Speare, Elizabeth George. 1958. *The Witch of Blackbird Pond*. Boston: Houghton Mifflin.

Sperry, Armstrong. 1940. *Call It Courage*. New York: Macmillan.

Spinelli, Jerry. 1990. *Maniac Magee*. Boston: Little, Brown.

Steig, William. 1969. *Sylvester and the Magic Pebble*. New York: Windmill/Simon and Schuster.

Steig, William. 1976. *Abel's Island*. New York: Farrar, Straus.

Steptoe, John. 1987. *Mufaro's Beautiful Daughters: An African Story*. New York: Lothrop, Lee and Shepard.

St. George, Judith. 2000. *So You Want to Be President*. Illustrated by David Small. New York: Philomel.

Taback, Sims. 1999. *Joseph Had a Little Overcoat*. New York: Viking.

Taro, Yashima. 1955. *Crow Boy*. New York: Viking.

Taylor, Mildred D. 1976. *Roll of Thunder, Hear My Cry*. New York: Dial.

Thurber, James. 1943. *Many Moons*. Illustrated by Louis Slobodkin. San Diego, CA: Harcourt Brace.

Tresselt, Alvin. 1947. *White Snow, Bright Snow*. Illustrated by Roger Duvoisin. New York: Lothrop.

Udry, Janice May. 1956. *A Tree Is Nice*. Illustrated by Marc Simont. New York: Harper and Row.

Van Allsburg, Chris. 1981. *Jumanji*. Boston: Houghton Mifflin.

Van Allsburg, Chris. 1985. *The Polar Express*. Boston: Houghton Mifflin.

Voigt, Cynthia. 1981. *Dicey's Song*. New York: Atheneum.

Ward, Lynd. 1952. *The Biggest Bear*. Boston: Houghton Mifflin.

White, E. B. 1952. *Charlotte's Web*. New York: Harper and Row.

Wiesner, David. 1991. *Tuesday.* New York: Clarion.

Wilder, Laura Ingalls. 1937. *On the Banks of Plum Creek.* New York: Harper and Row.

Williams, Vera B. 1982. *A Chair for My Mother.* New York: Morrow.

Wisniewski, David. 1996. *Golem.* New York: Clarion.

Yep, Laurence. 1975. *Dragonwings.* New York: Harper and Row.

Yolen, Jane. 1987. *Owl Moon.* Illustrated by John Schoenherr. New York: Philomel.

Young, Ed. 1989. *Lon Po Po: A Red Riding Hood Story from China.* New York: Philomel.

Zelinsky, Paul O. 1997. *Rapunzel.* New York: Dutton.

Zemach, Harve. 1973. *Duffy and the Devil.* Illustrated by Margot Zemach. New York: Farrar, Straus.

See also: ENGLISH EDUCATION, *subentry on* TEACHING OF; LANGUAGE ARTS, TEACHING OF; READING.

BIBLIOGRAPHY

APPLEBEE, ARTHUR. 1978. *The Child's Concept of Story: Ages Two to Seventeen.* Chicago: University of Chicago Press.

CARPENTER, HUMPHREY, and PRICHARD, MARI, eds. 1984. *The Oxford Companion to Children's Literature.* Oxford: Oxford University Press.

EGOFF, SHEILA; STUBBS, GORDON; ASHLEY, RALPH; and SUTTON, WENDY, eds. 1996. *Only Connect: Readings on Children's Literature,* 3rd edition. New York: Oxford University Press.

HARRIS, VIOLET J., ed. 1997. *Using Multicultural Literature in the K–8 Classroom.* Norwood, MA: Christopher Gordon.

HORNING, KATHLEEN T. 1997. *From Cover to Cover: Evaluating and Reviewing Children's Books.* New York: HarperCollins.

HUCK, CHARLOTTE; HEPLER, SUSAN; HICKMAN, JANET; and KIEFER, BARBARA. 2001. *Children's Literature in the Elementary School,* 7th edition. New York: McGraw-Hill.

HUNT, PETER. 1999. *Criticism, Theory, and Children's Literature.* Cambridge, MA: Basil Blackwell.

JACKSON, MARY V. 1990. *Engines of Instruction, Mischief, and Magic: Children's Literature in England from Its Beginnings to 1839.* Lincoln: University of Nebraska Press.

LEHR, SUSAN. 1991. *The Child's Developing Sense of Theme: Responses to Literature.* New York: Teachers College Press.

LUKENS, REBECCA J. 1999. *A Critical Handbook of Children's Literature,* 6th edition. New York: Longman.

LURIE, ALISON. 1990. *Don't Tell the Grown-Ups: Subversive Children's Literature.* Boston: Little, Brown.

MURRY, GAIL S. 1998. *American Children's Literature and the Construction of Childhood.* New York: Twayne Publishers.

ROSENBLATT, LOUISE M. 1994. *The Reader, the Text, the Poem: The Transactional Theory of the Literary Work.* Carbondale: Southern Illinois University Press.

ROSENBLATT, LOUISE M. 1996. *Literature as Exploration,* 5th edition. New York: Modern Language Association.

ROSER, NANCY L., and MARTINEZ, MIRIAM, eds. 1995. *Book Talk and Beyond: Children and Teachers Respond to Literature.* Newark, DE: International Reading Association.

SILVEY, ANITA, ed. 1995. *Children's Books and Their Creators.* Boston: Houghton Mifflin.

SUTHERLAND, ZENA. 1996. *Children and Books.* 9th ed. New York: Addison Wesley.

TOWNSEND, JOHN ROWE. 1990. *Written for Children: An Outline of English Children's Literature,* 4th edition. New York: HarperCollins.

SHELTON L. ROOT JR.
Revised by
BARBARA Z. KIEFER

CHILDREN'S PHYSICAL HEALTH

See: HEALTH EDUCATION, SCHOOL; IMMUNIZATION AND CHILDREN'S PHYSICAL HEALTH; NUTRITION AND CHILDREN'S PHYSICAL HEALTH; SLEEP AND CHILDREN'S PHYSICAL HEALTH.

CHILDS, JOHN L. (1889–1985)

Professor of education at Teachers College, Columbia University, John Lawrence Childs was a leading member of the New York Progressives from the 1930s to 1960. Childs was born in Eau Claire, Wisconsin, where he learned the value of hard work, which was for him both a moral and social obligation. Raised as a Methodist, he spent four years at the University of Wisconsin, Madison, graduating in 1911 with a degree in journalism. While at Madison he began working for the Young Men's Christian Association (YMCA). For three years he headed its Midwest chapter in Kankakee, Illinois, where he met and married his wife, Grace Mary Fowler, in 1915. The following year he sailed for China as a YMCA missionary working for most of the time in Peking (Beijing). During John Dewey's visit to China (1919–1920), he stayed for a short while with the Childses, and John Childs was impressed. Early in 1922 Childs returned to the United States, and in February 1923 began graduate work at Union Theological Seminary, which included two courses at Teachers College given by W. H. Kilpatrick. Childs returned to China eighteen months later. On his visit to China in 1927 Kilpatrick persuaded Childs to obtain his doctorate, and Childs moved back to New York.

Childs joined the faculty of Teachers College following the publication of his dissertation, "Education and the Philosophy of Experimentalism," in July 1931. In correspondence to Robert Miller, Kilpatrick described the book as "one of the very best pieces of thinking yet done in the field of the exploitation and criticism of Professor Dewey's ideas." Thus began Childs's close identification with the work of Dewey.

Almost immediately, Childs and Dewey coauthored two chapters in *The Educational Frontier,* edited by Kilpatrick. Several scholars noted that Dewey seemed to have flirted with social reconstructionism in these chapters. In a telling memorandum to Dewey, Childs wrote, "educational reconstruction and social reconstruction are correlatives, and, therefore, the two must develop together. Any attempt to work through the school problem–to say nothing of the educational problem as a whole– inevitably leads into a consideration of the prevailing economic and social situation." Dewey stepped back somewhat from this position; Childs was committed to social reconstruction, and in 1937 joined the board of directors of the *Social Frontier,* having been a regular contributor to the journal almost at its inception in 1934.

Dean William Russell was not altogether pleased with Childs's radical position, but promoted him to associate professor in 1935 and to professor in 1938. In 1935 Childs joined the American Federation of Teachers, in which he became an important player. Russell put him in charge of a select committee looking into the demands of striking cafeteria workers at Teachers College. The report exonerated the strikers, and it received some publicity in both the New York and the national press. Childs resigned from the union in 1937 on account of its takeover by communist sympathizers. He later rejoined and took a leadership role in its postwar activities. He achieved greater prominence when he was elected state chair of the Liberal party, a position he held from 1944 until early 1947. Childs's political activities were an extension of his philosophical ideals; they were moral necessities. This missionary had in effect changed his allegiance from the work of the gospel, albeit a social gospel, to the work of educational and social reconstruction. In his writings he made apparent his commitment to a morality based not in the supernatural or transcendent, but one embedded in human experience.

In 1950 Childs published his most significant work, *Education and Morals.* Perhaps the major point of the book is that morality always exists in the making of choices in genuine life alternatives. If there is no choice there is no morality involved. (He never engaged in discussion of the existential notion of choice.) Thus the educational enterprise is at root a moral enterprise because it is involves constant choices on behalf of students. For Childs, moral goods existed in the context of democratic values and aims. In this view he was at odds with Boyd Bode, with whom at this time he began an extended correspondence. Bode felt that the pragmatic educational agenda related to method and the reliance on intelligence; Childs believed that it also required a democratic outcome. He did not, as did George S. Counts, call for indoctrination, but he felt as strongly. Bode only went as far as to say that the schools should promote the processes of democracy but not expressly its aims.

In his last major book, *American Pragmatism and Education,* Childs devoted a chapter to Bode. The book is a delineation of the principles of pragmatism, and in the opening of the book he outlines its major tenets.

Thought is intrinsically connected with action; theories and doctrines are working hypotheses and are to be tested by the consequences they produce in actual life-situations; moral ideas are empty and sterile apart from attention to the means that are required to achieve them; reality is not a static, completed system, but a process of unending change and transformation; man is not a mere puppet of external forces, but through the use of intelligence can reshape the conditions that mold his own experience. (pp. 3–4)

If this statement sounds somewhat academic and remote from contemporary education, it is nonetheless an accurate and perceptive summary of pragmatic theory, and quite in line with Dewey's own views.

Childs's career was very much based on his interpretation and commentary of Dewey's work, and he was highly praised for both. He was a major speaker at Dewey's eightieth and ninetieth birthday festivities, and as well as the centenary celebrations; he wrote a chapter on education in Paul A. Schilpp's volume on *Dewey in the Library of Living Philosophers*; he was the recipient of the John Dewey Society medal in 1965, as well as many other awards. Childs retired from Teachers College in 1955 and spent much of the next decade as a visiting professor at several universities. Upon his final retirement he moved to Rockford, Illinois, where he died in 1985.

See also: CURRICULUM, SCHOOL; PHILOSOPHY OF EDUCATION; PROGRESSIVE EDUCATION.

BIBLIOGRAPHY

CHILDS, JOHN L. 1931. *Education and the Philosophy of Experimentalism.* New York: Century.

CHILDS, JOHN L. 1950. *Education and Morals: An Experimentalist Philosophy of Education.* New York: Appleton-Century-Crofts.

CHILDS, JOHN L. 1956. *American Pragmatism and Education: An Interpretation and Criticism.* New York: Holt.

CHILDS, JOHN L., and COUNTS, GEORGE S. 1943. *America, Russia, and the Communist Party in the Postwar World.* New York: Day.

DENNIS, LAWRENCE J. 1992. *From Prayer to Pragmatism: A Biography of John L. Childs.* Carbondale and Edwardsville: Southern Illinois University Press.

LAWRENCE J. DENNIS

CITIZENSHIP EDUCATION

See: CIVICS AND CITIZENSHIP EDUCATION.

CIVICS AND CITIZENSHIP EDUCATION

For more than 200 years—from the time of the country's founding to the early twenty-first century—Americans have believed that the primary purpose of U.S. schools is to educate young people for responsible citizenship.

Thomas Jefferson, James Madison, and others of the nation's founders realized that the establishment of well-constructed political institutions was not in itself a sufficiently strong foundation to maintain constitutional democracy. They knew that a free society must ultimately depend on its citizens—on their knowledge, skills, and civic virtue. They believed that schools must foster the qualities of mind and heart required for successful government within a constitutional democracy.

Americans continue to believe that schools have a civic mission. The 32nd Annual Phi Delta Kappa/Gallup Poll, conducted in the year 2000, asked respondents what they considered the most important purpose of the nation's schools. They ranked "preparing people to become responsible citizens" as number one. Other purposes such as "helping people become economically self sufficient," "promoting cultural unity," and "improving social condition" were mentioned but were considered of lesser importance.

Since the first Phi Delta Kappa/Gallup Poll in 1968, the public has not wavered in its conviction that the central mission of schools is educating young people for citizenship. This conviction exists whether or not respondents have children in school, and whether or not their children are in public or private school.

A National Education Goal

When the U.S. Congress passed the Goals 2000: Educate America Act (Pub. L. 103-227), it established eight national goals for education. Two of those goals dealt specifically with civic education. The law specifies that students will "leave grades four, eight, and twelve having demonstrated competency over challenging subject matter including . . . civics and government . . . so that they may be prepared for responsible citizenship." The Educate America Act also charges schools with seeing that all students are "involved in activities that promote and demonstrate . . . good citizenship, community service and personal responsibility." To achieve these goals, schools address citizenship in both the formal and informal curriculum.

Formal Instruction

All states require instruction in civics and government, but the amount and rigor of that instruction varies. Three-fourths of all states have statutes mandating instruction in specific civic topics. More than half of all states currently require students to take a government or civics course in high school.

The formal curriculum has three major tasks: providing students with civic knowledge, developing their civic skills, and fostering those dispositions or traits of private and public character essential for citizens in a constitutional democracy.

Civic knowledge. *Civic knowledge* can be defined as the range of factual information and understandings about civics stored in long-term memory. Formal instruction in civics and government seeks to provide a basic and realistic understanding of civic life, politics, and government. It familiarizes students with the constitutions of the United States and the state in which they live, because these and other core documents (e.g., the Declaration of Independence, the Federalist Papers, and landmark Supreme Court decisions) provide criteria that citizens can use to judge the means and ends of government. Formal instruction also emphasizes the rights and the responsibilities of citizens.

An additional purpose of the formal curriculum is to promote an understanding of world affairs. This includes awareness of how and why one's own security, quality of life, and economic well-being are connected to that of other countries, as well as to major regional, international, or transnational organizations.

Civic skills. If citizens are to exercise their rights and discharge their responsibilities they not only need to acquire a body of knowledge, they also need to develop intellectual and participatory skills. Intellectual skills essential for citizenship sometimes are called *critical thinking* skills. The *National Standards for Civics and Government* and the National Assessment of Educational Progress (NAEP) Civics Assessment

categorize these intellectual skills as: identifying and describing; explaining and analyzing; and evaluating, taking, and defending positions on public issues. The National Standards identify three participatory skills: interacting, monitoring, and influencing. These are skills that enable citizens to affect the outcomes of political processes.

Civic dispositions. *Civic dispositions* are the traits of public and private character essential to democracy. Through instruction and experiences that schools provide, students develop traits of private character such as moral responsibility, self-discipline, and respect for the worth and dignity of every individual. Schools are also concerned with developing traits of public character such as public spiritedness, civility, respect for the rule of law, critical-mindedness, and a willingness to listen, negotiate, and compromise.

The Informal Curriculum

Civic education is part of the informal, as well as the formal, curriculum. The informal curriculum encompasses the governance of the school community, the relationships among those within it, and extracurricular or cocurricular activities.

Research has consistently demonstrated the positive effects of students participating in the governance of their classrooms and school, as well as in cocurricular activities. The National Longitudinal Study of Adolescent Health has found that school engagement is a critical protective factor against a variety of risky behaviors—influenced in good measure by perceived caring from teachers and high expectations for student performance.

Students who serve as officers of student organizations are more motivated to learn, more self-confident, and exhibit greater leadership capabilities. Research also confirms that involvement in school activities increases civic engagement in later life. Cocurricular activities that enhance students' civic knowledge, skills, and dispositions include elections, debates, discussions, mock trials, and simulated legislative hearings. Students' understanding of how democracy works is also furthered by observing government agencies in action, as well as by interacting with government officials who visit their classrooms.

Community service is another cocurricular dimension of civic education. Community service learning has goals beyond motivating personal kindness in the society; service is viewed as a means of connecting what is learned in the classroom with "the real world" and with a better understanding of public policy. The National Center for Education Statistics estimates that 83 percent of high schools and 77 percent of middle schools have students participating in community service activities in the early twenty-first century.

Concerns and Issues

If Americans are agreed that the primary purpose of schools is to "educate people for responsible citizenship," then one would expect civic education to have a prominent place in the curriculum, but this is not the case. Reading and mathematics are the primary focus in elementary schools. Civic education is neglected at the secondary level as well, as a plethora of recent studies reveal:

- The NAEP Civics Assessment, also known as the "Civics Report for the Nation," found in 1998 that more than 30 percent of all students tested at grades four, eight, and twelve scored below a Basic level of understanding of civics and government. Another 39 to 48 percent scored at the Basic level, defined as a "partial mastery of the knowledge and skills that are fundamental to proficient work at a given grade." The National Assessment Governing Board, however, has said that the Basic level should not be considered an acceptable goal; rather, all students should attain the Proficient level. Even so, only 21 to 22 percent scored at the Proficient level. A mere 2 to 4 percent achieved the Advanced level signifying superior performance.

- A National Assessment of Educational Progress (NAEP) Trend Report found a trend toward less frequent social studies classes in grade four. In 1988, almost half of fourth grade nationwide reported daily classes, but in 1998 daily classes for fourth graders had dropped to 39 percent.

- A Council of Chief State School Officers survey found that almost all states regularly assess mathematics and reading, while about two-thirds assess writing. However, not even half of the states assess social studies, which includes civics and government.

Improving Civic Education

The need to improve civic education is recognized not only in the United States, but in other countries as well. Review and rethinking is underway in well-developed and long-standing democracies, as well as in some postcommunist countries. Studies conducted in twenty-four countries by the International Association for the Evaluation of Educational Achievement (IEA), confirm a universal or near-universal commitment to certain goals or themes. There is agreement that civic education should be cross-disciplinary, participative, interactive, related to life, conducted in a nonauthoritarian environment, cognizant of social diversity, and co-constructed with parents and the community, including nongovernmental organizations.

While there is general agreement with the goals enunciated in the IEA study, Americans are voicing some additional needs. The American Political Science Association, the National Alliance for Civic Education, and the Center for Civic Education have all called for an increase in the amount, quality, and visibility of civic education. These organizations want to dramatically increase high-quality pre-service and in-service training for teachers of civics and government. An additional goal that these organizations seek is to encourage the federal government to administer the NAEP Civics Assessment more frequently and with state-level results to make it more useful for improving state and local civic education programs. Two national commissions, the National Commission of Civic Renewal and the United States Commission on Immigration Reform, have urged that every state require all students to demonstrate a mastery of basic civic knowledge and concepts as a condition of high school graduation.

See also: GEOGRAPHY, TEACHING OF; HISTORY, *subentry on* TEACHING OF; NATIONAL COUNCIL FOR THE SOCIAL STUDIES; SOCIAL STUDIES EDUCATION.

BIBLIOGRAPHY

CENTER FOR CIVIC EDUCATION. 1991. *Civitas: A Framework for Civic Education.* Calabasas, CA: Center for Civic Education.

CENTER FOR CIVIC EDUCATION. 1994. *National Standards for Civics and Government.* Calabasas, CA: Center for Civic Education.

GUTMANN, AMY. 1999. *Democratic Education,* revised edition. Princeton, NJ: Princeton University Press.

LYNDON B. JOHNSON SCHOOL OF PUBLIC AFFAIRS. 1999. *The Civic Education of American Youth: From State Policies to School District Practices.* Policy Research Project Report Number 133. Austin: University of Texas Board of Regents.

MANN, SHEILAH, and PATRICK, JOHN, J., eds. 2000. *Education for Civic Engagement in Democracy.* Bloomington, IN: ERIC Clearinghouse for Social Studies/Social Science Education.

MCDONNELL, LORRAINE M.; TIMPANE, P. MICHAEL; and BENJAMIN, ROGER, eds. 2000. *Rediscovering the Democratic Purposes of Education.* Lawrence: University Press of Kansas.

NATIONAL CENTER FOR EDUCATION STATISTICS. 2001. *The Next Generation of Citizens: NAEP Civics Assessments—1988 and 1998.* NCES 2001-452. Washington, DC: National Center for Education Statistics.

NATIONAL COMMISSION ON CIVIC RENEWAL. 1998. *A Nation of Spectators: How Civic Disengagement Weakens America and What We Can Do About It.* College Park: University of Maryland.

NIEMI, RICHARD G., and JUNN, JANE. 1998. *Civic Education: What Makes Students Learn.* New Haven, CT: Yale University Press.

MARGARET STIMMANN BRANSON

CLAPP, ELSIE RIPLEY (1879–1965)

An expert in rural Progressive education in Kentucky and West Virginia, Elsie Ripley Clapp was director at the Arthurdale School in West Virginia; she documented her experiences in *The Use of Resources in Education* (1952) and *Community Schools in Action* (1939).

Elsie Clapp was born in the exclusive area of Brooklyn Heights, New York. Her father, William Gamwell Clapp, was a stockbroker and her mother, Sally Ripley Clapp, a gifted pianist. Clapp's life was shaped by the panic of 1893 (which destroyed her family's finances), by her rejection of the role of the Victorian woman, and by health problems.

She was educated at the Packer Collegiate Institute (1894–1899), Vassar College (1899–1903), and Barnard College, Columbia University (1908). She received a bachelor of arts degree in English from Barnard and a master's degree in philosophy from Columbia. Following graduation, Clapp began an extensive teaching career, having had previous experience at the Brooklyn Heights Seminary in Brooklyn, New York (1903–1907). She spent a short time at the Horace Mann School of Teachers College

(1908–1909), and served as an editorial assistant for the *Journal of Philosophy, Psychology and Scientific Method* from 1910 to 1913, where she met the American educator and philosopher John Dewey. Clapp took numerous courses with Dewey at Columbia, serving as a teaching/graduate assistant for him on occasion. It was John Dewey who suggested that she explore work in rural Progressive education because he knew that Progressive education had been largely centered in university lab schools, private schools, and urban public schools.

Beginning work with a committee assigned to help the children of strikers in the Patterson Silk Workers Strike, her first job was to locate day care for the children. Through her work she met social activists Margaret Sanger, Elizabeth Gurley Flynn, Carla Tresca, and John Reed. Clapp's social consciousness was awakened to the plight of the worker. Resuming her teaching career, she moved to Charleston, South Carolina, to teach at Ashley Hall (1913–1914), and from there, Jersey City High School (1914–1915); Brooklyn Heights Seminary (1915–1916); the Milton Academy for Girls (1921–1922); the City and Country School in New York (1923–1924); and the Rosemary Junior School in Greenwich, Connecticut (1924–1929). Through work at the City and Country School and the Rosemary School, Clapp was able to begin serious implementation of Progressive education ideas. This was followed by the highlights of her career, the Ballard Memorial School (1929–1934) and Arthurdale (1934–1936). After leaving Arthurdale, Clapp edited the journal *Progressive Education* from 1937–1939. She spent the war years researching in the University of North Carolina libraries and Teachers College in preparation for writing *The Use of Resources in Education.* She also assisted in teaching a seminar on rural education at Teachers College in 1946. Clapp's later years are difficult to document, particularly after the publication of *The Use of Resources in Education.* Clapp wrote the book to inspire teachers to learn from her experiences in rural education; the book is best recognized for Dewey's foreword, one of his last published writings. The later years of Clapp's life are characterized by the health problems that began in her youth. She spent her final years in Exeter, New Hampshire.

Clapp considered her most important contribution to education the linking of the school with the community. This was a complex undertaking at Arthurdale, the first federal subsistence project of President Franklin Roosevelt's New Deal. A pet project of Eleanor Roosevelt, Arthurdale was designed to improve the lives of displaced coal mining families in north central West Virginia. Eleanor Roosevelt believed a school modeled on the lines of Progressive education would best suit this community, and Elsie Clapp was recommended to become the director of school and community affairs. One of the first steps included integrating recreation and health concerns with the goals of the school. Clearly evident in her approach to education in the Arthurdale community is a central focus on Appalachian culture as the basis for creating self-identity and understanding. This embodied Dewey's belief that community was the starting point for democracy—for Clapp the school served as the tool for bringing together shared interests and talent to benefit the entire community. Unfortunately, no people of color were selected to be a part of this new community due to politics, prejudice, and Jim Crow laws. Clapp and her cadre of progressive educators left Arthurdale in 1936 because of declining private support. Their departure ended one of the most interesting and intriguing progressive experiments in rural education.

See also: COMMUNITY-BASED AGENCIES, ORGANIZATIONS, AND GROUPS; PROGRESSIVE EDUCATION.

BIBLIOGRAPHY

CLAPP, ELSIE R. 1939. *Community Schools in Action.* New York: Viking.

CLAPP, ELSIE R. 1952. *The Use of Resources in Education.* New York: Harper and Row.

PERLSTEIN, DAN and STACK, SAM. 1999. "Building a New Deal Community: Progressive Education at Arthurdale." In *Schools of Today, Schools of Tomorrow,* ed. Susan Semel and Alan Sadovnik. New York: Lang.

SAM STACK

CLARK, SEPTIMA POINSETTE (1898–1987)

An educator and civil rights activist, Septima Poinsette Clark was born in Charleston, South Carolina. Her father was Peter Poinsette, a former slave, and her mother was Victoria Warren Anderson Poinsette, a free woman who had spent her early years in Haiti. Although better known for her civil rights activism, Clark used her experiences as an educator as the basis for much of her activism, especially issues dealing with equity in teaching salaries, literacy, and citizenship.

In 1916, Clark completed the twelfth grade at Charleston's Avery Institute, a liberal arts school founded in 1865 by Charles Avery and the American Missionary Association. After passing the state examination, Clark accepted her first teaching position at the age of eighteen on Johns Island, South Carolina. She taught on Johns Island from 1916 until 1919 when she accepted a position teaching the sixth grade at the Avery Institute. In May 1920, Septima Poinsette married Nerie Clark, and shortly after a son, Nerie Clark Jr., was born. When Clark's husband died in December 1925, Clark sent her son to live with his grandparents in Hickory, North Carolina, so she could teach. Teaching did not pay her enough money to support her son, and most boarding houses did not allow children.

Clark's experience as a teacher provided firsthand knowledge of an oppressive system as well as possible solutions to problems of inequality, illiteracy, and poverty. Clark, like most African-American teachers in the South, faced inadequate schoolhouses, lack of transportation for students, short school terms, and overcrowded classrooms, as well as low wages. For the school year of 1915–1916, the value of schoolhouses in South Carolina for whites was more than $5 million compared to a little over $600,000 for blacks. The average expenditure according to enrollment was $17.02 per white child and $1.90 per black child (1916 State Superintendent Report, pp. 140, 146). Out of 1,176 school buildings for African Americans, most were made of logs and only two were brick buildings; 778 were in churches or lodge halls. In 1916, Clark received $35 per month as principal and teacher and her associate received $25 for teaching a class of more than sixty students each. In comparison, white teachers taught classes with no more than eighteen students. One teacher taught only three students. They were paid $85 per month.

Clark became an advocate for a teachers' salary equalization campaign as early as 1928. Later she worked on the issue with principal J. Andrew Simmons of Booker T. Washington High School (Columbia), NAACP lawyer Thurgood Marshall, and Harold R. Boulware, a South Carolina civil rights lawyer. Clark spent long nights convincing white and black teachers to show records of their pay. In 1945, Federal District Judge J. Waties Waring of South Carolina ruled that black teachers with equal education should receive pay equal to their white counterparts.

In 1935, Clark helped Wil Lou Gray, head of the South Carolina Adult Education Program, establish a program to help educate illiterate soldiers at Fort Jackson. Her experiences training soldiers to sign their checks, to read bus routes, and to learn to count were inspired in part by the citizenship schools Clark had designed at the Highlander Folk School and later Southern Christian Leadership Council. At Highlander in Monteagle, Tennessee, in 1956, Clark accepted a position of liaison between Highlander and Johns Islands residents to combat illiteracy and to teach skills necessary for true citizenship. Clark worked with Esau Jenkins, a Johns Island native, and community activist Bernice Robinson, of Charleston, South Carolina, to develop plans for the citizenship school classes. The Highlander loaned funding for the purchase of a building. Setting the front of the building up as a cooperative store, they used the back room of the building for Robinson to teach classes so as not to risk attracting attention from whites. In 1961, Clark accepted a position with the Southern Christian Leadership Council as director of education and teaching, focusing her attention on citizenship training, voting, and literacy. The program reached eleven states in the Deep South.

In 1956, forty years after her first teaching assignment, the South Carolina legislature passed a law that barred city and state employees from affiliating themselves with any civil rights organization. Clark was fired; she had openly confronted an unequal system, becoming an agitator for civil rights, requesting equal salaries for black teachers, and refusing to dissociate herself from the NAACP. When Clark lost her job at 58 years of age, she also lost her state retirement benefits. She spent two decades fighting for her benefits, which she finally received in 1976.

As an educator within an oppressive Jim Crow system, Clark's understanding of the connections among illiteracy, poverty, and power allowed her to link social reform and educational advancement. These were issues she spent her entire life addressing both as a teacher and a private citizen. In her autobiography, *Echo in My Soul,* Clark wrote: "In teaching [the poor and underprivileged] and thereby helping them raise themselves to a better status in life, I felt then that I would [also] be serving my state and nation, too, all of the people, affluent and poor, white and black. For in my later years I am more convinced than ever that in lifting the lowly we lift likewise the entire citizenship" (p. 51).

See also EDUCATION REFORM; MULTICULTURAL EDUCATION.

BIBLIOGRAPHY

CLARK, SEPTIMA POINSETTE, and LeGETTE, BLYTHE. 1962. *Echo in My Soul.* New York: Dutton.

Forty-Eighth Annual Report of the State Superintendent of Education of the State of South Carolina, 1916. 1917. Columbia, SC: Gonzales and Bryan.

McFADDEN, GRACE JORDAN. 1990. "Septima P. Clark and the Struggle for Human Rights." In *Women in the Civil Rights Movement: Trailblazers and Torchbearers, 1941-1965,* ed. Vicki L. Crawford, Jacqueline Anne Rouse, and Barbara Woods. Brooklyn, NY: Carlson.

VALINDA LITTLEFIELD

CLASSROOM MANAGEMENT

Classroom management is the orchestration of the learning environment of a group of individuals within a classroom setting. In the early 1970s classroom management was seen as separate from classroom instruction. Teachers' management decisions were viewed as precursors to instruction, and were treated in the literature as if they were content-free. The image was of a teacher first attending to classroom management, and then beginning instruction without further reference to management decisions. Research in the 1980s, however, demonstrated that management and instruction are not separate, but are inextricably interwoven and complex.

A teacher's classroom-management system communicates information about the teacher's beliefs on content and the learning process. It also circumscribes the kinds of instruction that will take place in a particular classroom. A classroom in which the teacher takes complete responsibility for guiding students' actions constitutes a different learning environment than one in which students are encouraged and taught to assume responsibility for their own behaviors. Content will be approached and understood differently in each of these settings. Furthermore, more intellectually demanding academic work and activities in which students create products or encounter novel problems require complex management decisions. This correlation between instructional activity and management complexity further reinforces the interrelated nature of classroom management and curriculum.

The interwoven nature of classroom management and classroom instruction is especially easy to see from a student perspective. Students have at least two cognitive demands on them at all times: academic task demands (understanding and working with content) and social task demands (interacting with others concerning that content). This means that students must simultaneously work at understanding the content and finding appropriate and effective ways to participate in order to demonstrate that understanding. The teacher must facilitate the learning of these academic and social tasks. Thus from the perspective of what students need to know in order to be successful, management and instruction cannot be separated.

As a result of this broadened definition of classroom management, research has moved away from a focus on controlling behavior and looks instead at teacher actions to create, implement, and maintain a learning environment within the classroom. Everything a teacher does has implications for classroom management, including creating the setting, decorating the room, arranging the chairs, speaking to children and handling their responses, putting routines in place (and then executing, modifying, and reinstituting them), developing rules, and communicating those rules to the students. These are all aspects of classroom management.

Creating a Learning Environment

Creating and implementing a learning environment means careful planning for the start of the school year. The learning environment must be envisioned in both a physical space and a cognitive space. The physical space of the classroom is managed as the teacher prepares the classroom for the students. Is the space warm and inviting? Does the room arrangement match the teacher's philosophy of learning? Do the students have access to necessary materials? Are the distracting features of a room eliminated? Attending to these and similar questions aids a teacher in managing the physical space of the classroom.

Teachers must also consider the cognitive space necessary for a learning environment. This cognitive space is based upon the expectations teachers set for students in the classroom and the process of creating a motivational climate. Effective teachers create and implement classroom management practices that cultivate an engaging classroom environment for their students. Two specific areas of cognitive space that teachers include in their plans are setting expectations (i.e., rules and procedures) and creating a motivational climate.

Setting Expectations

In both elementary and secondary classrooms, the start of the school year is crucial to effective management. A significant aspect of this beginning is the teacher's establishment of expectations for student behavior, which are expressed through rules and procedures. Rules indicate the expectations for behavior in the classroom, and for how one interacts with one's peers and the teacher. Procedures have to do with how things get done. Rules can be, and frequently are, developed with the students' help, which increases the likelihood of compliance.

Ultimately, with or without student input, the teacher must have a picture of what code of behavior is essential for the classroom to function as desired. Both rules and procedures must be taught, practiced, and enforced consistently. Included with the development of rules and procedures is the accountability system of the classroom, which must communicate to students how they are held responsible for the academic work that they do.

Researchers have confirmed that effective classroom managers begin the year by setting expectations. At the elementary school level better managers also consistently analyze classroom tasks, teach going-to-school skills, see the classroom through students' eyes, and monitor student behavior from the beginning of the year. These characteristics are similar at the middle school and junior high level, where better managers also explain rules and procedures, monitor student behavior, develop student accountability for work, communicate information, and organize instruction from the first day of school. Research has shown that teachers whose students demonstrated high task engagement and academic achievement implement a systematic approach toward classroom management at the beginning of the school year. Therefore, one of the critical aspects of managing classrooms effectively, or managing classrooms in ways to enhance student learning, is setting expectations.

Motivational Climate

An essential part of organizing the classroom involves developing a climate in which teachers encourage students to do their best and to be excited about what they are learning. There are two factors that are critical in creating such a motivational climate: value and effort. To be motivated, students must see the worth of the work that they are doing and the work others do. A teacher's demonstration of *value* shows students how their work is worthwhile and is connected to things that are important for them, including other learning and interests. *Effort* ties the time, energy, and creativity a student uses to develop the "work," to the value that the work holds. One way that teachers encourage effort is through specific praise, telling students specifically what it is that they are doing that is worthwhile and good. In combination an understanding of the value of academic tasks and the effort necessary to complete these tasks motivate students to learn.

It is possible to create a setting that appears to be well managed, where room arrangement, rules, and procedures are operating well, but where little actual learning takes place. However, when a teacher creates structure and order, as well as a learning environment in which students feel the excitement of learning and success, then the classroom can truly be said to be well managed. At the beginning of the year, teachers must set expectations and create a motivational climate for learning and combine this with orchestrating the physical space in order to both create and implement a successful classroom management system.

Maintaining a Learning Environment

A teacher's classroom management decisions do not stop after the planning and establishment that is crucial to beginning the school year. As the school year progresses, classroom management involves maintaining the learning environment through conscientious decision-making concerning students and the classroom.

Teachers in a classroom teach groups of children. Maintaining the learning environment, therefore, requires teachers to focus on group processes. Jacob Kounin's landmark findings from the late 1960s on the management of classroom groups identified that the means by which teachers prevent problems from occurring in the first place differentiated them as more effective managers. Kounin, whose work was reaffirmed by Paul Gump, a noted ecological psychologist in Kansas in the 1980s, identified several strategies that teachers use to elicit high levels of work involvement and low levels of misbehavior. These strategies are: (1) with-it-ness (communicating awareness of student behavior), (2) overlapping (doing more than one thing at once), (3) smoothness and momentum (moving in and out of activities smoothly, with appropriately paced and sequenced instruction), and (4) group alerting (keeping all students attentive in a whole-group focus). These tools help teachers to maintain the flow of instruction. A significant stumbling block to the flow of instruction is in attention to transitions between activities, lessons, subjects, or class periods. It is here that teachers are likely to feel that they are less effective in maintaining the flow of instruction. Effective transitions are structured to move students from one activity to another, both physically and cognitively. The goal of smooth transitions is to ensure that all students have the materials and mindsets they need for a new activity.

While effective managers work with groups of students, they also are attentive to students' individual behaviors and learning needs. Maintaining a learning environment requires teachers to actively monitor their students. According to classroom management research, active monitoring includes watching student behavior closely, intervening to correct inappropriate behavior before it escalates, dealing consistently with misbehavior, and attending to student learning. In terms of monitoring both student behavior and learning, effective managers regularly survey their class or group and watch for signs of student confusion or inattention. Maintaining effective management involves keeping an eye out for when students appear to be stuck, when they need help, when they need redirection, when they need correction, and when they need encouragement.

Teachers must also check for understanding, both publicly and privately. Maintaining a classroom management system requires the teacher to anticipate student actions and responses in order to be preventive rather than reactive. Excellent classroom managers mentally walk through classroom activities, anticipating areas where students are likely to have difficulty and planning to minimize confusion and maximize the likelihood of success.

Activities planned for these classrooms are paced to ensure that students have enough to do, that assignments reflect an awareness of student attention spans and interests, and that downtime is minimized between assignments or activities. The orientation of the classroom must be purposeful, with a variety of things to be done and ways to get those things done.

When Problems Occur

Though effective managers anticipate and monitor student behavior and learning, misbehavior and misunderstanding do occur. When inappropriate behavior occurs, effective managers handle it promptly to keep it from continuing and spreading. Though teachers can handle most misbehavior unobtrusively with techniques such as physical proximity or eye contact, more serious misbehavior requires more direct intervention. The success of intervention depends on orderly structures having been created and implemented at the beginning of the school year.

When students have misunderstandings about academic content or instruction effective managers look for ways to reteach content and to improve the clarity of their communication. In research studies teachers in classrooms that run smoothly score high on measures of instructional clarity. That is, they describe their objectives clearly, give precise instructions for assignments, and respond to student questions with understandable explanations. Classroom communication, teachers' clarity of instructions and understanding of students' needs, is particularly important in maintaining the interconnectedness of management and instruction. This communication is central as teacher and students make visible all of the aspects of the classroom that build a community. Maintenance of a learning environment combines a teacher's careful attention to group dynamics, individual student needs, and clear communication.

In order to create and support a learning-centered environment where teaching for understanding and the construction of meaning are valued, students must be very comfortable and feel that their contributions are valued. In addition, students must value the contributions of others, value the diversity within the classroom, and give their best effort because they see it as the right thing to do or something that they want to do. The uniqueness of each classroom and the variety and complexity of tasks that teachers face make it impossible to prescribe specific techniques for every situation. In each classroom there will be a variety of skills, backgrounds, languages, and inclinations to cooperate. Teachers, particularly beginning teachers who may not have the repertoire of experiences and skills they need to be able to teach diverse classes, require administrative support to identify and nurture the interconnectedness of instruction and classroom management.

A close look at how class activities evolve reveals the need for a classroom management system that is visible, established, monitored, modified, refined, and reestablished. While teachers work with students who have different dispositions and abilities, they must be prepared to create, implement, and maintain an environment in which learning is the center.

Research-based programs have been developed that aid teachers in coming to an understanding of what it means to be an effective classroom manager. Evertson and Harris, based upon the research of Evertson and others, have created one such educational program aimed at the professional development of teachers. Their program encourages teachers to create a conceptual and practical understanding of management and organization through exploration of teachers' expectations, student accountability systems, and instructional strategies. Freiberg and colleagues have developed another such program, which also creates a preventive approach to classroom management through attention to school-wide perspectives and student responsibility. Both programs have demonstrated their effectiveness in improving teachers' practice and students' academic achievement and behavior. Teachers empowered with an understanding of the complexity and multidimensionality of classroom management make a difference in the lives of their students.

See also: CURRICULUM SCHOOL; GROUP PROCESSES IN THE CLASSROOM; INSTRUCTIONAL STRATEGIES; MOTIVATION, *subentry on* INSTRUCTION; SCHOOL CLIMATE; SOCIAL ORGANIZATION OF SCHOOLS; TEACHING, *subentry on* LEARNING TO TEACH.

BIBLIOGRAPHY

BROPHY, JERE E. 1983. "Classroom Organization and Management." *The Elementary School Journal* 83(4):265–285.

Brophy, Jere E. 1998. *Motivating Students to Learn.* Boston: McGraw Hill.

Brophy, Jere E., and Evertson, Carolyn M. 1976. *Learning from Teaching: A Developmental Perspective.* Boston: Allyn and Bacon.

Bossert, Steven T. 1979. *Tasks and Social Relationships in Classrooms.* Cambridge, Eng.: Cambridge University Press.

Doyle, Walter. 1986. "Classroom Organization and Management." In *Handbook of Research on Teaching,* 3rd edition, ed. Merlin Wittrock. New York: Macmillan.

Doyle, Walter. 1990. "Classroom Management Techniques." In *Student Discipline Strategies,* Ed. Oliver C. Moles. Albany: State University of New York Press.

Doyle, Walter, and Carter, Kathy. 1984. "Academic Tasks in Classrooms." *Curriculum Inquiry* 14(2):129–149.

Duke, Daniel, ed. 1979. *Classroom Management.* Yearbook of the National Society for the Study of Education. Chicago: University of Chicago Press.

Emmer, Edmund T.; Evertson, Carolyn M.; and Anderson, Linda M. 1980. "Effective Classroom Management at the Beginning of the School Year." *The Elementary School Journal* 80(5):219–231.

Evertson, Carolyn M. 1985. "Training Teachers in Classroom Management: An Experiment in Secondary Classrooms." *Journal of Educational Research* 79:51–58.

Evertson, Carolyn M. 1989. "Improving Elementary Classroom Management: A School-Based Training Program for Beginning the Year." *Journal of Educational Research* 83:82–90.

Evertson, Carolyn M. 1997. "Classroom Management." In *Psychology and Educational Practice,* ed. Herbert J. Walberg and Geneva D. Haertel. Berkeley: McCutchan.

Evertson, Carolyn M., and Emmer, Edmund T. 1982. "Effective Management at the Beginning of the School Year in Junior High Classes. *Journal of Educational Psychology* 74(4):485–498.

Evertson, Carolyn M., and Harris, Alene H. 1992. "What We Know about Managing Classrooms." *Educational Leadership* 49(7):74–78.

Evertson, Carolyn M., and Harris, Alene H. 1999. "Support for Managing Learning-Centered Classrooms: The Classroom Organization and Management Program." In *Beyond Behaviorism: Changing the Classroom Management Paradigm,* ed. H. Jerome Freiberg. Boston: Allyn and Bacon.

Freiberg, H. Jerome, ed. 1999. *Beyond Behaviorism: Changing the Classroom Management Paradigm.* Boston: Allyn and Bacon.

Freiberg, H. Jerome; Stein, Terri A.; and Huang, S. 1995. "The Effects of Classroom Management Intervention on Student Achievement in Inner-City Elementary Schools." *Educational Research and Evaluation* 1:33–66.

Gump, Paul V. 1982. "School Settings and Their Keeping. In *Helping Teachers Manage Classrooms,* ed. Daniel Duke. Alexandria, VA: Association for Supervision and Curriculum Development.

Jones, Vernon. 1996. "Classroom Management." In *Handbook of Research on Teacher Education,* 2nd edition, ed. John Sikula. New York: Simon and Shuster.

Kounin, Jacob S. 1970. *Discipline and Group Management in Classrooms.* New York: Holt, Rinehart and Winston.

Weade, Regina, and Evertson, Carolyn M. 1988. "The Construction of Lessons in Effective and Less Effective Classrooms." *Teaching and Teacher Education* 4:189–213.

Carolyn M. Evertson

CLASSROOM OBSERVATION

Systematic classroom observation is a quantitative method of measuring classroom behaviors from direct observations that specifies both the events or behaviors that are to be observed and how they are to be recorded. Generally, the data that is collected from this procedure focuses on the frequency with which specific behaviors or types of behavior occurred in the classroom and measures their duration. There are several elements that are common to most observational systems.

- a purpose for the observation
- operational definitions of all the observed behaviors
- training procedures for observers

- a specific observational focus
- a setting
- a unit of time
- an observation schedule
- a method to record the data
- a method to process and analyze data (Stallings and Mohlman, pp. 469–471)

Prior to the use of systematic observational methods, research on effective teaching typically consisted of subjective data based on personal and anecdotal accounts of effective teaching. In order to develop a scientific basis for teaching, researchers began to use the more objective and reliable measures of systematic classroom observation. In the last quarter of the twentieth century, several hundred different observational systems have been developed and used in classrooms. There have similarly been hundreds of studies that have used classroom observation systems since the 1970s.

Although there are several types of observational procedures or techniques that have been used to examine effective teaching (e.g., charts, rating scales, checklists, and narrative descriptions), the most widely used procedure or research method has been systematic classroom observation based on interactive coding systems. These interactive coding systems allow the observer to record nearly everything that students and teachers do during a given time interval. These interaction systems are very objective and typically do not require the observer to make any high inferences or judgments about the behaviors they observe in the classroom. In other words, these low-inference observational systems provide specific and easy identifiable behaviors that observers can easily code. Some of the more commonly used observation instruments are the Brophy Good Dyadic Interaction System, Stallings Observation System, and the Classroom Observation Schedule. They all have been widely used in research studies and in teacher development projects designed to improve classroom instruction.

Some of the major strengths of using classroom observation allow educators to do the following: (1) permit researchers to study the processes of education in naturalistic settings; (2) provide more detailed and precise evidence than other data sources; and (3) stimulate change and verify that the change occurred. The descriptions of instructional events that are provided by this method have also been found to lead to improved understanding and better models for improving teaching.

A final strength of this research method is that the findings from these observational studies have provided a coherent, well-substantiated knowledge base about effective instruction. Many of the reviews and summaries of the classroom observation research, such as that of Herb Walberg (1991, 1995), have consistently found that a number of classroom behaviors significantly relate to students' academic achievement. Several aspects of classroom instruction such as conducting daily reviews, presenting new material, conducting guided practice, providing feedback and correctives, conducting independent practice, and conducting weekly and monthly reviews have been found to be significantly related to students' academic achievement. In other words, research using systematic classroom observation has provided us with a substantial knowledge base that has helped us understand effective teaching.

Purposes of Classroom Observation

Classroom observation has many valid and important educational purposes. This section summarizes three important purposes or areas where systematic classroom observation has been widely used: (1) description of instructional practices; (2) investigation of instructional inequities for different groups of students; and (3) improvement of teachers' classroom instruction based on feedback from individual classroom or school profiles.

Description of instructional processes. One of the fundamental purposes of classroom observation research is describing the current status of instructional practices and identifying instructional problems. As Tom Good puts it, "one role of observational research is to describe what takes place in classrooms in order to delineate the complex practical issues that confront practitioners" (p. 337). There have been many observational studies that have been specifically designed to describe specific educational phenomena. Large-scale observational studies such as Ken Sirotnik and Hersh Waxman, Shwu-Yong Huang, and Yolanda Padrón, for example, have examined instructional practices in elementary and secondary schools. Sirotnik examined 1,000 elementary and secondary classrooms and found that there was very little variety in teaching practices across subjects and grades. He found that the majority of class time was spent either with the teacher lecturing to the class or students working on written assignments. Waxman, Huang, and Padrón observed ninety sixth-grade and eighth-grade classrooms from sixteen inner-city middle level schools and found similar results to those of Sirotnik. Students were typically involved in whole-class instruction and not interacting with either their teacher or other students. Students rarely selected their own instructional activities, and they were generally very passive in the classroom, often just watching or listening to the teacher, even though they were found to be on task about 94 percent of the time. The teacher observation results revealed that teachers typically focused on the content of the task or assignment, responded to students' signals, communicated the task's procedures, and checked students' work. Teachers were observed spending very little time interacting with students regarding personal issues, encouraging students to succeed, showing personal regard for students, and showing interest in students' work.

Another example of descriptive, observational studies involves the extent to which technology is used in the classroom. Although there have been a large number of studies that have examined technology use in schools, most of these studies have relied on self-report data from administrators, teachers, or students. These types of data, however, are often unreliable and tend to be upwardly biased in the direction of over-reporting the actual amount of technology use. Therefore, it is important to observe the actual extent to which technology is used in classrooms and to look specifically at the technology used in classroom and used by individual students. In one such study, Waxman and Huang (1995) used systematic classroom observation to examine the extent to which computer technology was integrated into the curriculum of 200 elementary and secondary school inner-city classrooms. They found that there was no integration (i.e., use) of computer technology in the elementary school classrooms, and that students were observed working with computers only 2 percent of class time in middle school classrooms. Huang and Waxman (1996) also conducted systematic observations of 1315 middle school students from 220 mathematics classrooms in order to examine the amount of technology used. The descriptive results revealed that students were observed using calculators about 25 percent of class time, but they used computers less than 1 percent of class time in their mathematics classes.

Some other uses of descriptive observational studies have been to evaluate programs and more specifically, to evaluate the fidelity or degree of implementation of programs; to examine the extent to which higher-level thought processes are emphasized in schools; and to investigate the extent to which multicultural education is emphasized in urban classrooms. A final important use involves school effectiveness studies, such as Waxman and colleagues 1997 study, where classroom observation data have been used to investigate observable differences between effective and ineffective schools. Waxman and Huang (1997), for example, observed more than 700 students from four effective and four ineffective urban elementary schools that served predominantly African-American students and found that significantly more students from the effective schools were observed working in an individualized setting, interacting with their teacher, and working on written assignments. On the other hand, students from the ineffective schools observed in whole-class settings were found interacting with their teacher, interacting with others, reading, and working with manipulative materials significantly less than students from the effective schools.

Investigation of instructional inequities. Several studies, such as that of Elizabeth Fennema and Penelope Peterson, have found that some groups or types of students are treated differently by teachers in classrooms, and that these inequitable patterns of teacher–student interaction in classrooms result in differential learning outcomes for students. There have been many studies, for example, that have found gender imbalances in teachers' interaction patterns in the classroom. Jere Brophy and Tom Good's 1974 review of the research found that consistent sex-related differences exist in the classroom in teachers' interaction patterns. Boys, for example, typically have been found to receive more praise and criticism in the classroom than girls. They also found that teachers have more behavioral, procedural, and academic interactions with boys than girls. Boys have also been found to ask more questions in the classroom, and teachers have been found to ask boys more questions. Good and his colleagues (1987, 1988) have also conducted several observational studies that examined why low-achieving students in secondary schools ask fewer questions than high-achieving students. They also found that students from an upper-middle-class elementary school asked more questions than students from lower-middle-class schools.

Other studies have looked at both sex- and ethnic-related differences in the classroom. Hart examined the relationship between teacher–student interaction and mathematics achievement by race and sex. She found the following differences: (1) white and black male students had more classroom interactions than students from other groups; (2) a disparity in the type of interaction between white and black students; and (3) boys were involved in more public interactions with teachers than girls. In other words, it appears that patterns of teacher–student interaction may not only be influenced by the sex of the student, but also by the ethnicity of the student.

Padrón, Waxman, and Huang observed student behavior differences between resilient (i.e., successful) and nonresilient (i.e., less successful) elementary school students from low socioeconomic backgrounds. They found resilient students spent significantly more time interacting with teachers for instructional purposes, whereas nonresilient students spent more time interacting with other students for social or personal purposes. Resilient students were also observed watching or listening significantly more often than nonresilient students, whereas the latter were observed more often not attending to task. The percentage of time that resilient students were observed on task (85%) was much higher than that of nonresilient students (61%). The magnitude of these differences was both statistically and educationally significant and illustrates the instructional inequities that exist within classrooms.

Improvement of teaching practices. Research using observational methods has yielded important information that has practical implications for the improvement of teaching practices. One of the traditional problems hindering teachers' classroom instruction has been the lack of valid and accurate information that teachers could use in order to facilitate their professional growth. Many teachers, even experienced ones, are not always aware of the nature of their interactions with individual students. Consequently, one of the most important purposes of systematic classroom observation is to improve teachers' classroom instruction. Feedback from individual classroom profiles derived from systematic observations has been found to help teachers understand their own strengths and weaknesses, and have consequently enabled them to significantly improve their instruction. Through feedback, teachers can become aware of how their classroom functions and thus bring about changes they desire. This process typically involves having trained observers systematically observe teachers and their students in their classrooms and later providing teachers with information about their instruction in clinical sessions. This approach is based on the assumption that teachers value accurate information that they can use to improve their instruction.

There is growing evidence that feedback from systematic observations can be used to improve teaching. Several studies, such as that of Jane Stallings, have found that teachers could positively change their attitude and behaviors toward pupils after receiving feedback from classroom observations. Good and Brophy's 1974 "treatment study" exemplifies this type of research. In that study, teachers were given feedback based on forty hours of classroom observation. As a result of this "one-shot" interview where feedback was given, teachers' interaction patterns changed, and their attitudes toward individual students changed, too. Stallings, Howard Ebmeier, Good, and Good and Douglas Grouws have utilized similar strategies in other projects. In those studies, teachers were presented with individual feedback regarding their classroom instruction and then were found to change their behavior in desirable ways. All these studies have found that teachers can improve their classroom instruction given appropriate feedback and suggestions for improvement.

The overall findings from these studies suggest that feedback from classroom observations is a viable and effective mechanism for providing teachers with the information they need about their classroom behavior. This feedback is intended to create an "imbalance" in teachers' perceptions of their own behaviors. This imbalance exists whenever teachers find out that their attitudes or perceptions of their teaching differ from that of trained observers. Teachers in such a state of "imbalance" are motivated to do something about their behavior in order to restore themselves to a balanced condition. A similar notion is that self-awareness increases teachers' control of their actions and the possibility that they will modify them. In 1995 Waxman, Huang, and Padrón provided schoolwide feedback to middle school teachers that compared their school profile on classroom instructional behaviors to an overall districtwide average of these same behaviors. Feedback from these profiles was used to stimulate dialogue and discussion about instructional strengths and weaknesses in the school. The profiles also helped initiate discussion about specific instructional areas that needed to be improved in the school. It should be pointed out that these profiles provided some guidelines for practice, and they were not attempts to tell teachers what to do. These profiles provide teachers with concepts and criteria that they can use to reflect about their own teaching. The feedback session was not viewed as one where research findings should be applied into specific rules or guidelines for teachers to follow. Rather, the observational feedback was intended to be used as a guide for teachers with which they and their colleagues could reflect about their practices on their own and decide what action to take. Professional services and university courses are some of the possibilities that teachers could choose if they wanted to continue to collaborate with the researchers in order to help them improve their instruction. In summary, the use of feedback from classroom observations appears to be a potent strategy that can improve instructional behaviors in specific classrooms and schools.

Limitations of Classroom Observation

There have also been several criticisms and cautions related to the use of structured observation techniques, according to Sara Delamont and David Hamilton. The criticisms and limitations of using structured observation techniques are categorized into three subsections: (1) theoretical and epistemological criticisms; (2) methodological concerns; and (3) pragmatic concerns. This section also includes a brief discussion of the implications of classroom observation and some new directions.

Theoretical and epistemological criticisms. Although observational research has produced a substantial body of important findings that can lead to improved teaching practices, there is still a lack of consensus or lack of confidence regarding the research. There have been many theoretical and epistemological criticisms of classroom observational, process-product research such as that of Maurice Galton in 1988. Several critics, for example, have argued that this research is devoid of theory and consequently cannot explain why some instructional behaviors impact student outcomes. There are also related concerns about why some variables are selected to be observed at the exclusion of other variables. Because there is no model or theory behind the research, the critics argue that there is no justification for the selection of variables or meaningfulness associated with the interpretation of results. They further argue that the selection of events or behaviors may not be clear to anyone except the ob-

server or instrument developer. In other words, classroom observation research has not dealt with the theoretical assumptions of why a particular style of teaching or set of instructional variables influences student learning.

Tom Popkewitz, Robert Tabachnick, and Kenneth Zeichner (1979) state that this research approach has a behaviorist orientation that maintains "it is possible to identify, control, and manipulate specific outcomes of teaching by altering selected aspects of a teacher's overt behavior" (p. 52). They further contend that teaching is viewed, "as the sum of discrete behaviors and a change in one or several of these behaviors is assumed to affect the quality of teaching as a whole" (p. 52). Their most strenuous argument, however, concerns the notion that these teaching behaviors "are often viewed independent of the curricular context with which the techniques are associated" (p. 52). They are concerned that observers generally focus on isolated behaviors, without concern for the preceding and subsequent behaviors that they feel provide the context and meaning of the behavior. Another concern is that most observational systems are generally limited—they can be used only to observe covert behavior that can be quantitatively measured. Furthermore, these observational systems make it difficult to record complex instructional behaviors.

Methodological concerns. Most observational techniques have limitations. Some of these concerns or limitations are related to methodological issues that can interfere with the drawing of valid conclusions. One of the primary methodological concerns or source of invalidity that needs to be addressed regarding the use of systematic observational techniques relates to the obtrusiveness of the technique. Observer effects may occur because teachers and students are aware that their behaviors are being observed. The presence of an observer may change teacher or student behaviors, perhaps resulting in reactive effects. Teacher anxiety or teachers performing less well than usual can interfere with the drawing of valid inferences about what normally occurs in the classroom. On the other hand, there is also some evidence that indicates that teachers' instruction may be slightly better than usual when they are being observed. Although some researchers like Donald Medley, Homer Coker, and Robert Soar maintain that observer effects are not serious concerns, the possibility that this threatens the validity and reliability of data collected exists.

There are a number of methodological concerns that similarly need to be addressed. The reliability and validity of observational systems is a primary concern. Although many systems report inter-rater agreement or observer accuracy, they do not specify the reliability as it pertains to stability of teacher behavior or on the internal consistency of the scale. Validity is another important concern that needs to be addressed. Construct validity, for example, which focuses on the "theoretical integrity" of the behaviors, is particularly important. Criterion-related validity, or the extent to which the observational measures relate to a criterion measure, is rarely reported, and concurrent validity or the extent to which a particular instrument is related to other instruments is generally missing too.

There are other methodological concerns that are related to the actual amount of time that is necessary to obtain a valid observation period, as well as the appropriate number of observations that are required in order to obtain reliable and valid measures of instruction. Similarly, there are a number of methodological concerns related to the analyses of data. Most of these concerns address the issue of what the appropriate level of analysis (e.g., student, the class, or students within class) should be used when analyzing the observation data. Students are nested within classrooms, while classrooms are nested within schools. Prior teacher effectiveness research has often aggregated data to classroom-level analyses that may underestimate the importance of processes within classes because all the within-class variation is lost. Recent analytic developments, such as hierarchical linear modeling (HLM), allow researchers to disentangle these nested effects and investigate hypotheses about the effects of within- and between-school or class factors on classroom instruction or students' perceptions of their learning environments. Advanced statistical models, such as HLM, allow researchers to identify and separate individual effects from group effects, after statistically controlling for other explanatory variables. Such multilevel models can estimate how group-level variables (e.g., characteristics of the classroom or school) influence the way in which individual-level variables (e.g., students' classroom behavior) affect students' achievement.

Another concern related to prior classroom observation research is that it has typically been generic (i.e., generalizing across grade levels and content areas), rather than focusing on a given grade level and/or subject area. Similarly, the content of the lesson is often neglected as has the quality of the interaction that is being recorded.

Pragmatic concerns. A final category of limitations related to classroom observation are pragmatic concerns that focus on the practicality of conducting observational research. One of the primary pragmatic concerns of observation research is that it is costly to do because it requires extensive training and time. Some training programs for observers, for example, require as much as seven full days of intensive training before the observations are conducted in classrooms. Gaining access to schools and classrooms to conduct observations is another serious concern. Many school districts are reluctant to allow observation of teachers in their schools because they feel it would be too disruptive to the learning environment. Teachers have also been known to dramatically alter their instruction when observers are present in the classroom.

Another pragmatic concern relates to the misuse of classroom observation data. Classroom observations can be very useful as a formative evaluation procedure, but should not be used to provide summative decisions, such as those regarding a teacher's dismissal or rehiring. Similarly, classroom observations should not be tied to summative decisions like salary increases. Unfortunately, several school districts and state departments of education have misused observational research and translated findings into specific rules or standards that they have used in developing evaluation instruments. These misuses are more "accidents" of the research, however, rather than problems associated with the "essence" of the research.

The previously mentioned criticisms and limitations, however, do not necessarily detract from the value and utility of the observational method. Many of these criticisms are incidental aspects of some observational research. Nate Gage and Margaret Needels and others, for example, have refuted many of these criticisms and have provided several examples of how observation research has contributed to instructional theories. Medley has also argued that the previous methodological limitations of observational research were greatly reduced in the 1990s. He points out, for example, the impact that the laptop computer will have on classroom observation research. In addition to replacing traditional clipboards and stopwatches, the laptop computer will aid the precision and accuracy of researchers in recording events, as well as provide a detailed account of contextual items that occur during the observation.

New Directions

It is important to point out again that no one data source or methodology will sufficiently answer all critical educational questions. Multiple measures or indicators of instruction are needed to help capture a more comprehensive picture of what goes on in classrooms. Some of the new directions for classroom observation research include the following: (1) combining both qualitative and quantitative methods in observation systems; (2) developing observation instruments that are based on "standards" of pedagogy; (3) using student-centered observation instruments that allow for comparisons between groups of students within the class; and (4) using instruments that assess authentic, interactive instructional practices that have been found to relate to student gains on higher-level cognitive outcomes.

See also: ASSESSMENT, *subentry on* CLASSROOM ASSESSMENT; TEACHER EVALUATION, *subentries on* METHODS, OVERVIEW; TEACHING, *subentry on* METHODS FOR STUDYING.

BIBLIOGRAPHY

BROPHY, JERE E., AND GOOD, TOM L. 1974. *Teacher–Student Relationships: Causes and Consequences.* New York: Holt, Rinehart, and Winston.

DELAMONT, SARA, and HAMILTON, DAVID. 1986. "Revisiting Classroom Research: A Cautionary Tale." In *Controversies in Classroom Research,* ed. Martyn Hammersley. Philadelphia: Open University Press.

EBMEIER, HOARD, and GOOD, TOM L. 1979. "The Effects of Instructing Teachers about Good Teaching on the Mathematics Achievement of Fourth-Grade Students." *American Educational Research Journal* 16:1–16.

EVERTSON, CAROLUN, and GREEN, JUDITH. 1986. "Observation as Inquiry and Method." In *Handbook of Research on Teaching,* 3rd edition, ed. Merlin C. Wittrock. New York: Macmillan.

FENNEMA, ELIZABETH, and PETERSON, PENELOPE L. 1987. "Effective Teaching for Girls and Boys: The Same or Different?" In *Talks to Teachers,* ed. David C. Berliner and Barak V. Rosenshine. New York: Random House.

GAGE, NATE L., and NEEDELS, MARGARET C. 1989. "Process-Product Research on Teaching? A Review of Criticisms." *Elementary School Journal* 89:253–300.

GALTON, MAURICE. 1988. "Structured Observation Techniques." In *Educational Research, Methodology and Measurement: An International Handbook,* ed. John P. Keeves. Oxford: Pergamon.

GOOD, TOM L. 1988. "Observational Research . . . Grounding Theory in Classrooms." *Educational Psychologist* 25:375–379.

GOOD, TOM L., and BROPHY, JERE E. 1974. "Changing Teacher and Student Behavior: An Empirical Investigation." *Journal of Educational Psychology* 66:390–405.

GOOD, TOM L., and BROPHY, JERE E. 2000. *Looking in Classrooms,* 8th edition. New York: Longman.

GOOD, TOM L., and GROUWS, DOUGLAS. 1979. "The Missouri Mathematics Effectiveness Project: An Experimental Study in Fourth-Grade Classrooms." *Journal of Educational Psychology* 71:355–362.

GOOD, TOM L.; SLAVINGS, R. L; HOBSON-HAREL, K.; and EMERSON, H. 1987. "Student Passivity: A Study of Question-Asking in K–12 Classrooms." *Sociology of Education* 60:181–199.

GOOD, TOM L.; SLAVINGS, R. L.; and MASON, D. A. 1988. "Learning to Ask Questions: Grade and School Effects." *Teaching and Teacher Education* 4:363–378.

HART, LAURIE E. 1989. "Classroom Processes, Sex of Students, and Confidence in Learning Mathematics." *Journal for Research in Mathematics Education* 20:242–260.

HUANG, SHWU-YONG L., and WAXMAN, HERSH C. 1996. "Classroom Observations of Middle School Students' Technology Use in Mathematics." *School Science and Mathematics* 96(1):28–34.

MEDLEY, DONALD M.; COKER, HOMER; and SOAR, ROBERT S. 1984. *Measurement-Based Evaluation of Teacher Performance: An Empirical Approach.* New York: Longman.

NEEDELS, MARGARET, and GAGE, NATE L. 1991. "Essence and Accident in Process-Product Research on Teaching." In *Effective Teaching: Current Research,* ed. Hersh C. Waxman and Herbert J. Walberg. Berkeley: McCutchan.

PADRÓN, YOLANDA N.; WAXMAN, HERSH C.; and HUANG, SHWU-YONG L. 1999. "Classroom and

Instructional Learning Environment Differences between Resilient and Non-Resilient Elementary School Students." *Journal of Education for Students Placed at Risk of Failure* 4:63–81.

POPKEWITZ, TOM S.; TABACHNICK, ROBERT; and ZEICHNER, KEN. 1979. "Dulling the Senses: Research in Teacher Education." *Journal of Teacher Education* 30:52–60.

ROSENSHINE, BARAK V. 1987. "Explicit Teaching." In *Talks to Teachers*, ed. David C. Berliner and Barak V. Rosenshine. New York: Random House.

SIROTNIK, KEN A. 1983. "What You See Is What You Get: Consistency, Persistency, and Mediocrity in Classrooms." *Harvard Educational Review* 53:16–31.

STALLINGS, JANE A. 1980. "Allocated Academic Learning Time Revisited, or Beyond Time on Task." *Educational Researcher* 9(11):11–16.

WALBERG, HERBERT J. 1991. "Productive Teaching and Instruction: Assessing the Knowledge Base." In *Effective Teaching: Current Research*, ed. Hersh C. Waxman and Herbert J. Walberg. Berkeley: McCutchan.

WALBERG, HERBERT J. 1995. "Generic Practices." In *Handbook of Research on Improving Student Achievement*, ed. Gordon Cawelt. Arlington, VA: Educational Research Services.

WAXMAN, HERSH C. 1995. "Classroom Observations of Effective Teaching." In *Teaching: Theory into Practice*, ed. Allan C. Ornstein. Needham Heights, MA: Allyn and Bacon.

WAXMAN, HERSH C., and HUANG, SHWU-YONG L. 1996. "Classroom Instruction Differences by Level of Technology Use in Middle School Mathematics." *Journal of Educational Computing Research* 14:147–159.

WAXMAN, HERSH C., and HUANG, SHWU-YONG L. 1997. "Classroom Instruction and Learning Environment Differences between Effective and Ineffective Urban Elementary Schools for African American Students." *Urban Education* 32(1):7–44.

WAXMAN, HERSH C., and HUANG, SHWU-YONG L. 1999. "Classroom Observation Research and the Improvement of Teaching." In *New Directions for Teaching Practice and Research*, ed. Hersh C. Waxman and Herbert J. Walberg. Berkeley, CA: McCutchan.

WAXMAN, HERSH C.; HUANG, SHWU-YONG L.; ANDERSON, LASELLES; and WEINSTEIN, THOMAS. 1997. "Classroom Process Differences in Inner-City Elementary Schools." *Journal of Educational Research* 91:49–59.

WAXMAN, HERSH C.; HUANG, SHWU-YONG L.; and PADRÓN, YOLANDA N. 1995. "Investigating the Pedagogy of Poverty in Inner-City Middle Level Schools." *Research in Middle Level Education* 8(2):1–22.

HERSH C. WAXMAN

CLASSROOM QUESTIONS

When people really want to learn something, they ask questions. They ask questions to become skilled in using new software, or to figure out the norms of courtesy in another culture, or to master the fine art of parking a car. It is not surprising that for many, questioning is at the very heart of learning, the central skill in the teaching-learning process. Teachers have been described as "professional question-askers," and history records great teachers such as the Greek philosopher Socrates in terms of their unique questioning skill.

Questions can and have been used for a wide variety of educational purposes: reviewing previously read or studied material; diagnosing student abilities, preferences, and attitudes; stimulating critical thinking; managing student behavior; probing student thought process; stirring creative thinking; personalizing the curriculum; motivating students; and assessing student knowledge. The many uses of questions as described by Sari Rose and John Litcher, as well as the relative ease in recording and analyzing their use in the classroom, has led to extensive research of classroom questions. In 1912 Rommiett Stevens observed classroom life and the use of questions. She unearthed the fact that teachers were involved in a high frequency of question asking, asking approximately 395 questions each day. The majority of these questions, about two out of three, were asked at a low intellectual level, usually requiring little more than rote memory and recall. And they were asked not by the student, the person at the center of learning, but by the teacher. Reviews of research in the United States, the United Kingdom, Germany, and Australia, as well as in many developing nations, have shown similar results. To a great extent, teaching means talking and asking questions, and learning means following directions and answering questions. Much of the current research and teacher education has focused on altering these findings, and creating more challenging and meaningful classroom questions.

Types of Questions

One of the first directions for improving the quality of classroom questions was determining the intellectual level of teacher questions. Broadly conceived, content- or subject-related questions were grouped into two cognitive categories: lower order, for memory, rote, and simple recall; higher order, for more demanding and exacting thinking. The preponderance of lower-order questions was troublesome to educators, for it contradicted the notion of a thoughtful classroom, promoting important if not profound student insights. As a result, educators developed a number of classification systems to categorize question levels, the first step in promoting the use of more demanding questions in the classroom. Mary Jane Aschner and James Gallagher developed a widely used system that created four divisions, ranging from simple recall to more difficult thought, to creative thinking, and finally to evaluative thinking. In fact, numerous such systems have been devised, but none more influential than Benjamin Bloom's taxonomy.

In 1956 Benjamin Bloom headed a group of educational psychologists engaged in identifying the levels of intellectual behavior important in learning. The taxonomies they developed included three overlapping domains: the cognitive (intellectual), psychomotor (physical), and affective (attitudes and emotions). Each taxonomy is an organizational strategy in which lower categories are subsumed in higher ones. In the cognitive domain, knowledge, the lowest level in Bloom's taxonomy, must be mastered before comprehension, the second level, can be attempted. In fact, comprehension is an intellectual process that uses knowledge. These six levels have been adapted in formulating school goals, assessing learner progress, and developing questions. Bloom's six cognitive levels range from simple recall or recognition of facts through increasingly more complex and abstract intellectual tasks. The following brief definitions are followed by several sample verbs that reflect the appropriate intellectual activity:

1. Knowledge: Requires that students recognize or recall information. Remembering is the key intellectual activity. (define, recall, memorize, name, duplicate, label, review, list, order, recognize, repeat, reproduce, state)

2. Comprehension: Requires that students demonstrate sufficient understanding to organize and arrange material mentally; demands a personal grasp of the material. (translate, explain, classify, compare, contrast, describe, discuss, express, restate in other words, review, select)

3. Application: Requires that students apply information, demonstrate principles or rules, and use what was learned. Many, but not all, educators believe that this is the first of the higher-level thought processes. (apply, classify, solve, use, show, diagram, demonstrate, record, translate, illustrate, choose, dramatize, employ, operate, practice, schedule, sketch, write)

4. Analysis: Educators agree that this and all the following categories require higher-level thinking skills. Analysis requires students to identify reasons, uncover evidence, and reach conclusions. (identify motives and causes, draw conclusions, determine evidence, support, analyze, deduce, categorize, compare, contrast, criticize, differentiate, justify, distinguish, examine, experiment)

5. Synthesis: Requires that students perform original and creative thinking. Often many potential answers are possible. (write or arrange an original composition, essay or story, make predictions, solve problems in an original way, design a new invention, arrange, assemble, collect, compose, construct, create, design, develop, formulate, manage, organize, plan)

6. Evaluation: Requires that students judge the merit of an idea, solution to a problem, or an aesthetic work. These questions might also solicit an informed opinion on an issue. (judge, value, evaluate, appraise, argue, assess, attach, choose, compare, defend, estimate, rate, select)

While Bloom's taxonomy has facilitated gauging the level of teacher questions, sorting out the significance of these levels is more problematic. A meta-analysis of higher-order questions by Gordon Samson, Bernadette Strykowski, Thomas Weinstein, and

Herbert Walberg, among others, demonstrated only a weak link between higher-order question asking and higher-order thinking. Other researchers have discovered that lower-order questions can be as effective as higher-order ones. Factors such as student background, curricular goals, and the skill of the teacher can be influential in determining which level of question is most effective. Studies suggest that teachers may be more skilled in asking lower-order questions, that curricular goals stressing mastery and memory of content may be achieved more efficiently with lower-level questions, and that many lower-socioeconomic class students seemed to perform better with lower-level questions than higher-order ones. Other studies indicate that even when a teacher asks a higher-order question, students may answer at a lower level. The clarity and specificity of the teacher's question and the background knowledge of students are two reasons why higher-order questions may elicit lower-level responses. Determining what steps educators can take to promote more sophisticated and challenging student thought processes is a central concern of future research.

Beyond the taxonomy, William Wilen and other researchers have categorized several types of questions. Probing questions are follow-up questions asked after a student responds to the initial question. Probing questions require a student to think deeper than the original response, and to integrate new material. One type of probing is the Socratic question, which originated with the Greek philosopher whose skillful inquiry helped students recognize gaps and contradictions in their understanding. Teachers sometimes structure questions specifically for the purpose of diagnosing a student's needs and for bridging a learning gap, a questioning strategy called *scaffolding.* The term derives from the construction industry, where scaffolding is used to support a not-yet-completed building. Divergent questions often provide unique student insights, encourage the exploration of many possibilities, and do not produce a single correct answer. Affective questions concern attitudes, values and feelings of students, and although they reside in another domain, they are related to the levels described in the cognitive taxonomy. Defining and categorizing types of questions will likely continue in the years ahead.

Feedback

Teacher responses to student answers, often termed *feedback,* represent another rich area of educational

research and training. The most common teacher response is neutral acknowledgement, simply accepting a student response in silence or with minimal recognition. Educators John Goodlad, Theodore Sizer, and others have characterized the typical classroom intellectual climate as bland and unchallenging, and the preponderance of both lower-order questions and simple acceptance reactions from teachers undoubtedly contribute to this lackluster atmosphere. While teachers sometimes provide active help correcting and improving student responses, praise and criticism occur infrequently.

The silent time before feedback is given, a period called *wait-time,* has also been an important topic of investigation. Thomas Good and Jere Brophy have reported on the research of Mary Budd Rowe and others concerning two wait times in the questioning cycle. Wait-time I is the silent period that follows a teacher question but precedes the next utterance, typically a student answer or an additional teacher comment. Wait-time I can be thought of as "think" time, and if wait-time I is long enough, students have adequate time to volunteer to answer a question, as well as to think about the answer that they will give. Wait-time II, the second critical silent period, follows a student answer but precedes a teacher reaction. If wait-time II is long enough, both students and the teacher can carefully consider student responses. Unfortunately, research shows that wait-times I and II are rarely long enough for thoughtful classroom interactions, each typically less than one second in duration. Studies show that if wait-time I is increased to three to five seconds following a higher-order question, a number of positive results follow. Longer wait-time I leads to a higher rate of student participation, longer, more correct and more complete answers, higher achievement, and more on-task student talk. In addition, longer wait-time can attract low-participating learners into class interactions. Students with limited English proficiency, minority students, lower-achieving students, and females are typically among those who benefit from a longer wait-time. While wait-time II is less well known to educators, it is also important. By extending the silent period after a student response, teachers give students the opportunity to complete their answers and to build on each other's ideas. A longer wait-time II also gives teachers time to carefully consider student answers, and to formulate a more precise and helpful reaction to those answers.

Increased wait-time has also been linked to an increase in student-initiated questions. When children are young, their vocabulary is characterized by a high number of questions. In schools, however, children rarely formulate content-related questions on their own. It is ironic that although one typically links learning with asking questions, it is the teacher, not the learner, who is doing the asking. When students ask questions, they are typically procedural ("Will this be on the test?") or express confusion or lack of understanding of content. Research indicates that when students generate their own questions, their comprehension of a topic is enhanced. Although Barak Rosenshine, Carla Meister, and Saul Chapman have described several successful strategies in promoting student initiated questions, most classrooms have a dearth of such questions.

Effective Questioning Practices

William Wilen, Margaret Ishler, and Janice Hutchinson, among others, have synthesized the research on effective questioning techniques and suggested several helpful directions for teachers:

1. Effective questions are clearly phrased, reducing the possibility of student confusion and frustration. A major problem occurs when a teacher asks a series of run-on questions, while attempting to sharpen the focus of the original question.

2. Teachers should wait at least three to five seconds after asking a question that requires higher-order thinking (wait-time I), and three to five seconds after a student response to provide precise feedback (wait-time II).

3. Effective teachers encourage all students to respond, rather than depending on volunteers, or answering the question themselves. Longer wait time, probing questions, and a pattern of expectation for student responses are all helpful strategies in promoting student responses.

4. The research on student call-outs suggests that although call-outs need to be controlled, their response can be a helpful technique in promoting student participation among reticent and low-socioeconomic students.

5. The research on the effectiveness of higher-level teacher questions, those questions on Bloom's taxonomy that require analysis, synthesis or evaluation, is mixed. However, the consensus is that higher-level questions encourage higher-level student thinking.

6. Teacher feedback should be specific and discriminating. Students should be acknowledged for their contribution, praise should underscore genuine accomplishment, while criticism and remediation should point out areas in need of improvement (focusing on the behavior, skills, and knowledge, rather than the individual).

7. While researchers consider the frequency of teacher questions (well into the hundreds a day) as too high, there is an increasing emphasis on the need to encourage more student-initiated questions—an indication of student involvement and increased student comprehension.

See also: DISCOURSE; INSTRUCTIONAL DESIGN; INSTRUCTIONAL STRATEGIES.

BIBLIOGRAPHY

ASCHNER, MARY JANE; GALLAGHER, JAMES J.; PERRY, JOYCE M.; and AFSAR, SIBEL S. 1961. *A System for Classifying Thought Processes in the Context of Classroom Verbal Interaction.* Urbana: University of Illinois.

BEYER, BARRY K. 1997. *Improving Student Thinking.* Boston: Allyn and Bacon.

BLOOM, BENJAMIN, ed. 1956. *Taxonomy of Educational Objectives: The Classification of Educational Goals, Handbook I: Cognitive Domain.* New York: Longman Green.

DANTONIO, MARYLOU, and BEISENHERZ, PAUL C. 2001. *Learning to Question, Questioning to Learn.* Boston: Allyn and Bacon.

GOOD, THOMAS L., and BROPHY, JERE E. 2000. *Looking in Classrooms.* New York: Longman.

HUNKINS, FRANCIS P. 1995. *Teaching Thinking Through Effective Questioning.* Boston: Christopher-Gordon.

ROSE, SARI, with LITCHER, JOHN. 1998. "Effective Questioning Techniques: In Theory and Practice." In *Studies in Teaching*, ed. Leah P. McCoy. Winston Salem, NC: Wake Forest University.

ROSENSHINE, BARAK; MAISSTER, CARLA; and CHAPMAN, SAUL. 1996. "Teaching Students to Generate Questions: A Review of Intervention Studies." *Review of Educational Research* 66:181–221.

SAMSON, GORDON E.; STRYKOWSKI, BERNADETTE; WEINSTEIN, THOMAS; and WALBERG, HERBERT J. 1987. "The Effects of Teacher Questioning Levels on Student Achievement: A Quantitative Synthesis." *Journal of Educational Research* 80(5):290–295.

WILEN, WILLIAM. 1987. *Questions, Questioning Techniques, and Effective Teaching.* Washington, DC: National Education Association.

WILEN, WILLIAM; ISHLER, MARGARET; and HUTCHINSON, JANICE. 2000. *Dynamics of Teaching.* New York: Longman.

DAVID SADKER

CLASS SIZE AND STUDENT LEARNING

The class unit is the basic unit of organization for instruction; therefore class-size information should be foundational knowledge for educators. Yet between the first edition of the *Encyclopedia of Education* in 1971 (see John Reisert's entry on class size, pp. 157–160) and its second edition in 2002, understanding of class size and its actual use have arguably seen both the greatest and the least change among the fundamentals of education.

Class size and pupil-teacher ratio (PTR) are defined, computed, conceptualized, and used differently. Class size, the number of students in a class for whom the teacher is responsible and accountable, is determined by addition. A PTR is derived by dividing the number of students at a site, such as a school, by some representation of educators (e.g., teachers, administrators, specialists) serving that site. In a classroom with 30 students and one teacher, the class size is 30 and the PTR is 30:1. If two teachers serve those 30 students, the class size is 30, but the PTR is 15:1. Class size and PTR have changed much in thirty years but the terms are still used imprecisely as synonyms in research, critiques, policy, and in practice. Yet the distinctly different concepts provide far different outcomes.

Changes in the delivery of education initiated by the 1965 Elementary and Secondary Education Act (ESEA, or Pub. L. 89-10) influenced PTR greatly and class size only minimally. Among other things, ESEA targeted categorical funds to special audiences, such as students at risk of school failure. Title I teachers and aides (named after ESEA's major initiative) provided special services such as reading remediation in pull-out programs where students left regular classrooms for small-group instruction. Later legislation (e.g., the Education of the Handicapped Act, Pub. L. 94-142 [1975] and its extensions [the Individuals with Disabilities Education Act or IDEA] in 1990 and 1997) followed similar formats. According to the U.S. Department of Education's statistics for 1999, the spate of special teachers changed the overall kindergarten to grade 12 (K-12) PTR from 24.7 (1965) to 16.8 (1999). This change is readily seen in elementary grades (the area of most class-size research), where the average PTR decreased from 27.6 in 1965 to 18.6 in 1999.

Class-Size Research (1978–2002)

Interest in class size blossomed in the late 1970s. Gene Glass and Mary Lee Smith consolidated prior years of class-size research using meta-analysis to calculate the effects of many studies and pool the results. Indiana's statewide Prime Time project (1981) initially reduced class size in grades 1 and 2, and later expanded to include reductions in kindergarten and grade 3 reductions that could involve teacher aides, a PTR intervention. Texas passed House Bill (H.B.) 72 in 1984 to limit class size in grades K-2 to 22 and added grades 3 and 4 and a 20 student limit in 1986. The reasons for reducing class sizes include providing better instruction, more individual attention to students, and accommodating the growing diversity in public schooling.

In Tennessee, Project STAR (Student Teacher Achievement Ratio) was a statewide, large-scale longitudinal (1985–1989) experiment of small-class effects on the achievement and development of pupils in grades K–3. STAR expanded into the Lasting Benefits Study, Project Challenge, the Enduring Effects Study, and STAR Follow-up Studies to track students through the grades. By 2001, analyses had been conducted on STAR students who graduated from high school in 1998, including college admissions test results analyzed by the size of the K–3 class that the students had attended.

STAR involved 11,600 students and 340 teachers in 79 schools. Students were assigned at random to small classes (13–17 students), regular classes (approximately 22–25 students), and regular classes with a full-time teacher aide. The in-school design whereby each participating school had at least one of all three class types ruled out school-level variables. Random replacements for students who moved or were retained in grade maintained the cohorts in grades K–3. Grade-appropriate teachers were randomly assigned each year. Data were collected on pupil cognitive (e.g., test scores) and noncognitive (e.g., behavior, participation, attendance, self-concept) measures and teachers and aides were interviewed each year. Each year the small-class students exceeded the large-class students on all cognitive and most noncognitive measures. Gains were cumulative and were especially strong for students who had spent more years in small classes. Frederick Mosteller concluded: "The Tennessee class size project, a controlled experiment . . . is one of the most important educational investigations ever carried out." (p. 113).

Wisconsin began SAGE (Student Achievement Guarantee in Education) primarily in urban areas in 1996. SAGE later expanded to any district that met eligibility criteria. As in the early Glass and Smith works, Prime Time, and STAR results, SAGE evaluators found both cognitive and noncognitive gains. Like STAR, SAGE began in kindergarten and proceeded one grade per year, phasing in small classes, and results were similar. Compared to students in larger classes, small-class students achieved higher test scores and better behavior and discipline, and teachers felt that they were more effective and able to provide more individual attention. Minority and difficult-to-teach youngsters received greater benefits than did other students, echoing reviews of class-size research such as Harold Wenglinsky's 1997 findings that "fourth graders in smaller-than-average classes are about half a year ahead of fourth graders in larger-than average classes. . . . The largest effects seem to be for poor students in high-cost areas" (pp. 24–25).

In 1996 California began a massive voluntary class-size reduction (CSR) in grades 1 through 3 that included incentives to participate. Brian Stecher et al. (2001) found unanticipated consequences, including large-scale movement from poor and urban districts of certified teachers who were replaced by new, uncertified, or emergency-credentialled teachers. Modest student gains did not include the differential benefits for minority students found in other class-size studies. It remains to be seen if teacher mobility influenced this.

TABLE 1

Research and theory bases for small-class effects in early grades

The following lead to short- and long-range achievement benefits.

I. Learning
A. Task induction, students learn schooling expectations, and are socialized to school
B. Time on task, focused work
C. Engagement, participation, identification with school
D. Appropriate homework

II. Teaching
A. Individual accommodation
B. Early diagnosis and remediation of learning difficulty
C. Teach to mastery
D. Immediate reinforcement
E. Assessment (in-class)
F. Use of effective teaching methods
G. Cooperative learning

III. Classroom
A. Classroom environment (e.g. air quality, materials, crowding), space for learning centers
B. Family-like community
C. Inclusion, special needs, teachers can work with each student
D. Group dynamics
E. Opportunity for peer interaction
F. Classroom management
G. Less commotion
H. Controlled noise levels, seamless transitions

IV. Other
A. Increased parent interest
B. Teacher/student morale
C. Accountability and responsibility
D. Assessment (outcome)

SOURCE: Courtesy of author.

Translating Class-size Research to Practice

Many class-size studies collectively told educators much about schooling and identified that there were right ways to use small classes. On tests given in grades 3 and higher, studies showed that one year (grade 3) in a small class, and even two years (grades 2 and 3) yielded negligible test-score gains. For short-term and long-term results, students had to start small classes when they entered school (kindergarten or grade one). The treatment had to be intense (all day, every day) and for sufficient duration (at least three and preferably four years). Small classes are more preventive than remedial, as they help teach young students what is expected in schooling. By 2001 researchers had identified some two dozen research- and theory-based reasons why small classes provide superior student opportunities and outcomes (see Table 1).

The longer a student has small classes the better the outcomes, not just while in small classes, but through high school and beyond. Small-class K–3 students gained about a year's growth in all subjects tested over randomly assigned peers in larger classes. Small-class students had significantly higher graduation rates, lower retention in grade, and higher percentage of honors diplomas. Early small-class attendance reduced the college admissions test-taking gap between white and minority students significantly. In contrast classes with teacher aides (which reduced PTR but not class size) were particularly ineffective for minority male students, a finding that helps explain the mixed outcomes in Prime Time after aides were allowed as a small-class alternative.

Consideration of Critical Comments about Class Size

Small-class critics typically build on the comments of Eric Hanushek, whose work is typical of production function studies that use large, nonspecific databases not established for or from class-size research. Hanushek made two points: First, "pupil teacher ratios are not the same as class sizes," and second "the only data . . . available over long periods refer to teacher-pupil ratios" (p. 145). Thus, Hanushek's criticisms rely on PTR estimates and not on class-size work. His comments that small classes do not yield better student outcomes simply ignore class-size research findings such as early intervention, intensity, and duration. He also excluded Project STAR's results. Scholars criticized Hanushek's vote-counting methods and actually reanalyzed his data, obtaining different results. For example Rob Greenwald, Richard Lane, and Larry Hedges (1996) and Alan Krueger (2000) found that careful treatment of Hanushek's data and excluding "double counting" actually showed that small classes were associated with increased student outcomes.

Educators who use small classes for young students must balance costs against benefits and implement small classes in accordance with the research. The difference between class size and PTR in the United States in 1998 was about ten pupils. If a school had a PTR of 17:1, a teacher faced about twenty-seven students in elementary grades. Redeployment of personnel based on small-class benefits is one way to find personnel and space for the small classes sizes that support improved student achievement, behavior, and school participation.

John Reisert's 1971 plea to understand and use differences between class size and PTR remains. However, by 2001 there was experimental and anecdotal evidence that class sizes of about 14 to 16 in grades K–3 improve education outcomes of students, and the gains grow throughout the grades. There is no evidence that small classes in later grades are harmful. Much of the discussion is ideological

and not research-based. Glass (1992) said that "the controversy over class size has not subsided . . . educational research may . . . replace ordinary language with numbers . . . but it is not likely to reduce or eliminate the conflicts of interest and political positions that are played out in the school system" (p. 165).

See also: ELEMENTARY EDUCATION; SECONDARY EDUCATION, *subentries on* CURRENT TRENDS, HISTORY OF.

BIBLIOGRAPHY

ACHILLES, CHARLES M. 1999. *Let's Put Kids First Finally: Getting Class Size Right.* Thousand Oaks, CA: Corwin Press.

BOYD-ZAHARIAS, JANE, and PATE-BAIN, HELEN. 2000. "Early and New Findings from Tennessee's Project STAR." In *How Small Classes Help Teachers Do Their Best,* ed. Margaret C. Wang and Jeremy D. Finn, pp. 65–98. Philadelphia: Temple University Center for Research in Human Development in Education.

CHASE, CLINTON I.; MUELLER, DANIEL J.; and WALDEN, JAMES D. 1986. *PRIME TIME: Its Impact on Instruction and Achievement.* Final Report, December. Indianapolis: Indiana Department of Education.

FINN, JEREMY D., and ACHILLES, CHARLES M. 1999. "Tennessee's Class Size Study: Findings, Implication, Misconceptions." *Educational Evaluation and Policy Analysis* 21(2): 97–107.

FINN, JEREMY D.; GERBER, SUSAN B.; FARBER, STACEY L.; and ACHILLES, CHARLES M. 2000. "Teacher Aides: An Alternative to Small Classes?" In *How Small Classes Help Teachers Do Their Best,* ed. Margaret C. Wang and Jeremy D. Finn, pp. 131–174. Philadelphia: Temple University Center for Research in Human Development in Education.

GLASS, GENE V. 1992. "Class Size." In *Encyclopedia of Educational Research,* Vol. 1, ed. Marvin C. Alken, pp. 164–166. New York: Macmillan.

GLASS, GENE V., and SMITH, MARY LEE. 1978. *Meta-Analysis of Research on the Relationship of Class Size and Achievement.* San Francisco: Far West Laboratory for Educational Research and Development.

GREENWALD, ROB; LAINE, RICHARD D.; and HEDGES, LARRY W. 1996. "The School Funding

Controversy: Reality Bites." *Education Leadership* 53(5): 78–79.

HANUSHEK, ERIC A. 1999. "Some Findings from an Independent Investigation of the Tennessee STAR Experiment and from Other Investigation of Class Size Effects." *Educational Evaluation and Policy Analysis* 21(2):143–163.

KRUEGER, ALAN B. 2000. "An Economist's View of Class Size Research." In *How Small Classes Help Teachers Do Their Best,* ed. Margaret C. Wang and Jeremy D. Finn, pp. 99–130. Philadelphia: Temple University Center for Research in Human Development in Education.

MILES, KAREN H., and DARLING-HAMMOND, LINDA. 1998. "Rethinking the Allocation of Teaching Resources: Some Lessons from High-Performing Schools." *Educational Evaluation and Policy Analysis* 20(1):9–29.

MOLNAR, ALEX; SMITH, PHILIP; ZAHORIK, JOHN; PALMER, AMANDA; HALBACH, ANKE; and EHRLE, KAREN. 2000. "Wisconsin's Student Achievement Guarantee in Education (SAGE) Class Size Reduction Program: Achievement Effects, Teaching, and Classroom Implications." In *How Small Classes Help Teachers Do Their Best,* ed. Margaret C. Wang and Jeremy D. Finn, pp. 227–278. Philadelphia: Temple University Center for Research in Human Development in Education.

MOSTELLER, FREDERICK. 1995. "The Tennessee Study of Class Size in the Early School Grades." *The Future of Children: Critical Issues for Children and Youths* 5 (2):113–127.

REISERT, JOHN E. 1971. "Class Size." *Encyclopedia of Education,* 1st edition, Vol. 2. New York: Macmillan and Free Press.

STECHER, BRIAN; BOHRNSTEDT, GEORGE; KIRST, MICHAEL; McROBBIE, JOAN; and WILLIAMS, TRISH. 2001. "Class-Size Reduction in California: A Story of Hope, Promise, and Unintended Consequences." *Phi Delta Kappan* 82(9):670–674.

WENGLINSKY, HAROLD. 1997. *When Money Matters.* Princeton, NJ: Educational Testing Service (ETS) Policy Information Center.

WORD, ELIZABETH; JOHNSTON, JOHN; BAIN, HELEN; FULTON, B. DWAYNE; ZAHARIAS, JANE; LINTZ, NANNETTE; ACHILLES, CHARLES M.; FOLGER, JOHN; and BREDA, CAROLYN. 1990. *Student/ Teacher Achievement Ratio (STAR): Tennessee's K–3 Class Size Study.* Final Report and Summary. Nashville: Tennessee State Department of Education.

CHARLES M. ACHILLES

CLUBS

Many schools and community organizations sponsor clubs for children and adolescents. These clubs provide opportunities for youth to participate in activities, interact with peers in a supervised setting, and form relationships with adults. Some clubs focus on a specific area, thus allowing members to develop their skills and interests in that area. Other clubs provide an array of activities from which children and adolescents can choose.

Club Participation

Researchers have described how often children and adolescents participate in clubs, as well as the characteristics of young people that tend to join clubs. In 2001 Sandra Hofferth and Zita Jankuniene published the results of a study on how elementary school students spent their time after school. Using data from a longitudinal nationally representative random sample of U.S. residents, they found that although quite a few children reported belonging to youth organizations, only about 20 percent of the children actually attended clubs and youth organizations after school. On average, on any given day, these students spent between thirty minutes and one hour and twenty minutes at youth organizations engaged in supervised extracurricular activities.

Studies of high school students show that about 25 percent of adolescents join music-oriented clubs, such as choir or band, and 20 percent join academic or career-related clubs, such as a science club, a Spanish club, or Future Farmers of America. More children from middle-class families than from lower-class families report participating in school clubs. Participation is also higher in rural or small schools. One study found that club participants tended to be females from two-parent families with high socioeconomic status.

Why Participation Is Expected to Benefit Youth

There are a number of reasons that both scholars and parents expect young people to benefit from participation in clubs and youth organizations. These reasons have to do with the activities, roles, and relationships available to children and adolescents when they participate in clubs. Activities are important in several ways. For one, participation in a supervised constructive activity limits the time that is available for less constructive activity, such as television watching, or for getting involved in risky behaviors. For another, activities offered by clubs or youth organizations enable members to learn valuable skills. Many of the activities offered by clubs help students to extend and elaborate on the more formal knowledge learned in school.

Club membership provides an opportunity to participate in new roles. The leadership roles that are available in clubs provide a valuable experience that is not generally available to young people. Other roles, such as being a helper in a service club, a soloist in a music club, or an artist making scenery in a drama club, enable identity exploration.

Finally, relationships formed with adult leaders and with peers at the clubs are important. Adults and peers at these organizations can serve as models and as sources of social support, friendship, and caring. Several developmental theories point to the importance of adult mentoring for child and adolescent development. Mentoring relationships are important characteristics of clubs and youth programs. Adolescents who have an after-school relationship with a mentor are far less likely to use drugs or alcohol than adolescents who do not have such relationships. Peer relations might also benefit from participation in clubs. "Hanging out" unsupervised with peers contributes negatively to child and adolescent development. However, participation in supervised constructive activities provides adolescents with opportunities to gain social skills from positive interactions with peers.

Shirley Brice Heath has elaborated on the importance of extracurricular activities in the arts. She points out how arts groups offer young people activities, roles, and relationships that can contribute positively to their development. According to Heath, many youth art programs design environments that prepare youth for problem solving, conflict resolution, and productivity in work, family, and other community settings. Heath highlights the critical thinking, identity exploration, collaboration, organization, and pursuit of excellence that transpires when youth participate in artistic groups. Community arts organizations often help older youths to

elaborate their knowledge and skill by bringing younger participants into the group. By dedicating themselves to long-term projects, young people learn to stick with and complete projects, and they have the opportunity to produce creative works for audiences by putting on shows and plays. The racial and socioeconomic barriers that are breached by the work of such organizations is likely to benefit both youth and communities.

Benefits of Participation in Clubs

Researchers and club sponsors have been eager to learn how participation in clubs influences youth development. However, studies of the impact of clubs have been conducted mostly on small, local, and nonrepresentative samples of children and adolescents. Furthermore, many studies that have found differences between participants and nonparticipants in clubs and youth organizations have not examined whether such differences existed before the children and youths joined. It might be that joiners have preexisting differences that lead them to become involved in clubs and participate in youth organizations. Students who are drawn to participate in a science club, for instance, are likely to have been more successful academically prior to joining than nonparticipants. For these reasons, the studies must be evaluated carefully.

Studies of students' participation in extracurricular activities during high school have tended to focus on athletics. However, several studies have examined outcomes by type of extracurricular activity. One conclusion is that participation in fine arts programs appears to contribute to better academic performance and psychological well-being, even when taking prior academic performance and psychological functioning into account. Another conclusion is that young people can derive developmental benefits from participating in well-run organizations.

Jacquelynne Eccles and Bonnie Barber investigated the contributions of participation in school and community clubs to the development of approximately 1,200 adolescents from ten school districts serving working and middle-class families in or near Detroit. The researchers identified how much each adolescent participated in academic clubs (science, debate, math, computer, chess, foreign language) and performing arts organizations (drama, art, band, dance), whether at, or outside of, school. Church groups accounted for most of the activities that were grouped together with community service clubs in the social activity category, so any contributions of these activities are confounded with religious belief and practice and cannot be discerned. Although students who participated in the arts were less likely to use alcohol than other students, arts involvement did not change their drinking behavior during high school. Art participants also liked school more, had higher grade point averages during their senior year in high school, and were more likely to attend college full-time. However, only grade point averages actually improved as a result of participation. Art program participants liked school and intended to go to college before participating, and their levels of liking school and scholastic ambition did not change. Adolescents who participated in academic clubs were more academically skilled than other students before participating; however, the club activities also appeared to contribute to increases in the grade point averages of these students.

In a different longitudinal study, McLaughlin concluded that participation in effective programs provided multiple benefits. The National Educational Longitudinal Survey (NELS) followed a nationally representative sample of youths from 1988, when they were in eighth grade, through 1994. McLaughlin and her colleagues used NELS data to estimate general levels of self-esteem, academic achievement, future aspirations, self-efficacy, and civic responsibility of American youth. McLaughlin also gave youths participating in community organizations identified as effective a set of questions from NELS. Participants in effective programs were found to be more likely than nonparticipants to aspire to graduate from high school and to pursue further education. They also did better academically, compared to the national estimate. Adolescents who participated were more optimistic, had higher self-esteem, and expressed greater self-confidence than the national average, and they were more oriented toward serving their communities in the future. A longitudinal follow-up investigation found that the majority of participants in effective community programs were employed and active in their local communities during their twenties.

One study found that there was less juvenile delinquency and less alcohol and drug use among adolescents and adults in ten public housing sites that had Boys and Girls Clubs, compared to five public housing sites with no clubs. Adolescents who resided in public housing developments with Boys and Girls Clubs spent more time in activities that were healthy and constructive than did adolescents from housing developments without Boys and Girls Clubs. A study of two different girls-only programs at four Boys and Girls Clubs in Chicago supported the idea that relationships at the clubs are important contributors to participants' development. The fifty girls who participated in the study felt that the club provided a place for positive peer relationships and for working cooperatively with other girls to achieve goals.

Adult volunteer leaders or mentors at clubs might also benefit. Adult leaders of youth groups such as the Girl Scouts have expressed satisfaction with the experience because of positive youth responsiveness, as well as the usefulness and effectiveness of the programs.

Why Children and Adolescents Participate in Clubs

If clubs are beneficial developmentally, then it is important to understand why children and adolescents want to participate in them. Some researchers have examined the characteristics of clubs that children and adolescents identify as important and that motivate them to want to participate. One reason that clubs succeed is that they are familial—participants feel that they belong and are cared for at the club. Another reason that young people participate is that the available activities are rewarding—participants learn through participating and performing in the activities. Participants also have a sense of ownership, as they are expected to contribute to the planning, maintenance, and success of the organization. Adults at the clubs empower, support, and set high expectations for the participants, and the clubs are responsive to the needs and circumstances of their members.

Another study, using observations, surveys, and interviews, found that most (74%) of the 300 minority adolescents who participated in four affiliates of the Boys and Girls Clubs of America referred to the club as a home and mentioned relationships with the staff as important. Many of the adolescents felt cared for at the club and reported receiving both support and advice. Adolescents mentioned psychosocial benefits far more often than physical characteristics of the clubs.

Milbrey McLaughlin and Heath studied young people in thirty-four locations in low-income urban and rural areas over a twelve-year period from 1987 through 1999. Study participants were interviewed about what motivates them to participate in clubs and organizations. McLaughlin and Heath found that the effective organizations noticed the interests and strengths of participants and saw young people as resources. Effective programs were more than safe places to go—they were focused on activities like sports, arts, or community service. The programs offered adolescents opportunities to develop skills and interests, as well as to learn, plan, perform, or create products. Adolescents were also able to lead activities and to have some sense of ownership of, and responsibility for, the club. Adolescents also formed relationships with adults and peers centered on learning and developing skills. Effective programs provided participants with opportunities to improve through adult feedback, peer feedback, and self-evaluations; and they had safe nurturing environments that helped the adolescents to develop trust and security. These programs were also sensitive to community needs and circumstances in offerings and structure.

Emmalou Norland and Melissa Bennet studied a random sample of adolescent participants in Ohio 4-H programs. Using theory and previous research, they argue that program satisfaction is the best way to determine which adolescents will continue participating in a voluntary extracurricular activity such as 4-H. They found that a participant report of high-quality 4-H club meetings was the most important predictor of participant satisfaction. Other predictors of satisfaction that program planners can influence included opportunities to work with younger members and an ability to assume some level of responsibility. Parental support, but not direct parental involvement, was also found to be important to the adolescents.

Other studies of 4-H participants have underscored other program qualities that influence participation. For example, adolescents strongly value encouragement of leadership, community service, honesty, a strong work ethic, a healthful lifestyle, and the importance of family. Adolescents also valued organizations that met their needs to have fun, develop mature peer relationships, and learn about society. Some 4-H members were most satisfied when their leaders provided a balance between autonomy support (allowing for independence) and control.

See also: YOUTH ORGANIZATIONS: *subentries on* BOYS AND GIRLS CLUBS OF AMERICA, BOY SCOUTS OF AMERICA, CAMP FIRE USA, FOUR-H PROGRAMS, GIRL SCOUTS OF THE USA.

BIBLIOGRAPHY

BARTKO, TODD, and ECCLES, JACQUELYNNE. 1999. "Adolescent Participation in Structured and Unstructured Activities: A Person-Oriented Analysis." Paper presented at the Biennial Meeting of the Society for Research in Child Development in Albuquerque, New Mexico.

BERK, LAURA. 1992. "The Extracurriculum." In *Handbook of Research on Curriculum,* ed. Philip W. Jackson. New York: Macmillan.

ECCLES, JACQUELYNNE, and BARBER, BONNIE. 1999. "Student Council, Volunteering, Basketball, or Marching Band: What Kind of Extracurricular Involvement Matters?" *Journal of Adolescent Research* 14:101–43.

HEATH, SHIRLEY BRICE. 1991. "Community Organizations as Family: Endeavors that Engage and Support Adolescents." *Phi Delta Kapan* 623–627.

HEATH, SHIRLEY BRICE. 2001. "Three's Not a Crowd: Plans, Roles, and Focus in the Arts." *Educational Researcher* 30:10–17.

HOFFERTH, SANDRA, and JANKUNIENE, ZITA. 2001. "Life After School." *Educational Leadership* 58:19–23.

SAITO, REBECCA, and BLYTH, DALE. 1992. "Understanding Mentoring Relationships." Minneapolis, MN: Search Institute. ERIC Document Reproduction Service ED359295.

SCHINKE, STEVEN P. 1991. "The Effects of Boys and Girls Clubs on Alcohol and Other Drug Use and Related Problems in Public Housing." Final Research Report. ERIC Document Reproduction Service ED338739.

INTERNET RESOURCES

ASTROTH, KEITH. 1996. "Leadership in Non-Formal Youth Groups: Does Style Affect Youth Outcomes." *Journal of Extension* 34(6). <www.joe.org/joe/1996december/rb2.html>.

MCLAUGHLIN, MILBREY. 2001. "Community Counts: How Youth Organizations Matter for Youth Development." Public Education Network. <http://publiceducation.org>.

NORLAND, EMMALOU, and BENNETT, MELISSA. 1993. "Youth Participation." *Journal of Extension* 31(1). <www.joe.org/joe/1993spring/a5.html>.

SARVER, DANIEL; JOHNSON, EARL; and VERMA, SATISH. 2000. "A Tool to Assess the Worth of a

Youth Organization." *Journal of Extension* 38(3). <www.joe.org/joe/2000june/rb3.html>.

LEE SHUMOW

COALITION OF ESSENTIAL SCHOOLS

The Coalition of Essential Schools (CES) is a grass-roots network of approximately 1,000 schools and twenty regional centers around the country that seek to enact a set of ideas put forth by the American educator Theodore R. Sizer in *Horace's Compromise* (1984). Sizer found that, despite their differences in location and demography, American high schools, by and large, were remarkably similar and, quite simply, inadequate. He concluded that the typical American high school—with a huge array of unrelated courses taught in short, fragmented periods by teachers who face 150 students a day—promoted apathy and intellectual lethargy, and that the lesson such schools succeeded in teaching best, perhaps, was that school is deadly dull and has little to do with becoming a productive citizen or an educated human being.

Sizer considered how schools might be more wisely designed. Given the dismal historical record of major "top-down" reform initiatives over the previous fifty years, Sizer chose to approach reform not with a new and improved model to be imposed, but rather with a set of ideas that a school could employ in ways that suited its community. These ideas, referred to as the coalition's Common Principles, fall into four key program areas: school design, classroom practice, leadership, and community connections. In the area of school design, CES schools strive to structure schedules and staffing arrangements so that teacher–student ratios are low, teachers have significant time to collaborate, and all students participate in a rigorous intellectual program. In their classrooms, coalition teachers seek to emphasize depth of understanding rather than mere coverage of material, and they see their role more as a facilitator or coach than a deliverer of information. Coalition schools work to create democratic leadership structures, enlisting the active engagement of community members both in the governance of the school and in the education of students.

To aid K–12 schools seeking to adopt these ideas, CES has a two-tiered system of services. The regional centers support schools in the process of change by facilitating learning among schools in the region, providing carefully targeted opportunities for professional development, and offering technical assistance. Though CES regional centers vary in their particular program offerings, all are guided by the Common Principles and share similar strategies. Many CES centers, for example, set up one-to-one coaching relationships with the schools in their region; many sponsor meetings of teachers from different schools to serve as "critical friends" to one another; and many run an intensive summer institute for school faculty on whole school change, known as the "Trek."

The CES national office administers CES University, a series of professional development institutes offered around the country by and for educators from the CES network and beyond. The national office also organizes an annual Fall Forum, where thousands of teachers and administrators come together to learn and to share strategies and experiences. The CES national website serves as a repository of ideas and information and includes many active online discussion groups. *Horace*, the CES journal, seeks out important work and helps keep the network abreast of new findings in educational research. CES also conducts a program of research to track the results of CES schools and operates an advocacy program, to help inform educators and the public about the coalition's approach to schooling.

Several coalition schools have received national prominence. Perhaps best known is Central Park East Secondary School in East Harlem, New York, founded in 1985, and one of the charter members of the coalition. Many schools that joined the coalition more recently are showing equally impressive results, graduating and sending students to college at very high rates, and creating school communities with high levels of safety and trust.

The impact of the coalition's work can also be gauged by its effect on the school reform movement. Its ideas—creating small schools where students can be known well; graduating students on the basis of demanding, public exhibitions in which students present the results of their research to panels of community members; and insisting that curriculum must teach students how to learn rather than teaching disconnected facts—have become part of the language of school improvement. Such coalition phrases as "critical friends," "school coaches," "exhibitions of mastery," "less is more," and "teacher as coach" have become key components of many school reform efforts and state curriculum frameworks.

See also: INSTRUCTIONAL STRATEGIES; SECONDARY EDUCATION, *subentries on* CURRENT TRENDS, HISTORY OF.

BIBLIOGRAPHY

MCDONALD, JOSEPH P. 1996. *Redesigning School: Lessons for the Twenty-First Century.* San Francisco: Jossey-Bass.

MEIER, DEBORAH. 1995. *The Power of Their Ideas: Lessons for America from a Small School in Harlem.* Boston: Beacon Press.

SIZER, THEODORE. 1984. *Horace's Compromise: The Dilemma of the American High School.* Boston: Houghton Mifflin.

KATHERINE G. SIMON
HUDI PODOLSKY

COALITION OF ESSENTIAL SCHOOLS' COMMON PRINCIPLES

The Coalition of Essential Schools (CES) was founded in 1984 with the financial support of several national foundations as a secondary school reform organization. It built on the research conducted during the preceding five years by Theodore R. Sizer, Arthur G. Powell, and their colleagues in A Study of High Schools, research that was cosponsored by the National Association of Secondary School Principals (NASSP) and the National Association of Independent Schools (NAIS). The study's findings appeared in three volumes, *Horace's Compromise* (1984), *The Shopping Mall High School* (1985), and *The Last Little Citadel* (1986). The coalition was based at Brown University where Sizer was a professor and served as its chairman. NASSP and NAIS continued as cosponsors.

In light of the research, which had reflected the necessarily local character of effective secondary schools, CES avoided creating a "model" school design to be "implemented." Rather, CES set out nine "common principles," drafted by Sizer, that appeared to be essential in the functioning of a worthy high school. While each CES school accepts responsibility to address the practical implications of all of the principles, the shape of the expression of those ideas is developed with the character and strengths of that particular locality in mind. CES would assist with the process of adapting the principles to immediate situations by gathering all the schools into a "coalition" from which each school could systematically learn from others. The staff at Brown chronicled and assisted these associated local efforts; regularly issued a newsletter, *Horace*, which recounted good practices as they took form in individual schools; and authorized and obtained the funding of an independent ethnographic study, which focused on the process in which schools engaged in this effort at rethinking and restructuring, and of several field studies directed by Patricia A. Wasley.

In summary, the nine common principles are:

1. The school should focus on helping adolescents learn to use their minds well. The schools should not attempt to be "comprehensive."

2. The school's goals shall be simple: that each student master a limited number of essential skills and areas of knowledge. . . . "Less Is More" should dominate.

3. The school's goals should apply to all students.

4. Teaching and learning should be personalized to the maximum feasible extent . . . no teacher (should) have direct responsibility for more than 80 students . . . decisions (about) the use of students' and teachers' time and the choice of teaching materials . . . must be unreservedly placed in the hands of the principal and staff.

5. The governing practical metaphor of the school should be student-as-worker.

6. The diploma shall be awarded upon a successful demonstration of mastery—an "Exhibition" . . . that may be jointly administered by the faculty and higher authorities. . . . As the diploma is awarded when earned, the school's program proceeds with no age grading.

7. The tone of the school should explicitly and self-consciously stress values of unanxious expectation . . . of trust . . . and of decency. . . . Parents should be treated as essential collaborators.

8. The principal and teachers should perceive themselves as generalists first and specialists second.

9. Ultimate administrative and budget targets should include . . . substantial time for collective planning by teachers, competitive salaries for staff and an ultimate per pupil cost . . . not [to] exceed those at traditional schools by more than ten percent.

In 1998 a tenth common principle was added: "the school should demonstrate . . . inclusive policies (and) model democratic practices . . . explicitly challenging all forms of inequity and discrimination" (Coalition of Essential Schools pamphlet, *The Ten Common Principles*, 1998).

The initial group of twelve schools included several that have gained substantial public visibility, such as Central Park East Secondary School in East Harlem, New York, designed and launched by Deborah Meier; and Thayer High School in Winchester, New Hampshire, "redesigned" by Dennis Littky. Others such as the R. L. Paschal Essential School in Fort Worth, Texas, a small, autonomous unit embedded within the larger Paschal High School, survived and flourished by keeping a very low profile. As others joined, many had difficulty with what emerged as the two hardest principles to put into effect, the diploma based on a public "Exhibition" and the "no more than 80-1 student-teacher ratio." The Brown-based staff observed and reported on these matters, for example, in the former case with workshops, pamphlets, and books by Grant Wiggins and Joseph McDonald; and in the latter with Sizer's *Horace's School* (the chronicle of a fictional school, drawn with CES experience in mind, in employing the common principles) and *Horace's Hope* (the author's take on what he had seen and what independent evidence arising from the work suggested). Overall, the instability of leadership and of the "system's" own directions made the prospect of quick, uncontroversial, and sustained reform difficult.

From 1988 to 1993 CES engaged in a major joint effort with the Education Commission of the States and several of its member states in the Re:Learning project, an effort to connect the grassroots work of Essential Schools with policy reform consistent with CES and CES-like efforts. A substantive and positive residue of Re:Learning was the creation of state-based "centers," usually funded by a mix of private and public money, to forward the work. Political in-

stability, however, made major, highly visible, coordinated restructuring "from the schoolhouse to the state house" largely unsuccessful. In 1990 CES joined the ATLAS Communities Project, one of the New American School efforts, joining with Yale University's School Development Project, directed by James Comer; Harvard Project Zero, directed by Howard Gardner; and the Education Development Center, led by Janet Whitla. ATLAS activities have been funded largely at the federal and district levels.

In 1997 and on the retirement of Sizer from Brown University, CES, now numbering more than 1,000 members, established itself as a not-for-profit organization based in Oakland, California. Much of the close-in work earlier carried out by the Brown staff was shifted to state and regional "centers," these being themselves not-for-profit entities. An executive board, drawn from the member schools and the centers, directs CES's national voice, coordination, and program assessment efforts. A major independent study of "fully articulated" Essential schools (that is, those that have been able to actualize all the common principles) was underway in the early twenty-first century.

See also: COALITION OF ESSENTIAL SCHOOLS; SECONDARY EDUCATION, *subentry on* CURRENT TRENDS; SCHOOL REFORM.

BIBLIOGRAPHY

HAMPEL, ROBERT L. 1986. *The Last Little Citadel: American High Schools since 1940.* Boston: Houghton Mifflin.

KAMMERAAD-CAMPBELL, SUSAN. 1989. *Doc: The Story of Dennis Littky and His Fight for a Better School.* Chicago: Contemporary Books.

MACMULLEN, MARGARET M. 1996. *Taking Stock of a School Reform Effort: A Research Collection and Analysis.* Providence, RI: Annenberg Institute for School Reform.

MEIER, DEBORAH. 1995. *The Power of Their Ideas: Lessons for America from a Small School in Harlem.* Boston: Beacon.

MUNCEY, DONNA E., and MCQUILLAN, PATRICK J. 1996. *Reform and Resistance in Schools and Classrooms.* New Haven, CT: Yale University Press.

NEHRING, JAMES. 2002. *Upstart Startup: Creating and Sustaining a Public Charter School.* New York: Teachers College Press.

POWELL, ARTHUR G.; FARRAR, ELEANOR; and COHEN, DAVID K. 1985. *The Shopping Mall High School: Winners and Losers in the Educational Marketplace.* Boston: Houghton Mifflin.

SIZER, THEODORE R. 1984. *Horace's Compromise: The Dilemma of the American High School.* Boston: Houghton Mifflin.

SIZER, THEODORE R. 1992. *Horace's School: Redesigning the American High School.* Boston: Houghton Mifflin.

SIZER, THEODORE R. 1996. *Horace's Hope: What Works for the American High School.* Boston: Houghton Mifflin.

WASLEY, PATRICIA A. 1994. *Stirring the Chalkdust.* New York: Teachers College Press.

WASLEY, PATRICIA A.; HAMPEL, ROBERT L.; and CLARK, RICHARD W. 1997. *Kids and School Reform.* San Francisco: Jossey-Bass.

THEODORE R. SIZER

COGNITIVE AND INFORMATION PROCESSING

See: DEVELOPMENTAL THEORY, *subentry on* COGNITIVE AND INFORMATION PROCESSING.

COLEMAN, JAMES S. (1926–1995)

A major twentieth-century figure in the sociology of education, James S. Coleman was a social theorist and an empirical researcher with a prevailing interest in social problems in education—tackling issues that were sometimes unpopular. Richard Elmore describes Coleman as a "person who said what he thought and what the evidence said, regardless of whether he felt it was the right thing to say, or the socially acceptable thing to say, in other people's eyes. Even those who disagreed with him were always stimulated to think differently about the issues" (Schmidt, p. 11).

Career

Coleman was born in Bedford, Indiana, in 1926 and attended Purdue University, earning a B.S. in chemical engineering in 1949. Switching to sociology, he received his Ph.D. in 1955 from Columbia University, where his thesis, published in 1961, was a study

of adolescent society. His major work was done as professor in the Johns Hopkins University Department of Sociology (1960–1972) and at the University of Chicago in Sociology and the National Opinion Research Center (NORC) as a research director (1956–1959 and 1973–1995). He published more than thirty books and many articles. Besides being president of the American Sociological Association (1993–1997), he worked on the creation of the National Educational Longitudinal Study database, which he used extensively in his research.

Coleman made many important contributions to the sociology of education. First, in the mid-1960s, the so-called Coleman Report (1966) examined the effects of differentiated resources on student achievement, with the intention of showing that children attending impoverished schools (a disproportionate number of whom were African American) would perform badly. Second, in the 1970s, he analyzed the effects of forced racial integration (busing) on "white flight," becoming an advocate of school choice for impoverished families. Third, in the 1980s, he explored (with Sally Kilgore and Thomas Hoffer) the differential achievement of poor children attending private, Catholic, and public schools. Before his death in 1995, he treated schools as "output-driven systems," becoming a critic of the popular "portfolio analysis," which he believed produced inadequate measures of student performance and weakened incentives for teachers to improve their performance.

Contributions and Controversies

In 1964 Congress ordered the U.S. Commissioner of Education to investigate "the lack of availability of equal education opportunities for individuals by reason of race, color, religion, or national origin." The Coleman Report, the result of a national study of 600,000 students, 60,000 teachers, and 4,000 public schools, attempted to relate family background (including race and socioeconomic status) and school equity variables (including the integration of white and African-American children) to students' test results and their attitudes toward attending higher education.

Coleman found, surprisingly, that students' test outcomes were unrelated to the usual characteristics of schools (e.g., the quality of school facilities, programs, and teachers). Instead, the improvement in academic results among minority children was significantly linked to the quality of the student body—

as measured by the proportion of students with encyclopedias in their home and the proportion with high aspirations. He wrote, "These minority children have a serious educational deficiency at the start of school, which is obviously not a result of school; and they have an even more serious deficiency at the end of school, which is obviously in part a result of [a segregated] school" (1966, p. 22). Racial integration was, according to this study, the key social factor in improving student outcomes.

As for the policy effects of Coleman's research, Hallinan noted in 2000 that the findings of the landmark study "were among the most influential factors leading to the desegregation of the American public school system" (p. 76). Nevertheless, the study's heavy emphasis on the effects of family background on children's education lies in sharp contrast to prevailing opinion. Critics (e.g., Adam Gamoran, Walter Secada, and Cora Marrett in 2000), while admitting the significance of the Coleman Report, reproached it as "the most spectacular failure to connect the collective with the individual in an educational setting. Variation in school conditions [beyond racial integration] was largely unrelated to differences in student outcomes, as school-level effects were dwarfed by the powerful influence of home environment for student learning" (p. 37).

Although the Coleman Report was used extensively by integrationists, by the mid-1970s Coleman's research showed that forced busing of students for "racial balance" was actually compromising the education of bused students by the loss of middle-class (and largely white) students in urban schools. In a study of school choice, Coleman and colleagues (1977) explained that the equalizing effects of the common school are greatest when students from diverse backgrounds—who live in the same locality—attend school together. In his view, forced busing tends to "increase the gap in educational opportunity between those with money and those without" because affluent parents can "buy their way out" of bad schools either by moving to better neighborhoods, to the suburbs, or by enrolling offspring in a private school (p. 6).

Although the location of the school that students attend is largely determined by where they live, the same cannot be said for their parents' place of work. Coleman pointed out that technological and economic changes (e.g., access to automobiles, better commuter routes, and greater affluence) tend to make residential neighborhoods more racially and socioeconomically homogeneous.

Convinced that the quality of an educational experience is associated with the composition of the student body, Coleman asked whether parents, who could choose to live far from their place of employment, might also choose where their children attend school. He describes two methods for bringing about educational equality: court-imposed efforts to achieve racial balance (e.g., busing) and policies to remove economic restraints that decrease the ability of parents to make educational choices, by providing vouchers or through competition within the public school system (e.g., magnet schools, charter schools, and open enrollment/transfer plans). Coleman traced both approaches to the "egalitarian" impulse of achieving racial integration in schools, although he favored measures that expand rather than diminish parental options.

By the 1980s, Coleman (along with Kilgore and Hoffer, 1982a) analyzed the High School and Beyond (HSB) data set—the nation's largest longitudinal study of schools effects, involving 28,000 sample students attending 1,015 public and private schools. In 1980, sophomore and senior students from public and private high schools were tested in language arts, science, social studies, and mathematics. Using the data as a synthetic cohort, Coleman and colleagues found that Catholic schools upheld the "common school ideal"; that is, the effects of family background on achievement were lower in the Catholic schools. "Average" students were more likely to take rigorous academic courses, thereby producing better results. Thus, Catholic schools avoided the "stratifying" practices, in Coleman's words, of a "'public' school system that no longer integrates the various segments of the population of students, but appears no more egalitarian than private education, and considerably less egalitarian in outcome than the major portion of the private sector in America—the Catholic schools" (1982a, p. 196).

Social capital was defined by Coleman as "the set of resources that inhere in family relations and in community social organization and that are useful for the cognitive or social development of a child or young person" (1990, p. 300). He thus found an empirical referent for his social theory, based on a large-scale national survey: that the Catholic parish, which supported the parish school, united to improve the education of children: the corollary of the phrase, "it takes a village to raise a child." Coleman and Hoffer discovered that since Catholic high schools possessed more "social capital," their students tended to outperform public school pupils from similar backgrounds and neighborhoods. He further explained the importance of social cohesion that has diminished with social progress.

> Primordial social organization has depended on a vast supply of social capital, on a normative structure which enforced obligations, guaranteed trustworthiness, induced efforts on behalf of others, and on behalf of the primordial corporate bodies themselves, and suppressed free riding. The social capital has been eroded, leaving many lacunas. Perhaps the most important area in which erosion has occurred is in the regeneration of society through the nurturing of the next generation [e.g., education]. (1990, p. 651)

Coleman's research managed to stir up considerable controversy when he applied his theories and methods to the field of educational sociology. The work *Public and Private High Schools* (1987) written with Hoffer was perceived to threaten the hegemony of public schools and to elevate the effectiveness of faith-based (Roman Catholic) schools in the authors' attempt to help inner-city students. Its release brought negative reactions from the more liberal, public school establishment, as well as many of the radical equalitarians who had supported his earlier research on school integration.And a number of researchers, such as Jay Noel in 1982 and Karl Alexander and Aaron Palls in 1985, attacked Coleman's study of differing achievement in Catholic and public high schools. J. Douglas Willms, for example, reanalyzed the High School and Beyond data set and published the results in 1985, having studied 21,772 public and Catholic school students and using longitudinal data (sophomores and seniors). He determined that "no pervasive Catholic-school effect," was present although "we cannot be certain that the tests were sensitive enough to detect differences between Catholic and public school effects on students' achievement" (p. 113).

Redefining American Education

Coleman's work shows a pattern in which the process of social progress depends, to a large extent, on the extension of rights, choice, and resources to disenfranchised groups. He argues that any new "allocation of rights" results not simply from new

information but from a multistage process including: "information changes beliefs; the new beliefs show a conflict of rights; [and] the conflict of rights comes to be resolved by a change in one or the other right." (1990, p. 56)

For example, Coleman interpreted the 1954 *Brown v. Board of Education* court decision as vindicating the right of African-American parents not to have their children assigned to distant schools when schools attended by white children were closer. The findings from the Coleman Report suggested that children from poor backgrounds perform better academically when they attend school with children from more affluent families. In this case, African-American children benefit when they are bused to distant (integrated) schools. Thus, new information "brought into conflict the right to equal educational opportunity and the right of parents not to have their children assigned to a distant school on the basis of an arbitrary ground such as race" (Coleman et al. 1966, p. 56). Coleman thought a final resolution to the busing and integration issue had yet to occur.

Toward the end of his life, Coleman asked how educational systems might be more accountable, especially when evaluating students' academic achievement. In an essay published posthumously (1997), he advocated the principle of "output-driven" systems "in which the rewards and punishments for performance in productive activity come from the recipient of the product" (p. 25). He noted that educators sought alternatives to standardized testing, especially avoiding multiple-choice tests, for both good reasons (because there are more accurate methods of assessment) and bad reasons (such as the supposed stigma connected with poor scores or grades).

For instance, Coleman examined the increasingly popular method of alternative performance assessment, the use of portfolios. He contended that portfolio analysis, based on the idea that academic achievement is analogous to artistic or athletic performance, is attractive to many educators. In Coleman's judgment, however, the use of portfolios was subjective in nature, lacking in external standards, determined by teachers' vested interests, and without a stimulus for improvement. Coleman objected to such "soft" measures, stating that "the strongest drive toward performance assessment comes from the leveling impulse: i.e., from the aim of eliminating comparative evaluation in schools" (1997, p. 37).

Contribution to Education

Thus, in his last publications, as in his earlier ones, Coleman grounded his theoretical ideas in rigorous empirical data and an insistence on being able to measure academic results. Portfolios were to Coleman just another mushy example of educational predeterminism, rather than realistic, hard-nosed, data-based outcomes. To Coleman, nothing in social life was easy. For as he explained, "the threat [portfolios] pose is not inherent in performance assessment, but lies in the ease with which performance assessment can be made compatible with reduced performance levels by those who would eliminate competition in schools" (1997, p. 37). Even in death, Coleman managed to capture attention and stir controversy.

See also: GOVERNMENT AND EDUCATION, THE CHANGING ROLE OF; POVERTY AND EDUCATION; RACE, ETHNICITY, AND CULTURE.

BIBLIOGRAPHY

ALEXANDER, KARL L., and PALLAS, AARON M. 1985. "School Sector and Cognitive Performance: What Is a Little a Little?" *Sociology of Education* 58:115–128.

COLEMAN, JAMES S. 1961. *The Adolescent Society.* Glencoe, IL: The Free Press.

COLEMAN, JAMES S. 1990. *Equality and Achievement in Education.* Boulder, CO: Westview Press.

COLEMAN, JAMES S. 1990. *Foundations of Social Theory.* Cambridge, MA: The Belknap Press of Harvard University.

COLEMAN, JAMES S., and HOFFER, THOMAS. 1987. *Public and Private High Schools: The Impact of Communities.* New York: Basic Books.

COLEMAN, JAMES S.; HOFFER, THOMAS; and KILGORE, SALLY. 1982a. "Achievement and Segregation in Secondary Schools: A Further Look at Public and Private School Differences." *Sociology of Education* 55:162–182.

COLEMAN, JAMES S.; HOFFER, THOMAS; and KILGORE, SALLY. 1982b. *High School Achievement: Public, Catholic and Private Schools Compared.* New York: Basic Books.

COLEMAN, JAMES S., et al. 1966. *Equality of Educational Opportunity.* Washington, DC: U.S. Department of Health, Education and Welfare.

COLEMAN, JAMES S., et al. 1977. *Parents, Teachers, and Children: Prospects for Choice in American Education.* San Francisco: Institute for Contemporary Studies.

COLEMAN, JAMES S., et al. 1997. *Redesigning American Education.* Boulder, CO: Westview.

COOPER, BRUCE S. 1995. "In Memoriam: Tribute to James S. Coleman: The Man and His Research." *Journal of Research on Christian Education* 4(2):151–156.

GAMORAN, ADAM; SECADA, WALTER G.; and MARRETT, CORA B. 2000. "The Organizational Context of Teaching and Learning." In *Handbook of the Sociology of Education,* ed. Maureen T. Hallinan. New York: Kluwer.

HALLINAN, MAUREEN T. 2000. "On the Linkages between Sociology of Race and Ethnicity and Sociology of Education." In *Handbook of the Sociology of Education,* ed. Maureen T. Hallinan. New York: Kluwer.

NOELL, JAY. 1982. "Public and Catholic Schools: A Reanalysis of 'Public and Private Schools.'" *Sociology of Education* 55:123–132.

SCHMIDT, PETER. 1995. "James S. Coleman, Author of Landmark Education Studies, Dies." *Education Week* April 5:11–12.

WILLMS, J. DOUGLAS. 1985. "Catholic-School Effects on Academic Achievement: New Evidence from the High School and Beyond Follow-Up Study." *Sociology of Education* 58(2):98–114.

BRUCE S. COOPER
TIMOTHY S. VALENTINE

COLLEGE ADMISSIONS

Applying for admission to colleges and universities has evolved from a relatively straightforward process to a complex rite of passage that causes anxiety for many high school students. Increased media attention about college admissions during the late 1980s and 1990s facilitated the growth of a booming college admissions industry. Commercial test-preparation courses, independent counselors, annual college rankings by news magazines, and a wide range of guidebooks are now a routine part of the college admissions landscape.

Despite this plethora of advice on how to "beat" the admissions process, institutions of higher education vary greatly in their selectivity. Many community colleges, for example, have an open-access policy and admit any applicant with a high school diploma or its equivalent. On the other hand, the most competitive universities admit as few as 10 to 20 percent of their applicants.

Colleges establish enrollment goals based on considerations such as tuition revenue projections, financial aid budgets, housing availability, and the number of currently enrolled students. Since many applicants apply to more than one institution, not every offer of admission that a college extends will result in a student enrolling there. Colleges therefore admit more students than they hope to enroll. The percentage of students who accept an institution's offer of admission is known as a college's *yield rate*. Because this number is difficult to predict from year to year, some institutions maintain a wait list for applicants. If a college has not reached its target enrollment after regularly admitted applicants accept or decline their offers of admission, it may admit students on its wait list.

The Admissions Process

The admissions process is based on the submission of written applications and supporting credentials. In the late 1990s many colleges began offering the option of online applications, available through institutions' websites or through commercial third parties. While most students use application forms specific to a particular institution, a form called the Common Application reduces the volume of paperwork for students applying to participating institutions. Most institutions require an application fee, although students with severe financial hardships sometimes obtain fee waivers with the support of their guidance counselors.

Applications usually require submission of an official high school transcript, an official college transcript if the student has completed previous college coursework, a guidance counselor recommendation, teacher recommendations, and official results from either the SAT I or the ACT Assessment. Some selective colleges require the SAT II subject tests, which they sometimes use for placement purposes. In addition, many applications require one or more essays, and some colleges require interviews with admissions staff, alumni, or current students. Additional information may be required for transfer or international students.

Application Options

Many institutions have a strict admissions timetable to which applicants must adhere. Application deadlines can range from early fall of the senior year in high school to the summer before desired enrollment. The following are among colleges' most common application options, and an institution may offer one or more of these:

- **Regular decision.** Deadlines for submitting applications and supporting credentials for fall semester admission typically fall between December and March. Most institutions that follow this traditional schedule mail admissions decisions in late March or early April and ask students to notify them of their enrollment decisions by May 1.
- **Rolling admissions.** Some colleges offer a rolling admissions process, in which applications are reviewed and evaluated as they are received. These institutions notify students of their admissions status as decisions are made.
- **Early action.** Some colleges have a fall application deadline for students who wish to receive notification of their admissions status in December or January. Colleges may admit or deny these applicants, or they may opt to reconsider them under the regular decision process. Receiving an early offer of admission can be a relief for students, and students who are denied admission usually still have time to apply to other colleges. Some institutions ask that applicants apply for early action at only one college, while others do not have this restriction.
- **Early decision.** This process differs from early action in that students agree to attend the institution if offered admission. In addition, they must withdraw their applications from all other institutions if admitted. As students may apply to only one institution using this option, it is appropriate only for students who are certain about their first-choice college. In some cases, applying for early decision can have ramifications for financial aid.

Counselors generally recommend the early action and early decision options only for students with strong academic records through the junior year. Weaker applicants may improve their applications by retaking a standardized test or improving their grades during the fall of their senior year.

Some variations exist in the above timetable. In special cases, for example, highly qualified students may be permitted to enroll after their junior year in high school. Some colleges will agree to defer an offer of admission for students who wish to work or travel for a year between high school and college. Accepting a position on a college's wait list may prolong the college admissions process well into the summer before desired enrollment. Some institutions may admit a student with provisions (e.g., asking that he or she take a summer remedial skills course prior to being fully admitted to the college).

Offers of admission to high school seniors usually include the stipulation that the student must maintain satisfactory academic performance. Colleges may revoke offers of admission to students whose grades decline significantly during their second semester.

Application review procedures vary widely by institution. Some colleges have admissions officers independently rate applications, while others utilize committees comprising admissions personnel, faculty, or current students. Institutions are legally bound to adhere to their publicized admissions standards, honor their admissions decisions, and refrain from unjustifiably discriminating on the basis of race, sex, age, disability, or citizenship. At the end of the twentieth century, however, the legality of affirmative action, one of the most controversial practices in college admissions, began to be challenged in the courts.

Weight of Credentials

No particular set of credentials guarantees admission to the most selective institutions, as these colleges receive many more qualified applicants than they are able to admit. The process is subjective, and often several individuals will review each application.

Colleges usually identify the high school transcript as the most important credential. They consider rigor of coursework, grade point average (GPA), and sometimes class rank. Institutions typically publish their minimum expectations for applicants' high school curriculum. In evaluating the transcript, most colleges highly regard honors, Advanced Placement (AP), and International Baccalaureate (IB) courses. Some colleges look primarily at the number of years a student has studied each subject (e.g., three years of foreign language); others look to see that a certain course level has been attained (e.g., completion of Algebra II). Many col-

leges view applicants' coursework in the context of what their high schools offer. Most high schools send colleges a profile that includes information about grading practices, curriculum, extracurricular opportunities, and the socioeconomic environment of the school. This gives admissions officers a way to judge the work of students at high schools with which they are unfamiliar. Institutions vary as to whether they will consider GPAs and class ranks that are weighted for honors, AP, or IB courses; some recalculate GPAs to be consistent across applications. Likewise, institutions differ as to whether they include nonacademic courses, such as physical education or fine arts, as part of the applicant's GPA.

Standardized tests, especially the SAT and ACT Assessment, continue to play an important role in the admissions process at most colleges, despite concerns about the differential performance of disadvantaged students on these tests. Some institutions, especially public universities, use admissions formulas that combine standardized test scores and grade point average. Most institutions, however, consider standardized tests as only one aspect of a student's application. Standardized tests provide a uniform yardstick against which all applicants are measured—unlike grades, which may reflect differences in high schools' academic rigor.

Institutions look to counselor and teacher recommendations to better understand an applicant. While an outstanding counselor recommendation can hold great weight with an admissions committee, admissions officers recognize that guidance counselors may not know each individual applicant well. Teacher recommendations help with this situation, as teachers tend to have more face-to-face contact with individual students. Recommendations can help colleges to understand the challenges that applicants have faced and the extent to which students have contributed to their high school communities.

Good essays also help admissions officers better understand applicants or see a side of the applicant not evident in the rest of the application. Admissions officers judge essays with an eye toward content and quality of writing. Colleges expect essays to be the applicant's own work.

Applications usually include space for students to list their extracurricular activities. Some institutions allow applicants to submit videos, slides, or other materials that document special talents in areas such as sports or the arts, and many colleges give special consideration to applicants with extraordinary talents.

See also: ADVANCED PLACEMENT COURSES/EXAMS; COLLEGE ADMISSIONS TESTS; COLLEGE FINANCIAL AID; COLLEGE RECRUITMENT PRACTICES; COLLEGE SEARCH AND SELECTION.

BIBLIOGRAPHY

GUERNSEY, LISA. 1998. "Admissions in Cyberspace: Web Sites Bring Complications for Colleges." *Chronicle of Higher Education* October 9:A27.

HERNÁNDEZ, MICHELE A. 1997. *A Is for Admission: The Insider's Guide to Getting into the Ivy League and Other Top Colleges.* New York: Warner Books.

HOOVER, ERIC. 2002. "New Attacks of Early Decision." *Chronical of Higher Education* January 11:A45.

HOSSLER, DON. 1984. *Enrollment Management: An Integrated Approach.* New York: College Entrance Examination Board.

KAPLAN, WILLIAM A., and LEE, BARBARA A. 1997. "Admissions." In *A Legal Guide for Student Affairs Professionals,* ed. William A. Kaplan and Barbara A. Lee. San Francisco: Jossey-Bass.

MCDONOUGH, PATRICIA M. 1997. *Choosing Colleges: How Social Class and Schools Structure Opportunity.* Albany, NY: State University of New York Press.

SKRENTNY, JOHN D. 2001. "Affirmative Action and New Demographic Realities." *Chronicle of Higher Education* February 16:B7.

INTERNET RESOURCES

ACT ASSESSMENT. 2002. <www.act.org/aap>.

COLLEGE BOARD. 2002. <www.collegeboard.com>.

COMMON APPLICATION. 2002. <www.commonapp.org>.

NATIONAL ASSOCIATION FOR COLLEGE ADMISSION COUNSELING. 2002. <www.nacac.com>.

KATHRYN A. BALINK

COLLEGE ADMISSIONS TESTS

The ACT Assessment and SAT are the most popular college entrance tests administered in the United States.

The ACT

The ACT Assessment, formerly called the American College Test, is a standardized examination required by many colleges and universities in the United States for admission to their undergraduate degree programs. The test was developed in 1959 to measure the academic abilities of prospective college students and provided an alternative to the SAT. The ACT is a two-hour and fifty-five-minute multiple-choice exam that measures English, mathematics, reading, and science reasoning skills. Students are also required to complete two questionnaires that cover the courses they have taken, their grades and activities, and a standardized interest inventory. The test battery includes four parts: (1) a 45-minute, 75-item English test; (2) a 60-minute, 60-item mathematics test; (3) a 35-minute, 40-item reading test; and (4) a 35-minute, 40-item science reasoning test. Each of the tests is scored on a scale from one to thirty-six; the four scores are combined into a composite score of one to thirty-six. Most students who take the test score within the range of seventeen to twenty-three.

Most students take the ACT during the spring of their junior year or at the beginning of their senior year. Students are allowed to take the test more than once, and most colleges and universities count the highest score reported. Students may designate the colleges and universities to which their scores should be reported.

The SAT

The SAT, formerly called the Scholastic Aptitude Test and later the Scholastic Assessment Test, is an examination that is required by some of the higher education institutions within the United States for admission to their undergraduate degree programs. The SAT dates to the early 1900s when Ivy League schools formed the College Entrance Examination Board (College Board). The purpose of the board was to simplify the application process for students who were required to take a different entrance exam for each college they applied to. The SAT was designed as a standardized entrance exam for the College Board that required students to write out answers and compose essays.

In the early 1990s the test was redesigned to measure verbal and mathematical reasoning through multiple-choice questions. The revised SAT includes two separate divisions of the exam: the SAT I, which is a general test of verbal and math ability, and the SAT II, which tests knowledge in specialized subjects chosen by the student. The verbal and math portion of the test devotes seventy-five minutes to the verbal section and sixty minutes to the mathematics section. The verbal portion comprises three kinds of questions, as noted by Alexandra Beatty and colleagues in 1998: (1) analogy questions, which assess "knowledge of the meaning of words," ability to see a relationship in a pair of words, and the ability to recognize a similar or parallel relationship; (2) sentence completion questions, which assess "knowledge of the meaning of words" and "ability to understand how the different parts of a sentence fit logically together"; and (3) critical reading questions, which assess "ability to read and think carefully about several reading passages" (p. 18).

The mathematics section of the test assesses how well the students understand mathematics, how well they can apply what is known to new situations, and how well they are able to use the knowledge they have acquired to solve difficult mathematical problems. Each of the sections generates a score on a scale of 200 to 800, with the combined scores ranging from 400 to 1,600. Nationwide, average scores on both the verbal and math sections of the test are approximately 500.

Test Scores and Their Relationship to Admissions Selectivity

There is some misunderstanding pertaining to the validity and importance of college entrance test scores. While test scores weigh heavily in admissions decisions, they are not the only variable that is considered in admitting a student to even the most selective institution of higher learning. Most colleges and universities use the test scores as a means of assessing a candidate for admission. Other criteria included in this assessment are the high school grade point average (GPA), rank in class, record of extracurricular and service activities, letters of recommendation, applicant's essay, evidence of persistence, and interviews, which assist the college or university in determining the applicant's maturity, determination, personality, and character. High school GPAs are considered a "soft" measure because grading standards range as widely as they do in college. Nevertheless, GPAs are considered more important than test scores because they are inclusive of several years of performance, not just a few hours of testing.

The combination of high school GPAs and ACT or SAT test scores is very useful in determining admissions because it provides different kinds of information about the academic performance of students. Test scores and GPAs provide reliable and efficient information that is very useful to many admissions counselors. Test scores were not designed, however, to be a comprehensive approach to all factors that influence success in college. Admissions personnel rely as much on high school GPAs or class rank as they do on test scores, and the predictor of college success is higher for both numbers together than for either one alone.

The ACT and the SAT can be very helpful in assisting colleges in admissions selectivity when there are more applicants than the college can accept. The colleges believe that the tests are one excellent means of helping them to make a better selection of the candidates who apply. For instance, colleges that specialize in the liberal arts and humanities would seek students with higher scores in verbal aptitude and lower scores in mathematics aptitude, whereas engineering colleges would seek students with high scores in mathematics aptitude and lower scores in verbal aptitude.

Over the years, college entrance tests have improved considerably. Colleges and universities have determined that students who do well on the tests have the ability to succeed in college. These tests, however, are indicators only of a student's ability to do college work; they cannot measure perseverance and interest in learning.

See also: COLLEGE ADMISSIONS; COLLEGE ENTRANCE EXAMINATION BOARD, THE; COLLEGE FINANCIAL AID; COLLEGE SEARCH AND SELECTION.

BIBLIOGRAPHY

NATIONAL RESEARCH COUNCIL. STEERING COMMITTEE FOR THE WORKSHOP ON HIGHER EDUCATION ADMISSIONS. 1998. *Myths and Tradeoffs: The Role of Tests in Undergraduate Admissions,* ed. Alexandra Beatty, M.R.C. Greenwood, and Robert L. Linn. Washington, DC: National Academy Press.

OWEN, DAVID. 1999. *None of the Above: The Truth behind the SATs,* revised edition. Lanham, MD: Rowman and Littlefield.

WECHSLER, LOUIS K.; BLUM, MARTIN; and FRIEDMAN, SIDNEY. 1967. *College Entrance Examinations.* New York: Barnes and Noble.

SUSAN WEST

COLLEGE AND ITS EFFECT ON STUDENTS

Among the earliest systematic analyses of college outcomes are those of C. Robert Pace (1941, 1979); James Trent and Leland Medsker (1968); and Kenneth Feldman and Theodore Newcomb (1969). Focusing on both longitudinal changes and cross-sectional differences, this body of research generated some of the first significant impressions of the efficacy of college attendance. By and large, these studies explored basic distinctions between those who attended college and those who did not. Beginning with analyses of standardized achievement-test data and alumni surveys from single institutions, and progressing to syntheses of multi-institutional assessments, this early literature was quite convincing, albeit preliminarily, in its conclusion that postsecondary education made a significant positive difference in the lives of students, both during and following college attendance.

Early Work on the Impact of College

C. Robert Pace, whose pioneering work ranged from *They Went to College* (1941) to *Measuring Outcomes of College* (1979), concluded, after reviewing some fifty years of findings on college outcomes, that "college graduates as a group, of all ages and in all periods, more frequently possess knowledge about public affairs, people in the news, geography, history, humanities, sciences, and popular culture than do adults who had lesser amounts of schooling" (1979, p. 168). In addition to these gains in general education knowledge, the benefits beyond college, Pace observed, are apparent from reports of alumni who typically "have good jobs and good incomes, like their jobs, think their college experience was relevant and useful in their work, look back on their college years with considerable satisfaction, participate to a considerable extent in a variety of civic and cultural activities, and believe that college contributed to their breadth of knowledge, interpersonal skills, values, and critical thinking" (1979, p. 168).

Between 1959 and 1963 James Trent and Leland Medsker followed the paths of 10,000 high school graduates who either pursued postsecondary education or moved directly into the work force. Of these two groups, those who completed college following high school showed greater gains in autonomy and intellectual disposition. More specifically, college graduates were "less stereotyped and prejudiced in their judgments, more critical in their thinking, and more tolerant, flexible, and autonomous in attitude" (pp. 129–130). These outcomes were most evident, regardless of the type of institution attended, among those who graduated, followed by those who withdrew, those who sought employment immediately following high school, and those identified as "homemakers." *Exceptional changers*, that is, those who had experienced unusually high gains on these outcome measures, in comparison to *average changers* and *negative changers*, those who had experienced average gains or losses on these measures, were represented proportionally by more males than females and by students with higher levels of parental education and occupation. Exceptional change on a measure of social maturity was found to be related to "openness to ideas, tolerance of different points of view, and self direction" (p. 197).

Factors associated with negative change were "limited ability, limited education, a constricted socioeconomic background, over-dependence on a dogmatic or fundamentalistic religion, and an unenlightened, unstimulating, and autocratic family background" (p. 212). College graduates "emphasized general education as the most important purpose of education," in comparison to those who withdrew, who "placed more importance on vocational training" (p. 227). Trent and Medsker concluded that, "rather than effecting the changes, the college may facilitate change for many predisposed to it. But whether the process is facilitation or reinforcement, the specific catalysts for change have yet to be identified" (pp. 195–196).

Kenneth Feldman and Theodore Newcomb were the first to comprehensively catalog and analyze extant research on college impact. Their 1969 review attempted "to integrate a wide variety of studies of the effects of colleges on students over a forty-year period from the middle twenties to the middle sixties" (p. 2), with a particular focus on data relative to six value domains: theoretical, economic, aesthetic, social, political, and religious. They found the most consistent freshman-to-senior changes were that a higher relative importance was placed on aesthetics and a lower importance was placed on religious values.

Feldman and Newcomb's analysis is particularly instructive of the challenge in measuring attitude changes, especially in considering their extensity, intensity, and direction. Reliance on freshman-to-senior group differences to chart changes can mask any number of dynamics in the data that may implicate significant impacts. Group averages are influenced by the number of individuals who change (extensity) and the degree to which each of them changes (intensity). The largest changes would entail both high extensity and high intensity of effect, just as small changes would indicate low degrees of these factors. In between are intermediate changes, reflecting potential combinations of high intensity changes among few individuals or lower intensity changes among many.

Direction of change must also be considered, as six potential patterns may be apparent. First is the *accentuation* of an attitude, from a moderately favorable or unfavorable form to one that is strongly held. Second is the *regression* of an attitude, as indicated by movement to a more neutral position from a previously held favorable or unfavorable attitude. Third is the *conversion* of an attitude from a favorable to an unfavorable form, or vice versa. Fourth is the *maintenance* of an attitude, evident in the reinforcement or retention of an attitude in its current form (favorable or unfavorable). Fifth is the *neutralization* of an attitude when a favorable or unfavorable attitude dissipates toward a neutral form. Sixth and final is the *formation* of an attitude from a neutral position to one that is either favorable or unfavorable.

Nine Generalizations

Feldman and Newcomb concluded their analysis with nine generalizations regarding college impacts and the various experiences and factors associated with them. First, the authors state, "freshman-to-senior changes in several characteristics have been occurring with considerable uniformity in most American colleges and universities," namely "declining 'authoritarianism,' dogmatism, and prejudice, together with decreasingly conservative attitudes toward public issues and growing sensitivity to aesthetic experiences" (p. 326).

Second, they found that "the degree and nature of different colleges' impacts vary with their student

inputs, . . . those characteristics in which freshman-to-senior change is distinctive for a given college will also have been distinctive for its entering freshmen" (pp. 327–328). In other words, the most prominent changes among students owe much to an accentuation or reinforcement effect of their initial characteristics.

Third, the same accentuation effect that operates to distinguish one institution from another also differentiates students in one major from those in another. "Whatever characteristics distinguish entrants into different majors tend, especially if relevant to the academic field chosen, to become still more distinctive of those groups following the pursuit of the major" (p. 329).

Fourth, "the maintenance of existing values or attitudes which, apart from certain kinds of college experience, might have been weakened or reversed, is an important kind of impact" (p. 329). This insight underscores the potential effect an absence of "reinforcing or consolidating experiences" might have, such as the case of students who bid unsuccessfully to join an on-campus group (e.g., fraternity or service club) and subsequently develop "attitudes more closely resembling those of students with whom they continued to live" (p. 330).

Fifth, Feldman and Newcomb claim, "though faculty members are often individually influential, particularly in respect to career decisions, college faculties do not appear to be responsible for campus-wide impact except in settings where the influence of student peers and of faculty complement and reinforce one another" more on a professional than a personal level (p. 330).

Sixth, "the conditions for campus-wide impacts appear to have been most frequently provided in small, residential, four-year colleges . . . [where there is a] relative homogeneity of both faculty and student body together with opportunity for continuing interaction, not exclusively formal, among students and between students and faculty" (p. 331). Having human-scale opportunities for interacting around shared interests and characteristics is an apparent requisite for such outcomes.

Seventh, "college impacts are conditioned by the background and personality of the student" (p. 332). In terms of background characteristics, "the more incongruent a student is with the overall environment of his [sic] college the more likely he is to withdraw from that college or from higher education in general" (p. 332). However, personal characteristics, such as openness to change and a willingness to be influenced by others, can enhance the impact potential of the college experience.

Eighth, "attitudes held by students on leaving college tend to persist thereafter, particularly as a consequence of living in post-college environments that support those attitudes" (p. 332). This is particularly the case when students' habits of being open to new information and being influenced persist as new opportunities arise.

Ninth, "whatever the characteristics of an individual that selectively propel him [sic] toward particular educational settings—such as going to college, selecting a particular one, choosing a certain academic major, or acquiring membership in a particular group of peers—those same characteristics are apt to be reinforced and extended by the experiences incurred in those selected settings" (p. 333). This *accentuation hypothesis* asserts that "if students initially having certain characteristics choose a certain setting (a college, a major, a peer group) in which those characteristics are prized and nurtured, accentuation of such characteristics is likely to occur" (p. 335). From this point of view, the impact of college is related to the fit between a student and an institution.

Later Studies

Constituting a second wave of notable literature on the impact of college are the works of Howard Bowen (1977), Alexander Astin (1977, 1993), and Ernest Pascarella and Patrick Terenzini (1991). These more recent analyses are characterized by their more comprehensive scope, their attention to the myriad factors that contribute qualitatively to the college experience, and the depth of their synthesis of extant data. They also draw from theories that attempt to integrate the various components that contribute to college outcomes.

Howard Bowen, in *Investment in Learning* (1977), constructed a framework of higher-education goals related to outcomes for individual students. First, *cognitive learning outcomes* include verbal skills, quantitative skills, substantive knowledge, rationality, intellectual tolerance, aesthetic sensibility, creativeness, intellectual integrity, wisdom, and lifelong learning. Second are outcomes related to *emotional and moral development,* which include personal self-discovery, psychological well-being,

human understanding, values and morals, religious interest, and refinement of taste, conduct, and manner. Third is *practical competence,* including traits of value in practical affairs (such as need for achievement, future orientation, adaptability, and leadership), citizenship, economic productivity, sound family life, consumer efficiency, fruitful leisure, and health.

Reviewing the cumulative weight of evidence, Bowen concluded that "higher education, taken as a whole, is enormously effective" (p. 431) in terms of its contributions to positive individual and societal changes. On average, a college education "produces a large increase in substantive knowledge; moderate increases in verbal skills, intellectual tolerance, esthetic [sic] sensibility, and lifelong cognitive development; and small increases in mathematical skills, rationality, and creativity" (p. 432). In regards to affective outcomes, for example, college "helps students a great deal in finding their personal identity and in making lifetime choices congruent with this identity. It increases moderately their psychological well-being as well as their understanding, human sympathy, and tolerance toward ethnic and national groups and toward people who hold differing opinions" (p. 433). It also "greatly enhances the practical competence of its students as citizens, workers, family members, and consumers," in addition to influencing, in positive ways, "their leisure activities, their health, and their general ability to cope with life's problems" (p. 434). Significant positive changes in personality structures are also evident, namely in the "liberation of the personality as the most distinctive and important outcome" (p. 435), in becoming "more independent and self-sufficient" (p. 436), and in gaining a range of intrinsic values and interests.

Alexander Astin's two research compendiums stand as additional landmarks during this period in the study of college and its effect on students. First, in *Four Critical Years* (1977), and subsequently in *What Matters in College* (1993), Astin synthesized data gathered through the Cooperative Institutional Research Program (CIRP), surveying some 200,000 students from 300 postsecondary institutions of all types. Both of these volumes are rich in detail in their framing of the *inputs* (or characteristics of students at the point of entry to college), *environments* (various programs, policies, faculty, peers, and educational experiences to which students are exposed), and *outcomes* (students' characteristics after exposure to the environment) that figure into the mix of college-impact research. These three sources of data are placed within a taxonomy comprised of *outcomes* (cognitive versus affective), *data types* (psychological versus behavioral), and *timeframes* (during college versus after college).

Among the types of outcomes in this model are *cognitive measures,* including knowledge, critical thinking ability, basic skills, and academic achievement. These outcomes are reflected in both psychological data, relating to the "internal states or traits of the individual" and behavioral data, relating to "directly observable activities" (p. 9), such as certain aspects of career development, level of educational attainment, and vocational achievements (e.g., level of responsibility, income, and awards or special recognition). *Affective outcomes* incorporate those of a psychological nature, such as self-concept, values, attitudes, beliefs, drive for achievement, and satisfaction with college, as well as behavioral factors, such as personal habits, avocations, mental health, citizenship, and interpersonal relations. A temporal dimension considers that colleges and universities are interested in both short-term (during college) and long-term (after college) effects.

Overall, two decades of CIRP data show that, in the affective realm, "students change in many ways after they enter college," developing a "more positive self image, . . . substantial increases in Social Activism, Feminism, alcohol consumption, and support for legal abortions," as well as "increases in their commitment to participate in programs to clean up the environment, to promote racial understanding, and to develop a meaningful philosophy of life" (Astin, pp. 396–397). Cognitively, students report "substantial growth in most areas of knowledge and skills, especially in knowledge of a field or discipline" (p. 397).

Regarding factors that contribute to such changes, Astin tenders several general conclusions. First, "the student's *peer group* is the single most potent source of influence on growth and development during the undergraduate years." That is, "students' values, beliefs, and aspirations tend to change in the direction of the dominant values, beliefs, and aspirations of the peer group" (p. 398). Following the peer group, "the *faculty* represents the most significant aspect of the student's undergraduate development" (p. 410). Underlying all of this is the dynamic of student involvement and its potential "for enhancing most aspects of the undergraduate student's cogni-

tive and affective development" (p. 394). More specifically, "learning, academic performance, and retention are positively associated [proportionately] with academic involvement, involvement with faculty, and involvement with student peer groups" (p. 394). In addition, "living at home, commuting, being employed off-campus, being employed full-time, and watching television" (p. 395) tend to negatively affect these same outcomes. Last, it appears clear that "most effects of institutional type [e.g., public versus private, four-year college versus university, small versus large] are indirect; that is, they are mediated by faculty, peer group, and involvement variables" (p. 413).

Pascarella and Terenzini

The most comprehensive, systematic review to date on the question of college impact is found in Ernest Pascarella and Patrick Terenzini's tome, *How College Affects Students* (1991). Examining more than 2,600 empirical studies completed over a period of fifty years, the authors considered college outcomes in reference to: (1) verbal, quantitative, and subject matter competence; (2) cognitive skills and intellectual growth; (3) changes of identity, self-concept, and self-esteem; (4) changes in relating to others and the external world; (5) attitudes and values; (6) moral development; (7) educational attainment; (8) career choice and development; (9) economic benefits; and (10) quality of life after college.

Guiding their "narrative explanatory synthesis" of evidence regarding these outcomes were six fundamental questions. First, what evidence is there that individuals change during the time in which they are attending college? This question lies at the base of any comparisons between college attenders and nonattenders and is designed to ferret out data implicating outcomes or changes during the college experience. Second is the question: What evidence is there that change or development during college is the result of college attendance? In other words, can changes be attributed to the college experience itself, rather than other potential influences (e.g., maturation). Such changes are referred to as *net effects of college.*

The third question is: What evidence is there that different kinds of postsecondary institutions have a differential influence on student change or development during college? This query concerns whether different types of institutions (e.g., public, academically selective, small, or financially resourceful institutions) exert differential influences on certain outcomes. These are referred to as *between-college effects*. Fourth is the question: What evidence exists on effects of different experiences within the same institution? For example, do students who live in on-campus residences, select particular majors, interact frequently with faculty, or become involved in extracurricular activities change along these various dimensions to a greater extent than those who don't engage in such experiences. These changes are referred to as *within-college effects*.

Fifth is the question: What evidence is there that the collegiate experience produces conditional, as opposed to general, effects on student change or development? In other words, do different experiences affect different students in different ways? For example, are the outcomes apparent for men as well as for women? For majority students versus minorities? For first generation students? Such outcomes are identified as *conditional effects of college*.

The sixth question guiding Pascarella and Terenzini's synthesis is: What are the *long-term effects* of college? In this final probe, consideration for the durability or permanence of the collegiate experience is paramount. Are the effects of college attendance direct or indirect? That is, are they evident in the lives of students beyond the point of degree completion?

Subject-matter competence. Regarding verbal, quantitative, and subject-matter competence, the evidence for change during college is consistent and compelling. Accordingly, "students make statistically significant gains in general and more specific subject matter knowledge during their undergraduate years" (p. 107), with apparent changes in general verbal skills, general mathematical or quantitative skills, and specific subject-matter knowledge. However, the "net effect of college on verbal skills may be somewhat smaller and the effect on mathematical skills may be somewhat larger than that indicated by typical freshman-to-senior gains" (p. 108). Any evidence for between-college effects on these outcomes suggests that "measures of institutional 'quality' or environmental characteristics have [little] more than a small, perhaps trivial, net influence on how much a student learns during four years of college" (p. 108).

Research related to within-college effects on these outcomes has demonstrated that neither academic major nor small discussion-oriented class-rooms make any appreciable difference in mastery of factual subject matter, although well-sequenced, modular, and individualized strategies, when combined with frequent feedback and student involvement, do make a difference. Furthermore, greater degrees of teacher effort (in terms of command of subject matter, enthusiasm, clarity, organization and structure, and rapport), complemented by student effort, seem to enhance subject-matter learning. Concerning conditional effects, "there is little consistent evidence to suggest that either postsecondary education in general or the type of institution attended in particular has a differential effect on knowledge acquisition for different kinds of students" (p. 110). More consistent, however, is the evidence "that certain kinds of students learn more from one instructional approach than from another" (p. 110). With regard to long-term effects on these outcomes it seems rather clear that "college graduates have a more substantial factual knowledge base" and are more inclined to "engage in activities that are likely to add to their knowledge" (p. 111) than those whose formal education ends with the completion of secondary school.

Cognitive skills. The data in regard to cognitive skills and intellectual growth suggest that "students make statistically significant gains during the college years on a number of dimensions of general cognitive capabilities and skills" (p. 155), including oral and written communication, formal abstract reasoning, critical thinking, the use of reason and evidence to address ill-structured problems, and the ability to deal with conceptual complexity. Most of these gains seem to occur during the first two years of college. Research on the net effects of these outcomes suggests that college has a "net positive influence on diverse measures of critical thinking" (p. 156), reflective judgment, and intellectual flexibility, above and beyond the effects of normal maturation. Perhaps "college is the one [experience] that most typically provides an overall environment where the potential for intellectual growth is maximized" (p. 156).

Between-college effects on intellectual growth are sparsely documented and support the impact of institutional characteristics on general cognitive skills in only limited ways. Some evidence exists, however, to suggest that institutional selectivity and a "strong and balanced curricular commitment to general education" may make a positive difference on these measures. On the other hand, a "strong emphasis on fraternity or sorority life" may inhibit critical thinking (p. 157). Research on within-college effects suggests that various curricular emphases (as reflected in different majors) can influence reasoning processes differentially, as can varying emphases on teaching strategies (e.g., discussion-oriented problem solving), and specially structured interventions. The dynamics of such changes suggest that "cognitive development may be a gradual process characterized by a period of rapid advancement followed by a period of consolidation" (p. 159). Furthermore, such effects also appear to be partially a function of the social and academic integration of students. Evidence of conditional effects on the development of general cognitive skills is inconsistent and sparse, suggesting only limited influence attributed to differences in students or institutional characteristics. Finally, self-reports of impact suggest that college has important long-term effects on cognitive development and thinking skills, as do "intellectually and stimulating work environments" (p. 160), perhaps the kind that are more accessible to college graduates.

Identity. Changes on measures of identity, self-concept, and self-esteem during the college years consistently support a significant positive effect, although not dramatic, for students. The evidence tends to support generally linear gains in academic and social self-concepts, as well as "students' beliefs about themselves in such areas as their popularity in general and with the opposite sex, their leadership abilities, their social self-confidence, and their understanding of others" (p. 203). In addition, they gain in self-esteem. With the caveat that much of the research on the net effects of college on these particular outcomes is too often confounded by age and normal maturation, and absent controls for family background or other relevant characteristics, Pascarella and Terenzini concluded that "postsecondary educational attainment appears to be related positively to changes in students' ratings of themselves relative to their peers" (p. 204), in terms of both academic self-concept and social self-concept. Such effects, however, appear to be small, mostly indirect, and interrelated with other characteristics.

Concerning any between-college effects on these measures, it seems that "what happens to students after they enroll has greater influence on them than where they enroll" (p. 205). Although characteristics such as institutional size and selectivity may exert limited indirect effects, it appears that "there are few

changes in students' self-images and self-esteem associated with attending various kinds of colleges or universities" (p. 205). Research on within-college effects on these measures is even more scant, if not methodologically flawed. Despite other inconsistencies, the data do suggest that "levels of academic and social integration, particularly the degree of involvement with peers and faculty members, are positively related to gains in students' academic and social self-concepts" with peers being "particularly influential" (p. 206).

Support for any conditional effect of college on these measures is quite limited, although there seems to be evidence of a few sex- and race-related differences. All in all, the "effects of educational attainment on academic and social self-concepts are general rather than conditional" (p. 207). Concerning the long-term effects on these outcomes, the benefits of college seem to persist for at least seven to ten years, and probably longer. However, the authors caution educators to withhold confidence in the research in this domain, since the literature is novel and subject to many methodological constraints that warrant a more limited conclusion.

Relating to others. Focusing on changes in relating to others and the external world, Pascarella and Terenzini concluded that, with remarkable consistency, "students' relational systems change during the college years," including increases in "students' freedom from the influences of others, . . . in nonauthoritarian thinking and tolerance for other people and their views, in intellectual orientation to problem solving and their own world view in general, in the maturity of their interpersonal relations, in their personal adjustment skills and general sense of psychological well-being, and in their more globally measured levels of maturity and personal development" (p. 257). It is thought that "the early college years may be somewhat more influential than the later ones" in their effect on these outcomes, although a paucity of research on such questions precludes any firm conclusions in that regard. That these changes are reflective of net gains during college, however, can be claimed only about select but important areas. The authors state that "the weight of evidence therefore fairly clearly supports popular beliefs about the effects of college in helping to reduce students' authoritarianism, dogmatism, and (perhaps) ethnocentrism and in increasing their intellectual orientation, personal psychological adjustment, and sense of psychological well-being" (p. 259).

Evidence for between-college effects in this domain is mixed but suggestive of the claim that "where a student goes to college may make a difference in the kinds of change that are likely to occur in the relational facets of that student's psychosocial makeup. That difference, however, is likely to be slight." Furthermore, it appears that any "institutional effects [are] more likely to follow from differences in institutional context, such as the organizational policies, practices, and interpersonal climate—that students find on campus" (p. 261).

Research on potential within-college effects supports the positive influences of departmental environments, living-learning centers, and interpersonal contacts and relations with peers and faculty on these outcomes, but not necessarily academic majors. With regard to any conditional effects of college on these measures, the data are so limited as to warrant a conclusion only that "nothing can be said with confidence about college effects in any of the six areas reviewed that might be dependent on students' individual characteristics" (p. 262). Lastly, a review of the research on the long-term effects of college on graduates' relational systems offers only a few select influences in that regard.

Attitudes and values. One of the more voluminous agendas for research on college students over the decades has focused on charting changes in student attitudes and values in five general areas: (1) cultural, aesthetic, and intellectual; (2) educational and occupational; (3) social and political; (4) religious; and (5) sex and gender roles. Pascarella and Terenzini found that the evidence for change during the college years is both plentiful and consistent, in that "colleges, as their founders and supporters might hope, appear to have a generally liberating influence on students' attitudes and values. Without exception, the nature and direction of the observed changes involve greater breadth, expansion, inclusiveness, complexity, and appreciation for the new and different. In all cases, the movement is toward greater individual freedom: artistic and cultural, intellectual, political, social, racial, educational, occupational, personal, and behavioral" (p. 326). Research on the net effects of college in that regard support a consistent but modest influence "above and beyond the characteristics students bring with them to college," as well as independent of "changes that have occurred in the larger society" (p. 326).

While consistent evidence suggests that value changes are relatively independent of institutional structural characteristics, implicating few between-college effects, moderate evidence supports the observation that "selective, frequently private institutions . . . exert a relatively greater influence . . . on changes in students' aesthetic and cultural values and interests, their political and social values, and their religiousness" (p. 327).

Within-college effects on values and attitudes seem to be related more to "interpersonal associations students have with faculty members and peers, often in the departmental context, [but] more frequently in the residence halls." However, whether "these influences are exerted through the frequency of contact, . . . the nature of the contact, or the more contextual generalized presence of faculty members and other students who hold a certain set of . . . attitudes and values toward which new students gravitate over time" remains unclear (p. 328). In regard to the conditional influences on these changes, the "literature has little to say about the differential effects of college on values and attitudes for different kinds of students" (p. 329), although what changes do occur seem to persist into adulthood as long-term effects.

Moral development. Long considered an important goal of American higher education, the character education and moral development of students has only recently gained the systematic attention of researchers. Evidence to date suggests that "college is linked with statistically significant increases in the use of principled reasoning to judge moral issues," and that the college experience itself has a unique positive net influence on such development and may be accentuated differentially, from one institution to another, through the student peer context. Furthermore, the key to within-college effects in fostering moral reasoning may "lie in providing a range of intellectual, cultural, and social experiences from which a range of different students might potentially benefit" (p. 366), such as certain curricular or course interventions. Conditional effects in that regard are, in particular, more positive for those of high levels of cognitive development. Nevertheless, any influence in that direction seems to be long-term and consistent, and may even be linked ultimately to "a range of principled behaviors, including resisting cheating, social activism, keeping contractual promises, and helping those in need" (p. 367).

Educational attainment. The benefits of completing formal schooling, or educational attainment, have long been associated with occupational status and social mobility. Between-college effects are apparent in attending a four-year institution, rather than a two-year college; a private or small college, rather than a large one; and, for black students and females, institutions that enroll predominantly black and predominantly women students. College environmental factors, such as a "cohesive peer environment, . . . frequent participation in college-sponsored activities, and a perception that the institution has a high level of personal involvement with and concern for the individual student" (p. 417), also seem to contribute to such an outcome. So too does a strong institutional emphasis on supportive student personnel services, inasmuch as this contributes to higher persistence rates among students. In addition to successful academic achievement, significant within-college effects on educational attainment include "one's level of involvement or integration in an institution's social system" (p. 418), "social interaction with significant others during college, and the encouragement received therefrom," and living on campus, particularly in "living-learning residences that attempt programmatically to integrate the student's academic and social life" (p. 419).

In addition to part-time employment on campus, also linked to educational attainment are various first-year programs "designed to orient the student to the institution and to teach important academic survival skills" (p. 419). Research on conditional effects suggest that varying levels of social and academic integration may compensate for shortcomings in either, especially for "the persistence of students who either enter college with individual traits predictive of withdrawal or who have low commitment to the institution or the goal of graduation from college" (pp. 420–421). Ultimately, existing evidence offers strong support for the long-term generational effects of having obtained a college degree.

Career choice. "It is clear that students frequently change their career plans during college," and that they "become significantly more mature, knowledgeable, and focused during college in thinking about planning for a career" (pp. 487–488). In terms of net influence, one of the "most pronounced and unequivocal effects of college on career is its impact on the type of job one obtains" (p. 488), offering an advantage primarily through occupational status and prestige. Whether by socialization or certification a college education offers access to better-positioned, and potentially more satisfactory, employment. Included among between-college effects are the advantages to occupational status of a four-year degree, an elite institution experience, and to a lesser extent, enrollment in a large institution. Selective colleges also have modest effects on women choosing sex-atypical majors (e.g., engineering). Regardless of where students begin, their selection of a major/occupation tends to reflect the most popular choice at a given institution.

Within-college effects have included varying influences of academic major and achievement, extracurricular accomplishments, interaction with faculty, and work experience. Conditional effects on career choice and development have highlighted varying degrees of positive influence afforded to nonwhite men and women with regard to occupational status in the professions. Last, existing data on long-term effects have detected little direct intergenerational influence on career development, although it is quite clear that "attending and graduating from college is perhaps the single most important determinant of the kind of work an individual does; and the nature of one's work has implications for an array of outcomes that shape one's life" (p. 495).

Economic benefits. Study of the economic benefits has also attracted the attention of higher education researchers, particularly as this factor "probably underlies the motivation of many students who choose to attend college rather than enter the work force immediately after high school graduation" (p. 500). In terms of net effects, it appears that a bachelor's degree "provides somewhere between a 20 and 40 percent advantage in earnings over a high school diploma" and an estimate of financial return on such an investment is "somewhere between 9.3 and 10.9 percent" (p. 529).

Evidence of between-college effects supports the small positive influence on earnings of institutional quality and size, with larger and research-oriented schools having a modest effect. Major field of study and academic achievement have both demonstrated a positive within-college effect on early career earnings. Conditional effects have supported greater economic benefits of postsecondary education for women, especially blacks and other nonwhites.

Influences of institutional selectivity seem to be most pronounced for men from a high socioeconomic background in the private employment sector. Regardless, it appears that college may exert an indirect, positive intergenerational effect on early career earnings, through its influence on parental resources, type of institution attended, and educational attainment.

Quality of life. The final line of inquiry in Pascarella and Terenzini's synthesis focuses on indexes of quality of life after college, including effects of college on subjective well-being, health, committed relationships, family size, parenting, consumer and investment behavior, and leisure. In general, completion of a college education is associated in varying degrees with positive effects on each of these indicators. However, most of these effects seem to be indirect rather than direct, suggesting that a college education probably contributes to a number of intervening outcomes that, in turn, lead to a long-term or enduring positive effect on quality of life.

In summary, two generations of researchers have established the finding that positive individual effects of higher education are related directly to a myriad of factors, such as peer group involvement, interaction with faculty, and time devoted to learning, and indirectly related to a range of institutional characteristics, such as size and mission, inasmuch as they encourage or mitigate such dimensions of engagement. Overall, the impact of college depends much on student-institution fit and the kinds of learning experiences encountered along the way that serve to reinforce compatible characteristics. Cognitive, affective, and practical educational gains are a function, not so much of where a student goes to college, but rather what a student does once enrolled in an institution. In general, the literature appears conclusive in its observation that the greater the involvement, the greater the gain.

See also: AFFECT AND EMOTIONAL DEVELOPMENT; COLLEGE EXTRACURRICULAR ACTIVITIES; COLLEGE STUDENT RETENTION; COLLEGE AND UNIVERSITY RESIDENCE HALLS; MORAL DEVELOPMENT.

BIBLIOGRAPHY

ASTIN, ALEXANDER W. 1977. *Four Critical Years.* San Francisco: Jossey-Bass.

ASTIN, ALEXANDER W. 1993. *What Matters in College.* San Francisco: Jossey-Bass.

ASTIN, ALEXANDER W., and PANOS, R. 1969. *The Educational and Vocational Development of College Students.* Washington, DC: American Council on Education.

BOWEN, HOWARD. 1977. *Investment in Learning: The Individual and Social Value of American Higher Education.* San Francisco: Jossey-Bass.

FELDMAN, KENNETH A., and NEWCOMB, THEODORE M. 1969. *The Impact of College on Students.* San Francisco: Jossey-Bass.

PACE, C. ROBERT. 1941. *They Went to College.* Minneapolis: University of Minnesota Press.

PACE, C. ROBERT. 1979. *Measuring Outcomes of College.* San Francisco: Jossey-Bass.

PASCARELLA, ERNEST T., and TERENZINI, PATRICK T. 1991. *How College Affects Students.* San Francisco: Jossey-Bass.

TRENT, JAMES W., and MEDSKER, LELAND L. 1968. *Beyond High School.* San Francisco: Jossey-Bass.

C. CARNEY STRANGE

COLLEGE AND UNIVERSITY RESIDENCE HALLS

When the English colonized North America, they brought with them the educational traditions and concepts of England. In 1636 the Congregationalists founded Harvard University, using Oxford and Cambridge Universities as their model. With the exception of the Philadelphia Academy and the College of William and Mary, the original nine colonial colleges were founded by graduates of either Oxford or Cambridge. Although the original purpose of residence halls was to help build character and intellect, they also served the practical function of providing basic housing for students, who were as young as thirteen and fourteen years old and frequently traveled great distances to attend college. Living and boarding at a college was a necessity for many students.

Residential facilities on college campuses expanded greatly following World War II with the enrollment of veterans, and in the mid-1960s when the baby boomers began arriving on campuses. Today, more than 60 percent of all traditional-age college students attending a four-year college or university live in a residence hall for at least their first year of college.

Dormitory, or *dorm,* is the popular term used by students to refer to a residence hall. The term comes from the word *dormant,* meaning to sleep. Because these are places where students live, study, learn, and sleep, most student-affairs educators use the more inclusive term *residence hall.*

Purpose of Residence Halls

Although the need to house students is an important function of residence halls, it is not the most important reason for investing institutional resources in these facilities. If the only purpose of residence halls was to house students, off-campus apartment owners could do it equally well and with less cost. Organizing the peer environment in residence halls as a means of facilitating various aspects of students' cognitive and psychosocial growth and development is the principal reason for investing institutional resources in college residence halls.

The residential learning environment is an important vehicle for student learning. It focuses the students' time and energy on college, increases informal interaction with other students, and offers multiple opportunities for students to explore values, lifestyles, and interests in a supportive environment under the administration of student affairs administrators trained in the experiential education of students. Research has clearly demonstrated that living in a college residence hall during the first year of college adds significantly to a student's likelihood of remaining in college and graduating. Compared with students who live at home, students who live in residence halls have more interaction with faculty, participate in more campus activities, have a higher aspiration for graduate education, are more satisfied with college, and generally move beyond their peers who have not lived in residence halls in a range of psychosocial development areas.

Organization and Administration

The administration of college residence halls is usually organized into three major units: residence life programs, housing operations, and room assignments. The purpose of residence life programs is to provide educational programming, nonclinical counseling, and support for student learning. Educators who work in this area are primarily focused on improving the quality of student life, increasing student learning, and building community among students in the residence hall. Professionals who work in housing operations are principally concerned with the daily management, maintenance, construction, and cleanliness of residence halls. This is a complex responsibility because of the number of residence halls, the varying ages of the facilities, and the demands placed on the facilities by college-age students. Professionals who work in the area of room assignments are responsible for assigning students to the rooms, matching roommates, making room changes, and monitoring the occupancy of various facilities. Normally these three functions—residence life, housing, and assignments—are managed by a director of housing and residence life, under the supervision of the division of student affairs.

Residence Hall Staffing

Students spend approximately 80 percent of their time outside the classroom, and much of this time is spent in their residence. A wide range of social and behavioral issues arise in residence halls that demand the attention of college and university administrators. To assist students, and to maintain an educationally rich environment that supports the educational mission of the university, residence halls are usually well staffed by people trained to assist students. On every floor, students are likely to find an undergraduate student who serves as a resident assistant or resident adviser (RA). Students who serve in this role are trained in basic helping skills, have a wide range of information about institutional resources, have responsibility for providing educational programs on their floor, and assist with the enforcement of institutional policies designed to maintain a positive living environment. The most usual organization is one RA per floor, which most often consists of between forty and fifty students.

Also usually living within a residence hall is a hall director or resident director. This person may be a student affairs professional holding a master's degree in college student affairs administration, counseling, or a closely related field; or this person could be a graduate student. Hall directors receive more advanced training and are responsible for the RAs in the building and for the residents of the building. Their responsibilities usually include staff development of their RAs, student counseling, educational programming, enforcement of institutional policies in the residence halls, and may also include other functions such as academic advising, intramural sports adviser, and facilities management. In large residence hall systems, hall directors often report to an area coordinator. This person is a student affairs professional who has several years of experience in residence life and housing and who has responsibility for several residence halls. Responsibilities of area coordinators vary, but usually include hall director and RA selection, staff training, educational programming, community building, enforcement of university policies, crisis intervention, and student counseling. Sometimes these positions also include supervision of maintenance and security personnel. Area coordinators generally report to the director of housing and residence life.

Student affairs professionals who work in residence halls have strong affiliations with a number of professional associations. The Association of College and University Housing Officers-International (ACUHO-I) represents housing and residence life professionals. There are both regional and state divisions of ACCHO-I. Professionals in this field also are involved in national associations that represent student affairs administrators, such as the American College Personnel Association (ACPA) and the National Association of Student Personnel Administrators (NASPA).

Residence Hall Student Government

Most colleges have organized a system of student representation within the residence hall system. Common names for these representational bodies include residence hall government, resident hall council, and campus resident/student associations. These student associations usually have student representatives from every floor in a residence hall, which forms the hall government for that particular building. Representatives from each residence hall on campus form a campus-wide student association of residence hall students. Functions for these student associations vary, but they commonly include some responsibility for educational programming and social events, student input on residence hall policies, and mediation of grievances by residence hall students. Student judicial functions, such as hearing allegations of minor residence hall violations such as noise violations, guest hour violations, or other minor social policies, might also be run by student associations. The national association of students in residence hall government is called the National Association of College and University Residence Halls (NACURH). State and regional groups affiliated with this national association are active in most parts of the United States.

Types of Residence Halls

Residence halls are organized by the sex of the residents living in the facility and by the programmatic function of the residence hall. The most common is a traditional residence hall, which houses undergraduate men separate from undergraduate women. Coeducational residence halls house both men and women. Usually, men live on some floors of the building and women live on other floors, but other arrangements, such as men and women living on the same floor in separate rooms are not uncommon.

Living and learning centers, residential colleges, and learning communities are common forms of special assignment programs in which students live in a residence hall and take one or more of their classes with the other students with whom they live. These programs often require some type of application and selection process and are considered to be a combined academic and residential program with increased faculty involvement and increased student/faculty contact.

Residence hall programs are sometimes organized around a particular academic theme, such as engineering or nursing. Other theme residence halls include freshmen residence halls, honors residence halls, substance-free residence halls, or special lifestyle units based on racial or cultural similarities such as international living units, African-American living units, or Native American living units. The homogeneous assignment of students with common interests or characteristics forms the basis for the programming in that area and for the support services offered to students in the building. The effect of these special lifestyle units is generally to draw a closer relationship between the students' living environment and their learning and studying in the classroom.

Roommate Assignments

The most common form of residence-hall assignment is two students to the same room. Because many college students today come from homes where they did not share a room, the residence hall may provide the first occasion where students are asked to have a roommate. Positive roommate relationships are important for both the emotional and intellectual well-being of students. A number of schemes have been organized to increase roommate compatibility. Among these are assigning rooms on the basis of similar personal habits, such as smoking, neatness, or sleep habits, and matching students on responses to specially designed tests of personal habits and room use activities. Other systems for roommate assignments have included using the Meyers-

Briggs Personality Type Indicator, matching by birth order, and matching by demographic similarities. These systems are based on the premise that the more homogeneous the roommates, the greater the likelihood they will be compatible. Generally the research shows that the most successful form of roommate matching is self-selection where students have identified the person with whom they wish to live. Other forms, such as assignment by similar behavioral traits or by the Meyers-Briggs Type Indicator have also been shown to have some success in increasing roommate compatibility.

Facilities

The architectural design of a college residence hall has an influence on the students' patterns of interaction, on student satisfaction, and on the sense of community in a building. Research in this area shows that student satisfaction and similar outcome measures are inversely related to the size of a residence hall. Students who live in buildings with more students are generally less satisfied than students who live in buildings with a fewer number of students, and students who live in low-rise residence halls (five floors or less) are generally more satisfied than students who live in high-rise residence halls. This same relationship is true for students who live in residence halls with long uninterrupted corridors compared to students who live in residence halls with shorter corridors, suite-style living arrangements, or other architectural designs that break the living unit up into smaller, more manageable, functional areas. Large high-rise buildings are frequently credited with increasing feelings of alienation, hostility, and rootlessness in students, and they tend to inhibit students from establishing a sense of community. Architectural designs that organize students into smaller living units minimize these alienating factors and increase the likelihood that students will develop a greater sense of control over their living environment.

See also: ADJUSTMENT TO COLLEGE; COLLEGE AND ITS EFFECT ON STUDENTS; COLLEGE STUDENT RETENTION; LIVING AND LEARNING CENTER RESIDENCE HALLS.

BIBLIOGRAPHY

ASTIN, ALEXANDER W. 1977. *Four Critical Years.* San Francisco: Jossey-Bass.

ASTIN, ALEXANDER W. 1985. *Achieving Educational Excellence.* San Francisco: Jossey-Bass.

BLIMLING, GREGORY S. 1993. "The Influence of College Residence Halls on Students." In *Higher Education: Handbook of Theory and Research,* Vol. 9, ed. J. Smart. New York: Agathon Press.

BLIMLING, GREGORY S. 1998. *The Resident Assistant: Applications and Strategies for Working With College Students in Residence Halls.* Dubuque, IA: Kendall-Hunt.

BOYER, ERNEST L. 1987. *College: The Undergraduate Experience in America.* New York: Harper and Row.

CARTER, TRAVIS A. 1967. "The Effect of Roommate Ability on the Academic Achievement of College Freshmen." *Dissertation Abstracts International* 27(10):3302A.

COWLEY, WILLIAM H. 1934. "The History of Student Residential Housing." *School and Society* 40:705–712; 758–764.

JACKSON, GEORGE S. 1984. "The Impact of Roommates on Development: A Causal Analysis of the Effects of Roommate Personality Congruence, Satisfaction, and Initial Developmental Status on End-of-Quarter Developmental Status and Grade Point Average." *Dissertation Abstracts International* 36(9):4755B.

KUH, GEORGE D.; SCHUH, JOHN H.; and WHITT, ELIZABETH J. 1991. *Involving Colleges.* San Francisco: Jossey-Bass.

LAPIDUS, JACQUELINE; GREEN, SUSAN; and BARUH, EDLA. 1985. "Factors Related to Roommate Compatibility in the Residence Hall—A Review." *Journal of College Student Personnel* 26 (5):420–434.

LOZIER, G. GREGORY. 1970. "Compatibility of Roommates Assigned Alphabetically Versus Those Assigned According to Educational Goals or Extracurricular Plans." *Journal of College Student Personnel* 11:256–260.

NATIONAL INSTITUTE OF EDUCATION. 1984. *Involvement in Learning: Realizing the Potential of American Higher Education.* Report of the Study Group on the Conditions of Excellence in American Higher Education (U.S. Department of Education). Washington, DC: U.S. Government Printing Office.

PACE, LAWLIS T. 1967. "Roommate Dissatisfaction in a College Residence Hall as Related to Roommate Scholastic Achievement, the College and University Environment Scales, and the Edwards Personal Preference Schedule." *Dissertation Abstracts International* 28(8):2989A.

PASCARELLA, ERNEST T.; TERENZINI, PATRICK T.; and BLIMLING, GREGORY. S. 1994. "The Impact of Residential Life on Students." In *Realizing the Educational Potential of Residence Halls,* ed. Charles Schroeder, Phyllis Mable, and Associates. San Francisco: Jossey-Bass.

SAX, LINDA J.; ASTIN, ALEXANDER W.; KORN, WILLIAM S.; and MAHONEY, KATHRYN M. 1999. *The American Freshman: National Norms for Fall 1999.* Los Angeles, CA: American Council on Education, Cooperative Institutional Research Program.

TERENZINI, PATRICK T.; PASCARELLA, ERNEST T.; and BLIMLING, GREGORY. S. 1996. "Students' Out-of-Class Experiences and Their Influence on Learning and Cognitive Development: A Literary Review." *Journal of College Student Development* 40(5):610–623.

GREGORY S. BLIMLING

COLLEGE ATHLETICS

THE ROLE AND SCOPE OF INTERCOLLEGIATE ATHLETICS IN U.S. COLLEGES AND UNIVERSITIES

As entities of a university, athletic departments are visible representatives of higher education and should represent the same ideals that are facilitated throughout an institution. Athletic scandals negatively impact institutional reputations because a conflict in academic and athletic curricular aims becomes apparent. Athletic curricula should be educational in nature and, as such, should facilitate similar values to academic curricula within a diverse context. In this way, the aims of athletic curricula are compatible with academic aims. The integration of athletics and academics should, therefore, create an environment conducive to student-athlete growth.

The American educator and philosopher John Dewey defined growth as the "constant expansion of horizons and consequent formation of new purposes and new responses" (Dewey, p. 175). When values in one environment contradict those in another, growth is limited by confusion and inconsistency. Current trends in intercollegiate athletics often create conflicting curricular aims that deviate from the educational nature of intercollegiate athletics and the educational mission of universities. The infusion of commercialism, rising expenses, increasing salaries for coaches and administrators, and admissions exceptions and poor academic performance of student athletes are indicative of a shift from athletics as a diverse educational entity toward a professional model. Without being rooted in the educational mission of the university, intercollegiate athletics is difficult to justify.

Given the assumption that athletics can only be justified in higher education if inherently educational, the primary role of the athletic curriculum is to maximize the development of people—students become the focus of development, with coaches being the educators and designers of the athletic curriculum. As with academic programs, athletics has curricula, text, and pedagogy, and aims for student-athlete growth. A distinguishing difference, however, between the academic and athletic curricula is measures of student development. Whereas the academic curriculum has various levels of achievement and reward, typically illustrated by grades and degrees, athletics offers a very narrow definition of achievement: winning. Thus, athletic excellence is necessary to maximize the development of students. Athletics provides one of the few enterprises in academia where a group of individuals can strive together through adversity toward a shared vision while facing daily public scrutiny and accountability. If the vision is never achieved, development is limited. Without success, the athletic curriculum does not provide a significant reward, which is critical in maximizing the development of students.

The term *intercollegiate athletics* is defined as athletic contests between colleges. Colleges grant academic degrees upon completion of designed curricula. As college students, student athletes must attend classes; they must work to complete specific requirements in order to earn a degree; and they must have minimal academic success as determined and sanctioned by the NCAA if they are to continue participating in athletics. As their admission to college is based, at least in part, on academic credentials, athletes must be students. Thus, academic departments are directly involved in the application of athletics within a university: Student athletes must take academic courses. Subsequently, academic curricula influence student athletes. When academic and athletic departments have conflicting aims, problems arise that affect the entire institution. If the values facilitated by academic and athletic curricula were consistent, problems would be diminished.

American society values the elitism of academics and athletics in a manner that provokes conflict for participants in both domains. In essence, athletic elitism is a metaphor for academic elitism: Athletic teams aspire to be national champions, while their affiliate academic institutions seek national rankings. However, the means by which coaches and faculty achieve national reputations can create conflict for student athletes attempting to exist in both environments. Although both aspire to excel, the different measures of excellence for academics and athletics necessitates compromise by those who are placed in both settings.

NCAA Championships

The National Collegiate Athletic Association (NCAA) administers national championship contests annually. There are national collegiate championships in gymnastics, volleyball, water polo, indoor track and field, outdoor track and field, wrestling (men), fencing, rifle, skiing (men and women), gymnastics, ice hockey, rowing, water polo, and outdoor track and field and volleyball (women), among others. Division I championships include baseball, bas-

ketball, cross country, I-AA football, golf, ice hockey, lacrosse, soccer, swimming and diving, and tennis (men). Women compete for national championships in basketball, cross country, field hockey, golf, lacrosse, soccer, softball, swimming and diving, tennis, and indoor track and field. In addition to those sports in which the NCAA sponsors championships, NCAA sports also include archery, badminton, bowling, squash, synchronized swimming, and team handball. In order to participate, member institutions and their students must adhere to eligibility rules as established by the NCAA.

The Economics of Education

Although universities are educational organizations, they must be economically healthy in order to exist. Each department on a campus contributes to the profit or deficit of the university. Departments that operate with a deficit survive only because they are valued programs that the university is willing to subsidize. As a noneducational, extracurricular activity, it is difficult to justify underwriting an athletic department operating at a deficit. When viewed as a unique curricular experience for students, however, it becomes easier to justify the expense.

To remain economically healthy, institutions must continually reevaluate the worth of departments operating at a deficit. The result is an institutional hierarchy of financial worth that creates conflict between departments considered either curricular or extracurricular. For example, a French department was eliminated at a western U.S. university. Faculty within the department suggested that the athletic department, which also operated at a deficit, should be eliminated instead of the French department. They argued that French has an educational mission, and is therefore of greater value to the university than athletics. The business of education thus creates a context of departmental worth.

When viewed exclusively as an entertainment business, it is difficult to justify the economics of an athletic department within higher education. A former executive director of the NCAA has acknowledged that few athletic departments generate revenue, and most athletic departments are economic burdens on their institution. Universities are becoming more reluctant to economically support athletic departments because athletics are not financially productive businesses. Thus, the business of athletics can affect a university's business of educating—athletic departments operate at substantial deficits while being treated as extracurricular, noneducational programs. It is only when athletics are viewed as diverse educational experiences for students that athletics can be rationalized as a curriculum worthy of subsidy.

In a survey involving the NCAA's 298 Division I member institutions, Clarence Crawford examined the revenues and expenses of the NCAA and affiliate universities. Existing data from the NCAA were used for the study. Crawford found that "the NCAA had revenues of $152.5 million and expenses of $151.3 million for the year ending August 31, 1991. With an NCAA membership of over 800 four-year colleges and universities, this study utilized 298. Within these 298 schools exist 106 Division IA member schools—forty percent of which reported budget deficits" (Crawford, p. 3).

During the 1980s, athletic department expenses grew at a rate three times greater than inflation: a rate far surpassing revenues. A significant influence on these expenses was escalating tuition costs. "Between 1981–82 and 1986–87, tuitions rose between 20 and 37 percent in different types of higher education institutions" (Sherman, Tikoff, and Masten, p. 16). Thus, academic tuition revenues adversely affect athletic department expenses.

To offset deficits, many athletic departments are creatively recruiting corporate sponsors. These arrangements have raised questions regarding regulation, tax exposure, and the commercialism of intercollegiate athletics. In a study conducted by the National Association of College and University Business Officers, concern was expressed with respect to the potential "corrupting influence" (Lederman 1993, p. A27) of corporate relations with athletic departments. As athletic departments attempt to balance budgets, television networks and corporate sponsors are acquiring greater influence over athletic decisions. For example, men's basketball contests are played before televised audiences each weeknight. Was the decision to play during school nights made in the interest of economics or student athletes? It appears that the economics of sports are establishing a context for prostituting higher education and ultimately exploiting student athletes.

Member institutions reported in 1992 that "salaries and wages were the largest single expense for Division IA schools, accounting for 23 percent of operating expenses" (Crawford, p. 5). Grants-in-aid accounted for 17 percent of department expenses;

however, this figure changes significantly at private institutions. The economic emphasis on revenue-producing sports is reflected in the distribution of salaries among the most influential people in athletic departments. In 1992 the average base salary for the revenue-producing head coaches was $77,511 for football and $71,151 for men's basketball. Women's basketball head coaches were the highest paid coaches in non-revenue-producing sports. The average base salary for a women's head basketball coach was $40,482. These differences are exacerbated by additional income sources. Football and men's basketball head coaches averaged $25,568 and $20,162, respectively, from additional school benefits, while women's basketball head coaches averaged $4,943 in additional school benefits. Men's basketball head coaches averaged $39,338 and football head coaches averaged $32,835 from outside income, whereas women's basketball head coaches averaged $6,651. The total compensation averages for coaches were: football head coaches, $120,258; men's basketball head coaches, $114,993; and women's basketball head coaches, $46,005. Although these figures are substantial, coaches at prestigious programs are compensated with significantly greater salaries and benefits. During the 2000–2001 academic year, three football coaches received more than one million dollars in total compensation, and during the 2001–2002 academic year twenty-two football coaches will receive more than one million dollars for coaching at the Division IA level. The economic significance of revenue-producing sports begins with the athletic faculty.

Base salaries of academic faculty are comparable to athletic coaches. In 1993 the average salary for full professors at public and private doctoral institutions was $66,250, while the average salary for full professors at private institutions was $80,280. These figures are substantial, and compare to athletic faculty salaries. Similarly, faculty in prestigious programs are compensated with significantly greater salaries and benefits—particularly at institutions with medical schools. The economic significance of the elite athletic programs parallels elite academic departments.

There appears to be a cyclical perpetuation of status, reputation, and financial resources in athletics that is analogous to academia. The most reputable athletic programs have the greatest resources and attract the most athletically talented student athletes. For example, the difference in annual operating budget expenditures between the highest and lowest member schools in a Division IA conference was more than $16 million. It is obvious which athletic department had the more successful teams. Similarly, "the most prestigious institutions attract the best-prepared students from the most affluent and highly educated families, spend the most on their educational programs, pay their faculties the highest salaries, and charge the highest tuition and fees" (Astin, p. 11). The universities with the greatest reputations and resources annually garner the highest rankings, just as the same football and basketball programs are traditionally rated by pollsters in the top twenty. Resources foster success and success breeds resources.

See also: COLLEGE ATHLETICS, *subentries on* ATHLETIC SCHOLARSHIPS, COLLEGE STUDENTS AS ATHLETES, HISTORY OF ATHLETICS IN U.S. COLLEGES AND UNIVERSITIES, INTRAMURAL ATHLETICS IN U.S. COLLEGES AND UNIVERSITIES, NCAA RULES AND REGULATIONS.

BIBLIOGRAPHY

ASTIN, ALEXANDER. 1985. *Achieving Educational Excellence: A Critical Assessment of Priorities and Practices in Higher Education.* San Francisco: Jossey-Bass.

CRAWFORD, CLARENCE C. 1992. *Intercollegiate Athletics: Revenues and Expenses, Gender and Minority Profiles, and Compensation in Athletic Departments.* Hearings before the Subcommittee on Commerce, Consumer Protection, and Competitiveness of the House Committee on Energy and Commerce (ERIC Document Reproduction Service No. ED 345 639).

DEWEY, JOHN. 1916. *Democracy and Education.* New York: Macmillan.

GERDY, JOHN R. 1994. "How Televised Sports Can Further the Goals of Higher Education." *Chronicle of Higher Education* 12(7):A52.

LEDERMAN, DAVID. 1987. "Southern Methodist U. Revamps Governance. *Chronicle of Higher Education* 33:31–32.

LEDERMAN, DAVID. 1993. "Draft Report by Business Officers' Group Says Colleges Must Rein in Sports Budgets." *Chronicle of Higher Education* 39(46):A27–A28.

MAGNER, DENISE K. 1993. "AAUP Survey Finds Faculty Salaries Rose 2.5% in 1992–93." *Chronicle of Higher Education* 39(32):A19, A22–A26.

NATIONAL COLLEGIATE ATHLETIC ASSOCIATION. 2000. *2000–2001 NCAA Division I Manual.* Indianapolis, IN: National Collegiate Athletic Association.

SHERMAN, DANIEL; TIKOFF, VALENTINA K.; and MASTEN, CHARLES. 1991. *Issues in Public Higher Education. Background Papers Prepared for the Study of the Escalating Costs of Higher Education.* Washington, DC: Office of Policy and Planning (ERIC Document Reproduction Service No. ED 354 800).

SHULMAN, JAMES L., and BOWEN, WILLIAM G. 2001. *The Game of Life: College Sports and Educational Values.* Princeton, NJ: Princeton University Press.

SPERBER, MURRAY. 1990. "Despite the Mythology, Most Colleges Lose Money on Big-Time Sports." *Chronicle of Higher Education* 37: B1, B3.

ZIMBALIST, ANDREW. 1999. *Unpaid Professionals: Commercialism and Conflict in Big-Time College Sports.* Princeton, NJ: Princeton University Press.

BRADLEY JAMES BATES

HISTORY OF ATHLETICS IN U.S. COLLEGES AND UNIVERSITIES

Intercollegiate athletics in the United States has come to be regarded as higher education's "peculiar institution." This somewhat critical characterization results from the fact that although intercollegiate athletics is seldom listed as part of the central mission of a college or university, athletics have come to command inordinate visibility, resources, influence, and attention both inside and outside many campuses. Analyzing, explaining, and dealing with this disparity between official philosophy and actual practice presents a complex analytic task. To truly understand the present situation requires a reconstruction of college athletics' unique historical evolution.

Visitors to an American campus cannot help but be struck by the physical presence of the intercollegiate athletics enterprise. In the twenty-first century, it is not unusual for a major university campus to contain both a football stadium that seats 70,000 spectators and a basketball arena that accommodates audiences of 20,000. In the year 2000 many universities had annual operating budgets for athletics ranging between $30 million and $60 million. The success and pervasiveness of college sports described was not inevitable, but is the result of particular innovations and episodes over the past 150 years.

The Violent Birth of Intercollegiate Sports

Prior to 1850 intercollegiate sports played a marginal role in collegiate life. If there was a need for physical activity in the student regimen, college presidents and deans thought manual labor in the form of farming or clearing boulders from college lands fit the bill perfectly. Though admittedly both economical and expedient, students, not surprisingly, remained unconvinced that this was the type of physical release that their souls craved. Instead, collegiate student bodies increasingly devised their own elaborate (and often brutal) intramural contests known as "class rushes." These "rushes" usually involved some variation of football, which actually provided a pretext for a ritualistic and violent hazing of the incoming freshman by the sophomore class.

College officials struggled to curb these violent student traditions, but intramural sports persisted within the campus and eventually took a decisive turn toward sanctioned and refereed events in which a team representing one institution competed against its counterpart from another. Despite the increase in organization, administrators initially were not eager, generally speaking, to embrace such contests that they viewed as inappropriate distractions from serious scholarly work. Indicative of the administrative outrage at such elaborate contests was the telegram that the president of Cornell sent to officials at the University of Michigan in 1873 when he learned that student teams from the two institutions were planning to meet in Cleveland for a football game: "I will not permit thirty men to travel four hundred miles merely to agitate a bag of wind" (Rudolph, p. 374–375).

Whether or not Cornell's president won this particular battle, he and college presidents elsewhere lost the war of curbing intercollegiate athletic contests. With or without administrative blessings, college students formed athletic associations that included mechanisms for raising money, charging fees, sponsoring events, and selling tickets. And, by the 1890s, at many colleges, alumni groups joined with the student organizations to create formidable programs over which the college presidents and faculty exercised relatively little control.

Though college athletics would quickly be dominated by certain sports and by powerful institutions, the outstanding feature of college athletics in the late nineteenth and early twentieth centuries was its pervasiveness and diversity across American institutions. Although the oldest and largest institutions—Harvard and Yale—quickly gained the most attention in newspaper coverage and provided the largest athletic budgets, numerous other campuses made significant contributions as well. For instance, Springfield College in western Massachusetts, originally known as the International YMCA Training School, was where James Naismith invented basketball in 1891. Nearby, Amherst College initiated varsity baseball and incorporated calisthenics and physical fitness into the collegiate curriculum. By 1900 the popularity of collegiate sports was reflected by its adoption in even all-girls schools. Wellesley College, for example, acquired renown for having developed a distinctively female approach to such sports as crew, basketball, and physical fitness. Other examples of innovations in American college sports before the turn of the twentieth century include:

- First intercollegiate crew regatta (Harvard vs. Yale): 1852
- First intercollegiate baseball game (Williams vs. Amherst): 1859
- First intercollegiate football association (Harvard-Yale-Princeton): 1872
- First intercollegiate track and field association (Intercollegiate Association of Amateur Athletics of America, or IC4A): 1875
- First intercollegiate tennis match: 1883
- First intercollegiate ice hockey game (Harvard vs. Brown): 1895
- First intercollegiate gymnastics competition: 1899

The Maturing of a Collegiate Way of Life

As American higher education itself was largely nurtured in the Northeast, likewise in sports, this region also led the way in developing the intercollegiate sports that now seem so familiar. Heading into a new century, Yale dominated football and also came to be known as the "cradle of coaches" as it spread the Yale football gospel of strategy and sportsmanship across the nation. By 1910 Harvard obtained the national championship in football and asserted itself in numerous other sports. Harvard would also set the pace in terms of spectator facilities with the construction, in 1904, of Soldiers' Field—considered the finest, largest example of reinforced concrete architecture in the period. This regional predilection for architectural and spectator expansion continued when the Yale Bowl opened in 1914 with a grand design and a seating capacity of more than 70,000.

Although the eastern seaboard colleges initiated college sports, their models and lessons soon were emulated in regions across the country. In the mid-nineteenth century, faculty representatives from Midwestern universities formed the *Western Conference*—a formal group popularly known then and now as the *Big Ten Conference.* Within that conference, the universities of Michigan and Chicago set the pace with spectator appeal and winning teams.

The young University of Chicago was especially important as a leader in the structure and control of a high powered varsity sports program. Whereas many presidents had resisted and resented the ascent of intercollegiate athletics, the University of Chicago's administration embraced college sports. Chicago's young, brash president, William Rainey Harper, saw the athletic contests as an opportunity to connect the campus to the greater community and thereby generate goodwill, revenue, and attention for his model institution. The creation of a large stadium combined with a mass marketing effort that succeeded in generating popular appeal and large ticket sales. Harper found the ideal partner to help him carry out his brave new vision of commercialized collegiate athletics in Amos Alonzo Stagg. As coach and athletic director, Stagg, a Yale graduate and storied football hero, oversaw the University of Chicago's athletic department for forty years.

The importance of Stagg's tenure in athletics at Chicago lies in the fact that he (with the president and board's support) created a structure that gave substantial autonomy and influence to the athletic department within the normally complex and Byzantine university administrative structure. Though holding faculty status, Stagg's program budget was exempted from conventional bureaucratic procedures. He reported directly to the president and the board of trustees, with no oversight from academic deans or faculty budget committees. In addition, Stagg generated extra income for himself and his program by being allowed to use the university facilities to sponsor promotional events, host state high school track meets, and hold instructional camps. Such a situation made Stagg and his department the

envy of other athletic leaders who in turn pushed their own institutions to adopt similar procedures in order to create the winning programs that alumni and donors demanded.

New England colleges also played a crucial role in the evolution of administration and control of college sports. Harvard's hiring of Bill Reid as a well-paid, full-time football coach in 1901 represented a major escalation of professionalizing college coaches. After Reid's hiring, coaches across the country realized that if they won they too could demand the high salary and substantial benefits enjoyed by Harvard's head coach. During his long tenure at Yale as athletic director, Walter Camp seemingly perfected the financial and political control of an entire athletic program with little accountability to students, faculty, or academic administration. Camp also used his Yale position as the base from which to create an enterprising network of syndicated newspaper columns, annual guides, endorsements, and other lucrative, influential college sports publications.

The turn of the century did not mark simply heady days for the burgeoning athletic programs. Many students and some alumni resented that the emerging organizational scheme tended to give inordinate and enduring support to a few selected spectator (and hence revenue-generating) sports—namely, football—with relatively few resources being dedicated to numerous other varsity squads. Additionally, the power and popularity of intercollegiate athletics led directly to conspicuous abuse. Even at this early juncture, a lack of regulation and fair play both on and off the field left college athletics indelibly marked by corruption and a reputation that has plagued "big-time" college sports to this day. More significantly, as the games "professionalized," brutality often increased. At times, it seemed that the days of Roman crowds chanting for gladiatorial blood were returning.

At the turn of the century, the situation had deteriorated to the point that President Theodore Roosevelt summoned university presidents to the White House with an ultimatum that they eliminate brutality from the playing field or risk federal intervention. The violence did decrease, and the development of better protective equipment also aided in safeguarding the athletes, but the problems were far from solved. No standards were set in areas such as eligibility and scholarships, thereby blurring the line of definition for supposedly amateur contests between students. In an attempt to bring order to these increasingly popular competitions, the National Collegiate Athletic Association was formed in the early 1900s. This could only be considered a Pyrrhic victory, however, for the historic East Coast universities, which had the strongest athletic programs in the country, refused to cooperate and boycotted the organizational meeting with institutions from the Midwest and West. Consequently, intercollegiate athletics lacked any semblance of meaningful nation-wide coordination over the next half century.

Athletics Out West

As Frederick Jackson Turner postulated for the entire nation: Though born and raised in the East, Americans and their institutions are ultimately defined and refined in the West. Collegiate athletics certainly followed Turner's thesis as the rise of spectator and student interest in college sports spread to the Pacific Coast. Between World War I and World War II the geographical balance of power in dominance of college sports shifted. The June 1937 issue of *Life* magazine devoted to "going to college in America" included a feature article titled, "Sports Records Move West." The emergence of top caliber intercollegiate teams in the Midwest and on the Pacific Coast "left Eastern collegians clinging to a steadily dwindling share of athletic supremacy." This led the editors to observe that: "In the past two decades, athletic reputation has largely moved West and South" (*Life*, p. 72–73).

Increasingly, college sports became a symbolic litmus test of regional and/or ethnic esteem and assimilation. For example, in the 1920s in South Bend, Indiana, the University of Notre Dame gained national visibility by becoming a rallying point for American Catholic pride and affiliation. Its victories over established East Coast football teams and national symbols such as West Point provided American Catholics with a sense of accomplishment and belonging. This trend continued well into the 1960s, for example, when African Americans used sports to break color barriers, particularly in southern universities. The national basketball championship won by Texas Western in 1966 with an all-black starting five—over the perennially powerful University of Kentucky and its all-white squad—marked an important shift in recruitment and acceptance of black players.

Various regions of the country have also rallied around school sports programs. Since 1926 the annual intersectional contests between Notre Dame and the University of Southern California regularly attracted crowds of over 100,000, whether played in Los Angeles or Chicago, and provided victorious regions the enjoyment of martial bragging rights without the sacrifice of actual military battle. Starting in 1946 the annual New Year's Day Rose Bowl Game matched the champion of the Midwest's Big Ten Conference against the championship team from the Pacific Coast Conference—and thus provided victorious regions the enjoyment of martial bragging rights without the sacrifice of actual military battle. Tiny schools and forgotten regions could gain instant, if fleeting, national attention by successfully competing with national powers, such as when unheralded Centre College of Kentucky gained national headlines in the 1920s for spirited play—and an eventual victory—over Harvard's football squad in 1921. Finally, as with anything that has mass appeal, politicians endeared themselves to the electorate by associating with and supporting local schools. Perhaps the grandest example of such activities occurred when Huey Long, the indefatigable governor of Louisiana, pronounced in 1928 that Louisiana State University was the "People's University," and called on the people of the state to share in its wealth of championship teams and its magnificent football stadium.

From Chaos to Concern

Colleges and universities paid a dear price for the popularity of intercollegiate athletics. The strong, pervasive, and enduring appeal of varsity teams, combined with the quest by alumni, local boosters, and college officials for championship squads, meant that even by the 1920s the activities associated with recruiting and compensating college student athletes were largely unregulated chaos. This was most dramatically exposed in 1929 when the Carnegie Foundation for the Advancement of Teaching released its comprehensive study *American College Athletics,* written by Howard Savage. According to this report, meaningful reform in American collegiate sports could take place only if campus presidents replaced the "downtown crowd," comprising a city's businessmen, alumni boosters, and commercial interests, as the source of leadership and responsibility. The initial response of university presidents was outrage and denial, but when the Carnegie Foundation stood by its allegations and released more documentation, academic leaders showed some public signs of interest in reform. Shoring up conferences by adding regulations and a commissioner was one gesture. Ironically, conference reforms were often counterproductive because they merely gave official approval to such practices as training tables that provided college players with free meals daily, along with subsidies for athletes, and alliances with booster clubs that previously had been cited as the problems of unregulated college sports.

Immediately after World War II, the unresolved excesses of intercollegiate athletics gained unprecedented publicity. Returning armed-service veterans swelled the ranks of varsity athletics squads. Many presidents and athletic directors placed no restrictions on the number of athletic scholarships allowed, and some football squads included three hundred players for opening practice, with more than one hundred athletes on scholarship. Excesses were accompanied by illegalities. Between 1948 and 1952 exposés and successful prosecutions of student-athletes, coaches, and alumni boosters involved in point-shaving schemes and gambling cartels led to congressional hearings and a call for nationwide oversight by academic leaders. When organizations led by college presidents, such as the American Council on Education, failed to present a coherent plan, regulatory power was given to the National Collegiate Athletics Association—an organization whose primary charge had previously been to simply promote championship tournaments. Meanwhile, at the conference level, presidents and faculty delegates attempted to introduce standards of student conduct and eligibility into policies and practices. If New England colleges had been pioneers in the creation and expansion of college sports in the first half of the century, after World War II they again assumed a leadership role in the reform and removal of excess. Most noticeable were the codes and restraints demonstrated by the "Little Three"—Amherst, Williams, and Wesleyan. In 1956 the formal creation of the Ivy Group (League) provided a model of presidential and faculty oversight of college sports.

The economics of intercollegiate athletics was slowly but persistently altered in the 1950s due to the simultaneous appearance of two phenomena: (1) professional sports teams in football and basketball, and (2) the availability of radio and television for live broadcasts of sporting events. All college teams, ranging from the established powerful university squads to the small college teams, feared that the popularity of the National Football League and the National Basketball Association would cause declining attendance at college games. Small college squads faced a second threat: national and regional broadcasts of a few selected "big-time" college games prompted many long-time fans to stay at home rather than buy a stadium ticket on Saturday afternoons. The result was a shake-out in college sports programs over two decades in which a substantial number of institutions opted, or were financially forced, to drop football.

College Sports in the Age of Aquarius

In the late 1960s shifting cultural values forced widespread changes in sports policies and emphases. As other athletes demanded equality, granting athletic scholarships ceased to be confined to a handful of traditional revenue sports—namely, football and basketball. By 1970 athletic grants-in-aid were increasingly prevalent for such sports as track, soccer, lacrosse, hockey, wrestling, baseball, and swimming. Expanding the excellence and the number of squads tended to swell athletic department operating expenses, but the small fan base of these sports failed to cover the increased costs. Consequently, institutes of higher learning faced growing philosophical and economic problems within their athletic programs. The financial brinkmanship would be subjected to even greater—and unexpected—stress in the 1970s.

Much more vocally and powerfully than "minor" sports athletes, females increasingly sought equal treatment from institutions in regards to athletics. Their actions would lead to a dramatic change in intercollegiate sports: the inclusion of women as bona fide participants in varsity athletics. The Association for Intercollegiate Athletics for Women (AIAW), created in the 1950s, led the way in increasing financial support of female athletic programs and scholarships for women. This too placed institutions and athletic departments in dire financial straits, for female sports did not generate enough fan interest to be self-supporting. This largely became a moot point in 1972, however, due to the landmark Title IX legislation that prohibited, with some exceptions, discrimination by gender in provision of educational programs. Consequently, college athletics in many ways moved from the playing fields to the court rooms as individuals challenged institutional compliance with this federal mandate. Between 1972 and 1990 colleges and courts groped for a clear interpretation of precisely what was intended and required in terms of social justice and institutional compliance for women as student-athletes. In 1997 the Supreme Court upheld lower court rulings requiring Brown University to comply with Title IX guidelines on proportionality.

Originally, a school could demonstrate compliance in athletics in one of four ways: have a proportional number of male and female participants; have a proportional relationship between female athletes and female students; demonstrate increasing opportunity for females to participate in athletics; or show that female participation in athletics matched their interest and ability to participate. However, most subsequent court rulings have demanded that the most stringent of the four tests be met, insisting that schools have a proportional number of participants in men's and women's athletics and thereby a proportional number of scholarships for each gender. This rigorous interpretation of directives for compliance with Title IX legislation has proven difficult for institutions due to the disparity of income and male and female sports generate. For instance, many athletic departments rely on football to fund their entire operating budgets, but fielding a football team requires providing scholarships for more than sixty male students. Therefore, under Title IX directives, more than sixty female students must also be given athletic scholarships, which then requires athletic departments to create enough female sports to field sixty participants with the knowledge that these activities will not garner enough fan support to pay for their existence. Consequently, athletic directors nationwide have eliminated many non-revenue male sports, with the claim that athletics programs can no longer afford to fund them. The corollary is that athletic directors have viable alternatives to eliminating men's teams such as wrestling and swimming. The net result of these conflicting interpretations is that many intercollegiate athletics programs are held in suspense on their character and composition. Though difficult, failure to comply with Title IX directives can bring harsh and far-reaching repercussions; therefore academic leaders and athletic directors continue to review their intercollegiate athletic enterprise to ensure that women are equally represented.

Competing in a Brave New Century of Sport

The most conspicuous example of the problems of success and popularity that faced intercollegiate athletics in the late twentieth century can be seen in the 1991 and 2001 reform reports of the Knight Founda-

tion Commission on the Future of Intercollegiate Athletics. The absence of a government agency, combined with the limits of such voluntary associations as the National Collegiate Athletic Association to bring integrity to the governance of college sports, has prompted foundations to take the lead in promoting public discussion of the issues and problems. In 1991 the Knight Foundation panel, dominated by university presidents along with some executives and legislators, proposed that strong presidential involvement was the key to protecting the interests of student-athletes. A decade later, the emphasis was on cost containment as the essential ingredient in curbing the commercialism of intercollegiate sports. Whether or not such reforms have a widespread and enduring influence, intercollegiate athletics persist, for better or worse (or both), as a distinctive part of American higher education.

By the 1990s discussions about student-athletes had shifted from the question, "Are college athletics being paid?" to the proposition, "How much should college athletes be paid?" Such debates followed logically from research by economists who concluded that the National Collegiate Athletic Association had become a highly lucrative cartel, and that athletes participating in big-time programs were, in essence, often being exploited by their institutions and associations as "unpaid professionals." Furthermore, coaches in high profile sports enhanced their stature as celebrities rather than as educators, complete with endorsements and special contracts to supplement their base salaries. To increase the seriousness of these concerns, athletic programs at all institutions, including the most conspicuous ones, faced a paradox of prosperity: despite unprecedented revenues, most teams and programs were not financially self-supporting. Even at the Division IA level of NCAA competition, future funding of intercollegiate athletics faced a situation of dubious fiscal fitness.

The conventional wisdom was that overemphasis on intercollegiate athletics was most prevalent in the relatively small number of big-time programs at large universities. Yet significant, systematic research sponsored by the Mellon Foundation in 2000 suggested otherwise. William G. Bowen and James Shulman's study, *The Game of Life: College Sports and Educational Values*, complicated the profile with their finding that even at—or, perhaps, especially at—academically selective and relatively small-sized colleges and universities, the demands on student-athletes' time were substantial. Furthermore, at these institutions, usually regarded as apart from athletic excess, commitment to strong varsity sports programs tended to exert inordinate influence on such decisions as admissions and allocation of campus resources. Academic and public concern over the proper place of athletics in American colleges and universities remained problematic at most institutions at the start of the twenty-first century.

See also: COLLEGE ATHLETICS, *subentries on* ACADEMIC SUPPORT SYSTEMS FOR ATHLETES, ATHLETIC SCHOLARSHIPS, COLLEGE STUDENTS AS ATHLETES, NCAA RULES AND REGULATIONS, THE NATIONAL COLLEGIATE ATHLETIC ASSOCIATION, THE ROLE AND SCOPE OF INTERCOLLEGIATE ATHLETICS IN U.S. COLLEGES AND UNIVERSITIES.

BIBLIOGRAPHY

ATWELL, ROBERT H.; GRIMES, BRUCE; and LOPIANO, DONNA A. 1980. *The Money Game: Financing Collegiate Athletics.* Washington, DC: American Council on Education.

FLEISHER, ARTHUR A., III; GOFF, BRIAN L.; and TOLLISON, ROBERT D. 1991. *The National Collegiate Athletic Association: A Study in Cartel Behavior.* Chicago: University of Chicago Press.

LAWRENCE, PAUL R. 1987. *Unsportsmanlike Conduct: The National Collegiate Athletic Association and the Business of College Football.* New York: Praeger.

LESTER, ROBIN. 1995. *Stagg's University: The Rise, Decline, and Fall of Big-Time Football at Chicago.* Champaign-Urbana: University of Illinois Press.

MICHENER, JAMES. 1976. *Sports in America.* New York: Random House.

ORIARD, MICHAEL. 1993. *Reading Football: How the Popular Press Created an American Spectacle.* Chapel Hill: University of North Carolina Press.

RUDOLPH, FREDERICK. 1962. "The Rise of Football." In *The American College and University: A History.* New York: Knopf.

SHULMAN, JAMES L., and BOWEN, WILLIAM G. 2000. *The Game of Life: College Sports and Educational Values.* Princeton, NJ: Princeton University Press.

SMITH, RONALD. 1988. *Sports and Freedom: The Rise of Big-Time College Athletics.* Oxford: Oxford University Press.

SPERBER, MURRAY. 1990. *College Sports, Inc.: The Athletic Department vs. The University.* New York: Henry Holt.

SPERBER, MURRAY. 1999. *Onward to Victory: The Crises That Shaped College Sports.* New York: Henry Holt.

"Sports Records Move West." 1937. *Life* June 7, 72–73.

THELIN, JOHN R. 1994. *Games Colleges Play: Scandal and Reform in Intercollegiate Athletics.* Baltimore: Johns Hopkins University Press.

ZIMBALIST, ANDREW. 1999. *Unpaid Professionals: Commercialism and Conflict in Big-Time College Sports.* Princeton, NJ: Princeton University Press.

JOHN R. THELIN
JASON R. EDWARDS

ACADEMIC SUPPORT SYSTEMS FOR ATHLETES

College athletics are associated with many benefits for student athletes. Besides the thrill of actually competing and learning how both wins and losses parallel many of life's lessons, the single largest associated benefit of athletic competition for scholarship athletes is the opportunity of earning a valuable degree. Academic support systems for student athletes can improve academic success and graduation potential.

Components and Resources

Although the following components of an academic support system are certainly not inclusive, the items listed are fundamental and essential to the development of a good academic support system.

Student athletes. The better the academic quality of the students involved, the easier the job of academic support. But standardized test scores and high school grades cannot measure a student's desire or maturity. A poor high-school grade point average and low standardized test scores can be transformed into good college grades through dedication and an athlete's naturally competitive spirit. However, student athletes can also be somewhat pampered or sheltered before college, and the rigors of athletic demands and poor time management can contribute to academic underachievement.

Faculty. Faculty members are the true first line of communication regarding a student-athlete's academic performance. If communication and trust are fostered, everyone benefits. Faculty advisers must be the first source of academic advice.

Athletic counselors. Roles of athletic counselors vary, often involving eligibility issues, personal counseling and academic advice, and simply being a friend and cheerleader. Listening skills, trust, and respect are key ingredients to a successful relationship between a student athlete and a counselor.

Tutors. Tutors can play a part in the academic success of student athletes. Careful screening, knowledge of subject, clear and concise tutoring rules, a system of checks and balances that can be enforced and monitored, and regular evaluations are critical elements for success.

Computer resources. Maximizing a student's academic success without adequate computer support is difficult. The ready availability of computers for student athletes to use to complete academic assignments can be critical. Either the university or the athletic department can provide the computers. Dedicated machines for exclusive student-athlete use tend to be the growing trend. Having enough computers is essential. Many excellent academic support centers tend to have exclusive-use, desktop computers in an academic center laboratory, with additional laptops for use during team travel for competitions.

Nurturing study environment. Successful academic support centers tend to have a dedicated study area where student athletes can study in a quiet environment with easy access to both computers and tutors. Such a place becomes the defacto location to study for student athletes. Fostering the identity of this facility and insuring that disruptive behavior is not tolerated are essential.

Action Items

Many of the following action items are techniques and policies that can enhance the success of an student-athlete support center.

Good faculty contacts and relationships. Having 100 percent faculty support is a rarity, and in actuality probably is an impossibility. Some schools have close to 100 percent faculty support, while other athletic departments have few friends in the faculty ranks for a variety of reasons. Regardless of the current situation, athletic departments should work diligently to mend damaged relationships—and look to foster new ones. Simply stated, the student-faculty

relationship is fundamental because it is where academics and athletics meet. If communication lines are strong, initial problems can be recognized and improved before small problems become large ones. Regular telephone conversations, e-mail exchanges, early-semester warnings of academic shortcomings, mid-semester deficiency reports, and various surveys are all means that can be helpful in gathering information. It is important to recognize how critical this type of early-warning information is, and that it is available only from the student athlete or the professor. Appeals for this information should stress the value of recognizing any concerns and problems early. Faculty should be reminded that student athletes have routinely waived the rights to information privacy granted them under the Buckley Amendment (the Family Educational Rights and Privacy Act, or FERPA). The student-authorized waiver allows the release of valuable academic information to NCAA, conference, and university officials. Thus, a student athlete has generally accepted that professors can release this type of academic information to academic support staff.

Student-athlete stratification. Most academic support centers have limited resources, as well as student-counselor ratios that they consider too large. In a situation where resources are limited and maximizing staff efforts is important, stratifying the student-athlete population can be very useful and necessary. For example, upperclass students who have proven themselves to be responsible students will need less attention and effort than first-year students whose academic status is unknown. Devoting the most time and resources to those populations where these resources can result in the most benefits is only reasonable.

Regular counselor meetings. Athletic counselors should meet regularly with all students. Established, conscientious upperclass students may require only one or two meetings per semester or quarter. Freshmen and others on a so-called watchlist, and those deemed to be at risk by whatever criteria are used, should meet with their athletic counselors at least once a week, and preferably more often. Counselors can stand outside classes and count students attending class, or even attend random classes themselves, but the best way to monitor *knowledge intake* is to check a student's class notes regularly. Everyone has been in a class or a meeting in body only, with the mind wandering elsewhere. By checking a student's notes weekly (or more frequently), and by quizzing them from their notes, confidence levels about a student being both present and engaged in a class are increased. Making students understand that notes must be taken—on what is being done in class, and not only for test purposes—is a proven way to maximize both attendance and engagement. Even a crafty student will soon recognize that notes cannot be copied or created if they are going to be quizzed routinely, and anything less than attending class and taking notes requires more effort. Once this is recognized, a great academic leap will be achieved.

Study-hour incentives. Many college students view required study hours as being part of a high school mentality. Establishing a system with incentives so that a student athlete earns his or her way out of organized study hour requirements is essential. The conscientious student will recognize the relationship between performance and responsibility and will work to earn more freedom. Others will take longer and, unfortunately, some never learn.

The final aspect of study-hall hours is to insure productivity. These hours are not for socializing, sleeping, or playing computer games. Academic productivity (e.g., required note-taking from textbooks, homework inspection, and other techniques) must be monitored.

Subdivision of large assignments. Poor time management, competing assignments, or a feeling of simply being overwhelmed can lead to poor performance on a critical assignment, whether it be an English paper or a major project. Taking a larger assignment and dividing it into smaller, incremental, and more manageable assignments over a longer time period will enhance the final product and reduce student stress. The key is to start early and to require incremental progress reports.

Time management skills. Time management sessions that are developed internally or that rely on university personnel and resources are encouraged. The National Collegiate Athletic Association (NCAA) allows the preparation and distribution of free planners (a.k.a. *day timers*) by an institution, as long as it is fully generated in-house without any product endorsements or commercialization. These planners can aid time management and provide a good document that both student and counselor can inspect and use collectively. Finally, the distribution of the coming semester's planner coincides nicely with the return of a student's textbooks at the end of a semester. Thus, the student athlete has a plan-

ning document early to begin preparing and recording tasks for the upcoming semester.

Tutoring sessions. Because of the importance of good tutorial support, completion of tutor session forms by each tutor and end-of-semester evaluations by students of their tutors are recommended. The tutor-completed form can be a simple checklist with minimal narrative. If a completed tutoring session becomes part of the payment process for the tutor, then they become expected and routine. The tutor session form can also indicate other aspects of the session, such as punctuality, student preparation, attentiveness, and tutor recommendations for further work. They can also be used later to summarize the number of sessions by semester, subject, course, individual student, team, or student classification (e.g., freshmen).

Policy and procedures manual. Personnel change and ambiguity in policies and procedures can exist. A policy and procedure manual (PPM) cannot assure total elimination of possible confusion or differing interpretations, but "putting it in writing" will reduce the possibilities of confusion. The PPM is also a sensible way to document how an academic support center should function.

Opportunities to exchange ideas. Regularly scheduled meetings between students and counselors have already been mentioned. Other meetings, such as regular staff meetings, retreats, and student-athlete evaluations of their counselors, are critical. Facilitating communication downward, upward, and laterally is critical for all parties to remain informed and functioning cohesively.

Conclusion

Communication and trust are critical ingredients in the successful operation of any academic support center. These two attributes have been mentioned both explicitly and implicitly. But communication and trust at all levels leads to a more successful academic support system. However, no one action or series of actions can insure success. The ideas presented here will be beneficial when considered and implemented. An athletic counselor's fundamental responsibility is to provide the guidance and resources that will help each student athlete maximize his or her academic accomplishments.

See also: COLLEGE ATHLETICS, *subentries on* ATHLETIC SCHOLARSHIPS, COLLEGE STUDENTS AS ATHLETES, HISTORY OF ATHLETICS IN U.S. COLLEGES and Universities, NCAA Rules and Regulations, The National Collegiate Athletic Association, The Role and Scope of Intercollegiate Athletics in U.S. Colleges and Universities.

Robert E. Stammer Jr.

ATHLETIC SCHOLARSHIPS

The benefits of receiving an athletic scholarship from a university or college have evolved significantly since the origins of athletic grants-in-aid. National Collegiate Athletic Association (NCAA) guidelines provide member institutions with the autonomy to offer athletic scholarships to prospective student-athletes based on their athletic and academic abilities. The NCAA has minimum academic guidelines that categorize students as certified for participation as "qualifiers." Two other categories limit participation and financial assistance—"partial qualifiers" and "nonqualifiers." In an effort to create a competitively equitable financial context, the NCAA establishes specific limits as to the total number of grants-in-aid institutions are allowed to provide to prospective student-athletes. In addition to receiving financial aid, qualifiers receiving an athletic scholarship are certified through the NCAA to have access to numerous resources such as scholarships and academic support through both NCAA member institutions and the NCAA itself. Certification is required by an NCAA-approved certification agency that reviews coursework completed by high school prospects. The agency approves core units earned to ensure students meet NCAA minimum performance guidelines for qualification to participate in athletic competition.

Financial Support

Institutional financial aid is administered by each member institution and begins with "the cost of attendance (which is) an amount calculated by an institutional financial aid office, using federal regulations, that includes the total cost of tuition and fees, room and board, books and supplies, transportation, and other expenses related to attendance at the institution" (NCAA, p. 176). The NCAA categorizes sports into two areas of financial aid: head-count sports and equivalency sports. Head-count sports are those in which each student who receives financial aid is provided with the actual cost of atten-

dance as determined by the institution. Equivalency sports allow coaches to allocate different combinations of financial aid in various forms such as tuition, books, fees, housing costs, or meals. In addition to financial assistance provided by an athletic scholarship, the NCAA has alternative means of financial assistance accessible by student athletes in the form of its Special Assistance Fund. This fund ranges from providing expenses for family emergencies to a clothing allowance for need-based students. Student athletes receiving athletic aid are also allowed to work during academic semesters, earning up to a specified amount of money, and to work outside the normal academic calendar (summers and vacations).

Education

An athletic scholarship provides the means for students who compete athletically to attend an institution of higher education and ultimately earn a degree. The value of this education varies greatly, from the approximately $37,000 annual cost of attendance at private universities (in 2001) to less expensive tuition expenses at public institutions. The inherent value of a formal education in a postsecondary institution has been debated relative to the revenues generated by major collegiate sports and the ever-increasing salaries of head coaches. When viewed as a preparatory system for aspiring professional athletes, student athletes can be perceived as semiprofessionals who receive an athletic education of not insignificant value from skilled coaches. Additionally, if higher education sustains a pragmatic and philosophical justification for intercollegiate athletics as an inherently educational endeavor, then the value of the curriculum, both academic and athletic, provides satisfactory compensation for participation. Participation in a sport should be approached by the university as inherently developmental: the values acquired through engaging in athletic activities should be consistent with values learned in the academic curriculum and should primarily be aimed at maximizing the development of students. Thus, participation in athletics is itself the reward, as people grow through the experience.

Academic Support

Admissions advantages for student athletes have increased significantly over time. With the evolving weight given to athletic ability in the admissions process, institutions have been increasing their resources for supporting at-risk students. Most member institutions now provide an academic support center that focuses on the retention of student athletes through academic eligibility guidelines established by member institutions and the NCAA. Academic counselors, typically employed by the department of athletics, serve as guides to the academic curriculum for student athletes, while also assisting students in time management, class registration, tutorial sessions, satisfactory progress requirements, and graduate school opportunities. In many ways, these counselors mentor student athletes in ways in which coaches are unable to because they have a weaker power relationship with student athletes. Academic counselors do not determine student athletes' playing time, and thus, as guardians of student-athlete retention via academic eligibility, they often develop stronger relationships with students than faculty and can influence their academic decisions.

Academic counselors will typically establish a comprehensive system of monitoring for freshmen. Daily class checks and accountability for assignments make up much of the academic center's function. Once student athletes demonstrate that they have adapted to the curriculum, counselors will wean the students off their structure and allow more independence in terms of class preparation and registration.

CHAMPS/Life Skills

The NCAA, in an effort to encourage a holistic approach to educating student athletes, developed the CHAMPS/Life Skills program in conjunction with the National Association of Collegiate Directors of Athletics. This program, adapted by most members of the NCAA, attempts to maximize the total development of student athletes through engagement in career development, the academic curriculum, community service, counseling, leadership development, diversity training, and athletic development. This program utilizes campus resources while incorporating the unique challenges of intercollegiate athletics. Ultimately, the goal is to develop student athletes in every facet of their higher education experience. Perhaps the most utilized aspect of the Life Skills format is career development. Working with the university career center, most student athletes prepare for interviews and career fairs by capitalizing on career counselors and software programs made available to them through the program. Some institutions circu-

late booklets to alumni which contain senior student-athlete resumes in an effort to place them in productive and satisfying positions of employment.

Residential Affairs

An athletic scholarship for head-count sports allows the institution to cover the cost of residence during the student athletes' years of eligibility. Residential requirements vary significantly throughout higher education and range from mandatory dormitory requirements to off-campus housing subsidies. Each institution has a philosophical approach to residential education that ranges from significant emphasis (mandatory residency requirements) to commuter campuses. In the early 1980s, the NCAA eliminated athletic dormitories that were exclusively used by student athletes. The result is a more integrated campus community in terms of student athletes and their peers.

Coaching

An athletic scholarship provides student athletes with access to those who are experts in developing students in their sport-specific curriculum: namely, coaches. When viewed as educators, coaches utilize a diverse educational entity (athletics) to maximize the development of students. The athletic curriculum should not only facilitate improved athletic skill, but should encompass values such as leadership, discipline, competitiveness, and other holistic qualities that serve students outside the athletic domain. A significant component necessary to maximizing the development of student athletes is success. Without success, student athletes do not have the opportunity to work together toward a shared vision and actually experience the attainment of that vision. In athletics, success is narrowly defined: winning. Thus, winning is an essential part of the athletic curriculum.

As educators, coaches need to develop students not only in the skills of their specific sport, but must also utilize sport development to facilitate holistic growth in their students. Very few aspects of the academic curriculum introduce public competition and scrutiny in a way that invites adversity. Experiencing the dynamics of the athletic curriculum, including the intense competition within a narrow definition of success while facing scrutiny through various media outlets (talk radio, chat lines, newspapers, electronic media) offers a unique experience with the potential of elevating the student athletes' experiences in ways the academic curriculum cannot usually replicate. Thus, as creators of the athletic curriculum within higher education, coaches have a responsibility to their student athletes to facilitate their development.

Dining Services

Perhaps the greatest difference between students and student athletes is in their respective nutritional needs. Some athletes expend great quantities of calories, and therefore require replacement fluids for hydration and calories for physical development. Student athletes in sports where additional body weight presents a competitive disadvantage (gymnastics, cross country) are often placed in a situation where students predisposed to eating disorders struggle with their physical maturation and caloric expenditures. The NCAA allows each institution to provide, as part of an athletic scholarship, sufficient funds to cover three meals each day including one meal served by the athletic department training table to student-athletes receiving aid.

Sports Medicine

Student athletes participating on intercollegiate teams are entitled to institutionally provided medical resources. Typical of sports medicine and athletic training departments are team doctors and certified athletic trainers. The range of available resources extends from surgery to taping ankles. The nature of the sports medicine focus is injury prevention and rehabilitation.

Other Benefits

In addition to the previously mentioned provisions of athletic scholarships, student athletes receive equipment for competition and practice, coaches who specialize in strength development and cardiovascular conditioning, athletic department staff who market teams and individuals, and media relations staff who work with local, national, and sometimes international media. In addition, students may earn various achievement awards presented by their institution, conference, or the NCAA. Finally, the implicit value of team travel and experiencing the cultures of different institutions and regions provides student athletes with opportunities to grow socially as well as intellectually and athletically.

See also: COLLEGE ATHLETICS, *subentries on* ACADEMIC SUPPORT SYSTEMS FOR ATHLETES, COLLEGE STUDENTS AS ATHLETES, HISTORY OF ATHLETICS IN U.S. COLLEGES AND UNIVERSITIES, NCAA RULES AND REGULATIONS, THE NATIONAL COLLEGIATE ATHLETIC ASSOCIATION, THE ROLE AND SCOPE OF INTERCOLLEGIATE ATHLETICS IN U.S. COLLEGES AND UNIVERSITIES.

BIBLIOGRAPHY

BRADLEY, BILL. 1989. *The Role of Athletics in College Life: Hearings Before the Subcommittee on Postsecondary Education of the Committee on Education and Labor, House of Representatives, One Hundred First Congress, First Session.* Washington, DC: U.S. Government Printing Office.

DYSON, ERIC. M. 1994. "Be Like Mike: Michael Jordan and the Pedagogy of Desire." In *Between Borders: Pedagogy and the Politics of Cultural Studies,* eds. Henry A. Giroux and Peter McLaren. New York: Routledge.

GERDY, JOHN R. 1994. "How Televised Sports Can Further the Goals of Higher Education." *Chronical of Higher Education* 12(7):A52.

GERDY, JOHN R. 1997. *The Successful College Athletic Program: The New Standard.* Phoenix, AZ: Oryx Press.

GERDY, JOHN R. 2000. *Sports in School: The Future of an Institution.* New York: Teachers College Press.

LEDERMAN, DAVID. 1990. "Students Who Competed in College Sports Fare Better in Job Market than Those Who Didn't, Report Says." *Chronicle of Higher Education* 37:A47–48.

LEDERMAN, DAVID. 1998. "Players Spend More Time on Sports than on Studies." *Chronicle of Higher Education* 34:A33–34.

NATIONAL COLLEGIATE ATHLETIC ASSOCIATION. 2000. *2001 NCAA Division I Manual.* Indianapolis, IN: National Collegiate Athletic Association.

SHULMAN, JAMES L., and BOWEN, WILLIAM G. 2001. *The Game of Life: College Sports and Educational Values.* Princeton, NJ: Princeton University Press.

BRADLEY JAMES BATES

COLLEGE STUDENTS AS ATHLETES

Current thought regarding academics and athletics in higher education focuses on the academic performances of student athletes. The emphasis of the research literature concerning intercollegiate athletics is on the compromised admissions and subsequent inferior academic performance of student athletes in the revenue-producing sports of football and men's basketball. Consequently, the nucleus of research literature centers on the academic integrity of higher education institutions that participate in NCAA Division IA intercollegiate athletics.

In gauging academic outcomes of student athletes, most research relies on traditional scholastic measures. Empirical research objectifies student athletes by focusing on board scores, grade point averages (GPAs), and graduation rates, and depicts student athletes participating in revenue-producing sports as weaker students in high school, poorer students in college, and graduating at lower rates than other students. University graduation rates have emerged as the prevailing assessment tool of student athletes' academic engagement and as a measure of performance outcomes.

Graduation Rates

The most comprehensive research of academic performance of student athletes is conducted by the National Collegiate Athletic Association. The annual *Graduation Rates Report* utilizes institutionally submitted information detailing student-athlete graduation rates, undergraduate enrollment data, university grade point averages, and admissions data. This report describes in quantitative terms the academic performance differences between student athletes and other students, between student athletes in revenue-producing sports and non-revenue-producing sports, between students and student athletes in Division I schools, and between student athletes and other students by ethnicity. Although the findings show few significant deviations from year to year within each institution, differences between institutions are startling. For example, in the twelve-member Southeastern Conference, six institutions graduated less than 53 percent of their student athletes in 1999. Several NCAA institutions graduated less than 20 percent of the student athletes that entered their university during the 1986–1987 academic years.

The percentages become more alarming when students are separated by ethnicity and sport. For example, while Division I student athletes graduate at an average rate of 58 percent rate, only 51 percent of football players and 43 percent of men's basket-ball players graduate. Sixty-three percent of Division I Caucasian student athletes graduate from college while Division I African-American student athletes graduate at a rate of 45 percent. Sixty percent of Division I Caucasian student athletes that participate in football, and 53 percent that participate in men's basketball, graduate, while only 43 percent of Division I African-American student athletes that participate in football, and 37 percent that participate in men's basketball, graduate from college. These data demonstrate that student athletes in revenue-producing sports (football and men's basketball), especially African-American student athletes, graduate at lower rates than other students (including other student athletes), raising serious cultural concerns and questions regarding the support systems and admissions policies for student athletes participating in revenue sports.

These data are not surprising given the criterion by which football and basketball student athletes are admitted to universities (see Table 1). Football and men's basketball student athletes have lower entering board scores and lower core high school GPAs than other student athletes. Thus, NCAA data supports the contention that student athletes participating in football and men's basketball are given preferential admissions treatment by institutions of higher learning—a substantial statistical advantage that has increased over time. Once admitted, student athletes underperform academically and concentrate in certain fields of study. However, despite lower entering board scores and underperformance, student athletes, overall, fare as well as other students in terms of graduation rates. Additionally, viewing student athletes collectively portrays a universal characterization that is not applicable to all sports. Student athletes in non-revenue-producing sports elevate the academic means for student athletes in football and men's basketball. In other words, student athletes participating in non-revenue-producing sports have vastly different academic profiles than football players and men's basketball players.

The NCAA reports include the graduation rates for all students as a gauge of institutional academic integrity. Although the focus of the report is on student-athletes graduation rates, student athletes are measured against the graduation rates of their peers. The literature contains a consistent theme of discontent toward the graduation rates of student athletes, yet student athletes collectively graduate at rates consistent with their classmates. The 1999 NCAA

TABLE 1

Student-athlete admissions data: Four-year average, entering freshmen, 1990–1991 through 1993–1994

N is the number of students; SAT is total (verbal plus math) score.

Sport	N	GPA	N	SAT	N	ACT
Men						
Baseball	4,625	2.90	2,872	930	1,814	21
Basketball	3,062	2.66	1,936	840	1,209	19
Cross Country/Track	3,848	2.86	2,376	929	1,726	21
Football	12,935	2.67	7,433	862	5,681	19
Other	8,962	2.91	7,159	958	4,198	21
Women						
Basketball	3,496	3.11	1,964	890	1,595	20
Cross Country/Track	4,062	3.11	2,354	912	1,890	21
Other	11,611	3.13	8,091	946	4,198	21

SOURCE: Based on National Collegiate Athletic Association. 1994. *Official NCAA 1994 Graduation Rates Report.* Overland Park, KS. Page 615.

Graduation Rates Report shows that over a four-year period, student athletes actually graduated at a higher rate (58%) than their peers (56%). In Division IA, the most competitive level of the NCAA, student athletes graduated at a rate of 58 percent, compared to a rate of 59 percent for all students at Division IA institutions. In Division I-AAA, the least competitive level of Division I intercollegiate athletics, student athletes graduated at a 58 percent rate, compared to 50 percent of all students at those institutions, and Division I-AA student athletes graduated at a rate of 57 percent, compared to 54 percent of all students at those institutions. Collectively, then, student athletes do better than their peers in terms of graduation rates. However, the data reveal two distinct groupings of student athletes when assessing academic success: students who participate in revenue sports and those who participate in non-revenue-producing sports.

Focusing on football and men's basketball student athletes illustrates significant differences compared to other students. There is a distinct difference between the graduation rates, core high school GPAs, and board scores of student athletes who participate in revenue-producing sports and non-revenue-producing sports. Football and men's basketball student athletes not only graduate at lower rates than other students, they are poorer students than other student athletes.

Several empirical studies have examined the differences in academic performance between football and men's basketball student athletes and nonathlete students. The intent of these studies was to identify disparities in academic performance. As previously discussed, the primary source of data was collected by the NCAA from institutionally submitted student academic records. Mean scores are subsequently compared between independent groups. The scope of these studies was extensive. For example, data collected for the NCAA reports include all Division IA student athletes.

In a year-long study conducted by the President's Commission of the NCAA, student athletes were found to "spend more time on sports than on studies" (Lederman 1988, p. A33). Comparisons were made between student athletes and nonparticipating students in time-consuming extracurricular activities. This study involved forty-two institutions in Division IA and it found that "Football and basketball players spend approximately thirty hours per week in the sports when they are in season—more time than they spend preparing for and attending class combined. They also report missing about two classes per week" (Lederman 1988, p. A34). The result of admissions exceptions and athletic demands is that student athletes in revenue-producing sports graduate at a significantly lower rate than other students. At many universities, faculty are tolerating the continuation of academic programs "in which, for every student who graduated, nine others did not" (Weistart, p. 17).

The question investigated by Michael Maloney and Robert McCormick in 1993 was, "To what extent does intercollegiate athletic participation affect academic success?" (p. 556). Utilizing data collected on all students at a Division IA university, Maloney and McCormick discovered that the average grade for student athletes was 2.379, which was significantly lower than the average grade for the student body, which was 2.681. Using regression equations for grade estimates by semester, Maloney and McCormick found that "there is a negative season effect in the revenue sports" (p. 566). Football players received significantly lower grades during the fall season than other students. Student-athlete grades during the off-season improve significantly and are slightly better than nonathletes. However, the increase during the off-season is not sufficient "to recoup the losses during participation" (Maloney and McCormick, p. 566).

Conclusion

Universities are willing to compromise admissions criteria for athletic ability. The result has been institutional acceptance of lower graduation rates of student athletes who participate in revenue-producing sports. However, student athletes collectively graduate at rates comparable to their peers. The academic concession for athletic purposes amplifies an implicit institutional value on winning athletic contests in football and men's basketball, which are the primary users of "special admits" (students admitted with profiles significantly lower than the university average) and the teams with the lowest graduation rates.

See also: COLLEGE ATHLETICS, *subentries on* ACADEMIC SUPPORT SYSTEMS FOR ATHLETES, ATHLETIC SCHOLARSHIPS, HISTORY OF ATHLETICS IN U.S. COLLEGES AND UNIVERSITIES, NCAA RULES AND REGULATIONS, THE NATIONAL COLLEGIATE ATHLETIC ASSOCIATION, THE ROLE AND SCOPE OF INTERCOLLEGIATE ATHLETICS IN U.S. COLLEGES AND UNIVERSITIES.

BIBLIOGRAPHY

ADLER, PATRICIA A., and ADLER, PETER. 1991. *Backboards and Blackboards: College Athletes and Role Engulfment.* New York: Columbia University Press.

ADLER, PETER, and ADLER, PATRICIA A. 1985. "From Idealism to Pragmatic Detachment: The Academic Performance of College Athletes." *Sociology of Education* 58(4):241–250.

CRAMER, JEROME. 1986. "Winning or Learning? Athletics and Academics in America." *Phi Delta Kappan* 67(9):K1–K8.

GURNEY, GERALD S., and STUART, DEBRA L. 1987. "Effects of Special Admission, Varsity Competition, and Sports on Freshman Student-Athletes' Academic Performance." *Journal of College Student Personnel* 28:298–305.

LANG, ERIC L., and ROSSI, ROBERT J. 1991. *Understanding Academic Performance: 1987–88 National Study of Intercollegiate Athletes.* Paper presented at the American Educational Research Association convention (ERIC Document Reproduction Service, No. ED 331 880).

LEDERMAN, DAVID. 1988. "Players Spend More Time on Sports than on Studies, an NCAA Survey of Major College Athletes Finds. *Chronicle of Higher Education* 34:A33–A34.

LEDERMAN, DAVID. 1991. "College Athletes Graduate at Higher Rate than Other Students, But Men's Basketball Players Lag Far Behind, a Survey Finds. *Chronicle of Higher Education* 37(28):A1, A38–A44.

MALONEY, MICHAEL T., and McCORMICK, ROBERT E. 1993. "An Examination of the Role that Intercollegiate Athletic Participation Plays in Academic Achievement: Athletes' Feats in the Classroom." *Journal of Human Resources* 28(3):555–570.

McMILLEN, TOM. 1992. *Out of Bounds.* New York: Simon and Schuster.

NATIONAL COLLEGIATE ATHLETIC ASSOCIATION. 1988–1999. *Official NCAA Graduation Rates Report.* Overland Park, KS: National Collegiate Athletic Association.

SHULMAN, JAMES L., and BOWEN, WILLIAM G. 2001. *The Game of Life: College Sports and Educational Values.* Princeton, NJ: Princeton University Press.

WEISTART, JOHN C. 1987. "College Sports Reform: Where Are the Faculty?" *Academe* 73(4):12–17.

BRADLEY JAMES BATES

INTRAMURAL ATHLETICS IN U.S. COLLEGES AND UNIVERSITIES

The term *intramural* comes from the Latin *intra* (within) and *murus* (wall). In a collegiate setting, intramural usually refers to a formally organized program of activities, games, and sports designed to meet the needs of the entire college community. Campus intramural and recreational programs normally provide an opportunity for voluntary participation and/or competition among members of the same institution, and also for occasional competition between intramural groups at other institutions. Because participation is voluntary and open to all, intramural activities allow all students to experience the positive outcomes normally reserved for varsity athletes.

The intramural motto reads, "An activity for everyone and everyone in an activity" (Hyatt, p. 10), and the main purpose is student enjoyment. Intramural programs exist simply because students enjoy the activities and want them to continue. While there is no other necessary justification for the existence of intramural programs, there are many varied benefits, which have led to the secondary goal of providing educational experiences through physical activity. Several objectives related to this goal are:

- Physical development—personal fitness programs can help produce happier, healthier individuals.

- Mental development—many sports provide stress relief and require and enhance quick decision-making, interpretation, and concentration.

- Social development—being part of a team requires and fosters teamwork, cooperation, and sportsmanship.

- Skill development—intramural activities provide an opportunity to refine specific physical skills, an opportunity that may not have been available previously.

- Leisure-time development—these activities encourage a positive choice for filling free time, which may carry over to healthful life decisions.

History

There are a few early records of intramural events that eventually gave rise to formalized intramural offices and organizations, including an 1852 boat race between Harvard and Yale students, an 1857 Princeton University baseball game between freshmen and sophomores, and an 1859 baseball game between students at Williams and Amherst.

In 1913 the term *intramural* was first used at the University of Michigan, at which time the first for-

mal intramural departments were formed at Michigan and Ohio State. Many large state institutions soon followed, and in 1920 the Big Ten Intercollegiate Athletic Conference began holding annual intramural director's meetings. The first book on the topic, Elmer Mitchell's *Intramural Athletics,* was published in 1925. Mitchell was later a main force in developing Ph.D. and Ed.D. programs for physical educators. He also initiated *Research Quarterly* and was the first author of the *Journal of Health and Physical Education.* The first building dedicated solely to intramural activities was constructed in 1928 at the University of Michigan. The creation of the federal work-study program in 1933 established jobs for students in intramural departments and allowed many institutions to further develop their intramural programs.

The year 1948 marked the beginning of the first professional organization related to college intramurals. William Wasson, from Dillard University in New Orleans, toured twenty-five black colleges, studying their intramural departments. He then produced *A Comparative Study of Intramural Programs in Negro Colleges.* Wasson concluded that it would be very helpful to form a national organization to serve as a reference and resource for those involved in collegiate intramural programs. In 1950 there was a meeting of eleven black-college intramural directors, who named themselves the National Intramural Association (NIA). They later invited intramural directors from other institutions to join their group and eventually changed the organization's name to the National Intramural-Recreational Sports Association (NIRSA). In 1955 the first international conference was held, and in 1971 women were invited to join NIRSA.

Structure

Within an intramural department, each activity or team needs to be a separate program and function as a whole. Programs and activities do have relationships with each other, but they are not dependent upon each other for their existence, and no activity is more important than any other. A cooperative balance between intramural activities and varsity athletics is crucial, and it is important to recognize that both programs are meeting the needs of students, though of different populations and in different activities. The only pre-requisite for intramurals is a desire to participate, which often includes a broad range of duties, such as playing, coaching, managing, supervising, and officiating. The intramural office is typically responsible for the following:

- Organizing separate leagues for men and women.
- Creating opportunities for unstructured recreation (pick-up games).
- Providing structured and unstructured opportunities for coed recreation.
- Club teams (intercollegiate competition, but not selective the way varsity programs are).
- Special event planning.
- Extramurals (contests with another institution's club team or intramural team).
- Outdoor recreation.
- Recreational opportunities for faculty, staff, and families, including programs to integrate the entire campus.
- Cultural, creative activities.
- Special programs over the summer.

The intramural director is typically responsible for publicizing events, as well as coordinating activities, making policies governing participation, scheduling and supervising activities, ensuring that officials are trained, arbitrating any disputes between participants, purchasing and managing equipment, and overseeing and balancing the budget.

Typical Programs

The programs and activities offered at an institution are largely based on the size and type of the college and the diversity and needs of the college community. Intramural and recreation programs at large universities are much more standardized than those at smaller, private colleges. For the basis of comparison, examples are provided of current offerings at two very different types of institutions. Table 1 lists the intramural/recreation offerings at the University of Massachusetts, a large, public, East Coast university. Table 2 shows the intramural/recreation offerings at the California Institute of Technology, a small, private, West Coast college.

Benefits of Intramural Programs

Participation in intramurals has been found to have a positive effect on a student's self-esteem. As a student's recreation participation increases, his or her confidence also increases. College students are constantly required to cope with stress related to their

TABLE 1

Intramural/recreation programs at the University of Massachusetts

Intramurals	Season	Men, Women, Coed
Flag football	Fall/spring	M,W,C
Soccer	Fall/spring	M,W,C
Softball	Fall/spring	M,W,C
Field hockey	Fall	W
Cross country	Fall	M,W
Ice hockey	Fall	M,W
Volleyball	Fall/spring	M,W,C
Tennis	Fall/spring	M,W,C
Ultimate Frisbee	Fall	M,W
Foul shooting	Fall	M,W,C
3-point shoot-out	Fall	M,W,C
3-on-3 basketball	Fall	M,W,C
Holiday basketball	Fall	M,W
Quickball	Fall	M,W
Basketball	Fall	M,W,C
Wallyball	Spring	M,W,C
Swimming	Spring	M,W
Lacrosse	Spring	W
Wrestling	Spring	M,W,C

Club Sports
Bicycle racing
Fencing
Women's ice hockey
Rowing
Lacrosse
Women's rugby
Volleyball
Equestrian
Sailing
Wrestling

SOURCE: Courtesy of author.

academic life, and participating in intramurals can help balance a student's life and improve the quality of life. For some students, intramural activities can be the single common bond they feel with other students, and intramurals thus becomes the basis for developing a social network, which is crucial for persistence—an important goal of most institutions. Student participants also develop a sense of accomplishment when they become more adept at physical skills.

An intramural program is perhaps the most ideal location to foster moral development education, and this focus is the responsibility of the intramural administration. The overall atmosphere of a college intramural program should be fair, just, and geared toward moral growth. Participants should be clear that the focus is participation, teamwork, sportsmanship, and a sense of belonging. Any complaints or disputes should be handled by the administration with fairness and moral considerations in mind.

TABLE 2

Intramural/recreation programs at the California Institute of Technology		
Intramurals	**Season**	**Men, Women, Coed**
Volleyball	Fall/spring	C
Flag football	Fall/spring	C
Soccer	Fall/spring	C
Basketball	Spring	C
Softball	Fall/summer	C
Swimming/diving	Fall	C
Ultimate Frisbee	Spring	C
Track and field	Spring	C
Tennis	Spring	C
Club Sports		
Badminton		
Ballroom dance		
Cheerleading		
Cycling		
Cricket		
Dance troupe		
Fencing		
Floorball		
Ice hockey		
Racquetball		
Rugby		
Shorinji kempo		
Shotokan karate		
Soccer		
Surf/windsurf		
Table tennis		
Triathlon		
Ultimate Frisbee		
Volleyball		
Water polo		

SOURCE: Courtesy of author.

A campus intramural and recreation program has a unique opportunity to bring together all of the different members of the community, including students, faculty, staff, alumni, and families, for the pursuit of a common goal. The recreation center is often open up to eighteen hours per day and attracts a more diverse population than other facilities on campus. While students tend to be measured by their grade point average and the type of degree they earn, they are far more likely to value and remember the life skills and relationships they develop in college. An intramural office that values the education and development of the whole person has endless opportunities to meet the needs of the entire college community.

See also: COLLEGE ATHLETICS, *subentry on* HISTORY OF ATHLETICS IN U.S. COLLEGES AND UNIVERSITIES; RESIDENTIAL COLLEGES.

BIBLIOGRAPHY

CLARKE, JAMES S. 1978. *Challenge and Change: A History of the Development of the National Intramural-Recreational Sports Association 1950–1976.* New York: Leisure Press.

COLLINS, JOHN R.; GRAHAM, APRILL P.; KING, TERESA L.; and VALERIUS, LAURA. 2001. "The Relationship Between College Students' Self-Esteem and the Frequency and Importance of Their Participation in Recreational Activities." *National Intramural-Recreational Sports Association Journal* 25:38–47.

DALGARN, MELINDA K. 2001. "The Role of the Campus Recreation Center in Creating a Community." *National Intramural-Recreational Sports Association Journal* 25:66–72.

HYATT, RONALD W. 1977. *Intramural Sports: Organization and Administration.* St. Louis, MO: Mosby.

KLEINDIENST, VIOLA, and WESTON, ARTHUR. 1964. *Intramural and Recreation Programs for Schools and Colleges.* New York: Appleton-Century-Crofts.

MUELLER, PAT. 1971. *Intramurals: Programming and Administration.* New York: Ronald Press.

ROKOSZ, FRANCIS M. 1975. *Structured Intramurals.* Philadelphia, Saunders.

THEODORE, PHILIP A. 1999. "Promoting Moral Growth Through Campus Recreation." *National Intramural-Recreational Sports Association Journal* 23:39–42.

RACHEL M. MADSEN

THE NATIONAL COLLEGIATE ATHLETIC ASSOCIATION

The National Collegiate Athletic Association (NCAA) is a membership organization of colleges and universities whose fundamental charge is to "maintain intercollegiate athletics as an integral part of the educational program and the athlete as an integral part of the student body" (NCAA 2002). This governing body of intercollegiate athletics was initially constituted as the Intercollegiate Athletic Association of the United States (IAAUS) in 1906, following a call from President Theodore Roosevelt to eliminate the high numbers of deaths and injuries common to college football at that time. The first constitution of the IAAUS (which became the NCAA in 1910) was ratified by thirty-five colleges and universities in 1906. In 2002 NCAA membership included 1,036 colleges and universities and a number of other affiliates. Approximately 360,000 students participate in intercollegiate athletics at these member institutions each year.

Organization of the NCAA

Since 1973 NCAA colleges and universities have been organized into three divisions, each having separate championship events, legislative autonomy, and a distinctive governance structure. Division I (324 institutions in 2002) has the most stringent requirements for membership. These requirements involve minimum numbers of sports offered for men and women, minimum numbers of participants and events for each sport, scheduling criteria, and minimum and maximum financial aid awards for student athletes. Institutions with men's football teams are further subdivided within Division I into Division I-A and I-AA, based upon team competitiveness and attendance figures.

NCAA Division II (290 institutions in 2002) typically includes those schools with fewer financial resources devoted to athletics. Membership criteria for Division II are generally less strict than for Division I, especially in terms of minimum number of sports offered and minimum numbers of financial awards for student athletes. Division III members (422 institutions in 2002) do not offer any athletically related financial aid, but emphasize participation in intercollegiate athletics as an integral part of student life on campus.

Across divisions, the NCAA governance structure includes member institution presidents and chancellors, faculty, coaches, athletic department personnel, athletic conference personnel, and student athletes who work in conjunction with a national staff of more than 300 (based in Indianapolis, Indiana) to carry out the mission and functions of each division and of the NCAA as a whole. Many NCAA rules and policies are set by one or more of 120 NCAA committees that include approximately 1,000 representatives from member institutions. The NCAA Executive Committee, consisting of a small number of college presidents and chancellors from each of the three divisions, is the overarching NCAA governance body. Its responsibilities include dealing with key association-wide issues (including all legal issues) and strategic plans, ensuring that each divi-

sion is meeting its mission and the general mission of the NCAA, and overseeing the association's budget.

Each of the three divisions governs via its own committee structure, with a board of presidents and chancellors from institutions within that division serving as the highest-ranking committee and reporting directly to the NCAA Executive Committee. This board is called the Presidents Council in Divisions II and III and the Board of Directors in Division I. Many policy issues are first tackled within each division by a Management Council that reports directly to the division's board of presidents and includes athletics administrators, faculty, and student-athlete representatives. These governing bodies oversee a number of committees that each deal with a division-specific issue, such as championship events, academic standards, budget, legislation, membership criteria, student-athlete voice, and rules infractions. Additionally, there are a number of association-wide committees that focus on topics relevant to all member institutions, including competitive safeguards and injury surveillance, sport rules, opportunities for minority students and athletics personnel, sportsmanship and ethical conduct, research, and postgraduate scholarships.

Although the committee structures are similar across the three NCAA divisions, the methods for creating legislative policy have evolved differently within each division. In Divisions II and III, legislation is considered at each annual NCAA convention using a one vote per school process. Division I eliminated such a system in 1997, with all legislative policy subsequently decided upon by the institution presidents and chancellors constituting the eighteen-member Division I Board of Directors. This form of governance allows Division I to consider new legislation twice each year, as opposed to the once-per-year process used in Divisions II and III. NCAA staff members, led by the NCAA president, maintain the association's governance structure and carry out the policies set forth within each division.

Role and Function of the NCAA

The original 1906 constitution of the NCAA (IAAUS at that time) reflected a desire of the first delegates (primarily college professors) to regulate college athletics and ensure that athletic contests reflect the "dignity and high purpose of education" (Falla, p. 21). During the early years of the NCAA, this was carried out by assuming a role as the chief rules-making body for many sports, promoting ethical sporting behavior, suggesting that athletic departments be recognized as units of instruction within each university, and debating issues such as amateurism and eligibility for competition. Many of these functions and issues are still foci for the NCAA. However, the organization's role has expanded substantially over the years to include administration of national championships, education and outreach initiatives, marketing, licensing and promotion, communications and public affairs, membership/legislative services, and rules enforcement.

Although the first NCAA-sponsored championship competition (the 1921 National Collegiate Track and Field Championship) did not occur until fifteen years after the organization's conception, administration of national championship competitions certainly constitutes the most visible modern NCAA function. As of 2002 more than eighty national championships for men and women were being administered each year across twenty-two sports. These championship events include an estimated 44,000 participants each year.

As the national popularity of many of these competitions has grown, NCAA championship contests have become the focus of substantial media interest and merchandising efforts. By far, the most popular of these championships has been the Division I Men's Basketball Tournament. The television broadcast rights for this tournament were sold to CBS in 1999 for an average of $545 million per year over eleven years. Much of the money made on NCAA championship events (and their broadcast rights) is returned directly to member institutions to support athletic programs, with the remainder used to run the championship events and support other association-wide initiatives. The NCAA national staff includes a marketing, licensing, and promotions division that deals specifically with the promotion of the NCAA brand and NCAA championships.

Early in the NCAA's history, it was expected that member institutions would police themselves on adherence to constitutional principles—a policy known as the home-rule philosophy. In time, the need to provide some form of national oversight in the face of the growth of the business side of college sports forced a shift in NCAA ideals. The 1946 "Sanity Code" was a first attempt at establishing the NCAA as a body to deal with explication of rules to member schools and enforcement of those rules. Generally, the primary areas for oversight since that

time have included institutional control and responsibility, the amateur status of student athletes, academic standards, financial aid, and recruiting of student athletes. As the numbers of institutions in NCAA Divisions I, II, and III have grown and the governance structure and specific rules of each division have become more complex, the need to provide assistance to member schools in understanding and complying with national legislation has become a priority.

Membership Services

The Membership Services division of the NCAA national office has primary responsibility for assisting member colleges and universities in understanding and complying with NCAA and division-specific legislation. One function of Membership Services is to provide institutions and the general public with ready access to staff knowledgeable in NCAA rules and their interpretations. Numerous seminars and other educational initiatives are conducted each year to keep member institutions and other organizations (e.g., high schools) aware of rules and compliance issues. Membership Services (often in conjunction with NCAA counsel and federal relations liaisons) also assists NCAA governance bodies in evaluating current legislation and assessing ramifications of potential legislative changes.

The staff from this division also administers the NCAA's athletics certification and self-study program. This initiative requires that member schools maintain NCAA accreditation based on adherence to association principles and institutional control over athletic programs. In Division I, the certification program requires each institution to undergo a peer review of their athletic program at specified intervals.

Membership Services also coordinates the certification of individual student athletes as academically eligible for competition, based initially upon academic performance in high school and later on academic progress toward a degree at their college or university. Independent national assessment of whether athletes competing in NCAA-sponsored events are achieving reasonable academic performances has been a major association-wide initiative since the early 1980s.

Enforcement

In 1952, subsequent to the "Sanity Code," a rules enforcement mechanism was put in place that remains to this day. Member institutions, coaches, or athletes in violation of NCAA legislation or principles must face NCAA committees and staff charged with investigating and punishing transgressions. At the institution level, the NCAA reviews approximately fifteen to twenty major infractions cases and 1,500 secondary (much less serious and often self-reported) violations each year. Secondary violations often result in minor penalties that may be determined by the offending institution itself. Major infractions may lead to substantial penalties for a college or university, including recruiting limitations, loss of athletic scholarships, banishment of teams from competition in championship events, or even disbandment of a team and loss of some NCAA membership privileges. Violations involving individual prospective or enrolled student athletes are handled through similar mechanisms.

Education Services

Often lost amidst the substantial media attention afforded to the championship events, the big money aspect of college sports, and the rules violations is the substantial amount of education, outreach, and development initiatives undertaken by the NCAA through its Education Services division. This group is most directly charged with maintaining and enhancing the overall welfare of student athletes at NCAA member institutions. The division includes a sports sciences program that closely monitors trends in competition and practice injuries, informs rules committees of relevant injury data, administers drug education and drug testing programs, and promotes various wellness initiatives at the national level and through grants to member institutions.

Education Services also maintains the NCAA research staff whose mission is to collect, interpret, and disseminate data of interest to NCAA policymakers and member institutions. For example, the research staff collects data used by the NCAA to evaluate such diverse topics as the financial health of athletic programs, effects of academic reform legislation on member institution graduation rates for student athletes, and trends in minority hiring in athletic departments.

In conjunction with many of its championship events, NCAA Education Services staff organizes large-scale youth clinics that include sport instruction and life-skills discussions. The NCAA also is involved with the National Youth Sports Program (NYSP), which provides thousands of disadvantaged youths with education and enrichment activities each summer. Student athletes at member institutions are given opportunities to participate in NCAA life-skills programming and an annual NCAA-sponsored leadership conference. Other outreach activities involve promotion of athletic administration opportunities for women and members of racial/ethnic minority groups, and the administration of numerous scholarship programs for student athletes needing funding to complete an undergraduate degree or pursue graduate training.

As in its infancy, the NCAA is still involved in establishing competition rules for each sport, and in collecting and maintaining collegiate sports records and other historical data. Many of the issues that the NCAA deals with have been around since the advent of college athletics (e.g., recruiting violations, academic performance of athletes, competitive equity). However, there are also many issues that have come to the fore more recently, such as gender equity, the financial and commercial milieu of college athletics, and diversity issues. The one certainty is that the NCAA, in conjunction with its member institutions, will continue to evolve in scope and responsibility in response to the continued growth in popularity of intercollegiate athletics in the United States.

See also: COLLEGE ATHLETICS, *subentries on* ATHLETIC SCHOLARSHIPS, COLLEGE STUDENTS AS ATHLETES, HISTORY OF ATHLETICS IN U.S. COLLEGES AND UNIVERSITIES, THE ROLE AND SCOPE OF INTERCOLLEGIATE ATHLETICS IN U.S. COLLEGES AND UNIVERSITIES.

BIBLIOGRAPHY

FALLA, JACK. 1981. *NCAA: The Voice of College Sports—A Diamond Anniversary History, 1906–1981.* Mission, KS: National Collegiate Athletic Association Press.

INTERNET RESOURCES

BROWN, GARY T. 1999. "NCAA Answers Call to Reform: The 'Sanity Code' Leads Association Down Path to Enforcement Program." *NCAA News.* <www.ncaa.org/news/1999/19991122/active/3624n24.html>.

HAWES, KAY. 1999. "Championships Program Missing at NCAA's Birth." *NCAA News.* <www.ncaa.org/news/1999/19991108/active/3623n31.html>.

HAWES, KAY. 1999. "'Its Object Shall Be Regulation and Supervision,' NCAA Born from Need to Bridge Football and Higher Education." *NCAA News.* <www.ncaa.org/news/1999/19991108/active/3623n27.html>.

NATIONAL COLLEGIATE ATHLETIC ASSOCIATION. 1999. "NCAA, CBS Reach Agreement on $6 Billion, 11-Year Contract." *NCAA News.* <www.ncaa.org/news/1999/19991206/digest.html#1>.

NATIONAL COLLEGIATE ATHLETIC ASSOCIATION. 2002. "About the NCAA." <www.ncaa.org/about>.

THOMAS PASKUS

NCAA RULES AND REGULATIONS

The National Collegiate Athletic Association (NCAA) began with a meeting called by U.S. President Theodore Roosevelt in October 1905. In attendance were the presidents and football coaches of Harvard, Yale, and Princeton Universities. Roosevelt sought, among other things, effective regulation of college football, which in 1905 had seen eighteen deaths on the gridirons of the relatively few institutions fielding teams to play the still new and already popular sport. The meeting resulted in rules changes in football and a meeting of a group of college presidents that would become the thirty-eight-member NCAA in 1906. By 2002 the voluntary association of more than 1,000 U.S. colleges and universities governed intercollegiate athletics competition in more than fifty sports for both men and women.

The NCAA rules govern specific games, the conditions for institutional participation in the NCAA and its sanctioned leagues and championships, the recruitment and participation of individual student athletes, and the consequences for breaching NCAA rules. The *NCAA Manual,* which is updated for each of the three divisions annually (and four times per year online), encompasses the rules for which member institutions and individuals are accountable. By 2002 the manual had expanded to more than 500 pages as new rules continue to be legislated and old ones revised or reinterpreted.

As of February 2002 the NCAA had thirty institutions on probation for major rules infractions (those providing an extensive recruiting or competitive advantage, reflecting a general disregard for the governing rules, or for recurring violations). In 2000, when twelve institutions were sanctioned for major infractions, the NCAA processed to completion a total of 2,024 cases involving secondary infractions, an infraction defined as "isolated or inadvertent in nature, provides or is intended to provide only a minimal recruiting, competitive or other advantage, and does not include any significant recruiting inducement or extra benefit" (p. 311).

The number and complexity of NCAA rules, and the possible consequences associated with their violation, have led most Division I institutions to employ at least one full-time professional staff member and to establish an institution-wide infrastructure solely devoted to assuring up-to-date knowledge and compliance with NCAA rules. Further, the aspiring student athlete must attend to the rules as early as the ninth grade to be sure to achieve the necessary high school course work required to meet NCAA eligibility requirements.

Source, Structure, and Scope of NCAA Rules

The regulations for the governance of NCAA-sponsored intercollegiate athletics are encompassed in the *NCAA Manual* within thirty-three articles, which are organized in three sections: (1) the "Constitution," which covers the principles for the conduct of intercollegiate athletics that provide the framework within which all subsequent rules must fit; (2) "Operating Bylaws," which consist of principles and specific rules promoting the principles defined in the constitution; and (3) "Administrative Bylaws," which define policies and procedures to implement legislative actions of the association, NCAA championships, association business, the enforcement program, and the athletics certification program. Most rules and rule changes originate with recommendations from a number of internal committees, including the committee on infractions and the management council—a representative group of institutional and league athletics and faculty representatives of the specific division for revisions to the bylaws. However, depending on the nature of the proposed rule or revision, authority for rules and amendments may be delegated to the committee or may require approval beyond the management council.

The constitution provides a framework and defines limits for all subsequent regulations and future legislation. At its base is a two-part fundamental policy addressing the principle of amateurism, which is meant to assure that athletics is an integral part of the educational program, and the athlete is an integral part of the student body, thus establishing a "clear line of demarcation between intercollegiate athletics and professional sports" (NCAA, p. 1). The second part of the policy addresses the individual and collective responsibilities of member institutions to apply and enforce legislation to assure competitive equity, including "basic athletics issues such as admissions, financial aid, eligibility and recruiting" (NCAA, p. 1). Beyond the fundamental policy and purpose of the organization, the constitution includes five additional articles addressing the conduct of intercollegiate athletics, NCAA membership, organizational structure, legislative authority and process, and institutional control of intercollegiate athletics. The constitution designates the chief executive officer of the institution (rather than the athletic director) as ultimately responsible "for the conduct of the intercollegiate athletics program and the actions of any board in control of that program" (NCAA, p. 49). This responsibility is reinforced in the requirement that budgetary control falls to the institution within the realm of its normal budgetary procedures. The Constitution also spells out procedures for self-study and analysis to occur as part of a regular athletic certification process. Perhaps most important, this section of the constitution spells out the institution's responsibility for the acts of its staff members and any other individuals or agencies promoting the interests of the institution's intercollegiate athletics program.

The second article of the constitution contains principles for conduct of intercollegiate athletics, which anchor rules affecting prospective and current student athletes and institutions. The principle of student-athlete welfare, for example, requires athletic programs to protect and enhance the physical and educational welfare of student athletes. It requires an environment for the student athlete that: (1) is well integrated with the overall educational experience, (2) values cultural diversity and gender equity, (3) is healthy and safe, (4) fosters a positive relationship between the student athlete and coach, (5) exhibits fair, open, and honest relationships on the part of coaches and administrators towards student athletes, and (6) involves student athletes in matters affecting their lives. Other principles for the conduct of intercollegiate athletics include gender equity, sportsmanship and ethical conduct, sound academic standards, nondiscrimination, diversity within gov-

ernance, rules compliance, amateurism, competitive equity, recruiting, eligibility, financial aid, playing and practice seasons, postseason competition and contests sponsored by noncollegiate organizations, and the economy of athletic program operations. Each principle, briefly defined in the constitution, provides the philosophical basis for extensive and often complex subsequent rules in the operating and administrative bylaws.

The operating bylaws address ethical conduct (including gambling and the use of banned substances), conduct and employment of athletics personnel, amateurism, recruiting of student athletes, academic and general eligibility requirements, financial aid, conditions affecting awards, benefits and expenses for enrolled student athletes, the conditions and limitations of playing and practice seasons, championships and postseason football, enforcement, division membership, committees, and certification for institutional athletic programs. The administrative bylaws address rules in the governance of athletic programs, executive regulations, enforcement policies and procedures, and the policies and procedures governing the NCAA athletics certification program.

NCAA Eligibility Requirements

Imagine Sally Jones, a ninth grader who loves basketball. She knows that she wants to play college basketball, and therefore will try to do whatever is required to meet the admission requirements of her state university. In addition, perhaps unknown to Sally and her parents, she must also satisfy NCAA requirements and procedures in order to be eligible to compete in her first year in college.

The NCAA constitutional principle regarding eligibility specifies that "eligibility requirements shall be designed to assure proper emphasis on educational objectives, to promote competitive equity among institutions and to prevent exploitation of student-athletes" (NCAA, p. 5). It is designed to assure that when Sally gets to college she will be treated as a student first, and not simply as a commodity.

The subsequent bylaw related to eligibility, however, consists of thirty-seven pages in the *Division I Manual* detailing the conditions a student athlete must meet in order to be eligible to compete in athletics competition at a given institution. The rules related to initial eligibility are sufficiently complex that Sally and all other applicants must use an initial-eligibility clearinghouse contracted by the NCAA (in 2002 the contract was held by the American College Testing Service) to validate the information on which the initial eligibility determination is based. First, in order to qualify for eligibility, Sally will need to meet minimum grade point average (GPA) requirements in a set of thirteen designated core academic courses taken in high school. An index based on varying combinations of GPA and test scores on either the SAT or the ACT will determine the minimum that must be satisfied in each area. For example, if the core GPA is 2.0 (the lowest permissible for a qualifier), then the combined verbal/math score on the SAT would need to be at least 1010. If Sally's GPA in the academic core courses is 2.5 or higher, she will be allowed an SAT score as low as 820 to qualify for athletics financial aid, practice, and competition. If she is unable to meet these criteria, she might be able to be a *partial qualifier,*—a student who meets an index involving GPAs starting at 2.525 and going to 2.750 and above to balance SAT scores as low as 720. Partial qualifiers and nonqualifiers may attend the institution if accepted through normal channels, but they may not participate in the first year in intercollegiate athletics practice or competition (including club sports).

NCAA rules will dictate the maximum number of official campus visits Sally may make; when, how often, and under what conditions she may be contacted by coaching staff; conditions for campus visits, including where she may eat and under what conditions costs will be covered for her parents if they accompany her. If admitted, there will be conditions on summer school attendance and summer sport participation, when she must declare a major, the number of courses she must take to remain eligible, and permissible sources of financial support as she pursues her degree. Once on campus, her coaches will be responsible for certain rules, including when, how often, and for how long the team practices, and the number of contests in which she will participate. Violations of the rules could adversely affect both individuals and the institution.

Sanctions

Institutions typically self-report to the NCAA in the event they have reason to believe a violation of an NCAA rule has occurred. Information may also come through other channels such as opposing coaches or members of the public. In the case of a secondary violation, the institution prepares a report

on the situation, including corrective or disciplinary actions taken, if any. The *NCAA Secondary Violation Penalty Schedule* provides guidance for penalties for inadvertent secondary violations. For example, if basketball, football, or women's volleyball coaching staff members attended an opponent's contest, violating the regulation generally prohibiting in-person scouting of an opponent in these sports, the employing institution should issue a letter of reprimand to the involved coaching staff members. Many recruiting violations would necessitate the institution to issue a letter of admonishment to involved staff members, with notice that repeat violations will be forwarded to the NCAA for evaluation and imposition of appropriate recruiting restrictions on the institution. Examples of such violations include sending video materials to a prospect, placing institutional advertising in a high school game program or recruiting publication, failure to notify a prospect in writing of the five-visit limitation prior to a visit, providing a campus visit prior to receiving the prospect's test scores and/or transcript, allowing a media representative to be present during a recruiting contact by a coach, publicizing a prospect's campus visit, and putting a prospect's name on the scoreboard.

Major infractions involve an in-depth investigation process in cooperation with the institution. Major infractions may warrant penalties such as forfeiture of games involving ineligible players, probation, limiting television coverage, termination of responsible staff, dissociation of representatives of athletic interests, reduction of allowable grants-in-aid, financial penalties, and, in the worst case, effectively suspending an athletic program for a given period of time. Some examples of major infractions include providing extra benefits to student athletes or recruits, falsification of recruiting records, unethical conduct (including academic fraud), impermissible recruiting inducements, lack of institutional control and failure to monitor its athletic programs, provision of false and misleading information, hiring irregularities, fraudulent entrance examinations, impermissible observation of preseason activities, and impermissible tryouts.

Conclusions

The NCAA compliance effort is a well-intended attempt to respond to concerns related to ethics, commercialism, academic integrity, amateurism, exploitation of student athletes, racial equity and gender equity, disability accommodation, and other issues. An approach to ethical concerns based in legislated rules has perhaps created a structure so complex that it loses sight of the initial objective, and has, in turn, generated new concerns. The structure of NCAA rules continues to be challenged through the NCAA. The rules have also been challenged in the courts, including, for example, cases related to alleged racial discrimination in the use of test scores in initial eligibility determination, disability discrimination in disallowing test scores taken with accommodation for students with disabilities, anti-trust questions for denying access to prospective student-athletes, and for limiting salaries for restricted earnings coaches. Such coaches, prior to the court's prohibition as a result of this case, were limited by NCAA rules to a specific salary cap usually equivalent to a part-time salary even though they were employees of the hiring college or university. Others raise concerns about an athletic association determining academic policy at both the high school and college level. Time, however, will tell whether NCAA and member efforts to revise the rules structure will allow benefits from the order and ethical foundation provided by NCAA rules, while also simplifying the rules to reduce the volume of unintended violations. As the NCAA seeks to liberalize rules related to amateurism, it is useful to consider historian John Thelin's observation that "the initial impulse in each era was to deplore the illegal and unethical activities in college sports, then to proceed to make them legal. If there is an epitaph for the demise of educationally sound athletic programs on the American campus, it will read: 'the rules were unenforceable'" (Thelin, p. 222).

See also: COLLEGE ATHLETICS, *subentry on* NATIONAL COLLEGIATE ATHLETIC ASSOCIATION; TITLE IX, *subentry on* INTERCOLLEGIATE ATHLETICS.

BIBLIOGRAPHY

DUDERSTADT, JAMES J. 2000. *Intercollegiate Athletics and the American University: A University President's Perspective.* Ann Arbor: University of Michigan Press.

FESTLE, MARY JO. 1996. *Playing Nice: Politics and Apologies in Women's Sports.* New York: Columbia University Press.

FLEISHER, ARTHUR A., III; GOFF, BRIAN L.; and TOLLISON, ROBERT D. 1992. *The National Collegiate Athletic Association: A Study in Cartel Behavior.* Chicago: University of Chicago Press.

GERDY, JOHN R. 1997. *The Successful College Athletic Program: The New Standard.* Phoenix, AZ: Oryx Press.

GRIMES, PAUL W., and CHRESSANTHIS, GEORGE A. 1994. "Alumni Contributions to Academics: The Role of Intercollegiate Sports and NCAA Sanctions." *The American Journal of Economics and Sociology* 53(1):27.

JUSTUS, JANET, and BRAKE, DEBORAH. 1995. "Title IX." *Journal of College and University Law* 22(1): 48–62.

KNIGHT FOUNDATION COMMISSION ON INTERCOLLEGIATE ATHLETICS. 2001. *Report of the Knight Foundation Commission on Intercollegiate Athletics* (issued annually since 1991). Charlotte, NC: The Knight Foundation.

LAPCHICK, RICHARD E., and SLAUGHTER, JOHN B., eds. 1994. *The Rules of the Game: Ethics in College Sport.* Phoenix, AZ: Oryx Press.

SHULMAN, JAMES L., and BOWEN, WILLIAM G. 2001. *The Game of Life: College Sports and Educational Values.* Princeton, NJ: Princeton University Press.

SMITH, RODNEY K. 2000. "A Brief History of the NCAA's Role in Regulating Intercollegiate Athletics." *Marquette Law Journal* 11(1):9.

SPERBER, MURRAY. 1998. *Onward to Victory: The Crises that Shaped College Sports.* New York: Henry Holt.

THELIN, JOHN R. 1996. *Games Colleges Play: Scandal and Reform in Intercollegiate Athletics.* Baltimore, MD: Johns Hopkins University Press.

ZIMBALIST, ANDREW. 1999. *Unpaid Professionals: Commercialism and Conflict in Big-Time College Sports.* Princeton, NJ: Princeton University Press.

INTERNET RESOURCES

NATIONAL COLLEGIATE ATHLETIC ASSOCIATION. 2001. *2001-2002 NCAA Manual* (for Divisions I, II, and II). Indianapolis, IN: National Collegiate Athletic Association. <www.ncaa.org/library/membership.html#manuals>.

SUZANNE E. ESTLER

COLLEGE ENTRANCE EXAMINATION BOARD, THE

The College Entrance Examination Board, or College Board, is a national, nonprofit membership association with a mission of preparing, inspiring, and connecting students to college and opportunity. The College Board assists students in the school-to-college transition by helping them prepare academically for, and enter, colleges and universities. It also endeavors to aid international students in their transition to U.S. colleges; provide information on financial aid; help colleges identify, recruit, and place students; and assist educators in public policy development and advocacy. In addition, the organization sponsors educational research.

At its founding in 1900 the College Board had a membership of twelve institutions of higher education. The goal was to provide a common set of entrance examinations to be used by colleges to make admissions decisions. The first fifty secondary schools were admitted to membership in 1959. As of the beginning of the twenty-first century the association comprised more than 3,900 schools, colleges, universities, and other educational organizations.

Members and Governance

The College Board has three types of members. The first type, institutions, includes schools, colleges, and universities. Secondary and higher education systems are the second type. Finally, the third type of member, nonprofit organizations, encompasses agencies, associations, and education departments. Membership requirements differ according to type. Institutions of higher education, for example, must be accredited and document regular and substantial use of College Board programs and services such as the Advanced Placement (AP) Program, SAT, or College-Level Examination Program (CLEP). Members are elected annually at the College Board's membership meeting.

The College Board is governed by an elected board of trustees, officers appointed by that board, and staff appointed by the College Board president. The board of trustees includes faculty and administrators of secondary schools, colleges, universities, and other educational organizations. Appointed officers include the president, a president emeritus, secretary of the corporation, senior vice president for operation and finance, senior vice president for development, and vice presidents for government relations, research and development, communications/public affairs, academic initiatives, regions, chief of staff, teaching and learning, higher education services and international services, and human resources.

Programs and Services

While provision of national, uniform entrance examinations has always been an important function of the College Board, programs and services have expanded considerably throughout the years. The organization provides major programs and services in (1) college admission and enrollment (e.g., Admitted Class Evaluation Service, Preliminary SAT/National Merit Scholarship Qualifying Test [PSAT/NMSQT]); (2) guidance (e.g., Career Search); (3) financial aid (e.g., College Scholarship Service and Institutional Need Analysis System); (4) placement and advising (e.g., CLEP); and (5) teaching and learning (e.g., EQUITY 2000 and Pacesetter). These programs and services are described, and most are made available, on the College Board website.

Perhaps its best-known program, the Scholastic Aptitude Test was first administered in 1926, was renamed the Scholastic Assessment Test in 1992, and then became known simply as the SAT. Taken by more than 1 million students annually throughout fall, winter, and spring, the SAT is a standardized test required for admission by many colleges and universities. The College Board owns the SAT and contracts with the Educational Testing Service (ETS) to develop and administer the SAT and other standardized tests. There is no "passing score" on the SAT. Instead, individual institutions determine how to weight the SAT among other admissions factors including high school rank and grade point average, essays, and interviews. In 1929 the test was divided into verbal and math subtests. The three-hour SAT I: Reasoning Tests and one-hour SAT II: Subject Tests were developed in 1990. Subjects in the SAT II include writing, literature, U.S. history, world history, math, biology, chemistry, physics, and languages.

The PSAT was first administered in 1959 and was combined with the NMSQT in 1971. The PSAT/NMSQT is designed to measure critical reading, math problem solving, and writing skills. In addition to practicing for the SAT, students may also qualify for scholarships and other recognition based on their test scores. The PSAT/NMSQT is typically taken by high school juniors.

The AP Program, through which high school students can take college-level courses and earn college credit or advanced placement in over thirty subject areas, is among the College Board's other well-known programs. The first AP exams were administered in 1956.

The College Scholarship Service provides programs and services to help colleges, universities, and scholarship programs distribute student financial aid in an equitable way. Financial aid profiles and computer software programs are among the service's offerings.

Newer Ventures and Future Outlook

Former West Virginia Governor Gaston Caperton was named president of the College Board in 1999. Caperton launched the College Board website, a for-profit Internet venture that offers online SAT registration, practice tests, college searches, online college applications, career exploration tools, and information on college costs and financial aid. ETS has made a significant financial investment in the venture. Rival organizations contend that the site can provide only limited information because the College Board comprises member colleges and universities and would not, for instance, recommend that students and parents negotiate a financial aid package.

Caperton and the College Board will play an important role in the future of college admissions. Women and some minority groups have lower average SAT scores, and some claim the test is culturally biased. Furthermore, legal challenges to and the elimination of affirmative action programs in admissions on many campuses are changing the role of the SAT in admissions and therefore the role of the College Board as well. In several states and systems, including California, Texas, and Florida, some colleges and universities are reducing their reliance on the SAT and guaranteeing admission to students finishing in a set percentage near the top of their high school classes. In 2000 the president of the University of California system made a controversial proposal to the faculty there that applicants no longer be required to take the SAT. He proposed a set of admissions criteria that would provide a more holistic assessment of students, be less quantitative, and recognize a broad spectrum of achievement. If the plan is approved, California would be the first system with competitive admissions to drop the SAT requirement. Other states grappling with the same issues will likely pay close attention to what happens

there. Undoubtedly, the College Board intends to play an important role in any changes that take place. Its programs and services will continue to adapt to the growing diversity of its clientele.

See also: ADVANCED PLACEMENT COURSES/EXAMS; COLLEGE ADMISSIONS; COLLEGE ADMISSIONS TESTS; COLLEGE RECRUITMENT PRACTICES.

BIBLIOGRAPHY

COLLEGE ENTRANCE EXAMINATION BOARD. 2000. *College Board Annual Report.* New York: College Entrance Examination Board.

GOSE, BEN. 1999. "Historic Shift at the College Board as the SAT Faces Fresh Opposition." *Chronicle of Higher Education* 46(17):A51–A52.

WILDAVSKY, BEN; KLEINER, CAROLYN; HARTIGAN, RACHEL; PERRY, JOELLEN; MARCUS, DAVID L.; LORD, MARY C; and BOSER, ULRICH. 2001. "Reining in the Test of Tests." *U.S. News and World Report* 130(9):46–50.

INTERNET RESOURCE

COLLEGE BOARD. 2002. <www.collegeboard.com>.

MAUREEN E. WILSON

COLLEGE EXTRACURRICULAR ACTIVITIES

At the beginning of the twenty-first century, many colleges and universities have a broad educational mission: to develop the "whole student." On college campuses, extracurricular involvement is a key tool in this personal development. For the majority of college and university students, involvement in extracurricular activities plays an integral role in the collegiate experience. Students become involved in extracurricular activities not only for entertainment, social, and enjoyment purposes, but most important, to gain and improve skills. A wide and diversified range of extracurricular activities exists on U.S. campuses, meeting a variety of student interests.

Impact on Students

The importance of extracurricular activities on college campuses is well established. The primary goals of extracurricular activities focus on the individual student level, the institutional level, and the broader community level. These activities exist to complement the university's academic curriculum and to augment the student's educational experience. According to a 1993 article by Alexander Astin, almost any type of student involvement in college positively affects student learning and development. Extracurricular activities provide a setting to become involved and to interact with other students, thus leading to increased learning and enhanced development. Specifically, a student's peer group is the most important source of influence on a student's academic and personal development. By identifying with a peer group, that group may influence a student's affective and cognitive development as well as his or her behavior.

As the development of the well-rounded individual is a principal goal of extracurricular activities on college and university campuses, the numerous experiences these activities afford positively impact students' emotional, intellectual, social, and interpersonal development. By working together with other individuals, students learn to negotiate, communicate, manage conflict, and lead others. Taking part in these out-of-the-classroom activities helps students to understand the importance of critical thinking skills, time management, and academic and intellectual competence. Involvement in activities helps students mature socially by providing a setting for student interaction, relationship formation, and discussion. Working outside of the classroom with diverse groups of individuals allows for students to gain more self-confidence, autonomy, and appreciation for others' differences and similarities.

Students also develop skills specific to their career path and imperative for future job success. Students have opportunities to improve their leadership and interpersonal skills while also increasing their self-confidence. Extracurricular involvement allows students to link academic knowledge with practical experience, thereby leading to a better understanding of their own abilities, talents, and career goals. Future employers seek individuals with these increased skill levels, making these involved students more viable in the job market. Specifically, participation in extracurricular activities and leadership roles in these activities are positively linked to attainment of one's first job and to managerial potential.

Student involvement in extracurricular activities also positively impacts educational attainment. Ernest T. Pascarella and Patrick T. Terenzini's 1991

research indicates that extracurricular involvement has a positive impact on attaining a bachelor's degree and on educational aspirations. Students who are actively engaged are more likely to have higher educational ambitions than uninvolved students.

Finally, extracurricular activities focus on institutional goals, such as building and sustaining community on campus as well as student retention. As campuses become more diverse, students desire an environment in which they feel connected to others and to the university. Extracurricular activities provide a place for students to come together, discuss pertinent ideas and issues, and accomplish common goals. Within this community, where students feel comfortable with one another, learning and development are enhanced and student retention is positively impacted. According to Vincent Tinto's 1987 research, students will be more likely to persist in college if they feel they have had rewarding encounters with a college's social and academic systems. Through extracurricular participation, students frequently interact with peers who have similar interests, providing social integration into the college environment. As a result, involved students view their college years as a positive experience and feel they are a vital part of the university, resulting in higher retention rates.

Types of Extracurricular Activities

Because of the diverse interests of college students, the range of extracurricular activity offerings varies extensively, depending upon the size and type of college or university. Extracurricular activities range from primarily social organizations to governance organizations to intercollegiate athletic programs. Each activity offers students an opportunity to work with others and to gain essential life skills. Though numerous extracurricular activities exist, the following activities are those that are most commonly found on college campuses.

Student government. One of the most widespread types of extracurricular experience available on college campuses is student government. Students involved in governance organizations, such as student government and residence hall government, are typically elected by their peers to function as the "official voice" of students to university administration. These government participants often serve on campus-wide committees in an effort to represent the ideas and concerns of their fellow students. Student government functions include allocating funds to other organizations, planning programs related to student interests, providing forums for student issue discussion, and helping to build and sustain a successful campus community. Additional examples of campus governance organizations include honor councils, which seek to enforce a university's honor code, and judiciary boards, where students hear disciplinary cases and render verdicts.

Athletics. Almost every college and university in the United States offers some type of intercollegiate and intramural athletics. Student athletes may "try out" for intercollegiate sports teams such as volleyball, basketball, or lacrosse. Being a varsity athlete requires a great commitment of time and energy for practicing, conditioning, and competing. Intramural sports provide an opportunity for all nonvarsity student athletes to play a sport they enjoy, while competing against their peers. Typically, colleges and universities offer several intramural options including flag football, soccer, and tennis. Players at all skill levels are invited to participate, and often these activities may be quite competitive. For those students who particularly enjoy watching collegiate sports, many schools have student spirit organizations that allow students to attend sporting events, sit in a special student cheering section, and applaud the home team.

Academic and professional organizations. Academic major and professional organizations assist their members in acquiring experience in their chosen occupational field and in aiding in the job search. Students convene to discuss pertinent issues related to their field of interest and to learn job-related skills in an effort to be fully prepared for future success. Such professional organizations typically focus on one career area of interest. Examples of professional organizations include the American Marketing Association, Student Education Association, and the Mathematics Society.

Volunteer and service-related activities. Volunteer and service-related activities exist to help improve the local and worldwide community, an important goal of extracurricular activities. In the Alternative Spring Break program, students engage in community service projects, such as rebuilding homes, planting trees, or tutoring students during their college spring break. Additional service projects and organizations function throughout the year, including Alpha Phi Omega, Habitat for Humanity, and Circle K, which promote service and volunteerism during the college years. Service-learning programs offer students an opportunity to contribute to their community and, most important, to critically reflect upon their service experiences.

Multicultural activities. Multicultural activities focus on increasing awareness and understanding of various cultures and ethnic and racial backgrounds. Many schools sponsor festivals, concerts, lectures, and discussions that promote multicultural awareness on campus in which students may participate. In addition, involvement in these activities may be an important step toward positive racial, ethnic, or sexual-identity development. Examples of multicultural organizations include Black Student Union, Lambda (a gay, lesbian, bisexual, and transgender student organization), Muslim Student Association, and Russian Club.

The arts. Students interested in fine arts have a plethora of extracurricular opportunities in which they can actively participate. Activities including plays, musicals, and dance concerts offer a chance for students to demonstrate their dramatic abilities. Marching band, jazz band, orchestra, and singing groups allow students to pursue their musical interests at the college level. Pottery, sculpture, and mosaic classes and workshops are also offered for students to learn and enjoy.

Other activities. In addition to the specific extracurricular activities previously mentioned, other activities exist on many college campuses. Honorary organizations recognize student scholars, often in a certain academic discipline, who maintain a specific grade point average. Religious organizations offer students an opportunity to gather in fellowship with students of similar religious backgrounds. Media organizations on campus consist of print, television, and radio venues, and these activities may include writing or taking pictures for the school newspaper, serving on the yearbook staff, or working as a disc jockey for the campus radio station. Individuals interested in politics may join the College Republicans or College Democrats. Students who enjoy planning campus-wide events may participate in the Homecoming or Parents' Weekend committees. Greek organizations (fraternities and sororities) offer many social opportunities while also promoting service and leadership.

See also: COLLEGE AND ITS EFFECT ON STUDENTS; COLLEGE STUDENT RETENTION; LIVING AND LEARNING CENTER RESIDENCE HALLS; RESIDENTIAL COLLEGES.

BIBLIOGRAPHY

ASTIN, ALEXANDER W. 1977. *Four Critical Years.* San Francisco: Jossey-Bass.

ASTIN, ALEXANDER W. 1993. "What Matters in College." *Liberal Education* 79(4):4–15.

CHICKERING, ARTHUR, and REISSER, LINDA. 1993. *Education and Identity.* San Francisco: Jossey-Bass.

KUH, GEORGE D. 1995. "The Other Curriculum: Out-of-Class Experiences Associated with Student Learning and Personal Development." *Journal of Higher Education* 66:123–155.

MOORE, JODY; LOVELL, CHERYL D.; MCGANN, TAMMY; and WYRICK, JASON. 1998. "Why Involvement Matters: A Review of Research on Student Involvement in the Collegiate Setting." *College Student Affairs Journal* 17(2):4–17.

PASCARELLA, ERNEST T., and TERENZINI, PATRICK T. 1991. *How College Affects Students.* San Francisco: Jossey-Bass.

TINTO, VINCENT. 1987. *Leaving College.* Chicago: University of Chicago Press.

WHIPPLE, EDWARD G. 1996. "Student Activities." In *Student Affairs Practice in Higher Education,* 2nd edition, ed. Audry L. Rentz and Associates. Springfield, IL: Thomas.

AMY M. TENHOUSE

COLLEGE FINANCIAL AID

Despite the fact that college tuition rose much more rapidly than either consumer prices or family incomes during the 1980s and 1990s, few college students paid the full cost of higher education during this period. Those who attended public colleges and universities paid relatively low tuition, with state taxpayers funding much of the cost of running these institutions. Students enrolled in private colleges and universities generally paid significantly higher tuition, but that tuition was rarely high enough to cover costs, which have traditionally been subsidized by private donors.

Over half of all undergraduate students—and over 70 percent of those who attend full-time—receive financial aid to help pay their tuition. Most of this aid, which adds up to almost $70 billion a year, comes from federal or state governments or di-

rectly from the institutions. It may be in the form of grants (which do not have to be repaid), loans, or work. Some aid is based on financial need, while other aid is awarded on the basis of academic qualifications, athletic ability, or other personal characteristics.

Need-Based Aid

Historically, the driving force behind student financial aid has been the goal of providing access to higher education regardless of a student's ability to pay. The value placed on equal opportunity in American society, combined with the role of education in determining occupational and financial success, has created strong support for devoting both public and private funds to subsidizing students who would otherwise not have the means to continue education beyond high school. Although a decreasing proportion of student aid is based purely on financial circumstances, need-based aid remains the core of the financial aid system.

"Ability to pay" and "financial need" are not precise concepts, but an elaborate system has developed to direct funds toward those who need them most. The current approach to measuring need dates back to the mid-1950s, when a group of colleges established the College Scholarship Service of the College Board. They developed a standardized system of measuring family ability to pay, which allowed them to distribute their funds more equitably. This system has evolved over time and continues to guide the financial aid systems of many private nonprofit colleges and universities. Since 1986, Congress has legislated a formula for determining eligibility for federal need-based aid funds. This formula also provides the basis for aid allocation in many states.

Under both the congressionally mandated *Federal Methodology* (FM) and the formulas used by most colleges and universities, need is defined as the cost of attending college less the Expected Family Contribution (EFC)—which is determined by the need-analysis formula—a federal methodology that determines how much families/students can afford to pay and is used to allocate federal funds. (For students who are not dependent on their parents, only the student's financial resources are considered.) Students apply for aid by filling out the federal government's Free Application for Federal Student Aid (FAFSA), as well as any additional forms required by the schools to which they are applying. FM focuses on current income levels, family size, and the number of family members in college, though many institutions collect additional information from applicants and measure financial strength using a formula that, like the College Board's, relies on both income and assets in addition to relevant family circumstances.

Federal Aid

The federal government provides about three-quarters of its $48 billion of student aid in the form of loans. Half of this amount is in the form of subsidized loans to students. Students determined through the Federal Methodology to be eligible for need-based aid either borrow directly from the government (William D. Ford Direct Loans, usually called simply Ford Direct Loans) or take federally guaranteed loans from banks or other private lenders (Federal Family Education Loans, or FFELs). The government pays the interest on these subsidized loans while the student is in school.

In the 1990s, non-need-based loans became an important component of the federal student aid system. Forty percent of federal education loans are now in the form of unsubsidized student loans. Introduced in 1992, these loans are available without regard to financial need, and interest accrues on them during the college years. The federal government also provides non-need-based loans to parents of undergraduate students.

The largest federal grant aid program, the Pell Grant, is the main source of aid targeted directly at the most economically disadvantaged students. By the year 2000, almost 4 million students a year received an average of about $2,000 a year under the Pell program, which provided maximum grants of over $3,000. Funding for Pell Grants increased about 15 percent in real terms during the 1990s, but the growth was almost entirely in the number of recipients, not in the size of the average grant. In 2000, the maximum grant covered less than half as much of the cost of attending both public and private four-year institutions as was the case in the mid-1970s.

In addition to a variety of other smaller grant programs, the federal government provides about $1 billion in work-study aid, which subsidizes student employment during the academic year. Like Pell Grants and subsidized student loans, work-study funds are need-based and are distributed on the basis of eligibility as determined by the Federal Methodology.

Since 1998, the federal government has supplemented these explicit student aid programs with tax-based subsidies to college students. The Hope Scholarship and Lifetime Learning Tax Credits are nonrefundable tax credits that reduce the federal income taxes of students or their parents who are paying tuition. These credits benefit those who earn enough income to pay income taxes, but whose income falls below the legislated maximum. In other words, they are directed primarily toward middle-income students. The subsidies provided by these tax credits exceed the amount of federal grant aid to students.

State Aid

State subsidies for higher education come in the form of the relatively low tuition levels enjoyed by all students at public colleges and universities. However, states also have grant programs to assist students in covering their college costs. State grant aid grew much more rapidly than federal grant aid during the 1990s. By the year 2000, nine states spent less than $2 billion a year on student aid, but South Dakota was the only state with no program in place. At the other end of the spectrum, five states provided more than $200 billion a year to their students.

As is the case with federal student aid, the proportion of state aid that is based on financial need was smaller in 2000 than it was in 1990. Georgia has set a national example with its merit-based program and many states appear to be following suit. Nonetheless, more than 80 percent of state aid is dedicated to undergraduate need-based programs, and many states still have only need-based grant programs.

Institutional Aid

Financial aid funded directly by institutions grew very rapidly in the 1990s, particularly in private nonprofit colleges and universities, but also in the public sector. By 2000, about 20 percent of total student aid and almost half of total grant aid came from institutions. Financial aid, which used to be viewed only as a subsidy to students, is now frequently seen as serving multiple purposes. In addition to using it to make college affordable for more students, many colleges and universities are devising strategies to use aid dollars to attract particular types of students by influencing students' choices among institutions. Many schools have increased the proportion of their grants and scholarships they award to students based on academic or other personal qualifications. On public campuses, over half of the student aid is now based on criteria other than need. However, at private colleges and universities, about 80 percent of the student aid is still based on financial need as determined by a need analysis formula.

Financial Aid and Affordability

Student aid covers more of the cost of college for full-time students than for part-time students, and it covers more for lower-income students than for higher-income students. Grant aid reduces the amount students have to pay for education, while loans reduce liquidity constraints but impose repayment burdens after college. In other words, because of financial aid, different students pay very different amounts for the same educational experience. The student aid system is complicated, with aid coming from a variety of different sources and allocated based on a variety of different criteria. While it is difficult to measure precisely the impact of the aid system, it is clear that the availability of student aid has significantly increased the number of students who have the opportunity to continue education after high school, and also broadened the choice of institutions available to many students. Nonetheless, there is considerable evidence that financial aid has not succeeded in making higher education affordable for all qualified low-income students.

See also: COLLEGE ADMISSIONS; COLLEGE RECRUITMENT PRACTICES; COLLEGE SEARCH AND SELECTION.

BIBLIOGRAPHY

THE COLLEGE BOARD. 2000. *Trends in Student Aid, 2000.* Washington, DC: College Entrance Examination Board.

KING, JACQUELINE. 1999. *Financing a College Education: How It Works, How It's Changing.* Phoenix: American Council on Education/Oryx Press.

NATIONAL ASSOCIATION OF STATE STUDENT GRANT AND AID PROGRAMS. 2000. *30th Annual NASSGAP Survey Report.* Albany, NY: National Association of State Student Grant and Aid Programs.

NATIONAL CENTER FOR EDUCATION STATISTICS. 2002. *Federal Support for Education: Fiscal Years 1980 to 2001.* Washington, DC: U.S. Department of Education.

SANDY BAUM

COLLEGE RANKINGS

David Webster stated in 1986 that there are two elements that define college rankings. The first is that academic quality can be measured by selected criteria. For example, in many studies the reputation of the faculty and the selectivity of students are used as measures of an institution's quality. The second element is that using these measurements leads to an ordering of institutions. In other words, since quality is in short supply, there can be only one number-one school. Therefore, unlike classifications (e.g., Carnegie classifications), which group institutions by type, or guides, which give information on individual colleges (e.g., *Peterson's Guide to Four Year Colleges*), rankings order institutions from best to worst.

History of Rankings

This notion of ranking the academic excellence of U.S. colleges and universities is not new. For nearly 100 years various organizations have attempted to rank postsecondary institutions. In 1910 James Cattell from Columbia University offered rankings in *American Men of Science* that assessed the "scientific strength" of elite institutions by looking at the reputations of their science and social science faculty. Most early efforts applied the ranking to the college as a whole, rather than to individual departments. The rankings also tended to be based on what happened to the students after graduation instead of the accomplishments of the school's faculty. Cattell's work is an early exception.

E. Grady Bogue and Robert L. Saunders offered a brief history of graduate school rankings in 1992. They reported that the first graduate school study was conducted in 1925 by Raymond Hughes. He called on his fellow faculty members at Miami University in Ohio to draw up a list of quality universities and to identify national scholars in specific fields of study to serve as raters. Ultimately, in *A Study of Graduate Schools of America,* Hughes relied on forty to sixty raters to assess twenty disciplines for graduate study at thirty-six universities. He followed up this ranking with another in 1934 for the American Council on Education. In this report, he assessed fifty disciplines and increased the number of raters to 100. Graduate programs were not ranked again until 1959, when Hayward Keniston conducted his assessment of them. The list of schools was surprisingly similar to the work done by Hughes in 1925.

Two other well-known graduate school studies were done by Allan Cartter in 1966 and Kenneth D. Roose and Charles J. Anderson in 1970.

Since that time, there have been several other notable studies that assessed graduate education. One major study was conducted in 1982 for the Conference Board of Associated Research Councils. It was far more comprehensive than the earlier efforts—covering thirty-two disciplines at 228 institutions. Then, in 1995, the National Research Council's Committee for the Study of Research-Doctoral Programs assessed forty-one disciplines and 274 institutions using over 7,500 raters. These 1995 rankings included both reputational ratings based on the opinions of faculty and objective data that focused on student–faculty ratios, number of programs, and faculty publications and awards. In 1990 *U.S. News and World Report* began to offer their rankings of graduate and professional programs, focusing on business, law, medicine, and engineering.

In general, the early rankings efforts were not distributed widely. Most of these attempts were viewed only by "academic administrators, federal agencies, state legislators, graduate student applicants, and higher education researchers" (Stuart, p. 16). The audience, however, grew substantially when *U.S. News and World Report* began publishing rankings of undergraduate institutions in 1983. By the late 1990s, *U.S. News and World Report, Time* partnering with the *Princeton Review, Newsweek* partnering with Kaplan Testing Service, and *Money* magazine were selling an estimated 6.7 million copies of their special rankings issues annually. As Patricia M. McDonough and her associates illustrated in 1998, rankings have become big business. It should be noted that there are all kinds of college rankings besides those that look at academic quality. For instance, *Money* magazine determines the "Best College Buys" and the *Princeton Review* names the top party schools.

In spite of the numerous methods employed over the years, academic rankings have been amazingly stable (see Table 1). Curiously, there is just enough change to give the listings credibility. The number-one school may change from year to year, but, in general, schools near the top of the list decades ago are generally seen near the top of the list in the early twenty-first century. In 1991 Alexander Astin contended that the stability could be explained by "the fact that beliefs about the institutional hierarchy in American higher education affect our per-

ceptions of both graduate and undergraduate programs and are highly resistant to change" (p. 37), and that this "folklore" regarding an institution's quality affects students' college choices as well as the perceptions of institutional raters. Therefore, according to Astin, rankings reflect the myth of quality, rather than the reality of it.

The Pros and Cons of Rankings

Proponents of rankings contend that the main advantage to rankings is that they provide a way for families to make "sound economic decisions" regarding the education of their children. Rankings serve as a type of consumer report for families wishing to compare colleges and universities. Webster claimed that rankings bring to the attention of some families little-known schools that may be good choices for their children. Also, he found that ranking approaches have become more standardized, because *U.S. News and World Report* publishes its ranking methods.

McDonough and her colleagues offered several additional reasons for the public's interest in these publications. First, ever since the Watergate scandal, the American public has developed a skeptical attitude toward the country's national institutions. Therefore, as college admissions grow more chaotic, the public turns to these seemingly unbiased resources for help in their college searches. Thus, rankings help reduce the risk in a student's college choice. Second, the highly competitive race for places at the university further encourages families to seek objective, comparative data. Families believe the higher the ranking, the better the reputation of a college or university. According to Charles J. Fombrun, the college's "reputation is a cue to consumers of what they can expect; a reputation acts as a guarantee of quality" (McDonough, Antonio, Walpole, and Perez, p. 515). Third, students and families eager to bask in the glow of attending a highly ranked institution rely on these published reports to inform their college-going decisions.

In spite of these attributes, rankings are not without critics. Since the beginning, colleges have cried foul at the publication of rankings. For example, in 1986 Webster reported that the 1911 effort by the U.S. Bureau of Education was withheld by two U.S. presidents because of the outcry against it from college administrators. Today, the complaints are just as vociferous. Steven Sample, the president of the University of Southern California, called the

TABLE 1

U.S. News and World Report's top three liberal arts colleges for selected years between 1985 and 2002				
1985	**1987**	**1988**	**1990**	**2002**
1. Williams	Williams	Swarthmore	Amherst	Amherst (1)
2. Swarthmore	Swarthmore	Amherst	Swarthmore	Swarthmore (1)
3. Amherst	Carleton	Williams	Williams	Williams

SOURCE: Based on Webster, David S. 1992. *Change* 24(2):19 for 1985–1990 results and <www.usnews.com> for 2002 results.

rankings "silly" and "bordering on fraud" (Trounson and Gottlieb, p. A12). Theodore Mitchell, president of Occidental College, contended that "the rankings are 'a distortion of an institution's character and, at worst, a kind of tyrannical tool to get institutions to chase after a single vision of what good higher education is'" (Trounson and Gottlieb, p. A12). William Massy, director of the Stanford Institute for Higher Education Research, and Robert Zemsky, director of the Institute for Research on Higher Education at the University of Pennsylvania, went so far as to say that rankings encourage "the kind of competition that puts higher education at risk" (Webster 1992, p. 19). The criticisms even come from within the *U.S. News and World Report* organization. Amy Graham, an economist who was responsible for the list for two years in the late 1990s, stated that the methods for data collection are "misleading" and "produce invalid results" (Trounson and Gottlieb, p. A12).

Debra Stuart in 1995 offered a number of other common criticisms of rankings. First, "there is no consensus about how to measure academic quality" (Stuart, p. 18). Therefore, how does one make sense of the various rankings efforts? Additionally, Astin's concern regarding the stability of rankings suggests that myth and institutional perceptions may have as much to do with the rankings as the methods used to determine them. In fact, the methods for assessing quality reflect a bias toward institutional size, student test scores, and the number of "star" faculty. Astin and others question this definition of quality, because it has nothing to do with the student's college experience or learning.

Second, Stuart stated that raters are biased depending on their own affiliations and knowledge of institutions. Would the rankings be the same with different raters? Third, she suggested that there is a halo effect. For example, one highly ranked department at a college or university may provide suffi-

cient glow to allow other departments at that institution to be more highly ranked than is warranted. Fourth, the timing of assessments may affect the outcome. If studies are conducted close on each other's heels, then the results of one may affect the raters' views for the second. Also, if the studies are not done regularly, then the standing ranking may not reflect changes in the department, good or bad. And finally, the use of different sorts of methodologies makes comparisons between reports impossible.

Another criticism leveled at rankings is that colleges change their own processes and procedures to attempt to better their rankings. They do this because it is believed that high rankings positively affect admissions. Highly ranked schools have seen an increase in the number of student applications, a rise in the average SAT scores of entering students, and less need for financial aid offers to attract students. So, for example, the practice of early acceptance, which commits early applicants—who tend to be high achievers—to attend an institution if accepted, distorts selectivity and yield figures (i.e., the percentage of admitted students who actually accept admission offers).

The effects of rankings, however, are not limited to admissions. College administrators use the data to make decisions regarding resource allocations. Therefore the pressure is on for programs to do well, so departments may manipulate their reporting in a way to improve their placement on the list. For example, administrators at Cornell University removed students who had never graduated from their alumni lists "before computing the fraction of alumni who contributed to the university. This change . . . improved Cornell's reported alumni giving rate, a factor used by *U.S. News*" to assess quality (Monks and Ehrenberg, p. 44).

Yet, not all adaptations are seen as a negative. Webster in 1992 noted it is a virtue when institutions improve their facilities in their effort to improve their rankings. For example, the administrators at Texas A&M University acknowledge they use the rankings to spur changes, such as class size, with a goal of being ranked a top-ten university.

Central to much of the criticism is that the current rankings do not look at student learning in their assessment of an institution. As a result, an alternative to the *U.S. News and World Report* rankings has been developed. This National Survey of Student Engagement attempts to measure student learning and satisfaction. It hopes to create "national benchmarks of effective educational practices" (Reisberg, p. A67). Still in its infancy, it is unclear if this survey will usurp the *U.S. News and World Report* rankings or offer valuable supplemental information for prospective students, their families, and researchers.

Nevertheless, "academic quality rankings, despite all their faults, have . . . been useful, from their beginnings, in providing more accurate information about the comparative quality of American colleges, universities, and individual departments and professional fields of study than any other source" (Webster 1986, p. 9). Families have come to rely on these studies to make their college-choice decisions, so rankings are most likely here to stay.

See also: COLLEGE SEARCH AND SELECTION; HIGHER EDUCATION IN THE UNITED STATES, *subentry on* SYSTEM.

BIBLIOGRAPHY

ASTIN, ALEXANDER W. 1991. *Achieving Educational Excellence.* San Francisco: Jossey-Bass.

BOGUE, E. GRADY, and SAUNDERS, ROBERT L. 1992. *The Evidence for Quality.* San Francisco: Jossey-Bass.

EHRENBERG, RONALD G., and HURST, PETER J. 1996. "The 1995 NRC Ratings of Doctoral Programs: A Hedonic Model." *Change* 28(3):46–55.

GOSE, BEN. 1999. "A New Survey of 'Good Practices' Could Be an Alternative to Rankings." *Chronicle of Higher Education* October 22:A65.

HOOVER, ERIC. 2002. "New Attacks on Early Decision." *Chronicle of Higher Education* January 11:A45.

HOSSLER, DONALD, and FOLEY, ERIN. 1995. "Reducing the Noise in the College Choice Process: The Use of College Guidebooks and Ratings." In *Evaluating and Responding to College Guidebooks and Rankings,* ed. R. Dan Walleri and Marsha K. Moss. San Francisco: Jossey-Bass.

MACHUNG, ANNE. 1998. "Playing the Rankings Game." *Change* 30(4):12–16.

MCDONOUGH, PATRICIA M.; ANTONIO, ANTHONY LISING; WALPOLE, MARYBETH; and PEREZ, LEONOR XOCHITL. 1998. "College Rankings: Democratized College Knowledge for Whom?" *Research in Higher Education* 39:513–537.

MONKS, JAMES, and EHRENBERG, RONALD G. 1998. "*U.S. News and World Report*'s College Rankings: Why They Do Matter." *Change* 31(6):42–51.

REISBERG, LEO. 2000. "Are Students Actually Learning?" *Chronicle of Higher Education* November 17:A67.

STUART, DEBRA. 1995. "Reputational Rankings: Background and Development." In *Evaluating and Responding to College Guidebooks and Rankings,* ed. R. Dan Walleri and Marsha K. Moss. San Francisco: Jossey-Bass.

TROUNSON, REBECCA, and GOTTLIEB, JEFF. 2001. "'Best Colleges' List Released amid Criticism," *Los Angeles Times* September 7.

WEBSTER, DAVID S. 1986. *Academic Quality Rankings of American Colleges and Universities.* Springfield, IL: Charles C. Thomas.

WEBSTER, DAVID S. 1992. "Rankings of Undergraduate Education in *U.S. News* and *Money*—Are They Any Good?" *Change* 24(2):18–31.

WEBSTER, DAVID S., and SKINNER, TAD. 1996. "Rating Ph.D. Programs: What the NRC Report Says . . . and Doesn't Say." *Change* 28(3):22–45.

INTERNET RESOURCE

U.S. NEWS AND WORLD REPORT. 2002. "America's Best Colleges 2002: Liberal Arts Colleges—Bachelor (National) Top 50." <www.usnews.com/usnews/edu/college/rankings/libartco/tier1/t1libartco.htm>.

BARBARA F. TOBOLOWSKY

COLLEGE RECRUITMENT PRACTICES

College recruitment practices are as distinctive as the scope and breath of the more than 3,200 accredited colleges and universities in the United States. With more than 2.5 million students matriculating to a college campus for the first time each year, the role and responsibility of admission and enrollment personnel in higher education has become increasingly critical to the success of the institutions and the experience of the student.

Historical and demographic influences have allowed admission and recruitment practices to evolve and develop over the past 400 years of American higher education. During the first 300 years, admission duties were performed by a variety of college personnel and were primarily an orientation function, absent of any screening or recruitment. College presidents of the eighteenth and nineteenth centuries performed a dual role as recruiter and fundraiser. From the Civil War to World War II, America witnessed an increase in the number and variety of colleges. Enrollment growth ensued and denominational colleges were founded across the continent, while land-grant and state-supported universities brought a college education closer to the people. These actions translated into enrollment growth and recruitment efforts settled into an admissions role of screening and seeking a strong instructional fit for the student and college.

Origins of modern recruitment practices can be found in the mass expansion of higher education since World War II, emerging directly from the Servicemen's Readjustment Act of 1944 and the baby boom that followed. The rise in applications during the 1960s and early 1970s led many colleges to increase enrollments and concurrently expand capacity. The abundance of college enrollees reversed during the 1980s leaving colleges with increased capacity and a declining applicant pool. The prospects of declining enrollments prompted colleges and universities to adopt marketing practices used in business that centered around Phillip Kotler's emphasis on product, price, place, and promotion. College recruiting practices became reliant on market principles for success and matured into providing more information and increased attention to the prospective student.

Recruitment Theory and Practices

The recruitment funnel, where a high number of inquiries of prospective students from numerous entry points narrows to and moves toward application and ultimately a smaller number of matriculated students, is at the foundation of the college-recruiting theory. This funneling process is aided by recruitment efforts designed to move the prospect from casual interest to enrolling. The process is starting earlier and lasting longer. The inputs of a large number of inquiries result in a less but measurable number of applications, which ultimately yields a smaller number of enrollees. Database management, programmed marketing, and audience segmentation are designed to keep prospects engaged and moving through the funnel. Recruiting activities and market research allow enrollment managers to target prospective students at various stages of interest. Each contact should have a specific action-oriented, measurable task. A goal early in the funnel may be to encourage a visit, while a later goal may be to have an applicant commit to attend. Mail, telephone, electronic media, and personal contact are used to move the student from initial contact to matriculation. Publications are added at strategic times to inform and persuade. Analyzing demographic data, constructing surveys to measure attitude and preferences, use of geodemographic tools, and evaluating the efficacy of recruitment practices have allowed institutions to focus more personal attention on the prospective student.

Contemporary college recruiting practices are centered in the metaphoric recruiting funnel. Acknowledging that no one communication strategy will work with prospective students, college recruitment practices in the early twenty-first century seek to individualize the process. By segmenting the market, enrollment managers target prospects utilizing data that explains how students make college choice decisions. Students have become sophisticated consumers: they comb through massive quantities of direct mail, explore Internet websites, visit colleges, and even hire private counselors.

The most effective recruiting practices and strategies employed by enrollment professionals are visits to high schools in primary markets by a member of the admissions office, interaction on the Internet, hosting campus visits with prospective students, and offering merit-based scholarships. Live presentations by college personnel for prospective students at high schools and on-campus visits at colleges are practices that are considered strong inducements in choosing a college. The presence of friendliness, accessibility of faculty members, and attitude of administrative officials during the campus visit are highly valued. These are used regularly and are considered very effective strategies.

Secondary and less effective college recruitment practices are visits to secondary or test markets; college fairs and nights; using alumni to recruit; hosting off-campus meetings or social events for high school counselors; multimedia presentations; billboard, print, or broadcast advertising; and school promotional videos.

Use of direct mail has continued to increase as written communication continues to increase. Many colleges use mailing lists that contain information compiled by national testing agencies. Names are purchased that fit criteria selected by the college, such as geographical location and size of the college. Many private four-year colleges send eight or more written communications to prospective students. Analytical techniques and market research tools allow institutions to effectively target direct mail, off-campus visits and receptions, telemarketing, and financial aid awards.

Telephone contact is also used as a practice in student recruitment to augment existing correspondence and as a cost-effective method to track students through the funnel. Telephone recruitment calls made by students, admissions staff, faculty members, and alumni are effective. Institutions are increasingly using commercial vendors for prospect identification.

The use of technology to market institutions and counsel students adds new dimensions to college recruitment practices. The Internet, World Wide Web, and CD-ROMs have played a major role in recruiting students while reducing costs for their institutions. Significant elements of college recruitment practices are moving to the Internet and it is common for students to apply online. The Internet affords a prospective student unlimited and uncontrolled access to formal and informal information about any institution.

Nontraditional Enrollees

Many colleges that experienced growth since the late 1970s have expanded their markets to include adult, international, and transfer students. An institution that has recognized the growing importance of the transfer student market and has recruited transfer students successfully realizes that two out of five newly matriculated students nationally are transfer students. Publications and recruitment techniques targeted for adult or international students should portray the campus from the nontraditional student vantage point. Effective institutional recruiting activities aimed at attracting international students indicates that academic reputation and costs are the most influential factors in choosing to apply and enroll. Recruitment efforts abroad made by college representatives and the development of personal relationships are effective practices. Recruitment strategies should include simplified application forms and brochures specifically targeted to international students.

Ethics

The National Association of College Admission Counseling (NACAC) Statement of Principals of Good Practice defines ethical and accepted methods of student recruitment; institutional promotional techniques and admissions methods were adapted from the NACAC Code of Ethics and are clearly endorsed throughout higher education. Ethical issues are reviewed and revised annually. Joint statements, sharing the ethical values of the NACAC, have been issued and are recognized by all associations that govern the recruitment process in American higher and secondary education. Ethical standards include accuracy in the articulation of information and admission requirements and financial aid opportunities. Standards insist that admissions personnel are viewed as professionals and that their compensation take the form of a fixed salary rather than derive from any formula based on the number of students recruited.

Financial Aid as a Recruiting Tool

Financial aid has been increasingly used as a recruiting and marketing tool, especially for private institutions forced to compete with public institutions. Merit scholarships and non-endowed institutional funds are increasingly used to discount tuition and to make the college choice affordable. Enrollment managers are interested in net tuition income as well as in the number of students, and the use of leveraging financial aid awards has become important tool to increase enrollments. Although discussions continue over the appropriate mix between need-based and merit-based financial aid, colleges and universities use institutional funds to augment federal and state grant and loan programs. Private colleges are providing financial aid to a larger share of their students, and list in their view books the price of tuition before financial aid; public tuition continues to increase, not as the result of increased costs but because of changes in state fiscal policy. Institutional financial aid is used to increase enrollment goals and to change readily measurable student body characteristics.

The Future

Marketing and recruitment are likely to become even more sophisticated. Colleges will depend on a recruitment funnel that is tied to integrated marketing efforts and creates relevance long before the first contact is made. College recruitment practices will be increasingly integrated and coordinated throughout the campus to maximize recruiting initiatives. Traditional recruitment practices, augmented by Internet-based enhancements, will continue. The campus visit will remain a key component in the recruitment process. Mobilizing the total institution toward an integrated marketing enrollment program that fosters ethical, sound, and efficient recruitment practices will effectively serve prospective students and colleges.

See also: COLLEGE ADMISSIONS; COLLEGE ADMISSIONS TESTS, COLLEGE FINANCIAL AID; COLLEGE SEARCH AND SELECTION.

Bibliography

CROSS, ROBERT G. 1997. *Revenue Management: Hard Core Tactics for Market Domination.* New York: Broadway Books.

HOSSLER, DON. 1984. *Enrollment Management: An Integrated Approach.* New York: College Entrance Examination Board.

JOHNSON, ANNE LEWIS. 2000. "The Evolution of Enrollment Management: A Historical Perspective." *Journal of College Admission* 166:4–11.

KOTLER, PHILLIP. 1995. *Strategic Marketing for Nonprofit Organizations.* Portland, OR: Book News.

MCPHERSON, MICHAEL S., and SCHAPIRO, MORTON O. 1998. *The Student Aid Game: Meeting Need and Rewarding Talent in American Higher Education.* Princeton, NJ: Princeton University Press.

NATIONAL ASSOCIATION OF COLLEGE ADMISSION COUNSELING. 2001. "Statement of Principles of Good Practice." In *2001 NACAC Membership Directory.* Alexandria, VA: National Association of College Admission Counseling.

SEVIER, ROBERT A. 2000. "Building an Effective Recruiting Funnel." *Journal of College Admission* 169:10–19.

TAPSCOTT, DON. 2000. *Growing Up Digital: The Rise of the Net Generation.* New York: McGraw-Hill.

MICHAEL A. GRANDILLO

COLLEGES AND UNIVERSITIES, ORGANIZATIONAL STRUCTURE OF

The organizational structures of American colleges and universities vary distinctly, depending on institutional type, culture, and history, yet they also share much in common. While a private liberal arts college may have a large board of trustees, and a public research university nested in a state system no trustees of its own, the vast majority of public and private universities are overseen by an institutional or system-wide governing board. This somewhat paradoxical combination of distinctiveness and uniformity reflects the unique characteristics of individual colleges and universities, and the shared-task environment (including strategic planning, fiscal oversight, curriculum planning, and student affairs) common to American postsecondary institutions. Scholars of higher education view many aspects of private colleges and universities as significantly different than public universities. Yet the reliance on bureaucratic organizational structures and the belief in research, advanced instruction, and service at both types of institutions shape many aspects of public and private university governance structures in a fairly uniform manner.

The organizational structure of colleges and universities is an important guide to institutional activity, but not the only one. Scholars of higher education have developed a variety of multi-dimensional models of organizational behavior that also shed considerable light on college and university structure and process. Multi-dimensional models seek to explain organizational behavior across institutional types, and in various institutional activities. The models vary somewhat in the number of dimensions incorporated, from J. Victor Baldridge's three dimensions (bureaucratic, collegial, and political) and Lee Bolman and Terrence Deal's four-cornered frame (structural, human resource, political, and symbolic) to Robert Birnbaum's five dimensions (bureaucratic, collegial, political, anarchical, and cybernetic). These models are quite helpful in thinking about organizational structure and process within colleges and universities. The same institution may evidence a bureaucratic, hierarchical decision-making process in its central administration, and a collegial process in its academic senate. It is a combination of organizational structure and process that shapes college and university behavior.

Public and private colleges and universities of all types incorporate key authority structures, including a governing board, a president or chancellor, a cohort of administrative leaders, and an academic senate. In public institutions these core organizational entities collaborate with such external authorities as state and federal political leaders, community organizations, and members of the public, as well as business interests and philanthropic foundations. These external organizations routinely interact with and shape the policies and procedures of the university's internal organizational structures.

The degree of uniformity in private and public college and university organizational structures has been shaped by the nature of demands on the postsecondary system since the mid-twentieth century. Although the key governance structures of colleges and universities were present prior to the turn of the twentieth century, the full scope of the university's multifaceted organizational structure, most scholars agree, was not realized until after the rise of the research university, in the wake of World War II. In 1963 then-president of the University of California system, Clark Kerr, described the postwar American university as a *multiversity*. The term captured the increasingly complex organizational and governance structures required to negotiate its ever-expanding task environment.

Governing Boards

A university's governing board, also known as the trustees, regents, or board of visitors, possesses fundamental legal authority over the university. The authority of the governing board is vested in it by the state wherein the school resides or, particularly in the case of older, private institutions, by legally binding royal or colonial charters. Both public and private governing boards are generally constituted of citizen trustees. In the public case those trustees are often political appointees who serve as a fundamental link between the institution and state and national political structures.

In the United States the tradition of lay oversight of colleges and universities can be traced to the founding of Harvard College in 1636. Subsequent private colleges adopted this form of governance, which the U.S. Supreme Court deemed constitutional in its Dartmouth College decision of 1819. Public colleges and universities followed suit, although on the public side the role of governors in trustee appointments and the key role of legislative funding in institutional development has meant that the states play a central role in the governance of the institutions. The federal government has influenced the organization of higher education primarily through legislation—the Morrill Acts, the Higher Education Acts, and the G.I. Bill, for instance—that reinforced decentralized governance and, hence, the authority of institutional governing boards at both public and private institutions. As John Millet noted, "It has long been evident that it is the state governments rather than the federal government that carry the primary authority and responsibility for higher education in the United States" (p. 1).

Governing board members at public institutions typically arrive at the trustee table by one of four paths: direct appointment by the governor; ex-officio appointment; gubernatorial appointment subject to approval of the state legislature; and less frequently, election by popular vote. Public university board members represent the citizens of the state and the terms and conditions of their service are often defined by institutional charter or state constitution. Private boards are generally self-perpetuating, with new trustees chosen by the membership of the standing board. While private colleges and universities benefit considerably from public subsidies and support, private boards are not subject to the same degree of external scrutiny or intervention as are public boards.

The formal responsibilities of university governing boards are significant even as they are few in number. They include preservation of the university charter; institutional performance evaluations; fundraising; liaison with external agencies and political bodies; budget approval; oversight of campus policies and investment strategies; and, perhaps most important, hiring and evaluating the ongoing performance of the university president.

Because of their visibility, symbolic importance, and control over policies with significant political salience, public university boards became subject to increasing challenges from a variety of interests in the last two decades of the twentieth century. These challenges were accompanied by demands for nonpartisan board appointments and trustees that are more representative of the broader society, as well as calls for increased scrutiny of potential conflicts of interest. Boards were also challenged by governors and legislators concerned about issues ranging from rising costs to faculty ideology. A response to the heightened pressures on governing boards was a push for improved trustee education programs in several states in the pursuit of more open and effective governance processes. Given its myriad responsibilities and powers, a strong argument can be made that the board is the most powerful governing agent of the modern university.

The President

The liaison between a postsecondary institution and its governing board is the highest ranking executive officer, a president or chancellor. The president provides overall leadership to the institution and presides over its academic and administrative bureaus. The president generally works closely with a provost, who is responsible for academic affairs, and a chief financial officer, who oversees the institution's fiduciary operations. The president serves as the lead fundraiser, and as a key representative of the university and its academic community to external agencies and actors. Presidential duties include fostering a positive public image of the institution as a site of higher learning, maintaining a close relationship with the institutional governing board to further the president's agenda, and forging points of common cause and agreement with the entire university community and its constituents.

Since World War II the job of university president has become considerably more complex, and in many ways more constrained. Presidential authority has been eroded as boards and external actors have gained more legitimate roles in university governance. Presidential satisfaction has declined, and the average presidential tenure is shorter than before World War II.

No responsibility consumes the modern-day president's time and energy more than his or her role as the institution's principal fundraiser, a task made especially difficult because it requires extensive time away from the institution. While presidential fundraising has been a function of private universities for centuries, the emergence of significant public university fundraising in the 1980s and 1990s is a major development. Fueled by decreasing state and federal support in recent years, public universities have been forced to take on a more significant share of their own funding, with development playing a major role in this process.

Faculty

The formal governing body of the faculty at the institutional level is the academic senate, a body generally comprised of tenured and tenure-track faculty from the various disciplines and professional schools. The faculty senate and its attendant committees provide elected faculty liaisons to the university board and president. A primary function of the senate is to represent the voice of the faculty in matters of university governance.

Each school or college within a university is under the direction of a dean. A chairperson or department head supervises individual departments of instruction. Faculty members are ranked, in descending order, as professor, associate professor, assistant professor, and instructor. Faculty of various ranks may or may not be tenured, depending on the institution. Faculty members can be dismissed from their posts unless and until they have been granted tenure, a term denoting a measure of academic job security that is earned through a combination of demonstrated teaching, research, and service contributions. The faculty generally has significant influence over the hiring of new faculty members, tenure and promotion procedures, the university curriculum and graduation requirements, and admissions criteria.

While the role of the faculty in governance was at one time largely advisory, over time the faculty has become increasingly engaged in policy formation. In many cases the faculty possesses significant authority over academic affairs. Faculty representatives are often found on governing boards, in formal or informal (non-voting) positions. The formal authority of the faculty may be codified in institutional charters or in the standing rules of institutional governing boards.

A number of other factors and informal agreements shape the degree to which faculty are involved in institutional affairs. Many colleges and universities have a commitment to a process of shared governance that incorporates the faculty in various aspects of institutional decision-making. A collegial relationship between the faculty senate and the college or university president is a key component of shared governance, as is the relationship between the faculty senate and the institutional governing board. Faculty authority is also shaped by the strength and reputation of the institution's academic departments and departmental leadership, as well as the faculty's symbolic importance as teachers and producers of knowledge, and the legitimacy provided by individual faculty member's professional expertise.

National organizations also contribute to the legitimacy and organizational standing of the American professorate. Among these, the most prominent is the American Association of University Professors (AAUP). Established in 1915 to advance the collective interests, ideals, and standards of the fledgling university professorate, the AAUP has since that time become best known for its role in the defense of academic freedom and tenure. The AAUP's clearest articulation of this role can be found in its declaration, *Statement of Principles on Academic Freedom and Tenure* (1995). Over time the AAUP has developed initiatives on other aspects of faculty life, including shared university governance. In the last two decades of the twentieth century research on faculty turned attention to the rapid growth in the percentage of non-tenured and non-tenure track faculty in colleges and universities, a shift with significant implications for the organizational structure and governance of those institutions.

Administration and Staff

Internal university administration is composed of two interrelated administrative cohorts: one is responsible for the oversight and administration of academic affairs; the other is charged with institutional administration. The academic and institutional administrations are often in conflict with one another. The growth of the institutional administrative cohort after World War II has led to what some researchers perceive as disproportionate influence on the part of the institutional administration. The increasing growth and autonomy of the institutional administrative cohort also challenges the traditional perception of the overall mission of the university's administration as one of academic support and facilitation. As Amitai Etzioni (1964) has noted, there is an essential tension in organizations such as colleges

and universities that are driven by professional expertise but led by administrators. This has produced demands for a cohort of administrative leaders who can bring professional education and credentials to institutional managerial practice.

Within the academic administration, the president presides over a hierarchy that generally consists of a number of senior officers, including a university provost, and the deans of individual colleges and professional programs. Academic administrators are traditionally drawn from the faculty ranks, where departmental leadership positions serve as preparation for university-wide academic leadership roles.

The managerial cohort of the institutional administration is led by a chief financial officer and various senior executives. The chief financial officer provides leadership and direction to a host of administrative functions that generally includes student services, institutional support, maintenance and operation of the physical plant, and auxiliary enterprises. These individual units in turn encompass smaller departments responsible for more specialized services. The latter part of the twentieth century witnessed increased demands for greater efficiency, productivity, and entrepreneurial management at colleges and universities. Efficiency initiatives in particular, including outsourcing of institutional functions and the hiring of adjunct faculty, engendered significant internal conflict between the managerial and academic administrations.

Students

Historically students have not had a significant role in the organizational structure or governance of colleges and universities. During most of the nineteenth century, college administrations followed a practice of *in loco parentis,* an educational philosophy that led university administrators and faculty members to oversee the academic advancement and personal conduct of their students very closely. Over time a gradual loosening of the institutional academic and social oversight occurred, a result of the university's incorporation of the German university model that emphasized greater student and faculty freedom. The heightened social and intellectual autonomy available to undergraduates encouraged students to seek greater involvement in university governance and administrative affairs.

Student interest in university organization and governance increased significantly in the 1960s. In the aftermath of student unrest and demands for increased student involvement in campus affairs, a degree of student participation on university boards, search committees, and faculty senates has become commonplace. Many colleges and universities include a student representative in either an advisory or voting position on the board of trustees. In addition, students often have their own network of parallel undergraduate and graduate governance organizations headed by a student body president and elected representatives that have contact with university officials, such as the president and the board.

Future Prospects

As the American university moves into the twenty-first century, a number of factors, including the increased complexity of institutional functions, changing student demographics, demands for entrepreneurial behavior, technological innovations, and increases in external interest group interventions will significantly challenge existing organizational structures and processes. The rapid growth in demand for continuing education and the provision of distance programs by colleges and universities in particular has challenged traditional notions of the content and delivery of postsecondary education. A number of key political shifts, including a growing retreat from public funding of colleges and universities, demands for privatization of college and university services, and the use of the university as an instrument in broader national political struggles, will further complicate organizational arrangements. These political shifts entail considerably more institutional outreach to legislatures, governors, and key interest groups at the state and national levels, as well as additional staff in governmental and public relations. Finally, the rise of what Richard T. Ingram terms "activist trusteeship" and increasingly interventionist stances taken by public and private institutional governing boards may require increased collective action by internal cohorts. In order to preserve institutional autonomy and shared governance in a time of increasing political conflict, effort will also need to be directed to creating more effective organizational bridges between colleges and university leaders and institutional governing boards.

See also: ACADEMIC DEAN, THE; BOARD OF TRUSTEES, COLLEGE AND UNIVERSITY; CHIEF ACADEMIC AFFAIRS OFFICERS, COLLEGE AND UNIVERSITY; DE-PARTMENT CHAIRPERSON, THE; FACULTY SENATES, COLLEGE AND UNIVERSITY; GOVERNANCE AND DECISION-MAKING IN COLLEGES AND UNIVERSITIES; INSTITUTIONAL RESEARCH IN HIGHER EDUCATION; PRESIDENCY, COLLEGE AND UNIVERSITY.

BIBLIOGRAPHY

AMERICAN ASSOCIATION OF UNIVERSITY PROFESSORS (AAUP). 1995. *AAUP Policy Documents and Reports,* 8th edition. Washington, DC: American Association of University Professors Press.

BALDRIDGE, J. VICTOR. 1971. *Power and Conflict in the University: Research in the Sociology of Complex Organizations.* New York: J. Wiley.

BALDWIN, ROGER G., and CHRONISTER, JAY L. 2001. *Teaching Without Tenure: Policies and Practices for a New Era.* Baltimore: Johns Hopkins University Press.

BERGER, JOSEPH B., and MILEM, JEFFREY. 2000. "Organizational Behavior in Higher Education and Student Outcomes." In *Higher Education: Handbook of Theory and Research,* Vol. XV, ed. John C. Smart. New York: Agathon.

BIRNBAUM, ROBERT. 1988. *How Colleges Work: The Cybernetics of Academic Organization and Leadership.* San Francisco: Jossey-Bass.

BOLMAN, LEE G., and DEAL, TERRENCE E. 1997. *Reframing Organizations: Artistry, Choice, and Leadership,* 2nd edition. San Francisco: Jossey-Bass.

ETZIONI, AMITAI. 1964. *Modern Organizations.* Englewood Cliffs, NJ: Prentice-Hall.

FISHER, JAMES L., and KOCH, JAMES V. 1996. *Presidential Leadership.* Phoenix, AZ: ACE/Oryx Press.

GIEGER, ROGER. 1986. *The Growth of American Research Universities, 1900–1940.* New York: Oxford University Press.

HYMAN, HAROLD M. 1986. *American Singularity: The 1787 Northwest Ordinance, the 1862 Homestead and Morrill Acts, and the 1944 GI Bill of Rights.* Athens: University of Georgia Press.

INGRAM, RICHARD T. 1996. "New Tensions in the Academic Boardroom." *Educational Record* 77(2–3):49–55.

KERR, CLARK. 1963. *The Uses of the University.* Cambridge, MA: Harvard University Press.

MILLETT, JOHN. 1984. *Conflict in Higher Education: State Government Coordination Versus Institutional Independence.* San Francisco: Jossey-Bass.

PUSSER, BRIAN. 2000. "The Contemporary Politics of Access Policy: California after Proposition 209." In *The States and Public Higher Education: Affordability, Access, and Accountability,* ed. Donald E. Heller. Baltimore: Johns Hopkins University Press.

SLAUGHTER, SHEILA, and LESLIE, LARRY L. 1997. *Academic Capitalism.* Baltimore: Johns Hopkins University Press.

VEYSEY, LAURENCE. 1965. *The Emergence of the American University.* Chicago: University of Chicago Press.

BRIAN PUSSER
CHRISTOPHER P. LOSS

COLLEGES AND UNIVERSITIES WITH RELIGIOUS AFFILIATIONS

The landscape of higher education in North America first began to take shape at the start of the colonial period as religious communities and individual religious leaders realized the need to bring Western education to what was for them a newly discovered land. The motivation for the education varied. Some communities began schools as a means for training religious leaders. The first college, founded in Massachusetts Bay Colony, was Harvard. Evolving from a Puritan tradition now incorporated into the United Church of Christ, Harvard published a brochure in 1643, explaining the college's purpose as "to advance learning and perpetuate it to posterity; dreading to leave an illiterate ministry to the churches."

Religiously affiliated schools and colleges expressed their missions in different manners as they developed in the colonies and across the frontier; all pursued their work with energetic mission. For some, the educational mission was to assure that "children of the faith" had the opportunity to grow intellectually in remote locations across the frontier. For others, the mission was to create educational opportunity for all persons in order that they might develop their God-given intellect. Often the two approaches were combined, as noted in the challenge Methodist Episcopal Bishop Francis Asbury presented to every Methodist congregation in America in 1791: "give the key of knowledge in a general way to your children, and those of the poor in the vicinity of your small towns and villages" (Michael et al., p. 13).

Religiously affiliated colleges often combined the mission of education with the desire to train individuals in religious practice and to evangelize others. This mission is reflected in words by Disciples of Christ educator Alexander Campbell (1788–1866), "Colleges and churches go hand in hand in the progress of Christian civilization" (p. 61).

Religiously affiliated educational institutions often developed in response to social changes. For example, the world's first college charted to grant degrees to women was Wesleyan College in Macon, Georgia (1836). At the conclusion of the Civil War, the Freedman's Aid Society responded to absence of educational opportunity for newly freed slaves by creating institutes and colleges throughout the South. Many of these institutions continue their critical role in education in the early twenty-first century. Often church-related colleges began as academies or seminaries and then grew to college or university status. Many had short lives, closing as the result of social, demographic, political, and—quite often—financial reasons. Some colleges severed their relationship with the religious communities and continue in the twenty-first century as quality independent institutions. Among these are Vanderbilt University, Auburn University, University of Southern California, Oberlin College, and Princeton University. In 1881, 80 percent of the colleges in the United States were church related and private. In 2001, 20 percent of the colleges—approximately 980 institutions—had connection to a religious tradition. The "Digest of Educational Statistics, 2000," indicates that sixty-six religious groups in the United States currently sponsor colleges or universities. These institutions enroll more than 1.5 million students.

Characteristics

Religiously affiliated colleges and universities defy a monolithic description. They are as diverse as their religious traditions and the higher education scene in the United States. Although most are liberal arts colleges with enrollments between 800 and 2,000 students, church-related higher education also includes large research universities (Boston University, Notre Dame, for example), medical colleges, professional schools, two-year colleges, theological seminaries, and Bible colleges. Many religiously affiliated colleges regularly are highly ranked in various "best colleges" ratings in the United States.

Among the nearly 1,000 colleges and universities with religious affiliation are 65 institutions affiliated with the Jewish faith. Although most of these institutions are rabbinic and talmudic colleges and institutes, some are major well-known universities and colleges in the United States. Yeshiva University, founded in 1886 in New York City, is recognized as the oldest and most comprehensive educational institution under Jewish auspices in America. Yeshiva and Brandeis University, founded in 1948, regularly are listed among the top universities in the United States. Jewish educational institutions in the United States reflect a centuries-long commitment to learning. Like most religiously affiliated colleges and universities, Jewish colleges and universities offer degrees in several fields of study. Many Jewish colleges and universities have joined in partnership through the Association of Colleges of Jewish Studies, an organization committed to serving the educational and religious needs of the North American Jewish community.

While related to and supported by specific religious traditions, most colleges welcome students from a variety of faith traditions—or no faith tradition. The student bodies include representation from ethnic and international communities. The institutions' student-centered focus generally assures most students will graduate in four years.

The typical religiously affiliated college is residential, although some colleges have developed satellite learning and evening programs to meet the needs of nontraditional students. The residential approach is characterized by a commitment to a student-centered learning and living community where curricular and cocurricular programs combine to emphasize a holistic approach to human development and understanding. The colleges invest significant financial and personnel resources to foster personal worth and dignity within a diverse and just community, leading to an emphasis on lifelong learning, social responsibility, and service. Community service is an integral part of the colleges' philosophies.

The curricular focus on the liberal arts and a solid commitment to general education challenges students to integrate learning from a variety of disciplines. Most colleges require students to enroll in a prescribed number of hours of academic study in re-

ligion, philosophy, or ethics. For other institutions, the study of religion is optional. Cocurricular religious activities are present on all campuses. These include worship, fellowship, study of the sacred texts of the religious tradition, service, and religious support. At one time nearly all colleges related to the Christian tradition required weekly or daily attendance at chapel; such a requirement now is the rare exception rather than the rule. Campus religious programming is coordinated by a chaplain, usually a clergy or lay minister in the affiliated religious tradition. As a staff member of the institution, the chaplain participates in various administrative and programmatic aspects of the college's or university's life, thereby helping to infuse the concerns and perspective of the affiliated religious community into the greater life of the college. Although the institution and the chaplain may be from a particular religious tradition, cocurricular religious programs at most religiously affiliated institutions support programming reflecting the diverse religious needs of the student population. Many colleges arrange for representatives of other faith traditions to offer programs on campus.

Relationships

The nature and expression of the educational institution's relationship with religious bodies vary greatly. A few institutions are controlled by the denomination; others share only a nominal relationship. Some traditions have provisions for colleges to acknowledge an "historical" relationship, acknowledging the college's founding by a religious tradition while declaring there is no current, direct relationship with the religious tradition. Most religiously affiliated colleges regularly and actively engage in shaping a dynamic relationship reflecting on changing needs in society, the church, and education.

At least two religious traditions, United Methodist and Seventh Day Adventist, conduct regular reviews of their related institutions to assess their vitality and their expression of church relatedness. The University Senate, the United Methodist review agency, was founded in 1892, and is one of the oldest review agencies in the United States. The Association of Advanced Rabbinical and Talmudic Schools, although not part of a denominational structure, reviews and accredits several schools within the Jewish tradition.

The quality of the relationship between the religious community and the college is in constant redefinition. James Tunstead Burtchaell claims colleges and universities are disengaging from their religious foundations, becoming more secular in their approach to education. George M. Marsden characterizes colleges and universities as moving from a perspective of "Protestant establishment" to one of "established nonbelief," a move toward embracing secularization and diminishing religious tradition. Not all individuals agree fully with those perspectives. Merrimon Cuninggim describes relationships between Christian denominations and their colleges as being in a time when both church officials and college leaders are reassessing the nature of the relationship in light of trends in churches, in colleges, and in society. Conversations among church and academic leaders can lead to renewed understanding of what it means to be religiously affiliated. Cuninggim distinguishes three phases of the relationship between the college and the church traditions that founded them: (1) church as senior partner, college as junior partner, recognizing the college's need for the church's direct support; (2) a time of equality, when neither college nor church groups has an upper hand of the other in normal situations; and, (3) the college as senior partner, more in control of its own destiny. Most institutions fall in this final category and are no longer dependent on the church for financial resources and leadership.

Critical to discussions regarding the church–college relationship is understanding common and distinctive missions. Although each share a common genesis regarding their sense of mission and service, the primary mission of the church is addressing spiritual and communal needs and responsibilities; within that same call to service is the college's primary responsibility to provide quality education reflective of the sponsoring religious community's values. Churches and their colleges must respect and appreciate the distinctive mission of each partner. Understanding and expressing that relationship is an issue of constant concern.

Since the 1970s, Southern Baptists have engaged with their colleges, universities, and seminaries in often contentious discussions regarding relationship and control. Several institutions have opted to withdraw from formal relationships with the Southern Baptists in order to reduce control of the institutions. Catholic colleges and universities are engaged in discussion with the church's bishops regarding Pope John Paul II's *Ex Corde Ecclesiae,* a document outlining the church's position on the relationship

between the church and the teaching activity of its universities and colleges. The Presbyterian, United Methodist, United Church of Christ, and Nazarene churches are engaged in conversations with church judicatories and college and university leaders to clarify and affirm statements reflecting a partnership appropriate to the twenty-first century.

Since 1996 the Lilly Foundation-supported Rhodes Consultation on the Future of the Church-Related College has involved ninety church-related institutions in ongoing discussion regarding the church's higher education mission in the postmodern world. Faculty, chaplains, and administrators are engaged in critical reflection regarding how church-relatedness is expressed in the life of colleges and universities.

Leadership and Control

Nearly all religiously affiliated colleges and universities are legally independent institutions. Sponsoring bodies usually have representatives on the institution's board of trustees. This tradition assures there is representation from the religious body and the perspective of the religious tradition is heard. The number of seats specified for faith community representatives varies. In some situations, all trustees must be members of the sponsoring tradition; a few institutions have no specified spaces. In most instances, the percentage of representatives ranges from 2 to 60 percent. Often the regional judicatory leader and the local pastor from the area are ex officio representatives on trustee boards. In most cases trustees are elected by the college's board of trustees, however, the by-laws of some colleges require trustees to be confirmed by the sponsoring denominational body.

Although many presidents of the 980 religiously affiliated colleges and universities are members of the sponsoring religious tradition, such membership is not required at all colleges. Such latitude may seem contrary to religiously affiliated higher education. Colleges seek the best presidential candidate, based on a variety of capabilities. The vitality of a college's religious affiliation, however, depends significantly on the support and encouragement that its "faith tradition" receives from the college president and other senior leaders at the institution.

Some traditions require a higher degree of staff relationship with the sponsoring religious body or association. The Council for Christian Colleges and

Universities requires its ninety-five member colleges and universities to fulfill specific criteria. Among them is the requirement for a publicly stated mission based upon the centrality of Christ as well as a hiring policy requiring all faculty and administrators have a personal faith in Jesus Christ. Similarly, the Accrediting Association of Bible Colleges requires each member college to annually subscribe to a statement of faith.

Religiously affiliated colleges and universities also receive expressions of partnerships and support from their sponsoring tradition. Financial support for the institutions usually represents less than 1 percent of their budgets; this is a radical decrease from the 1980s. Several faith traditions also manage scholarship and loan programs for students of the tradition to attend an affiliated college. Occasionally funds are designated to support the college's outreach to previously underserved ethnic and economic populations. This assistance supports the colleges and their commitment to educational access.

Many religious groups provide structural and programmatic support for the colleges, offering consultative services, sponsoring workshops, and facilitating programmatic initiatives. Among the churches supporting their colleges in this manner are the Mennonites, Lutherans, Presbyterians, Nazarenes, United Church of Christ, Southern Baptists, Disciples, Catholics, and United Methodists. Associations of presidents in various religious traditions provide a network of support for these leaders.

Issues for the Future

Religiously affiliated colleges continue to have a significant role in the education life of the United States and the world. Their commitment to a just and value-centered living and learning community, with a commitment to the liberal arts and civic leadership, is a valuable alternative to other approaches to education. The clarification of the relationship between the college and their religious tradition will continue to be an issue. Some colleges will opt out of a relationship with the religious bodies. Many others will understand the relationship as a central part of their identity, giving the college a unique role as the provider of value-centered education, personal integrity, and social responsibility.

Other religiously affiliated institutions may disappear from the scene for another reason: financial resources. The smaller size of these institutions, the dwindling financial support from their denominations, and the absence of state subsidies afforded state institutions, places some of the colleges in precarious financial situations. The challenge will be for the colleges and the sponsoring religious groups to join together to secure the resources necessary to continue their significant educational role, reflected by the invitation of Saint Augustine, *Intellege ut credas; crede ut intellegas* (understand so that you may believe; believe so that you may understand), an invitation to unite the endeavor of intelligence and faith.

See also: HIGHER EDUCATION IN THE UNITED STATES, *subentries on* HISTORICAL DEVELOPMENT OF, SYSTEM.

BIBLIOGRAPHY

ASSOCIATION OF PRESBYTERIAN COLLEGES AND UNIVERSITIES. 1994. "To Be a Church-Related College/University." *A Point of View* 2 (October 20).

BEATTY, MICHAEL; BURAS, TODD; and LYON, LARRY. 1997. "Faith and Knowledge in American Higher Education." *Fides et Historia* 29:73–80.

BENNE, ROBERT. 2001. *Quality with Soul: How Six Premier Colleges and Universities Keep Faith with Their Religious Traditions.* Grand Rapids, MI: Eerdmans.

BOWSER, BETH ADAMS. 1992. *Living the Vision: The University Senate of The Methodist Episcopal Church, The Methodist Church, and The United Methodist Church, 1892–1991.* Nashville, TN: Board of Higher Education and Ministry of The United Methodist Church.

BRILL, EARL H. 1970. *Religion and the Rise of the University: A Study of the Secularization of American Higher Education, 1870–1910.* Ann Arbor, MI: University Microfilms.

BUFORD, THOMAS O. 1995. *In Search of a Calling: The College's Role in Shaping Identity.* Macon, GA: Mercer University Press.

BURTCHAELL, JAMES TUNSTEAD. 1998. *The Dying of the Light: The Disengagement of Colleges and Universities from Their Christian Churches.* Grand Rapids, MI: Eerdmans.

CAMPBELL, ALEXANDER. 1854. "An Address on Colleges, Delivered in the City of Wheeling, Va., 1854, Being One of a Series of Lectures in Behalf of the Erection of a New Church Edifice in That City." *Millennial Harbinger* 4th series, 4(2):61.

CARPENTER, JOEL A., and SHIPPS, KENNETH W., eds. 1987. *Making Higher Education Christian: The History and Mission of Evangelical Colleges in America.* Grand Rapids, MI: Eerdmans.

COOK, CONSTANCE EWING. 1998. *Lobbying for Higher Education: How Colleges and Universities Influence Federal Policy.* Nashville, TN: Vanderbilt University Press.

CUNINGGIM, MERRIMON. 1994. *Uneasy Partners: The College and the Church.* Nashville, TN: Abingdon Press.

DE JONG, ARTHUR J. 1990. *Reclaiming a Mission: New Direction for the Church-Related College.* Grand Rapids, MI: Eerdmans.

DITMANSON, HAROLD H.; HONG, HOWARD V.; and QUANBECK, WARREN A., eds. 1960. *Christian Faith and the Liberal Arts.* Minneapolis, MN: Augsburg.

FISHER, BEN C. 1989. *The Idea of a Christian University in Today's World.* Macon, GA: Mercer University Press.

GREELEY, ANDREW. 1995. *From Backwater to Mainstream: A Profile of Catholic Higher Education.* New York, NY: Oxford University Press.

HESBURGH, THEODORE M. 1994. *The Challenge and Promise of a Catholic University.* Notre Dame, IN: University of Notre Dame Press.

HOLMES, ARTHUR. 1975. *The Idea of A Christian College.* Grand Rapids, MI: Eerdmans.

HUGHES, RICHARD T., and ADRIAN, WILLIAM B., eds. 1997. *Models for Christian Higher Education: Strategies for Success in the Twenty-First Century.* Grand Rapids, MI: Eerdmans.

HULL, WILLIAM. 1992. "The Crisis in Baptist Higher Education: An Historical Perspective." *The Journal of the South Carolina Baptist Historical Society* 18:3–22.

LANGAN, JOHN, S.J., and O'DONOVAN, LEO J., S.J., eds. *Catholic Universities in Church and Society: A Dialogue on Ex Corde Ecclesiae.* Baltimore: Georgetown University Press.

MARSDEN, GEORGE M. 1994. *The Soul of the American University: From Protestant Establishment to Established Nonbelief.* New York: Oxford University Press.

MICHAEL, ELLIOTT T.; DILLARD, DIANE; LOEFFLER, RENÈE G.; and WEEKS, KENT M. 1976. *To Give the Key of Knowledge: United Methodists and Education, 1784–1976.* Nashville, TN: National Commission on United Methodist Higher Education.

MILLER, ALEXANDER. 1960. *Faith and Learning: Christian Faith and Higher Education in Twentieth Century America.* New York: Association Press.

NEWMAN, CARDINAL JOHN HENRY. 1982. *The Idea of a University.* Notre Dame, IN: University of Notre Dame Press.

O'BRIEN, DAVID J. 1994. *From the Heart of the American Church: Catholic Higher Education and American Culture.* Maryknoll, NY: Orbis.

PARSONAGE, ROBERT RUE, ed. 1978. *Church Related Higher Education: Perceptions and Perspectives.* Valley Forge, PA: Judson.

PATTILLO, MANNING M., JR., and MACKENZIE, DONALD M. 1966. *Church-Sponsored Higher Education in the United States.* Washington, DC: American Council on Education.

RINGENBERG, WILLIAM C. 1984. *The Christian College: A History of Protestant Higher Education in America.* Grand Rapids, MI: Eerdmans.

SANDIN, ROBERT T. 1992. "To Those Who Teach at Christian Colleges." In *Agendas for Church-Related Colleges and Universities,* ed. David S. Guthrie and Richard L. Noftzger Jr. San Francisco: Jossey-Bass.

SLOAN, DOUGLAS. 1994. *Faith and Knowledge: Mainline Protestantism and American Higher Education.* Louisville, KY: Westminster John Knox.

STEVENSON, LOUISE L. 1986. *Scholarly Means to Evangelical Ends: The New Haven Scholars and the Transformation of Higher Education in America, 1830–1890.* Baltimore: Johns Hopkins University Press.

INTERNET RESOURCE

U.S. DEPARTMENT OF EDUCATION. 2001. "Digest of Educational Statistics, 2000." <http://nces.ed.gov/pubs2001/digest>.

JAMES A. NOSEWORTHY

COLLEGE SEARCH AND SELECTION

The decision to attend a college or university and admission to an institution of higher education has important outcomes for individuals and for society. Most of the attention given to these decisions by researchers and by public policymakers has focused on how high school graduates (often referred to as traditional-age students) make their decisions. Attention has also been given to how the institutions make their decisions about the applicants they admit. There are many good reasons for the attention that has been given to these decision-making processes. It is clear that individuals, society, and colleges and universities benefit when more students choose to continue their formal education after high school. Economists have demonstrated that individuals who graduate from two-year and four-year colleges and universities typically have better jobs and incomes. College graduates are healthier and their quality of life is usually better. Society also benefits in a number of ways. Citizens with college degrees pay more taxes, vote more often, and contribute more to the civic life of a democratic society. Colleges and universities also benefit from students who enroll, namely, the contributions that students make to the intellectual and social life of each campus and the tuition dollars students and their parents pay to both public and private institutions. Public colleges and universities also benefit from the public funds that states provide to educate their citizens.

Beginning in the 1970s and continuing into the 1990s, there was a precipitous decline in the number of high school graduates. As a result, colleges and universities became more interested in understanding the factors that influence college choice. During the same time period, public policymakers focused more of their attention on encouraging lower-income and moderate-income high school graduates to pursue additional education after high school. These developments have stimulated a significant increase in the amount of research conducted on the college search and selection process.

Defining the College Selection Process

Since the 1980s the college selection process has become known as the student college choice, or the college choice process. The college choice process is complex and evolves over several years. During this longitudinal process individuals develop aspirations to attend a two-year or four-year college or university. After developing post–high school educational plans, individuals begin to gather information about the kinds of colleges or universities in which they might be interested, and finally they decide which institution to attend.

The college selection process for traditional-age students is often described as a three-stage process. The first stage is predisposition, which refers to the development of formal educational plans after high school. The second step is the search stage: the process of gathering information about colleges and universities as well as developing a list of colleges or universities to seriously consider. The final stage is called choice and refers to the final decision regarding which institution to attend.

Several researchers, such as Don Hossler and colleagues (1999), have devoted considerable attention to the college choice process. A number of factors and experiences can influence the predisposition stage of college choice. Most high school students have formulated their plans to continue their formal education after high school by the eighth or ninth grade. The most important factor that influences the decisions of students is extent to which parents consistently encourage their children to continue their formal education after high school. In addition, for children of parents who have attended college there is an increased likelihood of college or university attendance after high school graduation. High school students who earn better grades and who have friends who are planning to attend a college or university are also more likely to aspire to continue their formal education after they graduate. Finally, community norms and values also influence the development of postsecondary educational aspirations. Some communities value education more than others and these values are transmitted in subtle and complex ways to youth.

The search stage involves two simultaneous processes. One of these processes involves students learning more about the characteristics of different types of colleges and universities. The other part of this phase involves learning more about which specific institutions to seriously consider attending. Most students who are college bound enter the search stage during their junior year in high school. Some students start earlier and some wait until their senior year. This stage of the college decision-making process is complex. Not surprisingly, the students who spend more time investigating college options are more certain and confident about their deliberations during the search stage. Students from more affluent families and who earn better grades spend more time searching for college alternatives. It is also true, however, that students who earn better grades and who have parents who attended college are less certain about the kind of college or university they will eventually attend—more choices can create more uncertainty.

Most traditional-age students complete their choice stage during their senior year in high school. Typically seniors make their matriculation decisions in the spring or early summer. Making the final decision tends to bring a good deal more realism into the decision-making process. Students frequently drop more expensive, more distant, or more selective schools from their list. During the choice stage, peers and teachers, rather than parents, exert greater influence on the decisions of students. High school students who have consistently planned to attend college over long periods of time are more likely to follow through on their plans. Increased parental education, greater family income, and higher student grades increase the probabilities that high school graduates will attend colleges and universities that are more expensive, selective, and farther from home. Patricia McDonough's work on college choice also reveals that the norms and values of individual high schools influence the college destination of high school graduates. The attitudes and values of the faculty and other students within individual high schools can make a difference in determining the types of colleges and universities students are encouraged to consider. High school teachers and counselors can even help to channel students to specific colleges and universities. Informal and formal communication networks consisting of peers, teachers, counselors, and members of the local community influence which institutions are deemed to be good choices for graduates of individual high schools.

In addition, the marketing tactics of colleges and universities also have an influence on both the search and the choice stages. Colleges and universities that are more timely and personalized in all of their interactions with prospective students are more likely to exert a positive influence upon enrollment decisions.

Influencing College Search

In the last quarter of the twentieth century, public policymakers and college administrators have influenced the college choice process. Many public policymakers believe that the economic and political health and vitality of nations will be influenced by the number of its citizens who are well educated. The increasingly technological nature of many countries rests upon a foundation of well-educated citizens. In addition, public policymakers often measure the health of society by the extent to which all citizens, regardless of family background or ethnicity, have an equal opportunity to earn a college degree.

Irrespective of family background, parents can play an important role in the development of their children's plans for additional formal education after high school by providing consistent encouragement to their children over many years. Indeed, parental encouragement is one of the best predictors of college attendance. Parents exert another kind of influence on their children: More affluent parents view the college destinations of their children as an indicator of family status. For an increasing number of upper-middle-class and upper-class families, getting into a prestigious college has become an important outcome of the college choice process.

High schools can also play an important role in college choice. The kind of encouragement and college counseling provided in high schools has an impact upon student's decisions. High school teachers and counselors, as well as local community norms associated with issues like the value of higher education or the extent to which high school students are encouraged to leave the local area to attend a residential college or university can channel high school students toward or away from institutions of higher education as well as toward specific types of two-year and four-year colleges and universities.

State and federal governments can also play an important role in the college choice process. The amount of state revenue that is used to create and fund public colleges and universities influences college attendance rates in states. Generally, states with a higher concentration of colleges and universities have higher college attendance rates. In addition, lower tuition at public two-year and four-year institutions produces higher college attendance rates. The amount of state and federal financial aid programs also exerts an influence on college choice. Proportionately fewer state residents attend colleges and universities in states with smaller state financial aid programs.

It is also worth noting that the federal government, as well as several states and many local community groups, plays an increasingly important role in the college decision-making process. Federal and some state governments, in addition to local community foundations, have started programs to provide academic and personal support to encourage lower-income and moderate-income students to earn two-year and four-year college degrees. Programs ranging from the federally funded Gear Up program to the Twenty-First Century Scholar program in the state of Indiana to locally funded programs modeled after the Eugene Lang "I Have a Dream" program provide tutoring, social support, and financial aid to low-income students who focus upon academic goals, are admitted to one or more institutions of higher education, and enroll. These initiatives are attempting to expand educational opportunities for low-income youth.

The marketing, financial aid, and admissions policies of colleges and universities also influence the college choice process. Many four-year colleges and universities, both public and private, aggressively recruit students. They spend millions of dollars on publications, e-mail, CD-ROMs, and websites to attract and enroll students. Many campuses use financial aid, both need-based and merit-based, as tools to induce students to enroll. There is growing evidence that these tactics do influence which colleges and universities students consider and their final choice.

In 1999 Hossler, Jack Schmit, and Nick Vesper summarized the results of a nine-year longitudinal study of the college choice process and offered the following recommendations to families, educators, college enrollment professionals, and educational policymakers.

1. Parents should provide consistent encouragement to their children to continue their education after high school.

2. Parents should regularly ask questions about their children's plans, take them to visit campuses, and save for college.

3. Teachers and counselors should link college planning with curricular choices students make as early as eighth or ninth grade.

4. Teachers and counselors should plan group and/or individual college exploration and advising sessions for high school juniors.

5. Teachers and counselors should plan financial aid information sessions for students and parents.

6. Teachers and counselors should be well informed about postsecondary educational options so that they can offer good advice to their students.

7. Educational policymakers should encourage academic support programs and fund early college awareness programs.

8. Policymakers should try to constrain college costs.

9. Admissions professionals should provide information to prospective students at the times they are ready to receive the information—not when their institutions are ready to send it.

10. Most students are not ready for detailed information about postsecondary education until their junior year in high school.

11. College choice is a complex, longitudinal process: Parents, peers, teachers, counselors, and admissions recruitment activities influence college choice. Also, the amount of financial aid students are offered can influence their enrollment decisions.

Selecting Students

There are a wide variety of criteria used to decide who will be admitted to a college or university. At highly selective institutions only a small percentage of all applicants who apply are admitted. In highly selective public institutions the admissions criteria are usually very clear because freedom of information laws require them to disclose their admissions criteria. The selection criteria at highly selective private institutions are often less well known to students and their parents. At universities that are highly selective, admissions decisions are strongly influenced either by the academic performance of students at the secondary level and/or scores on either the SAT or the ACT Assessment exam. In some instances a composite score that combines these two academic indicators is used. More selective institutions require higher grades and/or test scores. At the other end of the continuum are institutions such as community colleges that have virtually open admissions. Students who are admitted may not even have to be high school graduates to enroll. Institutions that fall between these highly selective institutions and open admissions institutions call for an array of admissions selection criteria. Performance at the secondary level and/or standardized test scores are used, but students would not have to have been outstanding or even necessarily strong students to be admitted to some four-year institutions. It is important to note that at many colleges and universities additional nonacademic factors are used as selection criteria. These additional criteria might include such factors as special talents (athletics, music, and leadership abilities) and factors like socioeconomic status or ethnicity.

Important Issues Related to College Search and Selection

Since the 1980s several important public policy issues have emerged that are related to college search and selection. These issues include affirmative action, the tension between excellence and equity, merit-based and need-based financial aid, and the impact of prestige rankings on college choice. The most contentious are related to equality of opportunity. A continual strand of debate has focused upon the role of higher education in promoting equality. Some policymakers and scholars have argued that higher education should primarily be concerned with merit and excellence. Others have articulated a strong role for equity and access for all citizens. The debates in this arena often focus on admissions selectivity, affirmative action, and the appropriate role of standardized tests such as the ACT and SAT. Many institutions of higher education, as well as policymakers, educators, and families infer the quality of a college or university by the average of the standardized test scores of the enrolled undergraduate student body. Some ethnic minorities and many low-income students do not score as well on college admission standardized tests. For more selective colleges and universities that rely heavily on standardized tests to make admissions decisions, this means that fewer low-income and ethnic minority students will be admitted. This in turn leads to concerns about equal opportunity and access for students of all backgrounds. These issues are of special importance at public colleges and universities, where public funds are used to provide higher education for all citizens of the state.

In response, many institutions have developed affirmative action policies. These policies use locally developed standardized formulas that might include factors such as parental income, graduation from a secondary school with high concentrations of poverty (or low college attendance rates), or other more subjective criteria to make sure that all applicants have a more equal possibility of being admitted. In many states, however, legal challenges that dispute the legality of affirmative action policies have been mounted in state and federal courts. In *Hopwood v.*

State of Texas (1996), the court decreed affirmative action admissions policies to be unconstitutional. In two legal opinions involving the University of Michigan, one judge ruled the affirmative action admissions policies used at the undergraduate level to be legal (*Gratz and Hamacher v. Bollinger et al.,* 2001) and another judge ruled the affirmative action admissions policies used at the law school to be illegal (*Grutter v. Bollinger et al.,* 2001). Thus far, the outcome of these legal battles over affirmative action is mixed and contradictory. A final legal resolution for affirmative action admissions policies is unlikely in the near future.

Since the early 1990s there has been a growing public focus on the status and quality of different colleges and universities. Publications such as *U.S. News and World Report's America's Best Colleges* have ranked the quality of colleges and universities in the United States. This focus may result in more social and economic stratification among colleges and among the students who enroll in them. Wealthy and well-educated parents are increasingly using rankings publications as reliable indicators of institutional quality and prestige. These parents and their children believe that the colleges or universities that the children attend will determine their future prospects for good paying jobs in high-status occupations. Although research on college outcomes does not support these beliefs, societal pressures continue to reinforce the belief among many prospective college students that institutional selectivity, prestige, and rankings will exert a pervasive impact on the jobs they can get and their lifetime income. In this context, McDonough and colleagues have noted that the search and choice stages of college choice involve a series of high-stakes decisions. Parental pressures from some wealthy parents accentuate these concerns.

Concerns about student enrollment and institutional prestige have also had an impact upon colleges and universities. In the 1970s and 1980s the number of traditional-age students declined. As a result some colleges had to compete aggressively to attract enough students to survive this downturn in the number of traditional high school graduates. One of the methods employed to successfully compete was to offer campus-based financial aid to induce students to enroll. Later, more campuses started to use financial aid offers to compete for top students in order to enhance their prestige. Not surprisingly, many prospective students have demonstrated that they are responsive to financial aid offers. If some students are offered enough financial aid they will choose one college over another. Such financial aid competition has altered the college choice process. Many traditional-age students, and their parents, have become accustomed to the idea that they should receive financial aid, even if their families are wealthy and can afford to pay the full costs of going to college. There is a growing sense on the part of all parents that some sort of financial aid is an entitlement. This places ever greater pressure on colleges and universities to offer merit-based financial aid to prospective students.

As colleges and universities have invested more and more money in merit-based financial aid, the amount of need-based financial aid available to low-income students has not kept up with rising costs of college attendance. As a result of these trends, financial aid trends have also become part of the debate about access, equity, and excellence. Some educators and public policymakers assert that students who earn good grades should be rewarded with scholarships. Others point out that more students from more affluent families are more likely to earn good grades and as a result get more scholarships, while lower-income students who lack many societal and educational advantages receive fewer scholarships. Critics of merit aid trends argue that these developments only accentuate inequities existing in American society.

See also: COLLEGE ADMISSIONS; COLLEGE ADMISSIONS TESTS; COLLEGE FINANCIAL AID; COLLEGE RECRUITMENT PRACTICES.

BIBLIOGRAPHY

ANCRUM, ROBERT. 1992. *The College Application and Admissions Process.* New York: The College Board.

BECKER, WILLIAM. 1999. "The Role of Education and Training in Economic Development." In *Education in the Arab World: Challenges of the Next Millennium.* Abu Dhabi, United Arab Emirates: The Emirates Center for Strategic Studies and Research.

BOWEN, HOWARD R. 1977. *Investment in Learning: Individual and Social Value of American Education.* San Francisco: Jossey-Bass.

BOWEN, WILLIAM G., and BOK, DERECK. 1998. *The Shape of the River : Long-Term Consequences of Considering Race in College and University Admissions.* Princeton, NJ: Princeton University Press.

CABRERA, ALBERTO F., and NASA, STEVEN M., eds. 2000. *Understanding the College Choice of Disadvantaged Students. New Directions in Institutional Research, Number 107.* San Francisco: Jossey-Bass.

CARPENTER, PETER G., and FLEISHMAN, JOHN A. 1987. "Linking Intentions and Behavior: Australian Students College Plans and College Attendance." *American Educational Research Journal* 24(1):79–105.

CIOMPI, KATHRYN. 1993. *How Colleges Choose Students.* New York: The College Board.

HOSSLER, DON; BRAXTON, JOHN; and COPPERSMITH, GEORGIA. 1989. "Understanding Student College Choice." In *Higher Education: Handbook of Theory and Research,* Vol. 4, ed. John C. Smart. New York: Agathon.

HOSSLER, DON, and GALLAGHER, KAREN S. 1987. "Studying College Choice: A Three-Phase Model and The Implication For Policy Makers." *College and University* 2(3):207–221.

HOSSLER, DON; SCHMIDT, JACK; and VESPER, NICK. 1998. *Going to College: How Social, Economic, and Educational Factors Influence the Decisions Students Make.* Baltimore: Johns Hopkins University Press.

LEVIN, ARTHUR, and NIDDIFER, JENNIFER. 1996. *Beating the Odds: How the Poor Get to College.* San Francisco: Jossey-Bass.

LITTEN, LARRY H. 1991. *Ivy Bound: High-Ability Students and College Choice.* New York: The College Board.

McDONOUGH, PATRICIA M. 1997. *Choosing Colleges: How Social Class and Schools Structure Opportunity.* Albany: State University of New York Press.

McDONOUGH, PATRICIA M.; KORN, JESSICA; and YAMASAKI, ERICA. 1997. "Admissions Advantage For Sale: Private College Counselors and Students Who Use Them." *Review of Higher Education* 20:297–317.

PASCARELLA, ERNEST T., and TERENZINI, PATRICK T. 1991. *How College Affects Students.* San Francisco: Jossey-Bass.

PAULSEN, MICHAEL B. 1990. *College Choice: Understanding Student Enrollment Behavior.* Washington, DC: ERIC Clearinghouse on Higher Education and George Washington University.

STAGE, FRANCES, and HOSSLER, DON. 1989. "Differences in Family Influence on the College Plans of High School Males and Females." *Research in Higher Education* 30(3):301–315.

ST. JOHN, EDWARD P. 1994. *Prices, Productivity, and Investment: Assessing Financial Strategies in Higher Education.* Washington, DC: ERIC Clearinghouse on Higher Education and George Washington University.

ST. JOHN, EDWARD P., ed. 1995. *Rethinking Tuition and Student Aid Strategies.* San Francisco: Jossey-Bass.

TERENZINI, PATRICK T.; CABRERA, ALBERTO F.; and BERNAL, ELENA M. 2001. *Swimming against the Tide: The Poor in American Higher Education.* New York: The College Board.

INTERNET RESOURCES

THE COLLEGE BOARD. 2002. <www.college board.com>.

U.S. NEWS AND WORLD REPORT. 2002. "U.S. News and World Report's America's Best Colleges." <www.usnews.com/usnews/edu/college/ rankings/rankindex.htm>.

DON HOSSLER

COLLEGE SEMINARS FOR FIRST-YEAR STUDENTS

The successful transition from secondary school to the collegiate environment for students has been the topic of much research, many articles and books, international conferences, and a plethora of newspaper articles at the beginning of each new academic year. First-year seminars have become a common approach adopted by higher education institutions in their efforts to ease the transition to college for new students, and to systematically address unacceptable rates of student attrition.

The popularity of first-year seminars as a programmatic and curricular approach is grounded in the fact that a credit-bearing course offers a traditional and appropriate structure through which orientation efforts extend beyond the first week of classes. They also offer a way for student development and retention theories to be put into practice, and they provide a logical structure for encouraging (and intrusively demanding) active student involvement in learning and in the life and activities of the institution; for examining and discussing student/institutional fit; and for facilitating social and academic integration. First-year seminars are thus designed to meet both institutional and student needs.

Successful first-year seminars have been defined as those with long life and strong, broad-based campus support. They are likely to carry academic credit, be centered in the first-year curriculum, involve both faculty and student affairs professionals in program design and instruction. Instructor training and development is an integral part of the program, and instructors are paid, or otherwise rewarded, for teaching the seminar. In addition, upper-level students are involved in course delivery and conduct program assessment and disseminate the results to the campus community.

Types of First-Year Seminars

Most first-year seminars fall into one of five categories: extended orientation seminars, academic seminars with generally uniform content across sections, academic seminars on various topics across sections, professional or discipline-linked seminars, or basic study skills seminars. In addition, there are other types that do not fit neatly into any of these established categories, often combining elements from these five.

Regardless of type, first-year seminars are courses that, at their core, focus on the individual needs of new students. A seminar, by definition, is a small discussion-based course in which students and their instructors exchange ideas and information. While there are many variations among first-year seminars, they all aim to assist students in their academic and social development and in their transition to college. In most cases, there is a strong emphasis on creating community within the classroom.

Course Objectives and Content

More than half of all institutions with first-year seminars list the fostering of academic skills and a commitment to easing the transition to college as objectives of the seminars. More specific course goals include orienting students to campus resources and organizations; fostering personal development in students; developing critical thinking and writing skills; introducing general education requirements and/or specific disciplines; encouraging career planning; developing a sense of community on campus; increasing student interactions with faculty and staff; and developing support networks and friendships among classmates.

Course topics include study skills and time management, both of which are central to fostering good academic habits. Personal development and self-concept are also common course topics, as are career exploration, campus resources, transition to college, diversity issues, academic advising and planning, and wellness issues.

Pedagogy and Staffing

Instruction in first-year seminars differs from that of most first-year courses. Unlike many survey courses in traditional disciplines, most first-year seminars are taught in small classes of eighteen to twenty-five students per section. Seminar content also differs from most other freshman-level courses in that there is no set universal content. Because most first-year seminars are institution-specific, content will vary from campus to campus. Content is also dynamic in that it changes and evolves to meet the changing needs of both the students and the institution. Instruction in first-year seminars requires instructors who are interested in intense student content, and who both understand and embrace the unique goals, content, and processes inherent in first-year seminars.

Staffing for first-year seminar instruction varies from campus to campus. Very few seminar programs have a full-time cadre of faculty. More typically, instructors of first-year seminars are drawn from across the campus and may include faculty, administrative and student affairs staff, and undergraduate or graduate peer instructors. Frequently, a team approach is used, involving a pair, or small group, of individuals teaching a single section of the seminar.

Due to the fact that content for first-year seminars includes a focus on student success and transition, effective instruction in first-year seminars departs from the traditional lecture format. Students are expected to actively engage in discussion, share in the teaching as well as the learning in the seminar, and in some cases participate in the creation of the course syllabus. Instructors must therefore give up some of the traditional power associated with teach-

ing. Active-learning techniques are frequently employed, including experiential learning, collaborative projects, discussions, role play, cooperative learning, and oral presentation.

A common goal among many seminar programs is the development of a community of learners. Engaging in activities that establish and develop friendships and significant relationships within the class contribute to the development of powerful communities. Substantial two-way communication between instructor and student is widespread in first-year seminars and is often achieved through employing formal and informal feedback techniques, the incorporation of formative assessment measures, and including opportunities for significant reflection through journals and student writing.

Instructor Development

Instructors for first-year seminars are very likely to have access to development or training experiences to prepare them for this special type of instruction. Outcomes of effective instructor-training efforts include campus-wide faculty development, professional and personal development, the development of community among faculty and staff, development of faculty/student-affairs partnerships, improvements in teaching and learning, quality and consistency across seminar sections, and employee orientation, assimilation, and education.

First-year seminars provide fertile ground for the development of innovative teaching strategies. Teaching the first-year seminar encourages a rethinking of both teaching and the entire higher education enterprise. Many faculty who participate in a first-year seminar faculty development workshop and then teach a seminar bring new teaching techniques to their discipline-based courses. Furthermore, attending a faculty-development workshop and teaching a seminar can boost faculty morale, help faculty better meet the academic and nonacademic needs of students, and improve teaching in many other courses across campus.

Campus Collaboration

Many first-year seminar programs that were originally stand-alone courses are now linking with other campus initiatives. As new seminars are created, they are more likely to be part of a general education-reform effort. When seminars are linked with other campus programs, their institutionalization is more solid, and they are more likely to facilitate partnerships among various campus constituents. When both faculty and staff are involved in seminar design and instruction, the traditional gaps between faculty and staff are frequently ameliorated, or at least lessened.

Assessment

First-year seminars are, perhaps, the most assessed and measured of all undergraduate courses. Proving the value and worth of any educational innovation is key to sustaining the life of the innovation, especially in times of budget reductions and curricular reform. Assessment can document the effectiveness of a program, and also be used to continually improve the program. Institutional efforts examining first-year seminar programs have included a variety of assessment approaches. Through assessment efforts, first-year seminars have been proven to positively affect retention, grade point average, number of credit hours attempted and completed, graduation rates, student involvement in campus activities, student attitudes and perceptions of higher education, as well as faculty development and methods of instruction. They have also been shown to increase institutional engagement. Students enrolled in a first-year seminar are more likely to use campus resources, get involved in campus activities, and interact with faculty outside of class.

The modern first-year seminar is perhaps one of the most dynamic curricular innovations of the twentieth century. These courses have evolved to meet the changing needs of students and institutions, and they have the potential to continue to be one of the most adaptable and useful curricular staples during the twenty-first century.

See also: CURRICULUM, HIGHER EDUCATION, *subentries on* INNOVATIONS IN THE UNDERGRADUATE CURRICULUM, TRADITIONAL AND CONTEMPORARY PERSPECTIVES; GENERAL EDUCATION IN HIGHER EDUCATION.

BIBLIOGRAPHY

BAREFOOT, BETSY O. 1993. *Exploring the Evidence: Reporting Outcomes of Freshman Seminars.* Columbia: University of South Carolina, National Resource Center for The Freshman Year Experience.

BAREFOOT, BETSY O., and FIDLER, PAUL P. 1996. *The 1994 National Survey of Freshman Seminar Programs: Continuing Innovations in the Collegiate Curriculum.* Columbia: University of South Carolina, National Resource Center for The First-Year Experience and Students in Transition.

BAREFOOT, BETSY O.; WARNOCK, CARRIE. L.; DICKINSON, MICHAEL T.; RICHARDSON, SHARON E.; and ROBERTS, MELISSA. R., eds. 1998. *Exploring the Evidence Volume II: Reporting Outcomes of First-Year Seminars.* Columbia: University of South Carolina, National Resource Center for The First-Year Experience and Students in Transition.

FIDLER, PAUL P.; NEURURER-ROTHOLZ, JULIE; and RICHARDSON, SHARON. 1999. "Teaching the Freshman Seminar: Its Effectiveness in Promoting Faculty Development." *Journal of The First-Year Experience and Students in Transition* 11(2):59–74.

HUNTER, MARY S., and GARDNER, JOHN N. 1999. "Outcomes and Future Directions of Instructor Training Programs." In *Solid Foundations: Building Success for First-Year Seminars Through Instructor Training and Development,* ed. Mary S. Hunter and L. Tracy. Columbia: University of South Carolina, National Resource Center for The First-Year Experience and Students in Transition.

MARY STUART HUNTER
CARRIE W. LINDER

COLLEGE STUDENT RETENTION

Why do students leave college before completing a degree? This question is of interest not only to scholars, but also to employers, institutions, students, parents of students, and spouses. A student who leaves college before graduating paid tuition that will probably not be made up for through employment, for a person who lacks a college degree will have diminished lifetime earnings (compared to college graduates). In addition, there is a loss of tuition for the institution, a loss of a major in some department, and a loss of human capital—that is, the loss of highly trained individuals to enter the workforce or perform civic duties.

Retaining a student is fundamental to the ability of an institution to carry out its mission. A high rate of attrition (the opposite of retention) is not only a fiscal problem for schools, but a symbolic failure of an institution to achieve its purpose.

Defining Student Retention

There are two extremes of student retention. *Normal progression*, typical of a *stayer*, or *retained student*, occurs when a student enrolls each semester until graduation, studies full-time, and graduates in about four years. A *dropout*, or *leaver*, is a student who enters college but leaves before graduating and never returns to that or any other school. Between these two extremes are *transfers*, students who begin studies at one institution and then transfer to another. From the student's perspective, transferring is normal progress. From the perspective of the institution where the student first enrolled, the student has dropped out.

While it is easy to identify a stayer, a student who has left college could return at any time. Students who re-enroll after quitting school are called *stopouts*. Students often quit school due to a financial shortfall or a family crisis and return a year later. Other students might start school, drop out to work or to raise a family, and return years, or even decades, later. Someone defined as a dropout could become redefined as a stopout at any time. Other students become *slowdowns*, going from full-time attendance to taking just a few courses.

The previous definitions are from the perspective of a single institution. An important distinction must be made between students who meet their educational goals before graduating but do not receive a degree and students who enrolled intending to graduate but do not do so. For instance, a student might enter a college with the intention of taking three accounting courses to upgrade his or her status at work. When this is done, neither the institution nor the student fails, yet the institution would likely count the student as a dropout. Institutions that enroll large numbers of part-time students have to be very careful in understanding whether a low graduation rate represents institutional failure or institutional success. While a simple definition of retention or attrition may not be possible, an accurate description needs to consider the goals of the student upon entry.

Institutions often speak of *retention rates* or *graduation rates*. Institutions can calculate a meaningful retention rate only if they know the intentions of their students. Students who are not seeking a degree and leave school before graduation should not be counted as dropouts. Furthermore, overall retention or graduation rates are of little use to institutional planners. What is important is the retention rates for identifiable groups of students. When an institution has an overall graduation rate of 75 percent but only 15 percent of its Native American students graduate, the success of the majority masks problems in specific populations.

The following definition captures the essence of the problem of students leaving college prior to graduation: "A leaver or dropout is a student who enters a college or university with the intention of graduating, and, due to personal or institutional shortcomings, leaves school and, for an extended period of time, does not return to the original, or any other, school." In considering any definition, it is important to identify if the definition is from the perspective of the individual student, the institution, or from the economic or labor force perspective.

A Profile of Successful Institutions and Students

Students that have economic, social, or educational advantages are the least likely to leave college, while students lacking these advantages are the most likely to leave. Advantaged students are also likely to attend the most elite schools, and since these students are least likely to leave school before graduating, these schools have the highest retention rates. The reverse is also true. Community colleges, regardless of their quality or value, are the lowest status institutions and have the lowest rates of retention. To say that the most elite schools have the highest retention rates is partly a tautology, because one part of the definition of eliteness is the rate of retention. Nevertheless, eliteness and student retention run hand in hand.

The highest institutional retention rates in the country are above 95 percent, while the lowest may be only 10 percent. Typical graduation rates for elite schools may be 85 percent or higher; for average schools about 50 percent; and for non-elite schools 15 to 25 percent. Freshmen are most likely to drop out of school, while seniors are least likely to leave. For an average institution, freshman to sophomore year attrition is about 25 percent; sophomore to junior year attrition is about 12 percent; junior to senior year attrition is about 8 percent; and about 4 percent of seniors might leave school. Roughly half of an incoming class graduates in four to five years.

While there may be exceptionally high or low rates of retention for individual institutions, and individual students may defy expectations, retention generally follows these patterns:

1. The higher the degree offered, the higher the retention rates; the exception to this rule is that elite private liberal arts colleges have higher retention rates than many institutions offering masters or doctoral degrees.

2. The higher the quality of the institution and the more elite it is, the higher the retention rates.

3. Older institutions with longer traditions and larger endowments have higher retention rates.

4. Institutions where the majority of the students attend classes full-time, are of a traditional age (18–23), and reside on campus have higher retention rates than institutions where the majority of students attend part-time, are older or commuter students, and work full-time.

5. Predominantly white institutions that enroll a relatively high percentage of African-American, Hispanic, or Native American students will likely have lower retention rates than similar institutions enrolling fewer students from these groups; however, at many institutions minority students have higher graduation rates than majority students.

The characteristic profile of a student likely to remain in college and graduate in four to five years is implicit in this description of institutional retention rates. A typical retained student will enroll in college directly after high school (at age eighteen or nineteen); will attend, full-time, a selective four-year residential private college or university seeking a bachelor's degree; will come from a white or Asian family with educated parents with relatively high incomes (high socioeconomic status); and will have attended a high quality high school, taken college preparatory courses, received high grades in high school, and scored well on standardized tests. In addition, the student will intend to graduate, have a major and career goals clearly in mind, participate in numerous campus activities, enjoy being a student, feel that he or she fits in at school, and will have a positive attitude toward the school, the faculty, the courses taken, and the academic and social life of the college. The effects of these characteristics or circumstances are cumulative. The fewer of these attributes a student has, the greater the chances of the student withdrawing from college.

Theories of Student Departure

Scholars have long held an interest in student departure, partly because it is a complex human behavior; partly because it is related to other factors like status attainment, self-development, and the development of human capital; and partly because it is a place where theory can have an impact on practice. Retention studies are important to institutions because if institutions can maintain or increase their retention rates, they can survive, and possibly prosper.

Since student retention is by definition a process that occurs over time, theoretical models tend to be longitudinal, complex, and contain several categories of variables that reflect both student and institutional characteristics. *Theories of departure* provide an explanation of why students leave college. *Theoretical models* of departure are models based on theories, while *models of departure* identify factors assumed to be related to retention without providing an explanation of why the factors act the way they do. Theories, theoretical models, and models are used somewhat interchangeably in the literature.

Student retention models are complex because they contain a large number of variables, often set in a causal pattern. A variable could either affect retention directly, or it could affect some other variable that has a direct effect on retention. For example, high school grades could directly affect rates of retention (e.g., the higher the high school grades, the higher the rate of retention). High school grades could also be thought to affect retention indirectly; that is, the higher the high school grades, the higher the college grades—and the higher the college grades, the higher the rate of retention.

Since 1970, the main theoretical tradition in the study of student retention has been sociological, involving a search for commonalities of behavior that distinguish groups of students who stay from groups of students who leave. Psychological and sociopsychological approaches, concerned with how individuals assess themselves in an educational context, began to develop after 1980. In the decade of the 1990s there was an increasing interest in how economic factors affect retention and in how the cultural factors typical of subgroups of students affect retention decisions, particularly in terms of minority student retention. Other theoretical approaches have been taken, but have had little empirical study. Ernest Pascarella and Patrick Terenzini (1991) offer a summary of the literature on student retention and other associated outcomes from college.

Vincent Tinto's model of student departure has had the greatest influence on our understanding of student retention. His theory helped guide a large number of dissertations and empirical studies of student retention. The model posits that students enter college with family and individual attributes as well as precollege schooling. They enter with certain commitments, both to finishing college and to staying at their college. They enter an academic system that is characterized by grade performance and intellectual development, which together lead to academic integration, and they enter a social system where peer group interactions and faculty interactions lead to social integration. Academic and social integration work together to influence ongoing goal and institutional commitments, which, in turn, lead to the decision to remain in, or to leave, college. This model was later revised through the addition of commitments outside the institution and intentions to remain enrolled.

The explanatory theory underlying Tinto's model came most immediately from the research of William Spady (1971), who saw an analogy between committing suicide and dropping out of school. In both instances, according to Spady, a person leaves a social system. The French philosopher and sociologist Émile Durkheim had found that some people committed suicide because they lacked the values of the social system in which they participated, and because they were not supported by a group of friends. At the core of his model, Tinto borrowed Spady's use of Durkheim's two postulates to identify the concepts of academic and social integration. Academic integration was thought to be the result of sharing academic values, and social integration was viewed as the result of developing friendships with other students and faculty members. In Tinto's model, a student who does not achieve some level of academic or social integration is likely to leave school.

While Tinto's later model (1993) is similar in structure to his earlier ones, it offers another explanation of student departure: failure to negotiate the rites of passage. According to this theory, students would remain enrolled if they separated themselves from their family and high school friends, engaged

in processes by which they identified with and took on the values of other students and faculty, and committed themselves to pursuing those values and behaviors.

A second theoretical thrust came from John Bean, based on empirical and theoretical studies published in the 1980s, an explanatory model of student retention (Bean 1990), and a psychological model of student retention developed by John Bean and Shevawn Eaton (2000). Originally based on a model of turnover in work organizations, Bean's model evolved into one where the overall structure was based on a psychological model that linked any given behavior (in this case, retention) with similar past behavior, normative values, attitudes, and intentions. While based on psychological processes, the model was similar to Tinto's in that it was complex and longitudinal. The model differed from Tinto's original model in two important ways, however: It included environmental variables (or factors outside of the college that might affect retention) and a student's intentions, a factor found to be the best predictor of student retention. These factors were subsequently incorporated into Tinto's model in 1993.

Bean's model, describing traditional-age students, posits that background variables, particularly a student's high school educational experiences, educational goals, and family support, influence the way a student interacts with the college or university that the student chose to attend. After matriculation (as in Tinto's model) the student interacts with institutional members in the academic and social arena. According to Bean, the student also interacts in the organizational (bureaucratic) area, and is simultaneously influenced by environmental factors, such as wanting to be with a significant other at another school or running out of money. A student's interaction with the institution leads the student to develop a set of attitudes toward himself or herself as a student and toward the school. Academic capabilities (as indicated by grade point average), feeling one fits in at an institution, and loyalty to the institution are a secondary set of outcomes that are extremely important in determining a student's intentions to remain enrolled, as well as actually continuing enrollment. Bean and Barbara Metzner (1985) also developed a model of student retention for nontraditional students which reduced the emphasis on social integration factors since nontraditional (older, working, commuting) students have less interaction with others on campus than do traditional, residential students.

Bean and Eaton's (2000) model describes how three psychological processes affect academic and social integration. While attitude-behavior theory provides an overall structure for the model, self-efficacy theory, coping behavioral (approach-avoidance) theory, and attribution (locus of control) theory are used to explain how students develop academic and social integration.

These grand theories of student retention of the 1990s, which attempt to simplify a very complex action into a series of identifiable steps, are inadequate to deal with either specific populations or individual decisions. Because of this inadequacy, a series of articles was written to provide increased explanations of certain aspects of student retention. A collection of these partial theories, which provide a closer look at a certain aspects of student retention decisions, was published by John Braxton in 2000. This volume contains explanations of retention behavior based on economic factors, psychological processes, campus climate, student learning, campus cultures, ethnic differences, college choice, social reproduction, and power (critical theory).

Of these theoretical approaches, a number of studies of the economic influences on retention have been conducted, particularly by Edward St. John. Based on cost–benefit analyses, these studies examine how retention decisions are affected by ability to pay, family resources, student aid, perceptions of aid, and tuition.

Regardless of the particular approaches taken in a model, the general process of student retention remains the same: Both experiences before entering college and academic abilities are important; the way students interact in the social and academic environment once at college are important, as are factors from outside of the institution, particularly the cost of attending the college; and the attitudes a student forms about the institution and about his or her role of being a student at a particular institution (Do I fit in? Am I developing? Am I validated?) are also important aspects of a student's decision to remain enrolled.

Specific Factors Affecting Retention Decisions

There are literally hundreds, if not thousands, of specific reasons a student might leave college before graduation. Theoretical models classify groups of variables that are assumed to relate to some general underlying causes. For example, a general feeling of fitting in might be related to fitting in in the classroom, with one's roommates, with a team member or members of a club, with faculty members, with other students in one's major, with sports fans, and so on. Any list of factors associated with student retention will only be a partial list. The specific factors affecting retention decisions at colleges and universities vary from institution to institution and according to gender, age, and ethnicity. The following groupings are selected factors that are often looked at when doing retention studies of traditional residential students. When these factors are viewed positively by students they enhance retention, and when viewed negatively they decrease retention. Some of the factors that seem particularly important for minority and nontraditional students are noted here.

Background variables. These include parental support, parents' education, parents' income, educational goals, precollege academic success (high class rank, grade point average, standardized test scores), college preparatory curriculum, and friends attending college. For minority students, background variables include extended family support, church and community support, and previous positive interracial/intercultural contact, and for nontraditional students they include spouse support and employer support.

Organizational factors. These include financial aid, orientation programs, rules and regulations, memberships in campus organizations, involvement in decision-making, housing policies, counseling, the bursars office, ease of registration, and staff attitudes toward students. For minority students, organizational factors include role models in staff and faculty, a supportive environment, at least 20 percent minority enrollment, and not viewing rules as oppressive. For nontraditional students, parking, child care, campus safety, availability of services after hours, evening/weekend scheduling, and cost per credit hour are factors.

Academic factors. These include courses offered, positive faculty interaction (both in class and out of class), advising, general skills programs (e.g., basic skills, study skills, math, and English tutoring/help centers), campus resources (e.g., computer, library, athletic, college union), absenteeism, certainty of major, and academic integration. Factors affecting minority students include warm classroom climate and faculty role models, and those affecting nontraditional students include the expectation for individual faculty member attention.

Social factors. Among the social factors affecting retention are close friends on campus, peer culture, social involvement (e.g., service learning, Greek organizations), informal contact with faculty, identification with a group on campus, and social integration. For minority students, social factors also include a positive intercultural/interracial environment and at least 20 percent minority enrollment.

Environmental factors. These include continued parental support, little opportunity to transfer, financial resources, significant other elsewhere, family responsibilities, getting married, and a job off campus more than twenty hours per week. Factors affecting minority students also include the availability of grants.

Attitudes, intentions, and psychological processes. These include self-efficacy as a student, sense of self-development and self-confidence, internal locus of control, strategies of approach, motivation to study, need for achievement, satisfaction, practical value of one's education, stress, alienation, loyalty, sense of fitting it, and intention to stay enrolled. For minority students, self-validation is also a factor.

Enrollment Management and Programs to Increase Retention

Student retention is valuable to institutions because it assures a continued flow of revenues into the institution through the payment of tuition. It is also important for public institutions because institutional support is based on the size of the student body. *Enrollment management* provides continuity to the policies and programs that result in student retention. Enrollment management activities include attracting the right students, providing financial aid, easing the transition to college though orientation programs, using institutional research to gather and analyze data about students, using appropriate interventions for students lacking skills or needing guidance, conducting research to identify the factors associated with student retention, helping with job placement, and enlisting the support of alumni.

The Strategic Management of College Enrollments (1990), by Don Hossler and John Bean, describes the enrollment management process in some detail. Before the term was coined, however, programs to enhance student retention were already in place. Some of the more common ones are:

- Early outreach programs (into high school or junior high) to develop students' academic competencies.
- Bridge programs that provide study on campus between high school and college.
- Orientation programs to ease the transition to college that contain academic strategies, social support, and information about campus life.
- Programs for parents so they understand student life.
- First-semester courses that continue orientation and provide support and information about campus and freshmen interest groups.
- Advising and psychological or social counseling.
- Academic skills development (basic skills, time management, tutoring, course-specific skills).
- Monitoring students for early warning signs and intrusive counseling/advising.
- Social programming for informal socializing (parties, dances, mixers, community programs), and physical places for socializing (unions, lounges, places to eat, study areas that allow talking in libraries).
- Campus development (students interacting with administrators, faculty, and staff to improve the campus environment).
- Participation in campus organizations and activities.
- Programs celebrating cultural diversity, including events of particular interest to diverse groups.
- Sensitivity to ethnic and racial issues.
- Exit interviews.

Reentry Made Easy

It is unlikely that an institution can find a single, simple program that increases student retention, or that a single identifiable group is responsible for low retention rates. The application of resources to any student retention program has ethical implications because it favors one student or group of students over another. To be fair to all students, institutions must engage in ethical analysis before applying resources to any retention program. A central part of this analysis is that all groups of students be identified and included.

See also: COLLEGE AND ITS EFFECT ON STUDENTS; COLLEGE SEARCH AND SELECTION.

BIBLIOGRAPHY

BEAN, JOHN P. 1980. "Dropouts and Turnover: The Synthesis and Test of a Causal Model of Student Attrition." *Research in Higher Education* 12:155–187.

BEAN, JOHN P. 1990. "Why Students Leave: Insights from Research." In *The Strategic Management of College Enrollments,* ed. Don Hossler and John P. Bean. San Francisco: Jossey-Bass.

BEAN, JOHN P., and EATON, SHEVAWN BOGDAN. 2000. "A Psychological Model of College Student Retention." In *Rethinking the Departure Puzzle: New Theory and Research on College Student Retention,* ed. John M. Braxton. Nashville, TN: Vanderbilt University Press.

BEAN, JOHN P., and METZNER, BARBARA S. 1985. "A Conceptual Model of Nontraditional Undergraduate Student Attrition." *Review of Educational Research* 55:485–540.

BRAXTON, JOHN M., ed. 2000. *Rethinking the Departure Puzzle: New Theory and Research on College Student Retention.* Nashville, TN: Vanderbilt University Press.

CABRERA, ALBERTO F.; CASTENADA, MARIA. B.; NORA, AMAURY; and HENGSTLER, DENNIS. 1992. "The Convergence Between Two Theories of College Persistence." *Journal of Higher Education* 33:571–593.

DURKHEIM, ÉMILE. 1961. *Suicide,* trans. John A. Spaulding and George Simpson. New York: Free Press.

HOSSLER, DON, and BEAN, JOHN P. 1990. *The Strategic Management of College Enrollments.* San Francisco: Jossey-Bass.

PASCARELLA, ERNEST T., and TERENZINI, PATRICK T. 1991. *How College Affects Students.* San Francisco: Jossey-Bass.

SPADY, WILLIAM. 1971. "Dropouts from Higher Education: Toward an Empirical Model." *Interchange* 2:38–62.

ST. JOHN, EDWARD P., et al. 2000. "Economic Influences on Persistence Reconsidered: How Can Finance Research Inform the Reconceptualization of Persistence Models?" In *Reworking the Student Departure Puzzle: New Theory and Research on College Student Retention,* ed. John M. Braxton. Nashville, TN: Vanderbilt University Press.

TINTO, VINCENT. 1975. "Dropout from Higher Education: A Theoretical Synthesis of Recent Research." *Review of Educational Research* 45:89–125.

TINTO, VINCENT. 1987. *Leaving College.* Chicago: University of Chicago Press.

TINTO, VINCENT. 1993. *Leaving College: Rethinking the Causes and Cures of Student Attrition,* 2nd edition. Chicago: University of Chicago Press.

VAN GENNEP, ARNOLD. 1960. *The Rites of Passage* (1909), trans. Monika B. Vizedon and Gabrielle L. Caffee. Chicago: University of Chicago Press.

INTERNET RESOURCE

NATIONAL CENTER FOR EDUCATIONAL STATISTICS. 2001. <www.nces.ed.gov>.

JOHN P. BEAN

COLLEGE STUDENTS WITH DISABILITIES

ACCOMMODATING
  Troy R. Justesen
SPECIAL LEARNING NEEDS
  Frances K. Stage
  Magdalena H. de la Teja

ACCOMMODATING

Before the 1970s, more than half of the children with disabilities in the United States did not receive appropriate educational services that would enable them to have full equality of opportunity. More than one million of these children were excluded from the public school system and did not go through the educational process with their nondisabled peers. However, with the passage of the first federal eligibility program providing funding for special education and related services, more children with disabilities were integrated into regular classroom environments. This federal program, now entitled the Individuals with Disabilities Education Act (IDEA), ensures educational opportunities for children with disabilities in public elementary and secondary schools.

In the early twenty-first century, the numbers of students with disabilities successfully completing elementary and secondary school (among other improvements for this population) is largely due to the implementation of the IDEA, which increased access for many students with disabilities to the regular education classroom with the necessary special education and related services supports these children need to prepare for postsecondary education. The success of children with disabilities in primary education inevitably led to their desire to attend colleges and universities.

Postsecondary Students with Disabilities

Increasing numbers of children with disabilities are, in fact, entering postsecondary educational institutions. In 1999 the American Council on Education found that higher proportions of students with disabilities were enrolling in four-year colleges and universities than ever before. One in eleven first-time, full-time freshmen entering college in 1998 reported having a disability. Also in 1999, the U.S. Department of Education's National Center for Education Statistics (NCES) reported that an estimated 428,280 students with disabilities were enrolled at two-year and four-year postsecondary educational institutions. The numbers of students with disabilities transitioning from high school to higher education is expected to increase even more in the decades to come because of increased implementation of federal laws.

Federal Disability Laws Applicable to Higher Education

The protections and considerable modifications and services available under the IDEA to children with disabilities in primary education do not extend to education beyond the secondary level. The IDEA only applies to children with disabilities determined eligible for special education and related services from birth through their twenty-first birthday, and its protections and services end when the child leaves secondary school—either through aging-out or graduating with a regular high school diploma. The IDEA is not, however, a basic civil rights statute, but rather an educational eligibility program for children with disabilities who are determined eligible for services under the IDEA. The protections and services afforded to children with disabilities do not cross over to higher education. However, two federal civil rights laws specifically apply to colleges and universities; these are the Rehabilitation Act of 1973 and the Americans with Disabilities Act of 1990 (ADA).

The Rehabilitation Act

Before the end of the 1970s, there were only a small number of colleges and universities that provided access for students with disabilities. Many of these institutions were segregated colleges and universities that specialized in serving students with a particular type of disability, such as Gallaudet University, which focuses on educating students who are deaf. The benefits of the civil rights movement for African Americans, and the growing assertion by women for equality, directly influenced people with disabilities to advocate for their rights to equality and opportunity to participate in society, including access to higher education. Many of these early advocates for access to higher education were disabled war veterans and others with disabilities who were highly assertive in forcing federal attention to physical and academic access to colleges and universities. The efforts of these individuals with disabilities led to the passage of the Rehabilitation Act.

The Rehabilitation Act applies to any entity that chooses to accept federal financial assistance for any program or service, including higher education institutions. The specific provision of the Rehab Act that applies in higher education, with respect to otherwise qualified students with disabilities, is section 504. Subpart E of section 504 specifically applies to postsecondary education settings.

In basic terms, Subpart E requires any public or private college or university that accepts federal funds for any activity to provide "program accessibility" to campus programs and services. *Program accessibility* is a concept that allows recipients of federal funds, in this case colleges and universities, to make their programs and activities available to individuals with disabilities without extensive retrofitting of their existing buildings and facilities by offering those programs through alternative methods. In practical terms this means that campus buildings are not required to be made accessible to, and usable by, students or others with disabilities as long as the "program" is made accessible to individuals with disabilities. For example, if the second floor of a campus science building has no elevator and a course is offered on that floor that a student who uses a wheelchair wants to take, then the course must be relocated to a classroom that is accessible for the student. Under section 504, a campus is not required to make each of its existing facilities accessible to students with disabilities, though newly constructed campus buildings and facilities are required to be usable by all individuals with disabilities.

Congress intended the section 504 program-access requirement to enable individuals with disabilities to participate in and benefit from the services, programs, or activities of public entities in all but the most unusual cases. However, section 504 only applies to colleges and universities that accept federal financial assistance of some sort, and does not apply to those institutions that do not accept federal dollars. Moreover, section 504 was not adequately enforced and, therefore, did not increase the number of students with disabilities attending postsecondary education. A more comprehensive civil rights law was needed to implement access for people with disabilities in all facets of society, including higher education. Thus, the foundation for the Americans with Disabilities Act was developed, leading to its passage in Congress by an overwhelming majority and its enactment into law on July 26, 1990.

The Americans with Disabilities Act

The Americans with Disabilities Act (ADA) is the most comprehensive civil rights law protecting people with disabilities in history. In terms of higher education for students, the ADA applies to every public college and university and nearly every private college or university in America, with the exception of those institutions affiliated with religious entities or organizations. Examples of exempt institutions include Notre Dame University in Indiana and Brigham Young University in Utah. All public colleges and universities are covered under Title II of the ADA, and private colleges and universities are covered under Title III of the ADA. How the ADA applies to public institutions is very different than how private institutions are covered. Understanding these specific provisions of the ADA is critical to correctly implementing the act.

Basically, the section 504 and the Title II concepts of program accessibility are the same. However, Title II of the ADA extends the program accessibility concept to all public campuses regardless of the source of funding for any campus programs, meaning that existing buildings do not need to be altered to be accessible to students with disabilities as long as the program is accessible. This may mean simply relocating courses or offering services such as retrieving books from inaccessible areas of the campus for students with disabilities. Conversely, covered private campuses, under Title III, must actively remove architectural barriers in existing buildings and facilities where such removal is "readily achievable," or provide goods and services

through alternative methods where those methods are "readily achievable." In other words, a major distinction between public and private campuses is that private campuses must remove existing physical barriers whenever and wherever it is readily achievable to do so. This is a higher standard of access for private than public campuses. However, all public and private campus construction since January 26, 1992, must meet minimum federal standards for accessibility to incrementally add to accessible buildings over time.

Public and private campuses are also required to provide the necessary services and supports for students with disabilities to participate in campus activities, both academic and social. Services such as braille materials; providing sign language interpreters and readers; and allowing students with learning disabilities to take course exams in quiet environments may also be required, with certain technical stipulations, to the extent necessary for students with disabilities to participate in campus activities. However, students with disabilities must notify, and in some cases provide documentation of disability, prior to asserting the need for modifications, and they must not wait until the last minute. Furthermore, the level and extent of services that must be provided depend on whether the campus is public or private.

See also: PEOPLE WITH DISABILITIES, FEDERAL PROGRAMS TO ASSIST; SPECIAL EDUCATION.

BIBLIOGRAPHY

Americans with Disabilities Act of 1990. U.S. Public Law 101–336. *U.S. Code.* Vol. 42, secs. 12101–12213.

HENDERSON, CATHY. 1999. *College Freshmen with Disabilities: Statistical Year 1998.* Washington, DC: American Council on Education.

Individuals with Disabilities Education Act Amendments of 1997. U.S. Public Law 105–17. *U.S. Code 20.* Vol. 20, secs. 1400 et seq.

NATIONAL CENTER FOR EDUCATIONAL STATISTICS. 1998. *Fall Enrollment in Postsecondary Institutions 1996.* Washington, DC: National Center for Educational Statistics.

Rehabilitation Act of 1973, Section 504. U.S. Public Law 93–112. *U.S. Code.* Vol. 29, secs. 791–794.

TROY R. JUSTESEN

SPECIAL LEARNING NEEDS

Students with mental or physical disabilities increasingly contribute to diverse populations on college campuses. According to Cathy Henderson (1999), the number of full-time freshmen with a disability increased from 2.6 percent in 1978 to 9 percent in 1998. *Learning disability* is the fastest growing category of disability, and the most commonly cited in 1998 by freshmen (41%). Other disabilities cited included visual impairment (13%); orthopedic-related impairments (9%); speech impairments (5.3%); health-related disabilities, such as those resulting from cystic fibrosis, cancer, and multiple sclerosis (19%); and "other" disabilities (22%). This last category includes attention deficit disorder (ADD), attention deficit hyperactivity disorder (ADHD), and psychiatric disabilities. Twelve percent of freshmen reported hearing impairments in 1996.

Despite this wide array, students with disabilities are increasingly accessing, persisting in, and benefiting from higher education experiences. After examining National Center for Education Statistics (NCES) data, Laura Horn and Jennifer Berktold reported in 1999 that individuals with disabilities enrolled in postsecondary institutions are likely to be men, older, white, and pursuing an associate's degree at a two-year college (although four-year college enrollments are rapidly increasing). Faced with numerous challenges to being successful in higher education, students with disabilities are more likely than other students to leave college before attaining a degree. However, the Horn and Berktold study indicates that individuals with a disability who do attain a degree are just as likely to obtain employment, to be paid at a similar rate, and to enroll in graduate school as those without disabilities.

Most colleges and universities provide general learning assistance to increase student success. Since 1990, many campuses have focused on becoming learning-centered campuses that emphasize broad approaches to learning designed to create positive academic outcomes for increasingly diverse student populations. These new approaches, designed to improve students' views of themselves as learners, their motivation to learn, and their self-sufficiency as scholars, are especially important for students with special learning needs. (The term *students with special learning needs* is used to refer to students with learning disabilities, ADD, or mental health problems that interfere with their ability to function fully without assistance in the academic setting.)

The Rehabilitation Act of 1973 (Section 504) and the Americans with Disabilities Act (ADA) of 1990 prohibit institutions receiving federal funds from discriminating based on disability and are key to the success of students with special learning needs. These pieces of legislation define individuals considered to have a mental or physical disability and describe accommodations and modifications required by law. Case law over the years has also been instrumental in ensuring access and creating an environment geared toward success in higher education and in employment for individuals with disabilities. College campuses are required to recognize the federal imperative to provide equal access to learning for all students they admit and matriculate.

Most colleges and universities provide special support services as accommodations for students with disabilities. In 1998, 72 percent of two-year and four-year colleges and universities enroll students with disabilities (American Council on Education, 2000). Accommodations and modifications include removing architectural barriers; extended-time or alternative exam formats; and providing textbooks on tape, sign language interpreters, tutors, readers, note-takers or scribes, assisted or priority registration, and adaptive furniture, equipment, and technology. Colleges and universities continue to improve physical accommodation as they upgrade facilities and erect new structures. However, students with visual and mobility impairments may still find architectural barriers to easy access to campus, especially in older facilities. As innovative resources designed specifically for accommodation come on the market, particularly those geared toward computer accessibility, colleges and universities are required to continue to conduct accessibility audits and plan for needed modifications to provide access to learning for all college students.

Student Issues

Many students come to college unaware that they have ADD or a learning disability. After a semester or two of difficulties or placement on academic probation, they begin to recognize their particular learning needs. Sometimes they seek and receive formal diagnoses of their disabilities, while others conduct self-diagnoses. Even when students recognize their needs, they are often reluctant to seek help or disclose their needs to others. In 1998, Bradford Kruse, Tina Elacqua, and Ross Rapaport conducted a study of students with disabilities at a Midwestern university, but 79 percent of students declined to participate. The number of students with learning and mental health disabilities is growing, and these students face numerous obstacles in their efforts to become successful college students. The most problematic of these include:

1. A lack of diagnosis for many students with learning disabilities that would alert them to their own particular learning needs

2. A general lack of awareness of strategies and services that could be used by students with special learning needs

3. A reluctance on the part of students with special learning challenges to communicate their needs to others; this is especially true for students with invisible disabilities (e.g., ADD, ADHD, brain injury, dyslexia, mental illness)

4. A tendency of parents to attempt to intervene for their students, even though the most effective intervention is student self-advocacy

5. A lack of classmate acceptance of students with special learning needs

6. A lack of campus staff, equipment, and services to adequately serve this growing campus need

7. A faculty perceived by students with disabilities as having a general lack of awareness or even skepticism about the realities of learning challenges for college students and a reluctance by faculty to provide classroom accommodations

8. A general suspicion that students with a mental disability are being deceptive about their needs in order to secure accommodations related to classroom work

To overcome these difficulties and barriers, students must take responsibility for their own success, advocate for their own academic needs, provide documentation from a qualified professional about their disability to the designated office on campus responsible for services to students with disabilities, educate themselves about accommodations that are particularly helpful to them, and identify themselves to campus career centers and counseling centers and be ready to discuss their needs based on the disability and follow the advice given.

Additionally, if students inform faculty immediately about their special accommodation needs, fac-

ulty skepticism may dissipate. If students wait until academic problems arise, faculty may be suspicious of the students' veracity or motives. A useful strategy may be to give skeptical faculty the names of staff and other faculty who are knowledgeable and accommodating.

Students can use resources in the community to assist them in accessing and benefiting from a college education, including Vocational Rehabilitation Program offices, public agencies for a specific disability, Centers for Independent Living, special transit, mental health agencies, and high school counseling offices.

Campus Response

According to Bradford Kruse et al. (1998), students who receive accommodations report greater confidence and self-esteem, lowered anxiety and stress, greater ability to understand course material, and improved academic performance. On the other hand, students who do not receive needed accommodations are more likely to experience anxiety, stress, and academic failure. Actions colleges can take to empower students as learners include:

1. Educate academic advisors and counselors to the range of challenges faced by college students with special learning needs

2. Develop a network of successful upperclass students with special learning needs who can help facilitate workshops and informational meetings for faculty, staff, and students

3. Educate faculty regarding indicators of learning disabilities and mental health disabilities

4. Proactively educate faculty about reasonable accommodations they are required to provide in college courses

5. Widely publicize campus resources and referral procedures

6. Identify staff who can be contacted for advice regarding particular student challenges

7. Encourage faculty, academic advisors, and other staff to proactively respond when they identify students who might benefit from counseling, disability services, or other special campus services

8. Take full advantage of campus resources such as web-based courses to provide students access to learning services

In addition, campuses can keep advocacy groups for students with disabilities informed about distance-learning options and other campus resources known to promote learning to a broad range of students. Personnel in service offices for students with disabilities, student affairs offices, and others who work with students' special learning needs should be knowledgeable and able to advise students about assistive technology.

Future Issues

As colleges continue to recruit growing numbers of students with special learning needs, many outstanding issues need to be addressed, including:

- Students who had disability services in their pre-college education will come to expect and even demand them at college

- Adult students with disabilities who reached college age in the years before campuses were fully accessible will increasingly return to earn the college degrees once thought beyond their reach

- As diversity increases on campus, diverse learners with special needs will increasingly become a part of the student population

- More rural students with physical and mental disabilities will seek a college education; barriers to access for these students may include lack of adequate information about higher education opportunities, family resistance to their leaving home, and inadequate academic preparation.

Finally, the greater awareness that exists regarding disabilities, the more likely it is that campuses will meet students' needs. Steps taken by campuses to highlight the successes of upperclass students who have recognized and successfully worked with their learning needs, to develop and articulate the means of identifying other students' possible needs, and to provide widely publicized campus services can ensure that all students have the opportunity to learn.

See also: ADJUSTMENT TO COLLEGE; COLLEGE STUDENT RETENTION; PERSONAL AND PSYCHOLOGICAL PROBLEMS OF COLLEGE STUDENTS; SPECIAL EDUCATION.

BIBLIOGRAPHY

AUNE, BETTY P., and KROEGER, SUE A. 1997. "Career Development of College Students with Disabilities: An Interactional Approach to Defining the Issues." *Journal of College Student Development* 38(4):270–279.

DUNN, CAROLINE. 1995. "A Comparison of Three Groups of Academically At-Risk College Students." *Journal of College Student Development* 36(3):344–355.

EL-HINDI, AMEILA E. 1997. "Connecting Reading and Writing: College Learners' Metacognitive Awareness." *Journal of Developmental Education* 21(2):10–18.

HIRSH, GLENN. 1994. "Helping Students Overcome the Effects of Difficult Learning Histories." *Journal of Developmental Education* 18(2):10–16.

HITCHINGS, WILLIAM E.; LUZZO, DARRELL A.; RETISH, PAUL; HORVATH, MICHAEL; and RISTOW, ROBERT S. 1998. "Identifying the Career Development Needs of College Students with Disabilities." *Journal of College Student Development* 39(1):23–32.

HOCKLEY, DEAN G. 1990. "Planning Adaptive Computing Services in Higher Education: An Integrated Approach." Paper presented at Beyond Ramps: Accessing Higher Education through Technology: A Disabilities Services Conference for Higher Education, April, 1990, St. Paul, MN.

KRUSE, BRADFORD G.; ELACQUA, TINA C.; and RAPAPORT, ROSS J. 1998. "Classroom Accommodations for Students with Disabilities: A Needs Assessment." *Journal of College Student Development* 39(3):296–298.

LANCE, G. DENISE. 1996. "Computer Access in Higher Education: A National Survey of Service Providers for Students with Disabilities." *Journal of College Student Development* 37(3):279–288.

MARGOLIS, VICTOR H. 1986. "The Role of College Disabled Student Service Programs in Providing Access to the Microcomputer." *Bulletin of the Association on Handicapped Student Service Programs in Post-Secondary Education* 4(2):66–75.

MCCUNE, PAT. 2001. "What Do Disabilities Have To Do With Diversity?" *About Campus* May/June: 4–12.

ROBERTS, ELLEN R., and THOMSON, GREGG. 1994. "Learning Assistance and the Success of Underprepared Students at Berkeley." *Journal of Developmental Education* 17(3):4–14.

SCOTT, SALLY S., and GREGG, NOEL. 2000. "Meeting the Evolving Education Needs of Faculty in Providing Access for College Students with L.D." *Journal of Learning Disabilities* 33(2):158–168.

SILVER, PATRICIA; STREHORN, KREGG C.; and BOURKE, ANDREW. 1997. "The 1993 Employment Follow-Up Study of Selected Graduates with Disabilities." *Journal of College Student Development* 38(5):520–526.

STAGE, FRANCES K., and MILNE, NANCY V. 1996. "Invisible Scholars: College Students with Learning Disabilities." *Journal of Higher Education* 67(4):426–445.

STAGE, FRANCES K.; MULLER, PATRICIA; KINZIE, JILLIAN; and SIMMONS, ADA. 1998. *Creating Learning Centered Classrooms: What Does Learning Theory Have to Say?* Washington, DC: ASHE/ERIC.

INTERNET REFERENCES

AMERICAN COUNCIL ON EDUCATION. 2000. "Facts-in-Brief: Most Institutions Provide Special Services for Students with Disabilities." <www.acenet.edu/hena/facts_in_brief/2000/06_26_00_fib.cfm>.

HENDERSON, CATHY. 1999. "College Freshmen with Disabilities: A Biennial Statistical Profile." Washington, DC: American Council on Education. <www.acenet.edu/boolstore/pdf/College Fresh.pdf>.

HORN, LAURA, and BERKTOLD, JENNIFER. 1999. "Students with Disabilities in Postsecondary Education: A Profile of Preparation, Participation, and Outcomes." Washington, DC: National Center for Education Statistics. <www.nces.ed.gov/pubs99/1999187.pdf>.

FRANCES K. STAGE
MAGDALENA H. DE LA TEJA

COLLEGE TEACHING

College teaching is a very complex activity that cannot easily be defined or measured. Part of the reason is that teaching at any level cannot be divorced from the context in which it takes place and particularly from the teachers and learners who are involved. Good teaching in a graduate seminar in physics is not necessarily the same as good teaching in a large, introductory physics course, and it is certainly different from teaching in music or philosophy, or languages or medicine or business, whether in college or elsewhere. Another issue is that there is no single definition of good teaching. A major criterion of good teaching is, of course, the learning that results, but teachers cannot be held entirely responsible for student learning, and often, learning is as difficult to define and measure as teaching. Research on college teaching and learning has identified several factors that contribute to successful outcomes, but the presence or absence of these factors (often called dimensions, behaviors, practices, conditions, or principles) does not automatically mean that teaching is good or bad.

What is clear is that even though there are established general relationships between teaching and learning, each teaching and learning situation possesses unique characteristics and success is largely dependent on being able to capitalize on the conditions that promote learning and to avoid those factors that may impede it. The direct responsibility for success is shared by teachers and students, but this does not exempt institutions and academic units from some degree of responsibility for providing the tools, resources, and environments that allow teachers and students to maximize the benefits that result from their efforts. Indeed, the research shows how critical it is to create environments that promote and support success whether these are in traditional classrooms where teachers and students regularly meet face-to-face, or in new, virtual classrooms where teachers and students interact via the Internet and may never have such meetings.

A Short History

Since the 1950s there has been a tremendous amount of research on college teaching, and this work has become more comprehensive and productive, particularly since the early 1970s. Part of the impetus for this work came from faculty who were interested in understanding and improving teaching and learning in their classrooms. These faculty, however, were from all disciplines, and they did not have an organized body of research and theory upon which to base their investigations, experience in educational research, or criteria to guide their investigative methods and practices. Those with more specific training and experiences, for example psychologists and educational researchers, had a dual interest because research on teaching and learning not only served their own teaching but also contributed to the literature in their own disciplines. After World War II, the rapid growth of federal, state, and private funding in support of teaching and learning allowed these researchers to carry out large and comprehensive studies that formed the basis of research for the next half-century.

From another quarter, the social activism and student unrest during the 1960s fueled demands that a college education should be more relevant to students' interests and needs and more connected to real-world issues both in the personal realm of career preparation and the broad sociopolitical arena.

A third force was the growing interest in determining the extent to which higher education was fulfilling its roles. Institutional boards of trustees, state and federal governments, accrediting agencies, and others became more actively interested in the outcomes of a college education, and the matter of *accountability* became a more and more pressing issue as time went on. It was necessary to have ways of determining both what was happening (the instruments or processes of education) as well as what resulted (the consequences or outcomes of education). In the mid-to-late 1960s, landmark work began in the field of evaluation. Michael Scriven (1967) coined the terms *formative* and *summative* evaluation, with the former meaning evaluation for purposes of revision and improvement and the latter meaning evaluation for purposes of making decisions about the merit or worth of individuals, programs, units, or institutions. The evaluation of faculty performance and specifically of college teaching grew exponentially with early, major books on the topic contributed by Kenneth O. Doyle (1975) and John A. Centra (1979). The primary source of information for evaluating teaching was student-provided data from teacher/course evaluation questionnaires commonly referred to as *student ratings of teaching*. In a series of reports, Peter Seldin documented the growth of the use of student ratings, and by the mid-1990s well over 90 percent of higher education institutions in the United States were using student ratings as part of the evaluation of college teaching.

By the mid-1980s, it became apparent that typical classroom testing was not providing sufficiently detailed information about the nature and outcomes of teaching. More specific investigation was required to truly measure learning, and the *assessment move-ment* gained momentum. In their 1993 study, Thomas A. Angelo and K. Patricia Cross provided widely used guidelines for practice, and the quality of institutional assessment has become a primary criterion used by accreditation agencies not only to determine the extent to which student learning outcomes have been achieved but also as a mechanism to help teachers and programs develop better, more measurable objectives. Without clear specification of the intended outcomes, measurement becomes difficult. As the common paraphrase notes, "If you don't know where you're going, you won't know if you get there."

The Professional Roles and Responsibilities of College Teachers

Yet another factor has strongly influenced contemporary college teaching: the definition of the roles and responsibilities of college faculty. Ironically, the same postwar support for research that promoted more thorough exploration of college teaching also had a negative impact on college teaching. As early as the 1950s, the tradition of the faculty's equal responsibility for teaching, research, and service was called into question, and the discussion was not so much about teaching and research as it was about teaching versus research. In *The American University* (1968), Jacques Barzun decried the dichotomy, noting that universities recognized and rewarded even mediocre researchers more than great teachers. The prestige of institutions came more from their research and funding activities than from the quality of their teaching, with the result that promotion, tenure, and merit were determined more by one's scholarship than one's teaching. The Carnegie Foundation even made special classifications, separating *research universities* from other institutional types.

Nonetheless, there was motion in the direction of better balance. Books on teaching such as Wilbert J. McKeachie's *Teaching Tips* (in ten editions between 1951 and 1999) were widely disseminated, and in 1986, Lee Shulman proposed that expert teachers combined knowledge of their content with knowledge of pedagogy and developed repertoires of *curricular knowledge* that allowed them to most effectively teach in their disciplines. This conceptualization helped to establish the importance of pedagogical expertise in company with content knowledge. Another development was the creation in 1980 of the *teaching dossier* by the Canadian Association of University Teachers (revised in 1986) and the subsequent rise of interest in the *teaching portfolio* in U.S. institutions. The dossier or portfolio is a document that provides the opportunity for the teacher not only to present quantitative evidence of effectiveness such as student ratings but also to include a teaching philosophy, discussions and evidence of instructional innovations, assessment efforts, teaching-related service activities such as mentoring, classroom research, and related work.

The discussion of faculty roles and rewards leapt into general view with the 1990 publication of Ernest Boyer's *Scholarship Revisited: The Priorities of the Professoriate.* Boyer defined four kinds of scholarship: *discovery* (conducting traditional research), *integration* (making connections across disciplines), *application* (solving real-world problems), and *teaching* (transferring knowledge about both content and teaching to students and peers). The most widely discussed aspect of the *scholarship of teaching* is its emphasis on the formal and informal exploration of classroom processes and outcomes by faculty in all disciplines—in other words, the extension of the three other types of scholarship into the realm of teaching and the legitimizing of research on teaching. The American Association for Higher Education and the Carnegie Foundation have strongly supported developments in this area with efforts such as the Carnegie Academy for the Scholarship of Teaching and Learning and the Campus Conversations Program, initiatives designed to engage college teachers in dialogue and in projects that explore teaching and learning across the disciplines. Discussions of the scholarship of teaching promoted the importance of investigating college teaching, but it also added another criterion to the list of responsibilities of the expert teacher.

In a different conceptualization, James Bess and associates (2000) proposed that college teaching is so complex that its various roles cannot be expected to be filled by only one person. The authors identified seven *teacher subroles*—content research, instructional design, instructional delivery, discussion leading, content/activity integration, assessment, and mentoring—and argued that collaborating teams can provide more comprehensive service to students than can individual teachers. On an even broader scale, Raoul Arreola described the college teacher as a *meta-professional,* one who not only has expertise in a base profession within a given discipline but also is held responsible for myriad other skills, knowledge, and activities beyond pedagogy. These include advising, curriculum development, assessment, service, administration, leadership, team membership, strategic planning, communication, and entrepreneurship.

The contemporary college teaching profession thus involves much more than maintaining one's disciplinary expertise and delivering lectures. The responsibilities of the faculty member as a teacher are embedded in the context of a dynamic and multifaceted profession, but research on college teaching has not considered this kind of complexity in its investigations of the teaching role. In the following section, this complexity is reduced with the focus only on the findings of research that has explored what college teachers do, how they do it, and how it relates to various outcomes.

Principles of Good Practice, Dimensions of College Teaching, and Behaviors of Teachers

Despite the complexity of the profession, a good deal is known about generally successful practice, about the dimensions of college teaching, and about the specific behaviors of teachers. In 1987 Arthur Chickering and Zelda Gamson introduced "seven principles for good practice in undergraduate education." These were that good practice: (1) encourages student-faculty contact, (2) encourages cooperation among students, (3) encourages active learning, (4) gives prompt feedback, (5) emphasizes time on task, (6) communicates high expectations, and (7) respects diverse talents and ways of learning. These principles were drawn from a broad review of the higher education literature and were an attempt to provide general guidelines about effective practice. Classroom teachers, however, needed more specific information in order to be able to translate these principles into practice.

Early work on college teaching began by observing and recording teaching and by asking teachers and students about the characteristics of effective and ineffective teachers. The responses were generally similar and were categorized into smaller lists, and teachers and students were then asked to rank these characteristics or dimensions of instruction in terms of their importance.

At the same time, two other avenues of research were active. One area was in measurement and assessment, where ongoing efforts to more accurately determine the nature and amount of student learning provided new data about how students learn as well as about student achievement. Another was widespread research on student ratings of teaching. Because these student ratings were met with some resistance, they were the subject of intensive scrutiny. Numerous studies (over 2,000 studies on teaching and its evaluation by 1990) were conducted with an emphasis on examining technical and measurement characteristics such as their validity (the extent to which they measured teaching effectiveness as opposed to factors not associated with that effectiveness) and reliability (the extent to which they could consistently provide usable data). Herbert W. Marsh summarized these studies in a 1987 article. Marsh demonstrated that student ratings were reliable, valid, and useful indicators that both established college teaching as a complex and multi-dimensional activity and could provide useful data for formative and summative decision-making.

The obvious question was: How do the dimensions of teaching, student achievement, and student ratings relate to each other? Several studies correlated the dimensions with ratings or achievement measures such as tests or grades. Kenneth A. Feldman conducted an extensive review and meta-analysis (the reanalysis of data from other studies, compiled to provide a large set of results from a variety of similar situations), publishing the results in a 1989 *Research in Higher Education* article. He identified seventeen principal dimensions and ranked them with respect to the strength of their correlations with achievement and student ratings. There was a good deal of consistency in the findings. Teacher organization, presentation skills, the perceived outcome of instruction (i.e., learning or its results), and stimulation of interest in course content were the most strongly correlated with achievement and were also strongly correlated with ratings. Several other dimensions had similar rankings with respect to achievement and ratings and only three items had quite different rankings. Teacher helpfulness and teacher encouragement/openness were tied at fifth/sixth rank with respect to achievement but were only sixteenth and eleventh with respect to ratings. Intellectual challenge was ranked thirteenth with respect to achievement but fourth with respect to ratings. Feldman also arrayed the student and teacher rankings of the importance of the dimensions. The rankings were generally similar to each other with two exceptions: Students ranked stimulation of interest in course content in third position while faculty ranked it only twelfth, and students ranked intellectual challenge sixteenth while faculty ranked it sixth. The importance rankings were generally similar to the correlational rankings. Feldman attributed differences to the variety of the subdimensions that comprised the general dimensions and acknowledged that knowing the general dimensions did not identify specific ways in which teachers could develop and provide instruction that would be most effective.

Attempts to isolate specific behaviors were made by Harry G. Murray and Robert D. Renaud. Murray and Renaud broke down general dimensions such as clarity and organization into lists of *low-inference behaviors*—behaviors that could be directly observed and recorded. For example, rather than having an observer infer the teacher's degree of preparation based on other factors such as the use of class time, Murray and Renaud identified observable behaviors such as reviewing the topics of previous meetings; providing outlines; giving overviews of material to come; using headings, diagrams, and other organizing features; and summarizing frequently. Such behaviors could be learned and practiced by teachers in order to enhance organization and improve student learning.

The Future of College Teaching

No discussion of college teaching can omit the major changes brought about by two factors: the changes in the student population and the tremendous growth of distance and technology-based teaching and learning. The obvious differences between traditional, face-to-face instruction for young residential students and distance, computer-based, and other instructional formats for older learners are dramatic and have major implications for college teaching. Many of the methods and strategies for on-campus teaching simply do not transfer to older, off-campus learners. In effect, a major new agenda for research is necessary to test the extent to which what is currently known can inform teaching and learning in these new situations. If the premise of such differences is accepted, then another issue is raised: the extent to which current methods of measuring teaching effectiveness are usable. The best response at the moment is that simple replication of current methods of evaluation is not sufficient. New methods and instruments must be devised that take the changes into account and provide accurate information that can be fairly interpreted and used.

Summary

From the various avenues of research, it has been possible to develop useful guidelines for teachers, but these are not guaranteed techniques for successful teaching. No such list has yet been devised, and it would be foolish to presume that it will be, for no single technique will work in every situation, and even carefully developed sets of strategies may be more or less effective depending upon the context in which they are used. If anything is understood about college teaching, it is that to succeed it must be flexible and responsive to the teachers, students, and situations in which it takes place. In the future it is safe to assume that the combination of existing findings and what is learned in investigating new teaching and learning situations and tools will be required knowledge for all college teachers. This increased responsibility, in union with other expanding roles and responsibilities of faculty and ongoing changes in higher education, may drastically alter the profession of college teaching and the way it is practiced.

See also: FACULTY ROLES AND RESPONSIBILITIES; GRADUATE SCHOOL TRAINING.

BIBLIOGRAPHY

ANGELO, THOMAS A., and CROSS, K. PATRICIA. 1993. *Classroom Assessment Techniques: A Handbook for College Teachers,* 2nd edition. San Francisco: Jossey-Bass.

ARREOLA, RAOUL A. 2000. "Higher Education's Meta-Profession." *Department Chair* (fall):4–5.

BARZUN, JACQUES. 1968. *The American University.* New York: Harper and Row.

BESS, JAMES L., and ASSOCIATES. 2000. *Teaching Alone, Teaching Together.* San Francisco: Jossey-Bass.

BOYER, ERNEST L. 1990. *Scholarship Reconsidered: The Priorities of the Professoriate.* San Francisco: Jossey-Bass.

CENTRA, JOHN A. 1979. *Determining Faculty Effectiveness: Assessing Teaching, Research, and Service for Personnel Decisions and Improvement.* San Francisco: Jossey-Bass.

CHICKERING, ARTHUR W., and GAMSON, ZELDA F. 1987. "Seven Principles of Good Practice in Undergraduate Education." *Wingspread Journal* June (special insert).

DOYLE, KENNETH O. 1975. *Student Evaluation of Instruction.* Lexington, MA: D. C. Heath.

FELDMAN, KENNETH A. 1989. "The Association between Student Ratings of Specific Instructional Dimensions and Student Achievement: Refining and Extending the Synthesis of Data from Multisection Validity Studies." *Research in Higher Education* 30:583–645.

MARSH, HERBERT W. 1987. "Students' Evaluations of University Teaching: Research Findings, Methodological Issues, and Directions for Future Research." *International Journal of Educational Research* 11:253–388.

McKEACHIE, WILBERT J. 1999. *Teaching Tips: Strategies, Research, and Theory for College and University Teachers,* 10th edition. Boston: Houghton Mifflin.

MURRAY, HARRY G., and RENAUD, ROBERT D. 1995. "Disciplinary Differences in Classroom Teaching Behaviors." In *Disciplinary Differences in Teaching and Learning: Implications for Practice,* ed. Nira Hativa and Michele Marincovich. San Francisco: Jossey-Bass.

SCRIVEN, MICHAEL. 1967. "The Methodology of Evaluation." In *Perspectives of Curriculum Evaluation,* ed. Ralph Tyler, Robert Gagné, and Michael Scriven. Chicago: Rand McNally.

SELDIN, PETER. 1993. "How Colleges Evaluate Professors, 1983 versus 1993." *AAHE Bulletin* 12(October):6–8.

SHULMAN, LEE S. 1986. "Those Who Understand: Knowledge Growth in Teaching." *Educational Researcher* 15:4–14.

THEALL, MICHAEL. 1999. "New Directions for Theory and Research on Teaching: A Review of the Past Twenty Years." In *Teaching and Learning on the Edge of the Millennium: Building on What We Have Learned,* ed. Marilla Svinicki. San Francisco. Jossey-Bass.

MICHAEL THEALL

COLLIER, JOHN, JR. (1913–1992)

A founder of and one of the most significant contributors to the discipline of visual anthropology, John Collier Jr. applied still photography and film to cross-cultural understanding and analysis. He used photography for education in two ways. First, his principle work, *Visual Anthropology: Photography as a Research Method* (with Malcolm Collier, 1986 [1967]), defined the discipline for many years, and stimulated the creation of visual foci in anthropology departments nationally and internationally. The work offered methods by which photographs may sensitize students to cross-cultural nuance and allow them to find correlations between visual behavior, material culture, and cultural and psychological values. Collier's second key work, *Alaskan Eskimo Education: A Film Analysis of Cultural Confrontation in the Schools* (1973), applied visual analysis to a critique of "white-centered" education in Native American schools. Collier showed that irrespective of lesson content, teaching styles were ineffective if they were insensitive to indigenous cultural modes of learning.

Disabilities and Early Education

Collier's life-long commitment to visual communication and cross-cultural education was born in the unique circumstances of his youth. His father was John Collier Sr., indigenous-rights activist and commissioner of the Bureau of Indian Affairs under Franklin Roosevelt. As a boy, Collier Jr. spent many years living in and near pueblos of New Mexico, surrounded by Indian elders and the Western literary and political luminaries in his father's circle. A motor vehicle accident left Collier at the age of ten with a profound hearing impairment as well as motor and cognitive disabilities. He was thereafter unable to perform adequately in school, and he lost much of his father's regard. Both parents had been active in the home schooling movement, however, and Collier's mother Lucy took on the boy's personal education. Equally important were the Taos Indian elders who treated young Collier as one of their own and guided him in the ways of the Pueblo until he reached the age of puberty.

The near uselessness of formal, Western education for Collier contrasted starkly with his mother's tutelage and the silent life lessons he gained from Taos elders. Collier's subsequent training in painting and his mastery of still photography were achieved through apprenticeships, experiences of the type he would later call true education, not mere schooling.

Visual Anthropology and Cultural Blinders

Collier's complex disabilities, particularly with hearing, made him intensely sensitive to the visual world. The disabilities made it necessary for him to seek beyond words to alternative bases of knowledge. They made it possible for him to appreciate radical differences between Western worldviews and those of the pueblos. The "Indian experience," Collier wrote, "was in essence a pure nonverbal sensibility, and coming from a constantly talking intellectual society, [one might be] overwhelmed by this quietude" (1986, p. xix). Largely divorced from the words spun in his father's literary circles, Collier came to distrust theoretical constructs. Instead of seeing, he concluded, Westerners only learned to read. Collier's goal for training Western anthropologists and educators, then, was to liberate them from their cultural blinders, an inhibited dependence on print-based understanding. In its place he offered means to read cultural values visually. Visual messages are more reliable than those that people know how to express in words.

Photographs as Records and Elicitation Tools

Collier proposed two fundamental uses of photography with which nonverbal, cross-cultural meanings can be interpreted. First of all, the camera is an eye with a memory. Used systematically, photographs can track movement and change, can allow accurate counts and measurements, and can offer viable comparisons within and across cultures. Without principled method, the cross-cultural photographer will easily lapse into idiosyncratic or ethnocentric impressionism. In contrast, though, methodical documentation—time and motion studies, material culture inventories, and the recording of cultural processes—produces photographs that are researchable. In them, statistically representative data can provide reliable bases for understanding.

Collier's faith in the possibility that photos may disclose their visual memories in untroubled ways was shared by important contemporaries, including Gregory Bateson, Margaret Mead, Edward T. Hall, and Ray Birdwhistell. Collier expressed a modernist optimism about the possibility of photographic cross-cultural education. Later scholars, however, have rejoined that photographs, like all forms of representation in social science, are problematic. Statistical method may strengthen ethnocentrism by disguising it with the appearance of objectivity. Further, photographic depiction is rife with inegalitarian power relations.

Collier did not answer these criticisms directly, but dedicated enormous energy to disclosing inequality of power, particularly with respect to Native Americans. His second crucial application of photography to cross-cultural education scuttled the idea that pictures might somehow represent the world objectively or become neutral politically. In collaboration with psychiatric-anthropologist Alexander Leighton, Collier used culture-specific photographs in the place of Rorschach and Thematic Apperception Tests. Informants from different ethnic and class groups, shown the same collection of photographs, systematically identified different culture elements and projected different values on them. By comparing these contrasting responses, Collier could give a composite of how diversified communities interpret their visual world.

Cultural Vitality and Identity

Collier understood education in a very broad sense, as that which developed a child's well-being in the round. His study of Alaskan Eskimos (Inuit) weighed the emotional and psychological effects of Western-styled education on children, and concluded that most of it provided "humiliation instead of a stimulating fulfillment" (1973, p. 114). Credentialing, too, the "White backlash of conventional teacher training," could destroy the effectiveness of Eskimo educators (1973, p. 119).

Collier feared that despite its benefits, Western education undermined the cultural energy that is the greatest strength of Native American identity, and the greatest potential lesson for word-obsessed students. This energy is spiritual, something beyond the visible and audible. Yet, Collier felt, photography can help recover the pure intelligence that all may possess before onset of adult inhibition. Much of this energy and intelligence may be found in the enormous collection of photographs taken by John Collier Jr., stored in the Maxwell Museum of Anthropology at the University of New Mexico.

See also: MULTICULTURAL EDUCATION.

BIBLIOGRAPHY

COLLIER, JOHN, JR. 1973. *Alaskan Eskimo Education: A Film Analysis of Cultural Confrontation in the Schools.* New York: Holt, Rinehart and Winston.

COLLIER, JOHN, JR., and COLLIER, MALCOLM. 1986. *Visual Anthropology: Photography as a Research Method* (1967). Albuquerque: University of New Mexico Press.

COLLIER, MALCOLM. 1993. "John Collier, Jr.: Cultural Diversity and the Camera." In *Threads of Culture,* ed. Steve Yates and Robin Jacobson. Albuquerque: Museum of New Mexico.

MURPHY, JANE M., and LEIGHTON, ALEXANDER H. 1965. "Native Conceptions of Psychiatric Disorder." In *Approaches to Cross-Cultural Psychiatry,* ed. Jane M. Murphy and Alexander H. Leighton. Ithaca, NY: Cornell University Press.

PETER BIELLA

COMENIUS, JOHANN (1592–1670)

A prolific scholar on pedagogical, spiritual, and social reform, Johann Amos Comenius was born in the village of Nivnice in southeast Moravia (now part of the Czech Republic), and became a minister in the Unity of Brethren church, a Protestant sect. Political and religious persecution during the Thirty Years' War (1618–1648) drove Comenius from his homeland in 1628, and despite his earnest hopes for repatriation, Comenius never returned. He found refuge in Poland, England, Prussia, Hungary, and the Netherlands as a scholar and bishop of his church until his death in Amsterdam. Pained by the political and religious strife that plagued seventeenth-century Europe, Comenius authored more than 200 works as he searched for a method to alleviate human suffering while uniting all people and religions through a common appreciation of God.

Contributions

Comenius is best known for his innovations in pedagogy, but one cannot gain an adequate appreciation of his educational ideas without recognizing his religious and metaphysical convictions. Despite the prevalent human suffering of his day, Comenius remained optimistic about the future of mankind, as he believed in the immanence of God and the imminence of God's kingdom on Earth. As God's creations, humans were necessarily good, not corrupt. Comenius also felt that Christ's Second Coming would end human strife but that people themselves could act in ushering the new millennium by engaging in *pansophy,* or the lifelong study of an encyclopedic system of human knowledge. By seeing the harmony among everything in the universe, all human beings would come to acknowledge God's glory and presence in themselves and in nature.

Specifically, Comenius characterized human life—from the mother's womb to grave—as a series of educational stages in which objects from nature would serve as the basis of learning. In this, he was influenced by the writings of the English statesman Sir Francis Bacon, an early advocate of the inductive method of scientific inquiry. Comenius believed that true knowledge could be found in things as they existed in reality and when one came to understand how they came about. As a result, Comenius urged all people to recognize the interconnections and harmony among philosophical, theological, scientific, social, and political facts and ideas. That way, one could reconcile three seemingly distinct worlds: the natural, the human, and the divine. Comenius felt that disagreements among religious, scientific, and philosophic enterprises arose because each held only a partial understanding of universal truth—but that all could exist harmoniously through pansophic awareness. Viewing the human mind as infinite in its capacity (as the benevolent gift of God), Comenius advocated universal education so that the souls of all people would be enlightened in this fashion. Through universal education and pedagogy, pansophy would eliminate human prejudice and lead to human perfection—a state of being that God had intended for man.

Comenius found fault with many of the educational practices of his day. In particular, he disapproved of the scholastic tradition of studying grammar and memorizing texts. He lamented the haphazard and severe teaching methods in European schools, which tended to diminish student interest in learning. Finally, Comenius felt that all children—whether male or female, rich or poor, gifted or mentally challenged—were entitled to a full education, and he regretted that only a privileged few received formal schooling. For Comenius, all of these educational shortcomings were especially urgent, as they hindered mankind's progress to the new millennium. As a result, he attempted to remedy these problems by authoring a number of textbooks and educational treatises.

Works

Perhaps Comenius's most familiar work is the *Great Didactic*, which he originally wrote in 1632. As Comenius held the conviction that pansophy was necessary for the spiritual salvation of humankind, he reasoned that a good man (a rational being who understood God through nature), and ultimately a good society, could only be created if all people acquired encyclopedic knowledge. In order to guaran-

tee that this would occur, Comenius delineated a universal teaching method or standard set of pedagogical postulates that would facilitate an effective communication of knowledge between the teacher and student. Delineating four levels of schools lasting six years each, Comenius was one of the first educators to recommend a coherent and standard system of instruction. Indeed, Comenius suggested that the universality of nature dictated that all people shared common stages of intellectual development. As a result, he reasoned, teachers needed to identify their students' stages of development and match the level of instruction accordingly. Lessons should proceed from easy to complex at a slow and deliberate pace. Furthermore, Comenius argued that the acquisition of new material began through the senses—an idea that reflected the rise of empiricism in the seventeenth century.

Ultimately, Comenius believed that the purpose of learning was eminently practical: not for ostentatious displays of rhetorical acumen, but for preparing for the Second Coming of Christ. Comenius derided the educational legacy of the Renaissance with its focus on classical grammar and even the Reformation with its mechanical teaching of the catechism. By employing the methods presented in the *Great Didactic*, however, Comenius argued that teachers could ensure that they produced knowledgeable and virtuous students who would continue to learn throughout their lives. In this way, he viewed teaching as a technical skill; if performed correctly, one could guarantee the results.

In 1631, Comenius published *The Gate of Languages Unlocked*, a Latin textbook. In it, he recommended that teachers employ the students' native language as a necessary frame of reference for unfamiliar words to become meaningful. Comenius also advocated that teachers begin with simple lessons for students to master before proceeding to more complex exercises. It became the standard Latin textbook in Europe and America throughout the seventeenth and much of the eighteenth centuries. One contemporary scholar has suggested that the incremental organization and explicit goals of the text anticipated the principles of mastery learning.

In 1658, Comenius wrote another Latin textbook, *The World in Pictures*, one of the first reading books to incorporate illustrations. Enormously popular in Europe and America, it was printed in the United States until 1887. Again, reflecting Comenius's belief that all learning began with the senses, *The*

World in Pictures included numbered parts of illustrations, each of which corresponded to a word. It also presented a simplified vocabulary and specific examples to help students understand the relevant concept or rule. And like the *Gate of Languages Unlocked*, Comenius attempted to present lessons in a way that reflected the order of nature, although some scholars have noted that Comenius manipulated perspectives and exaggerated proportions to facilitate the lesson at hand. Some educators consider the *World in Pictures* a pivotal text in pedagogical innovation that opened the way for modern-day teaching instruments such as audiovisual aids and electronic media.

Frustrated by the fragmentation of European institutions of higher education, along with their tendency to impose knowledge authoritatively and discourage critical thinking, Comenius advocated the creation of a universal college. In *Way of Light*, which he wrote while visiting England in 1641 and 1642, Comenius outlined his vision for establishing universal textbooks and schools, a common language, and a pansophic college. Comenius believed that a pansophic college would contribute to the establishment of an intellectual and spiritual consensus in the world by propelling, steering, and coordinating the research of all scholars. This "college of light" would be located in a prominent and accessible locale and utilize a common language in order to facilitate the inclusion of all European scholars of prominence. It would also govern an ideal world and disseminate knowledge so that an understanding of God's creations and glory would not become the exclusive possession of the privileged. Such an institution would therefore unite all human beings in the world both culturally and religiously. Although the pansophic college never came about, Comenius's treatise inspired the establishment of the Royal Society in England (founded in 1662) and the Berlin Royal Academy of Sciences (founded in 1700).

Comenius's belief that knowledge and wisdom could be merged into a single pan-science drew the criticism of the French philosopher René Descartes, who sought to free science from theology in a quest to gain knowledge objectively. Indeed, Comenius's pansophic ideas fell out of favor by the late seventeenth century, as they became incongruous with the prevailing epistemological sensibilities of the Enlightenment.

In the past century, however, a number of educators revived the pedagogical elements of Comenius's legacy. They cited his emphasis on early childhood education and his aversion to corporal punishment as precursors to the German educator Friedrich Froebel's kindergarten idea. They lauded Comenius's call for universal education and a carefully graded system of schools. They noted his innovative use of learning aids such as the illustrations in the *World in Pictures* and his preference for focusing on actual things rather than rhetoric in education. Finally, they praised Comenius's desire to make learning enjoyable and more meaningful through the use of dramatic productions and other innovative methods.

Still, one must remember that these pedagogical innovations derived from Comenius's urgent desire for the alleviation of human suffering, the mending of political, epistemological, and spiritual divisions, and ultimately, man's gradual comprehension of God's will and glory.

See also: PHILOSOPHY OF EDUCATION.

BIBLIOGRAPHY

COMENIUS, JOHANN AMOS. 1673. *The Gate of Languages Unlocked, or, A Seed-Plot of All Arts and Tongues: Containing a Ready Way to Learn the Latine and English Tongue.* London: Printed by T.R. and N.T. for the Company of Stationers.

COMENIUS, JOHANN AMOS. 1896. *Comenius' School of Infancy: An Essay on the Education of Youth During the First Six Years,* ed. Will S. Monroe. Boston: Heath.

COMENIUS, JOHANN AMOS. 1967. *The Great Didactic of John Amos Comenius: Now for the First Time,* tr. and ed. Maurice W. Keatinge. New York: Russell and Russell.

COMENIUS, JOHANN AMOS. 1968. *The Oribs Pictus of John Amos Comenius.* Detroit, MI: Singing Tree.

LENK, KRYSTOF, and KAHN, PAUL. 1992. "To Show and Explain: The Information Graphics of Stevin and Comenius." *Visible Language* 26:272–281.

SADLER, EDWARD. 1966. *J. A. Comenius and the Concept of Universal Education.* New York: Barnes and Noble.

SMALL, MARY LUINS. 1990. "The Pansophism of John Amos Comenius (1592–1670) as the Foundation of Educational Technology and the Source of Constructive Standards for the Evaluation of Computerized Instruction and Tests." International Conference on Technology and Education, March 1990. ERIC. ED325079, microfiche, 1–11.

SPINKA, MATTHEW. 1967. *John Amos Comenius: That Incomparable Moravian.* New York: Russell and Russell.

SEVAN G. TERZIAN

COMMENCEMENT

The culmination of education for the high school student, the commencement ceremony, or graduation, is a major event and transition point for students, parents, and teachers. It is a time for students, parents, and teachers to celebrate their hard work and accomplishments. Students take pride in having met the graduation requirements that were established by their state and local board of education; parents celebrate the accomplishments of their children; and teachers and school administrators commemorate the fruits of their labors. Commencement exercises serve as a transition point for the individual members of the graduating class who will follow diverse paths into futures that may include higher education, the military, and the world of work.

The purpose for the commencement exercise is to acknowledge the students who have successfully met the requirements for high school graduation, usually with the presentation of a diploma. Graduation requirements differ from state to state and from school district to school district within a state. The accountability movement that took place during the 1990s resulted in more stringent requirements for high school graduation, leading to the creation of state tests that students must pass in order to earn a traditional diploma. States have responded to demands that high school graduates must be able to demonstrate mathematical and language skills needed for success in higher education and the workplace by creating a series of diplomas. The traditional diploma that was once awarded to all students who participated in the commencement exercise has been replaced in some states by differentiated diplomas and certificates. The new diplomas include the traditional diploma, diplomas for exceptional students whose handicapping conditions prevent them from meeting all graduation requirements, and certificates of attendance for students who have attended classes without passing all graduation requirements. By replacing the traditional diploma with awards that differentiate between students based on their achievement, high schools attempt to clearly designate the knowledge and skills of students who have completed study.

The typical commencement ceremony takes place in the school auditorium, gymnasium, or football stadium. Parents, friends, and teachers are usually seated in designated areas prior to the time scheduled for the ceremony to begin. School officials are typically assembled on a stage in front of the assembled guests, and special seating is reserved for the graduates between the stage and the audience. At the appointed time, the graduates march into the arena as music is played by the school band or over the public address system. Students may be dressed in matching caps and gowns; some students may wear special insignia that denotes membership in honor societies or other significant accomplishment. The ceremony usually includes speeches by the senior class president, the valedictorian, and a guest speaker. Instrumental or choral music may be included in the program. The culminating event is the presentation of graduates and the presentation of diplomas and certificates. Students are often called to the stage to receive their diplomas from the principal.

At some schools students are given responsibility for the program. At these commencement programs, students may talk briefly about their studies, discuss their accomplishments, or present a short play to dramatize some school experience. They may also recognize honor students or students whose accomplishments have been outstanding. The commencement program can include weeklong demonstrations and exhibits of student work prior to the ceremony.

Commencement planners encountered a number of challenges during the last two decades of the twentieth century. One of these challenges was finding a facility large enough to accommodate the families and friends of graduates who wanted to attend the celebration. Schools often use their school football stadium if one is available. This decision often solves one problem only to create another if weather conditions are not conducive to an outdoor ceremony. Since commencement programs typically occur in the spring, rain and lightning may force the program indoors. If weather does force the program indoors, the number of parents and guests who can attend may be limited.

Another potential problem for school officials is graduate behavior at commencement. Some students choose to celebrate by engaging in minor pranks at their commencement, such as throwing a beach ball around during speeches to handing the principal a marble as the diploma is presented. Students may also decorate their caps with decorations or a message. Educators who believe that commencement should be a formal ceremony have tried a number of strategies to prevent pranks from occurring and have enjoyed varying degrees of success.

During the second half of the twentieth century, United States courts handed down a number of rulings that defined the constitutional relationship between public schools and religion. None of those rulings directly addressed the constitutionality of prayer at public school commencement. The rulings did, however, limit prayer initiated by school officials in the classroom and at school events such as football games. Prior to these rulings, it was common practice for schools to invite a local clergy member to pray as a part of the commencement program. As schools wait for the United States Supreme Court to rule on prayer at commencement, some high schools are content to allow students to pray if they so choose while others expressly forbid students who make presentations from praying.

Some elementary and middle schools conduct an end-of-year ceremony that is similar to the high school commencement. These ceremonies typically include the presentation of awards and recognition of student accomplishments. They do not include the presentation of a diploma. Elementary and middle school ceremonies that closely parallel the high school commencement have been criticized as being inappropriate for students who may be tempted to drop out of school before high school graduation.

See also: SECONDARY EDUCATION, *subentry on* CURRENT TRENDS.

BIBLIOGRAPHY

BAGIN, DON, and GALLAGHER, DONALD. 2001. *The School and Community Relations.* Needham Heights, MA: Allyn and Bacon.

HUDGINS, HERBERT, and VACA, RICHARD. 1999. *Law and Education: Contemporary Issues and Court Decisions.* Charlottesville, VA: LEXIS.

KERMIT BUCKNER

COMMERCE OF EDUCATION

By the end of the twentieth century, the world economy had shifted in two important ways. First, the free flow of capital had created a high level of global interdependency. Second, production and distribution were no longer regionally bound within the nation-state. Trade agreements provide evidence of these trends. Educational commodities in the global marketplace are evident as services and goods. Though increasingly evident, however, the effects of a growing global economic interdependence are not well understood theoretically or empirically.

Reactions to these changes range from an acceptance of democratic and economic possibilities to a resistance to open-market trends. Proponents embrace the economic order because these initiatives move their country toward the free flow of information and capital. Opponents recognize a power imbalance, and fear a loss in national identity. The arguments rest on the standardization processes couched within trade agreements.

Trade agreements encourage countries to participate in international standards organizations with a view toward harmonizing the technical regulations of individual countries. Organizations engaged in standards development call for increased certification, accreditation, and rigorous assessment of these standards. Adherence effectively allows labor to move freely across national boundaries. More subtly, it seems that nonelected governance bodies (e.g., a trade agreement) can become imbued within the architecture of a country's educational system.

Trade Agreements and the U.S. Economy

Trade agreements typically deal with the commodification of raw materials and manufactured goods. There are few systematic studies that address the practical impact of trade agreements on education. This is because the notion of treating services as tradable commodities is new, both internationally and nationally. The General Agreement on Trade in

Services (GATS), concluded in April 1994, was the first broadly based international agreement on trade in services. In the 1980s the U.S. services sector moved into the competitive market, driven by the deregulation of telecommunications, financial services, banking, and transportation.

Trade agreements rarely address service sectors broadly, nor is education as a service generally addressed. For example, consider three ways in which education has been introduced in these agreements:

1. Global agreements, such as the General Agreement on Tariffs and Trade and the World Trade Organization (GATT/WTO), generally mention education, but only as a low priority service item.

2. Regional agreements, such as the European Community, the North American Free Trade Agreement (NAFTA), and the Association of Southeast Asian Nations (ASEAN), provide inconsistent structural recognition of education. For example, the Single European Act dealt with education issues only at the national level. However, when polled, a majority of Europeans felt that "testing, certification, technical standards, and science and research" should be handled at the European level.

3. Bilateral agreements, such as those between Japan and United States, open up markets for provisional time periods.

The dominant trend in every facet of the United States economy is the shift from the production of goods to services. In 2000 the U.S. export of private services totaled $278.6 billion, exceeding imports by $78 billion.

Educational services encompass both programs and ancillary services. Programs are defined as sets of curricular activities that may lead to a certificate or degree. These may include aspects of the following: elementary, secondary, postsecondary, university, vocational, and technical education; child care; special education; adult and continuing education; corporate training; distributed learning; and technology-based training. Ancillary services are a necessary component to managing the needs of individuals and the logistics of servicing equipment. Activities include: the design, marketing, and sales of testing, certification, test preparation, tutoring, and other enhancement programs; management consulting; and administrative and human resources.

Educational goods include the design, manufacture, and sale of textbooks, teaching materials, vocational and scientific equipment, software, videos, multimedia, school supplies, and furniture.

In 2000 U.S. exports of educational services totaled $10,287 million, which exceeded imports by $8,144 million and doubled the amount of exports in 1990 ($5,126 million). Asia and the Pacific Rim accounted for 55 percent of the 2000 export volume; Europe for 17 percent; and South America for 13 percent. In 1997 exports of educational goods included $11,600 million worth of textbooks and supplementary materials; $4,800 million in technology; and $3,000 million in testing and test preparation.

Educational Changes

Changes to educational systems are neither monolithic nor consistent. Changes in the content and form of educational services and goods occur at all levels and across cultures. The changes can roughly be categorized as being technological, organizational, social, or adaptive. These are not mutually exclusive categories, but provide a way to understand the complex interplay between global trade, the free-flow of information and labor, and the impact of trade on education. The role of technology in education can illustrate this complex interplay.

Information technology is one of the fastest-growing economic sectors in the global economy almost without exception in every country. That is, countries at all different phases of development recognize the importance of being technologically connected. This may include funding projects for telecommunications infrastructure, buying hardware and software, or any type of technology training. Countries like South Africa or the twelve newly independent states of the former Soviet Union represent countries in transition to a market economy. Examining the telecommunications trade occurring in these countries can provide a helpful framework for imagining how to de-commodify education in these countries. Telecommunications in Sub-Saharan Africa has grown to 8 percent of the total market of goods and services. In Botswana the leading sector for U.S. exports and investment is in telecommunications; in Cote d'Ivoire telecommunications is the third leading export sector; in Guinea telecommunications is the sixth leading export sector and in Nambia it ranks fourth. In all cases, telecommunications follows agriculture or civil infrastructure sectors; i.e., it is ranked more important than household goods. Advanced computer technologies in multimedia, real-time delivery and e-mail through Internet connections, and the ease of use of interface of personal computer systems can drastically alter the traditional form and content of education. U.S. educational technology funding went from $23 million in 1994 to $766 million in 2000. In 1996 the Technology Literacy Challenge was issued in order to provide a major commitment of resources to connect every classroom to the Internet, expand access to modern, multimedia computers; make high-quality educational software an integral part of the curriculum; and enable teachers to effectively integrate technology into their instruction. Some argue, however, that access to computers does not improve reading scores, but that access to books does, and that money spent on computers is therefore better spent on libraries and reading programs.

At the postsecondary level, the impact of technology on education is illustrated by the growth in distance education, which is perceived to overcome geographic barriers to access, and may reduce costs. On the one hand, the challenges involved in implementing distance education include the need to handle organizational, management, and educational changes over the short and long term; limited access to quality programming among certain populations defined by race, social class, or geography; the need for teachers to learn new approaches to teaching, monitoring, and mentoring to adequately serve their students; and the need for standards of quality for new programs. On the other hand, the move to commercialize and digitize curriculum delivery is dismissed as an attempt to de-skill and get rid of teachers with little consideration toward the pedagogical impact. This viewpoint sees automation as a strategy for reducing the need for highly skilled tasks that are expensive to maintain; in the field of education teachers are highly skilled at educational tasks. When their tasks become automated then the need for teachers with those skills is reduced, thus the expectation of what is wanted from a teacher, a teachers' skills bank, is that one can get by with or pay less for teachers who are less skilled. The general caveat is to warn against addressing people as information processors or to redefine complex human issues such as trust as simply information.

The digital classroom gives rise to new teaching and learning styles that can be more flexible and adaptable, yet it raises issues of equity and access that are not fully understood. Curricular changes are extrapolated to the entire university level with the creation of virtual universities. Western Governors University (WGU) illustrates the move from a *bricks and mortar* to a *clicks and mortar*, virtual institution. WGU is a collaborative effort of eighteen western states to create a fundamentally online higher-education program. The WGU plan ensures that it be "market-oriented, independent, client-centered, degree-granting, accredited, competency-based, non-teaching, high quality, cost-effective, regional, and quickly initiated."

In general, commercialism and privatization are advocated as organizational mechanisms to address controversies around how best to improve educational efficiency, cater to pluralistic preferences, make institutions more accountable, and reduce government spending. The phrase *school/business relationship* can be misleading, since such partnerships encompass everything from genuine altruism to cynical exploitation of the youth market. For example, at the K–12 level, a school may receive computer equipment in exchange for electronic marketing to students; or a school may receive free pizza from a specific pizza franchise if students read so many books. At the university level, partnerships include university connections to science parks that impact the processes of invention, innovation, technology transfer, commercialization, and enterprise. Many universities encourage faculty entrepreneurship, provide support systems, and promote university-industry links. These changes in the university environment effected by the increasing roles of knowledge and technological innovation can lead to healthy economic benefits, but excessive commercialization may undercut the mission of public universities. Knowledge generation no longer in the public domain becomes owned by or proprietary to corporations and individuals connected to technology transfer license agreements. The ability to advance scientific knowledge can be restricted by access to proprietary knowledge.

Theory

Globalism can be examined from several angles. In a general sense, globalism can refer to the process in which events in distant locales make a difference in the lives of people in a local area. Global processes have heavily influenced changes in technology, changes in capital, and changes in the mobility of labor. No one theory of globalization that tries to account for its effects can capture the inherent ambiguity of the multitude of ongoing processes. Some theories of globalization say it has a homogenizing effect, resulting from the imposition of capitalist logic. Other theories say it creates heterogeneity by circulating goods, ideas, and culture, thus creating new hybrid cultures that emerge from processes of globalization, e.g., youth subcultures. Others claim that globalism is functionally equivalent to modernity, but is a more neutral term.

However, globalization can be construed as a cover word for what used to be called *imperialism*. This is a Marxist formulation, describing capitalism as having reached the imperialist stage, though rather than imposing its will through force and colonization, it does so through the force of advertising and commodification.

It is not a question of whether or not the global economy will happen, but a question of the global economy on whose terms. What is at stake is both how globalization is theorized and how technologies are used to better understand the complex interdependencies between commerce and education.

See also: GLOBALIZATION OF EDUCATION; INTERNATIONAL TRADE IN EDUCATION PROGRAMS, GOODS, AND SERVICES.

BIBLIOGRAPHY

BRAY, MARK. 1998. "Privatisation of Secondary Education: Issues and Policy Implications." In *Education for the Twenty-First Century: Issues and Prospects.* Paris: UNESCO.

BROWN, JOHN SEELY, and DUGUID, PAUL. *The Social Life of Information.* Boston: Harvard Business School Press.

COLLINS, TIMOTHY, and DEWEES, SARAH. 2001. "Distance Education: Taking Classes to the Students." In *Rural South: Preparing for the Challenges of the 21st Century.* Mississippi State, MS: Southern Rural Development Center.

FEENBERG, ANDREW. 1999. "Reflections on the Distance Learning Controversy." *The Canadian Journal of Communication* 24(3):337–348.

HENRICKSON, LESLIE, and KIM, SONGMI. 2000. "Education as Commodity in the Global Marketplace." *International Journal of Education Policy, Research and Practice* 1(3):377–388.

HEYNEMAN, STEPHEN. 2000. "Educational Qualifications: The Economic and Trade Issues." *Assessment in Education: Principles, Policy, and Practice* 7(3).

KEARNS, MICHAEL. 1999. *The Education Industry: Markets and Opportunities.* Boston: Eduventures.

KIM, ANNA. 1997. "State vs. Market in Educational Open-Market Policy Making in Korea." Ph.D. diss., University of California, Los Angeles.

RUST, VAL D., and KIM, ANNA. 1997. "Free Trade and Education." In *International Handbook of Education and Development: Preparing Schools, Students and Nations for the Twenty-First Century,* ed. William K. Cummings and Noel F. McGinn. London: Pergamon.

TORRES, CARLOS, and MORROW, RAYMOND. 2000. *Globalization and Education: Critical Perspectives.* New York: Routledge.

INTERNET RESOURCES

MANN, MICHAEL, and BORGA, MARIA. 2002. "Detailed Services Transaction Guide." International Trade Administration. <www.ita.doc.gov/td/sif/TradeData2001.pdf>.

U.S. STATE DEPARTMENT. 2000. "Closing the Digital Divide." <http://usinfo.state.gov/usa/able/close.htm>.

WGA VIRTUAL UNIVERSITY DESIGN TEAM. 1996. "Western Governors University: A Proposed Implementation Plan." <www.westgov.org/smart/vu/imp.html>.

LESLIE HENRICKSON